POLITICS IN GHANA

WITHDRAWN

Politics in Ghana

1946–1960

DENNIS AUSTIN

*Research Fellow of the Institute of Commonwealth Studies, London University,
and of the Royal Institute of International Affairs*

*Issued under the auspices of the
Royal Institute of International Affairs*

OXFORD UNIVERSITY PRESS

LONDON   OXFORD   NEW YORK

1970

Oxford University Press

OXFORD LONDON NEW YORK

GLASGOW TORONTO MELBOURNE WELLINGTON

CAPE TOWN SALISBURY IBADAN NAIROBI DAR ES SALAAM LUSAKA ADDIS ABABA

BOMBAY CALCUTTA MADRAS KARACHI LAHORE DACCA

KUALA LUMPUR SINGAPORE HONG KONG TOKYO

SBN 19 285046 6

First published 1964 by Oxford University Press, London
Reprinted with corrections 1966

First issued as an Oxford University Press paperback
1970

Printed in Great Britain by
Fletcher & Son Ltd, Norwich

Contents

Nations, it may be, have fashioned their Governments, but the Governments have paid them back in the same coin.

JOSEPH CONRAD

Acknowledgements

Ti Koro nko agyina—'one man alone is insufficient for the full deliberation of an undertaking'. On completing this book I was very conscious of the truth of this Akan saying, for no single interpretation of a period of political history as important as that from 1946 to 1960 in Ghana can do full justice to the total scene. I was fortunate, however, throughout the writing of these chapters in being able to call on the help and advice of a number of people, and I should like to record my debt to them: primarily to Professor Kenneth Robinson, kindliest of Directors, who made it possible for me to work as a research fellow at the Institute of Commonwealth Studies, and to the Rockefeller Foundation which financed this study between 1959 and 1962. I should also like to thank Professor Thomas Hodgkin of the Institute of African Studies in the University of Ghana for his constant help and encouragement; the very many extra-mural students on whose knowledge I have drawn so deeply; and a number of my former colleagues in the University of Ghana: Mr Yaw Andoh, Miss Lalage Bown, Messrs Paul Bertelsen and W. B. Birmingham, Professor John Fage, Dr de Graft Johnson, Miss Polly Hill, Dr David Kimble, Messrs J. A. Nagba, J. H. Price, and Ivor Wilks, and especially Dr William and Audrey Tordoff for their unfailing generosity.

Those who helped in field work during elections and on visits to particular areas of the country are legion. There is no room to thank them all by name, but I should like to record my debt particularly to Messrs Lobaza Allen of Paga and Accra, Kwame Atiemo of Accra, John Abagre and W. A. Amoro of Bongo, Joseph Opuku-Ampomah, Antwi-Kusi, and Joe Mainoo of Kumasi, T. M. Goodland of Cape Coast, Evans Damoah of Dormaa Ahenkro, Eben Adam of Tamale, A. P. S. Termaghre of Lawra, C. K. Tedam of Paga, Patrick Amipare of Chiana, E. A. Mahama of Damongo, and E. H. Yeboah of Bekwai.

I should also like to thank Professor W. J. M. Mackenzie of the Victoria University of Manchester, Professor Hugh Tinker of the School of Oriental and African Studies, and Mr K. W. J. Post of the University College Ibadan for their comments on the text as a whole; Sir Charles Arden-Clarke and Mr A. J. Loveridge; Mr David Williams, editor of *West Africa* whose encyclopaedic knowledge of the Ghanaian scene has no equal in this country; and a number of leading Ghanaian figures: Nana Agyeman Badu Dormaahene, Dr J. B. Danquah, Messrs S. D. Dombo Duori-Na, Krobo Edusei, and K. A.

Gbedemah, Dr Kurankyi Taylor, Mr J. A. Tettegah, Mrs Nancy Tsiboe, and Mr John Tsiboe.

Finally, I should like to express my gratitude to the staff of the Institute of Commonwealth Studies and the Royal Institute of International Affairs: to Miss Patricia Devonald and Miss Philippa Gibson in particular for help in typing the several different drafts of the book, and to Miss Hermia Oliver of the research department at Chatham House for her patient skill and advice in preparing this study for publication.

D. A.

London.
September 1963

Abbreviations

AC:	Asanteman Council.
ACC:	Ashanti Confederacy Council.
AYA:	Asante Youth Association.
Coussey (Committee) Report:	GB, Committee on Constitutional Reform, Report. 1949.
CPC:	Cocoa Purchasing Co.
CPP:	Convention People's Party.
CYO:	Committee on Youth Organization.
Econ. Bull.	Economic Society of Ghana, Economic Bulletin.
Ewart Committee Report:	GC, Legislative Council, Select Committee appointed to Examine the Questions of Elections and Constituencies. Report. 1950.
FYO:	Federated Youth Organizations.
GC, LA/LC Deb.	Gold Coast, Legislative Assembly/Legislative Council Debates.
GCP:	Ghana Congress Party.
Ghana, Parl. Deb.	Ghana, Parliament, Debates, 1957–
Granville Sharp Report:	Ghana, Commission of Enquiry into the matters Disclosed at the Trial of Capt Benjamin Awhaitey. Report. 1959.
Jackson Commission Report:	Ghana, Commission appointed to Enquire into the Affairs of the Abuakwa State. Report. 1958.
Jibowu Commission Report:	GC, Commission of Enquiry into the Affairs of the Cocoa Purchasing Co. Ltd. Report. 1956.
JPC:	Joint Provincial Council of Chiefs.
Korsah Commission Report:	GC, Commission of Enquiry into Mr Braimah's Resignation &c. Report. 1954.
MAP:	Moslem Association Party (previously the Muslim Association).
MYC:	Muslim Youth Congress.
NA:	Native Authority.
NLM:	National Liberation Movement.
NPP:	Northern People's Party.
NT(T)C:	Northern Territories (Territorial) Council.
Sarkodee Addo Commission Report:	Ghana, Committee of Enquiry ... into Affairs of the Kumasi State Council &c. Report. 1958.
TC:	Togoland Congress.

Abbreviations

TCOR:	UN *Trusteeship Council Official Records.*
TVT:	Transvolta Togoland (now Volta).
UGCC:	United Gold Coast Convention.
UP:	United Party.
Van Lare Commission *Report*:	GC, Commission of Enquiry into Representational and Electoral Reform. *Report.* 1953.
Watson Commission *Report*:	GB, Commission of Enquiry into Disturbances in the Gold Coast. *Report.* 1948.
WYA:	Wassaw Youth Association.

NOTE ON GHANA NEWSPAPERS

The titles of Ghanaian newspapers changed in minor ways during the period under review: e.g. the *Accra Evening News* founded in September 1948, later dropped the word 'Accra'. To simplify the text, the following titles have been used throughout:

Ashanti Pioneer	*Evening News*
Ashanti Sentinel	*Ghanaian Times*
Ashanti Times	*Liberator*
Daily Graphic	*Morning Telegraph*

Glossary of Terms

THE inquiry to be followed in this study may be expressed in simple terms—namely, what can be learnt about politics in Ghana from a narrative of the events which took place between 1946 and 1960. Nevertheless, the various political parties and units of local administration which existed during these years require some preliminary definition if they are not to confuse the main body of the text, and to simplify the narrative given later, the reader is offered a short glossary of terms covering the main political divisions of the country.

The Colony: the thickly populated area between Ashanti and the sea, having a history of contact with western Europe since the end of the fifteenth century. It included the three municipalities, Accra, Cape Coast, Sekondi, where a relatively sophisticated population had grown out of a long history of mission education. A gold and diamond producing area, with a once flourishing cocoa industry until badly affected during the war years by the spread of the virus disease known as 'swollen shoot'. British jurisdiction rested on the 'Bond of 1844' (signed between a number of southern chiefs and the local colonial government) until 1874 when the area south of Ashanti was created the 'Gold Coast Colony'. A legislative council had already been established in Cape Coast in 1850: it was moved to Accra when the capital was shifted east in 1876.

Ashanti: the central forest region dominated by the Akan-speaking group of states forming the 'Ashanti Union' which has a notable place in the history of pre-colonial Africa. A series of wars in the nineteenth century against the British led ultimately to the exile of the Asantehene Prempeh I in 1896, and the imposition of Crown Colony rule five years later. The ability which had made Ashanti an unrivalled military power was then turned with equal success to peaceful ends: the region's rich timber resources were exploited, gold production increased (under concessions to British mining companies), and—once the matted undergrowth of the forest was hacked clear—cocoa farms planted.

Brong-Ahafo: the area lying to the west and north of Ashanti, of growing importance as a source of timber and cocoa. Under British rule the Brong (Akan-speaking) chiefdoms formed part of the Ashanti region. A separatist movement began to take shape after 1946, based on a traditional conflict with Kumasi, and in 1958 succeeded in obtaining a separate Brong-Ahafo region.

Northern Territories: the large savannah region north of the Black Volta, brought under British protection in 1901. A number of its individual chiefdoms—Dagomba, Mamprusi, Wala, Gonja—were of considerable size and antiquity; others were of so fragmentary a nature as hardly to deserve the name. An area of poverty and meagre communications, the majority of the people were engaged in subsistence farming, or growing yams for sale in the south; but there was also a substantial migration to the cocoa farms, mines, and towns of Ashanti and the Colony. Muslim beliefs were interwoven with the customs of many of the large chiefdoms.

Togoland: the trust territory formed by the division between France and Britain in 1919 of the former German colony. The northern section of the United Kingdom trust territory was administered as part of the Northern Territories; the southern section formed part of the Gold Coast Colony until 1952 when it was amalgamated with the small Colony chiefdoms east of the Volta river to form a Trans-Volta-Togoland region.

United Gold Coast Convention (UGCC): the first political organization to talk in practical terms of self-government, which it declared should be achieved 'in the shortest possible time'. Formed in August 1947 by a number of the 'intelligentsia' (q.v.) whose most active member was the lawyer, Dr J. B. Danquah; its general secretary from January to September 1948 was Kwame Nkrumah, who returned from London specifically to take up the appointment. It contested, and was defeated, in the first general election in February 1951, and was dissolved the following year.

Convention People's Party (CPP): the main nationalist party, formed in June 1949 by Nkrumah as a militant break-away movement from the UGCC, drawing its support from the 'commoners' or 'young men' (q.v.). It demanded 'Self-Government Now', successfully contested the 1951 election, and thereafter remained in office, winning an overall majority of the votes and seats in the two further elections of 1954 and 1956.

Northern People's Party (NPP): the northern-based party formed in April 1954 by S. D. Dombo Duori-Na, an educated sub-chief, and Mumuni Bawumia, secretary to the most powerful chief (and native authority) in the Protectorate. It contested the 1954 and 1956 elections, supporting the National Liberation Movement (q.v.) in the demand for a federal constitution. Merged with other opposition groups on 3 November 1957 to form the United Party.

National Liberation Movement (NLM): the Ashanti-based party formed in September 1954, led by Bafuor Osei Akoto of the Asantehene's court, Dr K. A. Busia of the University College, and a number of dissident CPP members. It demanded 'Federation'. Merged with other opposition groups to form the United Party.

Togoland Congress: formed in 1951 by the Ewe leaders S. G. Antor and Kojo Ayeke. It demanded (1) as an interim step, a separate legislature for the trust territory, (2) eventual integration with the neighbouring trust territory.

Moslem Association Party (MAP): formed by a majority (though not all) of the Muslim communities which numbered approximately 6·5 per cent of the population. The greater number of Muslims were in the north, but their political strength lay principally in the 'Zongo' or 'strangers' quarters' of the municipalities. The MAP began to enter politics during 1953–4. It too merged with other groups to form the United Party.

Ga Shifimo Kpee: 'the Ga Standfast Association': a protest movement which sprang up in mid-1957 in Accra, concerned with the poor housing conditions in the capital, and the influx of 'strangers' who were said to have crowded the Ga inhabitants out of their ancestral rights. The Ga Shifimo Kpee also formed part of the United Party.

The chiefs: a very mixed group. They included the powerful, autocratic rulers of a number of northern chiefdoms; the elected chiefs of Ashanti, Brong-Ahafo, and the Colony; and the irremoveable chiefs of the Krobo states in the eastern Colony, and of the small Ewe village communities. Once the centre of a rich culture, held in awe as the occupants of a sacred 'Stool' or 'Skin', and feared as the active possessors of state power. Until independence, most (but not all) of the Ashanti chiefs supported the NLM, many (but by no means all) of the northern chiefs helped to form the NPP.

The intelligentsia: the term used locally to refer to the small southern group of lawyers and businessmen who, from an early date, were active among the limited electorates of Cape Coast, Accra, and Sekondi, forming proto-nationalist associations like the Aborigines' Rights Protection Society (1897), the National Congress of British West Africa (1920), the Youth Conference movement (1930), and a number of municipal party groups. Their immediate concern after the Second World War was to replace the chiefs as the heirs of British rule, but with the founding of the CPP they were themselves displaced; they continued, however, as implacable opponents of Nkrumah and the CPP, adding a national element to the regional and local opposition parties.

The 'young men': also a local expression, often written in official reports as one word—viz. 'youngmen', used to describe the 'commoners', those who held no Stool office of importance. In earlier times there was also a large slave population, particularly in Ashanti, whose rights were at best indeterminate. The 'young men' were not necessarily young, any more than the 'elders' who surrounded the chief were old: the latter were counsellors, usually subordinate chiefs and holders of important Stools; the former were the commoners. The expression 'the young men' was also used more narrowly to refer to the educated commoners—storekeepers, petty traders, clerks, primary school teachers—who were likely to be among the younger generation.

To these political terms, one should add the basic statistical data:

Total area: 91,843 sq. mi., including 13,041 of the trust territory.

Total population: 4,118,450 .... 1948 census.

6,690,730 .... 1960 census, provisional est.

Population by regions, 1960:

Northern Ghana	1,282,164
Ashanti	1,108,548
Brong Ahafo	588,724
Southern Ghana	2,918,747
Volta (formerly Trans-Volta-Togoland) ..	782,547

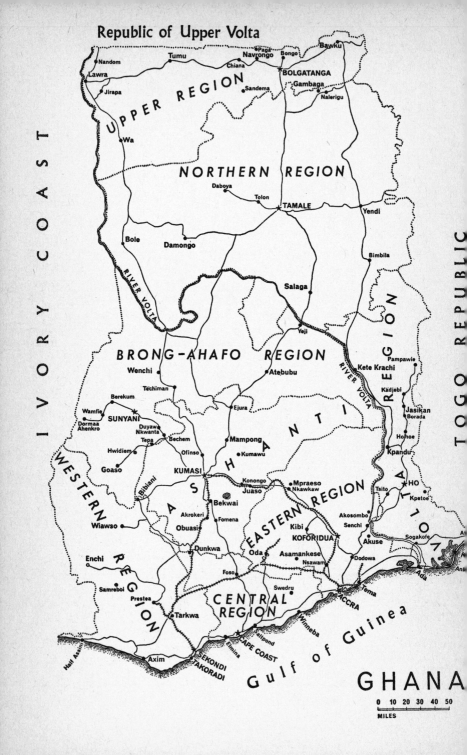

Republic of Upper Volta

IVORY COAST

TOGO REPUBLIC

UPPER REGION

Nandom
Lawra
Jirapa
Tumu
Paga Navrongo
Chiana
Sandema
Bongo
Bawku
BOLGATANGA
Gambaga
Nalerigu
Wa

NORTHERN REGION

Daboya
Tolon
TAMALE
Yendi
Bole
Damongo
Bimbila
Salaga
Yeji

RIVER VOLTA

BRONG-AHAFO REGION

Wenchi
Atebubu
Techiman
Berekum
Wamfie
Dormaa Ahenkro
SUNYANI
Duyawa Nkwanta
Tepa
Bechem
Ofinso
Hwidiem
Goaso
KUMASI
Bibiani
Akrokeri
Bekwai
Obuasi
Fomena
Wiawso
Ejura
Mampong
Kumawu
Konongo
Juaso
Mpraeso
Nkawkaw
Kete Krachi
Pampawie
Kadjebi
Jasikan
Borada
Hohoe
Kpandu

RIVER VOLTA

ASHANTI

VOLTA REGION

EASTERN REGION

Tsito
HO
Kpetoe
Akosombo
Senchi
Kibi
KOFORIDUA
Akuse
Sogakofe
Oda
Asamankese
Nsawam
Dodowa
Ada
Enchi
Dunkwa
Foso
Samreboi
Swedru
Prestea
Tarkwa
CENTRAL REGION
Saltpond
Winneba
ACCRA
Tema
Half Assini
Axim
SEKONDI TAKORADI
Elmina
CAPE COAST

WESTERN REGION

Gulf of Guinea

GHANA

0 10 20 30 40 50
MILES

I

Introductory Preview

THE narrative recorded in later chapters of this book describes the events which took place in the Gold Coast (now Ghana) from the introduction of the first post-war constitution in 1946 to the inauguration of the republic in 1960. In sum, it traces a familiar pattern of emancipation, and attempts have been made by several writers to bring together the universal characteristics which each particular nationalist movement in Africa and Asia has seemed to possess.[1] No such synthesis is attempted in this present volume. The setting is Ghana, and the account of these fourteen years should be seen as no more than an extended essay in Ghanaian history. In considering this history, however, the writer was made aware of a problem of a more general nature than those discussed in the main body of the text. It may be expressed quite simply by asking: why did a colony apparently so well endowed in its national life as the Gold Coast, for whose political future every prediction in 1946 was cast in the most favourable terms, suddenly enter a period of violent conflict—first between the colonial government and local nationalist leaders, and then between rival political groups—until by 1960 (after three years of independence) the new republic was ruled by a single-party régime whose leaders turned increasingly to harsh methods of control 'of a totalitarian kind'.[2] It was hardly the end foretold in 1946. Nor was it foreseen in 1954 (to take a point a little over half-way through these years) when the country appeared to be divided between two main party groups, each strongly based among its own supporters. It is this repeated failure in prediction, together with the causes which combined to

[1] Most successfully by T. L. Hodgkin, in *Nationalism in Colonial Africa* (1956) and *African Political Parties* (1962). See too G. A. Almond and J. S. Coleman, *The Politics of the Developing Areas* (1960); Rupert Emerson, *From Empire to Nation* (1960), I. Wallerstein, *Africa: the Politics of Independence* (1961).
[2] The phrase is Nkrumah's, in *Ghana: the Autobiography of Kwame Nkrumah* (1957), p. x.

produce the Nkrumah republic of 1960, which are examined in
these introductory pages.[3]

At first sight, the problem may be thought hardly worth discussing. It is not unusual for colonial governments to be surprised
by nationalist demands—indeed, it might be said that it is their
nature to be overtaken by such a fate—and since 1960 single-
party republics have become the rule rather than the exception
in Africa. Why, then, should it be supposed that the Gold Coast
would be different? Because for a long time the Gold Coast was
thought to occupy a special place among the British African territories. Among the handful of educated leaders in the Colony
area there was a level of political sophistication, and a history of
nationalist argument, of a degree unusual even in West Africa.[4]
In the central Ashanti region, African self-government, of a
highly developed order of political achievement, existed for more
than two centuries before British rule was imposed at the end of
the nineteenth century. And by 1946 the country as a whole possessed a number of advantages over its less fortunate neighbours
—advantages of size, wealth, educational attainment, administrative skill, and an air of confidence and stability—all of which
seemed likely to enable it to achieve an easy transition to self-
government. Thus Martin Wight concluded his study of *The
Gold Coast Legislative Council* in 1946 by remarking that 'the Gold
Coast people find themselves the pioneers of political advance
and the touchstone of political competence in Africa'—a verdict
endorsed by Margery Perham in her preface to Martin Wight's
book;[5] and the period of colonial reform inaugurated during the
war years was generally accepted as evidence, not only of the

[3] Nkrumah disliked the words, 'the Nkrumah constitution', when they were
applied to the internal responsible government constitution introduced in 1954.
But the presidential form of the republic introduced in 1960 may surely be so
described: it was tailor-made to suit the leader.

[4] For the early history of the intelligentsia leaders of the southern Colony, see
D. B. Kimble, *A Political History of Ghana, 1850–1928* (1963). There was an air of
unreality about many of the pronouncements of this small group of municipal
leaders, but the activities of the lawyers and businessmen in Accra, Cape Coast
and Sekondi helped to create a tradition of political agitation hardly to be matched
in Africa.

[5] 'Among African dependencies the Gold Coast has been chosen because it has
not only the longest constitutional history, except for its smaller neighbour, Sierra
Leone, but also because it seemed to be the most politically advanced. The Gold
Coast in 1946 has more than justified the expectations entertained when it was
selected for study in 1941. Even while Martin Wight has been writing this book, the
territory has made a most impressive constitutional advance'. (*The Gold Coast
Legislative Council* (1947), pp. 207 and vi.) Miss Perham's reference was to the unofficial majority constitution which linked the two southern regions, Ashanti and
the Colony.

pioneering road taken by the Gold Coast, but of the ability of its leaders to move along a path of moderate reform. Hence the astonishment of the officials at the riots which occurred in 1948, and at the speed with which a radical nationalist movement—embodied in the Convention People's Party—took shape the following year.

THE PERIOD OF COLONIAL REFORM

The dismay felt by the officials in 1948 was in proportion to the confidence they had expressed hitherto. Compliments scatter the pages of the Annual Reports of the post-war years, in which the Gold Coast was said to be 'a model colony', and 'a peace-loving country' which could look forward to an 'orderly and constitutional progress' towards self-government. Similar views were held by Alan Burns, Governor between 1941 and 1946, who expressed 'great confidence in these extremely sensible people. They know their limitations and they are very keen to take advice provided they know the man giving them advice is really sincere.'[6] Such statements were easy to understand, not only when they were made about the Gold Coast but when they were applied to British West Africa in general where the officials were free of the encumbrance of a European settler community, and able to administer their territories through, and with the help of, the local population. True, the officials might doubt whether there would be any final advance to so remote a goal as independence within their own term of office. But 'self-government' was recognized as a legitimate (if premature) demand long before the post-war nationalist movement appeared on the scene. Indeed, in the sense that African leaders participated in their own government, the movement towards local autonomy in the Gold Coast may be said to date from the earliest years of colonial rule—from 1850, when the first African unofficial members were appointed to the first legislative council of the southern Colony.[7] The pace of re-

[6] Address to Empire Parliamentary Association, 24 Oct. 1946. (Printed for private circulation only.)

[7] First established in 1850, the separate history of the Colony's legislative council dated from 1874 when the Gold Coast was administered apart (for the last time) from Sierra Leone. There were usually African representatives on the council during the latter part of the century. James Bannerman (a mulatto trader) was a member of the first council constituted on 30 April 1850; George Blankson, the Fanti merchant—a full-blooded African—was appointed in 1861, and John Mensah Sarbah, the Fanti lawyer and writer, in 1888. The chiefs did not appear until much later. For an account of Blankson's life, see the biographical sketch by J. M. Akita in the *Trans. of Gold Coast and Togoland Hist. Soc.* (1955), 1/5.

form in these early decades was extremely slow—interrupted at the beginning of the century by the addition of Ashanti and the Northern Territories, pushed forward by the First World War, interrupted again by the economic depression of the 1930s, and then urged forward at a quicker pace by the Second World War —but by 1946 it was possible to see some form of home rule as a not too distant prospect. By this date, too, a large part of Asia had begun to move towards independence. Ceylon, Burma, and India were almost free, and the effect of this vast upheaval within the empire was beginning to make itself felt not only on local African leaders but in Colonial Office thinking in London and among the officials of the West African Coast.

It was hardly necessary, however, to look overseas in order to justify the renewal in the 1940s of the movement of reform; there was ample evidence in the territory itself to support such a decision. For by 1946 the Gold Coast had acquired many of the prerequisites which it was then thought necessary that an independent state should possess. The number of children attending school, the degree of urbanization, the spread of road and rail communications, the increase in external trade, and the vast improvement in government revenue as world commodity prices climbed to heights unimagined before the war—all pointed in the same direction. The Gold Coast was being strengthened as a national unit not only in terms of the economy but (it seemed fair to assume) in political cohesion. The significance of the increase in the number of educated leaders will be examined a little later. For the rest, the evidence of national growth can be set down in tabular form:

1. Urban Population: Census Years 1921–60

	1921	*1931*	*1948*	*1960**
Accra	41,100	60,700	133,200	388,231
Kumasi	38,000	35,800	77,700	220,922
Sekondi-Takoradi	9,500	22,400	43,700	120,793
Cape Coast	14,900	17,700	23,000	56,730
Tamale	3,900	12,900	16,100	57,946

* Provisional figures.

Source: Census Reports.

2. Government Revenue & Expenditure, 1921/2–1959/60
(£'000)

	Revenue	Expenditure
1921–2	3,017	3,285
1926–7	4,051	3,634
1930–1	3,499	3,744
1946–7	7,568	6,630
1959–60	70,200	88,000

Sources: A. W. Cardinall, *The Gold Coast* (1931); *Annual Reports*; *Economic Survey, 1960.*

3. External Trade, 1921–60
(£'000)

Year	Exports	Imports	Cocoa exports	Cocoa percentage of domestic produced exports
1921	6,942	7,661	4,764	74·6
1930	9,911	8,856	6,970	70·3
1946	19,700	17,500	8,997	46·0
1960	115,983	129,617	68,779	58·8

Sources: Cardinall; *Annual Reports*; *Economic Survey 1960.*

4. Communications, 1921/2–1959/60

Year	Railway mileage	Motorable road mileage	Licensed vehicles in use
1921–2	276	2,241	470
1926–7	457	5,110	1,597
1930–1	500	6,738	1,884
1946–7	536	8,114*	
1959–60	591	19,236†	45,992

* 620 miles tar-sprayed.　　† 2,000 miles bitumen.

Sources: Cmd. 2744; Cardinall; *Annual Reports*; *Economic Survey 1960*; *Ghana Handbook of Commerce & Industry, 1960.*

NOTE: The Ormsby-Gore Report (Cmd. 2744) gave an excellent account of the early network of roads. His companion, J. E. W. Flood, was able to motor from Kumasi to Tamale, Yende, Navrongo, Wa, Bole, Kintampo, and back to Kumasi—a journey of 1,140 miles—in fourteen days. Surfaces deteriorated with the heavy volume of traffic during the Second World War and there was a particularly bad period after 1945. Road construction then became a principal feature of the CPP administration's development programme. But in this respect too—as in much else—there were colonial precedents. The main trunk routes were pushed across the river Volta at Yeji and Bamboi in the north and at Senchi towards the Togoland Trust Territory in the 1920s. In 1930 expenditure on roads totalled £1,164,000 (9·3 per cent of the total government expenditure; cf. Nigeria 3·8 per cent, Uganda 8·4 per cent, Kenya 6·7 per cent). The CPP spent 36 per cent of the 1951–9 £120 million development plan on communications. The railway entered Kumasi via the Tarkwa and Obuasi goldmining centres as early as 1903 to link the Ashanti capital with Sekondi; and again in 1923 to complete the link with Accra.

It was possible to add to this growing infrastructure of national unity an important social fact. Unlike most African colonies, the Gold Coast had an important central group of chiefdoms whose peoples spoke a common language and shared similar customs. Of the 4–5 million peoples in 1948—the date of the first post-war census—some 2–3 million were of Akan origin and spoke related dialects—*asante* (or *twi*) in Ashanti, *brong* in the western Ashanti chiefdoms, *akwapim-twi* in the hills behind the Accra plains, *fante* in the western Colony chiefdoms. Thus a substantial area of the central and southern regions of the country shared a common culture.[8]

On the one hand, therefore, there was the growing strength of the country as a national unit: on the other there was little apparent sign in 1946 of any growth of political consciousness. And the officials drew comfort from the contrast. Only in the municipalities, among the small group of lawyers and teachers, were

[8] To this Akan group of languages had to be added: *ga*, the language of the first settlers in Accra; *ga-adagme*, spoken in most of the states of the Accra hinterland; *ewe*, in the southern half of the trust territory and the south-east of the Colony; the different languages and dialects of the north—*dagbani, mampruli, wali, gonja, kasim, nankam, sissala;* and numerous 'pockets' of minor language groups spoken by subdominant tribal communities—*guan, vagala, cheripong,* and others. As late as 1960, the Ghana Broadcasting Service was using eight languages in its home services: English, *twi, fante, ga, dagbani, ewe, hausa* and Nkrumah's tongue -*nzima,* the language of the extreme south-west. The total picture is bewildering at first sight, but as early as 1931 Cardinall (p. 74) stressed 'the great underlying similarity between the various tribes' in language, religion, and social customs, adding: 'in that fact lies the possibility that the artificial Gold Coast may one day attain united nationhood'.

there any obvious signs of discontent. Elsewhere the dominant feature of the Gold Coast scene was a seemingly universal attachment to local chiefdoms, lineages, and village groups, and an absorption in local interests which was encouraged by the decentralized nature of the colonial administration under which Commissioners controlled their districts with a minimum of interference from Accra. The north was a remote region of primitive peoples; the Ewe villages of the Togoland trust territory were divided between those who accepted and those who disliked their attachment to the Gold Coast; the colony was parcelled out among separate chiefdoms; Ashanti was an ancient kingdom with a long history of conquest and rule over its neighbours: in short—although national ties were growing stronger, there seemed little danger of any sudden expression of nationalist unrest. So, at least, the officials reasoned. And the *Annual Report for 1947* contained a mild rebuke addressed to the lawyers of the coastal municipalities who in August 1947 announced the formation of a 'United Gold Coast Convention'.

A new movement [it noted] the 'United Gold Coast Convention' which may most conveniently be classified as a political party, sprang up during 1947 and declared as one of its main objectives the attainment of full self-government in the shortest possible time. The movement has not so far contributed to the solution of the practical and urgent problems facing the country but has confined itself to an appeal to nationalist feelings.

It may be thought that this was a prejudiced, official view. But the officials could have found confirmation—had they ever doubted their own judgement—in the categorical statement by Martin Wight. Writing from Oxford in 1946 as a careful (if distant) observer of the political scene, he considered that: 'Neither the Gold Coast nor even the Gold Coast Colony has yet attained that self-aware unity that is the essence of nationality.'[9]

Thus it was believed that time—the great enemy of careful, administrative reform—was still at the disposal of the colonial government, and under Alan Burns the officials busied themselves in preparing an administrative and legislative framework within which a 'self-aware unity' might develop. The most obvious need was for a political superstructure; the most obvious weakness, the lack of African officers in the senior ranks of the

[9] Wight, p. 183.

civil service. Burns addressed himself to both tasks with great
energy, and—against the background of the pre-war years—the
five years of his governorship constituted a period of almost unin-
terrupted reform. In 1942 African members were appointed to
the administrative service as assistant district commissioners and
to the Governor's executive council; the following year adult
suffrage was introduced in municipal elections (beginning with
the Kumasi Town Council). In 1944 the Colony native authorities were strengthened as units of local government; in 1946,
when Ashanti and the Colony were brought together under the
unofficial majority constitution, a regional territorial council was
inaugurated for the Northern Territories.[10] The crowning point
of these reforms was the 1946 constitution itself, with its 8 officials
and 24 unofficial members (18 elected, and 6 nominated), which
united the Colony and Ashanti in a single legislature and brought
the country as a whole to the clearly defined stage of representative government. Burns was well pleased: 'the people are really

[10] The first two members appointed to the executive council were Nana Ofori
Atta I and K. A. Korsah, to the administrative service (as assistant district commissioners), A. L. Adu, and K. A. Busia. Africanization—'Ghanaianization'—was
to become a succulent bone of contention. But in this respect too the Gold Coast
had more to build on and with than most African colonies. There were precedents
enough in a long line of African administrators, educationalists, judges, and doctors
for an administrative and judicial service staffed with locally recruited officers. The
first detailed Africanization scheme was the Guggisberg plan of 1925–6, which
aimed at increasing the number of Africans holding what were called 'European
appointments' from 27 to a total of 231 by 1946 when it was expected that the
establishment of such posts would be about 550. In fact, at that date there were
only 89 Africans holding senior appointments, among them: 3 puisne judges, 1
assistant colonial secretary, 2 accountants, 3 assistant district commissioners, 6
collectors of customs, 10 medical officers, 3 assistant engineers, 2 agricultural
officers. Schemes of training were set in motion by Burns, which again it was
hoped time would fructify. And indeed this was the case. The contrast between the
position at the beginning, at independence, and at the end of the fourteen years
under review was startling:

			African officers	Overseas officers
1946	..	..	89	960
1957	..	..	1,581	{ 1,138 mainly on pension 66 on contract
1960	..	..	2,883	660 on contract

The relevant documents are Ewart Committee *Report* (and Supplementary to the
Report), 1960; *Government Statement on the Report* (no. 4 of 1960); *Report of the Select
Committee on the Lidbury Report* (no. 3 of 1952) and a Gold Coast Government *State-
ment on the Africanization of the Public Service* (1954).

The way for entry by the north into the legislative council was prepared at the
end of 1946 by the setting up of a Northern Territories Territorial Council as a
regional deliberative assembly and a future electoral body. The Council met in December in the Dining Hall of the Senior Government School, Tamale: 15 chiefs,
all but two illiterate. A Southern Togoland Council was established in 1949 and
returned one 'territorial member' to the 1951 National Assembly. See below, ch. III.

happy', he told the Empire Parliamentary Association, on 24 October 1946, 'and really satisfied with the new Constitution they have gained'. Martin Wight compared the union of the southern half of the country with that of England and Scotland in 1707. The *Annual Report for 1947*, while criticizing the UGCC leaders for their nationalist claims, none the less affirmed that 'this major constitutional advance has been generally welcomed as conferring an important measure of self-government in a manner which will permit an orderly and constitutional progress towards self-government in the foreseeable future'.

In sum, the reforms which Burns introduced during these years amounted to a bold attempt to meet any widespread demand for political rights before it reached the final point of violent controversy. They were designed, in particular, to bring into closer partnership with the officials the two leading groups of local opinion in the country, namely, the chiefs as presidents of the reformed native authorities and the intelligentsia as representatives of the growing urban population. And in this respect, too, the Gold Coast was considered fortunate in having among the indirect-rule chiefs of Ashanti and the Colony, and among the lawyers and businessmen of the municipalities, a number of able and experienced leaders whom the officials were ready (by 1946) to see as potential heirs. To be sure, the Colony chiefs and the intelligentsia had been close rivals for power and position on the legislative council; and relations between the officials and the intelligentsia were often strained: the officials felt obliged from time to time to curb the pretensions of the municipal representatives as, on occasions, the latter liked to talk the language of anti-colonialism. But there was little sense of permanent hostility between any section of what constituted (by 1946) a triple ruling *élite*—the officials, chiefs, and intelligentsia.[11] One may perhaps

[11] One must except the personal relationship between Burns and Dr J. B. Danquah. See, for example, the remark by the former (in retrospect) on the elections to the 1946 legislative council: 'The Joint Provincial Council elected seven Chiefs, one clergyman and one lawyer; the clergyman was an excellent choice.' The lawyer was Danquah. Burns was much troubled during the latter part of his governorship by the 'Kibi murder trial'. Nana Sir Ofori Atta I, the *okyenhene* (paramount chief) of Akim Abuakwa died in August 1943 and a village chief, Akyea Mensah, was killed in ritualistic fashion probably in February 1944; his eight murderers were sentenced to death at the end of that year, but the defence succeeded in delaying execution at intervals throughout 1945 and 1946 until March 1947 when three of the condemned men were hanged. As Governor with the power of exercising the royal prerogative of pardon Burns had the unpleasant task of deciding whether so long a delay in the carrying out of the sentence should

quote here, as typical of the essentially moderate tone of the narrow stratum of opinion which the intelligentsia leaders voiced, the advice given at the end of 1929 by the Cape Coast barrister, J. E. Casely Hayford, to the delegates of the National Congress of British West Africa:

In these days when there is a natural tendency among the races of man to come together in their natural groups, it will be insincere for us to pretend that African nationhood does not interest us. If the principle that brought the National Congress into being is sound, the corollary must hold good that we are concerned in the pursuit of an African Nationality which will tend to focus world opinion upon African interests generally. But as a Congress we can only have sympathy with constitutional methods, remembering our fundamental policy which is to maintain strictly inviolate the connection of the British West African dependencies with the British Empire, and to maintain unreservedly all and every right of free citizenship of the Empire and the fundamental principle that taxation goes with representation.[12]

This was the reasoned voice of the intelligentsia at their most persuasive which the officials could listen to without alarm, however exasperated they (and the chiefs) might be by the intelligentsia's claim to speak for the country as a whole. The 1930s saw the beginnings of more general unrest when the Colony and Ashanti cocoa farmers collaborated in a series of cocoa hold-ups in an attempt to raise the low level of price paid by the European buying firms.[13] Their protests also coincided with a Youth Conference movement, and a radical penny press, started by Dr Danquah.[14]

---

temper justice with mercy. Danquah was one of the counsel for the defence. (See Burns, *Colonial Civil Servant* (1949), pp. 219–39.)

[12] Quoted in Magnus Sampson, *West African Leadership* (1949), p. 88. Casely Hayford was addressing the fourth session of the National Congress of British West Africa in Lagos, 1929. Founded nine years earlier to promote a federation of the four British West African territories, the Congress anticipated (in different form) many of the ideas of the later pan-African movement. Sampson (pp. 13–14), also of Cape Coast, also a lawyer, believed that: 'The dreams of Casely Hayford for an increasing share of the Aboriginal inhabitants of British West Africa in the political governance of their countries was realized after the 16th anniversary of his death [thanks to] the singularly distinguished and successful administration of His Excellency Sir Alan Burns. . .'.

[13] For the early history of the cocoa industry and the 1937–8 hold-up, see Sir Keith Hancock, *Survey of British Commonwealth Affairs* (1942), ii/2, pp. 209 ff., and the *Report* of the (Nowell) Commission on the Marketing of West African Cocoa, Cmd. 5845 of 1938.

[14] For the Youth Conference movement, which held its first meeting in 1930, see Wight, pp. 186–8. For a brief outline of the growth of a local press see Appendix A, p. 417 below.

But when the war broke out in 1939 there were fervent expressions of support for the government. The chiefs collected money for the Spitfire Fund. The Asantehene became an officer in the Home Guard. Recruiting officers were busy.[15] And, as the war continued, schemes of constitutional reform began to be discussed jointly between the Governor and the chiefs and intelligentsia of Ashanti and the Colony until, eventually, the Burns constitution was inaugurated. If, therefore, the central problem of colonial government in these post-war years lay in the need to move along a path of reform at the right pace and the right time, the Gold Coast government might well be thought to have made a shrewd, successful decision concerning its own rate of progress. 'We must carry the people with us', Burns told his audience, 'and it is no good trying to hurry the Africans'.[16] It seemed plausible in 1946 to suppose that he had succeeded.

It was not difficult therefore to sympathize with the officials when the riots burst suddenly upon them in 1948. It had been very easy to take part in the growing political life of the country, and yet remain unaware of the dangers which lay beneath the surface. When the eruption came, however, it was violent. Between 28 February, when the disturbances began in Accra, and 16 March, when they were finally brought under control, there were twenty-nine deaths and over 200 injured. Discontent on this scale was unprecedented. The military had to be brought in to help the small number of police. The country was placed under a state of emergency, and it was then that Gerald Creasy (Burns's successor) confessed to the legislative council on which so many hopes had been pinned that he had been 'overtaken by events'. Why was there this sudden, violent transformation of the political scene? What pressures had been building up in Gold Coast society?

THE DEMAND FOR SELF-GOVERNMENT

In April 1948 a Commission of Inquiry arrived in Accra.[17] With the hindsight available after the riots had taken place, the

---

[15] By the end of 1945 there were 63,038 men from the Gold Coast in the armed services of whom 41,888 had served overseas—6,000 in East Africa, 30,500 in Burma, 5,500 in the Middle East (GC, *Report on the Demobilisation and Resettlement of Gold Coast Africans in the Armed Services 1945*, no. 5 of 1945).

[16] Address to Empire Parliamentary Association, 24 Oct. 1946.

[17] Commission of Enquiry into Disturbances in the Gold Coast (Chairman: Aiken Watson), which published its *Report* (Col. No. 231) in June 1948.

Commissioners were able to list an impressive number of local causes of the disturbances—the return to civilian life of groups of dissatisfied ex-servicemen, the shortage of housing accommodation in the main towns, the steep rise in the price of imported consumer goods, and the methods adopted by the administration to check the spread of disease among the cocoa farms of the Colony. These were, indeed, important causes of discontent, and will be examined in some detail in a later chapter dealing with the actual events leading to the riots. But although the nationalist movement owed a great deal to local grievances of the kind described in the Watson *Report*, it would hardly have spread with the speed and force it acquired after 1948 had society itself not been particularly receptive to its appeal. The question raised at the end of the previous paragraph may thus be answered in general terms by saying that the disturbances of the post-war years needed to be seen not only in nationalist terms—as part of the general stirring of political consciousness throughout the African continent—but as marking a major shift of power within Ghanaian society. It is true that the grievances which sparked off the riots against the colonial government were particularly irksome. But the riots themselves were the violent herald of a struggle for power soon to be conducted by new leaders who drew their support from a much broader, more popular level than had hitherto been active in national politics, and the demands shortly to be raised by Nkrumah and the Convention People's Party implied a far greater upheaval in local society than the earlier struggle between the chiefs and the intelligentsia. They carried with them a strident protest not only against colonial rule but against the existing structure of authority in the Colony and Ashanti chiefdoms. There was, therefore, a significant ambiguity in the title of the new party. On the one hand, it meant the 'whole people'—as indeed a nationalist movement was bound to claim in its struggle against the colonial power. On the other, it stood for the 'ordinary people'—the commoners—as opposed to the chiefs and the intelligentsia.

It was not easy (even by 1960) to see the CPP as the vanguard of a clearly defined social class, since the general appeal of independence enabled the leaders to muster a broad front of support. (Moreover, opposition to the CPP tended to be expressed in tribal-territorial terms.) Nevertheless the demand made by the party for self-government was bound up with a struggle for power which had many of the characteristics of a class struggle—provided the words were widened in scope to connote a level determined as much by education, and by social standing within a traditional political system, as by economic criteria. And in order to examine this struggle—and to account for the sudden emergence in the Gold Coast at a national level of a new class of educated commoners—two predisposing factors needed to be examined: one, the growth of an elementary-school-educated generation; the other, a conflict (all too familiar to the officials at a local level and, therefore, underrated by them) between the chiefs and the commoners in the native authorities.

(a) *Nationalism and the Rise of the Elementary-School-Leavers*

The part played by the local mission and state primary school as a catalyst of nationalist growth hardly needs stressing. The simple calculation may be made—the more education, the more revolution: but this is not the whole story, since the critical factor may lie as much in the shape as in the size of the educational pyramid. The significant feature of the Gold Coast pattern was not so much the impressive number of pupils attending secondary school—although this fact in itself was remarkable—but the extremely broad primary base. (See tables below.)

It was among the elementary-school-leavers that the nationalist movement gathered force with such astonishing speed. By the end of the Second World War they had begun to cohere as a dis-

ELEMENTARY AND SECONDARY SCHOOL EDUCATION
AT DECEMBER 1948

1. Colony, Ashanti, Southern Togoland

	Govt & mission schools	Non-designated schools	TOTAL
Infant junior	136,516	97,089	233,605
Senior primary	47,295	1,818	49,113
	Total elementary education		282,718
Secondary & post-secondary			6,410
Teacher training			457

2. Northern Territories

	Govt & Mission Schools	Non-designated schools	TOTAL
Infant junior	3,374	47	3,421
Senior primary	549	—	549
	Total elementary education		3,970
Secondary	80	—	80

3. National Total

Infant junior	237,026 =	Standards I–III, age (approx.) 5–11 yrs.
Senior primary	49,662 =	Standards IV–VII, age (approx.) up to 16 yrs.
Total elementary education	286,688	
Secondary	6,490	
Teacher training	457	

NOTE: Figures exclude enrolment figures in private business and commercial colleges.

Source: Report of Education Dept., 1948–9.

tinct social group, marked out by the limited system of element-ary education through which they struggled to reach a minimum of qualifications—and thereby very different in outlook from the better-educated, older-established, intelligentsia class. Because the admission net was cast extremely widely—and not always by official hands—the result was that the primary-school base, as well as being broad, was also of a very indifferent quality, a fact not generally recognized by outside observers who were so much impressed by the excellent secondary schools in Cape Coast and Accra (from which many of the intelligentsia sprang and which gave the Gold Coast a deservedly famous name) that they over-looked the lamentable state of many village and small-town primary schools.[18] The education officers, however, were well aware of the situation:

[18] Note, however, the long history of secondary education in the Gold Coast: again an unusual feature of the African scene. It began in the 1880s in the Colony, when the Fanti Public Schools Company took over the local Wesleyan School in

. . . the basis of the educational system is the six-years' infant junior course. Selected pupils proceed to a further four years senior-primary course, but it is estimated for many years to come the Gold Coast will be unable to afford this course for more than a third of the number of children who complete the infant-junior course.[19]

By 1948 the position had been reached when 'in the Colony and Ashanti approximately half of the children of infant-junior school-going age and 20 per cent of those of senior-primary school-going age [were] at school',[20] while to this bare statement of fact the comment needed to be added:

> Despite all the war-time difficulties, the development of education went on throughout the 1939–45 period. On the one hand, there was a severe reduction in the amount of inspection and supervision possible, and on the other there was a rapidly increasing and insistent demand which showed itself in the opening of hundreds of non-assisted infant-junior schools. Of these many were started by local communities without reference either to recognised Educational Units or to the Education Department. No notifications of their founding were given and their existence was not registered. The majority were exceedingly ill-housed, and almost without exception staffed with untrained teachers.[21]

Cape Coast and appointed J. E. Casely Hayford as its first principal at the age of 23. The school became the uncertain forerunner of the great Cape Coast secondary schools, Richmond College (later St Nicholas's Grammar School, later again Mfantsipim) opened in 1909; Adisadel a year later. The Accra Royal School and the Accra Academy followed as private ventures before the First World War; Achimota opened its doors in 1926–7. By 1950 there were seven secondary schools in Cape Coast alone—Mfantsipim, St Augustine's, Adisadel, Holy Child School (for girls), Wesley Girls' High School, the Aggrey Memorial School, and the Ghana National School. Ashanti and the north followed much later—the first secondary school in Kumasi was Prempeh College in 1949, the first in Tamale was the Government Secondary School in 1952. But Kumasi had its very good Wesley Teachers' Training College in 1924, and boys came south for secondary education. A full list of political leaders educated at Achimota Training College alone would make impressive reading: it would include Nkrumah, K. A. Gbedemah, K. A. Busia, northerners like the Tolon Na and L. R. Abavana, the Ewe leader M. K. Apaloo, and the CPP Akim Abuakwa politician Aaron Ofori Atta, to take only a random selection. (Opposition spokesmen would have hastened to add that Dr Busia also went to Mfantsipim Secondary School.) *Primary* education in the Colony went back a very long way indeed. There is space here for only one interesting example. At the beginning of the nineteenth century Philip Quaque (1741–1816) of the local 'Torridzonian Society' opened the little Cape Coast Castle school for mulatto children where Joseph Smith, William de Graft, and John Martin were pupils; it was they who invited the Wesleyan mission to the country, which in 1838 engaged Thomas Birch Freeman. One of the fruits of Freeman's energetic career was the Wesleyan School in Cape Coast where Kwegyir Aggrey was educated. And it was Aggrey who taught Nkrumah at Achimota.

[19] *Report of Education Dept.*, 1948.   [20] Ibid.
[21] Committee to Review Gold Coast Education, 1941–6, *Report*.

This was the educational background of a great many of the leaders of the People's Party when it was formed in 1949.[22] The primary base was disproportionately large because of the reduced expenditure on education during the depression years of the 1930s, the result being that many who should have gone on to some form of post-primary schooling were unable to find a place. The total spent on education rose to just over £300,000 by 1930 but was cut back to £210,000 in 1933, and it did not reach the earlier figure again until 1941. Moreover, parents were unable to pay the fees even of those who might have gone to a secondary school, as the cocoa price fell and trade stagnated.

I continued my education at the Presbyterian Boarding School at Ada and finished up my Standard VII in 1934. I decided then to become a teacher. Unfortunately there was no room at Akropong Training College for fresh students in 1935 and I lost my chance. I then entered the service of the Union Trading Company as a store boy earning ten shillings per month as wages.[23]

The writer's case was typical and in these early post-war years the future leaders of the CPP still held relatively humble positions—relative, that is, to the lawyers, newspaper owners, and merchants among the intelligentsia. They were primary-school teachers, clerks in government and commercial offices, petty traders, storekeepers, local contractors, not very successful businessmen with a one-man, one-lorry transport enterprise or a small import-export trade. And their immediate following was still more humble. The junior-school leaver, and those who failed to complete the full senior course—who lacked the all-important Standard VII certificate—were hardly employable. Some remained in the villages, hoping for employment from a sub-native authority, or working on their uncle's farm; many more travelled to the 'capital town' of their local state, or to Accra, Kumasi, or Sekondi-Takoradi, where they struggled through adolescence in a series of unskilled jobs—as market-stall assistants, messengers

[22] An exception has to be made for Nkrumah—Achimota Training College, and Lincoln College, Pennsylvania; K. A. Gbedemah—Achimota Secondary School; Kojo Botsio—Fourah Bay College, Sierra Leone, and Oxford. The first central committee of the CPP in 1949 consisted of nine members: graduates 2; secondary school 3; elementary school 4.

[23] Stephen Dzirasa, *Political Thought of Dr Nkrumah*. Dzirasa was more fortunate than most: in 1944 he was given a Presbyterian Church scholarship to the seminary college in Kumasi. Later, he was elected to parliament for the CPP, became Resident Minister in Guinea, later Deputy Minister of Ext. Aff. until dismissed by Nkrumah in Feb. 1964.

in government offices, drivers' mates, or apprentices to a master carpenter or motor-fitter who had his 'workshop' under the trees on a vacant lot at the outskirts of the town. But although they were hardly able to follow even the simply-written pages of the CPP *Evening News* or *Morning Telegraph* they were none the less eager to absorb the simple precepts that the party wove into its nationalist appeal: 'We have the right to live as men'; and 'Seek Ye First the Political Kingdom, and All Things will be added unto it'. To these future party members, 'Self-Government Now' had not only an immediate but a practical end, and they gave the CPP their whole-hearted support.

It was from this broad social group of elementary-school-leavers that the leaders of the radical wing of the nationalist movement were drawn in 1949—locally rooted in the village, yet beneficiaries also of an educational system which, for all its short-comings, endowed them with a common language—English—and an awareness of common interests which cut across tribal boundaries. In 1948 they burst suddenly upon the political scene, attributing their grievances to the operation of colonial rule and sweeping aside the UGCC. But, although a new phenomenon in national politics, they were already a familiar element in the Colony and Ashanti chiefdoms, where they were persistent opponents of a native-authority system which offered them no outlet for their energies. For their part, the chiefs and elders watched the growth of an educated commoner class with mounting suspicion and from an early date the elementary-school-leavers were seen as 'malcontents' or 'agitators'—the two local expressions most commonly employed—who hastened to put themselves at the head of any attempt by the commoners to challenge the authority of the chief. Indeed, it was through such activities that the elementary-school-leavers were able to give the demand for self-government a broad base of support. And the CPP was to win its first election victory in 1951 over the earlier generation of political leaders, not merely because it outbid the UGCC in terms of 'Self-Government Now' rather than 'later', but because it enlisted in its ranks the general body of commoners—literate and illiterate alike. Thus, the roots of discontent which fed the strong vein of radicalism in the party went back over many years, to a familiar struggle between the chiefs and their subjects, and in order to explain the genesis of the CPP—and its sudden appear-

ance in 1949—something also needs to be said of the structure of
Akan rule in the Colony and Ashanti chiefdoms.[24]

(b) The Commoners of the Native Authorities

Like many African systems of government, Akan rule rested on
a broad measure of decentralized authority—a characteristic
masked in part by the vesting of great symbolic power in the
chief. In practice, power was exercised by the chief and his counsellors through a finely spun web of subordinate authorities held
together by kinship ties and bonds of fealty between the paramount chief, divisional (or 'wing') chiefs, and village heads. Even
within the Ashanti Confederacy there was a large measure of devolution of authority, and an ever-shifting balance of power between Kumasi and the outlying capitals of the Ashanti chiefdoms. The *asantehene* possessed rights of overlordship in respect of
war service and jurisdiction (though not in landholding); but the
individual Ashanti chiefs had their 'palatine privileges',[25] and
each lesser chief within the circle of authority of his superior was
a centre of power in his own right. In pre-colonial times, 'decen-
tralisation was the keynote of divisional administration—as it
was indeed of the administration of the Confederacy as a whole'.[26]
Throughout the Akan-speaking area, both in Ashanti and the
south, the authority of the chief was tempered by the need to gain
the consent of these intermediaries before it could be effective.

Akan rule had the further distinction, however, of being
grounded on a more popular conception of government than
was perhaps the practice in African societies. The commoners,
as well as the counsellors, or 'elders', not only had rights of their
own but were able to exert some measure of control over the
chief. Admittedly, the successor to a vacant 'Stool' had to be
chosen from among the members of a royal house, and the pro-

---

[24] The brief account which follows is drawn mainly from J. M. Sarbah, *Gold
Coast Customary Law* (1897); J. E. Casely Hayford, *Gold Coast Native Institutions*
(1903); Warrington's *Notes on Ashanti Custom*, compiled by a Committee of the
ACC appointed in 1934 'to lay down the old Ashanti custom as it obtained prior to
1900' and revised in 1941; R. S. Rattray, *Ashanti Law and Constitution* (1929); K. A.
Busia, *The Position of the Chief in the Modern Political System of Ashanti* (1951); W.
Tordoff, 'The Ashanti Confederacy', *J. Afr. Hist.* (1962), iii/3; and early accounts
by T. E. Bowdich, *Mission from Cape Coast Castle to Ashantee* (1819); J. Dupuis,
Journal of a Residence in Ashantee (1824); and F. Ramseyer and J. Kühne, *Four Years
in Kumasi* (1875). Akan government did not cover the whole country, or even the
whole of the Colony and Ashanti, but it was largely among its chiefdoms that the
'young men' or commoners of the CPP had their political origins.
[25] Bowdich, p. 256.   [26] Tordoff, p. 406.

cess of selection of a candidate was begun by the Queen Mother
—usually the aunt or sister of the former chief—who brought forward one of the eligible 'royals' for approval by the elders, that is,
by those who held important Stools within the state.[27] But the
'king-makers' had to be careful not to go against any strong expression of popular disapproval. And if, once installed, the new
chief misbehaved beyond a certain point, particularly if he
'abused the elders' by persistently opposing their advice, he
might be 'destooled' or forced to abdicate. In former times, the
office of chief—and the destoolment charges that might be
brought against him—were bound up with religious observances.
'Unconstitutional behaviour' often meant 'that the chief was no
longer fit to act as intermediary with the ancestors and must be
replaced by a worthier person'.[28] During the colonial period the
charges covered a much wider field until they bordered often
enough on the grotesque—charges were brought against the
chief not only on the grounds that he was ruling unjustly, or making improper use of native authority revenue, but because he was
'greedy' or 'insolent', or 'obese'. By the 1950s it was because he
had taken one side or the other in the struggle between the parties. A common principle, however, was evident throughout traditional and colonial times, namely, that once a chief had lost the
approval of his subjects he could, and should, be deposed; and
deposed not by an act of violence or rebellion but following a
known procedure of preferring charges against him. Moreover,
once deposed, a chief—though he might be treated somewhat
harshly in pre-colonial times—was allowed to live, and even to
return to the Stool should his successor be found even less satisfactory as a ruler. The principle also implied recognition that it
was not the chief, but the Stool, which was sacred. Unlike the
Egyptian pharaoh, the Akan chief never quite became a god. The

[27] The 'Stool' being the symbol and object which enshrined the unity and identity
of the state, or a family. Heirs to a Stool were traced matrilineally in most Colony
and Ashanti chiefdoms (though not in all), through a line of succession in two or
more royal houses from which chiefs were traditionally chosen. In some, the chief
might be a woman (though this was not usual). He (or she) might be quite elderly
(if in good health); he might, on the other hand, be quite young—even a schoolboy.

[28] Tordoff, p. 416. The same point was stressed by Rattray (p. 30). 'A chief
(*ohene*) was also by way of being an *ohene-okomfo*—a priest-king, whose safety and
well-being symbolised that of the state, since he was the intermediary between the
'*samanfo* (ancestral spirits) and his subjects.' The power of the chief (one should perhaps add here) did not rest on land ownership: his subjects held their land by right
of inheritance or (in the southern areas of immigrant cocoa-farmers) by purchase.

authority bestowed on him, though of a sacral nature and derived from his position as an intermediary between the living and the ancestors, could be withdrawn; whereupon—having been destooled—he lost the divinity he had acquired through his office unless he was re-elected. This distinction between the office and the office-holder could also be seen in the attitude adopted towards the 'royals' of a Stool before their election or after their destoolment. The potential chief lived a matter-of-fact life: a 'royal' might be a farmer or trader or (in more modern times) a motor mechanic or school teacher one day, and a chief (perhaps a paramount chief) the day after.

Nevertheless, despite these restraints on the power of the chief, he was undoubtedly feared—a fear heightened by awe and backed by grim penalties. Certainly this was true of pre-colonial times, when attempts to challenge his authority, though permissible in theory, were exposed to severe punishment in practice. They had indeed virtually to be successful before they were tolerated. 'Proceedings to destool a chief' in Ashanti—it was recorded—'might [and still may] be inaugurated by any commoner. . . . He would conduct an insidious campaign among the populace, until public opinion compelled the Elders to act. The chief would then be tried [but] if his accuser could not prove his case he would, in olden times, almost certainly have been killed.'[29] Chiefs *were* destooled, not only in the Akan states of the Colony, but in Ashanti:[30] but it was an undertaking not to be entered upon lightly. And the task was made more difficult in that the very structure of an Akan chiefdom imposed limits on the ability of the commoners to act: because the power of the chief was distributed among a number of subordinate authorities, criticism of his rule also had to be indirect. Thus in 1935, at the restoration of the Ashanti Confederacy Council, when the chiefs were asked to give their views of what had been traditional practice, they agreed that: 'at a meeting of the village Elders every young man has the right to be present and to speak. . . . If the young men as a whole express an opinion the Odikro [village head] is obliged to present their view at the next meeting of the Oman [general assembly]', but they also stressed the need for such views to be

---

[29] Rattray, p. 146.
[30] e.g. the Asantehene Osei Kwame (1771–*c*.1801) was destooled. So was Kofi Karikari (in 1874) for 'rifling the royal mausoleum' in Kumasi, and his successor, Mensa Bonsu, for 'extortion and cruelty' (Tordoff, pp. 415–16).

transmitted through intermediaries and through the proper gradations of authority from subordinate to superior.[31]

Such were the broad outlines of the division of power within Akan society in pre- and early colonial times. In sum, the chief was a powerful, even awesome figure; but he was subject to limits on his freedom of action. His subjects were free men, whose rights in the land they farmed were inalienable (except by themselves). They served the chief in time of war and in respect of such communal services they might be called upon to perform; they obeyed him not least because his authority was exercised more often than not indirectly, and because they saw the chief, and the Stool he represented, as both the guardian and symbol of the well-being of the state as a whole. How well, or how badly, Akan rule regulated local society can only be surmised; nor is it possible (on the evidence so far examined) to say what the relationship was between the chief (*ohene*), elders (*mpanyimfo*), and commoners (*mmerante*) in social or economic terms, or the extent to which they were antagonistic towards each other.[32] One characteristic, however, was noted by early visitors to the local state capitals—including Kumasi—namely, the existence of a turbulent and capricious mob of whom the chiefs and elders complained in despairing terms.[33] In pre-colonial times the balance

[31] Warrington, p. 17.

[32] The internal social or economic divisions of Akan traditional society are naturally difficult to assess. Polly Hill has begun to unravel some of the economic relationships which existed in late-traditional, early-colonial times among the farming and trading communities in southern and Ashanti society (see e.g. her article in *Econ. Bull.*, vi/1 (1962)). I. Wilks has begun to examine the structure of Ashanti traditional government, as in his paper on 'Some Developments in Akan Administrative Practice in the 17th and 18th Centuries', read to the Historical Society of Ghana in January 1959.

The phrases used earlier—*ohene, mpanyimfo*, and *mmerante* (chief, elders, and commoners) are those used to describe (in *twi* or *asante*) the three main social groups in the Akan areas. Similar expressions were (and are) used among the Fanti chiefdoms in the south, where the commoners also adapted the *asafo* organization—originally a body of fighting men around the chief—as a semi-permanent social and political organization through which they expressed their grievances. They formed 'the third estate or the common people . . . referred to politically as *mbrantsie* or "young men" to distinguish them from the *mpanyifu* or chiefs and elders', according to J. W. de Graft Johnson in his article on 'The Fanti Asafu' in *Africa*, 1932. The *asafo* he describes as a 'socio-political-military organisation'. The head of a company was a *tufuhin*, or 'chief of the gunners', a title bestowed later by popular usage on Nkrumah in a modern spelling—*tufuhene*. The commoners in Ashanti were also said to have their own local spokesmen—the *nkwankwaahene*—the 'leader of the young men'. See below, p. 24.

[33] Towns were rowdy places in traditional times. Bowdich (p. 250), on his visit to Kumasi, described the three most important groups at court as being the king, the aristocracy, and the general assembly of the 'Caboceers and Captains', but

of power between the different sections of Akan society was tilted
on the side of the chief because of the indispensable functions he
performed as a war leader, magistrate and priest. It was fundamentally disturbed, however, by colonial rule. And in respect of
the growth of popular discontent three broad stages may be noted.

1. In the early years of British administration, first in the
Colony, later in Ashanti, the power of the chiefs was deliberately
curtailed by the chief commissioners and their district officers.
The commoners on the other hand were not only more free to act
than at any time previously, but began to enjoy a much greater
sense of independence based on the income derived from the sale
of palm oil and cocoa and, led in many instances by the growing
number of educated young men, they seized the opportunity to
rid themselves of any chiefs they disliked out of what might well
be thought to have been a long pent-up emotion. By the end of
the First World War there was every sign that a considerable
struggle was in progress. In the Kwahu state in the Colony, for
example, 'the *asafo* company of young men' was reported by the
district commissioner in 1919 as having become 'a dangerous
and most undesirable element in the politics of Kwahu', and the
elders complained of 'the growing power of the youngmen which
is breaking the power of the chiefs'. In Ashanti: 'In the case of
Bekwai [a local market town] . . . the youngmen, that is to say,
the lower classes, those who were not elders, complained that they
were not consulted in the choice of Headchief . . . and to a man
they refused to serve him.'[34] The Kwahu and Bekwai examples
were only two in a long series of local conflicts described by the
officials, in which the elders were noted as siding sometimes with,
sometimes against, the chief until a position of near-anarchy existed in many of the smaller Colony states where, as Sir Gordon
Guggisberg complained: 'in the Central Province [of the Colony]

---

added that there was also 'the mob', or 'lower order' of Kumasi society, whom the
asantehene called 'the worst people existing, except the Fantees'. The *asafo* of the
southern towns were frequently a cause of riot in the early days of British rule when
the different companies put on their ceremonial dress and sallied forth to challenge
each other. Cape Coast had its special *akrampafu* company—the mulattoes—with
dark green tunics, cummerbunds, white drill jackets, helmets with a green
'puggaree' and black trousers with a red border. Each company had its flags and
drums (*akrampafu*=a drum and fife band).

[34] *Report on Ashanti for 1920*. On this occasion, the elders sided with the commoners. 'One cannot be a chief without subjects' (they were reported as saying).
'If we support the Headchief we shall be alone. The whole of the youngmen refuse
to serve the Headchief and we support them.'

practically the whole of the Paramount Chiefs, with exceptions that can be numbered on the fingers of one hand, have all been destooled or are on the point of being destooled by their people.'[35]

2. A second stage was then reached when the chiefs began to turn for help to the colonial government and were encouraged to do so by the very administrators who had formerly been suspicious of their power. By the 1920s theories of indirect rule were being grasped by the officials who saw in them a coherent, reasoned explanation of what they themselves now believed should be done in the rural areas. They began therefore to extend their protection to the chiefs, and to entrust them with new powers as presidents of native authorities. The most far-reaching reforms were brought about in the relative calm of the Northern Territories in 1934 with only minor opposition;[36] then—after many tentative beginnings—in Ashanti, where the officials worked hard to buttress the authority of the chiefs until, as Rattray observed: 'Every political office is familiar with the dictum, "the power and authority of the Paramount Chief must be upheld" '—a process culminating in the Native Authority Acts of 1935 and the restoration of the Confederacy under the Asantehene Prempeh II.[37] 'The present political unrest in some Divisions', the Chief Commissioner warned the first full meeting of the Council in 1936, 'is due to the inclination of some young men taking upon themselves the onus of electing their chief, and in fact endeavouring to administer their Divisions'; and the chiefs responded by attacking the locally chosen representatives of the commoners. They resolved unanimously that: 'The positions of *Nkwankwaahene* and *Asafoakye*, also *Asafo* should be abolished from the

[35] GC, LC Deb., Statement by the Governor, 3 Feb. 1925.

[36] There was little social basis for opposition to the chief in the north where only 4,000 children were attending school even as late as 1948 (0·42 per cent of the total northern population). Still, the northern protectorate was never hermetically sealed off from the rest of the country: carpenters, clerks, masons, came up from the south; labourers migrated southwards—over 100,000 in 1935–6. One might note too the remark of the Zuarungu chief quoted in the 1916 *Report on the Northern Territories*: 'Before I was made a chief, the people around here used to say—"When the Whiteman goes away, we will teach the Chief some sense".' Chiefs in such an area were very much government creations and their subjects never wholly forgot the fact.

[37] Rattray, p. 400. Stool treasuries were introduced into Ashanti on a voluntary experimental basis under an ordinance of 1927. (The first was in the Agona Division.) NAs were then established by law in the same year as the restoration (31 Jan. 1935) of the Confederacy.

whole of Ashanti in view of the fact that they are the cause of
political unrest in Ashanti.'[38] The *nkwankwaahene* was an unofficial title bestowed on the local 'spokesman' of the young men
(the *nkwankwaa* or *mmerante* being the main body of the commoners); the *asafoakye* was a similar title found in the southern
Akim states.[39] The Colony chiefdoms, on the other hand, remained a battle-ground until almost a decade later, when Burns
overhauled the courts (including the enforcement of the elementary requirement that fines and fees should be paid into a treasury), and introduced a comprehensive Native Authority Ordinance. The chiefs were then equipped (as Burns himself was prepared to admit) 'with considerable powers exceeding those which
the chiefs possessed under Native Custom', making it 'no longer
possible for a handful of malcontents to paralyse the activities of
a State' by 'fishing in the muddy waters of Stool intrigue'.[40]

It was not difficult to sympathize with Burns's attitude at the
time, many of the attempts at destoolment being engineered by
enterprising young men who were interested more in the profit
to be gained from Stool disputes than in commoner rights.[41] The
fact remained, however, that the attack launched by the chiefs on
the young men in the 1930s and 1940s resulted in the general en-
hancement of their authority at the commoners' expense. And
not all the criticisms voiced of their rule were unjustified. The

[38] ACC *Minutes*, Jan. 1936.

[39] Cf. Busia (p. 10): 'The commoners or young men (*mmerante* as they are called
in Ashanti), played an important part in the election [of a chief]. . . . They had a
recognised leader or spokesman, the *Nkwankwaahene* . . . whose position was of
political importance as it enabled the commoners to criticize the chief. The elders
and the chief formed the Government and were jointly responsible for any decision
they made . . .'. The title was also used to denote a chief-designate—one who had
not been formally enstooled or taken the oath of allegiance to his superior. The
position survived among a number of Brong chiefdoms into the 1960s when the
'spokesmen of the commoners' were still a powerful force in local politics, particularly over the allocation of land by the chief to 'strangers' who wished to farm in
the area.

[40] *Colonial Civil Servant*, pp. 203–4. Hailey's comment on the 1944 Native
Authority Ordinance was apt: 'The Paramount Chiefs have not in the past been
accustomed to see themselves as agencies of local government or as integral parts of
the machinery of government . . . and if today they have acquiesced in some measure of control, it is because acceptance of the status of Native Authority has seemed
preferable to the future indicated for them by the more radical outlook of the progressive section in Gold Coast politics' (*Native Administration in the British African
Territories*, Pt 3 (1951), p. 226).

[41] e.g. the 'Friends of Ashanti Freedom Society', led by Bankole Renner in
Accra, and O. S. Agyeman in Kumasi, which tried to prevent the restoration of the
Ashanti Confederacy in 1935, and (when this failed) brought embarrassing charges
against the Asantehene—to the effect that Prempeh had violated custom by being
circumcised.

European Superintendent of Agriculture, Wright, made a bitter attack on the chiefs in 1936.

Many of you here [he told the Ashanti Confederacy Council] are the most difficult obstacles on the path to progress. In the large percentage of cases where a chief was favourable to cooperatives we found that the members of the society, in a very natural manner, elected their chief as president of the society. That at first seemed an excellent thing. Unfortunately, experience has taught us that for farmers to elect their chief as president . . . spells certain failure . . . . Our strong enthusiastic and progressive societies are those where the chief is not included in the membership. Now why is this? I think I can give you an explanation. You object to having an independent organisation in your village, and a cooperative society concerns only the farmers. . . You resent this and it is this feeling of resentment which constitutes a very real bar to progress.[42]

A similar attitude on the part of the chiefs towards their own subjects was noticed during the great cocoa hold-up of 1937. The decision to withhold the main crop from the buying stations was taken by the general run of farmers—while the chiefs looked on, suspicious at first, then joining later, and wanting the farmers' associations disbanded as soon as the hold-up was over. Relations between the chiefs and the commoners were also strained in a number of districts by the steady movement of families out of their home areas to neighbouring and distant chiefdoms. The migration of cocoa farmers in the eastern province of the Colony, for example, led to very large tracts of Akim land being acquired by 'strangers' from the neighbouring Akwapim, Shai, and Krobo states, who paid tribute, but owed no allegiance, to the chiefs of the area. (Tribute was as high as a 1d. a cocoa tree, or 3s. 4d. a load of 60 lb., at a time when the price paid by the firms was under 10s. a load.)[43] And although some of the native authorities

[42] ACC *Minutes*, Jan. 1936. Unlike the Colony chiefs, however, the Ashanti rulers were chiefs with a bad conscience. By 1943 the Asantehene was warning his fellow chiefs that 'the present system of elections is very bad; some of the electors make their personal choice without the approval of the young men. I must explain that although the youngmen have no voice in the administration yet since they are the taxpayers it is always necessary that they should be consulted' (*Minutes*, Aug. 1943). There was an underlying unity in Ashanti, even between the chiefs and the educated young men, as the CPP was to discover in 1954.

[43] In the 1930s a load of cocoa was plucked from approximately 40 trees. For a pioneering account of the migrations of southern cocoa farmers, see Polly Hill, *The Gold Coast Farmer* (1956), and the series of monographs by her published by the Economics Research Division of the Univ. College of Ghana, 1958–60.

widened their councils a little to adjust the balance of representation to these and other changes, the changes came too late, and were too modest, to meet the growing complaints of the elementary school-leavers and the commoners in general.[44]

3. The effect was plain. Throughout the southern half of the country, the belief spread that the rights of the 'ordinary man' were being ignored—a belief expressed later by the CPP in the saying that 'chiefs no longer sit on Stools but on Gazettes'. The commoners did what they could to protest by defying the chiefs and making use of positions such as that of *nkwankwaahene* in Ashanti and the Colony *asafo* companies.[45] But the limits of such action were clear, for at best it had the negative success of destooling a chief only to find that his successor was also obliged to look for support to the district commissioner. And in the 1930s and 1940s, as the great flood of elementary-school-leavers flowed from the primary schools into the southern towns and villages, the commoners began to turn to new forms of organization. The instruments lay close to hand. Local scholars' unions, literary and debating clubs, youth movements, and improvement societies, had already begun to be formed in the state capitals and market centres at least as early as the 1920s. They were brought together

[44] e.g. by 1946 the Akim Abuakwa State Council in the Colony consisted of 40 members, including 'two representatives of the Scholars' Union, three of the Strangers' Community, the Legal Adviser to the Council [a barrister] and two representatives of the Church'; but (as Hailey observed) the great majority were 'Divisional Chiefs, sub-chiefs, or *Adikrofo*', and the Akim Abuakwa reforms were 'somewhat exceptional' (Hailey, p. 206).

[45] A particular example from the records of the ACC may help to illustrate the way in which agitation was often conducted. As late as 1944 a group of 'malcontents' who were dissatisfied with the management of the Nkoranza NA finances attempted to voice their complaints through the *nkwankwaahene*—despite the 1936 Order. They applied for permission to be present at the next meeting of the NA council; but being illiterate (or, probably, semi-literate) they wrote through a letter-writer who used—it was said—'unhappy and misguided words'. The leaders were brought before the local court and accused of 'undermining the chief', and eventually the case went before the Confederacy Council in Kumasi where it was recorded that one of the petitioners was 'though not so officially recognized [the] acknowledged leader of the "young men"'. The chiefs agreed that 'this would appear to have been the cause of much misfortune, for organized leadership of the *Nkwankwaa* or the common people, called *nkwankwaahene*, is abolished in Nkoranza'. The four leaders of the group were removed from Nkoranza to Kumasi by order of the Confederacy Council as being (in the stock phrase) 'the cause of political unrest and disorder'; and an appeal to the Chief Commissioner brought the uncompromising reply: '(1) No subsistence allowance will be paid to you. Over 15,000 strangers are able to make a living in Kumasi and you should be able to do likewise. (2) Your relatives can look after your farms. (3) It is most unlikely that you will ever be permitted to return to Nkoranza' (ACC, *Minutes*, 1945, App. 'U'). Here, undoubtedly, were three enthusiasts of a future People's Party.

in the first instance very often as friendly societies and social gatherings. But their members (including illiterates as well as 'scholars') also discussed local and national problems, including the general grievance of the educated minority that the structure of native-authority rule held no opportunities for a career open to such talents as the elementary-school-leavers possessed. And by 1948–9 each of these little societies was an active nucleus of an anti-chief, anti-colonial movement, quick to acquire new life as a radical commoners' party.[46]

Here, then, lay the long-term explanation of the upheavals of the post-war years: in the emergence of a new political class, radical in outlook, and urgent in expressing its needs. The commoners gave depth to nationalist demands, the elementary-school-leavers gave national direction to local grievances. And it was the long-term growth of an educated commoner class which enabled the CPP to spread so quickly after 1949. Formed as a homespun People's Party, its nationalist appeal struck home along a broad front among the disgruntled commoners: the youth societies became branches, and the malcontents party secretaries. The commoners flocked to these local leaders who, in turn, welcomed Nkrumah as a National Hero, like themselves of humble origin, and whom they recognized as a political organizer of very great ability. The particular grievances of the post-war years, therefore—though clearly important in bringing the unrest to the point of riots—only added fuel to a fire already smouldering and ready to burst into flame. The Ghana nationalist movement had its roots in the villages, among the commoners of the native authorities, many years before it found expression in a national People's Party, and the officials were taken by surprise because they underestimated the speed with which nationalist demands would spread once they became latched on to local discontents. In more general terms, the officials were taken by surprise because they were too closely allied with the chiefs and the intelligentsia; and—like them—they became victims of not only a national but a social revolution. Thus when, in due course, the administration responded to the riots by hurrying forward the re-

[46] There is a picture of the leading members of a typical 'Literary Society' in Nkrumah's *Autobiography*, facing p. 32. This was in Nzima—a relatively remote area—in the 1930s. It was through the Nzima Literary Society (says Nkrumah) that he 'met Mr S. R. Wood who was then secretary of the National Congress of British West Africa. This rare character first introduced me to politics' (p. 21).

forms already begun, and a first general election was held, the result was a foregone conclusion: the CPP was carried into office on
the votes of the commoners and the young men.

THE STRUGGLE FOR POWER

Once the first general election had been held in February 1951,
the officials, party leaders, and observers alike, had good grounds
for believing that the revolution was over. The commoners were
in office. Nationalism had won its first African victory. And in
July 1953 Nkrumah called upon the United Kingdom government to follow its declared policy of granting its colonies self-
government. There were, he said, no obstacles in the way:

> There is no conflict that I can see between our claims and the pro-
> fessed policy of all parties and governments of the United Kingdom.
> We have here in our country a stable society. Our economy is healthy,
> as good as any for a country our size. In many respects, we are much
> better off than many sovereign states. And our potentialities are large.
> Our people are fundamentally homogeneous, nor are we plagued with
> religious and tribal problems. . .[47]

This was how the country looked at the time. And in June 1954
the CPP was returned to power after a second general election.
Yet within a few months—by the end of 1954—a violent conflict
swept across Ashanti and part of the Colony, to add to the difficulties of the CPP in the north and Togoland. Thus the nationalist leaders, in their turn, were taken by surprise.

The primary cause was not difficult to discover. Just as the
colonial administrators in 1946 had exaggerated the extent of
division in the country because of their preoccupation with
native-authority affairs, so in 1954 the nationalist leaders overrated the strength of party loyalties because of their sweeping
victory in the 1951 election. But the excitement of that first contest was difficult to sustain, if only because the party's success had
been too easily won. The primary objective of the CPP was virtually attained within five years of the party's formation: the elementary-school-leavers were in power in Accra—in the new
ministries and a national legislative assembly; their followers had
gained control in the chiefdoms, where in 1952 a major reform of
local government had been carried through, the native authorities being replaced by new local authorities, two-thirds of whose

---

[47] GC, LC Deb., 10 July 1953.

members were elected on an adult suffrage, and only one-third
chosen by the state councils of the chief and his elders. In such circumstances it was difficult for the leaders to maintain control
over the rank and file, and still more so over the electorate as a
whole. And, as nationalist aims receded, local interests came to
the fore.

The CPP then found itself faced with a much stronger challenge than that provided earlier by the colonial administration.
Whereas in 1949 the leaders had set sail over a broad sea of discontent to run freely before the wind, they now had to grapple
with what was loosely (often misleadingly) described as 'tribalism': an amalgam of local interests and sentiment which drew
additional strength from particular grievances. As a result, religious minorities—notably the Muslims; ethnic groups—the Ewe
in southern Togoland; historic units—Ashanti; and administrative units—including the Northern Territories whose peoples
had acquired their own sense of local identity: all began to stress
the need for prior recognition of their own claims before the
country as a whole became self-governing until (by the end of
1954) the political scene presented a very different picture from
the early days of the nationalist party. The judgement once
passed by Martin Wight, that the Gold Coast lacked the 'self-
aware unity that is the essence of nationality', now seemed much
less antiquated than it had done in 1949. To be sure, none of the
dissident groups which tried to challenge the CPP was likely, by
itself, to worry the nationalist leaders. But the opportunity
afforded the small intelligentsia group which had continued to
oppose the CPP was not missed. Under a new leader, Dr K. A.
Busia of the University College, they hastened to add their support. They formed an alliance between the opposition parties,
placed themselves at its head, and called for revision of the 1954
constitution along federal lines, thus adding a national element
to the opposition and an impressive intellectual gloss to the demand for 'Federation' which the Ashanti cocoa farmers and the
northern chiefs could hardly have devised by themselves.

Although taken completely by surprise, the CPP leaders succeeded in rallying the party. They reaffirmed its appeal as a
nationalist commoners' movement, and gained support (even in
Ashanti) from those who disliked the alliance of the chiefs and the
intellectuals. They also used their powers as a government to ex-

ploit divisions among their opponents, and played skilfully on the alarm generated among the southern Fanti chiefdoms at the apparent resurgence of an Ashanti nationalism. In the struggle for power which occupied Ghanaian politics between 1954 and 1956 the party more than succeeded in holding its own. In the third election in July 1956 it won 72 of the 104 seats in parliament. This was a repetition of the earlier success in 1954. Nevertheless, the election was hard fought. No one doubted it at the time. In terms of votes, the CPP won only 57 per cent, and its opponents 43 per cent, of the poll in the 99 contested constituencies; it was also out-seated, and out-voted, in Ashanti and the north. And whether one counted votes or seats one fact at least seemed to stand out: it seemed clear that the country had travelled a long way from the single-party dominated election of 1951, and the first onrush of nationalist demands after 1949. Indeed, the grant of independence in March 1957 was based on this assumption. A series of meetings between the Secretary of State, the CPP, and the opposition (whose leaders quietly dropped the demand for federation), reached agreement on draft proposals for a new Order in Council whereby the unitary constitution which in 1950 had replaced the Burns constitution (and which in 1954 had been amended to provide for full internal self-government) was now recast. Legislative and executive control was retained at the centre; but interim regional assemblies were introduced, and entrenched clauses inserted to meet the demands of the opposition for constitutional and minority safeguards.

Once more, therefore, it seemed as though a new base for a stable political régime had been secured in the agreement between the CPP and the opposition, and that it might well support a majority–minority party system. The 1957 parliament began to function along familiar 'Westminster' lines. There were able party leaders on both sides. The country continued prosperous. It was also possible to argue that the lines of division between the commoners and the chiefs were becoming blurred and, therefore, blunted as many of the opposition chiefs hastened to come to terms with the government party, and the elementary-school-leavers acquired property and status beyond their early dreams. There seemed reasonable hope, therefore, that the violent scenes of 1954–7 might be forgotten, as those of 1948 had been during the first years of parliamentary rule.

THE SINGLE-PARTY REPUBLIC

Once again, however, appearances were deceptive, and for the third time in this brief span of years, the political scene was to change in dramatic fashion. As the CPP government asserted its sovereignty, the opposition (re-grouped as a United Party) crumbled, and the 1957 constitution was revised drastically by being shorn of its regional assemblies and constitutional safeguards. Then, in June 1959, Nkrumah revived a claim which had been allowed—perforce—to lapse. On the occasion of the tenth anniversary of the CPP, a large party rally in Accra was told: 'Comrades, it is no idle boast when I say that . . . the Convention People's Party is Ghana. Our party not only provides the government but is the custodian which stands guard over the welfare of the people.'[48] The corollary to this claim was drawn a year later by John Tettegah, general secretary of the Ghana TUC, who was reported as telling a local party rally that 'those who sit outside the ranks of the CPP forfeit their right to citizenship in the country. For it is only within the CPP that any constructive thing can be done for Ghana.'[49]

The actual events which transformed the agreed constitution of independence into the single-party republic will be discussed in a final chapter. Here, however, one may ask: what was there in

---

[48] The speech is printed in the *Evening News*, 16 June 1959. Nkrumah's claim that the 'CPP is Ghana' was implicit in the party objectives set out in 1949 'to win self-government for the chiefs and people of the Gold Coast': a nationalist party by definition seeks to represent the whole state. But it had disappeared during the party conflict of 1954-7, and it is interesting to compare two other quotations with the one given here, the first at the time when the CPP seemed unchallengeable, the other when it was on the defensive.

The first is from the *Evening News* of 3 Aug. 1952, during the 3rd annual Delegates' Conference, when 'Africanus' (Nkrumah ? Kojo Botsio ? Kofi Baako ?) examined 'the childish argument that the Gold Coast must obtain a stronger opposition' and claimed that 'we have in the Gold Coast (a) the elected Party of the People—CPP; (b) the party of the reactionary lackeys who still seem to have fooled some of the people, UGCC; (c) representatives of the British Government; (d) independent representatives. . . . As a party the CPP has filled and is filling the purpose for which it was founded, i.e. to fill the needs of all the people. Any other groups formed or forming will be artificial and non-representative. . . .'.

The second quotation comes from Nkrumah's speech at the 6th anniversary rally of the CPP in Accra in June 1955 at the height of the opposition challenge: 'I have always expressed both in public and in private that we need a strong and well organised Opposition Party in the country and the Assembly'; and: 'We must not forget that democracy means the rule of the majority, though it should be tempered by sweet reasonableness in the interests of the minority. In a parliamentary democracy legitimate constitutional opposition is part of its fabric . . .' (ibid. 14 June 1955).

[49] Ibid. 14 Apr. 1960.

general terms in the whole period between 1946 and 1960 which
led to this conclusion? There were several explanations—including two offered by Nkrumah in his *Autobiography* and in a number
of speeches after independence;[50] and it may be useful to discuss
Nkrumah's own views first. One was an argument drawn from
African principles—that single-party rule was a natural development of African society. The other, an argument from necessity—
that new states needed strong governments which were best provided for by concentrating authority within a single party.

The justification of single-party rule as a natural phenomenon
of African politics was far from simple. It implied, for instance,
that opposition to the CPP prior to independence was in some
sense unreal. This is indeed an argument put forward by Nkrumah in his *Autobiography*. Here the federation alliance—which
had held up independence for more than two years and had
gained a substantial percentage of the vote in 1956—is dismissed in retrospect as an 'uncooperative minority' which could
hardly have exercised the influence it had on current events but
for the backing provided by the United Kingdom government
and the tolerance shown towards it by the CPP.[51] Its continuance
after 1957 was dismissed as being motivated by 'a few disloyal
elements . . . who had striven to spoil the good name of Ghana
through tribalistic incitement, unconstitutional methods and
violence'.[52] Thus earlier assertions of the need for a 'strong and
well organised Opposition Party' were forgotten (or ignored)
and, instead, the theory was put forward that the concept of a
formal opposition was alien to Ghanaian (and African) practice.
Opposition (it now began to be argued) implied formal recognition of a principle of division that had no place in African society
which was corporate by nature, and communal in behaviour: it

[50] *Autobiography* and *I Speak of Freedom* (1961). The latter volume consists of a
number of speeches, linked together by a synopsis of principal events with the sub-
title: 'A Statement of African Ideology'.
[51] 'There can be few, if any, governments in the world who can have exercised so
much tolerance and devoted so much time to considering the whims of such an uncooperative minority, as my Government did during these years.' And: 'The
British Government were the only body who could have forced these obstruction-
ists to see sense, but they remained aloof, apart from giving publicity to the Ashanti
situation in both Houses of Parliament and through the Press. Thus their actions
actually served as a stimulant to the unrest in Ashanti. Unless the lawless element
felt fully confident of such backing, they would never have dared to persist in their
actions' (*Autobiography*, pp. 280 & 242).
[52] Address to annual Delegates' Conference, 2 Aug. 1959 (*Evening News*, 3 Aug.
1959).

was said that the new Ghana state, and the party, were 'essentially corporate in nature, and the TUC, farmers and cooperatives
as well as other elements must regard themselves as inseparable
constituents of a united whole'. Phrases were also borrowed from
abroad to emphasize the notion of a collective unity. ' "Let
flowers of many colours blossom, let various schools of thought
contend". But let discussion and criticism spring from absolute
loyalty and, thence, when the majority has decided, to the harmony of opposites which is the essence of democratic centralism.'
And the flourish was added: 'Long live unconquerable CPP,
Long live Katamanto Kwame Nkrumah, Teacher and Author of
the Revolution'.[53] Translated to Ghanaian soil, and set in a pan-
African context, these aphorisms were given the title 'Nkrumaism'—an 'ideology' which (it was asserted) 'emphasises African
originality' and 'teaches (*inter alia*) that African social concepts
are diametrically opposed to individual property rights'.[54] In
July 1960 the argument was formally embodied in a new republican constitution which was said to reflect the 'historical forms of
government in Ghana in the past'. The expression of an 'African
Personality' appeared in detail as well as substance, the seating
arrangements in the new parliament of 114 members being
altered from a Westminster pattern of opposed benches 'to form
the letter "U" ', because 'the previous arrangement was incompatible with our traditions': and—added Kojo Botsio, Minister
of State—'because the concept of an organised opposition was
unknown in Ghana's traditional ruling houses'.[55]

The difficulties in the way of accepting such arguments were
immense. It required an act of faith, rather than the exercise of
reason, to believe that a constitution designed by party leaders in
1960 for a modern state should owe very much to the traditional
institutions of a pre-colonial era. Was it Akan, Dagomba, Ewe, or

[53] *Evening News*, 31 July & 1 Aug. Two articles on the 'State of the Party'.
[54] Ibid. in article on 'Nkrumaism as an Ideology', 19, 20, 21 Nov. 1959. See
below, pp. 408–9.
[55] See too Nkrumah's broadcast on the eve of the April 1960 plebiscite to decide
whether Ghana should become a republic. 'In putting these [draft constitutional]
proposals before you, we have given much thought to the historical forms of government in Ghana in the past, and have always had in mind the need for a Constitution which befits our traditions.' And: 'under the proposed Constitution, the
Offices of Head of State and Head of Government are combined to give practical
interpretation to our conditions and traditional experience in the matter of government. . . . In effect, Ghana gives the world a unique and outstanding precedent in
the drawing up of a modern Constitution, based on the actual democratic demands
of party politics with the background of African circumstances.'

Ga patterns which had re-emerged? Perhaps such doubts would be considered frivolous or pedantic; it might be argued that there were underlying principles of African traditional rule which were able to find modern expression under African self-government. But if Akan government were taken as the model, then what appeared to be the collective uniformity of local society dissolved, on closer inspection, into a number of opposed groups, whether in state matters over Stool disputes, or in civil cases over land boundaries and private feuds. Indeed, had it been argued that the struggle between rival royal houses for the succession to a Stool provided an excellent training ground for the operation of a modern two-party system, it would have been hardly less plausible than the assertion that the obligations of a common allegiance to the chief implied acceptance of a uniform political system. In fact, it was difficult to believe that either assertion had much validity. 'African government' was too vague a concept to be of use in assessing particular forms of rule, and 'tradition' became a bottomless well of uncertain practice from which endless arguments could be drawn to justify whatever was thought desirable in current practice.[56]

It was noticeable, too, that the CPP leaders were unwilling to rely on the natural operation of what was said to be a liking for political uniformity within a communal society. On the contrary: they made a determined effort after 1957 to impress their authority on the country, partly through symbolic acts (as in the introduction of stamps and coins bearing Nkrumah's profile), more particularly through harsh measures of a legal and administrative nature, including the use (from 1958 onwards) of a Preventive Detention Act. They were very successful. Whereas in March 1957 the opposition was a solid feature of the political landscape, three years later it had all but disappeared as an

---

[56] It was possible to find some justification for regarding traditional African society as (in Sekou Touré's phrase) a *communaucracie*, e.g. in Rattray's description of Ashanti: 'Action, thoughts, certainly speech on all occasions were corporate affairs. It is not easy for us to realise what must have been the effect of untold generations of thinking and speaking not in terms of one's self but in relationship to a group' (p. 403). And Rattray saw Ashanti society as 'a true democracy'. But this somewhat romantic view of village life was very far removed from the single-party régime of the nationalist state. Nor would Nkrumah have agreed with Rattray. In 1950, having been mauled by the NLM, he was more inclined to believe that 'the unhappy history of Ashanti . . . has made the acceptance and practice of democracy in that part of the country more difficult than elsewhere' (*Autobiography*, p. 220).

organized force. CPP control over the country was almost complete, through the use of government-sponsored organizations like the Ghana Farmers' Council, the Ghana TUC, the National Co-operative Council, and the Women's League; and in April 1960 Nkrumah was given almost 90 per cent of the votes against Dr J. B. Danquah in the election for presidency. The single party was virtually in existence. But to argue from this mortal decline in the fortunes of the opposition a principle of African politics was to ignore the actual course of events between 1957 and 1960. Part at least of the explanation of the withering away of the United Party lay in the determination among the CPP leaders to see that it was blighted; and the outcome of the 1960 plebiscite reflected far more the power of the government to secure the results it wanted than an accurate measure of the degree of support for one side or the other.[57]

The other explanation advanced by Nkrumah of the course of events after 1957 lay in the need for strong executive control in a newly-independent state: 'Even a system based on social justice and a democratic constitution may need backing up during the period following independence by emergency measures of a totalitarian kind'.[58] The same argument appeared in the *Statement by the Government on the Recent Conspiracy* (December 1961)[59] which declared that 'the strains experienced by an emergent country immediately after independence are certainly as great as, if not greater than, the strains experienced by a developed country in war time' (p. 34). The argument is familiar and has a convincing air about it, although the analogy is not wholly clear; who is the enemy? The answer given by Nkrumah varied: sometimes it was 'neo-colonialism'—the malignant activities of former colonial powers—sometimes tribalism, sometimes both in unison. But the assumption behind either charge was the same, that Ghanaian society was dangerously open to attack from enemies within and outside the nationalist gate. Hence the need for a unifying nationalist party.

This was a very different assessment from that given by Nkru-

[57] In short, the detailed results of the plebiscite were not to be trusted except as a measure of the control which the CPP had over its agents—regional and district commissioners and party secretaries. See below, ch. viii.

[58] *Autobiography*, p. x.

[59] The occasion was the strike of railway and harbour workers in Sekondi in September of that year.

mah to parliament in 1953, and one may suppose that the federation issue raised in 1954 had alarmed the CPP leaders more than
they cared to confess. Moreover, by 1958 they had further cause
for alarm when it was found that sometime in June or July of that
year the general secretary of the United Party and a fellow opposition member of parliament had begun to explore the possibility
of staging an armed coup d'état against the government. It was
difficult to accept the evidence in its entirety. Nevertheless, a
Commission of Inquiry appointed to inquire into the strange conduct of an army major (and indirectly into that of R. R. Amponsah and M. K. Apaloo—the two opposition members of parliament) concluded that there had in fact been a conspiracy 'to
carry out at some future date an act for an unlawful purpose
which was revolutionary in character'. [60] Here was proof indeed, it
seemed, of the dangers of opposition. It was proof, too, to the
CPP leaders that 'totalitarian measures' were needed not only to
meet such threats, but to safeguard the nationalist party on which
(it was argued) the hope of a stable political system rested. Otherwise (again it could be argued) there was a danger that the as yet
half-formed national will would slacken, and open the way to
subversion. A disciplined mass party, however, would be able to
breathe national life into a divided society; it could mobilize the
resources of the country in an undivided, undistracted effort to
raise living standards until in time (under proper control) a
modern state would emerge, 'with electric street lights, a motor
road and other amenities'. [61]

[60] As full an account as it is possible to have of the strange episode of what became known as the 'Labadi T junction affair' will be found in Ghana, *Proceedings
and Report of the Commission appointed to Enquire into the Matters Disclosed at the Trial of
Capt. Benjamin Awhaitey before a Court Martial* (1959), the Government's *Statement on
the Report* and the rival *Statement* 'In Defence of Ghana' published by the United
Party. The three Commissioners—an Englishman, a West Indian, and a Ghanaian
—reached the unanimous conclusion quoted above. Two of the Commissioners also
said that there had been a definite intention to assassinate Nkrumah on 19 December 1958 at the airport before he left for India. The Englishman (Granville Sharp)
disagreed: he thought the conspiracy had been called off some time before December. The evidence produced at the inquiry was most puzzling, contradictory in
some parts, unbelievable in others. If ever intended, the proposed coup was of a
grossly amateurish nature, so clumsily devised that it is difficult to believe even the
handful of participants had any hopes of its succeeding. Extracts are printed as
App. B, below, p. 424.
[61] As a typical example of the fusion of traditional and modern ways, one might
quote the description in the *Ghanaian Times*, 27 Jan. 1960, of the party at work in a
rural area: 'The people of Bahanase in the Atwima No. 1 area near Kumasi at the
week-end celebrated their annual 'Fofie' festival at Behanase. The highlight of the
festival was a durbar which was attended by a large number of people including the

Such an argument needed no African gloss to justify it—although after 1960 it could draw a growing volume of evidence from the new African states to support its case. Indeed, it was hard to square with the earlier argument that single-party rule was a natural product of African society except on the grounds that it was 'natural' for African leaders to introduce harsh methods of control. There was a contrary chain of argument, however, reaching a very different conclusion from that drawn by the CPP leaders. It started from a denial that in 1957—or at any time before and after independence—the country was in danger of division. It stressed instead the underlying stability and cohesion of the state as a national unit, arguing that the very strength of the CPP as a nationalist movement reflected that unity. The argument recognized that the 1954–7 struggle was bitterly fought, but pointed out that—with one exception—the party disputes of those years did not carry with them any serious threat of secession. On the contrary, they were useful in helping to purge the country of its tribal spleen. The exception was important—the fact that a section of the Ewe people of the southern Togoland trust territory preferred to link themselves with the neighbouring Togo Republic. They had, indeed, registered their protest against CPP rule in March 1957 by a clumsy attempt at a local armed rebellion. But the revolt was limited to a narrow area of the trust territory, easily suppressed, and—so the argument ran—of a totally different order from that made by the other members of the opposition alliance. In Ashanti, the north, and the large Colony chiefdom Akim Abuakwa, the 1954–7 struggle needed to be seen not in over-simplified terms of Ashanti *versus* the Colony, or the north *versus* the south, but as an infinitely varied conflict in which districts, chiefdoms, and local groups of one kind and another—including the old conflict between the commoners and the chiefs—were opposed to each other in party guise. The opposition leaders, it was true, played dangerously at the time with the demand for federation and with talk of seces-

---

[CPP] District Commissioner, Mr J. K. Donkor. The local fetish priest, Obosomfuor Yaw Kye, commended the efforts of Mr Donkor in providing electric street lights, a motor road and other amenities in the town. . . . Obosomfuor Kye poured libation and said prayers against the proposed French atom test in the Sahara. He also sat in state and received homage from his people. He also rode in a palanquin amidst drumming, singing, dancing and musketry throughout the town.'

sion, but dangerously in the sense that they exposed themselves all too easily to the charge of subversion which the CPP was already anxious to bring. In practice, the results of the 1956 election, and the agreement reached over the 1957 constitution, killed federation stone dead—so quickly indeed that it was difficult to believe the opposition leaders ever seriously considered it a practical policy except as a means of effecting Nkrumah's downfall. And after 1957 (the argument concluded) the opposition was ready to play the role formerly attempted by the UGCC after 1951—that of a national critic. It still drew support from local interests—in Ashanti and the north in particular—but such were the threads of Ghanaian politics with which each side tried to weave a national support: they were not incompatible with a national outlook among the leaders, as may be seen from the readiness with which they took their place in the 1957 parliament.

In sum, the argument outlined here amounted to a plea for reconciliation—or, at least, for mutual tolerance—by the two party groups rather than the imposing by one side of its will on the other. It did not assert the need for a strict imitation of the Westminster pattern—of an alternating two-party system—but called in general terms for an acceptance by the CPP of restraints on its power and a similar readiness on the part of the opposition (sustained by areas of local control) to act cautiously. The new state, it could be argued, might then have been broadly based on a tolerant majority–minority system instead of being balanced precariously after 1960 on the rule of the Leader. What was needed—on this view—was, indeed, no more (but no less) than a strict observance of the rules formulated by Nkrumah himself on the eve of independence: the safeguarding of 'elections carried out in a fair and non-partisan spirit', 'freedom from arbitrary arrest', a 'free press', the right of any individual 'to join any trade union, political party, or other association of his choice', and 'provision . . . by law that any state broadcasting system is as free to put the Opposition's point of view as that of the Government'.[62] At a parliamentary level (Nkrumah added):

[62] GC, LA Deb., 12 Nov. 1956. The last provision was important in a country with a high proportion of illiterates, and where there was a readiness to be over-impressed by such devices as the wireless. The state broadcasting service was in fact denied to J. B. Danquah and the United Party in the April 1960 plebiscite campaign.

Minority rights would be respected. Opposition members in the Assembly would be able to raise questions which seemed to them in the national interest. The Opposition would have a guaranteed proportion of representation on Standing Committees and Select Committees of the Assembly. In matters of great national importance ... a tradition should be established that the Prime Minister of the day should consult with the Leader of the Opposition to secure, if possible, a concerted policy. [63]

In practice, most of these safeguards disappeared. The CPP brooked no bounds to its rule, and—in reply—the opposition began to move in the direction of conspiracy. Hence the clumsy attempt in the summer of 1958 to finance an armed coup d'état. Thus, by 1960—so the critic of CPP rule might conclude—the use of 'emergency measures of a totalitarian kind', and the clandestine activities of the opposition, had produced a situation which each side was able to claim had justified its actions: namely, conflict between a powerful ruling party closely identified with every aspect of public life, and the remnant of an oppressed opposition many of whose members were prepared to endorse any means by which the government might be overthrown. [64]

Neither argument, in the writer's opinion, was an adequate explanation of the post-independence period. The CPP case was too self-righteous: concentrating on the mote in its opponent's eye it ignored the beam in its own. The plea for reconciliation, on the other hand, ignored the history of the pre-independence struggle and misjudged the room for manœuvre which existed between the two parties. To see the history of these years in better perspective, other considerations have to be weighed: in particular, the influence on events exercised by Nkrumah (and the nature of the leadership provided by him); the nature of

[63] *I Speak of Freedom*, p. 79. During the November debate in parliament, Nkrumah went on: 'But questions of minority rights are not only concerned with the Opposition in the Assembly. They affect minorities also in the regions, and it is the duty of the government to see that in the various Regions any minority Party is given fair consideration in the regional machinery of government.' The fact is, that neither side trusted the other; the opposition did not trust the CPP nationally, the CPP did not trust the NPP and the NLM in the north and Ashanti.

[64] Cf. Alexis de Tocqueville: 'If ever ... free institutions ... are destroyed, that event may be attributed to the unlimited authority of the majority, which may at some future time urge the minorities to desperation, and oblige them to have recourse to physical force. Anarchy will then be the result, but it will have been brought about by despotism ...' (*Democracy in America* (1955), p. 198).

the CPP and its attitude to the power it had acquired; and the nature of the times in which these political struggles were conducted.

(a) Nkrumah as Leader

Consider, for example, Nkrumah's own background and character. It is difficult to believe that the moderate statements (quoted earlier) which recognized the need for an opposition, stemmed from conviction. They hardly tallied with the self-portrait drawn in the *Autobiography* and subsequent speeches, where he emerges as a leader singularly lacking in tolerance either of views other than his own or of organizations opposed to those under his control. Brought up in his early life as a Catholic, and profoundly influenced later in America by the writings of Marcus Garvey (the Negro Zionist), he spent his student days in London (he says) in search of a 'formula by which the whole colonial question and the problem of imperialism could be solved'—reading 'Hegel, Karl Marx, Engels, Lenin and Mazzini' in the process.[65] There was little interest in, or liking for liberal views, so far as one may judge from his *Autobiography*. Moreover, his understanding of the nature of authority was at the level of emotion and organization rather than ideas (whether liberal or illiberal); although nominally interested in theories of imperialism, his primary aim was 'to learn the technique of organization [for] ... I knew that whatever the programme for the solution of the colonial question might be, success would depend upon the organization adopted'.[66] He had—as his kindest critic has said—

the kind of intellect at the same time organising and practical, which enabled him to absorb, and turn to practical use, bits of theories that came his way and seemed likely to fit the context of the Gold Coast—collecting ideas and storing them against the future, as a squirrel collects and stores nuts. The essential eclecticism of this approach is worth stressing.[67]

He had, none the less, a single-minded pursuit of certain ends—self-government, national unity, pan-Africanism—to which he

[65] *Autobiography*, p. 45: 'I read Hegel, Karl Marx, Engels, Lenin and Mazzini. The writings of these men did much to influence me in my revolutionary ideas and activities.... But I think that of all the literature that I studied, the book that did more than any other to fire my enthusiasm was *Philosophy and Opinions of Marcus Garvey* published in 1923.'

[66] *Autobiography*, p. 45.   [67] Hodgkin, unpublished art. on Ghana.

brought a passionate advocacy. Power to achieve these ends was seen in personal as well as practical terms and the fashioning of a disciplined party went hand in hand with the expressed need for an extreme devotion to his own position as the Leader:

> Who is he that would become my follower?
> Who would sign himself a candidate for my affections?
> The way is suspicious, the result uncertain, perhaps destructive,
> You would have to give up all else, I alone would expect to be your
>   sole and exclusive standard,
> Your novitiate would even then be long and exhausting. . .[68]

The narrative which follows will also show Nkrumah as a clever tactical leader, who was quick to adapt himself to particular situations as they arose: the cautious revolutionary in 1949–50; ready on the other hand to respond in 1951 to the liberal governorship of Charles Arden-Clarke; playing the part of a frustrated parliamentary leader faced with an unreasonable opposition after 1954. But the extreme emotional attitude to power expressed in these verses from Walt Whitman was never exorcized, and from 1957 onwards it developed into the Nkrumaist cult which it was charitable, but misleading, to ascribe to popular zeal beyond his control. By 1960, certainly, it was clear that he had little interest in domestic politics and still less in the inter-party struggle of the immediate post-independence years. What mattered, it may be surmised, were external affairs. What was needed was a broadly based régime under the direction of a popularly elected leader. It was a Gaullist view of politics and the state which led quickly to the 1960 republic. And there was little doubt that the details of the new constitution, which vested power in a presidential executive, chosen either by plebiscite or by members of the National Assembly when standing for election, reflected Nkrumah's own views of the CPP as the unique expression of the national will and of himself as its sole interpreter. There was no attempt, therefore, by Nkrumah to check the movement towards a single-party republic or to moderate its emphasis on personal rule. On the contrary: if indeed the circumstances of the inde-

[68] Walt Whitman, quoted by Nkrumah as the frontispiece to his *Autobiography*. Note too the revealing comment: 'As I grew older . . . the strict discipline of Roman Catholicism stifled me. It was not that I became any less religious but rather that I sought freedom in the worship of and communion with my God, for my God is a very personal God and can only be reached direct. I do not find the need of, in fact I resent the intervention of a third party in such a personal matter. Today I am a non-denominational Christian and a Marxist socialist . . .' (pp. 11–12).

pendent state required an authoritarian régime, Nkrumah was more than ready to fill the role of an African Tsar.

(b) *The CPP as a Nationalist People's Party*

There was also little doubt that the party willingly endorsed Nkrumah's 'emergency measures of a totalitarian kind' when they were first introduced. His closest associates—K. A. Gbedemah, Kojo Botsio, Kofi Baako, Krobo Edusei—did not object,[69] and the government's readiness to exploit the advantages of power matched the general understanding of political control among the bulk of the party members. True, the CPP was avowedly a democratic party which had succeeded in engaging large numbers of men and women in political questions; it was also a commoners' party, opposed to privilege, and eager to defend the rights of the ordinary man. But the Assembly members and the general run of the party rank and file were democrats because they were commoners who 'spoke for the people', and the freedom they sought was conceived more in abstract terms of national independence than as a concern for individual rights. They were certainly no more tolerant than the leaders; and they had been trained in a harsh school. They knew little enough of the more liberal side to colonial rule, of the slow apprenticeship which had been designed for the chiefs and intelligentsia; and they carried over into independence a harsh view of power shaped by their experience of the native authorities. Akan government, to be sure, had imposed limits on the authority of the ruler: power could be withdrawn from the chief by those who bestowed it on him. And it might be thought that similar checks would reappear in the new relationship of the party to its leaders, and might modify the attitude of the CPP rank and file towards its rivals. But such a correlation between traditional and modern ways was by no means easy. In theory, perhaps, the transition from an elective chieftaincy to an elected parliament, or from the contests between rival royal houses to those between political parties, should have presented little difficulty. And, indeed, many Ghanaians (in the south at least) were quick to grasp both the mechanics and the significance of a general election. But there was no easy transfer to nationalist politics of the restraints

[69] Gbedemah objected when about to become a victim of the power he had helped to place in Nkrumah's hands.

embodied in the decentralized, hierarchical structure of traditional government. There was no time-honoured procedure or formula for the 'destoolment' of a party district commissioner; nor did the party rank and file have any entrenched rights, arising out of custom, against the power of the CPP central committee. The authoritarian aspects of traditional and colonial rule, on the other hand, were well suited to the nationalists' own assessment of their needs, and found full expression in the centralized framework of control devised for the party by its leaders.

One must recognize, therefore, that the very nature of the role which the CPP saw itself as performing pushed the leaders in the direction of the single-party republic. It is the main theme of this introduction that the CPP was a nationalist party engaged in a revolution on a number of fronts: an anti-colonial struggle against British rule, the seizure of power locally from the chiefs and the intelligentsia into its own hands, and a conflict between its own demands and local protest movements of a strong community nature. In no sense was the revolution long or arduous: but the total effect profoundly disturbed Ghanaian society. The CPP leaders exaggerated their part in the creation of a Ghanaian nation—they underrated the strength of the colonial state and ignored the limitations of their own appeal. Nevertheless, they could justly claim to have aroused and extended a sense of nationality which in 1946 was still inchoate. They could also take pride in the fact that they had succeeded not only in transferring power from colonial to local hands, but (in 1954) in resisting a bold attempt to cripple the centralized structure of authority which the party, and the colonial administration, had begun to construct. Parties with such claims are by nature monopolistic, and the CPP ran true to form. As a nationalist party, it sought to embody the whole nation. As a commoners' party, it demanded the undivided allegiance of the 'masses'. And as a party bent on modernizing and centralizing the machinery of state control, it was immediately hostile to any declaration of local interests. Minority rights were equated with tribalism, and both with subversion. Moreover, because its leaders owed their power to a successful revolution, they were over-ready to ascribe 'counter-revolutionary' intentions to any attack on their leadership. They lacked the ease and confidence bestowed by a long-established social order, and were quick to take alarm. He who

was not with the CPP was against it, and—the leaders added—so
much the worse for them. Hence the identification of the party
after 1957, not only with the 'general will of the nation', but with
the total power of the state. Leaders and rank and file alike found
it difficult, therefore, to accept the legitimacy of any organized
challenge to themselves, and rode roughshod over the opposition,
not because they underestimated its challenge, but because they
refused to believe that it had the right to exist. The refusal did not
spring, however, from an essential characteristic of Ghanaian or
African society but from the nature of the claims made by the
CPP. Single-party rule was achieved and defended not because
the leaders believed it to be the price to be paid for securing
the safety of the state but because it matched their own interpretation of the nationalist revolution to which they laid exclusive
claim.

(c) *The Circumstances of the Time*

The 1960 republic owed something also to the particular circumstances of the post-independence period. They were not pro-
pitious for the maintenance of a tolerant parliamentary régime.
For the CPP had scarcely ended its victory parades when it had
to face fresh outbreaks of local discontent, first in the former trust
territory, where a number of Ewe villages attempted to stage an
armed revolt against their absorption into an independent
Ghana, and then among the Ga community in Accra, who
formed a new political movement—the Ga Shifimo Kpee.[70]
Both protests came at a particularly dangerous time, when the
need was for a long period of quiet, and their effect was to renew
all the fears and memories of the pre-independence struggle. The
Ga revolt especially was a great shock to the CPP. It took shape
in the capital, in Nkrumah's own constituency, from within the
party's own ranks. And, like the Ewe and Ashanti and northern
parties, it broke a fundamental commandment of the governing
party—that 'tribalism' should have no place in an independent
Ghana: attempts by the Ga leaders to defend what they claimed
were important local interests were brushed aside therefore as
indefensible, for CPP dogma was perfectly clear (to the leaders)
on this point. Parties, by definition, were national organizations;
local associations, whether deliberately or unwittingly, were sub-

[70] See below, ch. VIII.

versive elements in the national life of the country, and needed to be dealt with ruthlessly.

During these same critical opening months the opposition showed that it too had learnt very little from its pre-independence days of the need for a prudent, cautious assessment of its own role. Instead, Dr Busia and his colleagues remained characteristically insensitive to the dangers of an unremitting hostility to the ruling party. Whether in practice the CPP would have behaved differently towards an opposition which adopted a more scrupulous attitude over the proper limits of its own stand may be doubted: but it was never put to the test; and the NLM–NPP–MAP leaders afforded the CPP every excuse to challenge their position on the grounds that they were deliberately promoting 'tribal and subversive' movements. The intellectuals who formed the active nucleus of the opposition alliance—Busia in parliament, Danquah outside it, and those who supported them—had already compromised their original stand as leaders of an anti-dictatorial, anti-corruption party when in 1954 they had given their support to the NLM—a movement which exhibited many of the qualities they had formerly deplored in the CPP. Admittedly, many of the more extreme proposals they sponsored—extending as far as talk of secession—had been more in the nature of counter-threats in the bitter verbal warfare between the CPP and the NLM than actual policies, but the annoyance and alarm they generated were real enough. The federation challenge had badly frightened the CPP. In 1957 many of the leaders, and most of the rank and file, were calling for retribution rather than reconciliation, and the support given by the opposition to the Ewe revolt and the Ga Shifimo Kpee (which was brought into the opposition alliance) fed this desire for revenge on the part of the CPP. It confirmed the general belief among the leaders in the need to eliminate their opponents, and strengthened their indifference to the harshness of the means adopted.

Finally, in order to understand fully the direction in which the CPP leaders moved after 1957 it is also necessary to take note not only of the relative strength of the governing party and the opposition but of the myth which the CPP leaders had woven so successfully around their origins that they, too, were held captive by it. Nkrumah especially, but many of those around him also, liked to describe the party as being 'the democratic instrument of the

people's will and aspirations',[71] or in similar phrases borrowed
from the general stock of revolutionary language. Rousseau,
Mazzini, Paine, Marx were pressed indiscriminately into the service of the party. And in 1949 it did indeed seem as if the CPP
embodied the general will of a nation about to be born; it was a
time when local interests were forgotten, and nationalist beliefs
found expression in a new People's Party. But it was unreal by
1957 to talk in these terms. The CPP had a large majority over its
opponents in parliament, and was widely supported in the country at large: but no more than that. Indeed, when the statistics
were examined of the voting figures in the three general elections
and successive by-elections, it could be seen that the party was
never actively supported by more than a quarter of the total adult
population: a sizeable minority voted against its candidates in
1954 and 1956; many never got to the polls; many eligible voters
failed to make the minimum necessary effort to have their names
entered on the electoral register.[72] It could be argued justly that
although many among the new electorate did not actively support the party, this did not necessarily mean they were opposed
to it. The fact remained, however, that the opposition was by no
means a negligible force at independence, nor the CPP as surely
based, even among its own followers, as its leaders would have
liked. Yet the fiction was maintained that the party was still—a
decade after its foundation—a movement to which 'the overwhelming majority of the nation' belonged,[73] and strenuous
efforts were made to re-establish the party as it had been in the
first years of its nationalist origins. By 1960 the leaders had seemingly accomplished their task: the *parti unique* was sole master of
the scene. Practice had been brought nominally into line with
theory, and was glossed by pointing to the theory. The reality was
different. For the CPP had 'swept the polls' during the 1951 election because it had been carried forward on a great wave of
nationalist excitement; but the apparently similar triumph by
Nkrumah in the presidential election of 1960 was reached only

[71] *Autobiography*, p. ix.
[72] In the 1954 and 1956 elections the party's candidates were supported by
approximately 60 per cent of the voters, who numbered approximately 60 per cent
of the electorate, which was approximately 60 per cent of the total population aged
21 and over. See below chs. IV and VII. The 1960 plebiscite (as has been stated) was
a guide not to popular support, but government power.
[73] Nkrumah, 'Address to 10th annual Delegates' Conference', *Evening News*,
4 Aug. 1959.

Introductory Preview 47

after opposition to the party had been crushed by the full weight of government power.

The forces at work at independence which combined to produce the new republic may now be summarized. Firstly, Nkrumah's own belief in, and taste for, autocratic rule of an extreme personal nature. Secondly, an initial willingness among the CPP rank and file to accept such a lead, since it matched both their own assessment of what was needed after the 1954–6 struggle and their understanding of the nature of political power.[74] Thirdly, the rash behaviour of the opposition, allied with (fourthly) the uncertainties of the political scene in the immediate post-independence months. And, fifthly, an extreme reluctance among the CPP leaders—arising partly from their nationalist origins, partly from the uneasiness with which they contemplated the situation at independence—to admit the legitimacy of any rival political group to themselves. None of these forces need have been of decisive importance. A leader more careful of individual rights could have led the CPP along more tolerant paths; a longer-established party, having a greater wealth of local talent than the CPP could call on, might have objected to the degree of power which the new republic vested in Nkrumah. An opposition more sensitive of the need to act prudently might have been able to keep open channels of criticism and dissent which, in the event, were choked by the concentration of power first within the single party and then in the hands of the president. If examples were wanted of what might have happened had these checks been applied they were there in other states whose leaders had resisted the drift towards authoritarian rule. Other ex-colonies in the past were able to preserve liberal, constitutional forms despite social and cultural differences at least as great as those which troubled the CPP leaders after 1949.[75] And not every nationalist government in the newly independent states has felt it necessary to deny

[74] After 1960, there were those who bitterly regretted that they had helped to place power in Nkrumah's hands, when—for K. A. Gbedemah, Ako Adjei, Tawia Adamafio and many others—

'Things sweet to taste, proved in digestion sour'

But it was then too late to recover what they (deliberately in many cases) had helped Nkrumah to take.

[75] e.g. in the older Dominions of the Commonwealth where (as Professor A. C. Brady noted) 'the success of representative institutions' demonstrated 'that homogeneity of culture and unity of thought are not prequisites for a democratic state provided that there is a determined will to accept readily tolerance and compromise' (*Democracy in the Dominions* (1947), p. 417).

the right of minorities to form their own party groups.[76] The avoidance of autocracy, however, requires a much greater effort than its adoption. And the effort was hardly attempted in Ghana. True, the state continued to be administered by a public service which had few equals on the African continent, and visitors to its shores were impressed not only by the level of administrative ability but the overall rate of economic growth—as, indeed, earlier visitors had been impressed by comparable developments in the Gold Coast. But while it was not difficult to pay tribute to the energy and ability of the new republic, or to recognize that an efficient administration and a steady expansion in the economy were prizes which eluded many of the other African states, it was also hard to believe that these achievements would remain unaffected by what was happening in the political life of the country. Indeed, the immediate effect of the shift towards autocracy was a melancholy succession of plots, reprisals, attempts at assassination, and repression. Between 1957 and 1960 the area of open discussion narrowed as the opposition was forced out of public life, the result being that the leaders who had held the CPP steady throughout its brief history then began to quarrel with Nkrumah and each other. Some clung desperately to office. Others fled into exile. Others again were held in prison under the Preventive Detention Act. The effect was to reduce political life to a barely discernible level of private conflict among his followers over the distribution of presidential favours. Thus the politics of intrigue succeeded the party disputes of previous years to confound the hopes of those who, looking back to the first reforms of the postwar years and the first general election in 1951, had confidently expected to see the development of a parliamentary system under liberal laws and a freely administered franchise.

[76] e.g. India and—a closer parallel perhaps with Ghana—Malaya, which became independent in August 1957. By 1960 the Alliance Party under Tunku Abdul Rahman was still only one (though the most important) of a number of competing party groups. Elections were still conducted fairly and freely contested; the trade unions and the press were relatively free from interference from the ruling party—a very different picture from Ghana—despite the long period of emergency rule in the Malayan peninsula after 1948.

II

The Early Years, 1946–51

THE five years dating from the introduction of the Burns constitution were the great watershed of Ghanaian politics when the 'model colony' run by the officials, chiefs, and intelligentsia was transformed into a national parliamentary system under the control of a People's Party. The rate of change astonished even those who were actively engaged in bringing it about, as first one group and then another sought to control the direction of events; and yet the process was a familiar one, whereby a period of stagnation was disturbed by reform, and reform slipped into revolution—familiar, too, in that the changes occurred partly as the consequence of the unsettled conditions which followed the Second World War. The period was also dominated by a number of prominent individuals—a reforming Governor, a nationalist lawyer, a revolutionary politician, but the central feature of these early years was the sudden outburst of rioting in February 1948: nothing was quite the same again in the political life of the country, neither the relationship between those who (as British power began to be withdrawn) were struggling for the succession, nor between the colonial administration and the general public. It was as if the entire political scene was suddenly distorted by an unexpected and violent eruption, with the result that when the dust settled and the lava cooled, a new landscape appeared. This is not an entirely accurate picture of what happened, since the future party-dominated state was to have many of the features of the former Gold Coast, but the February riots were sufficiently critical to stand at the centre of this account of the early nationalist period. One must discover first, therefore, why they took place.

The underlying cause of the major shift which took place in the political life of the country after 1946 has already been discussed, viz: the emergence of a new class of elementary-school-leavers who had a mass following among the commoners of the Ashanti

and Colony native authorities. There were a number of more immediate causes, however, and the most convenient starting point
of inquiry into the 1948 disturbances lay in the quickening of discontent among the Colony intelligentsia—the small group of
lawyers and well-to-do traders in the southern municipalities
whose most able representative was J. B. Danquah. By 1947 he
had gathered round him a group of companions who were dissatisfied with the reforms they had begun to applaud the previous
year. Their dissatisfaction stemmed partly from a natural ambition to push still farther the movement of reform already started; but they were also upset by what they considered had been
a change of attitude on the part of the chiefs to the distribution of
power under the Burns constitution. The intelligentsia had been
confident of the benefits to be gained from the introduction of a
new Order in Council precisely because the relations between
themselves and the chiefs were thought to be on a better footing
than at any time in the past. The passage of time had softened the
earlier disputes of the 1920s, and Danquah had worked hard
throughout the 1930s and the war years to form a common front
between the two sets of leaders. He had even been able to get the
agreement (on paper) of both the Colony Joint Provincial Council of Chiefs and the Ashanti Confederacy to the scheme of reform which he submitted to the Secretary of State during the
latter's visit to Accra in 1943,[1] and was able to help bridge the
gap between the chiefs and his fellow lawyers by virtue of his close
family relationship with Nana Ofori Atta II.[2] Moreover, the
means whereby the chiefs might yield gracefully to the educated
commoners were now available. For in 1942 the government had
accepted an amendment to the 1925 constitution making it possible for the chiefs of the Joint Provincial Council to elect non-
chiefs to the legislative council.[3] When, however, elections were

---

[1] Danquah's scheme embodied a limited ministerial system. Its approval by the
chiefs was perhaps less revolutionary than it seemed at the time. As Martin Wight
noted (p. 201): 'perhaps their agreement was in some cases due less to the merits of
the proposed constitution than to circumspection with regard to the press': but it
was an achievement in 1943 to have got the chiefs and the municipal members on
the legislative council to agree even on paper.

[2] Nana Ofori Atta I died in 1943 (after being on the Akim Abuakwa Stool since
1912).

[3] The intelligentsia had some cause to complain. In the nineteenth century the
unofficial members on the Colony legislative council consisted of African (and
European) merchants and lawyers. From 1911 onwards a balance was maintained
between the chiefs and the municipal members. However, by 1925—despite the
protests of J. E. Casely Hayford and others—the number of chiefs on the council

held in July 1946 for the new constitution there was an unexpected result. Only two commoners were successful when the Colony
chiefs met to choose their nine representatives—Danquah and
the Rev. C. Baeta. The remaining seven seats were taken by the
chiefs. The chiefs tried to gloss their decision by issuing a statement, saying:

> The Joint Provincial Council in allotting two of its seats to these
> gentlemen has been able not only to create a remarkable landmark in
> the political history of the country but also to disperse the allegations
> that the Chiefs were selfish as they were unwilling to cooperate with
> that section of the country known as the 'intelligentsia'.[4]

But the educated leaders had expected a much more generous,
and, in their eyes, enlightened, attitude. They knew that the legislative council in its new form was likely to become, or could be
made, a major source of power, and they feared the consequences
of not being its chief beneficiaries. As A. G. Grant, the Sekondi
timber merchant, was to tell the Watson Commission in 1948:

> We were not being treated right, we were not getting the licences
> for the import of goods, also we were not pleased with the way our
> Leg. Co. handled matters, because we had not the right people there.
> At one time, we had the Aborigines Rights Protection Society who
> were taking care of the country. Later on, they were pushed out and
> there was the Provincial Council of Chiefs. The chiefs go to the Coun-
> cil and approve loans without submitting them to the merchants and
> tradesmen in the country. Thereby we keep on losing.[5]

---

was double that of the municipal members. The change was justified by the
Governor, Gordon Guggisberg, who thought the 1925 constitution was 'far more
solidly based on the institutions which the people of this country have found suited
to them and far more likely to develop into something bigger and wider, than
any mushroom constitution based on the ballot box and the eloquence of politicians
over whom the people have no control except at election time' (*The Gold Coast;
a Review of Events of 1920–26* (1927), p. 24.) The justification was thought to lie
in the argument that the chiefs represented the greater numbers of the rural
population. The complaint voiced by the intelligentsia was that the chiefs were
'dummies'. 'The issue is one of life and death to us, for if you perpetuate the possibility of the return of dummies to the Legislature our national independence is
gone forever. Probably that is what has been aimed at all the time, to so gag the
people that while they have a machinery ostensibly of an advanced type, yet to be
truly and really voiceless in the affairs of their own country. . .' (*Gold Coast Leader*,
22 May 1926, quoted in R. L. Buell, *The Native Problem in Africa*, pt. i, ch. 51
1928). It was one of the ironies of colonial policy at this time that the officials wanted
to foster an 'African constitution', the African politicians wanted a modern parliamentary system.

[4] JPC, *Minutes*, Dec. 1946.
[5] Watson Commission *Report* and Minutes of Evidence submitted to the Commission.

Grant's complaint was a simple summary in homely terms of the long controversy between the chiefs and the intelligentsia. Hence their disappointment in 1946, amounting almost to a sense of betrayal, when the Colony chiefs showed that they were still unwilling to relinquish their place in national politics.[6] A great deal was now at stake: India, Burma, and Ceylon were almost independent, and the renewal of a period of local reform by Burns showed that the Gold Coast was moving, however slowly, in the same direction. But, if the 1946 constitution was merely the forerunner of still more fundamental changes to come, it was all the more urgent, in the eyes of the Colony leaders, that the 'right people' should be the beneficiaries.

It was with such thoughts in mind (and the prospect of ministerial office in view) that 'Pa Grant', the Sekondi timber merchant, discussed the possibility of forming a new political movement in his 'old offices on Poassie Road, Sekondi, in conference with three friends—Williams, Blay and Danquah'. By April 1947 the idea 'had germinated in a special conference held at Canaan Lodge Saltpond [a small coastal town] of about 40 representative leaders', and after 'months of preparation and propaganda' the United Gold Coast Convention was launched on 4 August under the direction of a Working Committee.[7] It was advertised as a nation-wide movement whose members proposed to restore leadership out of the hands of the officials into those of the 'chiefs and people', knit together existing organizations, and prepare for the time when the country would be self-governing. The desire for a national, all-purpose movement could be seen in the careful avoidance of the word 'party'; but it was avowedly political, and proclaimed its policy in phrases that subsequently became

[6] The intelligentsia were able to contrast the attitude of the Colony chiefs with that of the ACC which elected three non-chiefs and only one chief in the July election. (The chief came bottom of the poll.) The belief was still strong in Ashanti that the legislative council in Accra was no place for a chief—away from his subjects (and his enemies), and there was little conflict between the chiefs and the intelligentsia in Kumasi if only because the former were still confident of their power, and the latter still very few in number. The Ashanti quarrel (described later) was a straightforward conflict between the chiefs and the general body of the commoners.

[7] Foreword (by A. G. Grant) to the UGCC's *The 'P' Plan*, issued in January 1952. The leading members of the Convention were A. G. Grant, timber merchant, chairman; R. S. Blay, lawyer, vice-president; J. B. Danquah, lawyer, vice-president; R. A. Awoona Williams, lawyer, treasurer; W. E. Ofori Atta, graduate teacher; E. A. Akufo Addo, lawyer; J. W. de Graft Johnson, lawyer; Obetsibi Lamptey, lawyer. Later John Tsiboe, newspaper proprietor (*Ashanti Pioneer*), and Cobina Kessie, an Ashanti lawyer, were added from Kumasi.

famous: 'to ensure that by all legitimate and constitutional means the direction and control of government should pass into the hands of the people and their chiefs in the shortest possible time'. But if the long-term aim of the UGCC was self-government—and it was the first major association to talk in these terms —its immediate end looked back to the 1946 election. Its 'Aims and Objects' included the clause: 'to ensure that persons elected to represent the people and their natural rulers in the present Legislative Council shall be elected by reason of their competence and not otherwise'—a criterion which, it was supposed, would replace the chiefs by educated commoners. Similarly, when the Working Committee of the UGCC met for the first time on 20 September 1947, they resolved:

(a) that the Convention is of the opinion that the contact of chiefs and government is unconstitutional, and
(b) that in consequence their position on the Legislative Council is anomalous.[8]

This was the narrow constitutional issue taken up by the UGCC which, at the same time, raised the general question, where power should lie in a future self-governing Gold Coast—a question soon to be answered in language and terms hostile to the intelligentsia and the chiefs alike. For at the end of 1947 a new actor appeared on the scene who was destined not only to dominate the events of the years that followed his return to the Gold Coast but to destroy the UGCC as an active political force: Kwame Nkrumah. The irony of the situation was that the members of the Working Committee were the authors of their own downfall, for it was they who invited Nkrumah to return to the country. They had wanted a full-time secretary to run the Convention on their behalf and had looked round for a likely applicant. Ako Adjei, a young lawyer recently returned from England, was thought of; but he had already spoken to Danquah about a Francis— Kwame—Nkrumah whom he had known as a student at Lincoln College, Pennsylvania, and with whom he had worked in the African Students' Association of America and Canada, and in the West African National Secretariat in London. Ako Adjei was asked to write to Nkrumah about the possibility of taking up a post with the new movement. Nkrumah hesitated. Then

[8] UGCC, Working Committee, *Minute Book*, entry for 20 Sept. 1947.

the Working Committee, at their first formal meeting on 20 September, agreed to send Nkrumah £100 for his passage money, and he accepted. Travelling from London by sea, he arrived in December 1947, and was introduced to the Committee on the 28th. 'I am happy to be here with you at last', Nkrumah told the lawyers. 'At the moment I can't say anything more than to affirm that if you need me I am at your service.'[9]

Here was a meeting pregnant with fate, and much that happened in subsequent years in the politics of Ghana dates from this early association of Nkrumah with the intelligentsia of the UGCC. From their point of view they could hardly have made a worse choice, for Nkrumah was a very different sort of man from the members of the Working Committee. His first thought, he says, on receiving Ako Adjei's letter, was that it would be 'quite useless to associate myself with a movement backed almost entirely by reactionaries, middle class lawyers and merchants, for my revolutionary background and ideas would make it impossible for me to work with them'. His second, when he had Danquah's invitation, was that he would accept, although being 'fully prepared to come to loggerheads with the Executive of the UGCC if I found that they were following a reactionary course'.[10] These sentiments were expressed *ex post facto*, and the subsequent course of events cannot wholly be explained in these terms; but for the newly appointed secretary it was perhaps, as he himself was to describe it, 'rather like the dawn of action at the end of a long and intensive training'—in America and London, in the 1945 Manchester pan-African conference, and party organizations of one kind and another. Indeed, some of the members of the Working Committee sensed this difference between them and Nkrumah at their first meeting. Although the lawyer R. S. Blay expressed the hope 'that Mr Nkrumah would use the Convention as if it were his own organisation', his attitude was not shared by the whole Committee. Danquah, in particular, was suspicious. He asked Nkrumah how he was able to 'reconcile his active interests in West African unity (through the West African National Secretariat) with the rather parochial aims of the United Gold Coast Convention', and Nkrumah had to reassure the Committee, saying that he 'believed in TERRITORIAL BEFORE INTERNATIONAL solidarity'. He was questioned too about his

[9] UGCC, *Minute Book*, entry for 28 Dec. 1947.   [10] *Autobiography*, p. 62.

use of certain 'catch phrases'—in particular, the word 'Comrade'—which the Committee members feared 'might arouse the suspicions of the public as well as officialdom regarding the political connections of the Convention with certain unpopular foreign forms of government'.[11] This initial uneasiness was set aside later, and Danquah and Nkrumah campaigned together in the name of the Convention. But the Committee never quite overcame their ambivalence towards Nkrumah—hoping to use him, ready to accept (ready also to deny) what he might do in their name but possessed of a growing fear of what he might do without them.

Where did the UGCC, and Nkrumah, look for support? Primarily from the local youth societies which now existed in most of the Colony and Ashanti towns, whose members were ready to respond to any national movement able to present them with a simple programme of action—farmers, petty traders, drivers, artisans, school teachers, clerks and letter-writers—among whom were the growing number of elementary-school-leavers. Nationalist ideas were being canvassed, and many of the presuppositions which were to become the basic articles of belief of the CPP were beginning to be expressed in familiar, radical language:

Should we not fight for liberty? Are we not British subjects? Why should we be bound under unheard of restrictions and oppressions? Shall we not be free?
(a) Children weep and yearn for their snatched fathers.
(b) Schoolboys grumble and weep for freedom.
(c) For the first time in the history of this colony, Colleges have gone on strike for political interference.
(d) Farmers overleap restraint and burst from oppression.
(e) Professional men are wounded and the Government threatened them. . . .
Oh what a bitter time! Discontent is rife. . . . Where art thou, Justice? Bloodshed! Tyranny! Oppression! . . . Let us see Christian justice. . . . Welcome you Messengers of God . . . may your mission be just and peaceful, easy and successful.[12]

This *cri de coeur* was addressed to the Watson Commission immediately after they arrived in the country to inquire into the 1948 disturbances, and similar sentiments were voiced by the

[11] UGCC, *Minute Book*, entry for 28 Dec. 1947.
[12] Unpubl. letter to the Watson Commission by Kwasi Owusu, 12 Apr. 1948.

members of the local youth associations. For example, the Apowa
Literary and Social Club, in the western province of the Colony,
drew up a list of grievances for the Commission to study—among
them, the need to reduce the prices of imported goods, for industrialization, Africanization of the public service, cheaper education, a pipe-borne water supply, telephone and radio facilities—
and ended with the plea that 'since the Gold Coast Government
have failed to satisfy the needs of the people, self-government
should be granted as early as possible'.[13]

Farther north, the underlying unity of Ashanti had already
found expression in a wider association. For in August 1947—the
same month as the formation of the UGCC—an Asante Youth
Association, the 'AYA', had held its inaugural meeting in Kumasi. A local store-keeper, Atta Mensah, was elected secretary-
general, and told the fifty or more members present that 'the
hour has struck that the youth of Ashanti rally round in good
faith and in one body to do our duty in this age to promote the
social and political welfare of our dear land of birth'.[14] The main
burden of complaint voiced by the AYA was that of virtually
every petition by every local youth association, namely, the absence of any means of self-expression, whether locally or nationally. The remedy advocated was simple: self-government, not for
chiefs advised by officials, but under the control of the 'ordinary
man':

  1. We ask that this present Constitution be withdrawn. . . .
  2. We consider that the District Commissioner system in the Gold
     Coast is woefully undemocratic . . . (and) makes our chiefs semi-
     Government officials. . . .

---

[13] Unpubl. memo. submitted (to the Watson Commission) by Apowa Literary
and Social Club, Apowa Western Province, 16 Apr. 1948.
[14] AYA, *Minute Book*, 21 Aug. 1947. The leading members were Atta Mensah,
Bediako Poku (school teachers), J. K. Bonsu (a trader) and Krobo Edusei (employed by the *Ashanti Pioneer*). The AYA met at first fortnightly and then weekly,
and seems to have been formed side by side with the earlier Ashanti Students'
Union. The fact that its first meeting was held in the same month as the UGCC was
chance, but it quickly sought affiliation with other bodies in the south; e.g. with a
'Freedom Defence Society' in Accra, and with the UGCC at Saltpond. Cobina
Kessie (the Kumasi lawyer) was a member of both the AYA and the UGCC. So
was B. D. Addai, the Kumasi merchant, who was elected to the legislative council
for the Kumasi municipality in 1946. It was always much easier for any association
in Ashanti to come together and to move along a broad front than it was for a similar body in the Colony. By 27 April 1948 the *Minute Book* shows the AYA as having
98 members, including a few women. By 1949 its members were the mainstay of
the CPP in Ashanti—until 1954, when many of its rank-and-file membership went
over to the NLM.

5. The public vehemently disapproves the representation of Chiefs at the Legislative Council. . . .

26. . . . we want a complete upheaval of the present Constitution of the Gold Coast legislative council . . . the removal of our chiefs from the council, our economic deliverance, . . . and lastly but by no means the least, the attainment of SELF-GOVERNMENT within the next FIVE YEARS.[15]

Thus the UGCC complaint to the Watson Commission of the position on the legislative council of the chiefs under a native-authority system, and of the need for a more rapid advance to self-government, found a ready response among the youth societies. The AYA representatives told the Watson Commissioners:

The [Colony] Provincial Council and Ashanti Confederacy were made up of chiefs and the ordinary man had little or no say. The chiefs' decisions were often contrary to the wishes of ordinary men. They [the AYA] would like the present chiefs to wash their hands of political mandates.[16]

Here was further evidence of the commoner–chief conflict sketched in the previous chapter—of discontent, moreover, among the 'young men' in a part of the country where the power of the chief was deep-rooted. Each *omanhene* in Ashanti stood at the centre of a web of power extending into every sub-chiefdom, village, and family group, while over the chiefdoms as a whole stood the *asantehene*—a paramount of paramounts, representative of a long tradition of self-rule as the 'occupant of the Golden Stool', and a semi-sacred figure of whom (it was said) the Ashanti 'when they have to talk about him . . . do so in low tones, modulating gradually in whispers':[17] in short, almost a god. Yet by 1947–8 the Kumasi young men were prepared to press their claims against the Confederacy Council. Later, they were to assert their rights not only against the chiefs but against the intelligentsia as well—against the UGCC in the Colony, and the

[15] Unpubl. memo. presented by the AYA to the Watson Commission.
[16] *Mins. of Evidence* submitted to the Watson Commission. When the AYA was first mooted, its founders invited the Asantehene to become their patron. He refused, knowing full well the view taken by the young men of the way the chiefs were exercising their powers. Later, the AYA officers protested to the ACC that 'with a membership of 60, the Association was not compounded of outlaws nor anarchists. It was composed of patriots who had the steady advancement of Ashanti as their set goal' (J. K. Bonsu, the AYA president, to the Ashanti chiefs, ACC, *Minutes*, 18 Feb. 1948). But the chiefs were not deceived.
[17] Busia (p. 96).

small group of educated commoners in Kumasi who belonged to
the older, more established Asante Kotoko Society.[18] Meanwhile, in 1947–8, since their demands paralleled those of the
UGCC, a common front began to take shape: the youth societies
became branches of the UGCC, and Danquah and Nkrumah
began the task of knitting the multiplicity of local organizations
into a broad national movement.

To bring this growing discontent among the young men to the
point of riots, more urgent issues—capable of evoking mass discontent—were required. And by 1947 such issues existed. There
were two particular grievances which affected a large section of
the southern population—one, the plight of the cocoa farmers in
the areas affected by the swollen-shoot disease; the other, the
economic hardship of the urban population as the prices of imported goods rose and wages lagged behind. Each requires some
examination, before describing the actual sequence of events
leading to the riots, since together they helped to explain that
general distrust of the colonial government not only among the
elementary-school-leavers but the population at large which the
Watson Commission noted as 'the most serious problem which
the Administration has to face'.[19] The swollen-shoot issue is discussed first.

[18] In Ashanti (unlike the Colony) the very small group of better-educated commoners tended to side with the chiefs. The Kotoko Society had been formed in 1916
with the specific aim of securing the release from exile of Nana Prempeh I as well as
providing a meeting ground of educated opinion. It continued to exist after
Prempeh was repatriated (in 1924) until the early 1950s, its members growing
older, and its activities restricted more and more to occasional meetings of a good
fellowship nature. Among its early members were I. K. Agyeman, later secretary to
the Kumasi Council of Chiefs; J. W. K. Appiah, later chief secretary of the ACC;
and E. P. Owusu, a Kumasi store-keeper, who became Kumasihene in 1932 and
the Asantehene Prempeh II in 1935. *Kotoko*=porcupine, the emblem of Ashanti.
The attitude of the Ashanti chiefs towards the Kumasi intelligentsia may be seen in
the following extract:
Otumfuo: '. . . I wish to remind you two new members of the Ashanti proverb
which says that when a lad knows how to wash his hands he dines with grown-up
persons, hence you have this day been privileged to sit with your *nananom* (chiefs) in
Council to help our deliberations' (ACC, *Minutes*, June 1950, when two more
commoners (Cobina Kessie and M. T. Agyeman-Anane) were added to the seven
appointed at the restoration of the Confederacy in 1935). 'Otumfuo' is the Asantehene: that is, 'Almighty'.
[19] *Report*, para. 17. Much of the distrust was based on rumour, and rumour on
wild allegations. 'Putting it plainly', said Mr Frank Wood of the TUC, 'years ago
[we] were not accustomed to seeing European children with their mothers . . . in
the streets of the Gold Coast; . . . every mail boat, one or two hundred landed, and
some came by air' (Watson Commission, *Mins. of Evidence*). The increased number
of European families was thought to be a deliberate policy of 'population dis-
persal' by the United Kingdom government. It was also rumoured that cocoa

By the end of 1947 cocoa farmers in the south-east of the Colony (and many of their Ashanti counterparts) were on the point of open hostility to the government. The explanation lay not so much in the effect of the spread of the virus disease known as swollen shoot, though this was grievous, but in the measures taken by the administration to combat it. When the Watson Commissioners investigated the problem, they concluded that the mounting unrest in the cocoa-growing districts was 'to a great extent politically inspired',[20] but this hardly did justice to the anxiety among individual farmers as year by year the yield from their farms diminished or to the anger felt at each stage in the government's attempt to deal with the problem. The answer propounded by the experts who advised the officials was the cutting down of the infected trees, but to all but the most enlightened farmer (and he was not easy to find in 1947) the cure was worse than the disease. An infected tree was likely to be still bearing healthy pods, and might do so for two more crop seasons; to cut it down meant an immediate total loss. Yet the government was bound to act, and when persuasion was found inadequate it turned first to compulsion and then to direct action; when a farmer refused to 'cut out' the diseased trees on his farm, legislation was used to compel him, and when this too was ineffective, the government authorized the Agricultural Department to employ gangs of labourers whether the farmer agreed or not. By the end of 1947, despite the fact that $2\frac{1}{2}$ million had been destroyed of the total number of 400 million trees, it was estimated that there were nearly 45 million more infected, and that the rate of spread was a further 15 million a year. The government was right, surely, to take direct action. But although $2\frac{1}{2}$ million trees were only a little over a half per cent of the total number, in places they included the greater proportion of mature trees on a particular farmer's land which he and his pioneering forebears had planted; and although payment was made to enable farmers to replant, it was regarded as inadequate.[21] Moreover, nobody

---

plantations were being planted in East Africa, to the detriment of the Gold Coast farmer—a rumour which may have owed something to the East African Groundnut Scheme, something to the much debated argument after the First World War between Leverhulme and the Nigerian and Gold Coast governments over palm-oil plantations.

[20] *Report*, para. 265.

[21] The (Beeton) Committee of Enquiry which was set up in 1947 to review the legislation and provide compensation in respect of swollen shoot, opposed com-

was at all sure that new trees could, in fact, be planted successfully on an infected farm; the disease was a malignant growth,
difficult at first to detect, and a mystery even to the scientists at
the Cocoa Research Institute which had been established at New
Tafo in 1944. Farmers argued the case against cutting out in their
own way, saying that:

the disease was nothing new but would disappear if left alone for a few
years; it was only necessary to cut out the infected parts and not the
whole tree, for how could a diseased tree bear good fruit? What was
the point of cutting out the cocoa trees if the forest trees were left to
harbour the mealy-bug which was said to carry the virus? The
government was either wicked or foolish because labourers sent into
the farms cut down healthy as well as diseased trees unless bribed not
to. Was there, in fact, a secret motive behind government action? Did
it intend the deliberate destruction of the cocoa industry, and the
acquisition of land for some hidden end?[22]

Many of the more extreme flights of fancy indulged in by the
farmers were no doubt, as the Watson Commissioners inferred,
the result of a wild running propaganda which spread from village to village, but the effect was plain. Farmers talked of violent
resistance; head farmers met together to see what could be done
and turned to the educated leaders for help. Two examples may
be quoted here to illustrate the problem, one used by Danquah to
describe the anxiety of farmers in the eastern province of the
Colony where the disease was now rampant, and the other an extract from the minutes of the Ashanti Confederacy Council.[23]

---

pensation for the loss of diseased trees and instead recommended a replanting
grant of £12 an acre in two instalments within a period of four years. The JPC
wanted compensation at the rate of 2s. a diseased tree.

[22] See GC, Cttee of Enquiry into the Existing Organization and Methods of
Combat of the Swollen Shoot Disease, *Report*, 1951, from which the arguments
here are taken (this Committee was set up by the CPP government two months
after it took office). Memorandum after memorandum to the Watson Commission
took up the same points, e.g. 'We farmers do not deny that the swollen shoot must
be fought. An anti-septic for the killing of the germs must be sought instead of this
primitive method of cutting out which must bring no good results. The CUTTING
OUT OF COCOA TREES should stop. . . . My learned lords, learn of this! . . .
You know the number affected (45 million); we have been informed that the
disease affects not only cocoa trees but some forest trees. The order is that for every
affected cocoa tree, some others should be felled. . . . We must therefore reckon 322
million of cocoa trees to be felled. How much of the whole will be left?'

[23] Swollen shoot was first recognized in Ashanti in 1943 when an outbreak was
discovered south of Konongo. A cutting-out campaign was started in October
1945, and by June 1946 100,000 diseased trees had been cut out. 'Unfortunately'
(as the ACC *Minutes* record) 'in June 1946 opposition from farmers was so great

In 1947 Danquah was in close touch with the farmers' associations in his own state of Akim Abuakwa, and they came to him for advice:

Dr Danquah: Tetteh Kene, a Krobe man, a cocoa farmer, whose farm is situated at Bosuso . . . came to my office in a state of great trepidation. He was accompanied by an educated son who interpreted for him, for he spoke the Krobo language and I do not speak Adangbe. 'Sir', he said, 'they are destroying my plantation'. 'Who are destroying your plantation?' I asked him. 'The Agriculture people', he said. 'One clerk lives at Bosuso and a European lives at Bunso, and they entered my farm with a gang of labourers and cut down the trees—trees in full bearing. They cut them down, and when I protested they said they would take me to court if I stood in their way. Please master, save me, save my farm.'

I asked Tetteh Kene [said Danquah] if he had any paper on the subject for it is a habit of lawyers to begin with a writing on the matter in hand. Tetteh Kene said there was no paper. 'Have you not received any notice in writing that your cocoa trees are diseased and are to be cut down?'

'Nothing at all', he said. 'The clerk and the white man came there many months ago, and marked certain of my cocoa trees and told me to cut them down on the grounds that they were diseased. Those trees had pods on them, yellow pods and green pods, and they said I should cut them down. I cut them down, but they have come again, and again, and this time they did not ask me to cut down any trees, but they cut down the trees themselves, every kind of tree, one long belt from one end to the other. Can you, please, help me?'[24]

The other example is from Ashanti. In February 1948 the Confederacy Council met to discuss the Beeton Committee's *Report* on swollen-shoot legislation, and its own ordinance passed in June 1946. The debate in the Council reflected a growing alarm:

Kokofuhene: Trees die as a result of either old age or exhaustion of the fertility of the soil. The cocoa trees at Tafo are dead, due to old age and not due to any disease. I therefore oppose in strong terms, the idea of cutting down the cocoa trees in Ashanti, despite the Council's Order made in 1946.

Offinsohene: If Government would not find any way other than the drastic method of checking the disease by cutting, I would suggest that the cutting should cease. The germ is indigenous to the soil, and

---

that disease control had to be stopped' until the Confederacy Council was persuaded to pass its own control ordinance. The campaign was then renewed.

[24] GC, LC Deb., sess. 1947, issue no. 2, p. 77.

does not inhabit the cocoa tree alone. The order made by the Confederacy Council should be revoked.

Agonahene: I support Offinsohene.

Drobohene: I support the Kokofuhene. All orders made, whether by the Council or government, in favour of cutting down diseased cocoa trees should be revoked.

Wenchihene: I support Kokofuhene.

Berekumhene: I feel we should go and see what is being done at the West African Cocoa Research Institute about this disease before we take any decision...

Abeasehene: The trees should not be cut.

Sumahene: The trees are dying due to old age and soil exhaustion.

Nkwantahene: Those who have not been to Tafo before should be requested to go there. I am in favour of the cutting down of the diseased trees as the only method yet known to Science, of curing the disease. Perhaps when they go there, they will be able to advance reasons why diseased trees should not be cut down.

Beposohene: I am inclined to infer that cocoa has been planted somewhere in Europe; otherwise Government would not persist in cutting down our cocoa trees. I disagree.

Krontihene (Kumasi): Let us go to Tafo and gather reasons to support our contention that the diseased trees should not be cut down.

Hon. I. K. Agyeman: This is a question which has beaten me. I have no solution. It is, however, such an important affair that I would advise Nananom and the farmers to visit Tafo. It is not expedient to sit here and request Government to revoke orders already made.[25]

Later in the month, the chiefs travelled down to the Colony to New Tafo where they were shown round the Cocoa Research Institute by Dr C. J. Voelcker, its Director, but they were unimpressed:

Akyempemhene: We are in a disease farm. Show me a mealybug.

Dr Voelcker: If you are suffering from malaria, it does not necessarily follow that the mosquito can be seen on your body always.

Agogohene: Has the opinion of any other scientist, apart from those in Britain, been consulted?

Answer: This is the biggest research institute in the world, and it is being watched keenly. Let's drive to another farm—a typically infected farm....

Akyempemhene: Isn't it because of lack of shade that the trees are dying over there?

Answer: But these two trees are in the shade.

[25] ACC *Minutes*, Feb. 1948.

Berekumhene: How do you prevent the mealybugs from falling on healthy trees when the infected ones are being cut?

Answer: One healthy and strong man pulls the tree during the cutting, and it is made to fall away from healthy trees.

Berekumhene: Don't you see that these mealybugs drop from the leaves at every stroke of the axe and the chances are many that they fall on healthy trees?

Answer: Yes, I do agree with you.

Berekumhene: Do you realise that the wind can blow the mealybugs to healthy trees?

Answer: Yes. It is possible.

Berekumhene: What is the use of cutting then?

Agogohene: And when all the Swollen Shoot infected trees in the Gold Coast have been cut out will there be no possibility of an outbreak since these mealybugs inhabit other trees?

Answer: There will be outbreaks, but they will not be on such a grand scale.

Agogohene: What is the use of cutting down these trees then?....

Dr Voelcker: We have seen what happens with swollen shoot disease when it is not controlled. This afternoon we are going to walk through farms where the disease is under control by cutting off diseased trees. The Ashantis are known to be intelligent. You see things with your own eyes; this farm was attacked nine years ago, but it has been kept under control.

Assamanghene: Has any of these trees ever been infected?

Answer: One tree was infected, but was cut off 5 years ago.

Assamanghene: (Coming along with a pod) Aren't these mealybugs I see on the pod?

Answer: Yes, definitely they are.

Assamanghene: And you say this farm is not infected?

Answer: Take it from me that these trees are not infected.[26]

What stands out in these extracts is an extreme suspicion, even among the Ashanti chiefs (many of whom were cocoa farmers as well) who on other issues were in sympathy with the government. It was born of genuine hardship in the swollen-shoot affected areas among farmers many of whom feared the total loss of their livelihood. Nor were their fears unjustified. Consider, for example, the plight of the migrant cocoa-farmers of Larteh, the small hill town in the Akwapim hills which lie some twenty miles back across the Accra plains, who for several decades had been moving steadily westwards across the Densu river into the Akim

[26] Ibid.

lands. Their story is told by Polly Hill, who has done so much to
increase knowledge of, and sympathy for, the Ghana cocoa
farmer:

> From the point of view of the individual Larteh farmer the process
> of land acquisition was a benign spiral. Cocoa growing was, for most
> farmers, an expanding business into which a large proportion of the
> profits was constantly ploughed back, leaving other portions for the
> purposes of house building in Larteh and educational expenses. Land
> would have become scarce had it not been for the invention of the
> lorry. Labour would have become scarce had not northern and
> foreign labour been attracted from ever further afield. 'Management'
> was a factor which increased in supply owing to the higher survival
> rate of sons (who were often put in charge of lands) and to the ability
> and willingness of the supervising farmer to adapt himself to the lorry
> age. And the farmers were ready to improve access to their lands by
> making large investments, based on voluntary contributions, in roads
> and bridges.
>
> Then during the late nineteen thirties (or thereabouts, the exact
> date depending on locality), swollen shoot came and destroyed the
> whole process. Virtually all the cocoa on all the lands acquired during
> [the first phases of expansion, before 1900 to after the first world war]
> died of swollen shoot . . . and it seems reasonable to hazard the guess
> that all the Larteh lands taken together are today [1956] bearing no
> more than 5 to 10 per cent of what the production would have been
> had there been no swollen shoot. It seems that perhaps one-third of all
> the Larteh cocoa farmers are producing virtually no cocoa at all at
> present. . . .
>
> This depressing picture may remedy itself in course of time. Suc-
> cessful replanting in any area tends to have a snowball effect. There
> are areas where the young men of Larteh, as well as the older people,
> are working very hard to re-establish the old farms. No one suggested
> that there was any difficulty about the younger generation not want-
> ing to go in for farming, and in this sense the obstacles seem to be
> economic, not social. But whenever recovery comes the calamity has
> already been endured for a whole generation.[27]

The Larteh example was a dreadful one for the other farmers,
and although no doubt the sensible lesson to draw from its fate
was that the disease must be held in check, it was not the one that
those most affected were willing to draw. Polly Hill was able to

[27] *The Acquisition of land by Larteh Cocoa Farmers*, Cocoa Research Series, No. 14, published by the Economics Research Division, University College of Ghana, 1958.

quote an 'official observer [who] had this to say about the atmosphere prevailing immediately after the war in the swollen shoot
area: "It is a widespread economic depression which has affected
the social and moral life of the community . . . it has created a sen-
sation. The disaster is felt appallingly".'[28] The centre of the
catastrophe lay in the eastern Colony region, but the alarm it
generated was far-reaching, and although the government suspended compulsory cutting out in June 1948, by then it was too
late: the riots had taken place, the government was on the defensive, and the weight of argument looked as if it rested with those
who believed that the quickest way to reform was through direct
action.

In addition, the farmers had long memories of their own
efforts to defend their interests during the inter-war years when,
with the help of educated leaders, they had come together in the
1937 'cocoa hold-up' with a speed and determination that took
the administration and the European buying firms by surprise.
The history of independent action by the farmers went back
much further than the 1937 hold-up, the Director of Agriculture
noting in 1919 that 'the formation of Associations of Cocoa
Growers is being thought of especially among the older growers
. . . their one ambition . . . at the present time appears to be to enable them to ship their own cocoa'. There was a Gold Coast
Farmers' Association formed in 1921—'an organisation which
exported a hundred tons in the first year of its existence'.[29] And
the Ashanti Farmers' Union, and local associations in the Colony
like the Sika Mpoano (Cocoa) Akuafo Fekuw Ltd, and the
'Farmers' Committee of British West Africa', were still in existence from that earlier decade. Farmers in both regions had learnt
the value of joint action; and the experience gained in agitation
against the European firms was there to be turned against the
colonial government.[30] Thus in 1947–8 the farmers were more
than ready to meet the intelligentsia leaders in any criticism of
the administration: the UGCC took up the farmers' campaign
against cutting out, and the farmers gave their support to the de-

[28] Hill, *Gold Coast Cocoa Farmer*, p. 67.   [29] Buell, i. 814.
[30] The Asante Farmers' Union was started in 1937 with the help of B. D. Addai,
the Kumasi cocoa factor and trader) who was elected its 'Head Chief Farmer'. The
Sika Mpoano Akuafo Fekuw Ltd (Gold Coast Farmers' Association) was formed in
1939 by C. S. Oteng, the same year as Ashie Nikoe and John Ayew created the
Farmers' Committee of British West Africa. In each instance, attempts were made
to buy, ship, and sell the cocoa direct to agents in America and Europe.

mand for 'self-government in the shortest possible time'. William
Ofori Atta of the UGCC Working Committee (at this time principal of the Abuakwa State College) became Head Farmer of the
Akim Abuakwa Farmers' Union; others, like Ashie Nikoe and
John Ayew, were active leaders of long standing in attempts by
the Colony growers to market and ship their own cocoa. Throughout 1947 and early 1948 there were protest meetings among
farmers in the local state capitals of the cocoa-growing areas and,
as clashes occurred between individual farmers and the cutting-
out gangs employed by the Agricultural Department, the UGCC
leaders strove to turn the farmers' woes to political account
and to link them with a growing number of complaints in the
towns.[31]

They had high hopes of doing so. For if many of the cocoa districts were on the edge of revolt in 1947–8, the situation in the
main trading towns and municipalities was hardly less serious,
where a shortage of imported goods and an increase in the
amount of money available had sent prices rocketing. The explanation lay partly in the vastly increased cocoa price. The size
of the crop had gone down by a third (destroyed by swollen
shoot); but, whereas the 300,000 tons marketed in 1937–8 had
fetched only £5,300,000, the 200,000 tons of 1947–8 brought in
£41 million. The Watson Commission reported that 'the total
amount of money in circulation at present, about £18 million,
[was] about four times the pre-war amount'.[32] But the goods were
not there to buy even for those with money to spend: there was a
world shortage of shipping as well as of consumer goods, and the
Gold Coast had to take its turn. Thus the imports of sugar fell to
46 per cent of the 1937 figure, cotton piece-goods to 25 per cent,
kerosene to 45 per cent. The result was a widespread black market as well as a sharp rise in prices:

[31] The farmers were not always prepared to accept what the intelligentsia told
them. 'As I was going to Kibi', Danquah was later to tell the Watson Commission,
'I was tackled by a large number of farmers with their drums, and their faces
marked with red ochre. They said they had come to meet me and asked the reason
why I had signed the Beeton Report agreeing with the cocoa trees being cut down.
It took a considerable explanation to make them understand that I did not sign
the Beeton Report . . . but that my name appeared as the first witness.' This was in
February 1948 (Watson Commission, *Mins. of Evidence*).
[32] *Report*, para. 188. The big jump in the cocoa price came in 1947–8. The value
of the cocoa crop in 1946–7 was only £9½ m.; the following year it was £41 m.
The price paid per load of 60 lb. to the farmer went up from 15s. in 1945 to 27s. 6d.
in 1946, 40s. in 1947, and 65s. in 1948.

Selected Commodities: Costs and Supply

Landed costs	1939	1948	% Imports	1937–8	1948
Sugar, per cwt	18s. 7d.	58s. 2d.	Sugar	100	46
Flour, 95 lb bag	12s.	42s. 10d.	Wheat flour	100	37
Dutch blocks			Cotton piece-		
(48 in.)	16s. 9d.	48s.	goods	100	25
Cutlasses, per doz.	7s. 3d.	22s. 11d.	Kerosene	100	45

Source: Watson Commission *Report*, para. 195 & App. 17.

The effect was made worse by a system of petty retail trade which exaggerated the rise. Thus the price of sugar in the main stores was now 8*d*. a lb., compared with the pre-war price of 4½*d*., but when sold cube by cube on the small wayside stalls it was 3*s*.; the price of imported tinned fish and meat, candles, matches, and cigarettes was similarly inflated by a local system of multiple retail trade. The increase in the amount of money in circulation also affected the cost of local foodstuffs: when the Watson Commission looked at local commodity prices they found that 'the prices of staple foods on a number of urban and country markets [were] probably about 2½ times the pre-war level'.[33]

This steep rise in prices bore heavily on the daily-rated and salaried groups, as may be seen from the evidence accumulated of the plight of the unskilled labourer in Accra. The real wage index for these daily-rated, government employees dropped from 100 in 1939 (at 1*s*. 6*d*. a day) to 66 in November 1945. Small wage

Date	Daily wage	Money-wage index	Cost-of-living index	Real-wage index	Food-price index
1939 May	1s. 6d.	100	100	100	100
1945 Nov.	1s. 10d.	122	186	66	202
1947 Nov.	2s. 9d.	183	212	86	250
1948 Dec.	2s. 9d.	183	227	81	264

Source: W. B. Birmingham, 'An Index of Real Wages of the Un-skilled Labourers in Accra' and the table of statistics—reproduced here in shortened form—from *Econ. Bull.*, vol. 4, no. 3.

[33] Para. 192.

increases in 1946 brought the rate to 2s. 1d. a day, and the following year to 2s. 10d., but the index again fell to 86 by November
1947, and to 74 by August 1948. Other groups were similarly
affected, and savings and war gratuities were quickly eaten up.
The Governor's *Address to the Legislative Council* in 1947 included
figures which showed that the military authorities had opened
30,000 accounts for ex-servicemen's war gratuities with a total
deposit of £1,200,000, but 'of this amount there remained only
10 per cent in the bank at the end of the year'. A particularly
hard-hit section of the community was the drivers (many of
them ex-servicemen) who complained of the difficulty of getting
petrol except at black-market prices, and of restrictive trade
practices among the small 'Syrian' business community.[34] Another was the goldsmiths who found it difficult to obtain gold
either from the banks or the mining companies.[35] It was possible
to catalogue a number of similar discontented groups, and complaints flowed into the native authorities and district commissioners' offices. Early in 1948, the Colony chiefs met the Chamber
of Commerce and the Acting Colonial Secretary to see what
could be done to improve the system of price control, and the
youth societies held a rowdy series of semi-public meetings to
explore what means they, too, should adopt.

One fact was generally accepted. It might be difficult to understand what was happening, or what should be done, but everyone knew whom to blame: the European trading firms; and, in
particular, that much-maligned 'colossus'—the United Africa
Company.[36] The Gold Coast economy was still dominated by

[34] Most of the 'Syrians' were from the Lebanon. The near-monopoly that these
hard-working family businessmen had over the hire-purchase of lorries and
motor cars was greatly modified early in the 1950s when the big commercial companies (headed by the Compagnie Française de l'Afrique Occidentale (CFAO))
began to offer hire-purchase sales; but in 1947–8 there was very little the would-be
driver could do except fall in with the Lebanese conditions—high interest rates, the
adding of the cost of spare parts to the original price, and seizure of the vehicle at
the first failure to maintain the monthly payment. These were the main burden of
complaints among lorry drivers; yet without the Lebanese trader there would have
been little opportunity for the African owner-driver to start up on his own.
[35] See the Statement by the General Secretary of the TUC before the Watson
Commission: 'All this—the forbidding of local washing for gold—has thrown many
goldsmiths out of work; if you visit Accra you will find that the craft is dying out
gradually' (*Mins. of Evidence*). Local washing for gold was not in fact forbidden, but
many thought that it was.
[36] The phrase used by Hancock (ii.20): 'It [the United Africa Company] is the
commercial colossus of West Africa; yet it is only a subsidiary—no doubt a very
important subsidiary—of Unilever's.' The UAC was formed in 1929 by the
amalgamation of the Niger Company (bought out by Lever Bros. in 1920) and the

the overseas trading companies, and nationalist feeling drew no distinction between colonial rule and the activities of the European firms: to be against the one was to be against the other, and both were thought to be in league. 'The charge was clear: it was being alleged that importers, and particularly those associated with the hated organisation which flourished under the name of the Association of West African Merchants (AWAM) were deliberately keeping up prices of essential commodities to an outrageous extent'; and when the government took no action 'the suspicion not unnaturally grew up that, at all material times, there was some private arrangement between the powerful importers . . . and the Government'.[37] The attack on the European firms was made at two levels. In the first instance, local businessmen (many of them sympathetic with the UGCC) were eager to benefit from the boom conditions of the post-war period, but found it difficult to do so because the issue of import licences and the allocation of supplies among the importers were made on a scale determined by 'past performance'. The period taken was 1937–41—a decision favourable to the European companies which had been powerful enough to survive the lean depression years of the 1930s, and the African merchants were resentful. As a Kumasi businessman told the Watson Commission: 'there had been African traders for a very long time. Since the war, however, the "past performance system" was introduced. . . . This made it extremely difficult for many Africans who carried on business

African & Eastern Trade Company (formed by the merger in 1919 of Miller Bros. and F. & A. Swanzy). Its importance in the Gold Coast at this time may be seen from the figures quoted by F. J. Pedler in his *West Africa* (1951), p. 110:

> 1947–8: value of produce bought, £5,874,000
> value of merchandise sold, £11,637,000.

The total external trade of the Gold Coast in the same year (1947) was: exports, £22,007,000; imports, £26,184,000. In the cocoa-buying field the (Nowell) Commission on the Marketing of West African Cocoa *Report* (Cmd. 5845, 1938) found that 98 per cent of the trade was in the hands of 13 European firms (App. D). The Watson Commission was critical of the European companies, but it also felt obliged to comment: 'In fairness to the importing firms against whom feeling has been very high . . . we feel bound to say that we were greatly impressed by their efforts to find alternative supplies when other sources have dried up. . . . Without the extensive and intricate buying organisations of these firms, active in all the main exporting countries of the world, supplies of consumer goods . . . would have been far less and prices would have been even higher' (*Report*, para. 203). There were, however, very few Africans in 1947–8 prepared to believe such a statement, or who did not suspect that the European firms (headed by UAC), the overseas mining companies (headed by the Ashanti Gold Fields Corporation), and the colonial government were connected with each other.

[37] Watson Commission *Report*, para. 173.

long before the firms came to this country.'[38] Secondly, at a different level, the petty trader (and the general body of consumers) complained of the high prices and shortage of goods. The Apowa memorandum quoted earlier inveighed against 'Cartelisation and Trade Monopoly in European control' as the cause of 'high prices and unemployment'. The AYA representatives complained that

the Gold Coast African has been subject for a long time to economic oppression and exploitation. The economic oppression is evinced in the Export and Import Policy of the Government. . . . The AWAM, the *QUOTA* system, and the act of Past Performance, all of which are major roots of our present economic troubles, were born during the war, and therefore should be withdrawn immediately.

The Watson Commission was broadly sympathetic with the latter argument, pointing out that: 'During the war hardships were accepted cheerfully as part of the War effort but there was a general expectation that goods would become freely available again as soon as fighting was over; there is even now a widespread expectation that prices will return to their 1939 level.'[39]

In the immediate post-war years, accusations and argument continued along these lines until they suddenly found expression in a new movement and, again, one must take note of a particular individual. Little was clear-cut in Ghana politics, and although it was suggested earlier that it was possible to divide local society into the intelligentsia, chiefs, and young men, someone must now be introduced who did not fit easily into any single one of these categories. For in October 1947 Nii Kwabena Bonne II, Osu Alata Mantse—a businessman, an Accra chief, hardly a member of the intelligentsia, and still less a member of any youth society (although he drew his support from the young men)—began a boycott campaign that led directly (though unwittingly) to the riots.

Nii Bonne had very little formal education, but through his own energies he had become a wealthy contractor and trader. He

---

[38] *Mins. of Evidence*. The same point was made in a number of memoranda, e.g. by a Sekondi trader: 'The introduction of a system of importation based upon the criterion of Past Performance militated against free and open trade to all and sundry, giving the European established Houses practically a monopoly of the import trade; and . . . the practice set up by the Trading Houses whereby goods in bulk were sold to Asiatic and other foreign traders led to exploitation at outrageous prices' (memo. on 'Some Causes of the Disturbances').

[39] Watson Commission *Report*, para. 179.

also had a messianic sense of civic duty.[40] When the war ended, he disliked, and saw no justification for, the continuation of high prices in the Accra stores, and he considered that the fault lay in the organization of the country's trade:

we had neither a Government-controlled economy, with an efficient system of price control and regulation such as existed in England at the time, nor a liberal economy with free trade and genuine competition which would have cut down the profits of the middle men and importers and forced them to show real enterprise by taking their goods into the distant villages. Instead we had a virtual monopoly of the big firms and Syrian merchants who could fix their own prices. . . .

Using these arguments, Nii Bonne wrote to the secretary of the Accra Chamber of Commerce and proposed that they should issue a revised list of prices covering a large number of imported goods; he also called for a national boycott from Monday, 24 January 1948 should the firms take no notice of his appeal. When nothing happened in reply to his letter, an Anti-Inflation Campaign Committee was established in Accra with local committees in many of the Colony and Ashanti towns—in Kumasi for instance, Krobo Edusei was chairman, and Owusu Ansah secretary, of an Ashanti Boycott Committee; a watch was kept on the main European and Levantine companies,[41] and contact maintained between the committees by telegraph with Nii Bonne in Accra. The Colony and Ashanti chiefs promised their support at first for 'non-violent demonstrations in conformity with customary practice and as an indication of the country's utter disapproval of the trading methods of the Commercial establishments in this country':[42] but the fighting temper of what were

[40] Much of what follows has been taken from Nii Bonne's autobiography, *Milestones in the History of the Gold Coast* (1953). Nii Bonne was no novice in the hard task of public campaigning. 'Sometime in 1931', he says, he had had a dream 'that there was going to be great famine in the country, and I was directed to go and preach to the farmers, and fishermen everywhere to sell their harvests and catches at moderate prices.' He toured the Colony towns by motor car at his own expense and addressed meetings of chiefs, farmers, and fishermen with (he says) great success. His autobiography, a delight to read, gives a very good picture of the life of an able businessman and traditionalist between the wars. He was installed as a chief of the Ga people in July 1945.

[41] An exception must be made of A. G. Leventis & Co., a Cypriot trading firm (and no friend to the British-dominated Association of West African Merchants) which pledged support for Nii Bonne's campaign, and agreed to make 'substantial reductions' in its prices. As Nii Bonne commented, the company was 'duly rewarded in later weeks'. When the riots took place and the big trading stores were looted it was noted that the crowds spared the firm's property.

[42] ACC *Minutes*, Feb. 1948.

virtually committees of young men in the local market towns could be seen in their promises to Nii Bonne:

Yilo Krobo: The whole country will declare civil war on Monday 24th January. . . .

Cape Coast: We shall fight until success is achieved, no one will dare to enter any European store. . . .

Axim: Let us be united and we shall conquer our common foes, boycott will begin on Monday. . . .

Promises of help came from many quarters: 'one of the captains [sub-chiefs] declared [at Big Ada in the Colony] that on 24th January he would be at war with European and Syrian merchants, and as a captain he would "see to it that his army did a clean job of the boycott".' Nii Bonne asked the large crowd that welcomed him in Ada whether they meant what they said, and 'the audience shouted: "we shall do the job, do not worry, we shall be united and anyone who dares to buy any textiles, we shall know what to do with him".'[43]

The boycott came into effect on 24 January, and lasted nearly a month. It was directed against the sale of cotton prints, tinned meat, flour, biscuits, spirits—a wide range of imported goods, although most local committees seemed to have permitted some articles of necessity (soap, salt, matches, medicine) to be bought in small quantities. Then, on 20 February, agreement was reached at a meeting in the Chief Secretary's office between representatives of the Anti-Inflationary Campaign Committee, the Joint Provincial Council of Chiefs, and the Chamber of Commerce. The firms promised to reduce their gross overall profit margin from 75 to 50 per cent on non-controlled commodities for a three-month trial period; and on these terms (and because of local quarrels between the boycott committee and the petty-

---

[43] pp. 68–70. The arguments put forward by Nii Bonne and his helpers were expressed in simple terms. 'This cloth sold by the white man at eighty-four shillings per piece of twelve yards by forty-eight inches and sold at the black market for six pounds per piece cost the white man about forty shillings landed here in these days. If the white man sells at fifty shillings he would gain 10 shillings profit. If he sells it at eighty-four shillings he collects a profit of more than the print cost him. Is the white man not cunningly taking away your money for nothing? The people will reply, "yes, the white man is stealing our money by tricks". Nii Bonne will then say, "don't buy anything from the white man's stores and don't allow your fellow countryfolks to buy. If they do, swear the oath of the Omanhene on them and get them fined. Do this until the white men reduce their prices"' (an account of the boycott by the Cape Coast trader Amponsah Dadzie to the Watson Commission, quoted in Bonne, pp. 91–92).

traders' associations which had run short of goods on their own stalls) Nii Bonne and his committee announced that the boycott would be lifted as soon as the new prices were introduced on 28 February.

In the meantime—while the boycott was still in progress—the UGCC had also been active. During the latter half of January and the whole of February Danquah and Nkrumah travelled through the Colony and Ashanti chiefdoms, spreading the idea of self-government. It was difficult to say how successful they were. W. O. Essuman (acting general secretary of the Convention) told the Watson Commission that at the time of the riots there were only 13 branches and 1,765 paid-up members; and it was probably not until the riots had actually occurred and the leaders had been detained that support for the UGCC spread far and wide. (Thus the UGCC *Minute Book* showed that the number of branches had suddenly increased to 209 by August 1948.) But even before the riots, the Convention drew unprecedently large crowds in the main towns; the leaders made every grievance their own, and were wildly acclaimed. An attempt to link the boycott committee with the UGCC had to be dropped when Nii Bonne refused his support, but the failure was more formal than real: the local leaders of the youth societies and their followers were members of both movements and saw both as part of the mounting demand for self-government.[44]

On Friday 20 February—the day agreement was reached between Nii Bonne's Boycott Committee and the government— and a little over a week before the riots—a large crowd gathered in the Palladium cinema in Accra and heard Nkrumah, Danquah, and Ako Adjei give their support to another discontented group: the ex-servicemen. B. E. A. Tamakloe, general secretary of the Ex-Servicemen's Union, announced that the ex-servicemen would march in procession to the castle on Monday the

[44] Nii Bonne (pp. 90–91) resented overtures made to him by the UGCC leaders. 'I should mention . . . that early in February 1948, when I visited Koforidua to address a meeting there, Dr J. B. Danquah and one Sekyi Djan called on me and said that I had done a great deal of good work for the people of the Gold Coast and that if I would assist their movement they would make me Minister of Commerce when they came to power. I told Dr Danquah that he could not make me anything better than what God had made me.' This of course is Nii Bonne's story of the relationship between the two movements, but Amponsah Dadzie also told the Watson Commission that the arrest of the UGCC leaders after the riots 'was the direct result of their meddling into an affair [the boycott] from which they should have been wise to keep out'.

23rd to present a petition to the Governor.[45] The march was then postponed to the 28th and a rally arranged for the evening beforehand. At midday on Saturday 28 February the Union members (and their supporters) gathered at the polo ground to begin their march. By 3 p.m. the straggling procession of some 2,000 marchers had travelled the length of Christiansborg Road (abandoning the route authorized by the police) to reach the castle cross-roads: they were checked by a small detachment of police, warnings and threats were lost in a growing tumult, stones were hurled, and the European superintendent in charge of the police —snatching a rifle from one of his men—opened fire on the crowd, killing two and wounding four or five others. The centre of the excitement then shifted to Accra where crowds had already begun to collect, among them 'men of a rough type who seemed anxious to persuade the crowds in the streets that the stores were not in fact charging the agreed prices'.[46] By the middle of the afternoon the United Africa Company's offices and shops and a number of the European-owned stores had been set on fire, and looting continued late into the night; it flared up again the following morning when the gates of Ussher Fort prison were battered down and some of the prisoners released. News of the disturbances then spread to a number of outlying towns where similar scenes were enacted; and on Monday evening rioting broke out in Kumasi. By this time, however, a state of emergency had been declared throughout the country.

When the riots broke out Danquah and Nkrumah were in Saltpond. After Akufo Addo, the Accra lawyer, had telephoned an account of the disturbances, they motored quickly to the capital, met the local members of the UGCC, and sat together on the verandah of Betty House (Akufo Addo's residence) to discuss

[45] The petition is printed as App. 15 to the Watson Commission *Report*. Danquah's connexion with the ex-servicemen was partly through his son, who had served in the army in Burma. The government was particularly alarmed (after the riots) about the presence of a European at the rally—an employee of BOAC, who was said to be a communist. Danquah stoutly refuted the allegation by the government that he was connected with such people. 'I met [the European] in the left wing of the stage of the Palladium cinema [in December 1947 or January 1948]. From the phrases used by him in his chat with me I gathered he might be a communist. I asked him whether he was one and he replied that he was a Social Democrat. Being interested in neither the one nor the other, I left him and went back to my seat on the platform' (memo. submitted by Danquah to the Watson Commission, 16 Apr. 1948).

[46] Watson Commission *Report*, App. 10, 'Brief Narrative of Events' compiled by the Gold Coast Govt.

what should be done 'to take advantage of that day's tragic events and use that advantage as a fulcrum or lever for the liberation of Ghana'.[47] Eventually they decided to send telegrams to the Secretary of State and the world press. Danquah excelled all previous protests with a telegram of nearly 1,000 words in which he claimed: 'Civil Government ... broken down. ... Working Committee ... prepared ... to take over interim government', and demanded the dispatch of a 'special Commissioner ... to hand over Government to interim government of chiefs and people and to witness immediate calling of Constituency Assembly', ending with the words: 'God Save the King and Floreat United Gold Coast'.[48] Nkrumah's—addressed to the United Nations, the *Pan Africa* magazine in Manchester, the *New York Times*, the London *Daily Worker*, and the Moscow *New Times*—was more economical: it asked for the recall of the Governor and for a Commission to 'supervise formation Constituent Assembly'.[49] Nothing else happened, except the publication by Danquah in the local press of a manifesto addressed to the chiefs under the title: 'The hour of liberation has struck'. After a further ten days' hesitation, however, the government issued orders (11 March) for the arrest of the six leading members of the Convention and their removal to the Northern Territories as a suitable place of detention until the arrival of a Commission of Inquiry from London.[50]

When the government passed judgement on the riots it drew what seemed to be the obvious conclusion at the time, that the Working Committee and its general secretary had engineered the

[47] These are Danquah's own words. The 'noble band of the Working Committee of the United Gold Coast Convention ... on that fateful night of February 28th 1948 when Accra was burning and the imperialist agent had spilt the blood of men of Ghana sat together on a verandah in Betty House ... to plan to take advantage of that day's tragic incidents and use that advantage as a fulcrum or lever for the liberation of Ghana' (see *The Doyen Speaks: Some Historical Speeches by Dr J. B. Danquah* (n.d.). Danquah's description of the riots to the Watson Commission was vivid: 'I saw a horrible sight. All about the central part of the town I saw big cars—the first that struck me was a big car near the Insurance office—turned upside down and burnt. Another car near Chelleram I saw, and other cars too. I went through to the High Street and saw the whole of Kingsway Stores looted, glass broken. It was a terrible sight. I went through Station Road and found looting still going on in some parts'. The people 'were excited and rushing into the streets and taking some goods out. I saw policemen standing by doing nothing, and some of them, in fact, taking part in the looting' (*Mins. of Evidence*).

[48] Watson Commission *Report*, App. 14.   [49] Ibid. App. 13.

[50] The six detained were Danquah, Nkrumah, Akufo Addo, W. E. Ofori Atta, Ako Adjei, Obetsibi Lamptey. The two telegrams are printed in full as App. 13 & 14 to the Watson Commission *Report*. Danquah's was signed 'President, United Gold Coast Convention'. The signature was Pa Grant's, but the hand was Danquah's.

revolt: that their ends, 'while ostensibly the attainment of self-government by constitutional means, were in fact revolutionary'.[51] The officials did not doubt the fact, in the light of Nkrumah's activities in London, his liking for popular Marxist terminology, and the discovery by the police of his membership card of the British Communist Party. Other evidence also came to light. There was the extraordinary document known as 'The Circle', and a memorandum circulated to the other members of the Working Committee which advocated a programme of civil disobedience—'organised demonstration, boycott and strike'.[52] Two months later the Watson Commission came to a more cautious conclusion: the 'disturbances were planned but that there is no evidence to show by what persons or organisations they were planned'.[53] On a longer view still, the evidence looked even less conclusive. It was difficult to believe that the UGCC leaders were able successfully to plot a revolution (or to bring such grievances as existed to a predetermined end), although once the storm burst about their heads they were certainly capable of believing they could ride it. It might be thought that Nkrumah was of a different calibre, but this too was doubtful. As will be seen, a cautious judgement governed a bold imagination on a number of critical occasions: it was only with great reluctance, for example, that he agreed to head the second outburst of rioting in January 1950. It was not difficult to understand why the government should suspect the existence of a deep-laid plot. It had been taken by surprise, and had looked round, bewildered, for an explanation in wider terms than its own deficiencies. But coincidence probably played a larger part in the February riots than was allowed for at the time: the coincidence of the boycott, the mount-

---

[51] See the 'Brief Narrative of Events. . .' put out by the Government in March 1948, and printed as App. 10 to the (Watson) *Report*. By this time the government was thoroughly alarmed, far beyond what the evidence warranted. 'Further examination' (it claimed) 'of the activities of the Working Committee . . . showed additional links with the communist organisation overseas . . . [and] a danger of new forms of terrorism, quite alien to the spirit of this country, and fortunately not hitherto employed. These included assassination.' It also thought that the release of convicts from Ussher Fort Prison in Accra by a drunken mob was 'of a pattern familiar in communist disorders when the communists are seeking to seize power'.

[52] See App. 11 to the (Watson) *Report* and App. B to Nkrumah's *Autobiography*, 'The Circle' was drawn up by Nkrumah and used (he says) in London among West African students. It outlined a secret organization among a small band of devoted followers who should 'except as a last resort avoid the use of violence', with secret signs, fast days, and the threat of reprisals against traitors.

[53] *Report*, para. 85 (ii).

ing unrest in the rural areas, and the presence of a proto-nationalist group of ambitious lawyers. Thus the agreement reached between Nii Bonne and the Chamber of Commerce representatives on 20 February, whereby the firms undertook to reduce their profit margins (on certain commodities) by 50 per cent, had been popularly interpreted as a promise to cut the actual price of goods by half; in fact, prices fell by about a sixth, and the Accra crowd were in a resentful, ugly mood at precisely the time when tension was already high as a result of the boycott and when the ex-servicemen were gathering to parade their grievances. The waters in which the UGCC leaders sought to fish were already troubled, therefore, by events outside their control, and although by their fishing they added to the turmoil, this was not to say that they were ever in charge of a master plan, or responsible for the actual sequence of events from which, indeed, many of them drew back dismayed.[54]

The effect of the riots, however, was profound. At first the detention of the UGCC leaders raised their popularity to national heights, and the name of the ex-serviceman who was killed at the Christiansborg cross-roads—Sgt Adjetey—aroused genuine emotion among those who cared little enough for the Ex-Servicemen's Union. But the February riots were also responsible for the schism which took place between, on the one hand, the reformist intelligentsia and, on the other, the radical 'young men' who listened willingly to Nkrumah as he began to create his own following, nominally within, in practice opposed to, the Convention. Thus the early Jacobins gave place to the *sans-culottes*— in Ghana, the 'verandah boys'—and the revolution began to take a familiar course.[55] The UGCC leaders struggled to free themselves of Nkrumah without losing the popularity he brought them. They failed and, deserted by those who had formerly acclaimed them, they turned eventually to their earlier rivals, the

[54] Cf. George Padmore's account of the disturbances: 'What happened in Accra on [28 February 1948] was not initiated by the UGCC. The leaders merely fished in troubled waters and exploited the situation.' The telegrams sent to the Secretary of State were merely 'a piece of comic-opera politics' (*The Gold Coast Revolution* (1953), pp. 62–64).

[55] 'Verandah Boys'—those who slept on the verandahs of the rich because they had no home of their own, and no money with which to rent a room. One might recall here the remark by the Jacobin Père Gérard: 'When I first sat among you I heard so many beautiful speeches that I might have believed myself in heaven, had there not been so many lawyers present.' It might have been said by Nkrumah of the UGCC.

chiefs. Thus by the end of 1948 the leading figures of the Convention, and the more prominent of the indirect-rule chiefs, were sitting together on the Coussey Committee on Constitutional Reform. By the end of 1949 Nkrumah had formed a 'People's Party'. And by the end of 1950 the 'struggle for the inheritance' between the men of property and standing, and the young men of the CPP, had been sharpened and given precise shape by the impending general election. This fundamental shift in the leadership of the nationalist movement was the principal feature of the three years between February 1948 and February 1951. To describe it, one must see the effect of the riots on first, the chiefs, then the intelligentsia, and finally Nkrumah and the local youth associations.

As soon as the riots had taken place, the Standing Committee of the Joint Provincial Council—consisting of twelve paramount chiefs (plus the Ga Native Authority)—sent messages of loyalty to the king, in which they welcomed the measures taken by the government to restore order. At this particular juncture the UGCC leaders objected strongly. The chiefs' action was 'the last straw that could break the back of Gold Coast nationalism, a clear stab in the back'.[56] A similar scene was enacted in Kumasi, where the Ashanti chiefs affirmed their loyalty to the government, and took the elderly leaders of the Kotoko Society to task for having submitted a memorandum to the Watson Commission without the chiefs' approval. The memorandum had asked for a greater share in the government of the country for 'the youth', but the Asantehene pointed out that: 'The Youth have representatives on the Confederacy Council and all of them are members of the Kotoko Society. . . . I myself am a member of the Society; I have addressed the Society on two occasions, and have taken photographs with them'.[57] I. K. Agyeman, secretary to the Kumasi State Council, then hastened to apologize on behalf of the society, saying that its 'senior members' had not been consulted about the memorandum, all of them having been out of town when it had been drawn up, except J. S. Kankam who had made the mistake of signing without reading it.

The Ashanti chiefs then turned their attack on the young men of the Asante Youth Association and the boycott committees. Stories were abroad that some of the leaders had accepted money

[56] Danquah, *The Doyen Speaks*, p. 2.   [57] ACC *Minutes*, June 1948.

from the traders' associations, and the chiefs seized on the allegations to criticize Krobo Edusei, Owusu Ansah, and Atta Mensah
in harsh terms. 'You people are traitors, quislings and fifth
columnists', the Juabenhene informed them. 'You have betrayed
our trust. When you introduced yourselves to us last February
and sought our assistance, you made us to understand that you
were waging war against "blackmarketeers" . . . . The Council
therefore gave its support. Chiefs subscribed to your funds. You
promised always to consult the Council.'[58] Other chiefs took up
the same theme. Krobo Edusei, in particular, was criticized: the
future Minister of the Interior was now a local hero of the young
men, well known as the chairman of the Anti-Inflation Campaign Committee for his rough oratory and friendly invective,
and the chiefs singled him out for attack. The Adansihene accused him of having 'steadily amassed power'; the Akwamuhene
thought it was 'particularly distressing that Krobo Edusei whom
we entertain because of his jovial disposition should attempt at
wresting power from the natural rulers'.[59] The Asantehene himself spoke, widening the theme, and rebuking the leaders of the
AYA and the Boycott Committee alike:

Otumfuo: During the recent unrest in Ashanti, we maintained
silence, and watched you with a philanthropic contempt. We were
convinced—and we were not wrong—that you would reach nowhere. Here you stand belittled, accused of a heinous crime, a crime
compatible if not synonymous with theft. . . . Tell me by what power
you beat gong-gong and make your law?

To which Krobo Edusei replied:

As I have no power to do what I did, hence I have made overtures to
Nana Offinsuhene to plead with you for pardon for me.

The Asantehene then went on—so the *Minutes* record—to
comment

at large on the cause for which the disturbances were sponsored by the

---

[58] Ibid.
[59] When Owusu Ansah, the Anti-Inflation Committee secretary, protested (in-
cautiously) that the chiefs were misinformed, and that the Akwamuhene was
'tainted with hatred' for his fellow human beings, the Asantehene intervened saying
that Owusu Ansah had 'insulted my Akwamuhene, in my presence, and for that he
shall slaughter 4 sheep'. The usual custom was then followed:
Owusu Ansah: I beg for mercy, and for a reduction of the number of sheep to be
slaughtered.
Otumfuo: I reduce the number to 2 live sheep. I want to see the two sheep
slaughtered before I go on with the case (*Minutes*, June 1948).

youth. . . 'Self-Government'. He however deplored the intention of the youth to import a foreign system of government, instead of improving upon our own which foreign powers might envy. It might have been tainted with barbarism but it was not beyond polishing. Our form of Government, he said, knows nothing of Prime Ministers and Secretaries of State.

You people claim to be nationally conscious, and therefore undertook to fight against rising prices and black marketing. You claim to be waving the torch of emancipation, yet you have proved yourself to be after your own personal interests. What do you want us to make of your clamour for Self-Government?. . . The Secretary will inform the Government that the Anti-Inflation Campaign Committee has been dissolved in Ashanti and that if Krobo Edusei engineers another boycott or travels through Ashanti for funds, he should be arrested. The gong-gong to be beaten by chiefs should state in plain language that the recent reductions in prices have not been due to the efforts of Krobo Edusei.[60]

The Kumasi meeting was wild and noisy, attended by large crowds of onlookers in an excited mood, the whole episode recalling accounts of earlier scenes in the capital long before colonial rule when the chiefs went in fear of the Kumasi mob. But with the government once more firmly in control, and the police patrolling the streets, the Ashanti and Colony chiefs felt free to act. The young men were made to forswear their support for Nkrumah and the UGCC; fines were imposed on their leaders, and the renewal of the boycott (which had been planned for 28 May) forbidden.

The UGCC leaders hesitated a little longer than the chiefs, but after their release from detention they too moved to the defence of law and order; and in mid-1948 a new path of reform opened before them. The United Kingdom government accepted the recommendations of the Watson Commission that a local committee should be appointed to formulate proposals for a new constitution. This was clearly a step of great importance, and one that the intelligentsia understood very well. They were at home with committees and schemes of political reform; and they had no hesitation in responding to the government's invitation to join a 'Committee on Constitutional Reform' under the chairmanship of Mr Justice Coussey. Accordingly, six Conventionists accepted membership: B. D. Addai, E. Akufo Addo, J. B. Dan-

[60] *Minutes*, June 1948.

quah, G. A. Grant, Cobina Kessie, and E. O. Obetsibi Lamptey. In all, there were 40 members of this all-African Committee— 31 commoners and 9 chiefs, the right kind of proportion for the UGCC leaders, and from this point forward, the chiefs and the intelligentsia began to work amicably together. Nkrumah was not invited to serve on the Committee. It was, to say the least, unlikely in 1948 that the government should have invited the author of 'The Circle'. The decision was to his advantage, and in the struggle which developed between him and the UGCC Working Committee the odds were very heavily against the latter. The lawyers were now on good terms with those in authority, and absorbed in committee meetings. Nkrumah was under no such handicap. He was free to act within the Convention, without being affected by its association with the Committee and the government; and although anxious not to forfeit any prestige which the UGCC leaders might still have, he was also able to make use of the local youth societies (on which the Convention rested) as the basis of a new movement which would look to him personally for leadership.

Step by step, Nkrumah and the Working Committee now went different ways. In July Nkrumah opened the first 'Ghana College' in the Oddfellows Hall at Cape Coast to try and meet the plight of the Cape Coast secondary schoolboys who had gone on strike in February and had been dismissed.[61] The following month a national 'Committee on Youth Organization' (the CYO) was formed in Accra under two new leaders among the radical youth groups in the capital: K. A. Gbedemah (chairman), and Kojo Botsio (secretary).[62] In September the first issue of a daily news-sheet appeared—the *Evening News*—managed by Nkrumah, edited by Gbedemah, which was violently anti-colonial, anti-the-Coussey Committee, and anti-the-UGCC (despite Nkrumah's continued membership of the Convention). Later again, at the end of December 1948, Nkrumah summoned

[61] For the Ghana Schools and Colleges see Bankole Timothy, *Kwame Nkrumah* (1955), ch. 8, and Nkrumah, *Autobiography*, pp. 89–92. The idea was first put forward in the Working Committee of the UGCC.

[62] The CYO was never a tightly-knit body. Besides Gbedemah and Botsio, the executive included Krobo Edusei, Atta Mensah, and Bediako Poku of the AYA in Kumasi; Dzenkle Dzewu and Mrs Hannah Cudjoe; Kofi Baako, Saki Scheck and Kwesi Plange of the 'Ghana League of Patriots'; and R. S. Iddrisu and Eben Adam in Tamale. 'Youth' had to be interpreted liberally. Nkrumah was now 39, Gbedemah 36, and Botsio 33.

a Ghana Youth Congress in Kumasi which met in secret session. And—as a measure of the difference that now existed between the two sides—the declaration drawn up by the delegates to the Youth Congress may be contrasted with the statement issued by the UGCC Working Committee at the end of January 1949:

> Youth are everywhere in action against the forces of evil, suppression and repression, and we youth in the Gold Coast have not been found wanting. . . . We demand a constitution that would give this country nothing less than FULL SELF-GOVERNMENT NOW.[63]

> The country's hope for the design of a self-governing constitution is at present centred on the Coussey Committee and no one can tell how long it will take to come to the end of its report. . . . It is within the knowledge of those actively abreast with the making of Constitutions that it is an arduous task. In our present situation, until the Coussey Committee's Report is issued to the legislative council, is debated by that body, and received the approval or disapproval of the general public, there is nothing gained to fix a target date for the coming of the new constitution. . . . Our policy is that it should be at the earliest possible time and we counsel all patriots of the country to work steadfastly for the coming of the great event.[64]

No doubt the Working Committee was right in what it said, but the youth societies were not interested in the procedure of constitutional reform: they moved in the realm of absolutes; and in so far as their leaders had any policy, it began to be expressed quite simply as 'Self-Government Now', to be achieved immediately through the calling of a national constituent assembly: 'If by the first of April we haven't got self-government we shall begin to free ourselves according to our planned programme of action', said Saki Scheck of the Sekondi Youth Association at a local rally in January 1949. It was this view that the Working Committee was attempting to counter. Its lawyer members allowed their heads sensibly to rule their hearts: the CYO followed its heart.

Where did Nkrumah himself stand? He and the rest of the Working Committee stayed uneasily together, despite an atmosphere of increasing distrust and suspicion, until the middle of 1949. In August 1948, for example, he had been called before the Committee, and questioned by Akufo Addo:

[63] *Ghana Youth Manifesto*, 1948.
[64] UGCC, *Minute Book*; entry for 15 Jan., of a copy of a 'Press Release' issued to the general public.

Why do you persist in using the word Comrade as a term of address ? Why do you still continue connections with the West African National Secretariat ?

Why do you welcome the Watson Commission's laying the blame for the disturbances on the Convention ?[65]

He was then informed that he was suspended from the post of secretary. The next meeting of the Convention, three weeks later (in Nana Ofori Atta's house in Accra), coincided with the publication by Nkrumah of the *Evening News*, and Grant demanded his total removal from office. Blay and Ansah Koi (a medical practitioner) suggested he might be made vice-president. Akufo Addo and Danquah proposed, and others agreed, that he might be made honorary treasurer. Nkrumah refused—and, then, in November, accepted. At the end of the year, however, the Youth Congress met under Nkrumah's leadership in Kumasi and by February 1949—a year after the riots and the ex-servicemen's rally—the rift between the two sides could hardly be bridged. Nevertheless, Nkrumah and the Committee met again in a stormy meeting at which Nkrumah admitted that 'since August last year things had not gone well between himself and the Working Committee . . . the masses appreciated his contribution to the aims of the Convention [but] he had not been understood by the Working Committee as a body'. He had, however, 'promoted the youth organisation to rally all sections of the youth under the banner of the Convention [and] the Ghana Colleges were starting to "save the face of the Convention".'[66]

What the Committee thought of this explanation was not recorded. Its members found themselves in a humiliating Frankenstein situation, in which they would, no doubt, have liked to dispense with Nkrumah—'the humble and obedient servant of the Convention' as he had professed himself to be to the Watson Commission—had they not feared what he might do without them. They were now confronted with the growing demands put forward by the youth societies and, like the sorcerer's apprentice, they discovered that they had called up a force stronger than they liked which threatened to engulf them. Nkrumah was obviously responsible for a great deal of the propaganda which the *Evening News* and local youth rallies engaged in (much of it directed against the Convention). Yet to dismiss him was almost certain

[65] Ibid. entry for 12 Aug. 1948.   [66] Ibid. entry for 20 Feb. 1949.

to provoke a revolt among the youth groups from which the Convention drew the bulk of its support.

Thus it would be possible to plot a graph of events from the 1948 riots to the middle of 1949 in which the UGCC and the youth associations would be seen as starting from a common point but, month by month, event by event, diverging more and more widely; and by June 1949 the two lines on the graph would be far apart. At length, on 11 June, the Working Committee tried to stir itself. It issued the text of two resolutions: (1) membership of the CYO and the UGCC were incompatible; (2) Nkrumah was to be 'served with charges' because he had disregarded 'the obligations of collective responsibility and party discipline', had published opinions, views, and criticisms in the *Evening News*, 'assailing the decisions and questioning the integrity of the Working Committee', and had undermined the Convention, abusing its leaders and stealing its ideas.[67] At long last, too, the report appeared of a Committee of Inquiry into Headquarters Organization: appointed in August 1948, the Committee now produced 25 pages of typescript containing detailed recommendations for strengthening the Convention under a new general secretary and nine assistants.

The report was still-born. And once again, for the last time, the UGCC leaders were outmanœuvred. The CYO had met earlier in the month at Tarkwa, the mining town in the western province, where 'the discussions that took place', says Nkrumah, 'lasted for about three nights and proceeded into the early hours of the morning'.[68] During the conference the more experienced members of the youth movement—Gbedemah, Botsio, Dzenkle Dzewu, Krobo Edusei—had stressed the need to make a clean

[67] *Minute Book*, entry for 11 June 1949. One of the charges fabricated by the CPP against the Working Committee (and greatly resented) was that its members had accepted large sums of money from the U.K. government whereby they undertook to deflect people's interests from politics to sport. The accusation arose out of the visit (sponsored by the Colonial Office) of Sir Sydney Abrahams to advise on sport—a visit encouraged by Danquah when he met Abrahams at Lancaster House while attending the London Africa Conference in October 1948. The sum usually mentioned was £25,000. (This was the amount asked for in 1944 by Kojo Thompson (a member of the legislative council) of the representative on the council of the Chamber of Commerce as the price of stopping criticism of the Association of West African Merchants.) The accusation brought against the Working Committee may seem preposterous in retrospect (as indeed it was); but 1948–9 was a period of great emotion, when rumours were grasped at because there was a great willingness to believe them. The *Evening News* made a great issue of it (see Timothy, pp. 62–3. For the Kojo Thompson case, see Wight, p. 173).

[68] *Autobiography*, p. 100.

break with the UGCC; a younger section, led by Kofi Baako, Kwesi Plange, and Saki Scheck, evidently believed that the Convention still commanded wide support and, therefore, that the CYO should insist on Nkrumah's reinstatement as secretary in order to capture the UGCC from within. Eventually a compromise was reached: a new party should be formed, but one that would retain the name 'Convention'. And on Sunday, 12 June 1949, at the Arena meeting ground in Accra, before an audience of 'about 60,000 people', on behalf of

the CYO, in the name of the chiefs, the people, the rank and file of the Convention, the Labour movement, our valiant ex-servicemen, the youth movement throughout the country, the man in the street, our children and those as yet unborn, the new Ghana that is to be, Sergeant Adjety and his comrades who died at the crossroads of Christiansborg during the 1948 riots, and in the name of God Almighty and humanity

Nkrumah announced the formation of a 'Convention People's Party'. Kojo Botsio became its secretary, K. A. Gbedemah its vice-chairman, and Nkrumah its chairman.[69]

The final character in these opening scenes now appeared. Gerald Creasy left the country, and Charles Arden-Clarke arrived in August 1949—a strong Governor ready to negotiate but prepared also to act with resolution. Both qualities were necessary as events began to move towards a new climax. For in October the *Report* of the (Coussey) Committee on Constitutional Reform appeared. It proposed a form of semi-responsible government: an executive council of three *ex-officio* and eight representative ministers, and a nationally elected assembly. The Committee

[69] Ibid. p. 105. As soon as the CPP was formed Kojo Botsio sent a telegram to the Working Committee: 'Convention People's Party under the leadership and chairmanship of Kwame Nkrumah inaugurated in Accra Sunday 12 June 1949 aims at Self-Government Now for Chiefs and People of the Gold Coast, a democratic government and a higher standard of living for the people.' The Working Committee issued its own statement two days later: 'Saltpond 15/6/49. All members of the United Gold Coast Convention are warned that the Convention has no connection with the newly formed Convention People's Party . . . Pa Grant expects loyalty of all Conventionists. Formation new party at this juncture inimical to interests of country. . .'. On 26 June Nkrumah met the Working Committee, and arbitrators were appointed to examine the dispute between them. On 31 July an emergency conference of UGCC, youth groups, and the new CPP met in Saltpond; Nkrumah agreed to disband the CPP and resume the secretaryship of the Convention, provided a new Working Committee was elected. Argument broke out again, the delegates passed a vote of no confidence in the UGCC executive, and prevailed on Nkrumah to resign and lead the new movement. The CPP was to stay and the break was final.

had divided almost equally over the composition of the new legislature, and alternative schemes were suggested: (1) a bicameral
system comprising a Senate of chiefs and elder statesmen, and a
House of Assembly elected by poll-taxpayers, aged 25 and over;
or (2) a unicameral legislature, two-thirds elected on a popular
franchise, and one-third elected by the territorial councils of
chiefs. The UGCC members (and Nana Ofori Atta) also added a
minority rider to the *Report* in which they objected to the retention of reserve powers by the Governor, and proposed that the
new executive council 'apart from the Governor as chairman
[should] be composed only of elected members. . . '. As was to be
expected. however, the Secretary of State gave his approval to
the main body of the *Report*, and in favour of a unicameral system, whereupon the new Governor commended the *Report* to the
public at large as 'a very great constitutional advance',[70] while
strengthening the security forces in the main centres of population.

　It was unlikely that the UGCC leaders would oppose the
principal recommendations contained in the Coussey *Report*, and
doubtful whether they had any political power to do so. The important decision now rested with the CPP leaders, who were
faced with a difficult decision. The first paragraph of a six-point
programme adopted by the new party in June had been 'to fight
relentlessly by all constitutional means for the achievement of
"Self-Government Now" for the chiefs and people of the Gold
Coast'.[71] But where was the emphasis now to be placed? On Self-
Government Now? Or on the constitutional means? It was difficult to say how deep the division between the party leaders was,
but that they were divided was hardly in doubt, and Nkrumah
moved uncertainly between the need to retain support by a bold
appeal to nationalist principles, and the immediate practical advantages of compromise. Gbedemah, it might be noted, was now
in prison, convicted in October 1949 on a charge of publishing
false news, and the new Governor made it clear that any attempt
to force the government's hand would be dealt with far more

[70] Coussey Committee *Report* (Col. No. 248) and *Statement by His Majesty's
Government* (Col. No. 250). The Coussey proposals were indeed 'a very great
advance'. The 1925 Colony council of 14 (9 Africans, 5 Europeans) unofficial
members, and the Ashanti-Colony council of 18 unofficials, was to become a
National Assembly of 75 African members.
[71] The six points are given in Nkrumah's *Autobiography*, p. 101.

severely than in 1948. Thus a wavering line was followed. Nkrumah's first reaction to the Coussey *Report* was that expressed in the *Evening News* which warned its readers that the new constitution would prove a 'Trojan gift horse'. Nkrumah labelled it 'bogus and fraudulent', and began to talk of the need for 'Positive Action'—a civil disobedience campaign of agitation, propaganda and 'as a last resort, the constitutional application of strikes, boycotts, and non-cooperation based on the principles of absolute non-violence' to try and force the government to call a constituent Assembly.[72] This was obviously intended to disrupt. A month later, however, there was a shift of emphasis. Nkrumah summoned a 'Ghana People's Representative Assembly' in Accra on 20 November, consisting of party members, the CYO, trade unions, farmers' associations, ex-servicemen, and the local youth societies. The chairman of the Assembly was Pobee Biney, a locomotive driver and vice-chairman of the Gold Coast TUC. The delegates adopted a general resolution demanding 'immediate self-government, that is, full Dominion status within the Commonwealth of Nations based on the Statute of Westminster'; but it also approved a moderate draft constitution of a bicameral legislature (a Senate of chiefs and elders), an executive of twelve ministers, of whom one would be an *ex-officio* Minister of Defence 'appointed by the Secretary of State with the advice and consent of the Executive Council (cabinet)', and an assembly, directly elected 'without property qualification'. The Governor would retain a power of Certification and Veto, to be exercised on the advice and with the consent of the cabinet. A minority rider was then added—as if the CPP assembly were trying to provide an exact parallel with the Coussey *Report*—in which Kofi Baako and Saki Scheck of the 'League of Ghana Patriots' proposed the total exclusion of *ex-officio* members from the executive.

There was little likelihood that the Secretary of State or the Governor would accept these amendments (as, in effect, they were) to the Coussey *Report*, having already rejected the very similar minority rider submitted by the UGCC members; and in mid-December Nkrumah swung back to 'Positive Action'.

[72] The plan was outlined in *What I mean by Positive Action*, the pamphlet written by Nkrumah recording his meeting with the Ga State Council on 20 October. It contained a more moderate statement of belief than 'The Circle'. The main influence seems to have been C. V. H. Rao's book on the *Civil Disobedience Movement in India*.

Readers of the *Evening News* were warned that it was now imminent; and on Thursday, 15 December (having notified the Governor of his intentions), Nkrumah repeated to a large Arena crowd
what the *Evening News* had published the same afternoon:

> Get ready, people of the Gold Coast, the era of Positive Action
> rapidly draws nigh. The Coussey Committee has failed to grant the
> people of this country Full Self-Government; the Legislative Council
> has failed to demand self-government for the country; the Chiefs'
> Territorial Councils have failed to demand self-government for the
> country; and the British Government has tactfully refused to grant
> the country her true and legitimate demand for Self-Government....
>
> What the people of the country demand now is the calling of a
> CONSTITUENT ASSEMBLY through a General Election to de-
> termine a Full Self-Government Constitution for the country.
>
> The people of this country will be waiting patiently for two weeks
> from today, December 15, 1949, during which the British Govern-
> ment might announce through the Governor, the acceptance of the
> principle of a Constituent Assembly to be implemented without de-
> lay; otherwise, Positive Action may be declared any time after the said
> two weeks.
>
> People of the Gold Coast, get ready and be prepared; save and
> spend wisely and wait for the day, should it come.[73]

There was a note of uncertainty about this call to arms, and it
was easy to understand why Nkrumah should hesitate. The party
was daily growing stronger, although it was also becoming im-
patient: was the difference between the Coussey constitution,
and the outline drawn by the Ghana People's Representative
Assembly, worth a riot and the arrest of the party's leaders?
Might it not be possible to negotiate a compromise of honour—
to move from 'Positive' to 'Tactical Action'? When, therefore,
early in January, Arden-Clarke authorized Reginald Saloway,
the Colonial Secretary, to open negotiations with the party's
leaders, Nkrumah agreed to talk the matter over. If the account
of the meeting given by Arden-Clarke and Saloway is accepted as
an accurate description of what took place, Nkrumah was prepared—and at one stage agreed—to call off Positive Action, only
to be spurred on by his more ardent followers. The leaders, said
Arden-Clarke, were 'enmeshed in the coils of their own propaganda', and 'the tail wagged the dog'. Neither the party nor the

[73] *Evening News*, 16 Dec. 1949.

TUC, says Saloway, 'had any control over its wild men'.[74] Thus both portray a familiar situation when

> ... those behind cried 'Forward!'
> And those before cried 'Back!'.

Nkrumah himself is more reticent; in these meetings with the Colonial Secretary, the *Autobiography* relates: 'we went over the same ground and reached no agreement', and the New Year opened full of uncertainty, when 'nerves were on edge and the atmosphere was extremely tense'.[75] An announcement that Positive Action had started was twice reported and twice denied in the party's newspaper and, in the end, the issue was forced by the TUC which declared a general strike from midnight on Friday, 6 January, in sympathy with the government meteorological workers who had stopped work at the beginning of December. The CPP executive met throughout the night of Saturday, 7 January; but it was not until 5 p.m. the following day (Sunday, 8th) that Nkrumah announced to the Arena crowd that Positive Action should start from midnight.[76]

By Wednesday a general stoppage of work brought the crowds once more into the streets, but the government was quick to act and a state of emergency was declared throughout the country on the 11th. On the 17th a strict curfew kept the main towns quiet at night, and the extensive use of a new force of mobile police limited unrest in the main towns to sporadic outbursts of violence. On

[74] See two articles, one by Arden-Clarke, in *Afr. Aff.*, Jan. 1958, the other by Saloway in *Int. Aff.*, Oct. 1955. 'The party leaders had been officially informed and were well aware that they had a perfectly constitutional way of achieving power and gaining their objective, if their candidates at the forthcoming election were returned. I have good reason to believe that some at least of the party leaders would have preferred not to resort to 'positive action' but to await the results of the general election, of the outcome of which they were fairly confident. But they found themselves enmeshed in the coils of their own propaganda. The tail wagged the dog. . .' (*African Affairs*). Saloway says that he convinced Nkrumah that the forthcoming election would be managed fairly, and persuaded the executive committee of the CPP to follow constitutional methods. 'Nkrumah publicly called off "Positive Action" [and] tried hard to get the Trades Union Congress to call off the general strike, but the TUC no longer had any control over the wild men. [Moreover] Dr Danquah taunted Nkrumah with having sold himself to the Colonial Secretary and thus infuriated the rank and file of the CPP who forced Nkrumah to retract' (*Int. Aff.*, Oct. 1955, p. 47).

[75] *Autobiography*, p. 117.

[76] It was difficult to draw any clear distinction between the TUC and the CPP: H. P. Nyemitei, for example, was president of the Meteorological Workers' Union and assistant general secretary of the CPP: but Anthony Woode, Pobey Biney, and Turkson Ocran were leading figures in both the TUC and the Sekondi branch of the CPP who liked to interpret the nationalist movement in simple Marxist terms, and they constituted a small 'left-wing' trade union section of the party.

10 January Arden-Clarke addressed the legislative council in forthright terms, making it plain that 'when the time [comes] to apportion praise and blame I can see no need for the assistance of any commission of enquiry. I know of nothing that has occurred that cannot be dealt with justly and effectively by the Courts of this country and established disciplinary procedure.'[77] The arrest of the TUC and party leaders followed, culminating with that of Nkrumah, who had taken refuge in the Labadi suburb of Accra on 21 January. They were brought before the courts and convicted, some of promoting an illegal strike and attempting to coerce the government, others of sedition, Nkrumah being sentenced separately on three counts to a total of three years' imprisonment.

This is a useful point at which to bring the account of these early years to a close. The colonial government had asserted its authority on behalf of what was thought to be 'a very large body of moderate and responsible people who were utterly opposed to the methods of [the Convention People's Party]'.[78] The extremists were in prison, and the men of property began to speak out.

This is the time for the Government to strengthen its hands, check lawlessness and disregard for law and order. We have suffered enough, many lives have been destroyed and lost; valuable property has been damaged. This is the time for the government to strengthen its hands. Among the hooligans, there is not one responsible person in this country. No chief has asked for self-government, no responsible person in this country has asked for self-government and self-government is not attained overnight.[79]

Indeed, the intelligentsia and the chiefs were so sure (in Danquah's words, the 'wolf had been driven away'), that they began to quarrel again.[80] In an *Open Letter to Nananom in Council*, published in January 1950, the chiefs were rebuked by the UGCC; they were told that the reckless declaration of Positive Action by the CPP had unfortunately 'given opportunity for the reactionary forces in the country to strengthen their position not only

[77] *Governor's Address to LC*, 10 Jan. 1950.
[78] *Debate on the Governor's Address*, 19 July 1950.
[79] Ibid. I. K. Agyeman, elected in 1946 by the ACC.
[80] *Yepam pataku ansa na yeatu abirekyo fo* (In times of danger we drive away the wolf before we advise the goat). Quoted by Danquah in the *Debate on the Governor's Address*, 19 July 1950.

against the revolutionary and radical elements but even to question some of the plans of the progressive and saner groups'. The distinction was, however, unreal. The 'progressive and saner groups' were now an ineffective minority; and the 'very large body of moderate and responsible people' whom the Governor had sought to protect against the CPP hardly existed in face of the magnetic appeal of Self-Government Now. The young men (and the commoners in general) flocked to join the CPP, partly in the confident expectation that self-government would prove a sovereign remedy for all the grievances of the post-war years, partly because they saw in the People's Party a national movement that corresponded to their own efforts to assert their rights in the Colony and Ashanti chiefdoms. Building on these hopes in the early months of 1950, Gbedemah (released from prison) began to construct a network of party branches across the southern half of the country, and as the CPP gathered momentum the chiefs and UGCC leaders drew together again in mutual protection. The colonial government also began to revise its judgement. Its overriding concern now was to see the (modified) constitution devised by the Coussey Committee put to work, following a general election, in the hope that it would lead to a period of stability after the turmoil of the past two and a half years; but it was increasingly plain that there was little chance of achieving a settled administration unless the CPP leaders, including Nkrumah, were brought within the framework of the new reforms. The officials were willing to face the possibility of a CPP government. It remained to be seen whether the nationalist party was willing to form one should it win the election.

That such a prospect could be entertained showed how great a transformation had taken place. By 1950 the protagonists of the Burns constitution had been displaced so effectively that earlier arguments for and against indirect rule, for and against the chiefs and the intelligentsia, were no longer heard: they belonged to a seemingly vanished colonial order when the unofficials quarrelled among themselves and the officials ruled the country. Now, power was to be handed over in large measure to new leaders who had hitherto played no part in national politics. Thus it might be said that the 1948 rioters, and the young men who came together in 1949 to form the CPP, had destroyed and inaugurated more than they realized at the time, that in the brief span of five years the Gold Coast had crossed the gulf which separates a divided colonial society from one conscious of itself as a national entity. But does such a gulf exist? History knows few frontiers in time, and it has been argued already that the Gold Coast of 1946 concealed a much greater unity than was supposed at the time. (Its divisions were also to plague the nationalist leaders to an extent undreamed of in 1949.) Nevertheless, the events of these years, between the Burns and the Coussey constitutions, were of central importance in the evolution of a Ghanaian nation. They were as important in their way—in the mild setting of a liberal colonial régime—as those of 1789 or 1917, in that they marked a fundamental shift of power in local society. And if the subsequent upheaval in the Gold Coast was much less than seemed likely during these early years, it was because the revolution took place within a framework of rules and regulations watched over by colonial officials who were as much concerned with effecting the orderly demise of their own authority as the nationalists were with securing their uncertain hold on the country. Both, indeed, were soon to be cast in a new role—as umpires and participants in a novel electoral contest which was none the less significant because it was peaceful. A revolution by ballot is still a revolution. And the effect of the February 1951 election—the first to be held in the country, the first in Africa on an adult franchise—was to secure the primary aims of the nationalist revolution in a single irrevocable act.

THE BEKWAI SUB-PLOT

Two facts are clear from the foregoing pages. The first is that the years between 1946 and 1950 marked a clear departure from earlier forms of agitation. They stood at the beginning of party organization, when local branches were held together by a nationally directed policy and the emotional appeal of self-government. The second is that, though new in form, neither the UGCC nor the CPP came unheralded from a clear sky. Both built on the youth societies that existed in many of the towns of Ashanti and the Colony, and in many places these local associations continued to exist side by side with the newer party organization. There was usually the same nucleus of membership in both, and the division that took place in 1949 in the UGCC at a national level, between the militant rank and file and the less radical leadership, also took place in a number of local centres up and down the country. There was useful local material here for the historian to use. For the problem in trying to describe the quarrel that divided the chiefs, the intelligentsia, and the young men was, in part, a matter of getting the right focus. Too broad a picture and the details were lost. Too much detail and the picture as a whole disappeared. It may be helpful, therefore, to see the national scene played on a smaller stage. The narrative given earlier was of the main plot—the unfolding of events at the national and regional level, and the part played by the principal actors. The following account is of less epoch-making events in Bekwai, a small market town in south Ashanti.

Bekwai is an ancient Ashanti township and state, the whole district (of which the state forms a part) being known as 'Amansie', that is, 'the beginnings of the nation', and the chief of Bekwai—the 'Bekwaihene'—ranks high on the list of Ashanti chiefs. After the annexation of Ashanti in 1901 Bekwai town became an administrative centre and development was rapid. The missions opened schools in the town, first the Presbyterian, then the Methodist, Anglican, Catholic, and, in recent years, the Seventh-Day Adventist mission.

Year: 1948	Total population	Education	
		Less than full primary	Standard VII or over
Bekwai Town	4,506	598	382
Bekwai N.A.	24,660	691	435

Source: 1948 Census.

Trading firms from Kumasi, twenty-four miles to the north, built their stores around the market; the Sekondi–Kumasi railway ran through the town and increased its importance. (It was an important settlement in pre-colonial times, with a northern trade in cloth and salt through Kumasi to Salaga.) The district is also rich in oil-palms: hence the name 'ebe-Kwai'—meaning 'palm forest'. Cocoa was introduced from the turn of the century, but the spread of swollen shoot turned farmers back to foodstuffs, including a new venture, rice, to supply the expanding Kumasi market.

Distribution of Adult Males, Bekwai Administrative District, 1948

Est. male population aged 15 & over	Cultivation of cocoa*	Artisans, craftsmen, skilled workmen	Shop-keepers & traders	Unskilled workmen	Remainder
49,400	10,921 (22·1%)	4,898 (9·9%)	2,387 (4·8%)	9,707 (19·7%)	21,489 (43·5%)

* Plus 4,000 women engaged in cocoa farming. The large number of artisans and unskilled workers was largely accounted for by the gold-mining town, Obuasi, which was included in the large Bekwai administrative district.

Source: 1948 Census.

In general terms, the picture is of a prosperous, expanding, confident little state. Yet wars and riots figured prominently in its history. Although the Bekwaihene belonged to the same clan as the Asantehene and the near-by Kokofu chief, and although dynastic marriages have linked the Bekwai state with neighbouring chiefdoms, they have frequently fought each other. In the 1900 uprising which followed the exile of the Asantehene Prempeh I, Bekwai sided with the British, Kokofu with the rebels. In 1935 the chief and his elders agreed to form part of the restored Ashanti Confederacy. But they threatened to secede again in 1945. (This time, however, the Asantehene had the advantage of British approval, and the Bekwai chief was destooled.) Within the state itself, conflict was endemic. In 1919, for example, there was an ugly riot following a gambling quarrel between the immigrant Moshi people and the local townsfolk in which 10 were killed and 17 injured—the chief was destooled and sentenced to three years' imprisonment. And more than thirty years later, at the beginning of 1950, a dispute between the Bekwaihene and one of his sub-chiefs who ruled over a small group of villages at Jacobu again led to armed conflict. The government police brought in to restore order were stoned when trying to enter the area in the early hours of the morning; they were armed and opened fire on the villagers who fled. These were the Jacobu riots which held a brief prominent place in national politics.

Uneasy, then, lies the head that wears the crown of chiefly authority in Bekwai. In 1958 the chief had been three times destooled and four times enthroned; the following year he was again destooled. By 1960 there had been eight changes of chief since the First World War.[81] When a new chief was chosen from the royal family and placed upon the Bekwai Stool, he recited the state oath as follows:

> ... *Se enye amanmuopa na me ne mo be buo, se mede nananom kuro to sedie, se me de pe mmaa, se me Mpanyimfo ka asem kyere me na mantie, se me ye mo dom; se me ko gwane; ya me to Ntam Kesie* ... (If I do not administer the country efficiently in co-operation with you, if I gamble with my ancestors' estate, if I run after women, if I rebel against you, if I go to battle and escape from the battle-front, then I have violated the Great Oath) ...

This is after the Elders have warned him ... *mfa mpe mmaa; mfa nom mmorosa; mfa nye dom; ye ka asem kyere wo a, tie; mfa nnidi wo mpanyimfo atem; mfa oman nto sedie; yempe animguasie* ... (do not take advantage of your position to run after women, drink, or rebel against your elders; listen to our advice; don't be rude to or abuse your elders; don't gamble with state property. We do not want to be ashamed).

Such oaths and admonitions had little effect, and discontent with the chief began to take different forms. The educated minority formed their own associations, such as the Bekwai Kotoko Union in the 1920s, an offshoot of the Kumasi Kotoko Union Society. The *mmerante*, the largely illiterate commoners, pressed their claim to a greater share in traditional government. Both groups resented attempts by the administration to buttress the authority of the chief. Hence the Chief Commissioner's *Report* for 1920 which admitted that in Bekwai 'the "youngmen",

---

[81] (1) 1919–25: Kwame Poku, a schoolboy, and the main reason for his destoolment was insolence to his elders; (2) 1925–9: Kofi Buachie II, a farmer, and the main reason for his destoolment was that he was too mild; (3) 1929–36: Kwame Poku again, who had become a farmer; he was destooled for the same reason as before; (4) 1936–45: Yaw Gyamfi, a mason, and he was destooled for rebelling against the *asantehene*; (5) 1946–7: Yaw Buachie II, a driver, who abdicated because of general discontent with his administration by his subjects; (6) 1947–50: Yaw Gyamfi II, then a farmer, who abdicated with a compensation of £1,000 because of the Jacobu riots; (7) 1950–1: interregnum—Committee of Administration; (8) 1951–9: Kwame Poku IV, who had become a diamond prospector and was destooled for political reasons, having supported the NLM; (8) 1959: Yaw Buachie, who had changed his profession to become a timber contractor and farmer; he was opposed by two other royal candidates.

that is to say the lower classes, those who were not Elders, complained that they were not consulted in the choice of the Head-chief, that they did not regard him as a credit to the Stool, that people did not respect him in Bekwai itself, and when he visited the villages, and to a man they refused to serve him'.[82] These early divisions should not be exaggerated. There was no direct attack on the power of the chiefs before the Second World War; and the discontented commoners merely limited themselves to removing those they disliked; moreover, in the 1930s the chiefs, elders, and commoners—literate and illiterate alike—came to-gether to support the cocoa hold-up against the oversea buying firms. Nevertheless, it was clear that the system of native ad-ministration, with its traditionally constituted courts and in-efficiently managed treasuries, exasperated the educated com-moners, and, when strengthened and backed by the administra-tion, bore heavily on the ordinary villager.

Evidence of this resentment came to light in 1950 when the shock of the Jacobu riots brought about the collapse of the native authority. Somewhat unexpectedly, the administration turned to a small group of educated leaders in the town, and in March 1950 an order of the Chief Commissioner removed the powers of a native authority from the Bekwaihene and his elders and vested them in a Committee of Management. The Committee con-sisted of an (illiterate) wing-chief as chairman, effective control being exercised by a wealthy cocoa broker, a Presbyterian pastor, a teacher, and two leading store-keepers in Bekwai. They repre-sented the *élite* of the Bekwai state, the intelligentsia, who re-spected traditional authority but were dismayed at its inability to govern. They were now given an unusual opportunity to show what they could do—an opportunity comparable, in miniature, with that sought by the UGCC nationally—and there is an in-teresting record available of their views. They did not want revo-lution. As the Management Committee noted in its *Report on the Working of the Native Authority (1950)*, there was 'a growing tendency of an altered social relationship between the ruling authority on the one hand, and the plebeians on the other'; what was needed was to 'effect a necessary constructive reforma-tion in accordance with the rules of the Native Authority and in consonance with Native Custom, and to overhaul com-

[82] *Colonial Annual Reports: Ashanti 1920.*

pletely the machinery of Administration, to improve the present morbid state of affairs and to place the State on a sound solid basis'.

These were not the accents of revolution, but the committee none the less meant business. It inquired into the native administration court and treasury, and found there were no proper census records, no tally of levy payments, no account of contracts made, an omission to pay into the treasury certain monies, and 'a prodigiously extravagant expenditure on funerals by the Omanhene and the Elders'.[83] The court records also showed 'an abhorrent and glaring misapplication of justice'. The Committee checked the Stool paraphernalia—gold finger rings, silver neckplates, talisman sandals, umbrella crest, elephant tail, palanquin cushions, and so forth—and found many of them 'extremely dirty and needing repair'. Throughout 1950 the Committee tried to wrest order out of chaos, setting up sub-committees to look into market receipts, re-establishing the maternity clinic, reorganizing the lorry park and the system of toll collection, obtaining permission to remove the traditional court panels of elders and substituting a majority of lay members. Finally, it turned to Jacobu and the task of resettling the villagers, and in order to ease the burden of the work, the Committee turned to the young men. It

[83]
Bekwaihene's Office,
Bekwai, Ashanti,
14th April, 1950.
Sir,
Your letter dated 9th April has come to me and the Elders of the Bekwai Stool. With regard to payments for the Timber concessions, I beg to state as follows: That we received an amount of £50 from Mr John Myers and £100 from Kwami Owusu, making a total of £150.

2. This is how it was expended:

£					
9	0	0	was used in paying Mr S. E. Kusi-Appou (Stool debt)		
15	0	0	,, ,, ,, ,,	Asanhahene's Funeral Expenses	
30	0	0	,, ,, ,, ,,	Juabenhene's	,, ,,
8	0	0	,, ,, ,, ,,	Kokofuhene's	,, ,,
22	0	0	,, ,, ,, ,,	Akua Broni's	,, ,,
16	0	0	,, ,, ,, ,,	Bechem	,, ,,
3	2	0	,, ,, ,, ,,	Kofi Wuo's	,, ,,
7	5	0	,, ,, ,, ,,	Kofi Amoa's	,, ,,
14	10	0	,, ,, ,, ,,	Kofi Kunto's	,, ,,
15	12	6	,, ,, ,, ,,	Adjoa Saraha's	,, ,,
10	0	0	,, ,,	as an interest on £50 loan received from Kumasi for		

Funerals when the amount put down during the 1948 Estimate got exhausted.
I remain,
Yours faithfully,
(Sgd)   Yaw Gyamfi II
Bekwaihene

turned in particular to the 'Bekwai State Improvement Society', an association of educated, partly-educated, and illiterate young men-about-town.

The Improvement Society[84] was a comparatively recent creation, formed early in 1950 to meet the special situation of the Jacobu riots, but it had many of the features of its forerunners— the Kotoko Society in the 1920s, the Bekwai Literary and Social Club, a Scholars' Union and the Youth Movement. Membership was 'open to all true and indigenous citizens of the Bekwai State, literates and illiterates of and above the age of 21'. At its initial meeting it had an enrolment of ninety, with a wide range of occupations—primary-school teachers, clerks, the Presbyterian pastor, store-keepers, a goldsmith, carpenters, a tailor, farmers, and three driver-mechanics. There was an elected executive, and every member was 'dutifully and constitutionally bound to swear an oath of allegiance to the President'. No member was to 'institute any legal action against a fellow member without the consent of the executive'. No member was to 'have any underhand dealings with a fellow member's wife': it was considered to be a violation of the rules if any member 'took marriage' with the former wife of a fellow member. Offenders against the Society's rule were to be called before the executive and fined. There was also the provision (it existed in the earlier Kotoko Society) that a member who attempted to resign 'without reasonable cause' was to be deemed 'a TRAITOR and a TROUBLE MONGER . . . and liable to a fine of ten guineas'. Like many similar bodies, the Improvement Society also had some of the characteristics of a 'friendly society'. Thus membership carried death benefits: a gold ring for the deceased and £4 4s. for the relatives. In theory, it met weekly to discuss 'improvements' in the state— a better drainage scheme, the provision of market stalls and teachers' quarters, the duties and lapses from duty of the chief, and—in 1950—the resettlement of the now deserted Jacobu villages.

The Improvement Society was not the only association in Bekwai, as the writer found when he first visited the town in 1950. There was no clear-cut opinion, or clearly defined groups, among the townspeople, yet it was easy to note the difference in

---

[84] The writer is grateful to Mr Adjei Sarpong for letting him read the minutes and correspondence of the Improvement Society.

outlook, wealth, and education between the more elderly, more established members of the Committee of Management and the younger, more radical members of the Improvement Society. There were also differences which were to become important within the Improvement Society itself, between the more moderate and the more extreme. There was a reasonable group (so it appeared at least to the writer) of whom Adjei Sarpong (later, clerk to the Bekwai urban council) was a typical representative, which was prepared to join the newly opened extramural class in the town, and to form a local branch of the People's Educational Association.[85] An opposed group of out-and-out nationalists held back suspiciously, led by A. R. Boakye, a store-keeper and petty trader who gathered a personal support about him through an earlier Bekwai Youth Movement. Most of the young men were members of both the Improvement Society and the Youth Movement, as well as of the People's Education Association and a local Bekwai Literary Society. There was no chief (he had abdicated) and no agreement on who should be his successor. Finally, there was a branch both of the UGCC and the CPP. The UGCC branch had been formed at the end of 1947 by (among others) H. R. Annan, a wealthy cocoa broker who was now a member of the Committee of Management. Most of the young men had taken out a membership card, and national events were beginning to be discussed. Some of the young men who went regularly to Kumasi to replenish their stock of trading goods, or as teachers on holiday, had seen the riots and looting in March 1948. Some of them had earlier helped Harry Mensah, a retired native authority Inspector of Police, to organize a limited boycott of European goods, but the wild scenes of the Kumasi and Accra riots were mirrored in Bekwai only by crowds who gathered in the market place to discuss the news. Throughout 1948, however, the UGCC increased in membership and opened branches in the near-by towns—Essumeja and Kofofu—until, in June 1949, two representatives from Bekwai, both of them members of the Youth Movement as well as of the UGCC, travelled to Saltpond to attend the great debate between the UGCC Working Committee and the Committee on Youth Organization. They sided with Nkrumah, and very much liked the idea of a new People's Party

---

[85] Formed at Aburi in the Colony in 1949 as a movement similar to the Workers' Educational Association in Britain.

of the young men. On their return to Bekwai they told the others_,
what they had seen, and a majority of the teacher-clerk-petty-
trader class in the town agreed to transfer their allegiance from
the UGCC to the CPP, and to establish branches of the new party
in the district.

The UGCC leaders in Bekwai refused to join them. Men like
H. R. Annan, who thought and shared the hopes of their con-
temporaries in Kumasi, Accra, and Cape Coast, did not take
kindly to the idea of a local People's Party led by a group of petty traders and primary-school teachers. The more sober, more
wealthy, better educated, established leaders of Bekwai society
remained loyal, therefore, to the Convention, and opposed the
CPP as it began to extend its hold on Amansie. At first, however,
there was little to oppose, for even when the branches of the new
party were established, they were not very active. 'Positive
Action' in January 1950 had hardly any effect, although some of
the store-keepers judiciously closed their shops, and it was indica-
tive of the strength of local community feeling at this time that,
when the riots took place in Jacobu at the end of January 1950, a
new movement—the Improvement Society—was thought to be
needed to rally the young men, and to try and bring them and the
leading townspeople together.

As 1950 drew on, relations between the young men and the
Committee of Management grew more strained, and the Improvement Society itself was caught in a cross-fire of criticism. On
the one hand the more nationalist-minded young men in the
Bekwai area looked on the members of the Committee of Management as 'aristocrats', who were over-friendly with the district
commissioner and the local European manager of the United
Africa Company. They were also suspicious of any alliance with
those in authority, and critical, therefore, of the leaders of the Improvement Society because of their collaboration with the Committee of Management. But the society was also attacked from a
different quarter—by the elders of the native authority, who
wrote to its newly elected officers saying that they saw 'evil intentions' in such a body and 'objected to it *in toto*'. The secretary replied by pointing to the aims of the society—'to promote a true
spirit of citizenship among its members and render loyal service
to our Natural Rulers'—but the chief and his elders knew very
well that the society contained members who were hostile to the

exercise of any authority by the chief outside a narrow definition of customary law. [86]

These were local quarrels. But then a further element of conflict arose. By mid-1950 it was no longer possible to isolate Bekwai affairs, and a familiar process could be seen at work: the interaction of local and nationalist politics. Each of the local groups in Bekwai—the chiefs, the intelligentsia, the young men and rival groups among the young men—began to look farther afield for help in its own local affairs, and was encouraged to do so by outside interests. H. R. Annan and his fellow members on the Committee of Management gave their support to the Joint Territorial Council Movement in Kumasi sponsored by the Joint Provincial Council of Chiefs, the Asanteman Council, [87] and the Northern Territorial Council. [88] (Thus they drew near to the very traditional authority that they had earlier sought to curb.) The young men were also drawn into wider associations. In August 1950 the Youth Movement and the Improvement Society both sent representatives to a meeting convened in Kumasi by the Asante Youth Association, where they met similar delegations from the Offinso Unity Club, the Effiduase Youth Association, the Nsuta Scholars' Union, the Nkoranza Literary Club, the Mo Scholars' Union, and a dozen or more similar bodies which agreed to form a pro-CPP 'Supreme Council of Ashanti Youth' in opposition to the chiefs and the intelligentsia. Thus nationalist politics were bringing Bekwai and the whole Amansie district into the broad stream of the movement for self-government. And, as the date of the February 1951 election approached, it cast a long shadow before it, for Amansie became a constituency and its towns and villages had to choose a representative for the new Assembly. On this question—as the following chapter shows—the Amansie community (like many others) divided. The chief and his elders, and the Committee of Management and its supporters, went one way. The petty

[86] This somewhat clumsy phrase is necessary to emphasize what might otherwise be misinterpreted. Opposition to traditional authority was invariably limited to the exercise of power by one chief or another, or to action by the chiefs which went beyond 'customary practices'. These were difficult to define, and the interpretations varied, but it would have been difficult even as late as 1960, and quite impossible in 1950, to find anyone in Bekwai who would have agreed that the best solution to the problem of the chief's authority was to abolish chieftaincy as an institution.

[87] The Ashanti Confederacy Council was renamed the 'Asanteman Council' in 1950.

[88] See below, ch. III.

traders, letter-writers, goldsmiths, drivers, a majority of the farmers, and the more radical-minded among the teachers and clerks went a different way. The Improvement Society split, and disappeared; the Youth Movement was absorbed in the CPP; and henceforth national party associations dominated the Bekwai-Amansie scene.

III

The 1951 Election

TOWARDS evening on 9 February it became clear that the CPP had won a famous victory. The party's candidates had been successful during the previous day's voting in 29 of the 33 rural electoral colleges, and had won all 5 municipal seats; Nkrumah—while still in prison—had been elected for the Accra municipality with a vote of 20,780 against 1,451 for Ako Adjei, on whose advice the Working Committee of the UGCC had invited Nkrumah to return to the Gold Coast.[1] Admittedly, there were areas of the contest beyond the grasp of the party: the Northern Electoral College had elected its 19 members, the European Chambers of Commerce and Mines their 6 representatives;[2] there were still 18 'territorial seats' to be decided—11 in the Colony by the Joint Provincial Council of Chiefs, 6 by the Asanteman Council, and 1 by the Southern Togoland Council. And the party would have to accept the presence of three *ex-officio* members (both in the Assembly and the executive council), the retention by the Governor of reserve powers, and the appointment of European permanent secretaries to the new ministers. But none of these reservations had any effect on the jubilation of the CPP members after the first day's polling. Excited crowds of supporters thronged the streets, daubed themselves with white powder as a sign of victory, and danced their way through the

---

[1] Accra was a two-member constituency:

Adjei, Ako, barrister at law and journalist, UGCC	1,451
Bossman, Kofi Aduma, legal practitioner, NDP (National Democratic Party)	666
Hutton-Mills, Thomas, legal practitioner, CPP	19,812
Lamptey, Emmanuel Odarquaye Obetsibi, barrister at law, UGCC	1,630
Nkrumah, Kwame, politician and journalist, CPP	20,780
Ollennu, Nii Amaa, legal practitioner, NDP	742

[2] Four without voting rights. There was no contest for the three Mines' seats: nine members contested the Commerce section: the General Manager of the United Africa Company came first, John Christopulos Leventis (the Cypriot businessman) second.

victory rallies and picnics, exchanging the party's Freedom salute
and singing its hymn:

> There is victory for us
> There is victory for us
> In the struggle of CPP
> There is victory for us.

How had the party done it? What was likely to happen now that
the CPP had demonstrated its strength?

The election had been won during 1950 when local branches
of the CPP were formed as nationalist propaganda centres, but
there would have been no election to win without the parallel
effort by the administration to divide the country into constituencies, to have voters registered, and a polling staff briefed for election day. Throughout the year a twofold process could be observed: the party was extending itself across the country; the administration was constructing an electoral framework for the
party—and its rivals—to use. Sometimes the two came into conflict, but more often, as they worked towards a common goal, an
involuntary alliance developed between the party and the
officials. One characteristic, certainly, both had in common,
namely an ignorance of parliamentary elections; there was
hardly a member of the administration who had any detailed experience of conducting a national parliamentary contest (least of
all among a predominantly illiterate electorate) and everything
had to be done by trial and error. It was fortunate that a national
census had been held in 1948 and that by October 1950 its results
were ready for the officials who had to delimit constituency
boundaries and compile a register of electors; fortunate, too, that
their task had been made easier by the decision not to accept the
Coussey Committee's recommendations for the division of the
whole country into constituencies. Nevertheless, the problems
facing the officials were difficult enough, and before turning to
the actual contest, it is necessary to sketch the administrative
framework within which the election took place.

The translation into practical detail of the franchise recommendations in the Coussey *Report* had been entrusted to a select
committee of the legislative council.[3] It was urged to make recom-

---

[3] Ewart Committee *Report* (1950). The members of the committee were:
Kenneth Ewart (Chairman), Nana Amanfi III, Nana Kwame Gyebi Ababio,
E. O. Asafu-Adjaye, J. B. Danquah, Nii Amaa Ollennu. With the exception of the
chairman all had been members of the Coussey Committee also.

mendations for the holding of 'early elections' and did so at the
expense of the Northern Territories. 'There appeared to be universal support [in the north] for nomination', the Committee
declared (although this was hardly likely when one of the memoranda it received came from the Tamale branch of the CPP), and
it recommended that there should be a single electoral college for
the Protectorate based on the Northern Territories Council and
the existing native authorities.[4] For the rest of the country, however, the Ewart Committee gave precise form to the general outline framed by the Coussey Committee.[5] It made detailed proposals for the conduct of voting both in the municipalities and in
the rural primaries,[6] listed the basic qualifications (following
Coussey) for electors and candidates, and added an appendix
which—by outlining the boundaries of the new rural electoral
districts—made the appointment of a separate delimitation commission unnecessary. The *Report* was debated in July 1950 in the
legislative council, to which three representatives from the north
(J. A. Braimah, S. D. Dombo, and Yakubu Tali) were added as
'extraordinary members'; the following month the Gold Coast
(Constitution) (Electoral Provisions) Order in Council was
brought into effect by proclamation, the Elections (Legislative
Assembly) Regulations were published, and the date of the
rural primary elections announced for 5 and 6 February 1951.

[4] Danquah submitted a strongly worded minority report. 'I have to confess', he
said, 'that I cannot see how mere residence on the other side of the Northern Volta
should by itself make a person politically incompetent to exercise a franchise
granted by the King to the whole country. . . . The only instance of a qualitative
difference cited by my colleagues is the allegation that the south has been for centuries in contact with Europeans . . . whereas, until the second half of the nineteenth century, the only contacts which the northern people had with the outside
world lay to the further north and great caravan routes to the Sahara. . . . I find no
justification for the underlying assumption that contact of south Gold Coast with
Europe for centuries has innoculated the south with the idea of universal suffrage.'
He was able to quote from the Tamale CPP memorandum which admitted that
'because of the high percentage of illiteracy there might be some difficulty to get
efficient elections; but we contend that *if it is begun* it shall be improved as the
Years advance.'
[5] The only significant amendments were (1) the substitution of the Joint Provincial Council of Chiefs as a single electoral college for the eleven Colony territorial seats in place of the Committee's proposal of separate colleges based on local
states; and (2) the adoption of a uniform system of balloting for both the direct
(municipal) and the indirect (rural) elections.
[6] The Committee recommended two different systems of voting: (1) marking a
ballot paper over-printed with the candidate's name and coloured symbol for the
direct elections in the municipalities and the Rural Electoral Colleges, and (as a
temporary measure) (2) a multiple-box system—one box per candidate—for the
rural primaries. It was then decided that colour-printing was too long and expensive a process.

As soon as the Ewart Committee *Report* had been given legal expression, the administration considered how best to give it effect. The problems were formidable. Each rural electoral district and sub-district had to be demarcated—village by village and, in places, compound by compound; a register of electors had to be compiled for two-thirds of the country, and voting supervised in 2,000–3,000 primary elections, 31 electoral colleges,[7] 5 municipalities, 3 territorial councils, the specially constructed Northern Electoral College, and the 2 European chambers of commerce and mines. It was hardly to be wondered at that, in moments of despair in the new offices that now awaited their ministers, the officials said that the only members of the new assembly likely to be 'returned' on time were the three *ex-officios*. To see these problems in detail, it is useful to consider them under two heads, delimitation and registration.

THE DELIMITATION OF CONSTITUENCIES

How is an electoral map imposed on a country new to elections? A competent statistician, armed with the latest census figures, might (as the Ewart Committee put it) 'proceed with pencil and ruler to carve any country into any required number of constituencies on a parity population basis' but the Committee was not prepared to recommend such a course: 'such a division would cut ruthlessly across the boundaries of states and administrative districts, would have entirely to ignore ethnic considerations, and would certainly result in the grouping together of peoples who are mutually antipathetic'. Here the Ewart Committee raised one of the central questions of Ghanaian politics—the conflict of nationalist hopes and local interests. The nationalist ideal was to be expressed by Nkrumah later in the newly elected assembly—

> ... It is my view, Mr Speaker, that whatever the decisions of previous Commissions of Committees (and I have in mind the Coussey Committee in this regard) it is in the public interest that one logical principle should be applied generally in all Regions of the Gold Coast, in order to safeguard the intended result that people all over the country should have equal rights to representation according to popu-

---

[7] Two of the electoral colleges, Anlo and Akim Abuakwa, each returned two members.

lation. In a nutshell, Sir, I will not admit that one Gold Coast man from any area is better than a Gold Coast man from another area. . .[8]

But it is easier to define an ideal—to insist that the past should not press too heavily on the present—than to translate it into practical terms of constituency boundaries and sub-electoral districts. Outside the municipal areas (where ward boundaries had already been demarcated) lay a confusion of local chiefdoms and states built up by traditional rule, administrative decision, and legal argument, and the Ewart Committee was not prepared to override the local interests vested in these small administrative units. 'The boundaries of the future constituencies', it declared, 'must coincide as far as possible with the boundaries of the future Local Authorities'—and these were to be formed by a combination of native-authority areas. Parity of population between each electoral district gave way, therefore, before the need to get the electoral boundaries accepted. Ideally, dividing the total rural population of the Colony, the southern area of the Togoland Trust Territory, and Ashanti, by the number of proposed electoral districts, each rural constituency should have had between 83,000 and 84,000 inhabitants. In practice, the variation was large:

1. Colony and southern Togo-
   land average   ..   ..   97,570—21 rural constituencies
   Largest constituency   ..   141,094—Ga Adangme
   Smallest constituency   ..   60,535—Ahanta
2. Ashanti average   ..   ..   62,210—12 rural constituencies
   Largest constituency   ..   91,311—Amansie
   Smallest constituency   ..   48,082—Mampong South
3. Municipalities:
   Accra   ..   ..   ..   135,926—(2-member constituency)
   Cape Coast   23,346
   Sekondi-Takoradi   ..   44,557
   Kumasi   78,483

On the basis of Nkrumah's arguments, put forward three years later, it could be said that a person registered in Mampong South in Ashanti was 'worth' three times as much—politically—as anyone registered in the southern Ga Adangme constituency, but this was the price which the Ewart Committee thought it necessary to pay to get the acquiescence of the local states, each jealous

[8] GC, LA Deb., 6 Nov. 1953.

of its separate identity. It was wise to do so, for despite its tender attitude towards local feeling, the Committee still met with strong opposition in districts where it was unable to avoid a 'grouping together of peoples who are mutually antipathetic'. Protests were made up and down the country as chiefs, village heads, and the local youth associations objected either to being included in a constituency which combined them with those they disliked, or to being separated from those with whom they were traditionally associated. Some objected simply to the designation of a constituency. Thus Togbe Darke XI, an educated chief in the Ewe-speaking district on the east bank of the Volta, was later to declare that his people in the Awodome area of the Peki–Tongu electoral district had boycotted the 1951 primary elections 'because the government insists on calling us Peki people and we are not. We are Awodome people with equal rights with Peki people. No one in the state registered so there was no election. . . . That means that there will be eight vacant seats in the Peki–Tongu electoral college.'[9] The objection was quite simply to the name, in the belief that the inclusion of the Awodome state in a constituency called the Peki–Tongu Electoral District implied its subordination to the Peki people—a much disliked rival group across the near-by range of hills. Similar protests were made by other states, some small, some large, whose peoples suspected ulterior (and to them unpleasant) motives in the combination of states within the new framework of an electoral district, and it was reasonable to suppose that, had the Ewart Committee not made the maximum use of these local boundaries, there would have been a far louder outcry. It could also point out that the principle of 'one man, one vote' had already been abandoned by the Coussey Committee when it decided that the north, despite its much larger population, should have the same number of representatives as Ashanti—i.e. nineteen—in the new Assembly.

The only effort made to achieve parity of representation was at the level of each sub-electoral district. Where the Coussey Committee *Report* had suggested a round figure of not less than 200 delegates for each electoral college, the Ewart Committee submitted the working rule of one delegate for every thousand in-

[9] A statement made immediately after the rural primary elections on 6 February (*Daily Graphic* 8 Dec. 1951).

habitants.[10] It was confident that the task of defining the boundaries of each group of 'one thousand inhabitants' could be done by the chiefs themselves,[11] but officers charged with the duty of supervising the division flinched before its execution. 'Before the exercise began', A. C. Russell, the Judicial Adviser to the Government, wrote in an 'Eve of Election Report', 'it had been thought by many people reckoned as good judges, that the "breakdown" would be almost impossible'; it was finally completed 'with very much less effort than had been expected [but] how it was done, I still fail to understand.'[12] Throughout the latter half of September and the early part of October 1950 district commissioners[13] paced out the boundaries with native-authority clerks, defining disputed areas by villages, trees, bush paths, streams, and vague phrases like 'the villages of Kojokrom, Nyame-Bekyere, Chichiwere and the surrounding territory'. They found hamlets unknown at district headquarters and not recorded in the census; they had to repeat in simple terms, at village level, what the Ewart Committee had already tried to explain to the state authorities, that what they were doing was 'solely for electoral purposes and did not affect the ownership of land or jurisdiction':[14] gradually, however, the new electoral map took shape, and by the middle of October the task was complete, the boundaries being published in each state council area before registration began on 1 November.

REGISTRATION

It was decided that registration should be voluntary: an eligible elector had to make an application, at a given place and within a stipulated period, to have his (or her) name entered on the register. The qualifications and disqualifications in 1950 may be set down briefly:

[10] Electoral Provisions Ordinance No. 29, 1950: 'Each rural sub-district shall so far as is practicable comprise an area containing approximately one thousand inhabitants' (s.3(3)).

[11] 'We have consulted many chiefs in the Colony and Ashanti', said the *Report*, 'and we are informed from all sides that there should be no difficulty in each State Council dividing its state into the necessary number of sub-constituencies, each containing roughly one thousand inhabitants, and we consider that this task should be entrusted to them.'

[12] 'Eve of Election Report' by A. C. Russell, Min. of Local Govt. files.

[13] A district commissioner or assistant district commissioner had been appointed in August 1950 as a Registration Officer for each municipality and rural electoral district.

[14] *Report on the First Election to the Legislative Assembly of the Gold Coast*, 1951.

Qualifications:

(a) British subject or British-protected person. Aged 21 and over.[15]

(b) In the rural districts, six months' residence within the constituency; in the municipalities, six months' ownership, rental or occupancy of assessed premises within the constituency.

(c) In the rural districts, payment of local tax 'if liable thereto' for the current or preceding year.

Disqualifications:

(a) Being sentenced to death or imprisonment for a term exceeding twelve months or convicted of any offence involving dishonesty within the previous five years.

(b) Being a lunatic.

(c) Being convicted of an offence in connexion with elections.

(d) Being registered as a voter in any other constituency.

This was theory. In practice the number of electors was limited not only by the actual terms of the regulations but by the difficulty of applying them. The problems involved were partly technical, partly political. For example, in a country where baptismal or birth certificates covered only a fraction of the total population it was not always possible for a young man or woman to convince the registration officer that he (or she) had reached the age of twenty-one. It was also difficult to prove that the basic rate had been paid when tax receipts were easily misplaced and native-authority records badly kept. The larger problem, however, was that of a prevailing suspicion of government intentions, and it was to meet this difficulty that a tacit alliance developed between the CPP members and the colonial officials. Their interests coincided, and it was through the efforts not only of nearly 2,000 administrative officers and junior staff that electors were

[15] The Coussey Committee had sought to 'minimise the dangers in the wide and rapid extension of the franchise' by recommending an 'election in two stages' for the rural constituencies, and restricting the grant of 'universal adult suffrage' to 'males and females of twenty-five years and over . . . who should have paid or contributed to the payment of rates or have paid levy or annual tax'. Had its proposals been implemented they would have disfranchised the 21–24 age-group in the municipal areas. Kwesi Plange, who was elected for the CPP at a by-election in Cape Coast in June 1950 shortly before his 25th birthday, argued this point in the legislative council until the unofficial members agreed that the age for electors —but not for candidates—should be 21. Plange was over 25 by February 1951, and therefore able to stand again in the general election.

registered,[16] but with the help of many more voluntary helpers in the local branches of the party. The official *Report on the First Election* paid handsome tribute to the party which the government had once described as 'a subversive organisation without any real support from the people', saying that 'during the period of registration the Convention People's Party was the only political party which was noticeably active, and there can be no question that the high rate of registration in certain areas was in large measure due to its enthusiasm and its co-operation with the registration staff'. Because the administration was still under suspicion, and the CPP in its first flush of enthusiasm, the latter had sometimes to give its sanction before the officials could act. Thus a senior official at Winneba, a small coastal town, reported that: 'The people will often ask the [Junior Assistant Registration Officer] if he is CPP; if he says "yes", they will register; if he says "no" he is suspect of being a government detective and sent away.'[17] Collaboration along these lines sometimes took an extreme form, whereby officials handed out registration forms in bulk to branch secretaries, until the point was reached—from which the administration then tried to draw back—when people 'imagined that the party was carrying out a rival registration'. A report was sent from Akuse, a market town on the river Volta, that 'the people say that they will register only with the CPP, and not the government'. From the Kisi district, between Cape Coast and Sekondi, the Junior Registration Officer reported: 'at eight villages I had a nil registration. When I go they turn me out: they say that they will not register until they have CPP registration forms.' A CPP branch secretary in Nkawkaw, in the Kwahu area, was said to have registered over 200 electors, and similar stories came from other districts.

The colonial government and the nationalist party also joined hands in conducting a sustained campaign of advertisement. The government used leaflets, loudspeaker vans, film strips, wireless announcements, gramophone records in English and half-a-dozen vernaculars—the full weight of government propaganda —to urge the people to register.[18] The CPP used its local rallies

---

[16] Colony and Southern Trans-Volta, 1,222; Ashanti, 625.

[17] Unpubl. report by the Senior Registration Officer, Winneba (Min. of Local Govt).

[18] 77,000 pamphlets were printed in English, 280,000 in the vernacular, a 'Constitution Corner' inserted daily in all the local newspapers, a training course

and propaganda tours. The *Evening News* printed a daily caption:
'PAY YOUR LEVY! REGISTER AND VOTE AT THE
GENERAL ELECTION': and editorials warned their readers
that

should anybody fail to register his or her name today then that body
forfeits his or her own liberty. This is the hour calling all real and duti-
ful citizens of this country to their duty. . . . We have endeavoured in
all respects to explain in the best way possible the qualifications a voter
must have; we have also explained the way registration will have to be
conducted. . . . To our literate brothers and sisters we say that a great
and onerous duty hangs on them to educate our unfortunate illiterate
brothers on this vital issue. . . . It is this registration that will prove that
we should have our S.G. now or wait in further squalor and discontent
for the next hundred years.[19]

The CPP Newsletter, published daily in the *Evening News*, told
party officials to 'go round their various constituencies and see
that in the rural sub-districts the illiterates are educated that it is
the government which will register their names, and so they must
obey the registration officers when they come round to write their
names'.[20] Registration became a main item of local propaganda,
and in Akim Oda town (in the Colony)

on Sunday October 15th twelve of the party members volunteered to
spend the whole of their following week in the service of their country,
and formed themselves into three sections, each under the leadership
of a propaganda secretary, to trek to the outlying villages to win more
members into the party and explain the procedure designed by the
government for the general election. . . On Sunday October 21st, all
three sections under their leaders, looking hale and hearty, returning
to Oda having enrolled 238 new members, and convinced over 150
men and women to pay their State tax for registration.[21]

The party's help was undoubtedly needed, especially in areas
where (as the *Report on the First Election* admitted) there had been
a persistent refusal to pay the rate for a number of years, or where
strong local issues predominated. Thus in the southern half of the
Togoland Trust Territory the period of registration coincided

---

devised for 100 instructors to tour the country in fifteen teams, each with its cine-
projector, maps, diagrams, gramophone records in English, Twi, Fanti, Ewe, Ga,
and Hausa. A full picture of the efforts made by the Public Relations Department
is given in the *Gold Coast Bulletin*, 31 Jan. 1951.
[19] *Evening News*, 1 Nov. 1950.   [20] Ibid. 3 Nov. 1950.
[21] Ibid. 5 Nov. 1950.

with the appointment of an enlarged Standing Consultative
Commission for the two (British and French) Togolands, and the
Ewe 'unificationists' argued that to register for a Gold Coast
election meant approval of the link between the British colony
and the trust territory. The administration made a serious mistake in the farming areas affected by swollen shoot when it used
members of the Cocoa Rehabilitation Department as registration staff. Moreover, the hostility aroused by the delimitation of
constituency boundaries tended to be confirmed by registration,
and chiefs who disliked the final shape of an electoral district
objected no less to the registration of names. 'In some instances',
said the *Report*, 'no-one would register until the chief had given
his support', and misunderstanding was deliberately 'fostered by
sub-chiefs who sensed a diminution of their traditional powers'.
Elsewhere the number who registered was low because those
who did not wish to serve the chief also refused to pay the local
levy: in Saltpond, for example, a highly sophisticated area
politically (the scene of the famous meeting at which the CYO
broke from the UGCC), only 380 registered out of an estimated
2,100 because of 'internal political disagreements with the *omanhene* which resulted in an almost complete cessation of levy payment'. In the Agona district of the Colony only 12 per cent of the
eligible population registered because of the large number of
'immigrant' Gomoa farmers from farther south who cultivated
land in Agona but did not consider that they 'belonged' to the
state. Thus the final registration figure was only 40 per cent of the
total possible electorate. The difference between the Colony and
Ashanti and between the municipalities and the rural districts
may be seen from the following table:

Area	Estimated population*	Eligible electorate	Registered	Per cent
Colony (incl. S. Togoland)	2,153,310	1,095,190	350,525	32
Ashanti	784,210	398,590	220,658	55·4
Municipalities	290,230	141,480	90,275	64·1
TOTAL	3,227,750	1,635,260	661,908	40·5

* As at 1 Jan. 1951.

Sources: 1948 Census and the 1951 *Report on the First Election*.

It would be wrong to take these very low registration figures as a reliable measure of the support which existed for the party. Enthusiasm went beyond understanding of electoral procedure, and the CPP had very little time in which to translate goodwill into practical support. It was still struggling to shape itself into a national organization when it was faced with the problem of conducting an election campaign, and although this helped the party by enabling it to direct its efforts to a single immediate end, it also meant that everything had to be done in a hurry. With its leader and many of its national figures in prison at one period or another during the twenty months between June 1949 and February 1951, it did well to spread its appeal so widely through Ashanti and the south. How this was done was something of a mystery even to its organizers. Its appeal to the 'Common Man', and for 'Self-Government Now' ran like a flame through the Colony and Ashanti chiefdoms and branches were formed in many instances without the knowledge of the national headquarters. The CPP had a number of assets, however, in 1949–50 which greatly helped it to evoke a mass enthusiasm, and we should look briefly at these.

It was able, for example, to make full use of a 'cult of martyrdom' through the succession of party leaders who entered or were released at convenient intervals from prison. It was the party's good fortune that Gbedemah went to prison at an early date (17 October 1949) and not as a result of Positive Action in January 1950: thus Nkrumah going in, met Gbedemah coming out.[22] Throughout 1950 there was a procession of victims in and out of the Accra, Kumasi, and Sekondi prisons: as the Positive Action leaders came out after serving their three- or six-month terms, others went in on convictions for libel and sedition. G. K. Amegbe, for example, regional chairman of the CPP in Transvolta, was arrested in August for publishing an article which accused Britain of arming and inciting northern tribesmen under the guise of 'a "reserve constabulary" to dignify the blood bath to come'.[23] August saw H. P. Nyemitei (acting general-secretary of the party) arrested and acquitted,[24] and T. Hutton-Mills[25] and

[22] Gbedemah was sentenced to six months' imprisonment for publishing false news.
[23] The article was taken from an American magazine, *The Index*.
[24] And first president of the Meteorological Workers' Union.
[25] One of the very few lawyers in the party, elected with Nkrumah for Accra in February 1951.

K. O. Quarshie of the *Evening News* released. The latter carried a
message from Nkrumah to the party members at their first annual
conference in Cape Coast (on 5 August 1950) saying that: 'The
battle is nearing an end. All I ask of them is grit and determination and unflinching loyalty to the Party. In this lies the strength
of the Party. Our slogan is organisation and "cipipification" of
the whole country.' In September Saki Scheck—editor now of
the *Takoradi Times*—went to prison. So the catalogue of martyrs
continued, and those who were released were fêted, awarded a
'Prison Graduate cap', and extolled in the party press.

AKUA ASAABEA GRADUATES FROM THE
UNIVERSITY OF JAMES FORT PRISON

Know ye, by all these presents, that our worthy Sister and Com-
patriot, Miss Akua Asaabea hath this 17th day of July in the year of
our Lord one thousand nine hundred and fifty, in the third year of
Ghana's campaign for Self-government, been admitted a Graduate
of the University of James Fort Prison after having successfully completed a course in 'Patriotism' . . . and that from henceforth she shall
have full power to append after her name, the insignia, 'P.G.' (Prison
Graduate).[26]

In Kumasi Krobo Edusei (propaganda secretary of the party in
Ashanti) was released at midnight on 18 November after his
nine-month sentence with a great crowd thronging the gate to
welcome him. The following day he addressed an audience in
Prempeh Assembly Hall on 'Imprisonment Intensifies the
Struggle', and Gbedemah—with the help of Kwesi Lamptey, the
national acting deputy chairman, from Sekondi—awarded him
his 'P.G. cap'. Five days later an even larger crowd in Accra welcomed Kojo Botsio (the general secretary) and A. R. Dennis
(national propaganda secretary) when they were released from
James Fort Prison (again with a message from Nkrumah), and
there was a mass procession through Accra to the party headquarters in Kimberley Avenue. Such ceremonies did a great deal
to keep interest and excitement alive, and throughout 1950
Gbedemah used the image of the imprisoned Nkrumah and his
colleagues not only to arouse a mass sympathy among the electorate but to maintain a wavering discipline in the party during

---

[26] *Evening News*, 18 July 1950. At this time the 'campaign for self-government'
was still being dated from the formation of the UGCC in 1947.

the struggle (described later) that sprang up over the nomination of candidates.

Secondly, the CPP was able to build on earlier associations and movements—the UGCC, the CYO, the Asante Youth Association, trade unions, farmers' associations, and local bodies like the Bekwai Youth Movement and the State Improvement Society. The TUC was shattered after the general strike in January 1950, but there was a rank-and-file membership (many of them dismissed employees) who were eager to help, and branches still existed in the main towns. In the rural areas the CPP found entry for its appeal through the numerous farmers' associations that still existed. Ashie Nikoe (of the Farmers' Committee of British West Africa) was a member of the CPP central committee. And in mid-December 1949 he and John Ayew had formed a national Ghana Farmers' Congress out of the Farmers' Committee, the Sika Mpoano Akuafo Fekew Ltd, and the Asante Farmers' Union. Nkrumah had addressed its inaugural meeting, and two members of the executive were arrested during Positive Action. Almost a year later (October 1950) the Congress met again in the Mikado cinema at Nkawkaw to be addressed by Kwesi Lamptey and Ohene Larbi. The farmers' representatives condemned the work of the Cocoa Rehabilitation Department, objected to the Cocoa Marketing Board Ordinance, under which 'the entire Cocoa Industry . . . had as it were, been nationalised and converted into state property', and complained that 'lack of scientific training had resulted in the ruthless destruction of healthy cocoa trees with ripe pods on them' by gangs of untrained labourers.[27] The CPP took up these (and other) complaints and recruits hastened to join. Once the farmers accepted a nationalist party as the political expression of their own grievances it spread through the southern rural areas like fire through a dry wood, as indeed Danquah had foreseen would happen.[28] There was an

[27] Ghana Farmers' Congress, *Minutes*, Oct. 1950. 'Under the Gold Coast Marketing Board Ordinance, the entire Cocoa Industry once owned by peasantry had as it were been nationalised and converted into State property with no compensation whatever. General economic conditions of the peasantry were deplorable owing to systematic exploitation.'

[28] See Danquah's statement in his monograph on the cocoa hold-up and boycott of 1937–8 in his *Liberty of the Subject*. He believed that the deliberate intervention by the government to prevent the NAs from siding with the farmers did 'irreparable harm to Government prestige, and by throwing the farmers back on their own resources . . . has thereby rendered it possible for the masses to build up a solid foundation for future mass action, not necessarily economic but possible political,

initial hesitation on the part of the farmers: the October Congress addressed a long telegram to the Secretary of State which included the demand for 'direct representation for farmers in the forthcoming Legislative Assembly'. But by December 1950 the farmers had agreed to sponsor candidates through the CPP.

Thirdly, the CPP had the great advantage of being presented with a series of 'trial runs' before the main election in February. Municipal elections were held in Accra in April 1950, in Cape Coast early in June, and in Kumasi at the beginning of November; in June 1950 there was a by-election at Cape Coast for the legislative council brought about by the death of George Moore. In each election the CPP was successful; each helped to test its organization and add new members to its branches.[29] Thus the first propaganda vans, equipped with loudspeakers, were used in the Accra municipal elections in April, despite protests from the older party groups on the grounds that they intimidated the electorate. The Kumasi municipal elections were particularly useful to the CPP, for it was there that local leaders tried out many of the devices used later with good effect in the general election—writing with raw plantain over the roads, streets of flags and bunting, mass processions, and propaganda vans illuminated in the party colours with festoons of lighted bulbs.[30]

---

and possible in a more delicate and dangerous field.' This was true, although it was not Danquah but the CPP which seized the opportunity presented by the farmers' grievances.

[29] The administration also learnt to improve its handling of elections. Only one polling station was opened in each ward in Kumasi, with the result that there were long queues and a number of disgruntled would-be voters at the close of polling. Most of these defects were put right before 1951. The Kumasi elections were a remarkable victory. The CPP won five of the six wards and would have won the sixth if their candidate, Young-Sidi, had not been disqualified; their opponents, sponsored by a People's Democratic Party (formed in June 1950), were given 37 votes against 6,210 for the CPP. (There were 13 votes for two independent candidates.) The *Evening News* enjoyed itself at the expense of a Mr Brobey who had 1 vote 'commonly attributed to his wife'. The change in the temper of local politics may be seen in the size of the poll compared with former elections in the municipality: e.g. in 1947 when there had been only 1,014 votes in four contested wards.

In the Accra municipal elections, CPP candidates (including one woman, Mrs Olabisi Renner) won all 7 seats against candidates sponsored by the UGCC, the local Mambii Party, and the Rate-Payers' Association.

Kwesi Plange and J. E. Hagan won the by-elections in two wards of the Cape Coast municipality. Then Plange went on to win the legislative council by-election with 1,246 against 730 votes for two Independents. The conservatives had indeed been routed in their high places. 'Is the CPP still a "minority and irresponsible group"?' the *Evening News* demanded; 'tell it not in Ghana, publish it not in the streets of Britain. For the very elements of heaven and earth will curse your bones even when you are dead and gone. We will continue Forward Ever, Backward Never.'

[30] Much of the success of the Kumasi elections was due to Beattie Casely Hayford,

Fourthly, there were a number of immediate causes of complaint in 1950 which added to the general unrest. A new source of discontent was found for the perennial grievance over the rate of 'Africanization' of the public service. (Admittedly the few leading Ghanaian civil servants were by no means sympathetic with the CPP, but it was a general point of nationalist honour in 1950 that the European 'civil masters' ought to be replaced as quickly as possible.) The government announced the names of the permanent secretaries for the new ministries that were to be established—and all six were European. There was an immediate outcry, in the legislative council, the Joint Provincial Council, the Asanteman Council, and the *Evening News* which attacked the appointments officer by officer. The government tried to make amends in October by announcing the appointment of A. L. Adu as Commissioner for Africanization to be 'responsible for . . . ensuring that the maximum of suitably qualified African candidates became available for appointment to the higher grades of the public service', and it appointed six African principal assistant secretaries to work side by side with the permanent secretaries; but this did nothing to stop the attacks.[31] There were other grounds for complaint which, in sum, helped to arouse mass support for the party. The maize harvest was bad, for example, at the end of 1950, and a vicious black market developed in the large towns as imported corn reached the retailers. There were anti-tax riots in the Keta district early in November, in which six villagers were killed. A new daily newspaper, a subsidiary of the London *Daily Mirror*, appeared on 2 October as the *Daily Graphic*, and Nii Bonne once again launched an (unsuccessful) boycott to try and protect the local press. Later in the month an article appeared in the London *Daily Telegraph* (and was widely reproduced in the Gold Coast press) written by two visiting British Members of Parliament who saw the red hand of Moscow at work in the CPP.[32] In Kumasi the Asantehene came under

---

whose father, Archie Casely Hayford (son of J. E. Casely Hayford) won the municipal election in Ward A against B. D. Addai, and the whole Kumasi constituency in the general election. The advantage of using raw plantain to inscribe the party's slogans on roads and buildings lay in the fact that it did not wash away in the rain.

[31] 'Once more the Government has offered us a toothless gift horse', said the (CPP) *Morning Telegraph*, and the *Evening News*.

[32] See the remarkable article by L. D. Gammans (Conservative) and Wing Commander Cooper (Labour), 'Red Shadow over the Gold Coast', in *Daily Telegraph*, 17 Oct. 1950.

attack when the Confederacy Council agreed that the Geology Department of the University College might investigate the floor of the sacred Lake Bosumtwe, and the rumour spread that the chiefs were selling the lake. In November it was announced that the Judicial Committee of the Privy Council had rejected Nkrumah's appeal against his conviction. Thus the storm clouds of 1948 were not yet dispersed, and the CPP was the beneficiary of every local and national discontent voiced against the colonial government.

On 28 December, however, the government announced the dates of the forthcoming general election: 5 and 6 February for the primary elections; 8 February for the rural electoral colleges, the Northern Electoral College, and the municipalities; 10 February for the territorial councils. The CPP warned its members to read the *Evening News* daily to enable the national headquarters to guide the country to victory; the officials once more renewed their efforts. The period of preparation and waiting was over, and interest shifted to the constituencies where the candidates were already at work.

The actual conduct of the election raised a number of questions, viz: how did the party choose its candidates? How did it raise its campaign money? What was happening to its rivals— the UGCC and the chiefs? The evidence was not always available to show what was happening beneath the surface of events, but from newspapers and the resolutions of local party congresses it was possible to obtain a fairly reliable picture of the CPP and its opponents as they entered the election campaign.

The nomination of candidates by the CPP national executive became a contentious issue towards the end of 1950. Part of the difficulty lay in the fact that the machinery of party organization was still in the process of being put to work: the interim constitution drawn up in 1949 had not yet been ratified and, although the central committee of nine members (and the national executive committee of about thirty) had been given provisional powers, many of the leading members were still in prison. Nor were there any precedents for the party to follow in choosing its candidates; only certain obvious limitations to what the centre could do. In effect, the general working rule adopted was the simple one that rewards should go to those who had stood by the party in 1949 and during Positive Action. There were two kinds of would-

be supporters who were 'scrambling for adoption', said Gbedemah early in December when the nomination struggle was at its
height: there were those 'who were convinced of the party's programme and became members' and those 'who enrol with the intention of getting into the Assembly on the party's ticket'. The
former were the true nationalists, and 'anybody who has not
stood by the party in its darkest moment will not be supported by
the party. We must be sure of their loyalty to the party when they
enter the Assembly.'[33] The rule was easier to devise than to apply,
and by the end of 1950 it was clear that the party had started on a
long controversy which was to stay with it until the end of the
decade. Society was still extremely parochial, and the party
(though strongly nationalist) reflected its divisions. Thus there
developed a conflict of authority between the Accra headquarters and the regions, and between both and the constituency
executives, which seriously damaged the party in 1954. The
problem was first voiced in November 1950. H. P. Nyemitei,
acting general-secretary, issued a *Statement*, saying that: 'it is the
duty of the national executive of the party to adopt candidates
for the elections and not the local branches. When the time comes
for the election the executive will make known universally the
candidates they would put up for the electoral colleges.' This was
much too sweeping, and there were widespread protests. A
second *Statement* was then issued (on 8 December) which placed
the executive's claims on a more acceptable basis.

The constituencies [it said] have a free hand in making their
selections but the National Executive Committee must approve their
choice. It would only be as a last resort when a constituency had persistently sent in an unsatisfactory choice that the NEC would, in the
interests of the party's efficiency and prestige, select a candidate from
the area or outside it for the constituency.

There were a number of reasons for this carefully worded statement. There was known to be disquiet in Kumasi where Casely
Hayford, a Fanti, had asked for the nomination. (This was as-
suaged by placing J. E. Jantuah, the alternative Ashanti candidate, in the Kumasi North rural constituency.) A similar conflict, based on 'length of service to the party', arose in Sekondi-
Takoradi between Kwesi Lamptey and Ashford Inkumsah

[33] *Daily Graphic*, 8 Dec. 1950.

(P.G.), and was settled in much the same way by placing Inkumsah in the Ahanta rural area. The national executive could usually influence the decision by coming down on one side or other of a divided branch executive provided it had a clear picture of the local issues. But its knowledge must often have been incomplete, and in three of the thirty-three rural constituencies (Sunyani North West, Wenchi, Mampong North) the election was fought between rival party members who stood as 'Independents'. The conflict within the party was much less serious in 1950 than it was to become during the second election in 1954—these were the years of the high tide of nationalist advance when the party (not yet in office) displayed a strong moral fervour that helped to bind national decisions on the local executives—but the struggle was there, and the leaders fought hard to contain it. It was proposed to announce the final list of candidates in Accra on Sunday 10 December, but the West End Arena crowds which turned up to applaud and criticize were disappointed. Krobo Edusei and others were 'capped' (or 're-capped'). Anthony Woode (now general secretary of the TUC) declared that candidates which had the support of the TUC would work loyally through the party: but the only announcement made about the candidates was that there would be an all-night meeting of the executive committee. Later that afternoon a growing crowd of party supporters gathered outside the headquarters in Kimberley Avenue. The propaganda vans (newly painted in the party colours) stood by, and the Women's Section members danced and sang in the courtyard; but Boi Doku, national acting propaganda secretary, had to plead with the crowd that they should be patient, and eventually they settled down to wait out the night. Inside the meeting, Gbedemah warned the constituency delegates of the need for party discipline, saying that those who found themselves unable to accept the executive's decision must resign,[34] but it was not until dawn was breaking that an 'official list' of candidates was read out to the dwindling numbers who still waited below in the street. Nor did agreement in Accra carry the party as a whole. Arguments still continued in the constituencies, and Paul Tagoe (released from prison on 14 December) carried yet another message from the leader: 'Kwame Nkrumah Chairman of the Convention People's Party serving a term of imprisonment, has

[34] *Evening News*, 11 Dec. 1950.

advised me to do my best to bring unity in the rank and file of the party because it has been rumoured in prison that party members are quarrelling over the selection of candidates to the new assembly.' The executive then had to meet once more on the 23rd to amend its previous list, and to try and persuade those who had not been chosen to stand down.

The difficulties which the leaders faced over the selection of candidates needed to be seen in perspective. It was much to the credit of the party that the national executive committee was able to lift the controversy to a national level, and to reach agreement on a final list. Admittedly by far the greater number of candidates selected were local figures: the national executive committee had to accept this restriction on its freedom of choice: but within these limits the leaders were able to appeal to a remarkable loyalty (over and above local interests) which held the party steady and gave it a national focus. To see the practical effect of this overriding loyalty which the nationalist party could command it was necessary to see the struggle as it was fought out at constituency level, and an account is available of the conflict in Bekwai-Amansie.

Within the Amansie district—now a constituency—the basic structure of the party followed much the same pattern as that between the local chiefdoms and their subordinate villages. In theory, the party existed on a basis of equality. Thus each town and group of villages had its branch which was said to be equal to every other, and each branch sent two representatives to a Constituency Conference in December 1950 to choose a candidate for the February election. In practice, the local 'state capitals', such as Bekwai, Kokofu, and Essumeja, were more active than the villages, and Bekwai (the administrative headquarters) was the most active of the towns. Thus, the delegates at the Constituency Conference agreed, first that Bekwai should continue to be the constituency headquarters, secondly that although as many members as possible should be elected from the outlying towns and villages the key figures of chairman, secretary, propaganda secretary, and treasurer should be held by those who lived in Bekwai. These were sensible arrangements, and not greatly disputed. It was when the question arose of choosing a candidate that the party divided sharply. The members of the Bekwai Youth Movement (within the CPP) wished to sponsor the petty trader and drug-store keeper, A. R. Boakye. Those in the Improvement Society (at this time also in support of the CPP) were less certain. Some of its leaders pushed their own claims; others looked round for an alternative candidate. Ambition, local interests, traditional fears, personal rivalries, all began to play their part, and had already been voiced before the Delegates' Conference at crowded meetings in the 'Social Centre' in Bekwai, a dark, cavernous, concrete-and-wood structure above a cocoa storage depôt, overlooking the main street, from which a long flight of wooden steps led to a narrow open balcony. It was here that the dispute had been fought out among the executive members. Each branch in the Amansie district had its representatives on the constituency executive, but there had been little pretence at any show of credentials: the meetings were crowded and noisy with a swarm of party members and 'sympathizers' packing the rooms and balcony, and (at the beginning) a total failure to agree on a single name.

The strongest candidate was Richard Boakye. He had been to the all-important Saltpond meeting the previous year where the decision had been taken to break from the UGCC; he was well known locally, as an active social campaigner, who had helped to organize the Bekwai Lions football team, the Presbyterian choir, the Youth Movement, a Literary and Social Club, harvest festivals, and the like. He was 'of the people', as a former clerk in the Swiss Union Trading Company at Konongo, a cocoa buyer for the United Africa Company in Bekwai, and now a drug-store keeper and vendor who travelled the rural areas with his medicines. He had a passionate belief in 'Self-Government Now', was much attracted by Nkrumah at Saltpond, and aroused by the Positive Action riots in Kumasi where at the famous 'Dunkirk' meeting in January 1950 he had seen Atta Mensah and others roughly handled by the police. He was a good orator in *twi*, an effective, rough-voiced speaker in English; in 1950 he was 30, hardly an educated man, despite his Standard VII school-leaving certificate, and unrelated to any chiefly family in Amansie: in short, a very typical CPP figure. He had been elected the Amansie constituency chairman; he was a deservedly popular figure, and an able organizer in a party that was beginning to stress the value of discipline and organization.

Unfortunately for Boakye, however, there were several points against him in general, and one in particular. He was not a 'local man' but from the Juaben state on the other side of Kumasi. This accident of birth freed him from local ties and quarrels but also faced him with local challengers. It was probably the most important charge against him, but it led to others, based on what was said by some to be a lack of political judgement on Boakye's part, a defect which might make it difficult for him to represent (and speak up for) Amansie at a national level. There were (it was argued) other candidates—from the area—who were at least Boakye's intellectual equal, more temperate, less fiery, who might do better. So at least it was said by those who pressed their own claims, or the claims of those whom they preferred to the constituency chairman. Eventually the choice was narrowed to four: Boakye, Adjei Sarpong of the Bewai Improvement Society, J. D. Wireko, the able state secretary of the neighbouring Essumeja chiefdom, and S. K. Forson, a Catholic teacher from Kokofu. But although each could rely on the support of his own immediate following, none had a constituency-wide appeal, and voting among the thirty-odd members of the constituency executive at its meetings in the Social Centre usually gave Boakye fourteen and eight to his nearest rival. On this basis, and because Boakye could show that he had loyally served the party, the Constituency Conference confirmed, and the national executive committee endorsed, his candidature.

Once this was done, the other claimants dropped out of the picture. Nevertheless, the decision of the national executive committee did not stop all opposition to Boakye's candidature, and those who had objected strongly to an 'outside candidate' remained divided between party and local loyalty, particularly when a new opponent appeared—a local 'scholar' with family connexions both in Bekwai and Kokofu, who might easily have been among the founders of the party had he not still been abroad in 1949. This was K. A. T. Amankwah: only 27 years old, an ex-Mfantsipim student, who had been awarded a scholarship by the Asanteman Council to Fourah Bay College in Sierra Leone, whence he had gone to King's College, Durham, and taken a degree in economics, followed by a course in public administration at Oxford. These were high qualifications indeed. To be sure, Amankwah was now assistant secretary to the Asanteman Council, and willing to stand as a candidate for the Asante Kotoko Society with the backing of the Bekwai intelligentsia and the chiefs; but he was also known to hold popular, nationalist views. Even within the CPP, therefore, Amankwah had his supporters (especially in Bekwai and Kokofu) who liked the look of so favoured a 'local son'.

When, however, the election was held, the deciding factor in the constituency was not the particular standing of either contestant but the nationalist appeal of the party. Had Amankwah stood for the CPP he would have won: had Boakye not been accepted he would have lost.[35] The choice of candidate was important—the CPP made sure of Amankwah in the 1954 election by bringing him within the party as its candidate when the large Amansie constituency was divided in two—but less so than the fact that the CPP stood for self-government and the 'Common Man'. When Gbedemah listed the qualifications of an ideal candidate the order in which he placed his three criteria was: 'service to the party, ability to take an intelligent part in debate, and possession of a high standard of morality in the community'.[36] It was the first of these qualifications—'service to the party'—interpreted in the broad sense of playing an active part in the nationalist movement from 1947 onwards—which had determined the choice of Boakye in Amansie, and once he was accepted by the national executive committee he was sure of a place in the new assembly. A majority of the executive and branch officers campaigned on his behalf in the name of Nkrumah and the CPP; the electorate voted for him as the party's candidate. And this was generally the case throughout the Colony and Ashanti. A candidate such as Krobo Edusei, for example, a former reporter and debt collector for the *Ashanti Pioneer*, was chosen for Kumasi North West because of his 'service' in the boycott campaign in 1948, in the Asante Youth Association, and during Positive Action in 1950—a service confirmed by his nine months' imprisonment; Mate Johnson—formerly a letter-writer and an ex-policeman—was chosen for Manya Krobo in the eastern Colony area because of his pro-CPP stand against Nene Mate Kole, the paramount chief; Pobee Biney, a locomotive driver, not because of his trade union backing but because of his efforts in spreading

[35] Had Amankwah stood for the CPP the margin of the party's victory would almost certainly have been greater. As it was, Amankwah gave Boakye a good fight: A. R. Boakye (CPP) 57, K. T. Amankwah 27.
[36] *Daily Graphic*, 2 Dec. 1950.

the party through the Denkyira rural area. All these three very representative candidates—like Boakye in Amansie—were chosen because they had played a notable part in the early days of the nationalist movement, and it was the party which brought them to the assembly.

How did the party finance its election campaign? Nothing is more obscure in the operation of a party machine than the raising of funds, and the CPP was no exception. One fact was clear: it raised very little through regular membership subscriptions. What, after all, was a member? 'As for Komenda' (a coastal fishing town), the author was told late in 1950, 'we are all CPP here'. The same was said of the near-by town of Kissi: but when asked what it cost to belong to the party, the local branch secretary replied that members should buy a membership card and give what they could to the 'Fighting Fund', and, on these terms, the party gained a nominal recruit. The 'Fighting Fund' was based on a flat rate of 5s. a man and 3s. a woman; in addition there was usually a charge of 1s. or 6d. for attendance at rallies. But money was slow to come into the national headquarters, and the subscription list read out at the first annual conference in July 1950 was not encouraging.[37] In this respect, however, the local branch was probably better equipped (in 1950) than the national headquarters. Much of the propaganda was carried out at local expense, for the party was not yet in power and therefore unable to draw on those sources of income that a governing party can command; nor was it able in 1950 (as it was later) to attract large sums from those who wished to stand well with the party—the well-wishers and the frightened who quickly helped to meet the £500,000 appeal fund launched early in 1958. Indeed, it was still struggling to establish itself in different parts of the country. It did, however, have the enthusiastic support of its rank-and-file members—an enthusiasm which led bands of young men and women to spend week-end after week-end travelling into the villages, at their own expense, to make the party known and its candidates acceptable. Moreover—their loyalty called upon—Ghanaians were extremely generous in *ad hoc* contributions during rallies or in response to personal appeals. Thus a CPP 'harvest festival' (in December 1950) raised over £100 for the (Colony)

[37] It included Accra £40 17s., Winneba £6, Obuasi £3 18s., Prestea £10. Bogoso £6 1s., and smaller amounts from other districts.

Nsawam branch of the party, when a service held in the Methodist Church was followed by a collection outside immediately afterwards, and similar sums were obtained through rallies, football matches, and dances, by other branches. These were the 'financiers' of the party in its early days—local farmers, fishermen, and traders who had the good cause at heart, to whom the CPP was much more than an instrument of political action, and something approaching a new order of society which commanded their whole-hearted affection and what little spare money they could set aside.[38]

This was the most striking feature of the 1951 election—the force and vigour of a nationalist movement in full cry, and if the CPP drew a large part of its strength from existing organizations, it touched them all with its own magic. The 'Prison Graduate cap' was only one example of a spectacular showmanship[39] which took over the rich ceremonies accompanying the election of a chief and the organization of the *asafo* companies, and gave them fresh life in party form. A party flag—red, white, and green; a party salute—the uplifted arm and the open palm; and the cry of 'Freedom';[40] propaganda vans picked out in red, green, and white; cloths, handbags, and belts in the party's colours, the sale of framed photographs of Nkrumah, processions, picnics, dances, rallies, songs and plays,[41] ensured that the party was seen to exist in as personal and colourful a form as it was possible to devise. The *Evening News* excelled itself in daily captions and articles exalting the party, with phrases taken from the Bible and books of quotations to express an extreme devotion. 'Chameleon organisations shall pass away but the Political Holy Ghost, CPP, shall stay for evermore. Long live Kwame.' And 'Oh Dynamic Cii Pii

[38] e.g. Kofi Suarenuah's creed in 1950: 'I believe in the Convention People's Party, The Dynamic Political Party, The Liberty of the Masses, The Progress of the Nation, The Resurrection of Ghana, And Freedom Everlasting.' Suarenuah's home town was Lawra, in the extreme north-west of northern Ghana, though he worked in the south.

[39] Another was the title D.V.B.—'Defender of the Verandah Boys' awarded to Archie Casely Hayford who defended the CPP Kumasi leaders (and Nkrumah at Cape Coast) and to others, including Mrs Olabisi Renner and the two English lawyers, C. S. Rewcastle and R. Milner, who defended Nkrumah at Accra.

[40] The Freedom Salute was said to have been introduced by Dzenkle Dzewu, the party treasurer, who left the party in 1952 and in 1958 was placed in preventive detention.

[41] e.g. By the 'Axim Trio', one of whom—J. E. Dadson, elected in 1951—became Government Chief Whip in 1957. The 'Trio' presented a number of amusing skits on the administration and the chief, as in 'A D.C. and his Good Friend', and more serious performances: e.g. 'Kwame Nkrumah is Mightier than Before'.

Pii, Sanctify them through thy truth; thy word is truth'.[42] These
were extravagant variations of the slogans that the *Evening News*
proclaimed daily: 'We prefer Self-Government with danger to
servitude in tranquillity', 'We have the right to live as men', 'We
have the right to govern ourselves'. As the election date drew
near, the registration campaigns gave place to propaganda urging voters to support the party, and engine drivers, lorry- and
taxi-drivers entering the main towns whistled and hooted the
rhythmical slogan 'Cī Pī Pī, Běkǒ Āssēmblēe'.[43]

This cheerful flamboyance did not conceal the hard work of
organization that lay behind the party, or the effort that was put
into preaching its name and message up and down the country.
The following weekly 'diary' of events, taken at random from the
Evening News for July 1950, provided some measure of the energies and devotion among the CPP leaders in its early years:

> July 2nd—rally at Obuasi, Ashanti.
>
> 6th —rally and lecture by C. F. Amoo-Gottfried at Tamale, Northern Territories.
>
> 8th —rallies at Korle Gonno and Mamprobi in Accra, with a report on party organization by Councillor Ashong.
>
> 8th —rally and lecture by Kwesi Lamptey at Koforidua in the Colony.
>
> 9th —new branches opened in the Obutu district, Colony.
>
> 9th —rallies at Dompoasi, Fomena, Obuasi in Ashanti.
>
> 9th —Anomabu branch inaugurated rallies in the Edubiasi district of the Colony.
>
> 9th —'monster rally' at the Arena, Accra: Rev. Osabutey Aguedze on 'Democracy in Theocracy', R. S. Iddrisu (regional chairman, Northern Territories) on 'The CPP and the North'; K. A. Gbedemah on 'The CPP and the General Elections'.

Four days after the Arena meeting, Gbedemah left Accra for a
'twelve-day tour of the western province', opening branches,
bringing in new members, and settling disputes. There were
plenty of willing helpers. The Ashanti regional headquarters

---

[42] Other religions were pressed into the service of the party: 'with the advent of Christianity and western civilisation', said Nii Akwaa Mensah II, Nai Wulomo of Accra, addressing a CPP rally, 'we have been taught to disregard our way of living—a setback to our culture and an opportunity to the imperialists and their agents. . . . We have too much adopted the Christian way of life and if we could do as our forefathers did there was no reason why we should not force the imperialists to go bag and baggage from our God-given land' (*Daily Graphic*, 12 Dec. 1950).

[43] 'CPP will go to the Assembly'.

dispatched thirty-nine propaganda secretaries into the rural constituencies with party membership cards; Atta Mensah conducted his propaganda in Kumasi by travelling constantly on the
municipal buses and exhorting the passengers to vote CPP.
Rallies were crowded with enthusiastic audiences, and usually
included a lecture—where possible by a party leader or a close
ally such as the then immensely popular Nigerian barrister,
Prince Onotu Emeni—and the demands made by constituency
and branch organizations kept the leaders continually on trek
through the southern constituencies. Across the Volta—to the
north and east—the CPP found the going more difficult, although the Tamale branch members did what they could to influence those who were most likely to be delegates to the Northern
Electoral College; but the party members were few in number
and unable to arouse enthusiasm among the chiefs and their educated advisers for a southern-based People's Party. The Ewe-
speaking peoples of the trust territory were also suspicious of the
new party. The CPP had scarcely begun to enter the territory,
although it had (on paper) a fully fledged regional organization
for Trans-Volta-Togoland, and when it began to open branches
there it encountered a rival (Ewe) nationalism of much longer
antecedents. Thus when G. K. Amegbe, the regional chairman,
opened the CPP branch in Ho early in October 1950 he was challenged by J. M. Dumoga, president of the Togoland Youth
Association: on what grounds, he was asked, was a party movement in the Gold Coast entering 'an associated territory'?[44] But
the north and Trans-Volta were the frontier areas of nationalist
advance, and when the party drew back to its own campaign
country in the south its hold was unassailable.

Early in 1951 the CPP headquarters issued its election manifesto, *Towards the Goal*, which set out the party's nationalist aims
in simple terms; the constituency executive and branch members
carried its message into the urban and rural areas, and the elec-

---

[44] *Ashanti Pioneer*, 17 Oct. 1950. A protest note was sent to Gbedemah saying that
while the Gold Coast Ewe might wish to join a Gold Coast party this was not true
of the Togoland Ewe who had their own end to secure. Gbedemah was an 'Anlo
Ewe' from the crowded Ewe districts in the south-east of the Gold Coast Colony.
For the Ewe question, see below, ch. VI.

A Northern Territories Progressive Society existed in Tamale, but it was not
very active—'a potential sleeper in the race of man' according to the *Evening News*,
which ascribed the lack of support for the CPP in the north to the autocracy of the
officials and the chiefs 'who were not encouraged to ride in cars but flattered to use
the old-fashioned horse for travelling'.

torate responded by voting for those who undertook to support the party's candidate in the Electoral College.

CPP MANIFESTO 1951
Towards the Goal

1. *Constitutional.* The Coussey Committee let the country down by prolonging white imperialism. The CPP will fight for self-government NOW.

2. *Political.* An upper house of the Legislature, known as the Senate, shall be created for the Chiefs.

    Universal suffrage at the age of 21.

    Direct elections with no property or residential qualifications for candidates. . .

3. *Economic.* A five year Economic Plan. . . .

    (i) Immediate materialisation of the Volta hydro-electric scheme.

    (ii) Railway lines to be doubled and extended.

    (iii) Roads to be modernised and extended.

    (iv) Canals to join rivers.

    (v) Progressive mechanisation of agriculture.

    (vi) Special attention will be given to the swollen shoot disease; farmers will be given control of the Cocoa Industry Board funds. . . .

    (ix) Industrialisation will be carried out with all energy.

4. *Social.* Education:

    (i) A unified system of free compulsory elementary, secondary and technical education up to 16 years of age.

    (ii) The University College to be brought up to University status.

    (iii) A planned campaign to abolish illiteracy.

    Family Assistance:

    A free national health service.

    A high standard housing programme. . .

    A piped-water supply in all parts of the country. . .

    A national insurance scheme.

The manifesto warned electors that hard work was necessary: 'even under self-government taxation will still be levied'; it called for discipline and unity, and incorporated party beliefs in a number of easily quoted maxims: 'The CPP is a Party of the

People. In ourselves we are nothing; it is the people who give us strength.' 'The CPP has been built on service, sacrifice and suffering.' 'Seek Ye first the Political Kingdom and All Things will be added unto it.' And: 'Vote wisely and God will Save Ghana from the Imperialists.'

It was not difficult to understand why these proposals and sayings should draw the electorate to the CPP. They blended emotion with self-interest. There was the appeal to the heart—to the loyalty of those who prefered self-government to servitude, an appeal, too, to local pride and an 'Africanism' which (after 1951) took the whole continent for its province. Secondly, there was the projection of the CPP as the party of the Common Man—the 'Party of the People'—an appeal which was given an immediate reception among not only the elementary-school-leavers in the youth societies but the commoners within the native authorities, each group seeing the district commissioner and the chief as joint instruments of colonial rule. Thirdly, there was the promise of immediate, material benefits as soon as self-government was attained, when the common man would be able to enjoy all the blessings which it was supposed existed in a country able to control its own affairs. With the removal of the imperialists, there would be an end to the enforced destruction of the cocoa farmers' trees, and a return to a market price for kerosene, cloth, matches, rice, yam, plantain, and tinned fish, as to enable the ordinary man to live within his income while he enjoyed the amenities of pipe-borne water, free schooling, cheap houses, smooth roads, more hospitals, industrialization and a 'mechanized agriculture'. This was the Goal that the party set before its members and its members before the electorate. All three aspects of its appeal were incorporated in the demand for 'Freedom', and freedom meant not just the rejection of colonial rule and its agents but carried with it the positive ideal of national unity under popular leadership.

The constituency executives and branch officers had to translate this general message of hope into terms understandable at a local level. How this was done in Bekwai Amansie may be seen in the following account:

When we go on rallies we would tell the farmers that they should vote for CPP for Self-Government Now. When the Europeans first came they helped us and we were grateful. Now we find they are cheating us. We said we wanted more schools for our children. Also prices were too high. Now Kwame Nkrumah has come to tell us how to get our self-government and we must form a branch of CPP. The country is rich. We have our cocoa, timber, gold, so many things. Only we are poor. The farmers understood us very well and told us of their needs. We promised that the CPP would put all things right.

This is what we told the people. We would go to the village by lorry, a group of us, fifteen or twenty. Some times we would hire a band to attract the people. We would greet the chief, but if the chief would not listen we would preach in the market place whether the chief wanted us or not. We told them that they should listen to the young men and not only the elders. The chief often helped us and beat gonggong to call his people, but we always had a member in the village who would welcome us. When we had preached CPP to them, we would leave that village and go to the next. We spent many weekends like this, not caring for our profit but to help party members in prison, and to get self-government for Ghana. We went to Kumasi for party discussions and to Accra.[45]

One may note here, too, the report by the chairman of the Constituency Conference in December 1950:

REPORT OF THE CONSTITUENCY CONFERENCE HELD FROM 2nd–3rd DECEMBER 1950

On Saturday the 2nd inst. the long talked of Constituency Conference began with a picnic in the afternoon, music being provided by the Senfi Brass Band. Members, supporters and sympathisers of the party merrily danced to the tune of the ever popular song 'Obiara Ntumi Kwame Nkrumah'. The picnic which started at 2.30 p.m. came to a close at 6 p.m. In a cool and refreshing atmosphere a very successful dance was staged under the banner of the CPP from 9 p.m. to 3 a.m.

Early on Sunday, in spite of the energy exerted the previous night at the dance, the delegates and supporters were seen moving to and fro in hasty preparation to the Special Delegates Conference which was to start at 9 a.m. Barely at 9 a.m. the Conference Hall had been packed to its capacity leaving no breathing space. This occasion was graced with the presence of Councillors Archie Hayford, Jantuah and Donkor, while P.G's Amoo, Krobo Edusei, Fori Dwuma and under-graduate Atta Mensah were no small figures to be left out unmentioned. At the meeting the Chair was occupied by councillor Archie Hayford.

In the chairman's address, he pointed out that he was glad that the

---

[45] Account given to the author by a member of the Amansie West constituency executive. 'Chief' here is the *odikro* (village head).

Convention People's Party which was at one time reckoned as a Party of irresponsibles is now proving its worthy merits in the municipal councils of Accra, Cape Coast and Kumasi. The advisability of getting a suitable station as the Amansie Constituency Headquarters was discussed. After some deliberations it was agreed upon that Bekwai be set aside as the Party's headquarters.

Funds for running the party's constituency was then brought for discussion and after a heated argument, a final decision was arrived at that on all enrolments the out stations should subscribe fifty per cent out of their share of 6d. from the enrolment fee of two shillings to feed the Constituency Headquarters.

It is interesting to mention that at this juncture one Mr Appiah, who had been moved by the speeches of the chairman freely donated one pound to help build an office for the party and to carry on with the struggle for S.G. Now. So was Mr Osei Frimpong stirred, that he donated five guineas.

To see that the party is run on an efficient basis, it was suggested that a full time Secretary and a Propaganda Secretary be employed. Mr Kofi Akuwuah was popularly elected propaganda secretary while Mr Efrifa was elected Secretary.

Their rate of pay was to be determined by the Constituency Executive which was scheduled to meet on Saturday the 9th inst. Honorary appointments made were: Chairman, Mr A. R. Boakye, Vice Chairman, J. K. Nyarku, Treasurer, R. E. Brace.

Voluntary contributions of £5 (Five pounds) per each branch were made to help Build up the party and this plus offers made by generous members, supporters and sympathisers amounted to £70. 10s. (Seventy pounds, ten shillings).

The football match scheduled to take place at the Gyemfi Park between the Famous Cape Coast Majestics XI and Kumasi Evergreen XI successfully came off before Spectators numbering well over two thousand strong. Krobo Edusei took the kick off. The scores were Cape Coast Majestics 1, Kumasi Evergreen 4.

The teaming crowd would not rest satisfied to let this Sunday pass off without their hearing the 'London Hyde Park Wizard' Kwesi Lamptey, supported by Krobo Edusei, Atta Mensah, Councillors Jantuah, Archie Hayford, Donkor, dilating on speeches of significance. (The Government and the Jacobu shooting incident.) The lecture closed at about 9.30 p.m.

In all 90 branches attended with two representatives each.

Recorded by (A. R. Boakye) CHAIRMAN.

As the date of the election drew near, the CPP intensified its campaign. The party flag hung above every town and almost every large village in Ashanti and the Colony: its propaganda agents were to be seen travelling the rural areas by lorry, teaching the villagers how (and which way) to vote, settling disputes at a local level between candidates for the rural primary elections and trying to ensure that the delegates to the electoral colleges would be party members. But their opponents, too, were not inactive.

The intelligentsia and the chiefs began to draw together in 1950. What was left of the UGCC met at Saltpond early in April, and drew up a Ten-Point Programme (incorporated later in its election manifesto) as a basis for agreement between the anti-CPP groups. At the end of May, the handful of elderly members of the Aborigines Rights Protection Society met in Cape Coast to plan its fifty-third anniversary and to examine what the young men were doing, and both the UGCC and the ARPS (under W. E. G. Sekyi) agreed that the chiefs were now the most effective rallying point of sensible opinion in the country.[46] There was much to forgive on both sides between the chiefs and the intelligentsia, but—the times had changed—and there were obvious advantages in collaboration. It began to look as if the CPP might well win a majority of the seats in both the municipal and rural constituencies, and the prospect of CPP rule was a bleak one for the intelligentsia and the traditional ruler alike. Nkrumah's remark that if the chiefs did not co-operate with the masses, the time would come when they would 'run away and leave their sandals behind' was widely quoted; and the members of the Working Committee of the UGCC knew that they, too, had nothing to hope for, and much to fear, in Nkrumah's rise to power. There was, however, still room for manœuvre. The chiefs and the intelligentsia might not be able to stop the CPP in the open constituencies, but the chiefs had eighteen 'territorial seats' of their own,[47] and, if the delegates to the Northern Electoral College could be won over, the number would be increased to thirty-seven, almost a half of the (75) African seats in the proposed Assembly. Here was an alternative route to the Assembly if things went badly at the polls. As A. G. Grant told the press in November 1950: 'Our aim is not just to present candidates; we must

---

[46] For a sympathetic sketch of the Cape Coast lawyer W. E. G. Sekyi, see Wight, pp. 74–75.
[47] i.e. The Joint Provincial Council of Chiefs 11, South Togoland Council 1, Asanteman Council 6, Northern Territories Electoral College 19.

really get first class people into the Assembly'—and precisely how they got there did not matter.[48] The UGCC leaders were more adept at manœuvring with blocks of possible support dependent on influential leaders than in scouring the villages and market places for votes, and now that it was clear the old alliance of chiefs and officials was coming to an end, the chiefs, too, were ready for a broad front of opposition to the CPP.

In this way the idea arose of a Joint Territorial Council movement. A preliminary meeting in August between representatives of the UGCC, and of the Ashanti and Colony territorial councils, led to a full meeting in Kumasi in October. It was well attended: 4 representatives (2 chiefs, 2 non-chiefs) from the Southern Togoland Council, 4 chiefs from the Colony, 9 members from the Asanteman Council (5 of whom were chiefs) and 6 northerners led by J. H. Allasani, Yakubu Tali (Tali-Na), and shrewd traditional heads like the Navropio. A strong contingent was present from the UGCC, the National Democratic Party in Accra, and the People's Democratic Party in Kumasi. The Asantehene was elected chairman, and the opening speeches on 18 October set the tone of the meeting. J. H. Allasani (later to be an ardent supporter of the CPP and minister in Nkrumah's cabinet in 1954 and 1956) spoke on behalf of the Dagomba District Council. He disliked the party system (he told the conference, amidst general applause) because it set age against youth: it was 'dangerous and possibly nauseous to the vital integrity of the people as a whole', because parties were 'foreign practices' that disregarded 'our own traditional institutions and culture'. He wholeheartedly supported the idea of a national congress.[49] Other speakers took up the same theme, using phrases drawn from the vocabulary of intelligentsia argument which condemned the CPP for having broken the 'common front' of national unity established in 1947. The following ten days were spent discussing national events in which the members attempted a neutral stand. They agreed to protest against the 'Gammans–Cooper article' in the London *Daily Telegraph*; they forwarded a petition to the Governor and the Secretary of State praying for the release of Nkrumah and Nana Kobina Nketsia.[50] Their dislike of the CPP was manifest,

---

[48] *Daily Graphic*, 14 Nov. 1950.   [49] *Daily Graphic*, 19 Oct. 1950.
[50] Chief of British Sekondi, imprisoned in 1950 for defiance of the emergency regulations, released in 1951. These resolutions of the Conference were largely tactical moves following an angry meeting between the chiefs and a small number of

however, and I. K. Agyeman told the conference that he had 'never before come across any bad organisation such as the CPP. The CPP must be killed, otherwise the chiefs should not bother to do anything good for the country.'[51] On the 27th the Asantehene himself spoke. Through one of his senior linguists, Bafuor Osei Akoto, he (and the Queen Mother, Nana Ama Serwah Nyarko) swore the great triple oath of Ashanti (*ntamkessie miensa*) that he had not sold Lake Bosumtwe to any person, and that the fixing of the cocoa price at £3 10s. a load had nothing to do with him or the chiefs.[52] The CPP was wrong, the Asantehene complained, to set themselves against the chiefs for 'we all want self-government, and I do not understand why some people say that some of us, the chiefs, do not want self-government and that they will destool us'.[53]

The conference closed on 29 October, after appointing a steering committee (with A. A. Y. Kyerematen and J. E. Baiden as joint secretaries) to arrange a further 'Gold Coast National Congress' for 29 December. A final appeal was issued 'to the whole country and to every national group, party or association to co-operate with the Committee in the supreme bid for national unity, and to bring sanity and a reasoned measure of political action into the Struggle for Home Rule'. The following month (13 November) the steering committee urged 'the Territorial, State and Divisional Councils' to 'make use of their special machinery of information' to make sure that their people registered and voted in the elections. On 19 December, however, the proposed National Congress was abandoned. The decision was taken, instead, to oppose the CPP where the party was thought to be most vulnerable, in the rural chiefdoms within each constituency. Late in 1950 and early 1951, therefore, a number of local alliances were concluded between the chiefs and the intelligentsia: the state councils of chiefs agreed to 'sponsor' a candi-

CPP members on 24 November. The CPP group, led by Kwesi Lamptey, warned the chiefs that if they were not patient they would cause an explosion, and told them that the idea of a National Congress had already been carried out by the CPP at its Ghana People's Representative Assembly. If the chiefs were sincere, said Lamptey, they should demand the release of Nkrumah; and in reply, the chiefs 'prayed' for his release.

[51] *Daily Graphic*, 25 Oct. 1950.
[52] The cocoa price was now 70s. a load of 60 lb, and one of the items of CPP propaganda in Ashanti was that the 'real price was 90s., and that the government and the chiefs kept the difference'.
[53] *Daily Graphic*, 28 Oct. 1950.

date whom the UGCC, or the Asante Kotoko Society, or one or other of the smaller party groups, then 'supported' as its candidate. National policy, in so far as it was an issue, was embodied in the election manifesto of the UGCC—*Plan for the Nation*:[54]

Constitutional: The present constitution is a watered-down version of the Coussey recommendations; it is 'a step, but not our last step, in the struggle for self-government', which must be achieved 'by all legitimate and constitutional means'.

Political: The chiefs must, in spite of themselves, be saved for the Gold Coast, by removing the Governor's power to grant or withdraw recognition from Chiefs recognized by their people.

Remove civil servants from the top level of 'field administration', and place the character and structure of the civil service under the control of the Assembly. Civil servants must cease to be the 'Civil Masters' of the country.

Economic: A Ten-Point Programme—to ensure that the optimum diffusion of private enterprise and ownership of property shall be developed alongside the maximum attainment of personal liberty, within the framework of the WELFARE STATE:

   (i) An end to Government's extravagant spending and appointments, and to the lowering of the dignity of the Chiefs;
  (ii) An end to the political officers system and to the 'Go-Slow' policy in education;
 (iii) A reduction in the importation of light manufactured goods, which should be manufactured locally under a five-year plan;
  (iv) A national bank;
   (v) An active and adequate road building programme;
  (vi) Scholarships for industrial and technological training to show results, within five years;
 (vii) The raising of the standard of living, improvement in housing, water supply, primary education, health, lighting, clinics, literacy and culture;
(viii) The safeguarding of agriculture and land products, a rationalized cocoa industry, diversified agriculture, development of the Volta and of base metals; . . .
   (x) Development of the rural life of the people.

[54] Adapted from J. H. Price, *The Gold Coast Election* (Bureau of Current Affairs pamphlet, no. 11, 1951).

Finally the UGCC *Plan for the Nation* urged the electorate to 'elect to the new Assembly the best men for the job, the best men in the true sense, irrespective of party, tribe, religion and class'.

In general, there was very little difference (except in the language used) between the CPP 'Goal' and the UGCC 'Plan', and it was both the strength and weakness of the UGCC leaders that they stood close (yet opposed) to the CPP. They, too, demanded self-government—indeed, they could claim to have started the post-war nationalist movement, and by 1950 Danquah in particular could look back over more than twenty years of political agitation since he returned to the Gold Coast as a young barrister in 1928. The UGCC lawyers were 'patriots', therefore, even if they found it difficult to accept the age of the 'common man'. In challenging the CPP, however, they were on difficult ground, for it was not easy to see why the demand for 'Self-Government Now under Nkrumah' should be less desirable than that of 'Self-Government in the shortest possible time under Grant or Danquah. If the bid was for self-government, the more radical section of the nationalist movement held all the cards: indeed, it had stolen the pack. The intelligentsia also found it difficult to explain why they should suddenly ally themselves with the chiefs, their former rivals in the Colony. It was true that the Akan chiefs were not quite the 'feudal overlords' of CPP propaganda: in theory, at least, they drew their power from the people, and as the officials transferred their approval from the chiefs of an indirect-rule system to the new CPP administration, the theory became closer to practice. (Hence the alliance of the young men and the Ashanti chiefs at the end of 1954 in the NLM.) But the position was different in 1950–1. The election was popularly seen as a challenge to colonial rule of which the chiefs had hitherto appeared as local agents, and the conservative element in the UGCC was inevitably—if unduly—emphasized by its alliance with the local state councils of chiefs and elders.[55]

Although the principal protagonists during the pre-election months were the CPP and the UGCC, smaller groups proliferat-

---

[55] The UGCC had its radical and conservative 'wings': Danquah was a radical, Francis Awooner Williams a conservative. The difference comes out clearly in the *Minute Book* of the Working Committee of the UGCC, in remarks by Awooner Williams (during the quarrel between the Convention and the CYO) like: 'Although we are for unity, we should not allow ourselves to be dictated to by the masses' (entry for 14 May 1949).

ed. Of these, perhaps the oddest was the Ghana Freedom Party
started by a European, Charles Deller, in May 1950: it sought
self-government by 1 June 1953, and published an elaborate
Crusade for Ghana Freedom manifesto which included the aims of a
National (Powdered) Milk Scheme, a Ghana Foreign Legion,
and a bicameral legislature with 'resignation from the Senate to
be accomplished by the application for membership of the "Aburi
hundreds" which will be set up as an Honorary Order for that
purpose'. A month later two other parties appeared: a National
Democratic Party in Accra, formed by Dr F. V. Nanka Bruce and
Nii Ama Ollennu through an amalgamation of the local Mambii
Party and the Rate-Payers' Association; and a People's Democratic Party in Kumasi formed by Cobina Kessie, Ben Tamakloe, and Agyeman Anane. The tone of the NDP was set in an
Election Statement, by its secretary Enoch Mensah, saying that 'in
the ranks of the National Democratic Party will be found tried
and proved politicians some of whose records go back thirty
years'. The Kumasi People's Democratic Party announced that
it stood for 'law, order and peace, protection of persons and property and respect for native institutions', and the elimination of
'fanatacism, insubordination, boycotts and looting'. October
1950 saw the momentary appearance of a Gold Coast Labour
Party formed by S. H. K. Cleland of the (Obuasi) Mineworkers'
Union, Fred Loo of the P. W. D. Employees' Union, and John
Tsiboe, managing proprietor of the *Ashanti Pioneer*; it was proposed that it should collaborate with a National Labour Party in
Accra thought up by Kwame Kessie Adu: Nii Bonne was interested but, by the end of 1950, he had his own Liberal Party.
Then, as the dates of the election approached, these phantom
groups faded and (except for the National Democratic Party
in Accra) disappeared, leaving the field clear for the CPP, and
for the candidates of the UGCC and/or the Asante Kotoko Society.

The rural primary elections were held in the Colony, Southern
Togoland, and Ashanti on 5 and 6 February, the rural college
elections two days later. The Coussey Committee had believed
that the combination of an indirect system of elections, and an
'adult suffrage' limited to those who had paid their local levy,
would be a moderating influence on the temper of the election: but this was not borne out in practice. Many of the rural

primaries (it is true) were not contested because, as the official *Report* commented,

in the majority of cases the person to represent the subdistrict was agreed upon at a village meeting in accordance with the usual custom and to the satisfaction of the majority without any need to resort to the ballot box [and] many subdistricts simply chose their normal spokesman such as the local headman, a leading farmer, or other respected citizens and in the rural-areas more often because of his public standing than for his politics.[56]

Nevertheless in the electoral colleges party canvassing was intense, and there were a number of stories of how electors were plied with drink and presents, or locked in a room while the constituency secretary appealed for support for the party candidate.[57] All but one (Winneba) were contested. There was a grand total of 89 candidates. The final results were:

Opposition 4 seats, 763 votes in 32 Colleges
CPP   29 seats, 1,950 votes in 32 Colleges, and 1 seat unopposed.

[56]	Sub-Districts	No. without nominations	Total of uncontested elections	Total contested
Colony and Southern Togoland	1,736	43	1,232	461 (21 constituencies contested)
Ashanti	730	5	534	191 (12 constituencies contested)
	2,466	48	1,766	652

Source: Report on the First Election, 1951.

[57] The administration learnt this lesson very quickly. In April 1953 there was a by-election for Kumasi East (when Fori Dwumah resigned to go to England to study accountancy) and the electoral college had to be reassembled on 27 April. Its 66 members met on 30 April to choose between three candidates—C. de Graft Dickson, CPP (who had stood against the party in February 1951), E. Ohemeng, Ind., and M. B. Osei, Ind. The report of the Assistant Government Agent in Ashanti Akim noted that: 'there were a great many allegations that attempts had been made to suborn, bribe or intimidate members of the Electoral College before the election took place . . . although nothing to suggest that any malpractices occurred which substantially affected the results of the election. . . . As usual no member . . . actually came forward to complain. . . . It is however undoubtedly true that great efforts were made by all three candidates and their organisations to contact members of the Electoral College and this again underlined the importance of doing away with the present system of indirect election which might well have been designed to maximise corruption and intimidation.' The Chief Regional Officer concurred: 'I entirely agree that the direct vote should replace the electoral college system' (4/6/53. C.R.O. to the Permanent Secretary, Min. of Defence and External Affairs, Min. of Local Govt. files). De Graft Dickson, later Minister of Defence, was elected with 47 votes against 10 and 8.

In the municipal seats (also contested on 8 February) the administration had learnt a useful lesson from the council elections, and polling was both easy and orderly, at the rate of thirty an hour in the early morning,[58] despite the fact that more than half the electorate could not read the name on the ballot paper, and had to 'whisper' the name of the candidate to the Presiding Officer. (The CPP had been uneasy over this, and some of its educated members posed as illiterates to test the neutrality of the officials but no serious allegations were brought.) There was remarkably little tension on polling day if only because it was obvious that the CPP would win, and only nine convictions for infringements of the regulations in the whole of the four constituencies. Of the 90,725 registered electors, 47·2 per cent went to the polls. The CPP won all five seats, and over 90 per cent of the votes:

		Votes	*Seats*
CPP	.. ..	58,585	5
Opposition ..	..	5,574	0

Thus by the evening of 8 February the CPP had won 34 of the 38 popularly contested seats. The remaining 4 had gone to the opposition—2 for the UGCC in Akim Abuakwa, and 2 anti-CPP independents in the southern section of the Togoland trust territory. It was indeed a famous victory. And yet it was not quite as sweeping as it seemed at first. In Accra over 2,000 electors turned out to vote against the nationalist party, against 20,000 for the imprisoned leader; and in the thirty-two contested rural electoral colleges, the non-CPP vote went up to 20 per cent. Why?

Even in 1951, at a high point of nationalist fervour, the CPP was opposed from three different directions (although the attack might be launched as a joint enterprise between any two of the three) by groups which continued to resist the party's leadership in subsequent elections. In this first contest, in order of importance (an order that shifted subsequently) they were: local bodies (external to the party) usually supported by the chief and his elders which sought to protect their own particular interests from control or absorption by the nationalist party; the intelligentsia opposition; and dissident movements led by rebels within the

[58] Polling was 7 a.m.–6 p.m., changed in later elections to 5 p.m. to permit the ballot boxes to be sealed and started on their journey to the counting stations in daylight.

party's own ranks. These were to be consistent points of attack, and may be illustrated by examples taken from the municipal and rural constituencies.

The anti-Nkrumah vote in the Accra elections was compounded of the first and second of these three groups. The contest was different from that in the three other municipalities where the CPP met with only nominal resistance: 8,358 in Kumasi against 570; in Cape Coast 3,287 against 324; in Sekondi-Takoradi 6,621 against 191. In the Accra two-member constituency a growing concern among the Ga people led them to cling to their rights and traditions in a town where the population was becoming more and more cosmopolitan,[59] and reinforced the intelligentsia-UGCC dislike of the CPP. Thus Obetsibi Lamptey and Ako Adjei, the Ga lawyers and members of the Working Committee of the UGCC, were able to pick up 1,630 and 1,451 votes. Three years later Ako Adjei was standing in Accra East for the CPP, but the Ga vote, and the distaste for the party among the more educated sections of the population persisted, to break out in the Ga Shifimo Kpee (Ga Standfast Association) in midsummer 1957, and in the large minority vote against Nkrumah in the April 1960 plebiscite.

Similar local protests were recorded in the rural areas, not as yet of great weight, if only because the CPP had not yet taught the rest of the country the value of concerted action: but in the Wassaw district of the Colony, a Wassaw-Aowin Youth Association put up a strong challenger to the party's candidate: E. K. Dadson (CPP) 77; S. A. Arkah (WAYA) 30. The anti-CPP Ewe vote was still more significant, although again less than it was to become by 1954 since those who disliked the association of southern Togoland with the Gold Coast were still undecided, in 1951, whether to boycott or to oppose. Nevertheless, the CPP candidates in the Akpini-Asogli and Tongu areas were defeated, and the election of P. K. Adjani and Gerald Awuma, both sponsored by the local state councils of chiefs, were the first hesitant steps in the much stronger campaign mounted in 1954 by the Togoland Congress Party.

The most obvious points of local resistance to the CPP in 1951

[59] *Accra: 1948 Population*
Ga & Ga Adangbe .. 66,619
Others 58,804
(1948 *Census* and Ione Acquah, *Accra Survey* (1958), ch. 2.)

were in fact the state councils of chiefs through the backing they were able to give to a particular candidate. Although the chiefs were slow to move in face of the 'young men's party', and discouraged by the poor start to the Joint Territorial Council movement, they were not inactive. They set about things their own way, using their state council machinery of wing-chiefs and councillors, and prevailing on local figures of importance to stand. D. J. Buahin, an education officer in Sunyani (Ashanti), was persuaded by Nana Yiadom Boakye Owusu II (Berekumhene), the local paramount chief, to file his nomination papers as a member of the Asante Kotoko Society. [60] The Asanteman Council and the Kotoko Society sponsored K. A. T. Amankwah in Amansie. The Mampong State Council backed the Rev. S. C. Nimako against Atta Mensah. [61] This assertion of local and traditional interests could be seen most clearly, however, where the chief was himself a candidate. Three paramount chiefs stood for election on the 8th: Nana Sir Tsibu Darku of the small state of Asin Atandasu in the Colony, Nana Akompi Firim III of Kadjebi in the Akan-speaking area of southern Togoland, and Nana Agyeman Badu of the Dormaa state in western Ashanti. In Wenchi, in north-west Ashanti, the paramount chief Nana Kusi Appeah placed the full weight of his authority behind his elder brother, Dr K. A. Busia. The CPP opposed their candidature and influence in bitter terms. Bediako Poku dispatched a telegram from Wenchi to: 'The Governor, Christiansborg, 5/2/51. Wenchihene using intimidation and assaults on villages refraining casting votes for his brother. Stop. Four CiPiPi members arrested. Stop. Being inhumanly treated in cells.' The Dormaahene, a former government school teacher, who became a steadfast supporter of the CPP after 1954, was accused by the CPP Ashanti regional chairman, J. K. Donkoh, of 'strongly intimidating people, especially the members of the CPP, and even going to the extent of Assassination if they did not promise to vote for him'. An open letter from Sekondi in the Colony to the Chief Secretary asked whether Sir Tsibu Darku was standing 'as chief or as a man', for: 'if the chiefs can come down and contest with the

---

[60] With moderate success: John Gideon Awuah (CPP), produce buyer, 48 votes; Daniel Joseph Buahin, former education officer (Asante Kotoko) 13 votes. Having been forced to resign from the education service Buahin became a timber merchant —a serious loss to the administration, an acquisition to the business community.
[61] S. G. Nimako, 19 votes; Atta Mensah, 30 votes.

people, then there is no reason why the Government should make separate allocation of seats for chiefs'.[62] The Asin Atandasu contest, in particular, dramatized the commoner–chief opposition:

Alfred Pobee Biney, ex-locomotive driver, Sekondi, CPP
(nominated by a trader, fitter and farmer)   51
Nana Sir Tsibu Darku Kt, OBE, Omanhene of Asin Atandasu[63]
(nominated by a fellow paramount chief, a divisional chief
and the Denkyira State secretary)   13

From the chiefs' point of view, the mistake they made in trying to challenge the CPP lay in the belief that if they controlled the votes in their own traditional area, the chiefs of the neighbouring district could be relied on to do the same. But this did not happen. If a chief campaigned *against* the CPP, his neighbour was most likely to canvass *for* the party. Thus, the Dormaahene and the Kadjebihene had the support of most of the representatives from their own state in the electoral college: but in the very large electoral districts of 1951 their votes were insufficient to carry the constituency as a whole.[64] Nevertheless, these commoner-traditional contests are worth recording if only to show that the 1951 elections were far from being 'a race with one horse', and that the party did not have everything its own way.

Secondly, there was the challenge from the UGCC. When the administration marked down the opposition in 1951 as making only a 'half-hearted attempt to compete', saying that it was led by 'elder statesmen of more moderate views [who] were unwilling to enter the rough and tumble of politics', it was not only over-

---

[62] This and the previous two quotations are extracts from the 1951 election files in the Min. of Local Govt. These allegations of intimidation were investigated and rejected by the government, and temporarily forgotten in the general excitement of victory.

[63] Nana Sir Tsibu Darku, enstooled in 1930, was better educated than most of the chiefs, having gone to Adisadel College, Cape Coast. His state was small but his career was impressive: awarded the King's Medal for Chiefs in 1939, the MBE in 1941, the OBE in 1944, knighted in 1948; a member of the legislative council from 1932, of the executive council from 1943, and a member of the Coussey Committee. He abdicated from the Stool in September 1951, but continued to sit as a territorial member in the legislative assembly until 1954. Sir Tsibu Darku had his revenge: it was Pobee Biney, who later quarrelled with the party, and Sir Tsibu who made his peace with Nkrumah to become, after independence, chairman (first) of the Tema Development Corporation and then of the Cocoa Marketing Board. And in August 1962 he was re-elected paramount chief of Asin Atandasu.

[64] The Dormaahene had 19 votes against 36 for B. Yeboah Afari (CPP) who ran a small part-secondary, part-commercial school in the chief's own town. The Kadjebihene had 29 votes against 37 for Joseph Kodzo (CPP), a primary school teacher.

simplifying a complicated pattern of opposition, but being less than fair even to the 'elder statesmen'. A number of the UGCC leaders and their supporters were humiliated—Cobina Kessie in Kumasi East, A. A. Y. Kyerematen in Mampong North, J. W. de Graft Johnson in Saltpond failed to get any votes at all in the rural electoral colleges. But, when allied with tradition, the intelligentsia could still show fight. Both Danquah and William Ofori Atta succeeded in Akim Abuakwa where the CPP was unable as yet to match the combination of respect for the two candidates and the ability of the Akim Abuakwa chiefs to muster support on their behalf. The contest was close in this two-member constituency since the CPP, through Ashie Nikoe, was able to draw support from the migrant cocoa farmers in the Akim states; nevertheless, the CPP candidates were defeated:

William Ofori Atta, principal Akim Abuakwa State College, UGCC	87
Joseph Boakye Danquah, barrister, UGCC	95
Gershom Ashie Nikoe, farmer, CPP	85
John Edmund Turkson, trader and farmer, CPP	83

(*Note:* there were two spoiled papers—one unmarked, the other 'wrongfully recorded', according to the senior district commissioner who presided over the electoral college.)

If by themselves, therefore, the intelligentsia were no match for the nationalist party, they might still look for allies. The Akim Abuakwa results, and the alliance concluded elsewhere between the chiefs and local associations, showed that opposition to the CPP could not be disregarded completely. The function of the small group of intellectuals (as they saw it) was to maintain a position of attack, however feeble, until such time as other sources of strength became available to them; they did not accept their defeat in the election but bided their time, and held themselves ready to shape any local grievance which might develop into a common front of opposition.

The third ingredient in the anti-CPP alliance—the dissident elements within the party's own ranks—was much less conspicuous in 1951 than in the next election. The party was still new and its loyalties not yet strained; but, although the argument over nominations had been settled effectively, the possibility (at least) of rebellion could be seen. In the opposition to Boakye in

Amansie, in similar conflicts between would-be candidates else-where—all devoted party members up to the point of the election —the party was experiencing its first uneasy movement of internal dissent.

In sum, the party leaders would have had little to worry about in 1951 had they been faced with nothing more serious than the opposition expressed in the popular voting. But the Northern Electoral College had also chosen its nineteen members; and on 10 February the three territorial councils were to meet in Kumasi, Dodowa (in the Colony), and Ho (in Trans-Volta) to elect their eighteen members. Virtually nothing was known of the election in Tamale except that some of the northern delegates who had attended the Joint Territorial Council conference in Kumasi had been returned to the Assembly. Two days later, however, the territorial elections in Ashanti and the Colony produced a number of familiar figures, and it may be helpful to look first at the way in which the chiefs voted.

There was keen competition: 53 candidates for the 11 Colony seats, 31 for the 6 in Ashanti, and 6 for the single Southern Togoland seat.[65] The decision to hold the elections two days later than the popular vote in the constituencies meant that those who thought they might fail on the eighth were able to reinsure themselves by putting their names forward for the tenth—the explanation given in the *Report on the Election* was the 'wish of the Council members to be in their own States during the holding of the popular election'. Fourteen of the ninety candidates had tried and failed against CPP candidates in the constituency elections. Three were now successful—Nana Sir Tsibu Darku, K. A. Busia, and C. W. Tachie Menson, the Sekondi businessman,[66] and it was well known that many of their colleagues were also opposed to the People's Party. Over half of the territorial members were representative either of the old-guard intelligentsia (e.g. Magnus Sampson, secretary to the Joint Provincial Council), the new intellectuals (e.g. K. A. Busia), or the indirect-rule chiefs (Nana Ofori Atta, Nene Mate Kole of Manya Krobo, Nana Kwame Gyebi Ababio from Essumeja in Ashanti). The exasperated contempt with which the party members viewed the

[65] The elections were conducted on a card vote, in which each chief cast a number of votes proportionate to the population of his state.
[66] Who had been given 3 votes against 51 for A. E. Inkumsah (CPP) in the Ahanta (Colony) constituency.

chiefs' representatives was seen shortly after the Assembly met, when Nana Ofori Atta tried to argue that the 1950 constitution was unsatisfactory because it fell short of full self-government:

Nana Ofori Atta: We demanded full self-government but this constitution is not representative of full self-government...
Assemblymen: You!....[67]

The charge usually levied at the territorial members was that they had entered the Assembly 'through the back door', and Krobo Edusei mocked Busia's election on these grounds, for Busia had lost not only in Wenchi but on the first count in the Asanteman Council election. He was placed seventh (level with D. J. Buahin): then Dr I. B. Asafu Adjaye announced that, although elected, he did not wish to take his seat, and Busia was given his place.[68]

Thus of the eighteen members elected by the territorial councils only a small minority was sympathetic to the CPP—notably F. Y. Asare for the Southern Togoland Council[69] and the Rev. Francis Fiawoo (later Deputy Speaker in the Assembly) and Dr Ansah Koi (later minister in Nkrumah's first administration) for the JPC—and at the close of polling on 10 February, it was possible to reckon that the CPP would have the support of (at best) 39 in the new Assembly of 80 voting members. If the party took office, it would be able to include on its side the three *ex-officio* members; it was also likely that the two special members for the Chambers of Commerce and Mines would normally vote with the government, or at least abstain on any issue outside their immediate interests. Even so, the CPP would be delicately placed, and it was clear that much would depend on the nineteen members from the north, where the special electoral college had already met under the presidency of the Chief Commissioner in Tamale, the regional capital. The list of successful candidates had been published, but who they were, and what stand they were likely to adopt, was hardly known.

There were 120 electors in the electoral college—the 16 mem-

[67] GC, LA Deb., 25 Apr. 1951.   [68] Ibid.
[69] There was the same uncertainty in the territorial council election as in the (Ewe) rural constituencies. 'There was evidence of an attempt by elements of the Togo Union to prevent any election and pressure was put on some members not to attend the meeting' (*Report ... on the Administration of Togoland under U.K. Trusteeship for the year 1951*, para. 126). The necessary quorum was obtained, however, and Asare (a pharmacist) was elected.

bers of the Northern Territories Council, and 104 additional delegates chosen on a population basis by district councils based on grouped native authorities. There were thirty-four candidates for the nineteen seats. But (as the *Report on the First Election* noted) the members found 'considerable difficulty . . . particularly illiterate electors, in deciding how they should cast the nineteen votes', for few of the candidates were known personally to all of them. Because of the distribution of population in the north, the very large Mamprusi Native Authority dominated the college with forty-two representatives,[70] but this did not greatly affect the voting, and the final result was a reasonable distribution of northern seats:

Area	Delegates	Candidates	Representatives†
Dagomba–Nanumba	25	5	5
Gonja–Volta	13	4	1
Lawra Confederacy	10	5	1
Mamprusi	42	9	6
Northern chiefdoms*	16	3	2
Wala/Tumu	14	8	4
	120	34	19

* Kassena–Nankanni and Builsa.

† The highest vote (73) was given to the Tali-Na, the second highest (67) to J. H. Allasani, both from Dagomba. Two candidates tied for nineteenth place: E. A. Mahama, a school teacher at Damongo, and Seidu Wala, Katua-Na (a sub-chief at Wa); the Chief Commissioner who presided over the electoral college gave his casting vote to the chief. This was one of the considerations that led E. A. Mahama later to join the CPP: elected in 1954 and 1956, he was regional commissioner, Northern Ghana, in 1960.

Those elected fell within a single broad category. Only one paramount chief—the Wa-Na—stood for election (and was elected), and the typical northern representative was either an elementary-school-educated teacher or native-authority secretary—in either case a person of some standing in his own locality, perhaps a chief in his own right, and usually a close adviser of the paramount chief of his state. Their leaders were very able men—such as J. A. Braimah, Kabachewura, a minor chief and secre-

[70] In 1951 the Mamprusi NA included the subordinate NAs of the Frafra Confederacy and the north-east Kusai chiefdoms.

tary to the large Gonja Native Authority; Yakubu Tali, Tali-Na, a sub-chief within the Dagomba chiefdom and a former teacher; J. H. Allasani, a former headmaster of a Catholic school in Kumasi, and closely associated with the Dagomba paramount chief at Yendi; Mumuni Bawumia, a former teacher, and in 1951 clerk to the large Mamprusi Native Authority. Most of them were already known to each other through the government Boys' Middle Boarding School in Tamale; a few (like J. H. Allasani and the Tali-Na) had received some further education in the south. All were men of authority among their own people, very experienced at threading their way through the maze of chieftaincy disputes, though quite ignorant of nationalist politics. Because the CPP could get very little foothold among them, the local branch chairman and secretary in Tamale—R. S. Iddrisu (a transport owner) and Eben Adam (a drug-store keeper)—had declined to stand for election, knowing their certain defeat; and only Ayarna Imoru from Mamprusi, and Ayeebo Asumda from Zebilla, could be regarded as (at most) party 'sympathizers'. Voting in the college had been influenced entirely by the individual merit or tribal affiliation of a particular candidate, or by stories of the iniquities of nationalist politicians in the south. In one important respect, however, the CPP was fortunate. Its leaders were soon to become the dominant partners in a new administration, and all the nineteen northern members had a great respect for those in authority. They had it for the local chief and district commissioner, and, in the opening years of the CPP-*ex-officio* alliance, they were prepared to give the same respect to the central government in Accra—a loyalty confirmed when J. A. Braimah (who was justly held in high regard among them) was offered and accepted a place in the new executive council. By 1953–4 this respect was greatly diminished and, in its place there developed a 'northern consciousness' which found expression in a Northern People's Party; but this lay in the future and in 1951 the nineteen northerners were prepared to give their votes to the CPP government, if only because it was the government.

Thus, with northern support, the CPP was assured of a good working majority, and, when Nkrumah was released from prison, on 12 February, it was clear that there was nothing to stop him forming a government should the Governor invite, and the party allow, him to do so. There was little doubt on either side. In

1949–50 the administration had made a number of miscalcula-
tions but it quickly amended its arithmetic. It had underrated
the CPP and overrated the influence of the chiefs and the intelligentsia. It had underestimated the extent to which the elementary-school-leavers in the Colony and Ashanti chiefdoms
were ready to work together; it had discounted the possibility
that, once nationalist ideas had taken hold of the young men in
the towns, they would be carried swiftly into the rural areas. In so
far as the officials had formed any mental picture of the kind of
government likely to be formed under the constitution outlined
in the Coussey proposals, almost certainly they had seen as its
leading figures chiefs like Nana Sir Tsibu Darku, Nene Mate
Kole, Nana Ofori Atta, Nana Kwame Gyebi Ababio, and the
UGCC leaders from the municipalities; it was recognized that
extremists might succeed in getting elected, but the general
temper of the government was expected to be of a moderate disposition, with sufficient power (backed by the officials) to curb
those who might try and force the pace of reform. By the end of
1950 this picture was so obviously false that the administration
had little difficulty in discarding it. A different note was then
struck by Arden-Clarke, who did not hesitate to use the courts
and the police to suppress violence and illegal acts, but also made
clear his readiness to accept far more sweeping measures of reform than had been contemplated earlier. Arden-Clarke recognized that:

> Nkrumah and his party had the mass of the people behind them and
> there was no other party with appreciable public support to which we
> could turn. Without Nkrumah, the Constitution would be still-born
> and if nothing came of all the hopes, aspirations and concrete pro-
> posals for a greater measure of self-government, there would no
> longer be any faith in the good intentions of the British Government. . .
> the Gold Coast would be plunged into disorders, violence and blood-
> shed. [71]

Nkrumah grasped the same point: that unless the CPP accepted
office, notwithstanding the limitations of the 1950 constitution, a
chance would be lost that might not easily be regained.

It was felt that had we not accepted office by virtue of our majority
in the Assembly, but had embarked on non-cooperation and re-

[71] *Afr. Aff.*, Jan. 1958.

mained in the Opposition, we would merely have been pursuing a negative course of action. It was moreover the opinion of the Party Executive that by taking part in the new government, we were at least preventing the 'stooges and reactionaries' from taking advantage of the position. Governmental positions could also help us to obtain the initiative in the continuing struggle for full self-government.[72]

The last point was undoubtedly true. Once in office, the CPP stayed in, and this may well have been the happy fate of any successor government during the fat, harvest years of the first decade of party rule.

Within twenty-four hours, therefore, of Nkrumah's release from prison, the Governor invited him to become Leader of Government Business, and to submit the names of the eight representative ministers for approval by the assembly. The nationalists were in office; the election was over. The total cost of this first trial of strength had been £50,000—a small price to pay for an election which had given the country a government and from which much had been learnt that would be of use in future contests. What form such contests would take, it was difficult to see. One fact, however, was sure: a majority among the small group of intellectuals (hitherto led by Danquah) was certain to be against the CPP. They were now embittered beyond the point of reconciliation for, as Grant complained:

> By June 1949, Dr Kwame Nkrumah, expatriated by the Convention in 1947 to take up the secretaryship, had for reasons that are now obvious to all, so sabotaged the effort of the principal leaders of the Convention and so discredited me and all my principal colleagues that he was able to mislead the masses to follow him. . . . He filched our name, our 'S.G.' policy, our branches and even our colours—to establish a separatist group—the Convention People's Party. . .[73]

To this small band of lawyers and professional figures, therefore, the CPP was a treacherous breakaway movement, and what had been sauce for the UGCC goose would be good sauce for the CPP gander if ever the occasion arose. Provided, however, the CPP

---

[72] *Autobiography*, p. 142. Similar phrases had been used in the 1951 election manifesto: 'Only the youth and progressive people in the country who are not party to the [Coussey] proposals can conscientiously fight for their eradication. To remain any longer merely as political agitators from the platform would spell national disaster.'

[73] George Grant, in Foreword to UGCC's *The 'P' Plan*. Only one of the leading UGCC members joined the CPP—Ako Adjei.

rank and file recognized the need for loyalty to the leaders, and provided the leaders refrained from quarrelling among themselves, there seemed little that the intellectuals, or the chiefs, could do to challenge the new government. A cautious observer might, indeed, have questioned the permanence of a revolution which had been accomplished so easily, but such pessimism would have been brushed aside. All the advantages seemed to lie with the CPP: all the disadvantages with its opponents.

IV

The CPP in Office, 1951–4

THESE first years of CPP government have been given a modest title appropriate to the position in which the newly elected party found itself. Its election victory, following the introduction of a modified form of the Coussey constitution, transformed the 1946 Colony-Ashanti legislative council into a parliamentary system along party lines, but the CPP was not yet fully in control—even of itself. It had a majority in the reconstituted executive council, and a substantial minority of the seats in the Assembly; but it still had to serve a period of apprenticeship under official control, and its own organization fell far short of the demands made on it by the party constitution—to act as a 'vigorous conscious political vanguard... for the establishment of a democratic socialist society'. For the day-to-day conduct of affairs the 1950 constitution worked surprisingly well: the need to co-operate produced a working alliance between the CPP ministers who knew nothing and the officials who knew very little of the working of a parliamentary system, while between Nkrumah and Arden-Clarke there developed a 'close, friendly, and if I may say so, not unfruitful partnership'. Nevertheless, as this chapter will show, the possibility of crisis was always there. As Arden-Clarke himself was to comment (half-humourously): 'That Coussey constitution lasted three and a half years. During that time we lived in an atmosphere of perpetual crisis.'[1] The

---

[1] Arden-Clarke, in *Afr. Aff.*, Jan. 1958. Immediately after the 1951 election, the Extra-Mural Dept of the University College arranged a conference on 'Parliamentary Government' for the newly-elected assemblymen. The writer was chairman for a senior government official who tried to explain what lay behind the preparation of government estimates and the drawing up of a budget. It slowly dawned upon the largely CPP audience that the budget they would be asked to approve had been prepared before they were elected—while many of them indeed were still in prison. They would have none of it, therefore: they wanted their own, and not an 'Imperialists' budget. Order was restored only when it was suggested that the new government could, if it wished, introduce an 'anti-imperialist', supplementary budget in the 'autumn', and thereafter goodwill prevailed once more. This was very characteristic of the 'atmosphere of perpetual crisis'.

difficulties of the period were embedded in the nature of the change from colonial to nationalist rule: on the one hand, the CPP had to move from an attitude of violent opposition to colonial control to acceptance of what was still a colonial framework of authority; on the other, minority groups in the country—hitherto protected by the decentralized character of colonial rule—had to adjust their own claims to those of the nationalist movement as a whole. Neither Nkrumah nor Arden-Clarke foresaw how difficult this process of readjustment would be. It was, indeed, easy to be misled by the sweeping success of the CPP in the February elections into supposing that the party was fully in control of the country, and on the basis of such a premise, to conclude that all that remained was for the United Kingdom and Gold Coast governments to conduct a series of detailed negotiations before the final grant of self-government. But the premise being faulty, the conclusion proved to be false. Although the CPP leaders had been remarkably successful in making articulate a general dissatisfaction with colonial rule, they were to find it a far more difficult task to keep this discontent within bounds, and prevent it from being turned against themselves.

The new Assembly met on 20 February 1951 and, six days later, Nkrumah became Leader of Government Business, appointed by the Governor and confirmed by the votes of the Assembly members.[2] Presided over by a Speaker,[3] the eighty voting members were expected (as suggested by the formal 'Westminster' design of the chamber) to divide into a government and an opposition, but it was difficult in practice to draw any sharp dividing lines between those who were wholly for, and those who were wholly against, the coalition of party members and officials who formed the new executive. The thirty-four elected CPP members were reinforced by five 'sympathizers' among the territorial council and northern members and, with the three *ex-officio* members, they formed a reasonably disciplined group—although occasionally a ministerial secretary had to be reminded that he was now part of a government.[4] There was also the small

[2] 78 votes for; 1 against (GC, LA Deb., 26 Feb. 1951).
[3] E. C. (later Sir Emmanuel) Quist, appointed president of the former legislative council in 1949, a choice which helped to assure the officials and the Independents of the sobriety of the nationalists.
[4] When J. B. Erzuah, ministerial secretary to the Min. of Education and Social Welfare, put the case for greater social development in his constituency he had to be reminded that he was now responsible for seeing to it:

group of UGCC members led by Danquah, Busia, and Nana
Ofori Atta which tried to behave as a national opposition. It was
outnumbered, however, by the non-party members—particularly the northerners—who liked to defend the *status quo*, as expressed in the 1950 constitution, and to decide each issue as it
arose from a neutral standpoint. Among the more articulate of
the northern members, for example, was J. A. Braimah from the
large Gonja state, who, though appointed as a member of the
executive as Minister without portfolio, regarded himself (at
least in theory) as a non-party northerner:

Mr Braimah: ... I wish to make the position of the Northern Territories quite clear. We do not belong to any party and we are not bound
to follow any party line of action. To hate one party and to favour the
other is not our policy, so when we support or reject any motion tabled
by a member of a party, we do so clearly on the merits of the motion
and not for party reasons.[5]

In the early years of the new administration this potential danger
to the nationalist aims of the party members was slow to show itself. It was held in check by a long habit of obedience to those in
authority, helped by the composite character of the new executive. Thus it was not until the end of 1953, when a further period
of reform was under discussion, that a number of leading northerners began to move away from this automatic acceptance of the
power of the central government to consideration of the need for
a local 'People's Party' of their own.[6]

The executive council rested on a similar compromise between theory and practice.[7] The Governor was still a source of

---

Mr Erzuah: ... my people asked me to ask this Government to assist them.
Minister of Justice: Mr Speaker, I beg to point out to the Honourable Member
that he is a member of this Government, and a Ministerial Secretary! (Laughter).
Mr Erzuah: Mr Speaker, I beg to break off (GC, LA Deb., 3 Apr. 1951).

[5] Ibid. 25 Apr. 1951. The motion in question was Danquah's, calling for a select
committee to examine Dominion constitutions and to report on the terms of a constitution suitable for a self-governing Gold Coast. It was defeated by 65 votes to 6,
with 8 abstentions.
[6] See below, p. 184.
[7] It consisted of the Governor, Arden-Clarke; 3 *ex-officio* Ministers of Defence
and External Affairs (R. H. Saloway), Justice (P. F. Brannigan), Finance (R. P.
Armitage); 8 party ministers: Nkrumah, K. A. Gbedemah (Health and Labour),
A. Casely Hayford (Agriculture), Kojo Botsio (Education and Social Welfare),
T. Hutton-Mills (Commerce and Industry), Dr Ansah Koi (Communications and
Works); and a representative of the Asanteman Council—E. O. Asafu-Adjaye
(Local Government), and the north—J. A. Braimah (without portfolio). Ansah
Koi was also a representative of the Colony Territorial Council.

independent power with a right of veto and certification (together with responsibility for defence, external affairs, and matters affecting the Togoland Trust Territory). The change of
name from Leader of Government Business to Prime Minister
on 21 March 1952 did not greatly alter the situation, since it still
left executive responsibility divided, the Governor being responsible to the Secretary of State, the *ex-officio* members to the
Governor, the representative ministers to the Assembly. Once
again, however, the system worked well enough in practice. In
August 1952, for example, Nkrumah wished to remove Dr Ansah
Koi, a representative of the Colony Joint Provincial Council and
a party member, from the executive council. The decision was
taken at an evening meeting of the CPP ministers. Nkrumah saw
Ansah Koi, who refused to resign; both he and Nkrumah then
appealed to the Governor, who supported Nkrumah, and Ansah
Koi resigned under protest. His successor was appointed by the
Governor on Nkrumah's advice, and confirmed by a comfortable
majority in the Assembly.[8] Thus it was always possible for Nkrumah to assert his authority provided the Governor and the Assembly recognized—as in practice they did—his right to do so.

　　Acquiescence by the CPP leaders and the Assembly rank and
file in this cumbersome process was at first sight surprising in view
of their militant behaviour in 1949–50, but one must remember
that the party itself was still barely two years old, and that the
leaders were still feeling their way to power. A minority on the
national executive—as will be seen—wanted to push the revolution forward at a quicker pace, but the majority of the Assembly
members, and the constituency rank and file, were perfectly
satisfied with the opportunities that now opened before them.
They were quite content to compromise on the immediate means
to achieve the end to which they had pledged themselves in 1949,
provided 'Self-Government Now' was not postponed too long.
And they accepted without much difficulty Nkrumah's argument that the party should move from 'Positive' to 'Tactical
Action'—a phrase which helped not only to placate the party's
followers but to disarm the officials. This readiness on the part of
the nationalists to compromise once they were in office was also
understandable when one looked at the material circumstances
of these first years of CPP rule. They were particularly favourable

[8] There were 46 votes for A. E. Inkumsah (CPP), 15 votes against him.

to a period of consolidation, and it may be helpful to examine what these circumstances were before looking more closely at the party itself.

The outstanding feature of these years was the growing prosperity of the country as the world price for cocoa climbed higher and higher.[9] From this increase in wealth flowed a number of advantages. It made possible, for example, the alleviation in part at least of the post-war distress of the rural and urban areas. Gbedemah introduced a more generous wage and salary structure for the civil service following the recommendations of the Lidbury Commission. A *Statement* by Nkrumah in the Assembly (April 1951) supported by a similar announcement by the European Chambers of Commerce led to the reinstatement of the employees dismissed as a result of Positive Action, and the daily wage of the unskilled labourer went up in April 1952 by a third to 4s. 6d. These were useful gains, even if the advantages were offset to some extent by the rise in local food prices; then these too were held in check by the end of 1952. It was also clear that the Ten-Year Development Plan of £11½ million drawn up in 1948 was far too modest a document; it was replaced in 1952 by a new Five-Year Plan (together with an Accelerated Plan for Education) of £120 million, a sum considerably in excess of the amounts spent in the whole of the period between the two world wars.[10] Moreover, the worse effects of the wartime shortage of administrative officers had been mended, and with a quick grasp

[9]
Cocoa Prices, 1937–52

Year	World price (£ per ton)	Price to the Farmer (£ per ton)	(s. per load = 60 lb)
1937–8	29·4	14·4	7s. 6d.
1945–6	49·8	27·0	14s. 6d.
1946–7	155·0	51·3	27s. 6d.
1947–8	238·0	74·7	40s. –
1948–9	139·0	121·3	65s. –
1949–50	190·0	84·0	45s. –
1950–1	208·0	130·7	70s. –
1951–2	285·0	148·3	80s. –
1952–3	301·0	130·7	70s. –

Sources: Economic Survey & B. J. Wills, *Agriculture and Land Use in Ghana,* p. 199.

[10] Guggisberg's Ten-Year Development Plan of 1919 had proposed an expenditure of £24 million, but this had been cut back to £16½ million after the depression of 1920–3.

of the need to reach out into the villages the government established an impressive social welfare department. Its 'community development teams' fanned out into the rural areas with such success that the beginnings of local-welfare projects of one kind and another—a new latrine, a new school house, an improved water supply, the concreting of the open drains which ran through town and village alike—were to be seen in almost every district in the Colony and Ashanti. And the party reaped the benefit.

The increase in government revenue also helped in the considerable expansion of the civil service, whereby 'Africanization' was promoted without losing the services of the overseas officers. The rate of growth may be expressed quite simply:

Public Service, Senior Officers

	Overseas officers	Africans	Per cent of Africans
1949	1,068	171	13·8
1954	1,490	916	38·2

Thus the number of African officers (including the appointment or promotion of 180 senior executive officers) went up steeply; but so did the senior service establishment as a whole.

There were also substantial gains to be had at a local level, and in 1952 the party rank and file were given their own share of self-government. A major reform of the native-authority system was set in train through the establishment of new local authorities, with a two-thirds elected, one-third traditional membership. The CPP then repeated, in the elections to the new authorities, its 1951 victory. The actual running of the new local government system was never very satisfactory: it led to frequent quarrels between elected and traditional members, and to anti-tax riots in a number of districts where the newly elected party members allowed their zeal for reform to outrun the readiness (and often the ability) of the electorate to pay.[11] None the less, the local-

[11] The worst riots were in Anloga, in the south-east of the Colony, where in January 1953 a local councillor was murdered, the local Government Agent (a European) stabbed, and houses (including the Rev. Fiawoo's) burned. Four months later—9 May 1953—an excited crowd gathered at Elmina on the coast to protest against the enforcement of the Elmina-Eguafo local council rate; a riot followed in which the local Superintendent of Police, Edgar Brooks, a constable who tried to defend him, and (in the police inquiries that followed) eleven villagers were killed.

government reforms of this period, like those at the centre, helped to absorb the energies of the party. There was less pressure for further reform on the party leaders, and a greater readiness to accept the gains already made. The (British) district commissioner became a 'government agent'—a change of name which (like the replacement of the officials of the colonial secretariat by permanent secretaries to the ministers) helped to persuade the newly elected councillors of the need for advice from those they had formerly criticized in bitter terms. The commoners within the Colony and Ashanti chiefdoms also benefited, for they were able to exercise much greater influence over the elected party members than they had been able to do over the chiefs and elders of the native authorities.

In view of its election campaign the party was also compelled to do something about the control of swollen shoot, many of its members having come to the Assembly with a mandate from the farmers to protect the cocoa industry from the Agriculture Department. Among the first acts of the new government, therefore, was one (in April 1951) suspending the policy of compulsory cutting out for a trial period of one month (thus confirming the worst fears of its overseas critics). But the party leaders were also prepared now to believe what the administration had been trying to tell them for a long time, that if the farmer did nothing to check the spread of the disease, there would soon be no cocoa for him to harvest and no money for national development. The new administration followed good colonial practice, therefore, and appointed a local committee of inquiry to examine not only the effect of previous legislation but the actual methods used by the colonial government in its cutting-out campaign. The committee set to work and produced its *Report* in which the members agreed with both the experts and the politicians.[12] They recognized the

---

These were the worst incidents in a number of protest meetings. The increases were sometimes very large: e.g. at Atwima No. 2 local council in Ashanti, where the council put the rate up from 12s. for a man, 6s. for a woman, to £2 and £1. There was a riot here, too, on Christmas Eve 1952; in the end the council was forced to resign *en bloc*.

[12] GC, Committee of Enquiry into the Existing Organisation and Methods for the Control of Swollen Shoot Disease by the Compulsory Cutting Out of the Infested Cocoa Trees, *Report* (Govt Printer, 1951). The CPP showed the same ability to be right after the event as the colonial administration. 'Investigation on the matter [of swollen shoot] confirmed my former fears that the only solution was to cut down the affected trees' (Nkrumah, *Autobiography*, p. 152). These fears were not in evidence during the election campaign.

need to cut down the diseased trees, but warned the government that 'if the general policy of compulsory cutting out is pursued there will be general unrest and possibly public disturbances in the country'. Farmers who testified before the committee had 'uttered threats of violence against anyone who might attempt to carry it out' and appeared convinced that 'the object is to wipe out the cocoa industry from the Gold Coast'; moreover, 'the surveying and demarcation of farms has led to the fear that the farmers' land is to be confiscated'. The committee then went on to criticize the methods adopted by the government. The 'approach had not been very sympathetic'; the use of the police to enforce cutting out had been 'very damaging to good relations between the farmers and the control staff', and there should have been 'a more direct method of approach through the farmers' unions and chief farmers'. Witnesses had complained that 'the Government had held meetings with the Chiefs but not with the farmers'.

This was the kind of comment that the CPP liked to make, and with Ashie Nikoe of the Ghana Farmers' Congress among the committee members, the *Report* was likely to contain material of this sort. This did not mean that its findings were wrong, however, even if (as was likely) they were exaggerated, and the government had no hesitation in accepting the *Report*.[13] It then abolished the Cocoa Rehabilitation Department, suspended the compulsory cutting-out policy indefinitely, and substituted for it a sustained campaign of propaganda under the heading 'A New Deal for Cocoa', using local party groups as well as the new community-development teams to explain the need for voluntary co-operation with the cutting-out gangs. Meanwhile, the world

[13] It accepted a number of particular recommendations made by the Committee, including the abolition of the Cocoa Rehabilitation Dept and the placing of its functions under the Dept of Agriculture. The Committee also suggested—and again the influence of Ashie Nikoe may be detected—the 'establishment by ordinance of the Gold Coast Farmers' Association'. The early years of CPP swollen-shoot control were still further complicated by statements put out by Dr R. E. G. Armattoe (a Gold Coast Ewe) that he had discovered a cure for swollen shoot but was not prepared to say what it was until the government approached him in a respectful manner, a bizarre episode that closed with Armattoe's death in Germany at the end of December 1953. Acceptance by the government of the need to cut out infected trees was greatly helped by the report of the three scientists sent out in 1948 by the U.N. (from Canada, Hawaii, and Holland) who eventually concluded that 'the cutting out of diseased trees is the only measure of control'. There was the hope, too, that the use of an insecticide—hannane—which was particularly effective against the mealy bug that harboured the virus would lead to a reduction in the number of trees that might have to be cut down.

price soared still higher. The Cocoa Marketing Board paid farmers the unprecedented price of 80s. a load for the main 1951-2 crop, and was still left with a substantial margin of profit from which to pay an increased sum in compensation for each tree cut down.[14] The effect of this careful mixture of propaganda and reward was seen in October 1952 when the government authorized the Department of Agriculture to resume cutting out on a compulsory basis. Here was a return, apparently, to the dark days of 1948. But although the attempt at persuasion had failed, the policy was reintroduced without serious protest, and in sum, the New Deal for Cocoa was a good illustration of the general advantages which the new government enjoyed. It was much more closely linked through its party branches with the village population than the colonial administration had been, and it had at its disposal far more resources—of wealth, staff, and voluntary helpers—than its predecessor had been able to call upon.

Thus in the early years of the new administration the CPP appeared to be firmly established. It drew after it a large following, and there was a great pride among its members in the achievement of the 1951 election and the sight of African ministers with their attendant Europeans, a feeling, too, that history was being made once more on the African continent. Nevertheless, as the excitement of the election receded, the new régime was increasingly disturbed. The leaders stood uncertainly in a middle course of reform in which, if they went too slowly, they were open to the accusation that they had lost their nationalist spirit, while, if they pushed ahead too fast with their demand for independence they were in danger of losing control, not only over areas of the country where the population had little understanding of the nationalists' programme, but of the loose-knit, sprawling party itself. The result was that the leaders found themselves faced with a triple threat. To begin with, there was a minor revolt within the party's executive, based on a rejection of the need for a period of transition before independence; it was easily suppressed and, indeed, made to look inept once the government reopened negotiations with the United Kingdom government. Secondly, however, as the leaders renewed their demand for self-government, they encountered a growing indiscipline among the con-

[14] Compensation was now paid at the rate of 4s. for every live tree cut down, and 2s. a year for three years towards the cost of replanting.

stituency rank and file. Thirdly, opposition grew, not only within the CPP, but among regional and sectional groups external to the party. Each of these attacks will be described later, but in order to measure their importance some account is needed in general terms of the CPP as it existed during these years.

The formal outline of the party was set out clearly in the constitution drawn up in 1949 and approved by the second annual conference at Ho in southern Togoland in August 1951.[15] It proposed a number of aims and objects:

National

I. SELF-GOVERNMENT NOW and the development of (Gold Coast) Ghana on the basis of Socialism.

II. To fight relentlessly to achieve and maintain independence for the people of (Gold Coast) Ghana and their chiefs.

III. To serve as the vigorous conscious political vanguard for removing all forms of oppression and for the establishment of a democratic socialist society.

IV. To secure and maintain the complete unity of the Colony, Ashanti Northern Territories and Trans-Volta. . .

VIII. To establish a Socialist State in which all men and women shall have equal opportunity and where there shall be no capitalist exploitation.

International

I. To work with other nationalist democratic and socialist movements in Africa and other continents, with a view to abolishing imperialism, colonialism, racialism, tribalism and all forms of national and racial oppression. . . .

II. To support the demand for a West African Federation and of Pan-Africanism by promoting unity of action among the peoples of Africa and African descent.

To carry out these policies, the leaders erected a neat pyramid of authority, headed by the Leader who was empowered to choose a central committee of nine to act as the 'directorate' of a broad national executive committee. Both committees were said to be answerable to the National Conference made up of representatives from the constituency organizations, a Women's Section of the party, a Youth League, and affiliated organizations.

[15] *Constitution of the Convention People's Party, 1951.*

The Conference was expected to 'lay down the broad basic policy and programme of the Party for the ensuing year', and its decisions were to be 'binding on all members of the Party and affiliated organizations'. Thus although the central committee and the national executive were given particular powers, such as 'approval of candidates for Central and Local Government elections', and made responsible for the day-to-day conduct of party affairs, they were also expected to keep within a policy approved in advance by the annual conference—approved, that is to say, by representatives of the numerous local organs of the party, including the village (or ward) branch which the constitution singled out as being 'the basic organisation of the Party'.[16]

This was the formal structure of the CPP, which bore as little relation to the way in which the party worked in practice as most constitutions do to the parties they purport to describe. The nationalist party was still inchoate in 1951. The 1949–50 struggle had been too short—its election victory too easily gained—to shape the party into an adequate instrument of control, and nothing was clear in practice as to the relationship between its various sections. Nkrumah had been made Life Chairman, but he had yet to adopt the role of 'unique Leader'. Others had helped to form the party in 1949 and directed its fortunes while Nkrumah was in prison; and they were not disposed to leave policy-making entirely to the joint efforts of Nkrumah and Arden-Clarke. Similarly, the central committee itself had not yet become the all-powerful body that it was to be by the end of the 1950s. There were important figures within the national executive who were not members of the central committee, while the latter body was soon to be weakened by dismissals and resignations: the distinction between the two committees was blurred, therefore, and there was a tendency for major items of controversy to be thrown to a wider audience still. Thus down to 1953 the annual conference was still a battleground of conflicting opinion. The delegates carried vivid memories of the great debates at

[16] A 'Parliamentary Committee of the Party' also existed (on paper), consisting of the Assembly members and others nominated by the national executive committee. It was to be 'under the direct supervision and control of the Party Leader who will report to the National Executive and the Central Committee on the work of the Party in the Assembly'. This did not mean that the members of the Assembly were unimportant or that they were subordinate to the national officers of the party who were outside the Assembly. On the contrary, they were the most important link (at that time) between the headquarters and the constituency executives.

Saltpond and Tarkwa which had led to the formation of the CPP, when decisions had been argued out and forced on the leaders, and a belief in the right of delegates to participate in decisions reached by the party was still strong.

Such was the state of the party at the national level immediately following the first general election and, coupled with the uncertainty of the constitutional position, it led to the first stirrings of revolt among the leaders. Under pressure from the small opposition group in the Assembly, Nkrumah had already challenged the UGCC leaders and the chiefs in September 1951 to join him in staging a second round of Positive Action. The challenge was not taken up, and it was difficult to believe that Nkrumah meant it to be taken very seriously.[17] It was, however, an indication of the pressure for further reform which had already begun to build up within the party itself, and at the end of 1951 a small group of discontented individuals within the national executive began to criticize the party on moral grounds and to urge the need for a more resolute attitude towards independence.

The contrast between the party as a revolutionary movement of African socialists, and as the dominant partner in the 1951 administration, was all too evident. Many of its leading figures had settled down in office, as ministers, Assembly members, officials of the Cocoa Marketing Board, and party secretaries. Rumours of corruption and malpractices circulated freely, centred in the belief that money and favours were changing hands between foreign contractors and the party leaders. The stories grew throughout 1951 and 1952 and were investigated eventually by a Commission of Inquiry when J. A. Braimah confessed to the Governor that as Minister of Communications and Works he had accepted £2,000 from Aksor Kassardjian, an Armenian contractor working in the north.[18] Long before the Commission was

---

[17] Nkrumah, *Autobiography*, pp. 145–6.

[18] See Korsah Commission *Report* (1954). The inquiry was a major one, distressing to those who knew and liked Braimah, but the facts were both plain and extraordinary. Braimah resigned in November 1953, saying that he had heard 'rumours of bribery and corruption', his 'own experiences made [him] feel that some of the allegations deserved to be investigated' and (said Braimah) 'I felt I had a special mission laid upon me to give opportunity for the rumours and allegations to be investigated'. Braimah spent only part of the money, giving his driver £300, and buying a wireless and a radiogram for himself. Kassardjian had lived in the Gold Coast for some fifteen years, becoming a contractor in 1950. He was, as those who knew him well could testify, an extremely generous man who had already given £500 to the Coronation Fund and the Lord Mayor's Flood Relief Fund in London. He told the Commission that he had given the £2,000 to Braimah for 'election

appointed tales similar to those recounted by Braimah were being discussed in the country. The refusal of the CPP ministers to live in the bungalows provided for them in the outskirts of Accra, the large houses which they built and drew rent allowance for in town, the flamboyant style of living of many of the party members, stories of the need to buy contracts from ministers and ministerial secretaries, and the failure of an Anti-Bribery and Corruption Committee were produced as evidence of the distance the party's leaders had travelled from the early days of 1949. The danger had been foreseen by Nkrumah himself who had pointed out that there was a

risk in accepting office under the new constitution which still makes us half-slave and half-free. . . . The temptation there is that it is easy for one to identify oneself with such a constitution and thereby be swayed by considerations of personal temporary advantage instead of seeking the interests of the people. Hence we call for vigilance and moral courage, to withstand the evil manœuvring of imperialism. Now bribery and corruption, both moral and factual, have eaten into the whole fabric of our society and these must be stamped out if we are to achieve any progress.[19]

These were stirring words, but many found it difficult in 1952 to see what was being done either about the 'evil manœuvring of imperialism' or the bribery and corruption. Moreover there were several stories of how the Prime Minister himself had borrowed £1,800 from A. Y. K. Djin (chairman of the Finance Committee of the CPP) *via* Ohene Djan (a ministerial secretary) to pay for the importation of a Cadillac.[20]

---

expenses'. Radiograms had a curious fascination for Gold Coast politicians at this time. Krobo Edusei, for example, had three: one from Holland, another from Denmark, and the third from Sweden.

[19] 'Message to Members of the Assembly'. Nkrumah also announced that 'There must be no fraternisation between our Party members in the Executive Council and the European officials, except on purely official relations; for what the imperialists failed to achieve by strong-arm methods they will hope to bring off by cocktail parties.' This ruling was quickly (and sensibly) abandoned.

[20] Korsah Commission *Report*, paras. 89–93. The Commission reached the conclusion (para. 347) that 'allegations of general misconduct among those holding high office . . . were not substantiated', but was critical of individual members, e.g. of Krobo Edusei, whose conduct was said (para. 218) to have fallen 'below any acceptable standard for men in the public service and . . . is strongly to be deprecated'. As the result of evidence submitted to the Commission, two ministerial secretaries (among others) were later sentenced to terms of imprisonment. The contrast between the way in which the CPP ministers and ministerial secretaries now lived and the conditions under which many of those who had elected them to office, could be startling. Compare, for example, the account given in the Korsah

If there were many who saw these failings as a betrayal of what the party stood for in 1949, others again were resentful because they had been denied what they considered should have been their proper share of the advantages of office, and criticism of the party's morals might not, by itself, have been very important had it not been linked with other charges of a more political nature. Opposition began to be expressed over the government's negotiations for the financing of the Volta River project, the rate of Africanization of the public service, and the relationship which existed by 1952-3 not only between Nkrumah and Arden-Clarke but between the ministers in general and their European civil servants.[21] The more vehement of the government's critics objected also to the growing adulation of Nkrumah, and contrasted it with the period of collective leadership in 1949-50.[22] Each of these different strands of discontent—reinforced by charges of peculation and 'easy living'—found outlet in the demand for a more rapid advance to independence, based on a growing concern among a small radical group within the party lest the govern-

---

Report of Krobo Edusei's large, three-storied house in Kumasi with Busia's description of housing conditions in Sekondi: 'Sixteen rooms, 52 occupants, no kitchen, two bathrooms, one latrine. Rent 10*s*. to 20*s*. . . . Three rooms meant for kitchens had been converted into living rooms and let at 10*s*. a month. One room with floor space of 9¾ feet by 7 feet was occupied by a man, his two wives, and three children, and stored with all their belongings and food' (*Social Survey of Sekondi-Takoradi*, Accra, 1951).

[21] The Volta River scheme aroused a great deal of controversy. Designed to harness the flow of the Volta in the form of hydro-electric power, and to smelt the country's large deposits of bauxite into aluminium, the difficulty was then, and for many years afterwards, who was going to pay for it? By 1952 it had reached the stage of detailed discussions between the Ghana, British, and Canadian governments. Bediako Poku, later to be general secretary of the party, warned the government that it might lead to 'a second Abadan . . . it might mean economic enslavement' (GC, LA Deb., 23 Feb. 1953); Cecil Forde organized the Swedru branch of the People's Educational Association to protest publicly against it; de Graft Johnson published articles trying to show that the scheme could and should be financed locally; the AYA protested to Nkrumah, asking him to suspend the scheme 'in the name of the people of Ghana, the children yet unborn, in the name of Sarbah and others'.

The rate of Africanization at permanent secretary level was a further cause of disquiet among this small critical group. In January 1953, T. K. Mercer—later the Gold Coast's first Commissioner in London—was reported in the *Ashanti Pioneer* (13 Jan. 1953) as telling a CPP rally, with Nana Kobina Nketsia IV in the chair, that the country's development plan was being upset by the expatriate civil servants; 'We must take the key ministries from the hands of the European Civil Servants immediately'.

[22] 'Kwame Nkrumah is our Leader, admitted', Kwesi Lamptey was reported in the *Evening News* in August 1951, 'we cannot make him a tin god or a Hitler impervious to criticism'. By 1952 the expression of such views in the party's newspaper was unthinkable.

ment should compromise once more on the issue of Self-Government Now. A *Statement* made by Nkrumah in October 1952 had asked the members of the territorial councils and party groups in the country to send in recommendations for a new constitution, but nothing was said of the need for a timetable for independence, and those who had seen Nkrumah hesitate when half in, and half out of, the UGCC were not convinced that he was prepared to force the hands of the officials.

These uneasy movements of unrest took shape at an early date. The first to resign from the party in protest against the rate of advance towards self-government was Kwesi Lamptey in August 1951; he had hitherto been an important figure in the party—its acting national vice-chairman in 1950 and a ministerial secretary in February 1951. Within a year he had been joined by Dzenkle Dzewu and Ashie Nikoe, both members of the original central committee, and others—among them, Saki Scheck, B. F. Kusi, H. P. Nyemitei, and Nuh Abubekr—who had also stood high in the early organization of the party.[23] The defections were discussed by Kwame Afriyea, the party's general secretary, in his address to the third annual conference of the party at Sekondi in August 1952. The growth of a critical group within the national executive was traced back to December 1951 when 'an attempt was made to disrupt the solidarity of the party by Messrs Dzenkle Dzewu, Mate Kole, H. P. Nyemetei (all National Officers at the Secretariat) and E. S. Nartey, Eastern Regional Secretary'.[24] The delegates were told that the matter had been discussed in January 1952 at an emergency meeting of the national executive which had taken a 'modest view of the offence and allowed these men to apologize [but] their subsequent demeanour and activities had proved to be detrimental to the Party'. The executive had met again, therefore, on 12 April in Kumasi, and by a majority vote decided to expel Dzenkle Dzewu, H. P. Nyemetei, Mate Kole, K. A. Twumasi Ankrah, Sydney Brown, and E. S. Nartey. A month later the executive was obliged to meet once

[23] The original members of the central committee were: Nkrumah (chairman); Kojo Botsio (secretary); K. A. Gbedemah, N. A. Welbeck, Kwesi Plange, Kofi Baako, Krobo Edusei, Dzenkle Dzewu, Ashie Nikoe. Saki Scheck was at one time private secretary to Nkrumah, assistant general secretary to the CYO, and editor of the *Takoradi Times*. H. P. Nyemitei was acting general secretary of the CPP.

[24] 'Text of the Third Annual Report of the CPP, delivered by K. A. Afriyea', *Evening News*, 6 & 7 Aug. 1952.

more, and there was a further round of expulsions, including
Ashie Nikoe, J. G. Swaniker, K. G. Kyem, Kojo Nkrumah, and
Saki Scheck.

By the middle of August 1952 criticism of the party leadership
for having compromised over the issue of immediate self-government had spread to a further group whose leaders brought the
argument into the open at the third annual conference at Sekondi. The critics were headed by Kurankyi Taylor, an able,
ambitious lawyer, de Graft Johnson, an extra-mural tutor in the
University College, Cecil Forde (later editor of the *Ghanaian
Times*), Eric Heymann (later editor of the *Evening News*), Anthony Woode, president of the Ghana TUC, and Turkson Ocran,
the TUC general secretary. While the conference was sitting, the
Evening News warned the delegates against disturbing the unity of
the party by forcing a demand for self-government.

> This week-end is a very difficult one in the life of the Convention
> People's Party. . . . By reason of the fact that the Party has grown so
> large both in membership and the number of branches, it is expected
> that the delegations attending the Conference will be unusually
> enormous. . . . No doubt delegates are going to raise burning issues
> which will entail very serious discussions. We expect, however, that
> in the usual CPP way of tolerance, the exercise of patience, and the
> display of sweet reasonableness, great and grave issues will be deter-
> mined with ease and in the interest of our dear country. . . . One would
> be expecting too much of human nature—in fact, the impossible—to
> suggest that every vital decision arrived at will satisfy every delegate.
> But in the usual democratic way, we expect the minority will accept,
> without much ado, the decisions of the majority.[25]

These were unusually hesitant words for the *Evening News* to employ. But the admonition was repeated by Nkrumah in his
'Address to the Conference on Constitutional Reform'. The delegates were warned that these differences within the party 'if not
checked, can lead to serious consequences. There will be chaos
and confusion unless we work according to the principles of
democratic centralism which we have all accepted and here it is
vital that members, especially party leaders, improve their
political education. . . .'[26] The Life Chairman himself came under
attack from individual delegates, and Kurankyi Taylor presided over the final session of the conference on Sunday, 3 August,

[25] *Evening News*, 2 Aug. 1952.   [26] Ibid. 7 Aug. 1952.

when a six-man committee was appointed to work with Nkrumah to draw up the party's own proposals. Kurankyi Taylor was chairman of the committee, which was carefully balanced between the radicals—Kurankyi Taylor, J. C. de Graft Johnson, and J. E. Jantuah—and the loyalists—Gbedemah, Botsio, Archie Casely Hayford. Thus a temporary truce was concluded, and the *Evening News* (more perhaps in hope than with conviction) told its readers that 'those who were grumbling at the CPP for not jumping to wrestle S.G. for the people of this country must surely see the tactical plan of the Party in its move to lead the country into "Canaan".'[27]

These were quarrels and suspicions over a necessarily difficult situation which Nkrumah, Gbedemah, and Botsio saw in better perspective perhaps than their critics.[28] The open argument which went on at Sekondi was also interesting evidence of the much greater freedom of discussion within the party in 1952 than at any time subsequently, or, from a different point of view, of the weakness of party discipline during these years. It was difficult, however, to view the attempt by Kurankyi Taylor and others to force the pace of reform as a serious threat to the leaders. Nkrumah, Gbedemah, Botsio, Krobo Edusei were immensely popular still, having the prestige of the 1949–50 struggle behind them; and the bulk of the party members in the constituency were reasonably content (so far as one could judge) with the gains already made. The critics were small in number and, although able to excite party feelings on one side or the other, had little weight behind them. Moreover, their ability to exert such influence as they had on the rank and file derived from an uneasy suspicion that independence was still a long way off; and it needed only the renewal of the movement towards self-government to enable Nkrumah to recapture the initiative. This happened towards the middle of 1953. Early in April the government published a White Paper which embodied the views of the territorial councils and local political groups, and in July Nkrumah

[27] *Evening News*, 7 Aug. 1952.
[28] This is open to argument. Had independence been granted in 1953 or 1954 the subsequent troubles might have been avoided. On the other hand, they might well have crippled the new state. In the end, it took the country roughly ten years, 1947–57, to gain its independence—an incredibly short period compared with India or Ceylon, a comparatively long term compared with, say, Tanganyika: but then Ghana was a forerunner in Africa and pioneers necessarily move more slowly.

devised a formula whereby the Assembly was asked to approve the proposal:

that Her Majesty's Government as soon as the necessary administrative arrangements for independence are made, should introduce an Act of Independence into the United Kingdom Parliament declaring the Gold Coast a sovereign and independent state within the Commonwealth; and, further, that this Assembly do authorise the Government to ask Her Majesty's Government, without prejudice to the above request, to amend as a matter of urgency the Gold Coast (Constitution) Order in Council 1950, in such a way as to provide *inter alia* that the Legislative Assembly shall be composed of members directly elected by secret ballot, and that all Members of the Cabinet shall be Members of the Assembly and directly responsible to it.[29]

A certain ambiguity was retained over the actual timing of the stages proposed, but the motion was endorsed wholeheartedly by the Assembly. And in October an event took place which further strengthened Nkrumah's hand. The United Kingdom government suspended the constitution of British Guiana, Dr Jagan's People's Progressive Party went out of office, and colonial rule was resumed.[30] The events were widely reported in the Gold Coast, and although Nkrumah may have been dismayed on his own account, it enabled him to stress the wisdom of 'Tactical Action' in dealing with the British. The critics were silenced and, later that month (October), Kurankyi Taylor was expelled from the party; Turkson Ocran was relieved of his duties as general-secretary of the TUC to make way for a young trade unionist of (at this time) more moderate views, J. K. Tettegah,[31] and both he and Anthony Woode were suspended from the party. These abrupt decisions were followed by a statement by Nkrumah in the Assembly in February 1954 which explained and justified the non-employment of communists in the civil service.[32] The following month the TUC renewed its membership of the International Confederation of Free Trade Unions from which it had disaffiliated in August 1953, and professed support for its aims.

[29] GC, LA Deb., 10 July 1953.
[30] The Progressive Party had been elected on 27 April and was dismissed on 9 October.
[31] One of the charges now levelled at Anthony Woode was that he had attended the Vienna meeting of the WFTU in March 1953. Tettegah was formally elected full-time secretary of a (temporarily) united TUC at its eleventh annual conference in September 1954.
[32] GC, LA Deb., 12 Feb. 1954.

This sharp rebuff to the party's critics was accompanied by a major attempt to strengthen party organization in order to exercise a closer control from the headquarters. The CPP was an open party, based on an unrestricted membership, and it attracted a growing army of followers. Within eighteen months of taking office, membership was up to 700,000, the number of branches to something over 500,[33] and it had become necessary 'to plan to cope with the tremendous growth of the Party in order to ensure a more solid, militant and disciplined organisation able to bear the task it had undertaken on behalf of the country'. So Kwame Afriyea told the third annual conference at Sekondi in 1952, and over the ensuing months a number of reforms were introduced.

Money was a continual problem. 'The finances of the party have not been too healthy of late', Nkrumah told the Sekondi conference. 'Funds have not come in commensurate with the growth of the party.' The general secretary was more specific. 'Soon after the Annual Delegates' Conference in August last year [1951] a sudden depression in the finances of the National Headquarters occurred.' The balance sheet submitted to the 1951 Ho conference had shown a credit balance of £788 (with stock valued at £128), but this sum had been used up; meanwhile there had been 'a slow down of dues'—the 'main source of income of the party'. Also, 'where dues are regularly collected, with the exception of a few branches, the portion that is due the National Headquarters is always withheld'. The Assembly members had promised to contribute a percentage of their salaries to the party and, 'on the whole', said Afriyea,

> the Ministers have shown a keen sense of responsibility although there are still some outstanding arrears to pay. Only a few of the ministerial secretaries have arrears to pay, although in some cases heavy. But it is much regretted that most of the back benchers are very hesitant in paying their contributions and at times the Life Chairman is compelled to assist in the collection of the contributions.

In theory, party funds were derived from the 'proceeds of functions (dances, football matches etc.), voluntary subscriptions, appeals, donations, bequests, sale of literature, badges and other things approved by the National Executive, admission

---

[33] 3rd Ann. Report of CPP, *Evening News*, 6 & 7 Aug. 1952.

fees of individual members and organisations, and monthly dues. . . .'[34] There was little doubt, however, that from 1952 onwards, the party drew on more lucrative sources than the contributions of its members. For example, a number of Levantine merchants, many of whom had been eager to enrol as special constables in 1948 to put down rioters, hurried forward with offers of good will. Although evidence of such activities was naturally hard to obtain, some of the stories which were in circulation were confirmed. Thus the Armenian contractor Aksor Kassardjian told the Korsah Commission in 1953 that 'he had given in all £200 in separate sums of £100 each to the Convention People's Party'.[35] Before the same Commission Nicholas Paidoussis—a Greek contractor—testified that he, too, had subscribed. Ohene Djan (when ministerial secretary to the Ministry of Finance and Chairman of the Central Tender Board which approved the issue of contracts) had told him (said Paidoussis) that 'all other companies and firms had given generous donations or contributions to the party'; so he had handed Ohene Djan a cheque for £100.[36] Many of these very minor transactions were of course gifts to influential party members in the hope of government favours, but some may have spilled over into party funds in the form of general donations to ensure good will.[37] A much stronger ally, however, than the Lebanese and Syrian community had already appeared at the end of 1952, when the 'Cocoa Purchasing Company' (CPC) was established by the government as a subsidiary of the Cocoa Marketing Board with an authorized share capital of £2 million. Originally designed to challenge (and eventually replace) the large overseas buying firms, it was empowered the following year (August 1953) to relieve what was believed to be a chronic indebtedness on the part of the cocoa farmer. A Loans Agency began to issue individual loans to farmers within a limit first of £150 and then (by February 1954) £1,500 until by September 1954 the government had approved

---

[34] *CCP Constitution 1951.*   [35] Korsah Commission *Report*, para. 238.
[36] Ibid. para. 283.
[37] This was not true, however, of the £100 given to Ohene Djan. The cheque was made out in the name of his companion, Miss Freda Abdullah, who cashed it for him. It was entered on the firm's books as 'payment for a pump' for, as Mr Paidoussis told the Commission, he was 'a married man and his wife was not in the country at the time, so he was afraid that if Miss Freda Abdullah's name appeared in the ledger and it was known that he had paid money to her his wife might not understand'. Thus 'what a tangled web we weave, When first we practise to deceive'.

the release of funds to the Company via the Marketing Board to the extent of £1,900,000. This was an impressive sum, and critics of the party were quick to point out the close relationship between the CPP and the CPC. A. Y. K. Djin, for example, was acting managing director of the Company and chairman of the finance committee of the CPP; Martin Appiah Danquah, a director of the company, was general secretary of the party's ancillary organization, the United Ghana Farmers' Council. Without exception, the directors of the company were leading party figures. The nature of the relationship between the CPC and the party was expressed in characteristic terms by Krobo Edusei in the Assembly early in March 1954:

> The CPC is the product of a master brain, Dr Kwame Nkrumah, and it is the atomic bomb of the Convention People's Party. As honourable members are aware, the Prime Minister in his statement to the CPP told his party members that organisation decided everything and the CPC is part of the organisation of the Convention People's Party.[38]

It was difficult to estimate how much (or how little) the party drew from such sources. The (Jibowu) Commission of Inquiry into the Affairs of the Cocoa Purchasing Company (appointed in 1956) concluded that CPC vehicles had been used by the CPP for electioneering, and that some of the Company's funds had gone towards 'securing votes from farmers prior to the election on 15 June 1954'. At the very least, the network of agents and buying stations which the Company established with the help of the United Ghana Farmers' Council must have relieved the party of a great deal of the burden (and expense) of propaganda in the cocoa areas.[39]

Access to funds of the Cocoa Purchasing Company, and to those of the newly created public corporations like the Industrial Development Corporation, did not stop the leaders calling for greater efforts from the members themselves—it was clearly in the interests of party organization to do so—and Gbedemah told the fourth annual delegates' conference in Tamale in August 1953 that they still lacked sufficient funds to fight the forthcom-

[38] GC, LA Deb., 3 Mar. 1954. Krobo Edusei was now Government Chief Whip and Ministerial Secretary to the Minister of Justice. He was dropped from the government after the publication of the Korsah Commission *Report*, but reinstated after the 1954 election.

[39] Jibowu Commission *Report* (1956), which is summarized below, p. 341 n. 25.

ing second general election. It was announced that the sale of party badges, contributions from the assemblymen, membership dues, donations given at party rallies, had brought the party's finances to £4,255, but that not less than £30,000 would be needed for the second general election. In fact, by June 1954 (the date of the election) sufficient money had been acquired. The party was well equipped with lorries, propaganda vans, and paid agents; glossy, coloured portraits of Nkrumah framed to form a country-wide election poster were printed and imported from abroad, and Gbedemah was able to issue a cheque for £5,200 to the Attorney-General to meet the £50 deposit of the party's 104 candidates.

An attempt was also made to improve the administrative structure of the party. Regional liaison committees were created, representative of the constituency executives but controlled by secretaries paid for and appointed by Accra. The committees were expected to 'organise branches in the districts, cities, towns and villages within the region [and] coordinate their activities and work', advise the national secretariat on questions of regional 'affiliation, disaffiliation, dissolutions or expulsions', and, in general, 'manage, control and guide the work of the Party in Regional and Local Government bodies. . . .'[40] In Accra itself, the headquarters organization was streamlined, and a secretariat established of up to a dozen national officers and staff.[41] It was now too that a number of ancillary organizations were brought into close association with the main body of the party: a Ghana TUC appeared, as the 'industrial wing' of the party;[42] an African

[40] 3rd Ann. Report of CPP, *Evening News*, 6 & 7 Aug. 1952.

[41] This was actually a reduction in number from an over-staffed headquarters. It was now, however, that the CPP began to develop its 'departments'—propaganda, foreign affairs, parliamentary, education, local government, women's section, farmers, co-operatives, economic affairs, and so forth.

[42] A note on trade union history may be useful here. The first Trade Union Ordinance was passed in 1941, although tribal and occupational groups—fishermen, goldsmiths, palm-wine sellers, women market traders, &c—went back a long way in the form of craft guilds and friendly societies. The first union to register was the Western Province Motor Drivers' Union, although the Ashanti and Northern Drivers' Union had already been formed in 1931 and had staged a strike in 1937. By December 1951 the paid up membership of the sixty-six active unions registered was 44,092—approximately a fifth of the total (male) wage-earning population. The history of the TUC was extremely involved. The first Congress collapsed after the general strike of January 1950, and between 1951 and 1953 there were two splinter groups. The Gold Coast TUC was resuscitated by the United Africa Company Employees' Union, and a Ghana TUC (sponsored by the CPP) formed out of a Dismissed Employees' Association. The two came together in 1953, and J. K. Tettegah was elected full-time secretary at the 11th annual congress in September

Chamber of Commerce was formed in May 1953.[43] A Ghana Farmers' Council was launched in July.[44] The Women's Section began to hold its own delegates' conference and to improve its local branches. N. A. Welbeck formed a new group of adolescents within the Youth League, known as the 'Youth Falcons', who paraded at party rallies dressed in red caps, white shirts (or blouses) and green shorts (or skirts).[45]

The strengthening of the party during these years in order to spread its power through as many channels as possible was a constant preoccupation on the part of the leaders. Again and again, the structure was examined, amended, and added to, in an attempt to produce a militant, disciplined body of followers out of a strongly localized society. The difficulties were immense. For although there was still great support for the nationalist aims proclaimed in 1949, and 'Freedom' and 'Self-Government' were powerful concepts still among the commoners of the Colony and Ashanti chiefdoms, the CPP depended in practice on the ability of the leaders to bind together a vast collection of local (often conflicting) loyalties. And the very strength of the CPP as a mass party was also a main source of weakness. If the analogy were not faintly ridiculous in so warm-blooded a country, one might say that between 1951 and 1954 the CPP showed, as does an iceberg, only its surface structure to the casual observer. Thus, although Nkrumah, Gbedemah, Botsio were leaders of obvious ability, and Hutton-Mills, Casely Hayford, E. O. Asafu Adjaye were educated men who could outline policy to the officials with a fair

---

1954. The movement divided again in 1955 with the formation of an anti-CPP Congress of Free Trade Unions. After 1957 the Free Trade Union Congress disappeared and the Ghana TUC expanded until it reached the point of having 72 affiliated unions, and a membership of 154,000. It was then that the TUC was remodelled (ostensibly) on the lines of the Israeli Histadrut. A limited number of centrally controlled, automatically financed, national unions were created, and compulsory membership imposed on every salary and wage-earner in the country (see below, ch. VIII).

[43] The Chamber of Commerce held its first meeting in the Accra Community Centre on 10 May with representatives of (allegedly) 104 firms. The president was E. Ayeh Kumi, the secretary-treasurer W. A. Wiafe, both prominent CPP businessmen who had worked their way up from 'petty trading'.

[44] The Ghana Farmers' Council included A. Casely Hayford, Kojo Mercer (chairman of the Cocoa Marketing Board), A. Y. K. Djin (managing director of the CPC), R. R. Amponsah, B. E. Dwira, and D. E. Asafu Adjaye.

[45] The general secretary also told the delegates that the 'overseas branches of the CPP' were doing well in London, America, and Nigeria. The CPP was 'encountering success in its attempt to capture initiative and mass support. A great part of Northern Nigeria has been captured by the Kano branch. Over 30 branches have been established in the east and west.' This was, of course, wholly illusory.

show of understanding, this front rank of leadership masked the essential nature of the party. In the constituencies, the rank and file were continually exposed to pressure from the infinity of local interests in the country. Thus towards the end of 1953, at precisely the time when the Nkrumah, Gbedemah, Botsio triumvirate had what seemed good grounds for confidence, when criticism within the national executive over the pace of reform had been crushed, and negotiations resumed for a further advance towards independence, when the country was prosperous and considerable reserves were accruing to the Cocoa Marketing Board—precisely at this seemingly high point in the party's fortunes the leaders encountered further difficulties of much greater weight than any experienced hitherto. Stirred by the prospect of a further series of reforms, regional and local interests began to be expressed in growing volume by members of parliament, constituency secretaries, local youth associations, and—eventually—by rival parties.

The immediate cause of a sudden outburst of local discontent was the redelimitation of electoral districts carried out in 1953 by the (Van Lare) Commission of Enquiry into Representational and Electoral Reform. Like its predecessor (the Ewart Committee of 1950) the Commission tried to avoid giving offence by using, as far as possible, the boundaries of the local chiefdoms in drawing its electoral map of the whole country, but it was unable to avoid grouping together many of the small states of the Colony within a single constituency. In doing so, it provoked an anguished petition[46] (one of many) from the chiefs and people of the tiny Aowin state in the Colony who objected to their merger with the peoples of the larger, neighbouring Amenfi state, on the grounds:

1. That the Aowin State is an entirely independent State.
2. That the customs, language, tabooes and the like are by no means akin to those of the Amenfi. . .
5. That since the ratio of voters of the Amenfi and the Aowin States is 2–1,[47] it is evident that for a thousand years the Aowin State would never be represented in the Legislative Assembly by any

---

[46] Submitted to the Van Lare Commission but not published.
[47] Amenfi-Aowin Electoral District:

Wassaw Amenfi local council	..	..	..	21,500
Aowin local council	..	..	..	10,441

person of Aowin birth since the Amenfis have the advantage over us when it comes to the question of voting.

6. That the continuance of the government insisting on the Aowins forming part of the Amenfi constituency is an indirect way of merging the Aowins into the Wassaw Amenfi State and thereby losing forever the identity of the Aowins.
8. That since 'blood is thicker than water', and since the fact that our Assembly man will ever remain an Amenfiman against our will, we must never expect close contact from any Wassaw Amenfi member of the Assembly. . .
10. . . . That the situation wrongly nurses inferiority complex among the Aowins while it nurses superiority among the Wassaw Amenfi people. This is indeed a pathetic affair.
12. . . . That in as much as we the people in the Gold Coast wish to govern ourselves however small the country may be, so do we Aowins desire to have our own representative in the Legislative Assembly.

The party leaders did what they could to resist this extreme particularism. In the debate on the Van Lare *Report*, Nkrumah told the Assembly members that 'people all over the Gold Coast should have equal rights to representation according to population' now that the country was 'moving forward into an era in which tribalism, as an aspect of colonial "divide and rule", no longer holds sway'.[48] The argument lay at the heart of the nationalist case, but it was much easier to assert its claims from Accra than from the regional and state 'capitals' in the country. Far more important claims than those put forward by the Aowin people remained to be voiced, and were argued in angry terms by the Ashanti members of the Assembly in November 1953.

The Ashanti complaint was straightforward. In the proposed new legislature of 104 directly elected members the Ashanti region (including at this time the Brong Ahafo chiefdoms) were entitled (by population) to 21 seats, an increase of only 2 over the 1950 figure, and an actual decrease when taken as a percentage of the new total. The north was to go up from 19 to 26, the Colony to 44, the Trans-Volta region to 13.[49] Yet Ashanti produced more than half of the country's cocoa and a substantial part of the country's gold and timber exports; it contained the large bauxite deposits for the Volta River Project; and, the argu-

[48] GC, LA Deb., 6 Nov. 1953.
[49] 1950 figures: North 19, Colony and Trans-Volta 37, Ashanti 19.

ment which lay at the heart of the Ashanti protest, its rulers had formerly held sway over a great part of the Gold Coast. Accordingly, in a long and bitter debate that lasted (on and off) from 6 to 17 November, the Ashanti members in the Assembly pressed the demand for 30 seats in the new legislature:

B. F. Kusi [ex-CPP]: . . . If in 1900 we had the support of all sections of the country we could have fought the British Empire and driven the British away and it would have been unnecessary for us today to agitate for self-government. . . . Another point is sentiment—(interruption). Yes, I will explain that to you—All Ashantis express the sentiment that Ashanti is a nation and that fact has been accepted. We are not a region at all; we should be considered as a nation. . . . Population alone does not make a country. . . .

Krobo Edusei [Ministerial Secretary to Ministry of Justice]: I have got mandate from CPP members in Kumasi to ask for 30 seats. As I have already stated, this matter cropped up during the Coussey Committee meeting and the only compromise which was arrived at was that Ashanti should be given one-fourth of the representation. . . We are not asking for more: we are asking for 30 seats . . . we Ashantis are not preaching tribalism or anything of the sort; we are only agitating for our legitimate right . . . and, Mr Speaker, with your permission, I am going to read to Honourable Members one of the most important telegrams that I have received. . . .

KROBO EDUSEI, ASSEMBLY, ACCRA—LIVING AND DEAD GODS AND ALL SPIRITS OF ASHANTI EXPECT YOU TO PROVE YOURSELF TRUE DESCENDANT OF WARRIOR AMANKWATIA SECURE THIRTY SEATS FOR ASHANTI HISTORY AWAITING YOU ALSO—G. K. ADAI

. . . We are loyal! Our chiefs are humble to the government. . . . But this is a demand which is being made by the whole Ashanti nation. . . . We do not want to cause any riot; we do not want to secede from the Colony; we want to march abreast with them. . . .

Atta Mensah [Ministerial Secretary to the Ministry of Communications and Works]: It has been suggested somewhere that the intention of Ashanti in asking for these thirty seats is that should Government refuse to accede to our demand we would break away and form a federal government. Such false and malicious statements . . . are most unfortunate. It is not our intention whatsoever to wreck the smooth unity which Ashanti has contributed in a large measure to build. On this question of delimitation, as I have said, there is no difference of opinion as far as the CPP and the [Opposition] are concerned in

Ashanti. Among the rank and file of the CPP, among the leaders of the [Opposition] in Ashanti, among the rank and file of the Ashanti Youth Association, from the Chief to the *ahenkwaa*, from the common man to the aristocrat, there is no division on that issue, that is, our demand for 30 seats.

C. E. Osei [Representative of the Asanteman Council] : . . . Ashanti's position is 25 per cent of the total seats. . . . The Transvolta Togoland area which has eight seats now will have an increase to 13, the Northern Territories from 19 to 26. (Some Honourable Members : By population)—What do you mean by population? Look here, my friends, there is no Government that can stand because it has population alone; it must have money backing it. . . . (Some Honourable Members: Shame! Shame!) (Uproar)—You must be prepared to buy our good will. (Uproar).

W. E. Arthur [CPP Rural Member, Colony] : . . . I want to remind my brothers from Ashanti that they were not taking part in the administration of this country in the early days and it was only as late as 1946—if I am correct—that they were invited to take part in the Government. And so I should not claim too much. (Mr Krobo Edusei: 'Talk sense!') I am talking sense, Mr Speaker, they must understand that Ashanti is a conquered territory. (Interruption) (Some Honourable Members: Shame! Shame! Shame!) (Uproar).

Nana Boakye Danquah [Akyempimhene, an important Kumasi chief] : . . . On a point of order, Mr Speaker. The last speaker has said that the Ashantis were conquered and I would like him to prove to this House in what way or manner they were conquered. We were never conquered.

Mr Arthur: We all know the history of this country and that—

Mr Bediako Poku [CPP]: On a point of order Mr Speaker. An expression has been made by the Honourable Gentleman who just sat down that Ashantis were conquered. If Ashantis were conquered, he should know that the Ashantis also conquered the people of the Colony in those days. The Ashantis were not conquered by Fantis! (Uproar).

Mr Arthur: . . . If he insists I will prove that it was conquered, and it was through the efforts of the people of the Colony that King Prempeh I—(Interruption).

Mr Speaker: What has that got to do with this debate?[50]

What indeed? But when Nana Kwame Gyebi Ababio, Essumejahene, moved that the Electoral Provisions Ordinance 1953 should be amended 'to provide for the election of 28 mem-

---

[50] Extracts are taken from different days of the debate between 4 and 17 Nov.

bers from the rural electoral districts of Ashanti'—in addition to
two from the Kumasi municipality—Gbedemah tried to stop a
division of the house. 'I think it is very wrong for Honourable
members to press the point to a division', said Gbedemah, for 'the
Honourable the Prime Minister has said that he is very anxious
to keep the unity of the country together'. 'We want it', said
Bediako Poku, and the Question was put and lost. All but three
of the Ashanti representatives who were present voted for the
amendment: Asafu Adjaye, Minister of Local Government, ab-
stained; so did Casely Hayford who was in the unhappy position
of being a Fanti elected by the Kumasi municipality. Yeboah
Afari voted *against* the amendment, and this, too, was a significant pointer to the future, for Yeboah Afari represented the large
western Brong constituency (Sunyani) whose peoples viewed
any increase of Ashanti–Kumasi power with alarm.

This strong Ashanti protest over the Van Lare *Report* was a
dark shadow falling across the nationalist scene, which lifted
throughout the period of the election until the end of 1954 when
the CPP–Ashanti quarrel broke out in full fury following the inauguration of the NLM. Meanwhile, similar conflicts (of a more
local nature) broke out within the CPP branches throughout
Ashanti and the Colony over the nomination of candidates: the
members of the national executive quarrelled among themselves,
the constituency executives were divided, village groups com-
peted against each other on behalf of local favourites, rebel candidates appeared in defiance of the national executive and the
central committee until, in Ashanti especially, the CPP trembled
on the brink of division.

One last feature of these early years needs to be discussed. In
addition to dissent within its own ranks, the CPP had to resist
attacks from rival party groups which joined together to oppose
the government. This further challenge to the party was always
present after 1951 in the small opposition group led by Danquah
and Busia in the Assembly, but it was given much greater weight
a little before the second general election by an alliance between
the intellectuals of the former UGCC and the leaders of a Northern People's Party, the Moslem Association, and the Togoland
Congress.

The break between the intelligentsia and the CPP in 1949 continued after the 1951 election. The former still held aloof, under

a new name and a new leader. Because the UGCC was thought to be outworn (in a sense, discredited) after the disappointment of the election, a new start was called for, and on 4 May 1952 a Ghana Congress Party was publicly launched in Accra with K. A. Busia of the University College as its leader. It declared its aims in modest terms as being to supply 'an effective opposition to the CPP government' in order, one day, to offer the country 'an alternative government'.[51] The GCP continued in the same traditions as the UGCC, in that it tried to ally itself with the chiefs (Busia, for example, standing in relation to Wenchi and its chief Nana Kusi Appea, as Danquah stood in relation to Kibi and Nana Ofori Atta) while stressing its appeal to moderate, intellectual opinion. Like the UGCC, it too had a tendency to be weakened by disputes among the leaders and, in trying to provide a rallying ground for every shade of anti-CPP activity, the new party became instead a battleground between dissident ex-CPP radicals and those whose education and outlook led them quite genuinely to dislike the authoritarian ways of the CPP. Thus Dzenkle Dzewu, Ashie Nikoe, Mate Kole, H. P. Nyemitei, Saki Scheck, B. F. Kusi, Kwesi Lamptey—leaders of the early inner party revolt against the CPP leaders—joined hands with Busia and the lawyer-merchant rump of the UGCC—Danquah, Obetsebi Lamptey, Akufo Addo, N. A. Ollennu, W. E. Ofori Atta, B. D. Addai, H. R. Annan. There were numerous quarrels among this ill-assorted group,[52] and Busia was obliged to caution his followers at an emergency delegates' meeting at Bekwai, Ashanti, in March 1953. The GCP, he said, was a party of 'lofty ideals' that existed 'to combat tendencies, even actual activities, which if allowed to continue unchecked might lead to the establishment of a dictatorial or totalitarian system of government'. Unhappily, there were 'already among us politicians who are shouting that they wanted immediate self government for the Gold Coast. . . . We must be careful of such politicians. They are not true patriots.'[53] An air of uncertainty hung over the party,

[51] *Ashanti Pioneer*, 6 May 1952.

[52] e.g. Kwesi Lamptey was suspended in 1953, then reinstated in March 1954; Obetsebi Lamptey (the Accra lawyer) was expelled after a quarrel with the leaders, and went off to start his own 'Ghana National Party'.

[53] *Ashanti Pioneer*, 17 Mar. 1953. Dr Busia's view of Gold Coast politics at this time may be found in his article in *Parl. Aff.*, v/4 (1952). Several sentences stand out: '. . . the present constitutional experiment is the child of agitation, and it is to the "agitators" that power was delivered. No one . . . could mistake the revolution-

which was never wholly masked by the insistence of its leaders that, in the long run, quality would tell:

> ... Congress is out. It will show the country the right way. It will meet the CPP squarely and defeat it. ... We cannot sit down and allow our country to be so run and ruined by men who think of themselves only and who compromise principles without the least compunction. ... The Congress flag, Blue for Unity, Gold for our Mineral Resources, and Green for our vegetable resources was hoisted [at Bukom Square, Accra last Sunday]. Of course the Congress means business. We cannot allow this fooling and thieving to go on any longer or else we are all doomed. I am again repeating that in Congress the CPP has met its match and no doubt, its Waterloo! The great array of intellectual giants behind the party, the response of the chiefs and farmers and the joy and support of the thinking man at the birth of Congress give evidence of the strength of the new party. This Ghana must be saved from a one-party evil, the evil of dictatorship.[54]

The hope expressed by the GCP leaders was forlorn. The party lacked any solid base of support except where it was able to draw strength from local interests intimately associated with individuals within the party. Thus its strongest points of support were at Wenchi because of Busia's relationship with the Wenchi Stool, at Kibi because of Danquah's connexion with the Ofori Atta family, and among relatively sophisticated areas of the population—Cape Coast in particular—where an old 'intelligentsia' tradition continued whose members responded to Busia's call for a stand against 'demagogy'. The only major success of the GCP during these years was, in fact, the entry into the

---

ary character of the Convention People's Party. ... There was the deified "charismatic" leader in the person of Nkrumah; the fanatic band of propagandists; the fanning of the discontents of the people; the scapegoat found in the "imperialists" and "stooges"; the party picnics, the flags and slogans; the defeat of opponents by vilification; ... backed by popular enthusiasm and the hope for immediate material benefits. ... With the rejection in [1951] of the Chiefs and the older leaders, with a large number of the best educated youth in the civil service, the field was left clear for demagogues and seldom has demagogy been paid as high dividends as in the Gold Coast today.' The article is entitled: 'The Prospects for Parliamentary Democracy in the Gold Coast'.

[54] Tawia Adamafio's 'Jottings by the Wayside' in the *Daily Echo*, 6 May 1952. By 10 May the *Daily Echo* was comparing the CPP and Nkrumah with the Nazi Party and Hitler. Later Tawia Adamafio joined the CPP to become, by 1960, its general secretary and, later, Minister of Information; in 1962 he was arrested under the Preventive Detention Act. This picture of the GCP as the rising hope of the unbending intellectuals was often put by Busia who was reported by the *Ashanti Pioneer* (5 Nov. 1952) as saying, during the inauguration of the Essumeja branch of the party, that 'we would not have offered the post of an office messenger to Krobo Edusei if the Ghana Congress Party had been in power'.

Assembly as the member for Cape Coast of an Independent-pro-Congress candidate, Kofi Amponsah-Dadzie who, though defeated at the polls by N. A. Welbeck (at this time propaganda secretary of the CPP), brought an election petition against his opponent and succeeded (August 1953) with the charge that Welbeck was not a registered voter in the municipality. The *Ashanti Pioneer* and the GCP celebrated the occasion, but it was a legal victory that did the party little good and merely confirmed the CPP leaders' belief in the trickery of lawyers and the law.[55] In general, the CPP paid little attention to the GCP, which it nicknamed the 'Ghost Party'. The rank and file enjoyed themselves at its expense, staging an elaborate mock burial of their nominal rival, with hearse, coffin, effigies of the leaders, and a funeral oration.[56] As a token opposition which posed no threat to the ruling party, the GCP was well within the limits of tolerance permitted by the CPP between 1951 and 1954. Indeed, its existence was probably an additional, though minor, help to the CPP leaders in their insistence on the need for vigilance and discipline.

The most serious challenge to the CPP came from the area

---

[55] The by-election (following the death of Kwesi Plange) was an interesting one. Amponsah-Dadzie was well known locally as a 'poor man's lawyer' (though not qualified in any formal sense), as the negotiating adviser for the Motor Union, and an important figure in the local *asafo* organization—the *Oguaa Mpontu Kuw*. Welbeck was not personally popular in the municipality, and there were two other contestants for the party's nomination: Kweku Ackon, principal of the Ghana National Academy in Cape Coast, and K. O. Thompson, a former chairman of the Cape Coast CPP. It was said that at the party election Welbeck and Ackon tied with 8 votes each with a single ballot for Thompson. Then a second ballot gave the nomination to Welbeck. Ackon decided to stand as an Independent and was expelled from the party on 11 June. (A second Independent, J. Aggrey-Fynn withdrew at the last minute.) Out of 11,515 registered electors only 3,186 voted and 66 of these were spoiled papers. The result was close: Welbeck, 1,546, Amponsah-Dadzie, 1,135, Ackon, 439. Amponsah-Dadzie filed his petition, accusing Welbeck of using bribery, undue influence, threats, and impersonation, and of not being a registered voter in the municipality. Then Amponsah-Dadzie was convicted in September of saying that Nkrumah should be stoned if he came to Cape Coast, and was bound over in the sum of £100 to keep the peace for twelve months.

[56] 6 May 1952. Note, too, the amusing, schoolboyish glee with which the *Evening News* celebrated the demise of the opposition paper *Talking Drums*: 'I was present at the funeral and there I saw the chief mourners in grey tails and toppers—the same tails and toppers which missed the ministerial coach and bungalows. . . . As the Oxford and Continental intonation of Dr Armytoad filled the air, Bourgeoise shouted "Quality! Quality!"; and great crocodile tears rolled down the cheeks of Dr Damquack. . . . "Earth to earth, ashes to ashes" intoned Armytoad, and with one accord they all jumped into the open grave." (A full account is given in *Afr. Aff.*, July 1953.) Occasionally, however, fate took a hand. On 28 July 1953 Bafuor Obuobi, *odikro* of Odumase in Akim Abuakwa, took part in the mock interment of a coffin supposedly containing the body of Danquah. Two days later the sub-chief died and Danquah sent £2 2s. to the funeral ceremony.

where its appeal was least understood and its organization weak-
est: the north. Dissatisfaction among the northern members in
the Assembly came to a head in February 1954 following J. A.
Braimah's resignation as Minister of Communications and
Works. In a series of discussions in Accra, the 'Aims and Objects'
of a northern political movement were drawn up, and early in
April representatives from the various district councils of the
Protectorate met at the Tolon-Na's house in Tamale to approve
the outline constitution of the new party. The Northern People's
Party was then inaugurated during the week-end 10–11 April
1954 at a public rally in the regional capital.

The NPP was formed to ensure:

1.   (i) (*a*) That there is respect for the culture of the people of the
             Northern Territories (Protectorate)
        (*b*) their political and social development
        (*c*) their just treatment and
        (*d*) their protection against abuses.
     (ii)   A progressively increasing share in the administrative and
             other services of the country; . . .
     (iv)   That by all legitimate and constitutional means the con-
             trol and direction of government in the country as a whole
             shall pass into the hands of the Chiefs and their people as
             soon as they are capable to assume full responsibility and
             to press for the immediate development and progress of
             the Protectorate.
2.   To take all possible steps to see that only people who actually have
     the interests of the Protectorate at heart, and not carpet-baggers,
     represent them in the Legislative Assembly.[57]

Here was a second regional protest against the government—
regional, not tribal, the Protectorate being no less of an artificial
unit when it was formed in 1901 than the country as a whole.
How was it that the very different chiefdoms of the north were
able to come together in 1954? Why should they want to do so?

Although divided among themselves—chiefdom against
chiefdom, rulers against subject peoples—the different communities in the Protectorate were conscious of their 'northern-ness'
simply because they were not southerners. The colonial government had tried to foster a sense of regional unity with the establishment of a territorial council in Tamale in December 1946,

[57] NPP, *The Constitution, Aims, and Objects, 1954.*

partly for administrative convenience, partly to provide a base from which the north could enter a national legislative framework, but there were a number of contributory causes. The emergence of a small, closely-linked group of educated northerners from the Tamale Middle Boarding School and the Teacher Training College, the resentful attitude invariably shown by southerners posted as clerks or teachers to the north, and the frequently harsh treatment in Ashanti and the Colony of northern labourers, house servants, and watchmen—coupled with the obvious poverty of the region—helped to produce a strongly-held belief that the north was not only different from the south but in danger of being subjected to its over-hasty, over-radical politicians.[58] Distrust of the south among the chiefs and their educated advisers, and anxiety at the impending withdrawal of British protection, deepened as southern-based parties tried to spread their influence across the Volta.[59] In 1948 the illiterate chiefs of the Northern Territories Territorial Council had listened without comment to the chief commissioner when he warned them that the riots in the south had followed 'a careful plan which had been centrally organised' and 'we must not let our people who have grievances here become the instruments of dangerous agitators'.[60] By November 1949 the Council had been radically altered: its members were mainly educated chiefs and commoners and they dissociated themselves forcefully from the 'Self-Government Now' resolution adopted by the CPP People's Representative Assembly in Accra on the grounds: 'first, it has

[58] A long historical connexion existed between Ashanti and the north in trade and military conquest before 1901. Northern contacts with the south were then interrupted but were resumed with still greater impact during the later years of colonial rule. Thus an almost isolated town like Bawku, in the north-east of the Protectorate, was brought into close contact with Tamale, the regional capital, after the bridging of the White and Red Voltas, and by 1954 as many as 30 or 40 lorries were to be seen in the market place of this frontier town. The urban population grew steadily: Tamale had reached 16,000 in 1948, Yendi 8,000, Bawku 7,000, Wa 5,000, Bolgatanga 3,600. There was a constant stream of migrants to and from the south: the *Report of the Labour Dept for 1951-2* estimated that in that year 169,117 migrants went south across the Volta ferries, and 173,582 made the return, northbound journey—miners, farm labourers, cattle drivers, PWD workmen. But increased contacts of this sort, while they helped to draw the country together, also created points of friction. For an account of pre-colonial Ashanti-northern relations, see Ivor Wilks, *The Northern Factor in Ashanti History* (Univ. College of Ghana, Inst. of Afr. Studies monograph, 1961).

[59] During the week that included the inauguration of the NPP, Dr Busia's GCP came up to Tamale to offer its help; so did Dr Renner for the MAP; and on Friday, 16 April, Nkrumah started a week's tour of the Protectorate.

[60] NTTC, *Minutes*, Mar. 1948.

extreme views; secondly, no society or political party from the
north was represented; thirdly, if the people of the Northern
Territories could have their way, which is greatly doubted, they
will not be prepared for full self-government until in about 10 to
15 years at the earliest.'[61] Later again, the Council produced a
memorandum which stated that 'the people of the Gold Coast
should be cautious of the speed at which they advance towards
complete independence' and that 'undue haste . . . seems to be
unwarrantable'.[62] Its views were ignored by the CPP government, and by 1954 J. A. Braimah, having resigned from the
government, was drawing comparisons with India, saying:
'When the time for self-government came, those regions in India
which were in the same position as we are today, were left by the
British to the nationalists. A similar case confronts us today and
we have to fight on our own.'[63] Braimah's own position lent force
to his words. Here was an able, widely-respected northerner, a
chief (albeit a minor one), an employee of the large Gonja
Native Authority for eighteen years, so misled by the wickedness
of southern politics that he had allowed himself to accept the
offer of £2,000 from a foreign contractor. Such were the dangers
of nationalist politics and of unguarded contact with the south!

How strong the northern party was in practice, and whether
the CPP would be able to combat its hold on the chiefs and their
advisers, remained to be seen. Its ability to challenge the nationalist party could hardly be doubted, however, as the leaders began to enlist support from those most likely to influence the newly
enfranchised electorate in the twenty-six northern constituencies. The Northern Territories Council acted as an effective
headquarters organization.[64] The national executive of the party
was drawn from a wide area of the Protectorate—S. D. Dombo
Duori-Na, an educated sub-chief from the north-west (Lawra)
district; Yakubu Tali Tolon-Na, an important Dagomba chief
from the western Dagbani-speaking area; J. A. Braimah from
southern Gonja; Mumuni Bawumia, state secretary and adviser

[61] NTTC, *Minutes*, Jan. 1950.
[62] NTC *Memo. on Constitution Reform*, Mar. 1953.
[63] *Ashanti Pioneer*, 7 May 1954.
[64] The close connexion between the NPP and the NTC was obvious to anyone
who saw the party at work. Its first propaganda broadsheet gave, by an oversight,
the postal box number of the regional administration, which had allowed the NTC
to use one of its offices. (As a result the Council lost its office there, and went to the
Social and Cultural Centre.)

to the Na Yiri, the Mamprusi paramount; B. K. Adama and
Jato Kaleo from the western Wa chiefdom; Adam Amandi from
the north-east Kusasi district.[65] They had the support of traditional heads in their area, and they knew—none better—how
to make use of local divisions and ambitions. These very considerable advantages derived from an intimate knowledge
shared by the leaders of the local balance of forces in the different
chiefdoms and districts; but the NPP also learnt from its southern-
based rival, and the leaders adopted all the paraphernalia and
techniques of a mass party: a flag, a salute (a clenched fist), a
slogan ('United We Stand' or 'Unity'), the holding of rallies
wherever a large enough audience could be found, the use of
propaganda vans, and the sale of a membership card.

A second ally, both of the GCP and the NPP, was the Moslem
Association Party, formed among the 'Zongo' (immigrant)
peoples of the main towns. The Muslim connexion with Kumasi
in particular was an ancient one. Its leaders had served at the
Asantehene's court as scribes, traders, military advisers, and
teachers, until displaced in the nineteenth century by European
trade, missions (including mission schools), and political control.[66] Thus the Muslim communities saw themselves as a
minority whose earlier advantages had gone and whose remaining privileges were under attack, and a Gold Coast Muslim Association had been formed in 1932 as a welfare and social organization which exercised its influence through tribal unions and
marketing associations. The Muslims were not a united community, being divided between the French-speaking Zabrama[67]
people and the Hausa in Accra, and between the Gao[68] and
Hausa in Kumasi. And in 1950 the elderly, wealthy leaders of the
Association—led by Imam Abbas of Accra and Alhaji Amadu

---

[65] The first officers of this party were: chairman, Duori-Na; vice-chairman,
Mumuni Bawumia; general secretary, F. Derrimanu; propaganda secretary,
Imoru Salifu.

[66] See e.g. the interesting account, given by Dupuis (p. 95) of a conversation with
the 'Bashaw' or 'Caboceer' of the Muslims in Kumasi under the Asantehene Osei
Bonsu. 'My avocations at Coomassy', said the Bashaw, 'are several; but my chief
employment is a school which I have endowed and which I preside over myself.
God has compassionated my labours and I have about seventy pupils and converts
at this time. Besides this, the king's heart is turned towards me, and I am a fa-
foured servant. Over the Moslems, I rule as Cady, comformably to our law; I am
also a member of the king's council in affairs relating to the believers of Sarem and
Dagomba; and I trade with foreign countries through the agency of my friend Abu
Becr.' See also Wilks, *The Northern Factor*.

[67] From Upper Volta.   [68] From the Soudan (now Mali).

Baba, Zerikin Zongo in Kumasi—were opposed by a Muslim Youth Congress, led by Z. Shardow in Accra and Mallam Muta- wakilu, the CPP joint constituency chairman in Kumasi.[69] Sep- tember 1953, however, saw the first direct Muslim participation in politics in the Accra municipal elections. (The immediate cause lay in the extension of the franchise in local-government elections to the immigrant communities, whether they came from French or British territories.) The Muslim Association sponsored seven candidates in the Zongo wards, won 2 of the 27 seats on the municipal council, and a seventh of the total vote. It repeated its challenge in February 1954 in the Kumasi Town Council elec- tions: again 7 candidates were put up and 4 were successful in the 24 wards. The following month it contested the Sekondi-Takora- di municipal elections with three candidates: none was suc- cessful but (as in Kumasi) its candidates won a sixth of the vote.[70]

The Muslim Association became the Moslem Association Party early in 1954, and was violently anti-CPP. 'True Moslems can never be friends with the CPP. The Moslem Association is prepared to hold the devil by the throat until everybody is free in this country', Alfai Larden, chairman of the Kumasi branch of the party, wrote to the *Ashanti Pioneer*,[71] thus demonstrating again the narrowing circle of definition of self-government. The leaders were anti-CPP on a number of grounds. They were on the side of age and traditional authority, whereas it seemed clear in 1953–4 that the CPP was not—indeed, it had sponsored a Mus- lim Youth Congress in opposition to the Association. In particu- lar, a large number of Moslems resented the restrictions placed

[69] The Muslim community in Kumasi was locally divided over the building of a new mosque which led to fierce quarrels. The protagonists were the Hausa leader, Alhaji Amadu Baba, and Mallam Mutawakilu of the MYC. 'The aims and objects of the so-called Congress are treacherous and do not in any way seek the welfare of the Zongo community and we condemn it outright', said a letter in the *Ashanti Pioneer* in Oct. 1953, purporting to come from the Kumasi Zongo Volunteers (a free-lance vigilant organization which was very active in 1948–9 when Kumasi was troubled by armed gangs of thieves), the Zongo sheep sellers, the Kumasi Motor Drivers, the Arabic Students' Union, and 34 tribal heads. Mutawakilu was on to a good thing, however, when he began to criticize the collection and safe- keeping of the mosque fund, collected largely from the butchers in Kumasi, and held by Alhaji Amadu Baba.

[70] The figures are given by J. H. Price in 'The Role of Islam in Gold Coast Politics', West African Inst. of Social & Economic Research, *Proc. of 3rd Ann. Conference, 1954* (Ibadan).

[71] 9 Jan. 1954. Both Alfai Larden and Alhaji Amadu Baba were deported in 1957.

by the CPP-controlled municipal councils on Moslem traders in the markets, in general, there was the suspicion that minority communities, especially those which contained a high proportion of immigrants, would be roughly treated by a local nationalist party. The MAP was not a widely spread movement since its members were too thinly spread in the rural areas to provide an effective groundwork of organization; its leaders were also handicapped both by their foreign origin and by their inadequate grasp of English. [72] None the less, in the Zongo areas of the southern towns, where the Moslem community was strongly grouped, the rallying cry of 'Islam' was used with great effect to enlist support on behalf of a particular candidate, and the MAP was able to bring a useful militancy to the more gentle methods of the Congress Party.

The third challenge to the CPP came from the east, from the Togoland Congress. In sum, the arguments put forward in 1953–4 by S. G. Antor, its secretary-general, amounted to the demand for an Ewe homeland under Ewe control. The Congress opposed the integration of British Togoland with the Gold Coast and sought instead its unification with the neighbouring French trust territory to reconstitute in effect the boundaries of the former German colony. Its members were strengthened in their bid by the certain prospect that self-government for the Gold Coast would raise the problem of the future of the trust territory, but the arguments used by Antor and his followers also continued a long and complicated dispute among the Ewe-speaking peoples which went back some years before the formation of the CPP. [73] The dispute had taken shape between local associations like the Togoland Union, formed in 1943 by Kofi Dumoga and Victor Anku, and the different sections of the more powerful All-Ewe Conference, under Daniel Chapman and Ephraim Amu. The basic dilemma was easy to state. Ewe unity could be promoted by the integration of the British trust territory with the Gold Coast (thus confirming the existing administrative union between the

---

[72] The Muslims were therefore prepared to accept 'outside' leaders like the former CPP leader Bankole Renner in Accra and the Ashanti lawyer Cobina Kessie. The more western-educated Muslims belonged to the Ahmadiyya sect, but except in isolated districts (as in Wa in the north where tribal differences were mixed with Orthodox Maliki-Ahmadiyya differences, and both with CPP-NPP rivalries) the Ahmadiyya deliberately held aloof from politics.

[73] It is examined with great skill by J. S. Coleman in *Togoland*, a pamphlet published in 1956 by *International Conciliation* for the Carnegie Endowment.

two) but only at the expense of the Ewe under French rule. Or it might be promoted (through agitation at the United Nations) by the unification of the two halves of the trust territory, but only at the expense of the large number of Ewe who lived in the south of the Gold Coast. The difficulty was how to decide which of these policies was the most likely to achieve the ultimate union of all sections of this energetic and able people—and under whose auspices. But the Ewe under British rule were also divided by fierce disputes among themselves. Thus the Anlo Ewe in the south-east of the Gold Coast, whose local capital town was the coastal trading centre, Keta, were closely related by common trading interests, marriage, and kinship to the Ewe groups in and around Lomé, capital of French Togoland. But they were greatly distrusted by the Ewe of the British trust territory to the north who feared, and were resentful of, the greater progress made by their more sophisticated, better-educated, wealthier kinsmen. (Gbedemah and Chapman were two of a number of such leaders from the Keta-Anlo area). Even the Ewe in the trust territory were divided among themselves, and from their kinsmen immediately to the west of the trusteeship border, by quarrels arising over land ownership or ancient, traditional animosities. The conflict between these several Ewe communities had come to head some time between 1947, when a meeting at Tsito, a small town just outside the trust territory, proved to be the last amicable conference between the leaders, and 1949, when a further meeting at Borada, a town in the trust territory, ended in disarray. As J. W. K. Dumoga was later to comment: 'such was the confusion [at Borada] that when a Committee was appointed after the meeting to draft some resolutions nobody knew exactly what it was they wanted to do'[74]—a confusion which was common in Ewe politics and did much to explain why the CPP, which knew what it wanted, was able to divide its opponents. It was after the Borada conference, however, that the Togoland Union merged with a Togoland Youth Conference, a Farmers' Union and the 'United Nations Association of Togoland'—each under Ewe control—to form the 'Togoland Congress'.

How strong was the Togoland Congress in 1953–4? Its appeal

[74] The quotation comes from a series of articles on the Togoland question in the *Ashanti Pioneer* (Sept.–Oct. 1953) by 'Brother Culture' (=J. W. K. Dumoga, Kofi Dumoga's brother).

was limited, since its declared aim—the reunification of the two Togolands—was open to a number of objections. It was not easy, for example, to see why the frontiers of a former German colony should be regarded with such affection as a possible homeland. Admittedly the Ewe were not the only people to be divided by the Anglo-French boundary, for the Chakosi, Kotokoli, and B'Moba in the north also spread eastwards into the French trust territory; but examples of this kind were outnumbered by the chiefdoms and tribal communities which had been divided by the Anglo-German frontier of 1886 and reunited after the First World War. Thus the Togoland Congress was opposed on the basic issue of unification-integration by the Northern People's Party (in other respects, its anti-CPP ally) whose leaders wished to retain the administrative unity of the Gold Coast and British Togoland. The position in the northern area may be illustrated as follows:

| | ←── INTEGRATION ──→ | | |
| | | ←── UNIFICATION ──→ | |
	Gold Coast North	*British North Togoland*	*French North Togoland*
B'Moba	1,600	29,200	54,200
Chakosi	500	10,200	8,900
Kotokoli	13,300	7,000	51,500
Dagomba/ Nanumba	130,600	41,700	..
Kusasi	70,700	22,400	..
Busanga	19,800	7,500	..

.. = None recorded.

Source: Figures from Spec. Report on the Togoland Unification Problem, *TCOR*, 5th gen. sess., Oct. 1955.

In the second place, as a number of the All-Ewe Conference leaders had argued, a unification of the two Togolands would mean that the Ewe-speaking states of the two trust territories would then be divided from the large Ewe communities in the south-east of the Gold Coast (in the Tongu and Anlo states and the coastal trading town of Keta):

	←——— INTEGRATION ———→	
		←——— UNIFICATION ———→
	Gold Coast Colony	*British Southern Togoland*	*French Southern Togoland*
Ewe & allied groups	376,000	137,000	369,000

Source: Figures from Spec. Report on the Togoland Unification
    Problem, *TCOR*, 5th gen. sess., Oct. 1955.

Thirdly, even in the southern half of the British trust territory, the
Ewe were only one (though the largest) among a number of other
communities, including not only the small Togoland remnant
tribes but immigrants (mainly Akan-speaking) from the Gold
Coast, whose ties were still with kinship groups in Ashanti and
the Colony. Thus the population statistics for southern British
Togoland showed that out of a total of 232,000 only 139,000
were Ewe.[75]

Fourthly, it was difficult in 1953 to see the unificationist movement as having any hope of success. French rule, if not irremoveable, at least seemed able to resist any challenge short of a
united effort by the Gold Coast and the people of both trust territories. Hence the persuasive nature of the CPP argument which
stressed the need for a united, independent Gold Coast and
(British) Togoland as a first stage in the struggle to liberate
(French) Togoland.[76]

None of these arguments swayed the leaders of the Togoland
Congress. Strongly conscious of their own communal ties, they
saw each move of the CPP government as part of a slow smothering of Ewe national identity. The fierce temper of the propaganda
used may be seen in an early issue of the pro-Congress *Togo-*

[75] *TCOR*, 5th spec. sess., 24 Oct.–14 Dec. 1955, suppl. 2.
[76] The most active nationalist party in Togo was the Comité de l'Unité Togolaise.
It was formed initially by Montaigne (Commissaire de la République) in 1939 to
counter Nazi claims for a restitution of the colony to Germany. It was reshaped in
1941 by Augustino de Souza and Sylvanus Olympio, when it lost all official connexion. In the immediate post-war years Sylvanus Olympio was also an active
member of the All-Ewe Conference and supported the demand for Ewe unity. By
early 1951, however, he and other Togoland Ewe leaders had swung round in
support of unification.

land Vanguard (for 12 October 1951) during its brief existence:

It seems that the present Gold Coast is out more for territorial aggrandisement than for self-government. Togolanders are not against the restoration of the lost Ghana Empire provided she [Togoland] would be given her place as a separate country in West Africa, such as Gambia would have, when the whole of West Africa or Africa becomes a federal state. In short Togoland could Federate with the Gold Coast but not to be Annexed.... [But] Togoland has become a double slave to the Gold Coast people and a slave to the Administering Authorities.

Togolanders! please gird your loins.... Gold Coasters! Keep out of the way for us to fight for our own rights.... Don't obstruct or you will be termed Black Imperialists avid for the acquisition of colonies!

Early in 1953 the Congress leaders were presented with a useful piece of propaganda. A 'most secret document' fell into their hands, with the title 'The Future of Togoland under United Kingdom Trusteeship'. Supposedly (and most probably) drawn up by the CPP, the document set out ways 'to ensure that the Territory emerges from its Trust Status not later than the Gold Coast attains full self-government and that it becomes an integral part of a self-governing Gold Coast'. The means to be employed were the presentation of petitions to the United Nations by selected pro-CPP Ewe representatives, generous financial subsidies for the development of the territory, and a vigorous campaign to secure places for CPP members on the newly established local authorities. There was nothing in the document that was not known about CPP intentions but its publication by Antor caused a stir among local politicians and excited Ewe opinion in the trust territory. The Congress leaders called it a 'vulgar and treacherous document' and protested volubly to the United Nations Trusteeship Council. Its effect, however, was wholly to their advantage since it stiffened support for Congress candidates in the 1954 election, and embarrassed those who hoped to stand for the CPP.[77]

Presented with this catalogue of difficulties which faced the government on the eve of the second general election, the reader

---

[77] A parallel appeared in 1960 when the Ghana government produced a secret document which contained a map of the independent Togo republic enlarged by the detachment from Ghana of its Ewe-speaking areas. Responsibility for its authorship was denied by Olympio's government in Lomé which announced that the document was the unauthorized work of a Togolese official in Paris.

may marvel at the fortitude with which the CPP went on its way. The heroic role played by the leaders in 1949–50 was increasingly difficult to sustain as they sat in their ministerial offices; many were corrupt, none (from the Prime Minister to the local party officials) had emerged unscathed from the Korsah Commission *Report* on Braimah's resignation. The leaders were under attack from rebel candidates in the constituency executives, the party as a whole was challenged by the opposition alliance of the Ghana Congress Party, the NPP, the MAP, and the Togoland Congress. Yet the ruling party retained a number of very great advantages. In the first place, Self-Government was still a rallying cry. Indeed, the very sight of the large houses and cars owned by the ministers and party executives was a token of the more generous (and more widely distributed) benefits that it was hoped would follow independence. And although the charges of corruption levelled at the CPP leaders were generally accepted as valid, they did not offend the public at large to anything like the extent the opposition hoped. Secondly, wealth (in Ghana) did not necessarily bestow status: the CPP was still a commoners' party. Despite their houses and cars, its leaders had not ceased to talk the language of the village market and the urban housing estate; their appeal to the ordinary man for support still carried weight —particularly in view of the renewed activities of the small intelligentsia group and their conservative-looking allies. Thirdly, the CPP had the advantage of its three and a half years in office— an asset of inestimable benefit which invested the leaders with all the authority of a successor government, and many who had no particular love or distaste for the party were prepared to accept its rule as an established fact. The change was noticeable in the attitude of the officials. They now looked kindly on the CPP as the only organization to which power might conceivably be entrusted, and it was they who urged on Nkrumah the need to bring to a conclusion negotiations for the continued employment of overseas officers in the public service, the establishment of a local Ghana army, and the ending of the United Kingdom trusteeship over Togoland. Thus the stage had been reached when the nationalist leaders, the colonial officers, and the United Kingdom government were all in agreement, and when the forthcoming election was seen as the last act of an unexpected partnership which thereafter (it was assumed) would be dissolved.

A NOTE ON PARTY MEMBERSHIP

The broad social base of the CPP during these years may be illustrated quite simply, first by an analysis of its representatives in the Assembly, secondly by examining the membership of a typical rural constituency executive:

CPP Assembly Members, 1951: Age & Education

	Age at 31 Dec. 1950	Education		
		University	Secondary or 4-year teacher training	Elementary (Std VII)
Ministers (6)	44·5	5	1	–
Ministerial secretaries (10)	34·2	1	7	2
Other Assembly members (23)	36·7	2	5	16

NOTE: The CPP had 39 party members—34 by election from constituency seats, plus Dr Ansah Koi, the Rev. Fiawoo, and F. Y. Asare elected from the territorial councils, and Ayarna Imoru and Ayeebo Asumda from the north.

CPP Assembly Members, 1951: Occupation

	Ministers (6)	Ministerial secretaries (10)	Other Assembly members (23)
Lawyer/doctor	3		
Businessman	1		
Teachers:			
Secondary school	1	3	
Elementary school		1	3
Politician/journalists	1		1
Store-keepers/traders		2	8
Clerks			3
Ministers of Religion			2
N.A. employees		2	
Pharmacists		2	2
Letter-writers			2
Locomotive driver			1
Stage artist			1
	6	10	23

Thus the CPP leaders were well able to lead a People's Party. By local standards, the ministers, ministerial secretaries, and Assembly members were well above the national level of education: they were those who had not only completed the full range of infant-junior and senior-primary schooling but (a third of them) had obtained some form of higher education. Nevertheless, they were still only the more fortunate among the broad stratum of elementary-school-leavers, and the list of occupations showed very clearly the 'common man' basis to the CPP. The table above is not wholly accurate. It would have been impossible to give any detailed account of the occupations of many of the leading CPP figures, for many had held a bewildering number of jobs: e.g. J. K. Donkor from Kumasi—an ex-clerk, ex-public letter-writer, ex-debt collector, ex-native-authority policeman, who in 1950 managed a 'house and property agency' and a small trading bar in Ashanti New Town. Many of the store-keepers had spent some time as teachers, many of the teachers had petty-trading interests on the side; E. K. Dadson of the comedy stage team (the Axim Trio) also owned a small printing press in Tarkwa.[78] This willingness to experiment in finding a livelihood was reflected in the range of interests that the assembly members laid claim to: J. E. Hagan, for example, who was educated for ten years in a Catholic primary school and then up to the fourth form at Adisadel College, Cape Coast, stated that he was 'interested in commerce, transport, politics, football, socialism, international brotherhood, history and citizenship'.[79] Few of them had held office in any native administration; few of them, before 1951, would have been considered (in local parlance) as 'big men' in terms of wealth or prestige.[80] Indeed, in so far as they were known at all, it was as 'agitators' or 'malcontents' within a local youth association, active in any attempt to destool the chief or to investigate the running

---

[78] A vocational eclecticism was true of many; e.g. K. A. Gbedemah, who taught science at a secondary school (Accra Academy) 1939–43, started a sweet factory, ran a timber and transport business, and was a contractor in a small way until 1948 when he became a 'professional politician and journalist'; e.g. J. A. Ayinibisa from the north who went to the Tamale Middle Boarding School, and became an 'Interpreter, Registrar, Treasurer, Store keeper, Miner, Farmer, Carpenter, Bicycle Repairer, Painter, Grass-Weaver, mason and roofer' [information supplied by Members of the Assembly to the Speaker's Office].

[79] In 1950 he was president of the Ogua (Cape Coast) Youth Association, President of the Catholic Youth Association, Treasurer of the Cape Coast Football Association, founder-member of the UGCC in 1948 and of the CPP in 1949, Cape Coast branch. He was also a store-keeper for the Swiss Union Trading Company and a petty trader.

[80] There were one or two exceptions. The Rev. Fiawoo (a CPP territorial council representative) and the Rev. Osabutey Aguedze were experienced headmasters and respected pastors of their church. J. E. Jantuah was at one time assistant secretary of the Asanteman Council with a Cambridge School Certificate (1941), a Teacher's Certificate (1944), and a two-year diploma course at Oxford (1946–8).

of the native-authority treasury. The relatively large number of petty traders (and of those with trading interests of one kind or another) followed from this: to manage a small provision store (in which the biggest turnover was in cheap medicines) was the easiest way to earn an independent livelihood.

To see the popular base to the party at its broadest extent it was necessary to go into the constituencies, to a rural area such as Amansie East where the party had already spread out from the market town, Bekwai, into the surrounding villages. In 1954 the constituency executive consisted of twenty-four members drawn from branches based on the new local-authority areas which, in turn, were based on the traditional chiefdoms and sub-chiefdoms of the district. The membership was as shown in the table overleaf.

The average age of the members was between 35 and 45 with a good number above 45; the officers were considerably younger than the ordinary members. (These were general statements, age being a hazy computation by individuals from events that had happened in their early years.) All but two were Ashanti, and although there were a number of 'strangers' in the Amansie—Fanti teachers and clerks, northern labourers on the cocoa farms—party leadership in the constituency was firmly in Ashanti hands.[81]

What did the executive do between 1951 and 1954 in such an area? It was supposed to meet in Bekwai once a month, but it did not usually achieve this; the average number of meetings was seven or eight in a year, the members paying their own travelling expenses when they could not persuade the constituency treasurer to disburse part of the small fund kept for headquarters expenses. The executive officers kept a close watch on matters affecting the chief and his councillors, and on

---

[81] The position was different in the southern wards of the Kumasi municipality, where a majority of the constituency officers were non-Ashanti:

Kumasi South Constituency Executive, 1954

	Occupation	Origin	Education	Age
Chairman	Master carpenter ⎫	Fanti	Self-educated	52
Vice-Chairman	Clerical worker ⎭		Std 7	40
Secretary	Councillor	Ashanti ⎫		28
Asst. Secretary	Clerk	Ashanti ⎬	Std 7	37
Treasurer	Councillor	Ashanti ⎭		38
Propaganda Sec.	Petty trader	Fanti	Std 3	36
Leader of Women's Section	Trader, leader of the plantain sellers	Banda	Illiterate	32

CPP Constituency Executive Amansie East

Office	Occupation	Education
1. Chairman	Bar keeper & contractor	Std 7
2. Vice-Chairman	Cocoa factor	Std 7 plus 1-year secondary
3. Secretary	Letter-writer	Std 7
4. Asst. Secretary	No permanent job	
5. Propaganda Secretary[1]	Teacher	4-year teacher training, Achimota
6. Treasurer	Cocoa factor	Std 7
7. Committee member	Cocoa broker	Illiterate
8. ,, ,,	Driver	Std 7
9. ,, ,,	Petty trader	Std 3
10. ,, ,, [2]	Cocoa farmer	Std 7
11. ,, ,,		Illiterate
12. ,, ,,	Cocoa broker/farmer	Std 7
13. ,, ,,	Cocoa broker	
14. ,, ,,	Sand & gravel contractor	Std 3
15. ,, ,,	Chief farmer (local president of Farmers' Association)	Illiterate
16. ,, ,,	General farmer	Illiterate
17. ,, ,,	Clerk, District Council Treasurer	Std 7 & local govt school
18. ,, ,,	Cocoa broker	Illiterate
19. ,, ,,	Driver	Std 7
20. ,, ,,	Food farmer	Illiterate
21. ,, ,, [3]	Contractor	Std 3
22. ,, ,,	Teacher	2-year teacher training
23. ,, ,,	Goldsmith	Std 7
24. ,, ,,	Member Legislative Assembly	

[1] D. C. Addae, who resigned in 1954 and joined the (Ashanti) NLM and, later, the United Party.

[2] Kodjo Fordwo, who was later suspended by the executive when he opposed its policy in the destoolment case against the Kokofuhene.

[3] Kwaku Appiah, a local contractor from the small nearby town of Amoaful, well-known as generous supporter of the party, who donated a propaganda van to the constituency in 1954—hence his nickname 'Kasserdjian Appiah' after the wealthy Armenian contractor—a largely self-educated man of about 40 (in 1954).

local development schemes formulated by an advisory committee to the Government Agent, but their main concern was with the elections to the new local and district authorities.[82] (Through its control of a majority of local councils, the party won 23 of the 37 seats on the Amansie District Council.) The officers were also busy extending the network of party contacts through which they liked to work. Party organization seemed slipshod, particularly by 1952–3, when dues were infrequently paid or, if paid, never reached the constituency treasurer, but appearances were often deceptive: there seemed to be a Ghanaian way of doing things which, incomprehensible in theory, often worked in practice, and in regular visits to Bekwai the writer ceased to marvel at the apparently haphazard way in which affairs were conducted. Much was done through 'association'. Thus the constituency secretary was a member of a number of local bodies (also ill run, so far as one could judge) grouped around the party— the Youth Movement, the Cocoa Farmers' Union, the Rice Farmers' Association, the Drivers' Union—and by these means he and others were kept responsive to local opinion. It was this sensitivity to local opinion, however, which constituted the main threat to the party. The Amansie executive could translate into homely terms what the party stood for and, from time to time, what the national headquarters thought ought to be done, but they were also open to all the stresses and divisions of Amansie society.[83]

[82] Pressure on the party from local opinion was often effective. In January 1953 the party forced the resignation of its councillors in Kokofu because of strong feeling in the district over the proposal to increase the local levy from 15s. to £2 10s.

[83] A particular example may help to illustrate the quarrels that were endemic in Amansie society. In 1950 branches of a People's Educational Association were opened in three main towns, Bekwai, Essumeja, Kokofu, and the members agreed to support a joint extra-mural class in Bekwai. It was not very successful (partly because of the dispute between the Bekwai State Improvement Society and the Youth Movement) and the teachers, clerks, and traders who attended from Essumeja (three miles away) and Kokofu (five miles away) proposed to transfer the class to the main centres of interest. Eventually this was done, but at a price: the Bekwai minority fell away completely, and the new class had to be held on alternative weeks in Essumeja and Kokofu, to avoid a further split.

V

The 1954 Election

THE second general election was to disappoint a great many hopes. Intended (by the CPP, the colonial officials, and the United Kingdom government) to open the way for the final grant of independence it resulted in further conflict, not only between the CPP and the alliance of local opposition groups, but within the nationalist party itself. The election stood thus at a turning-point in the fortunes of the CPP, looking back to the early years of single-party rule after 1951, and forward to the violent quarrels of the pre-independence period. It was also further proof of the delicate balance in Ghanaian society between national and local interests, in which, hitherto, the emphasis had been on the larger, general issue of independence. But whereas a period of nationalist agitation may unite a colony in the early stages of its struggles, an election designed to produce a sovereign government is likely to lead to fierce local disputes. And so it proved in the Gold Coast between May and June 1954.

Neither the CPP nor the officials foresaw the danger. So sure were the party leaders that the nationalist struggle was drawing to an end that they turned to wider horizons. They announced a new destiny for the party—to implement a pan-African programme whereby the rest of the continent would be liberated from British, French, and Portuguese rule, and then united. At the end of 1953 a meeting of West African nationalists in Kumasi called for the creation of 'a strong and truly federal state [of West Africa] capable of protecting itself from outside invasion and able to preserve its internal security';[1] and early in 1954 the *Evening News* began an intensive campaign of propaganda, stressing Nkrumah's pre-eminence not merely as a national, but as an African, leader. The same air of optimism governed British

[1] The Kumasi meeting during the week-end of 7 and 8 December was not well attended: but it included Dr Azikiwe, Mrs Ransome Kuti, Chief H. O. Davies, and Mallam Aminu Kano from Nigeria, W. F. Conton as an *ex parte* representative from Sierra Leone, and a journalist from Liberia. The final statement incor-

thinking. The Gold Coast officials and the United Kingdom government were hardly likely to endorse every item in the nationalist programme. But they too were confident that the transfer of power would be effected without much difficulty if (as seemed likely) the CPP were to repeat in a second general election its 1951 success. A precise timetable for the transfer was impossible, since it was not yet clear what conclusions the United Nations General Assembly would reach concerning the future of the Togoland trust territory.[2] But a breathing space after the election would not come amiss either for the CPP or the officials. Nkrumah needed to reassert a closer control over the party: the administration required a limited period for the orderly transfer of the Governor's discretionary powers. In the meantime it was agreed between the Gold Coast and United Kingdom governments that an interim measure should be introduced, and in April 1954 a new Order in Council was promulgated to provide for the grant of full, internal self-government as a 'final stage' before independence.[3]

It was at this point, however, that the CPP began to falter, and a dangerous quarrel developed over the nomination of candidates as local interests were asserted in defiance of the authority of the central committee. The leaders sought desperately to steady the party, but despite the urgency of their appeal to nationalist loyalties, despite, too, the chorus of praise for Nkrumah as 'Africa's Man of Destiny', the unpleasant fact remained that (as the date of the election approached) the nationalist party was deeply divided. Its constituency executives split into warring groups, and 'rebel candidates' appeared. An unexpected oppor-

---

porated a resolution that a West African state should 'identify itself with the Commonwealth of Nations': but this early attempt at a pan-African meeting on African soil took place before the sudden rush of independent French-speaking states in 1960.

[2] The UN Trusteeship Committee discussed the Togoland problem in November 1953, and heard petitioners from British and French Togoland, most of whom were opposed to integration with the Gold Coast. A resolution was then adopted, sponsored by Brazil, India, Indonesia, Liberia, the Philippines, and Syria, which declared that a decision on British Togoland should not take place until after the French and British territories had 'attained self-government or independence'. The UK representative, Mathieson, spoke strongly in favour of integration, an advocacy which may have upset the anti-colonial countries. The following year, however, the Trusteeship Committee changed its mind.

[3] The Gold Coast (Constitution) Order in Council, S.I. 1954, No. 551. The new constitution provided for the progressive reduction and transfer of the Governor's discretionary powers, partly to the prime minister, partly to a Gold Coast Public Service Commission, and Judicial Service Commission.

tunity was thus afforded the opposition parties. And, heartened
by the prospect of division within the enemy's ranks, they hastened to strengthen their bid to rescue the country 'from the degradation and ruin which threaten it as a result of the inefficient,
incompetent, nepotic, corrupt and nefarious Government of the
CPP'.[4]

Before turning to these conflicts, something must be said of the
electoral framework within which they took place. The decision
to hold a second general election called for a further effort by the
administration, and a useful starting-point for a brief survey of
the problems involved was the fourth term of reference given the
Van Lare Commission on Electoral Reform: 'the division of the
Gold Coast into approximately one-hundred-and-three electoral
districts, comprising: (*a*) approximately seven municipal districts . . . and (*b*) approximately ninety-six rural electoral districts'.[5]

THE DELIMITATION OF CONSTITUENCIES

Some of the problems raised by the delimitation of constituencies in 1953 have already been discussed, in particular the demand put forward by Ashanti for thirty seats. That the Ashanti
case was only one of many similar grievances may be seen from
the (Van Lare) *Report*. When the Commissioners considered the
task of sweeping away the multiplicity of primary electoral
boundaries, and replacing them with single-member constituencies throughout the country, they moved cautiously. Particular
districts were excluded from, or included in, a constituency 'at
the express request of those concerned', and there was no rigid
adherence to the principle of parity of population between electoral districts. The Builsa constituency, in the extreme north of the
Northern Territories, was allowed to rise to over 51,000 inhabitants, while Tumu (its neighbouring constituency) fell to 30,000 so
as to preserve the linguistic and traditional distinction between the
Builsa and Tumu (Sissala) peoples. Wenchi West in Ashanti, with
its thinly populated outlying districts, numbered 32,000; Amansie
East was a compact area with a good network of roads, and the
number went up to over 50,000. Similar examples of the care

[4] 'Joint Declaration' by the GCP, MAP, NPP, Togoland, and other minor
political groups in May 1954 (*Ashanti Pioneer*, 9 May 1954).
[5] Sess. Paper no. 1 of 1953. The Commission increased the number of rural
constituencies to 97, making the total 104.

taken to observe traditional state boundaries could be found throughout the country to show that the strength of local feeling was hardly less after the first general election than before it. Indeed, as was clear from the Aowin state protest quoted earlier, local interests had been stimulated by the prospect of a greater number of representatives in a National Assembly. The task of the Van Lare Commission was somewhat easier than that of its predecessor, however, if only because it had over a hundred constituencies to delimit, and could therefore satisfy a greater number of local interests. It was thus able to arrive at a greater uniformity in size of population between the new electoral districts. The average population of each rural constituency was now 39,218: the largest, Ahanta-Shama in the Colony, had 53,006; the smallest, Ho East in Trans-Volta, had 30,055. (The Cape Coast municipal constituency was slightly smaller with 29,571.) The range was only 23,000, compared with over 93,000 in 1950, and of the total of 97 rural constituencies, 47, or nearly half, fell within the range of 10 per cent above or below the overall average.

The 104 constituencies demarcated in this way carried the country through the two general elections of 1954 and 1956 and the 1960 plebiscite. But although they reflected the CPP government's belief in equality and uniformity, neither of these qualities was evident in the party's attitude towards the Commission's recommendations on the qualifications of electors and candidates:

Qualifications:

In general terms, the qualifications required in 1954 were the same as those needed in 1950:
  (a) A British subject or British-protected person or anyone serving in the armed forces or the police. Aged 21 or over.
  (b) Ownership of immovable property or six months residence in the ward in respect of which the application is made.
  (c) Payment of the 'basic rate' unless specifically exempt.

Disqualifications:

  (a) Being sentenced to death or imprisonment for a term exceeding twelve months or convicted of any offence involving dishonesty within the previous five years.
  (b) Being a lunatic.

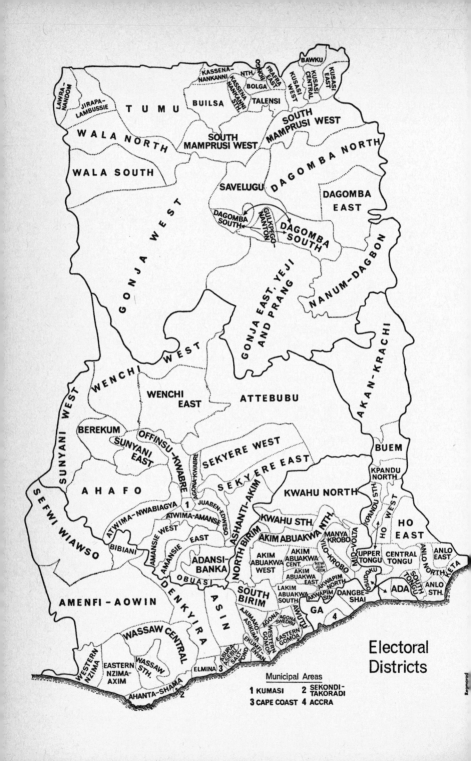

Electoral Districts

Municipal Areas
1 KUMASI
2 SEKONDI-TAKORADI
3 CAPE COAST
4 ACCRA

(c) Being convicted of any offence in connexion with elections.

(d) Being a registered voter in any other constituency.

The surprising feature was the retention of the basic-rate qualification—justified by the Van Lare Commission on the grounds that 'the rate payment is generally understood and accepted and we consider that this proof of civic responsibility ... is desirable and justified'. The CPP government not only approved this limitation on the qualifications for electors, but imposed others of its own on those suggested for candidates. The Van Lare *Report* recommended that the age-limit for candidates should be brought into line with that for electors and lowered to 21 years and over, but despite the emphasis by the party on youth, despite too the fact that the younger party members (like Kofi Baako) had been ineligible to stand in 1951 and were only just eligible in 1954, Nkrumah refused to accept the Commission's recommendation. He gave his reasons in the Assembly.

> The Government in considering this question took note of the customary position of persons aged 21 in the community, that at that age they were not necessarily mature members of the community and were not in fact so regarded. It is amazing how much these few years make in bringing an adult to maturity.[6]

These were unexpected sentiments from the former organizer of the CYO, but the minimum age qualification of 25 years for candidates was retained and was still there—as late as 1960.[7]

Two other matters troubled the Van Lare Commission when it discussed the qualifications of candidates. One was the question of residence. The Commissioners decided in general terms that, although a prospective candidate needed to qualify as an elector, he should also be free to file his nomination papers wherever he wished, and the subsequent Electoral Provisions Ordinance tried to meet this vague requirement. It failed, however, to make it clear whether a candidate should actually be enrolled as an elector or merely entitled to enrol, and the issue was put to test a little before the June election. A petition was brought against Nkrumah's and Gbedemah's candidature on the grounds that they had registered in the ward of the Accra municipality which

[6] GC, LA Deb., 6 Nov. 1953.

[7] Candidates also had to be literate in English. The 25 years minimum-age qualification was another illustration of the confusion inherent in the expression—the 'young men'.

contained the party's headquarters, instead of in the ward where they resided; the petition was admitted, and their names were struck off the electoral register. Neither, therefore, was able to vote in the elections—a humiliation which might have been more serious had the Supreme Court not also ruled that their disqualification as electors did not prevent them from standing as candidates. In theory, then, a candidate was free to stand not only where he wished but with the minimum of preparation. In practice, the number of non-local candidates was very small: no non-northerner could hope to succeed in the north, no non-Ashanti in the rural areas of that region, and an Ashanti would be unacceptable in the south. Only the candidates in the large towns—Nkrumah (from the Nzima district) in Accra Central, Casely Hayford (from Cape Coast) in Kumasi South—could appeal to a population sufficiently mixed to enable national interests to supersede local loyalties.[8]

The other issue that puzzled the Commission was the vexed question of chiefs. There were to be no 'territorial members' from the regional councils of chiefs in the new legislature, and no second chamber. Should a chief not have the right to stand in a constituency? It might be unwise—and Nana Ofori Atta declared that he would not even consider standing for election—but should it be illegal? The difficulty was thought to be not the danger to chieftaincy from chiefs being subject to party attack in the constituencies, but the possibility of intimidation: a chief had 'a special authority over his subjects which might be used to influence them to vote on his behalf'. On the other hand, he would probably do so anyway behind the scenes, and the Commission found it difficult to define a chief. For example, should the Duori-Na, a sub-chief from the extreme north-west of the northern re-

---

[8] For more detailed examination of the position *vis-à-vis* local and non-local candidates see below, ch. VII. The Van Lare Commission had to consider a related problem when the CPP members—R. S. Iddrisu, G. K. Amegbe, C. F. Amoo-Gottfried, and S. A. Dzirasa—wanted the incorporation of a 'right of recall', defined by the Commission as meaning that a member who changed party sides in the Assembly should be obliged to resign and stand for re-election. The non-CPP members—W. B. Van Lare, S. D. Dombo (Duori-Na), J. Sarkodee-Addo, N. A. Ollennu—and the ex-CPP member Victor Owusu—thought that any such provision would be 'a dangerous and undemocratic procedure'. The CPP members added a minority rider to the *Report*, recommending the introduction of 'a right of recall' as 'an operative convention', which the government declined to accept. Had it been introduced, it would probably have worked to the disadvantage of the CPP in 1957 when many of the opposition members of parliament crossed to the government side.

gion and a member of the Van Lare Commission, be debarred? The members confessed themselves divided but eventually recommended that no provision should be made to disqualify a chief *qua* chief from being a candidate. This problem, too, was more difficult in theory than in practice, since the chiefs quickly learnt the lesson of the 1951 election: no paramount chief again stood for election, but instead they confined their partisanship to support for others.

REGISTRATION

In the re-registration carried out at the beginning of 1954 the overall figure rose by 10 per cent to just over half the adult population:

Est. population (mid-1954)	Aged 21 & over	Registered	Per[9] cent
4,535,500	2,376,602	1,225,603	50·4

As in 1950, the CPP canvassed energetically for support during the three weeks' registration period:

THE GAME HAS STARTED[10]

GHANAIANS, if you believe that the common men must rule this country; if you believe that you too have a right to live a free citizen although condemned and described by the Ghana Congress Party leaders as 'verandah boys', 'street boys', 'hooligans', 'strangers', and unfit for even the post of a messenger, then Register NOW!

Your wives, your cousins, your mothers, fathers, grandfathers and grandmothers, sisters, brothers, friends, comrades, fellow-workers MUST be registered. The Game has started. Play well your part. This

---

[9] These statistics are only approximate. The estimated population is taken from the *Digest of Statistics* for 1954. It includes non-Commonwealth, non-African immigrants not in the army or police; and these, according to the 1948 census, numbered about 3 per cent of the total African population. Those 21 and over in the *Digest* were given as being a little over 50 per cent, but this was doubtful: they were more likely to be under 50 per cent, for the young outnumber the old in most African countries. But the figures given here are a fair guide to the numbers actually participating in the election.

[10] There was a nice confusion of imagery in a similar passage from the *Evening News* at this time:

'A CALL TO THE PEOPLE

The Trumpet Sounds. The silent drums summon the broad masses of the people to register their names and win freedom once and for all for the beloved fatherland. Loud as a bell, the call vibrates in those sonorous tones so classically recorded in Captain Rattray's scholarly work "Ashanti". 104 Freedom! Register, Ghanaians!! The messages resound across the farthest reaches of the land like an oracle.'

is the turning point in African history. Be a pride to Ghana by Registering your Name on the List of Honour and VOTE FOR Convention People's Party for FREEDOM. Break your chains for all time! Down with imperialism for ever. Long live the Revolutionary Vanguard of the African Liberation Movement—Great CPP.

One last comment is needed on the electoral regulations and the preparations for the elections. When the Van Lare Commission looked at the actual method of voting it considered three possibilities: (1) 'marking the paper' by literates and (for illiterates) the 'whispering vote' used in 1951 in the direct elections in the municipalities; (2) the multiple-box system used in the rural primaries where the candidates' names and symbols were affixed to separate ballot boxes concealed behind a voting screen; and (3) the recommendation by the Ewart Committee (which had not been adopted) that electors, whether literate or illiterate, should put their mark in secret on ballot papers over-printed with the candidates' symbols and then 'post' them publicly in a single ballot box. The Commissioners disliked (1) because of the distinction it drew between literate and illiterate voters and the abondonment of secrecy involved in the 'whispering vote'. They rejected the third possibility because they believed that the number of 'shaky' and 'sprawling' crosses might be such 'as to render the ballot papers liable to challenge by counting agents'. They argued instead from the 'convenience of the voter', and declared the second of the three methods, the multiple-box system, was 'simple, easily understood, and reasonably safe from abuse'. Accordingly, the *Report* recommended that 'ballot papers should not be required to be marked by the voters [but] a separate box, clearly marked with the name, symbol and colour, should be provided for each candidate'. This was the Ghanaian—and British African—technique for adapting the franchise to a predominantly illiterate electorate.

The *Report* went farther than this. It said that 'there would be advantages in allocating symbols and colours to political parties for uniform use by their candidates throughout the country', and recommended that each candidate should be allocated 'a distinctive symbol on a coloured background at the time of the acceptance of his nomination'. Control by the national executive of each party over its candidates was usefully strengthened in this way, since those who wished to stand had to present a letter of authorization from the national headquarters to the returning officer before being allowed to use the party's symbol. The blanket use of a symbol meant, too, that the CPP (for example) could tell its supporters to 'vote for the red cock' for Kwame Nkrumah and independence, and indeed a simple election poster appeared throughout the country early in June which displayed a large coloured portrait of the Leader, the red cockerel symbol, the words 'Vote CPP to complete the job' and, at the bottom, a space for the insertion of the name of the local candidate.[11]

The CPP stood in need of help along these lines. When Nkrumah came to the 1954 election in his *Autobiography* (p. 208) he described how it

was with disappointment and anger . . . that I discovered that eighty-one party members had put themselves up to stand against official candidates. I called these people 'rebels'. Firm action had to be taken. It was vital that the Party should not be allowed to become disorganised or to be weakened by the split that this would ultimately bring about.

The comment touched the central feature of the election, and if a title were needed for this second contest it should be the 'Independents' Election'. Of the total of 323 standing for election, 160 were Independent candidates, or, to be exact, there were 160 candidates who did not stand under a symbol allocated to a party.

---

[11]   *Party symbols*   *Independents' symbols*

1954:

CPP =Red cockerel on white ground

MAP=Star and crescent, white on green ground

NPP =Clenched right fist in black on white ground. (Issued only in Northern Territories)

GCP =Blue elephant on white ground

Togoland Congress=yellow five-pointed star on white ground

Anlo Youth Organization=two crossed white keys on green ground. (Issued only in Keta and Anlo electoral districts)

Ghana Action Party=house crossed by red linguist stick on green background. (Issued only in Eastern Region)

Ghana Nationalist Party=black elephant on red ground. (Issued only in Accra Region)

Oman Party=yellow rising sun on blue ground. (Issued only in Cape Coast electoral districts)

1. White fish—blue ground

2. White butterfly—orange ground

3. White palmtree—red ground

4. White cooking pot—black ground

5. White house—yellow ground

6. White crossed paddles—blue-green ground (issued in coastal electoral districts only)

7. Yellow Jaguar car—white background

Some were 'Independent' in the generally accepted use of the word, and did not belong to any party, but well over half their number were CPP 'rebels' who had failed to get the party's nomination. The Independents were not confined to, or even concentrated in, a particular region. There were 36 out of a total of 80 candidates in the north alone, although the explanation in the more remote constituencies was the inability of the leaders of each little chiefdom to see the election in terms wider than their own local state. The overall position was as follows:

	Candidates of parties	Independents	Total	Seats
Colony	64	75	139	44
Ashanti	34	38	72	21
Trans-Volta	21	11	32	13
North	44	36	80	26
	163	160	323	104
(Municipalities)	(13)	(5)	(18)	(7)

NOTE: 'Parties' include the 2 candidates for the Anlo Youth Organization, and the 2 candidates (1 apiece) for the Ghana Action Party and the Ghana National Party.

Why were there so many Independents? The immediate explanation was a simple one. There were now 104 constituencies to be contested, an increase of 66 over the number in 1951; and the difficulty of selecting candidates divided the parties—the Ghana Congress Party and its allies as well as the CPP—in a large number of them. A stream of claims and objections flowed into the parties' headquarters. A choice was made, an objection lodged, the decision upheld (or, what was worse, changed) and the disappointed party member then stood as a 'rebel' Independent. The extraordinary readiness on the part of many candidates to believe that they had a reasonable chance of success usually owed something to the strong communal ties which bound many would-be candidates to a large family or clan group, these deceived them into thinking that, because they had a good following of some hundreds in their own district, it could be broadened into something much wider—of some thousands—in the constituency as a whole. But it must be remembered that this was only the second general election to be held in the country. In a narrower sense, it was the first country-wide election to be held by direct ballot in single-member, territorial constituencies; and the Aowin petition which had sought particular representation for a small tribal group was now reproduced in similar claims throughout the country in the hope of obtaining the party's nomination for a local candidate. A place in the new Assembly was a source of pride to a district. It also carried with it the hope of material benefits, not only for the successful candidate, but for the particular district in which he was born. For to have one's own village candidate elected could affect the siting of a local court, a district council headquarters, a new school, a borehole, a power station. In short, a candidate was an investment, and the dividends could be high. A number of these disputes between would-be candidates will be examined later, but it is sufficient here to state that, although the 1954 election might seem—and, in the long run, was—the narrow gate through which the country would pass to independence, its immediate effect at con-stituency level was to splinter the nationalist party into rival groups.

There was a further explanation of why this 'splintering' should have taken place. In the 1951 election, the battle lines had been clear, and the party leaders had been able to call for disci-pline in the struggle for national independence: but in mid-1954 it looked as if the conflict was over. Where, after all, was the enemy? The chiefs and the intelligentsia were discomforted; the British and the CPP had become negotiators.

The discussions which have led to the satisfactory settlement now reached [said the Minister of State for the Colonies, Henry Hopkin-son, in the House of Commons] have been cordial and constructive. It is proposed that a General Election should be held under the new Constitution in June. I am confident that when there is an All-African Government it will prove as friendly, co-operative and responsible as the present one. Under these changes, the powers retained by Her Majesty's Government are the minimum which they must retain so long as they have any responsibility for the Gold Coast. These changes must therefore be regarded as the last stage before the Gold Coast assumes full responsibility for its own affairs.[12]

---

[12] H.C. Deb., vol. 526, col. 1625, 28 April 1954. It was during this debate that the

Under this benign sky it was difficult for the CPP to persuade its
followers of the need for a strict discipline. Its appeal thus lacked
the emotion and urgency of 1950. It could hardly campaign once
again for 'Self-Government Now' and, instead, it devised the
clumsy phrase: 'to shorten the transitional period to independence'. No longer was there a martyred leader in prison: on the
contrary, he was now to be seen in his Cadillac—a change in the
party's fortunes which the *Ashanti Pioneer* of 8 January 1954 noted
sardonically:

the masses should be reminded that the CPP entered the Legislative
Assembly as tramps in N.T. smocks. Today, within barely three
years, they are riding not in buses, not even in taxis, but in luxurious
American saloon cars. A good number of them have built mansions
and go about in tails and toppers.

Whether this worried the 'masses' in 1954 as much as the readers
of the *Pioneer* would have liked may be doubted. Indeed, the picture drawn here of the new rulers helped to explain why there
should be so many candidates and claimants for the party's
nomination. Assembly membership carried with it a basic salary
of £960 a year, and there were many who thought that they, too,
deserved their 'tails and toppers'.

The CPP leaders tried to meet the danger of a growing complacency over the need for discipline by widening their propaganda. The election campaign was launched in military terms:
'Operation 104', and an attempt was made to strengthen the
threefold appeal of 1951 (the national aims, the bid for support
from the 'common man', and the promise of material benefits) by
adding a fourth element—the portrayal of Nkrumah as the
Leader, and the party as the instrument, of African redemption.
The four main points of CPP propaganda in 1954 may be seen in
extracts from their *Manifesto* and the *Evening News*:

I VOTE CPP TO COMPLETE THE JOB
How to Shorten Transition to Independence

The torch of independence now rests in our hands. It now depends
on the broad masses of people in this country, by voting into power a

---

distinction was drawn between 'full responsibility within the Commonwealth' and
'full membership of the Commonwealth', the former 'a matter for the United Kingdom Government and Parliament', and full membership of the Commonwealth
'a matter for consultation between all existing members of the Commonwealth'.
The distinction was drawn again in May 1956. The point is discussed briefly by
K. C. Wheare in his *Constitutional Structure of the Commonwealth* (1960), pp. 123-4.

national movement already committed to the achievement of independence by advanced political strategy, to shorten the transition between the proclamation of full internal Self-Government and complete Independence within the Commonwealth of Nations. This is the
real issue before the people of this country to decide at this critical
stage of our struggle.

II FORWARD WITH THE COMMON PEOPLE

... The advances made in the field of education stagger imagination.
The introduction of free primary education has doubled the school
population in two years! The University College has been expanded
and the College of Technology has been established at Kumasi. In all
these fields more has been done under its leader Kwame Nkrumah
than any previous Government.... But the semi-CPP Government has
done more than that ... the outlook of our people has changed out
of recognition. A spirit of liberty, of national consciousness, per-
vades the country, and the *Common People* have come to feel that they
are as good as the so-called aristocrats who have ignored and
despised them. ... In barely three years, Kwame Nkrumah has
changed the whole 'bogus and fraudulent' Coussey Constitution,
moulding it to accord with the advancement of the COMMON
PEOPLE.

III MATERIALISE YOUR DREAMS THROUGH
'OPERATION 104'

When we think of the glory that was Ghana and the splendour that
was Songai we are filled with enthusiasm to help in the struggle. ...
The wealth and opportunities of our country are bounteous and it is
our responsibility to join forces under 'Operation 104' to defend and
redeem ourselves. We are quite satisfied the Convention People's
Party has successfully fulfilled its mission. ... Given a further opportunity Kwame Nkrumah and his able lieutenants shall waste no time
in translating our dreams into realities. ..

These general promises of independence and prosperity were
reinforced with specific appeals to farmers, trade unionists,
market-women's groups, fishermen, and so on, in much the same
style as in 1951. The *Manifesto*, however, did not include any
specific guarantee to the cocoa farmers of a higher load price. Instead, it promised to 'give the cocoa industry—the basis of our
economy— ... all the attention and encouragement it deserved'. It promised loans, and a general programme of rural
welfare:

EVEN THE COCOA TREES WILL YIELD 104 FREEDOM
All Ghana Farmers Declare Faith in Nkrumah

Every Cocoa Farmer in this country knows that his destiny and the future of his great industry hinge on '104 Freedom' completely. Won under the banners of the common man's own CPP. Ask any farmer at all in this country and he will tell you. Our eyes have seen for the first time in history the Cocoa Marketing Board's 4,000 ton 'M.V. Virgo' the first of three ships chartered for carting our cocoa. The farmers' own organisation, CPC, will have 250 tons loading space allocated to it on this new ship. Not only that. Here is a resolution just passed by the United Ghana Farmers Council to Nkrumah:

That we assure you that once your government has been the first to give loans to farmers to extend and re-claim their pledged farms, we are going to register in our thousands and vote you and your men into power again, for we believe that with you as Prime Minister of this country, the needs of the Gold Coast farmers shall be fulfilled. . . . And so say all of us.

It was in order to strengthen this (by now) familiar propaganda that a fourth element began to be emphasized—the portrayal of Nkrumah as not merely the 'Hero of the revolution' but 'Africa's Man of Destiny'. The *Manifesto* itself appeared with Nkrumah's head superimposed on a map of the continent with the words: '*Our victory in the forthcoming General Election is Africa's hope*. We . . . are determined to be FREE and to use our position as a free independent sovereign state to help in the redemption of all Africa.'[13] A rally was held in Accra at the beginning of April to introduce the *Manifesto*; and in speeches and leaflets to mark

---

[13] OPERATION 104, p. 19. See too: 'A Soliloquy by Jehu Appiah':
    So Nkrumah is really the hero of Africa
    And who designed the cover of the CPP Manifesto,
    His heart on the South with his starry eyes
    Gazing over the four West African colonies—his mother land?
    Alas! Only the Gold Coast on the map is inserted
    But already, 'I am the monarch of all I survey', he has whispered
       in his mind.
The 'African Nkrumah' appeal was always part of the CPP, as the early editorials of the *Evening News* showed; but it grew in force as the country approached independence. It may be worth quoting here, however, from the *Evening News* the Christmas appeal of 1950 which was very much in the style of 1954 and the post 1957 period: 'Gird your loins in readiness for the crown that awaits us after this multitude of sacrifice and struggle. Kwame Nkrumah, the Messenger of Destiny, leads on before us like a Pillar of Fire. He is born to suffer and conquer through suffering. Lo, Brother Blackman, engaged in the fight against Man's inhumanity to man. You who peep across a thousand international frontiers on the continent to this budding Mecca of political autonomy! Watch Africa's greatest Hero. . . .'

the occasion, the role of Nkrumah and the CPP as the leaders of Africa was stressed again and again:

IV ALWAYS FIRST

The Convention People's Party took the lead in the struggle since June 1949 and has kept that lead.

Today the party is the hope of all Africa and the Black World; the party will continue fighting for African irredentism, till we too can live like free men in our own God given land.

Therefore Vote CPP in June 1954 and support Kwame Nkrumah to complete this NOBLE TASK.

There is VICTORY FOR US

FORWARD EVER, BACKWARD NEVER.[14]

Today the name of the Convention People's Party and of its great leader Kwame Nkrumah is world famous. . . Yes, the names . . . are the hope of FREEDOM to all oppressed peoples of Africa and of African descent everywhere, while on the other hand the slogan 'CPP-104 FREEDOM NKRUMAH' strikes fear, despondency and alarm in the hearts of tribalists, racialists, communalists, imperialists, and other reactionaries—white as well as black. . . . Now the GOAL IS IN SIGHT. It is only Kwame Nkrumah, the tried and experienced Captain, and his crew of 104 that can pilot the mighty ship 'GHANA' into the port of FREEDOM. . .

VOTE for KWAME and his dynamic CPP—the fighting Vanguard of the African Liberation Movement.

FORWARD TO VICTORY! 104—FREEDOM!![15]

This was the broad sweep of the election appeal which the party leaders placed before the electorate. Before it could reach the ordinary voter, however, it had to be taken up and re-broadcast by the outer ring of party members. The *Evening News* claimed to have a circulation in 1954 of 20,000, but even if a readership of three or four members to each copy sold is assumed, this was still far from a mass circulation, and in order to carry the electorate as a whole, the leaders had first to carry the constituency executives.[16] It was at this level that the first break in party

[14] 'Launching of Electioneering Campaign', 4 Apr. 1954. Party leaflet announcing a rally to introduce the manifesto.
[15] *Manifesto*, p. 4.
[16] The leaders failed to carry the Ashanti constituency executives in one important respect. The careful avoidance in the *Manifesto* of any promise to raise the cocoa price was not observed by many local branch members. In Amansie it was generally assumed that the election would be followed by a higher cocoa price, an assumption encouraged by local party propaganda. See below, pp. 253-4.

discipline occurred. It was not difficult to produce agreement on the demand for independence, or an enthusiastic response to the appeal for the liberation of Africa: but when it came to choosing between rival candidates for the party's nomination, the local branches and constituency executives found a great deal to divide them. It was fortunate that the country was small, and that the steady improvement in communications—roads, bridges, telephones, postal services—had brought Accra so much nearer in time to each constituency headquarters that it was possible for Nkrumah personally to visit over two-thirds of the 104 constituencies. It was even possible to bring all the rival candidates and their supporters to Accra for discussion. Nevertheless, by April 1954 the party began to divide into obstinate, local groups which remained unmoved by appeals for discipline and unity, and this unrest was communicated to the electorate as a whole.

Uneasy movements of dissent among the local executive members had already shown themselves during the Cape Coast by-election in June 1953, and again during the Kumasi municipal elections in February 1954; but, from the beginning of May, warnings against indiscipline, and appeals for unity in the forthcoming election, began to be sounded from the national headquarters in letters to constituency secretaries, and in the *Evening News*. Members were exhorted to stand firm, remain loyal and await their turn for reward:

Since our opponents are no problem to us, we must stress the necessity of maintaining strict Party discipline and a keen sense of mission and national responsibility within our ranks. The Assembly is not the only place for service of one's country. Those whose nominations fail to gain national approval should take it easy and remember that the destiny of their country, yea, of all Africa is entrusted to the great CPP. What the country needs today is a UNITED VOICE during the transition to complete independence. That is why the CPP MUST CAPTURE all the 104 seats and we shall not tolerate the treachery of blacklegs and traducers within and without the ranks of great CPP. Stand firm, Party members! Remember there is more beyond for all who will keep the faith and set the banner flying.
104 Freedom! 103 No Mistake!
Vote the Common Man's way to shorten the transitional period to independence.[17]

[17] 2 May 1954, repeated from time to time in different issues.

As the date of the election drew near—10 June in part of the north, and 15 June in the south and remaining districts of the north—the party's pronouncements grew more insistent and shrill. The number of claimants for the party's nominations at the beginning of May reached 1,005, and there would have been more, said the *Evening News*, 'if it had not turned out that some very staunch, qualified and able party members decided to withdraw'.[18] There was now a fierce scramble to get into the Assembly. And for the first time, the phrase 'election contractor' was heard—local agents for would-be candidates who undertook not merely the hard work of canvassing, but the delicate task of approaching members of the local constituency executive to incline them towards a particular applicant. It was no secret that many constituency executives were open to persuasion, or that the most effective form of persuasion was money. In 1954 this was regarded as an 'abnormal situation', and the national headquarters (directed by the central committee) acted promptly. It insisted that disputes should be fought out at the centre, and the constituency secretaries were told by Gbedemah to send to Accra not one or two names for the national executive to approve, or choose between, but as many names as the local officers thought should be considered. It was this decision by the central committee that opened the gates to a flood of applications. The headquarters justified its decision in a series of election statements. It explained that, 'in arriving at the final choice for each constituency and, by Jove, some constituencies had about twenty applicants, the best tests were made; in other words every stone was turned to ensure that the choice was the best or about the best which could be made in the circumstances'.[19] Hence the decision by the central committee 'that the constituencies should collect and send to the Headquarters as many applications as would be forthcoming for final selection not out of idle fancy or because it wanted to "rob" local leadership of its "inalienable democratic title" but from necessity'.

We are agreed that in NORMAL circumstances the constituencies should have selected one or even two candidates for the blessing of the Headquarters. But when the leaders found that an ABNORMAL situation had arisen in very many constituencies they had to decide as they did in order to prevent the party from being broken to pieces. If

[18] 8 May 1954.   [19] *Evening News*, 4 May 1954.

the constituencies in this instance had been allowed to select the candidates many awful things might have happened quite apart from the fact that persons who had been bitterly opposed to the party could then jump into the party offering constituency executive members very huge and fantastic sums of money to buy their candidature.[20]

Since it was unlikely that many of the constituency executives would have been able to agree unanimously on a candidate by 22 May, the last day for nominations, a firm decision by Accra may actually have helped to swing the loyalists behind the party. None the less, the fact remained that many of the local executives resented the transfer to Accra of what was regarded—at least in the early years of the party—as a local prerogative. It robbed them of their importance; it deprived some at least of an opportunity of gain, and they felt aggrieved. In Ashanti especially, where the regional committee and its executive were fully established, the feeling of being by-passed, or of being overridden, by the Accra headquarters was particularly strong. When the central committee decided on the extreme step of holding a mass rally to expel the rebels it was in Kumasi that the expulsions were carried out; and when, added to the disappointment among those who were not selected, the feeling of resentment in Ashanti at what was regarded as the high-handed attitude of the national headquarters was to play an important part in precipitating the large-scale revolt at the end of 1954.

In the meanwhile the *Evening News* and the *Ashanti Sentinel* (the party's newly established paper in Kumasi) stressed that every decision taken by the national executive had the sanction of the Life Chairman, and laid emphasis on the need not only for party discipline but for a personal loyalty to Nkrumah. Thus, in addition to a natural tendency to see power in terms of loyalty to a particular person, there was the added need in 1954 to keep the sprawling mass of the party together as it entered the final weeks of the pre-election campaign; and Nkrumah became a national arbiter whose judgement, it was hoped, would be accepted as final. Accordingly, the first approved list of candidates was read out to the Arena crowd in Accra on Sunday 2 May amidst an elaborate ceremony built around the leader:

Riding in a Jaguar car wearing a *batakali* [Northern smock] and his P.G. cap, the Osagyefo arrived at about 4.15 p.m. accompanied by

[20] Ibid. 15 May 1954.

K. A. Gbedemah, Kojo Botsio and T. Hutton-Mills all wearing P.G. caps. The gigantic crowd suddenly burst into deafening applause when the Osagyefo Tufuhene was lifted high in a white 'palanquin' with the CPP Tricolour at the back amidst the firing of muskets. . . . The long procession wended its way through Knutsford Avenue to the Arena as the conspicuous State umbrella, made in red, white and green velvet cloth, continued to 'dance' jubilantly over the head of Ghana's chosen leader. The climax was reached when the Wonder Boy arrived at the arena. Everything was kept moving and everybody was rushing to behold his leader. The masses victoriously responded as their amancipator waved majestically and confidently at them. Before the Man of Destiny delivered his soul inspiring speech preceding the release of the 104 candidates he stated that the hand of God is in our struggle otherwise we could not have reached where we are now.[21]

It was in such extracts that something of the fervour which the CPP still retained in 1954 could be seen, in its skilful weaving together of a traditional and modern symbolism. After Nkrumah had spoken to the Arena crowd at its dusty meeting-ground— open to the sky, fenced by a dilapidated palisade, and with a simple wooden platform guarded by the party's women 'police' and strong-arm followers—he was 'led to the gate of the Arena where a bullock had been slaughtered and customarily bathed his feet in the blood after the Nai Wulomo [fetish priest] had poured libation asking blessings for Kwame Nkrumah'.[22] The more ardent of the party's followers were arrayed in the 'Nkrumah cloth', overprinted with the leader's portrait. The party's favourite hymn—'Lead, Kindly Light'—the party's Victory Song, Christian prayers, libations, brass bands, flags and banners carried the day forward, and the national officers were there in strength to show their confidence and trust in the Leader. Yet this spectacular showmanship failed to hide the tension that lay beneath the surface of party loyalty. The May meeting was enthusiastically applauded, and the leaders acclaimed; but it made very little difference to the disputes that continued to divide the

[21] 4 May 1954. Note too the election appeal used in a propaganda leaflet in Accra: 'This is your man, voters of Accra Central, the Sun of Ghana, Star of Africa, Man of Destiny, Hope of the Common Man, Wonder Boy of Africa, the giant surrounded by opposition dwarfs for whom you must vote. The destiny of Africa is bound with the destiny of Ghana, the destiny of Ghana is interwoven with the success of the Convention People's Party and the success of the CPP is deep-seated in the winsome personality of Kwame Nkrumah. Therefore, voters of Accra Central, vote for Kwame Nkrumah.'

[22] *Evening News*, 5 May 1954.

party. Both before and after the first list of candidates was selected, deputation after deputation arrived in Accra from the constituencies to protest against or affirm their support for a particular candidate.

On what basis were the 104 candidates finally selected? The
basic rule was still that of 'past performance' in the service of the
party, but it was increasingly hard to define. Even the practical
ruling which the central committee tried to apply that the existing legislative assembly members should be re-elected did not
help much, for some of the former M.L.A.'s who had left the
party had to be replaced, and others were in disfavour. Kwesi
Lamptey, Nuh Abubekr, and B. F. Kusi had resigned; two
(Ohene Djan and Atta Mensah) were still in prison. Others were
rejected by the central committee as being too critical and (in
these early days) too radical in their insistence on the socialist
aims of the party: neither Pobee Biney nor Anthony Woode (the
Sekondi trade unionists) was re-nominated.[23] In the end, of the
34 party members elected in 1951, only 23 were selected to stand
again in 1954, leaving more than 80 seats for the central committee and the constituency executives to quarrel over, and the
candidates finally approved were chosen from very mixed motives. Because the central committee was anxious to strengthen
its intellectual side—a persistent hope in the party's history—it
was now prepared to sponsor Ako Adjei (Ll.B.) in Accra, K. A.
T. Amankwah (B.A.) in Amansie, and E. O. Asafu Adjaye
(Ll.B.) in Kumasi South, all of whom had opposed the party in
1951. It also insisted on re-nominating Krobo Edusei, the party's
strong-armed man in Ashanti, despite the scathing comment
passed on his conduct as a ministerial secretary by the Korsah
Commission, whose *Report* appeared at the end of April.[24] In

[23] Nor was Bediako Poku who represented Wenchi between 1951 and 1954, and
who was later to become the party's general secretary, but Bediako Poku's name
appeared in the first list issued on 2 May. He then agreed to stand down in face of
the stronger candidature of C. E. Donkor, who had the backing of the rival royal
house to the Busia family in Wenchi and who might have stood as an Independent
had he not been chosen. The change was made on 10 May. The CPP was naturally
keen to win Wenchi, and although Donkor lost it was only by 11 votes in a 7,500
poll. In the 1960 Wenchi by-election Donkor was elected by an overwhelming
majority.

[24] The direct effect on the electorate in Sekyere East (Krobo Edusei's constituency) of the *Report's* judgement—that Edusei's conduct in his dealings with a German business firm fell 'below any acceptable standard for men in the public service
and is strongly to be deprecated'—was probably nil: but it gave his opponents
within the party an excellent opportunity for challenging his nomination. Fortu-

other instances, however, the constituency executives made the
running, and the central committee had somehow to decide between the names which the warring sections of the local executives sent to Accra. There was no effective machinery to cope
with such a situation. The national executive, or to give it its full
title, the national executive committee[25]—was too cumbersome
and divided a body to reach any clear-cut decisions, and the final
lists of nominations were almost certainly drawn up by Nkrumah, Gbedemah, Botsio, and a small group of advisers. These
inner-party counsellors included officials like Boi Doku, the national propaganda secretary, and one of the party's few permanent officials who did not want an assembly seat, and a small
number of key party members in each region—Krobo Edusei for
Ashanti, Kofi Baako for the west, Emmanuel Korboe for the east,
F. Y. Asare and Wellington Kuma in the southern Togoland
Trust Territory, R. S. Iddrisu and L. R. Abavana in the north.
But the party was now too diffuse, and the number of electoral
districts too great, for the central committee to have the close personal control and knowledge that Gbedemah had been able to
exercise over the 38 constituencies in 1951.

The problem facing the committee—how to choose a loyal
winner—could be seen in its simplest form in the north, where
the national headquarters was most ignorant of the balance of
forces. One example (of many disputed constituencies) was
Gulkpe-Nanton which included Tamale, the regional capital.
The central committee relied for much of its information about
the southern constituencies of the Northern Territories (including Gulkpe-Nanton) on R. S. Iddrisu, the Dagomba transport
owner in Tamale, who made several journeys to the south in
April and May to advise about candidates. But Iddrisu was not
always a reliable informant. There was rivalry between himself
as the local regional chairman, and Eben Adam (a former school-
teacher and, in 1954, a drug-store keeper) as the regional secretary; and on Iddrisu's advice Adam's name was kept off the list of
candidates until its revision in mid-May. Then the weight of protests from Tamale (from Eben Adam himself, and the younger

---

nately (for Krobo Edusei) there were four Independents against him and he was
re-elected with a 2,000 vote lead over his nearest rival.

[25] In 1954 the national executive committee still consisted of the members of the
central committee, national officers, and representatives elected (one each) from
the former thirty-eight constituency executives.

constituency executive members) led the central committee to change its mind. Because Iddrisu had been promised the Gulkpe-Nanton constituency, Adam was given a place in the constituency immediately to the north—Savelugu; but this merely spread the area of confusion still wider, for it provoked an immediate outcry from the candidate originally selected for Savelugu—Sumani Bukari. He too made the long journey to Accra; but now the central committee refused to listen. So Sumani Bukari defied the party, stood as an Independent—and, because of the strength of his personal following in the constituency—was elected. Moreover, the division in the Tamale branch of the CPP between those who supported R. S. Iddrisu, and those who would have preferred Eben Adam, so weakened the party in Gulkpego-Nanton that Iddrisu, too, was defeated.[26] The Tamale dispute was a remote one perhaps, remote at least from Accra: but a similar situation arose in Wenchi East, in Ashanti, where the central committee again changed its mind, substituted one candidate for another, and so bewildered not only the electorate but the local branches (whose members canvassed some for one candidate, and some for another, in the name of the CPP) that the party lost the seat to a rebel candidate. Indeed, the central committee did better where it stood firm on its original decision. There were so many local candidates (each representing a particular group of villages) that, where the overall national appeal of the party was clearly expressed, it often carried the official candidate through. In almost every constituency, however, there were angry scenes in packed constituency executive meetings, and the central committee must often have been at a loss to know what to do.[27]

[26] It is doubtful whether either Eben Adam or R. S. Iddrisu could have won in Tamale in 1954 without the support for each other which each refused to give. So Alhaji Osmanu got in on a MAP/NPP ticket. In 1956, however, when the CPP was more united, and the local quarrel between Iddrisu and Eben Adam had been patched up, Iddrisu defeated Alhaji. Then, when R. S. Iddrisu died in 1960, Eben Adam was elected (unopposed).

[27] Even in what should have been a straightforward constituency like Amansie East divisions appeared. Boakye was readily approved by the central committee for re-nomination, but the local executive was divided. The Kokofu and Essumeja branches tried to push the candidature of a local Kokofu bookseller, and the complaint was revived that Boakye was 'really from Juaben and not from Amansie'. This move failed, for the bookseller refused to stand as an Independent: then J. P. Acquah from Dadiase in Amansie (a clerk in Kingsway Stores, Kumasi) was persuaded to put his name forward, grossly misled by election 'contractors' in Bekwai and by those who wanted to annoy Boakye. (One of the election 'contractors' was the 'Chief Driver' in Bekwai who claimed quite erroneously to have the votes of

Eventually a revised list of candidates was ready, and issued by the central committee on 19 May. 'After a careful scrutiny, taking into every consideration, CPP presents with the full blessing of Kwame Nkrumah, Life Chairman of the party, the names of the 104 candidates for election to the Legislative Assembly.' There should be 'no more pressure groups, no more resolutions': the 'interesting inner party struggle which manifested itself in the past few weeks over the issue of nominations has come to a HALT'. So the *Evening News* told its readers.[28] But still the local quarrels continued, and by the middle of May the central committee was obliged to impose a stricter discipline. Thus, when Adu Amankwa Boahen, the secretary of the New Juaben (Colony) constituency executive, refused to accept the decision of the central committee, he was removed from office by the local officers on instructions from Accra, on the grounds 'that he was undertaking undermining activities against the party's candidate, the Rev. S. G. Nimako, and attempting to create confusion among party members'.[29] Similar quarrels divided the party in other constituencies, and at the end of May the central committee uttered a solemn, general warning that continued opposition would invoke sterner measures. Telegrams were then dispatched to all the 'rebels' and their supporters, warning them that if they persisted, they would face expulsion,[30] and Nkrumah issued a special statement from Accra:

STATEMENT BY THE LIFE CHAIRMAN

In a number of constituencies, some party members have filed nomination papers to stand election as independent candidates seek-

---

the taxi and lorry drivers.) This too was a forlorn attempt and, at the last, Acquah would have been glad to stand down; but the election went forward, and he was given the ludicrous vote of 43 out of a total poll of nearly 9,000. Nevertheless, opposition to Boakye produced the (relatively) high vote of 1,741 for S. B. Darquah, the GCP candidate, against 6,211 for Boakye. But, then, Darquah was from Bekwai with good family connexions in the near-by towns of Kokofu and Abodom. In the neighbouring constituency, Amansie West, K. A. T. Amankwah was given the rousing vote of 6,125 against 570 for the GCP candidate, and 461 and 56 for two Independents.

[28] 11 May 1954.

[29] *Evening News*, 21 May 1954. The New Juaben Party did not like it, however, and the statement issued by the local committee added that 'this action has nothing to do with the membership of the said Adu Amankwa Boahen who still enjoys every facility as a member in our dynamic Party'.

[30] A typical telegram read: 'Please withdraw your candidature for the Election not later than May 31st in the interests of your country's independence or face expulsion from the Convention People's Party. Kwame Nkrumah.'

ing election into the Legislative Assembly. There are several such CPP members.

I have instructed Constituency Executives and officers to advise the 'independents' to withdraw their nomination papers not later than the 31st day of May.

I have also caused letters and telegrams to be addressed to the individuals concerned advising them to withdraw their candidatures in the interests of the party and of the country.

I have to warn that if by Friday the 28th May any one of these party members who are standing in opposition to the official CPP candidates fails to withdraw his nomination, I shall be compelled to ask the Central Committee on behalf of the National Executive to expel him for indiscipline and disloyalty.

The forthcoming General Election is too important to trifle with and we must do nothing which may weaken the solidarity of the party which has demonstrated that the future of our country depends so much on its unity at this time.

I must take this opportunity to exhort the Constituency organisations to give their full and unflinching support to the official party candidates and organise effectively for the party's victory.

May 24, 1954   Kwame Nkrumah

These warnings, and more subtle pressures involving the offer of comparable benefits if a 'rebel' stood down, had some effect. J. E. Homiah withdrew in Wassaw Central, and the CPP candidate (S. E. Ackah) was then declared elected unopposed. The CPP western region chairman (J. E. Baidoo) withdrew his name in Sekondi-Takoradi, leaving the contest as a straight fight between John Arthur (CPP) and Pobee Biney (a more stubborn 'rebel'); so did J. H. Ankrah in Cape Coast, leaving a straight fight between Welbeck (CPP) and Amponsah-Dadzie (GCP); so (in Agona Kwabre) did Victor Owusu—later, to be one of the leaders in the Ashanti National Liberation Movement—leaving J. E. Jantuah (CPP) to contend with a second strong 'rebel' candidate and a Moslem Association Party member. These were useful gains, but a hard core of 'recalcitrant opportunists, careerists and freedom-saboteurs'[31] refused to listen either to appeals or threats. And on Whit Sunday, the 6th of June, four days before the election opened in the north and nine days before the main polling day, a national condemnation of the rebels was staged at

[31] *Evening News*, 25 May 1954.

a rally in the Subin Valley meeting ground in Kumasi. The party's leaders turned up in full force, and Nkrumah—'feeling rather as an executioner must do when he has to carry out his distasteful job because of duty and justice'[32]—formally read out of the party the names of 81 rebels.

These quarrels among the party members, and between the national headquarters and the constituency executives, were a good measure of the weakness of the nationalist party. It was easy to be misled by the leaders' strident use of a vocabulary of terms borrowed from Marxist and nationalist writings into supposing that the CPP was in fact as the leaders portrayed it—a close-knit, disciplined force, capable of mobilizing local opinion behind any cause it chose to sponsor. There was some truth in this claim: the party did, indeed, rest on a broad base of support, and it had succeeded in generating a widespread enthusiasm for its 1949 programme. It was a 'mass party'. But this very fact carried its own dangers, for once the foundations of its mass support began to shift, cracks appeared very quickly, and the whole structure of party organization looked in danger of toppling. This was how it seemed in April–May 1954. The main lines of fracture were now visible between local territorial groups of one kind and another— regions, chiefdoms, villages—which sponsored 'rebel' candidates in defiance of the central committee, and the leaders had to fight a hard battle to retain control over the infinite variety of such disputes. Admittedly, by early June, it began to look as if they had succeeded: at least the party was able to enter the election with an official list of almost 104 candidates. Nevertheless, the CPP was obviously in difficulties, and in consequence the opposition alliance of the Ghana Congress Party, the NPP, the MAP, and the Togoland Congress was obviously much better placed than had seemed likely a twelve month earlier. How skilful had the leaders been in exploiting the divisions which had appeared within the CPP? How successful were they in putting across their own appeal?

Criticism of the CPP by the Ghana Congress Party followed

---

[32] *Autobiography*, pp. 208–9. What did expulsion mean? It was difficult to say in detail, and many of those expelled found their way back to the party. The *Evening News* found refuge in abuse. 'To be expelled from the National Liberation Army means your services are totally useless to the nation, useless to the people and useless to the whole African world. Renegades, you have exposed yourselves to be traitors of the first order. Wicked Souls. . . Big Traitors and fat headed outcasts! Shame on you! O Shame!! Black quislings!!!'

familiar lines, expressed in general terms by 'Brother Culture'
(J. W. K. Dumoga) in the *Ashanti Pioneer* of 22 May 1954 who
argued that the current adulation of Nkrumah was 'an invitation
to the people of the Gold Coast to accept the dictatorship of a
führer whose will should become law, and thus prove to the
world that we do not understand the democracy which we have
been talking about'. Much the same sentiments were expressed in
the *Election Manifesto* issued by the GCP early in April, which
accused the CPP leaders of trying to impose on the country a corrupt dictatorship. The only specific bid for support by the party,
however, was the promise of more money for cocoa farmers. 'The
present world price of cocoa and the forecast for the next year'
(the *Manifesto* stated) 'justify an increase in the price paid to the
farmer. Accordingly we shall increase the price of cocoa.' Exactly how the party proposed to do this and, at the same time,
'bring down the cost of living' was not made clear—indeed it was
hardly possible to correlate the two—but its criticism of many
aspects of CPP policy (of its housing programme, for example,
which had involved a great deal of expenditure on prefabricated
Dutch and Swedish houses with very little result) was both
moderate and telling. Indeed, the whole tone of the proposals
outlined in the *Manifesto*—for an expanded health service, a
better phased educational policy, the encouragement of local
business enterprises, and the improvement of the output and distribution of locally produced food—was eminently sensible, and
hardly open to challenge, except on the grounds that a moderate
view of the CPP's own programme of wide social and economic
benefits was likely to attract only moderate support. This basic
characteristic of the party was indeed its chief handicap. Thus
the *Manifesto* demanded 'full self-government' and criticized the
CPP leaders for 'having failed to achieve self-government for the
country, even though as the first predominantly African Government they had the power to achieve this'. But such statements
called for a much greater belief in the ardent spirit of the Congress leaders than in fact existed, for the 'image' popularly held
of the party was hardly one of militancy. With its usual optimism,
the *Ashanti Pioneer* (5 April 1954) called the GCP election appeal
a 'fighting manifesto'. 'It is profoundly realistic, down to earth,
devoid of any glamorous and fantastic promises and lying propaganda'; but, in the circumstances of 1954, this was merely an-

other way, perhaps, of saying that it was unlikely to appeal to the electorate.

The main problem facing the GCP leaders was the impossibility of finding an alternative programme to the CPP's demand for self-government—a difficulty pointed out by Nkrumah himself. 'Until independence', he was said to have told a visiting journalist, 'there is only one political platform—that is, independence—and I happen to be occupying it.'[33] The observation was just—as long as the nationalist base was not narrowed to a region or re-defined (as in Togoland) in other terms—and there was nothing in the early part of 1954 that the GCP leaders could do about it. There still hung about them the sour smell of defeat, whereas the CPP had the prestige associated with success; and the general impression left by the Congress on all but a narrow band of supporters was one of hapless indecision. In the Colony and Ashanti chiefdoms, where there was a wild confusion of CPP, CPP rebel, and Independent candidates, the leaders failed even to unite the non-CPP vote under a single banner. In Ekumfi-Enyan, for example—a southern coastal constituency, J. W. de Graft Johnson, the lawyer and former UGCC member, stood as an Independent against M. B. Pokoo-Aikins for the GCP, regardless of the fact that on almost every issue they were in full agreement; there were two other Independents, a CPP rebel, and an official CPP candidate.[34] Such quarrels were frequent among those who tried to oppose the CPP, and when Kwesi Lamptey tried to form a Sponsors' Group, to try and hasten the formation of a more closely-knit alliance between the anti-CPP candidates, the attempt ended with Lamptey standing as an Independent. When nominations closed, therefore, the party had only 22 candidates in the field.

Nevertheless, the GCP leaders could claim to have kept alive the possibility of opposition, and to have offered a national lead (however feeble) to the local and regional parties: thus Busia helped to lead the opposition in the new Assembly. Nor could the GCP be accused of wanting to subvert independence. Its leaders could claim to be 'patriots', even if they were opposed to the main nationalist party; and Danquah in particular could

[33] Quoted by Arden-Clarke in *Afr. Aff.*, Jan. 1958.
[34] Voting was: S. K. Otoo (CPP rebel) 2,754; W. E. Arthur (CPP) 1,991; J. W. de Graft Johnson (Ind.) 407; M. B. Pokoo-Aikins (GCP) 85; J. G. Oppon (Ind.) 31; S. K. Sampson (Ind.) 204.

point to a long and distinguished record of nationalist agitation. Indeed, the party continued the remarkably persistent 'intelligentsia' tradition which looked back to the Cape Coast and Accra lawyers of the last decades of the nineteenth century, and might fairly be regarded as being still in the main stream of nationalist politics. On these grounds alone, the GCP may be said to have had, and was usually recognized as having, a significance greater than its own capabilities warranted.

The Northern People's Party was in a different category altogether. It opposed the CPP not on principle but out of self-interest—a much more solid ground of support—and it had a region of twenty-six constituencies as its field of operation. In April–May 1954 it was by far the strongest challenger to the CPP that had yet appeared. This was partly because the CPP had not yet had time to cross the Volta into the Northern Territories in anything like the strength it had in the south; partly, however, because the social base of its support did not exist in the northern chiefdoms. When, for example, the writer was in the western districts of the Protectorate early in June 1954, and asked who was likely to win the Wala North constituency, the reply came:

> It is fairly clear that the NPP candidate will have the best chance. Because, as we can see, he is more enlightened than either of the two other candidates. He is of royal descent and in addition to this he is the oldest. He is physically better built and has an impressive appearance. His language is full of logic and conviction. He stands for a party the chiefs and people favour. . . . The CPP candidate is a driver with no special education. He is a native, it is true, but he spent much of his time on the coast. He is a very ordinary man. . . . The Independents are from very poor families and not much known in the constituency.[35]

Thus the radicalism and 'verandah boy' appeal of the CPP, that often held the party steady in the south, were a disadvantage in the north where the common man was still firmly under the authority of the chief. It was only by competing with the NPP on its own terms, and by asserting its authority as a government to back its appeal as a party, that the CPP later succeeded in splintering—and eventually breaking—the NPP.

The basis of the northern party was a skilful combination of tribal authority and an educated leadership. The NPP slogan,

---

[35] Letter to the author from a member of the NPP branch in Wa.

'the North for the northerners', was mainly important because it helped to create a strong feeling of unity among the leaders (despite the artificiality of the Protectorate as an administrative unit). Its electoral strength in the constituencies rested on local issues. Or, expressed more exactly, it rested on the ability of the leaders to win over to their side locally influential figures to whom it was necessary to explain the issue between the CPP and the NPP in homely terms. Such a task required patient, repeated canvassing among the chiefs, headmen, *tendanna* (priests of the earth god), wealthy cattle owners and traders of the northern constituencies. The arguments used played on local fears and individual ambitions, and had to be supported by the presentation to the right person of a suitable gift which (by 1954) included not merely the handful of kola-nut of earlier times but whisky and money. Propaganda of this nature demanded an intimate knowledge of the balance of authority in each constituency between rival chiefs and lineages, or between the individual who was influential behind the scenes and those who could be safely ignored because they were unimportant locally. And in this extremely complicated art of political manœuvre the NPP leaders had a clear advantage over their southern-based rivals.[36] In addition, they had a convenient headquarters' organization in the standing committee of the Northern Territories Council in Tamale, and capable helpers like J. A. Nagba (chief secretary to the Council) whose access to a typewriter, duplicating machine, paper, and telephone, enabled the NPP to function in a surprisingly efficient way—surprising, that is, to those who knew nothing of the work of the Northern Territories Council or the ability of its members.

Did the NPP gain any strength from Islam? This was doubtful. Islam rested easily on these northern chiefdoms, and although a number of the candidates (on both sides) were Muslims their religion was much less important politically than their social position as confidants of the local chief. Nor were they all Muslim: in the Lawra-Nandom and Kassena-Nankanni areas, where the White Fathers had their missions, a majority of the population (and of the candidates) was Christian. Religion played no part, therefore, in the differences between the parties,

---

[36] For an account of electioneering in a northern constituency see the appendices to this chapter and to ch. VII.

or in the appeal made by either side to the electorate, and the NPP *Election Manifesto* made no reference to it.

The main burden of the *Manifesto*, which parodied the CPP's by being labelled 'Operation 26', was an appeal for support on the grounds that it was necessary to keep the south at arm's length while the relationship between the two halves of the country could be put on an equal footing. To achieve this feat, the NPP demanded a special £8 million development plan for the north to be spent over six years 'during the period of internal self-government'. The money would help to build bridges, 'accelerate the accelerated plan for education', 'expand the mechanised farming scheme at Damongo', bring back the Veterinary Department from Accra to Pong Tamale, increase the number of dispensaries and hospitals, and 'finance a full review of the long projected railway extension from Kumasi to Tamale'. The British (said the *Manifesto*) had neglected the region, the southern politicians had shown themselves to be indifferent: yet 'the North contributes directly to the revenue of the Gold Coast by providing labour for the mines, cocoa farms, and other industries'. Secondly, as might be expected, the *Manifesto* called for increased support for the chiefs. It proposed 'substantial grants for the salaries of Chiefs and other traditional authorities' to preserve 'this sacred trust in our heritage', and commented that 'on the question of Chiefs taking sides in politics . . . it would be suicidal for any Chief to stay indifferent'. Thirdly, the *Manifesto* outlined a settlement of the Togoland problem whereby:

1. Northern Togoland will be integrated into the Gold Coast since that is the unanimous wish of the Chiefs and people of this section of the Trust Territory.
2. In the matter of Southern Togoland we shall allow the people themselves to determine their own future.

The document then concluded with the general hope of 'full self-government for the Gold Coast within the British Commonwealth', within which

the ordinary man, earning a living and striving to bring up a family will be free from the fear that some grim police organisation, under the control of a single party, will tap him on the shoulder and pack him off without fair or open trial to bondage or ill treatment

brave words, which did not always match the energetic campaigning of the NPP in its own strongholds where the full weight of the local state authority was used to curb the (CPP) opposition.

The NPP put up fifteen candidates in the twenty-six constituencies, and had the support of Independents and MAP candidates in a further nine—a remarkable feat for a party formed only three months beforehand. But, although it was clearly a stronger movement in the northern constituencies than the CPP, the latter was not entirely without resources. By its very success the NPP raised enemies against it, and the CPP was able to woo them to its side. Rivals to a pro-NPP chief, local leaders who saw the possibility of substantial rewards through support for the ruling party, individuals who were prepared to support a local candidate and who did not mind (or even understand) what particular label they adopted, became 'CPP' because their opponents were NPP. They used exactly the same methods of propaganda as the NPP, but placed them at the service of the nationalist party. As their knowledge of the north grew, the CPP leaders were able to use their authority as the party in power with still greater effect.[37] Even so, they did well in 1954 to secure candidates like J. H. Allasani (who had the backing of a number of the Dagomba chiefs), E. A. Mahama (supported by the Yabumwura, the Gonja paramount), L. R. Abavana (adviser to perhaps the shrewdest of the northern chiefs, the Navropio), Ayeebo Asumda in Kusasi, and Imoru Egala in Tumu.[38] There was not the slightest difference between the NPP leaders and the small pro-CPP group. J. H. Allasani, for example, had swung round from hostility to support; but foresight, ambition, and (for some) a personal prediliction for the CPP, drew these northern leaders away from the NPP. If, therefore, there was little doubt that the northern-based party would win a substantial number of seats and votes, there was little doubt too that the CPP was still in the fight.

Because the NPP covered the north so effectively, its ally the MAP did what it could to concentrate its efforts on the Zongo wards of the southern towns. Here there were migrant labourers, traders, and cattle drovers—many of them from the French-

[37] See below, ch. VII.
[38] For local, tactical reasons, Egala fought the campaign as an Independent. He became a minister in the new CPP administration immediately after the election.

speaking territories to the north of the Gold Coast—who lived together in poor conditions and held fast to their religion as a distinctive feature of their communal life, and the MAP was strongly supported by these stranger-communities. In Kumasi there was also a long-established community of Ashanti Muslim converts, particularly in the Suame district where the MAP flag—green with a white crescent—fluttered above a great number of the tumble-down houses and motor-repair shops. Looked at nationally, however, the party had little weight of members behind it. The Muslim communities were too scattered in the rural areas to be able to exercise any independent influence, and the MAP was able to put up only fifteen candidates in the country as a whole with little overall control even of these.[39] Its *Manifesto* appeared late in May 1954, and was a poorly printed, ill-written document which called for recognition of Muslim interests in the country while denying that 'the creation of Pakistan shall ever be the aim of policy of the Moslem Association Party'.[40] It reaffirmed the traditional alliance between the Muslims and the chiefs, and declared that 'chieftaincy shall be restored to its ancient dignity' should the MAP form part of a new government. It wanted 'Arabic training centres' for Muslims, denied that it had any intention of dividing the country, refused to 'dupe the electorate with sugar coated promises couched in traditional mob oratory', and concluded by calling for a general development plan to promote as many fields of welfare as the MAP leaders could think of. As was noted earlier, the Muslim community as a whole was not fully behind the party, since the CPP was able to make use of many local, internal quarrels—between the Hausa and Gao communities, and between the MAP leaders and those who (though not necessarily young) sided with the Muslim Youth Congress. The MAP also lacked—or thought that it lacked—leaders of its own with sufficient education to stand for election. Thus although it sponsored the elderly Alhaji Osmanu in Tamale,

[39] For example, S. P. Tayo (a Muslim butcher) stood in Salaga against the NPP leader, J. A. Braimah, to be given 293 votes against Braimah's 4,286. Alhaji Osmanu was a strong MAP candidate in Tamale because of the backing given him by the NPP and the dispute within the local CPP executive. The difference between the scattered Muslim vote in the rural areas and the relatively high vote in the town wards could be seen in the results. The total MAP vote for candidates in 8 southern rural constituencies was only 3,096 compared with Accra West—3,039; Kumasi North 2,878; Sunyani West (with a large Muslim community in Sunyani town) 1,409.

[40] This was the bizarre charge that the CPP liked to bring against the MAP.

it agreed to let the Ashanti lawyer Cobina Kessie, and the Ga lawyer Bankole Awooner Renner, represent it in Kumasi and Accra. The greatest asset that the party had was its militancy. 'You the youth are the soldiers. We the elders are the powder, the bullets and the machine guns. If you want anything, tell us and we shall do it for you', Alhaji Amadu Babu, the Kumasi Muslim leader, was reported in the *Ashanti Pioneer* as telling a meeting of the MAP.[41] The military imagery was characteristic. But ardour without numbers was a poor electoral asset, and the MAP was under the further disadvantage that many of its members were unable (officially at least) to vote because they were not British subjects or Protected Persons. At best, therefore, the leaders could only hope that its candidates might be able to benefit from divisions among the CPP candidates in the municipalities.

Allied with the GCP, the NPP and the MAP was the Ewe-based Togoland Congress, whose leaders in the trust territory wanted a 'homeland' under Ewe leadership. Since this was a difficult platform from which to contest a Gold Coast election, the Congress leaders—S. G. Antor, Kojo Ayeke, and the Rev. F. R. Ametowobla—tried (ostensibly at least) to spread their appeal on a territorial rather than a tribal base. Thus the *Election Manifesto* called for a separate legislature for the trust territory to mark its different international status, and the Congress looked for allies in the northern section among the minority communities of the Mamprusi and Gonja chiefdoms. They made common cause (for example) with the B'Moba Youth Association led by J. P. Kona in eastern Mamprusi, as well as among the non-Ewe states of the southern section of the territory.[42] Accordingly, the leaders raised a number of grievances common throughout the two sections of British Togoland—the very bad state of the roads,

---

[41] 23 Sept. 1953.

[42] Mr Kona and the B'Moba Youth Association were surprisingly active, but some of their difficulties in challenging the authority of the dominant northern chiefs could be seen in 1955 when the Association presented a memorandum to the U.N. Visiting Mission. The memo. was signed by the B'Moba chief, the Bunkpurugu-naba, and his sub-chiefs, and demanded a separate legislature for British Togoland and the ultimate unification of the two trust territories. The following morning, however, the Na-Yiri, the paramount chief of the Mamprusi and overlord of the B'Moba, was able to show the Mission a letter he had received from the Bunkpurugu-naba in which 'the latter stated in apologetic terms that he had been misled by Mr Kona and assured the Na-Yiri of his continued loyalty'. The final words of the letter were 'Separation down—Integration up'. See the Special Report on the Togoland Unification Movement, *TCOR*, 5th spec. sess., 24 Oct.–14 Dec. 1955, suppl. 2.

the danger of flooding should the Volta dam be constructed, the poor water supplies and health services, the general poverty and illiteracy of the northern peoples and, in the south, the enforced sale of cocoa through the Gold Coast Marketing Board (at a time of high cocoa prices in the neighbouring French trust territory). These were practical points of discontent that might well be thought to attract more than Ewe support for the Congress.

Nevertheless, even when the undoubted neglect of the trust territory was placed in the scale alongside the Ewe appeal of the Congress, it was difficult to see how it could hope to win more than the three constituencies which formed its own (Ewe) stronghold—Kpandu North, Ho East, and Ho West. It was opposed in the north by its national ally, the Northern People's Party, whose leaders drew support from the dominant Mamprusi chiefs of the area. In the south the non-Ewe states of the Krachi, Nkonya, Likpe, and Santrokofi peoples (whose ties lay westwards with the Gold Coast) looked with suspicion on all Congress propaganda. Nor was the CPP a party which was easily challenged with the charge of neglect. It had made it clear (particularly in the early half of 1954) that it meant to force the pace of economic development—and equally clear that it was more likely to reward its friends than its opponents. Thus a special grant of £1 million for development projects in the Trans-Volta region (which included the southern section of the trust territory), the laying of the foundations of a high-level suspension bridge to replace the ferry crossing at Senchi on the river Volta, government subsidies for regional and district councils, and suggestions from time to time of the likelihood of a place for party members on one or other of the new public corporations—were strong inducements which drew support away from the Congress. The Ewe leaders were likely to win—and win comfortably—in the Ewe heartland of southern Togoland, and they might pick up a strong minority support elsewhere; but it was difficult to see what more they could hope to achieve, either in the June election or in the plebiscite that would one day have to be held.[43]

[43] The CPP, like the colonial administration before it, had done what it could to minimize the fact of the separate status of the trust territory. Hence the creation of Trans-Volta-Togoland region, consisting of the southern section of the trust territory and the Ewe states of the south-east of the Gold Coast. The region was divided into 13 constituencies, the boundaries of which overlapped the boundaries of the

With these parties which appealed to intelligentsia, regional, religious, and ethnic interests could be grouped the Anlo Youth Organization, the Wassaw Youth Association, and the non-rebel Independents. Some of these local associations were genuinely representative of local grievances, others were formed by individuals who relied on an entirely mythical body of support miscalculated usually on the strength of their family backing. The 'unattached' Independents were a mixed group who differed considerably in their chances of being elected. Kwamena Ocran in the western region of the Colony was a strong candidate because he was backed by a lively Wassaw Youth Association which still kept itself free of the embrace of the nationalist party. W. A. Amoro in the extreme northern constituency (Bongo) was in a strong position since he had the support of the chief and a majority of the heads of the ruling families in that remote cluster of lineages. At the other end of the Independent scale were the 'one-man parties' like that started by Dr Ansah Koi, whose chances even of saving his deposit were justly regarded as minimal.

In sum, the opposition parties—except in the north—were an unimpressive group, ill led and poorly equipped. By contrast, the overall strength of the CPP could be seen in its ability to find candidates in almost every constituency: but their number was less than a third of the total, and the final list of nominations showed how widespread had been the scramble for seats in the new Assembly:

---

trust territory. Similarly, in the north, the boundaries of some of the 26 constituencies overlapped the Northern Territories–northern Togoland trusteeship boundary. The electoral pattern was extremely complicated but:

A. There were 6 constituencies *entirely* within the trust territory: Southern Togoland —Kpandu North, Buem, Akan Krachi. Northern Togoland—Nanum-Dagomba East, Kusasi.

There was 1 constituency *almost* wholly within the southern trust territory: Ho East.

There were 7 constituencies *partly* within the trust territory: Southern Togoland —Ho West, Kpandu South. Northern Togoland—Gonja East, Dagomba South, Dagomba North, South Mamprusi East, Kusasi Central.

B. The Trans-Volta region had 13 constituencies, 6 of them in, or partly within, the southern trust territory; and 7 in the Ewe-speaking districts of south-east Gold Coast.

Southern Togoland: Akan Krachi, Buem, Kpandu South, Kpandu North, Ho West, Ho East.

South-East Gold Coast: Keta, Anlo East, Anlo North, Anlo South, South Tongu, Central Tongu, Upper Tongu.

	Colony (44 seats)	Ashanti (21 seats)	TVT (13 seats)	North (26 seats)	Total (104)	Munici-palities (7 seats)
CPP	44	21	13	26	104	7
Unattached Independents	16	6	3	26	51	2
'Rebels'	59	32	7	5	103	3
NPP	—	—	—	18	18	–
MAP	5	4	1	5	15	2
GCP	13	9	—	—	22	3
TC	—	—	6	—	6	–
AYO	—	—	2	—	2	–
Ghana National Party (GNP)	1	—	—	—	1	1
Ghana Action Party (GAP)	1	—	—	—	1	–
	139	72	32	80	323	18

NOTE: The number of Independents has been reduced to 154 by adding the two pro-CPP candidates (Imoru Egala and W. P. Yelpoe) and the three pro-NPP candidates (J. A. Braimah, Yakubu Tali and C. K. Tedam) in the north, and the pro-Togoland Congress candidate (Rev. F. R. Ametowobla) to the party lists.

In the last few weeks before the election the officials were hardly less uneasy than they had been in 1951. They were again venturing into the unknown with these first direct, rural elections, and there were a number of bizarre accounts after polling day of what had happened, particularly in the more remote Protectorate villages where the illiterate peasant (and his wives) encountered the hazards of a multiple-box system of voting.[44] The administration did what it could to publicize the electoral system. It was they who insisted that, because of the shortage of available polling staff, the election should be conducted over

[44] e.g. the voter in South Mamprusi West who, faced with two boxes in the secrecy of the polling booth, tore the ballot paper in half, and placed a half in each box; e.g. the voter who 'stayed a little too long in the booth [says a local official report] and when asked what she was doing, said that she was finding difficulty in opening the box to put the paper in'; e.g. the sub-chief 'who stayed in the polling booth to await the arrival of his people to instruct them which symbol to vote for. . . '. Papers were often placed beside the box, or in front of the box; and the half-light of a northern hut made voting especially difficult where, as in Gonja South, there were seven boxes to choose between.

two days (10 and 15 June) in the north. They were also handicapped by a lack of skilled assistants, with the result that the
registers of electors were inefficiently drawn up at local level and
difficult to use. The *Report on the Gold Coast General Election 1954*
admitted that: 'Generally speaking, Returning Officers had
great difficulty with their registers which were in many cases
badly prepared and from which it was often impossible to trace
an elector's name.' Very often, the difficulty was a simple linguistic one. For example, if a southern Fanti-speaking clerk
working as a registration officer in Ashanti asked an illiterate
Ashanti farmer his name, he might be told that it was 'Kwabena'.
When asked for a second name, the farmer would, perhaps, add
'Mensah'. Thus the name should have appeared in the register as
Kwabena, Mensah. But the clerk might also write down:
Cobina or Kobina, Mensah; and he might turn it round until it
became Mensah, Kwabena, Cobina or Kobina. All these variations were legitimate, the distinction between pre-names and
cognomen being irrelevant, and the variation in the spelling a
matter of slight shifts in the two Akan languages—*fanti* and
asante.[45] When, however, the farmer came to vote, and said that
his name was 'Kwabena', the Ashanti presiding officer or polling
assistant might look in vain under 'Kw', and unless the farmer
could produce his registration receipt he might be turned away
from the polling booth. Admittedly, this was unlikely in 1954, the
Ashanti farmer being a stubborn man and more than a match
for an assistant, but there was always the danger that a dispute
between the would-be voter and the polling staff would lead first
to altercation between the candidates' polling agents, and then

[45] 'Kwabena' is a male day-name—born on Tuesday; 'Mensah' means 'the third
child'; since there is one chance in seven of being born on Tuesday and a good
chance of being the third male child, there may be a number of Mensah Kwa-
bena(s) or Kwabena Mensah(s). A similar linguistic confusion was possible over the
other day-names Kojo or Cudjoe for Monday, Quarshie, Kwesi or Kwasi for Sunday, and so forth, which were written differently in *twi, fanti, asante, ewe* or *ga*. In
the immigrant wards of the large towns, two or three names out of five on the
register were often the same—page after page of electors being put down as Alhas-
san Dagomba, or Atinga Frafra, or Seidu Wala—a common pre-name linked with
the general name of the tribal group to which the new residents belonged, as if
whole districts of Manchester or Birmingham were to be settled by immigrants who
(to the outside world) described themselves as Neil Campbell or John Jamaica.
Even in the north, confusion was rife. Thus the Government Agent's Report for
Dagomba South noted that 'a number of people in the Kumbungu area were refused a vote as it was quite impossible to trace their names as the original registration was done by non-Dagomba clerks who wrote down the names as they sounded
to them' (*Report on the Gold Coast General Election, 1954*).

to violence among the crowd of party supporters who thronged and jostled each other outside the school compound or court house where polling was taking place.

Because the officials were uncertain of the temper of the electorate, the bars were kept closed in the main towns, and extra staff and police drafted to possible areas of trouble. And although both polling days were orderly these were sensible precautions. The 1954 election was the lull before the more critical struggle between the CPP and the NLM; and Mr P. H. Canham, the administrative officer in charge of the election, was merely being wise before the event when he warned the government in his *Report* on the election that it could not automatically rely on a repetition of its good fortune.

It is submitted [wrote Canham] that, although the General Election arrangements (both in 1951 and 1954) worked well on the whole, it would be unwise to expect these arrangements to work equally well in future. . . . The *cadre* of experienced Government Agents . . . is diminishing rapidly. It will increase again in five to ten years but it is precisely during this immediate future that a number of vital elections (and perhaps plebiscites also) may be expected.

And the further warning was added: 'The Police Force is quite inadequate to cope on a General Election day with even minor disturbances if they occur simultaneously.'

This was undoubtedly true, as the events of the next two years were to show. But by the close of the second day's polling (when all the boxes were opened) 706,720 voters had cast their ballot successfully, in a 60 per cent poll. In proportion to the total adult population, the number voting was (approximately) 31 per cent.

(1) Total Adult Population	(2) Registered	Voters	% of (2)	% of (1)
2,376,602	1,225,603	706,720	59·4	30·7

NOTE: Allowance has been made for 3 uncontested constituencies in calculating the percentages.

As the voting returns began to come in, it was clear that the CPP would be returned with a comfortable majority, and in terms of its efforts during the campaign and on polling day, it deserved no less. Its Nkrumah posters had been displayed throughout the country—behind the bar in the Youngsters' Canteen in Bolgatanga (the northern trading town), on the Takoradi dock front, on the Kumasi Post Office (illegally), and on the palm trees that shade the Accra beaches. In respect of the basic equipment of organization—propaganda vans to exhort the voters, and lorries to carry them to the polling booths—it was far ahead of its rivals. It had a national organizer of genius in K. A. Gbedemah, who was in overall charge of the campaign. It still had many local executive officers who continued to work loyally on behalf of the official candidates—arranging rallies in the evening and at week-ends, raising local funds to buy petrol for the party van, and urging the national headquarters to supplement the basic grant of £50 per constituency for election expenses. It was able to bring the full backing of a government to whatever local propaganda was devised to bind the electorate to the party—the promise of a new school, the allocation of funds to a local development com-mittee, or the offer of an introduction to a minister in Accra, with examples in virtually every southern constituency to show the close alliance of party and government power.[46] And it had money. It had access nationally, through bodies like the Cocoa Purchasing Company, and locally, through the newly constitut-ed local authorities, to funds denied its opponents who (outside the north) were dependent largely on private subscriptions. The heavy cost of fighting an election in Ghana was 'a truth univers-ally acknowledged'. For although the election regulations laid down appropriate penalties for bribery and treating, there was no legal limitation on the amount a candidate could spend; and a great deal of electioneering which in the United Kingdom be-longed to the nineteenth rather than the twentieth century was accepted as normal practice in Ghana where personal relations, or a service rendered by someone to a friend, were made secure by the bestowal of a suitable gift. What expenses of this kind might amount to in practice could be seen from a rough estimate of election costs given the writer by an (unsuccessful) contender in a northern constituency:

[46] e.g. the removal, on orders of the government in 1953 of the district council headquarters and the important Native Court 'A' from Kibi (the Akim Abuakwa capital) to New Tafo, within the immediate jurisdiction of a pro-CPP sub-chief—a demonstration of the power of the central government on behalf of the local CPP. As Danquah complained, the decision 'led to the position of the Paramount Chief (at Kibi) being undermined, and it exposed him and his other chiefs to hatred, ridicule and contempt . . .' (Jackson Commission *Report*, 1958; see also H. K. Akyeampong, *The Akim Abuakwa Crisis* (Accra, n.d.)).

	£	per cent
Initial payments to chiefs and headmen to ensure support for his candidature	100	11·6
Payment for entertainment of headmen and villagers, including drinks, kola and hiring of musicians	300	34·6
Gifts of cloth to influential leaders	80	9·2
Petrol for himself and agents; and car repairs and hiring of lorries on polling day	200	23·2
Payment to helpers, and 'donations'	160	18·5
Miscellaneous, including a small number of handbills	25	2·9
	865	100·0

When this list was shown to a (successful) contestant in one of the Accra constituencies his only reaction was to comment dryly that 'the candidate was fortunate to have escaped so lightly, and might have done better had he spent more'.

Given, therefore, its constituency organization, its funds, its nationalist *élan*, and its new appeal to the electorate to free Africa by their example, the CPP deserved to win. And it won handsomely: with 72 of the 104 seats, well distributed between the regions.

The description of this second election as 'the Independents' election' was also justified in the results. It is true that only sixteen Independents were elected—eleven, if J. A. Braimah, the Tolon-Na, and C. K. Tedam were associated with the NPP, the Rev. F. R. Ametowobla with the Togoland Congress, and Imoru Egala with the CPP.[47] But in nearly every constituency, the issue was closely fought, and 22 of the seats—more than a fifth—were won on a minority vote. These included constituencies as far apart as Sekyere West in Ashanti,[48] Savelugu in the north,[49] the Colony mining constituency Bibiani,[50] and Anlo North in southern Trans-Volta.[51] In all, the Independents—rebels and 'un-

[47] The criteria being the known views of the candidate and the absence of any competing candidate from the party concerned.

[48] Sekyere West: Osei Bonsu (CPP) 4,114; R. B. Kwakwa (Ind.) 2,640; K. Agyarko (Ind.) 1,624; O. Amanfo (Ind.) 520; A. E. Ofori (Ind.) 128.

[49] Savelugu: Sumani Bukari (Ind.) 1,755; J. Bukari Harruna Bogundona (Ind.) 938; Eben Adam (CPP) 751; Alasani Mahama (Ind.) 675.

[50] Bibiani: J. K. Essien (Ind.) 1,766; J. A. K. Essel (Ind.) 1,476; C. D. Arthur (CPP) 1,375; J. B. Ajileye (MAP) 87.

[51] Anlo North: N. K. Maglo (Ind.) 3,133; J. K. Quarshie (CPP) 2,053; G. A. Atitsogbui 878; J. G. Husunukpe (Ind.) 670.

attached' together—polled between a fifth and a quarter of the total: 156,401 votes, or 22 per cent. These figures were a good indication of the many divisions which were beginning to appear in the nationalist party; and although, given time, many of the Independents were likely to drift over to the side of the ruling party, the CPP remained dangerously open to attack in the immediate post-election months.

Moreover, the party suffered its first regional defeat. The NPP won twelve, and would control sixteen, seats in the new Assembly; the CPP won only eight.[52] Here too was a dangerous pointer to what could happen, given an effective combination of educated leaders, the use of traditional authority, and the appeal to regional interests. Since the CPP was very much a movement of success, any check to its progress was likely to encourage other elements of discontent within its rambling, ill-articulated structure, and the example set by the north was one that, before the year was out, Ashanti was quick to copy.

The Togoland Congress did what was expected of it. That is, it succeeded in its own strongholds, and did well wherever it could translate its Ewe nationalism into votes: Kpandu North, for example, which included the expanding commercial town, Hohoe, returned S. G. Antor, the Congress general secretary, with 8,221 votes against 2,903 for Wellington Kuma[53] for the CPP. Of the 13 seats of the Trans-Volta region, the CPP won 8; the Togoland Congress won 3 (including Ho West where the nominal Independent, the Rev. F. R. Ametowobla, was returned with an easy majority). The Anlo Youth Organization won Anlo South in the Ewe districts of the south-east;[54] and a CPP rebel was returned for Anlo North. When the voting figures were added up throughout the region the CPP was seen to have slightly less than half of the total: 46,547 against a combined non-CPP vote of 46,866. If allowance is made for the unopposed CPP seat (Upper Tongu) then the party might fairly be said to have won a clear majority of

[52] That is, adding to the 12 NPP seats those of the three pro-NPP Independents (J. A. Braimah, Tolon-Na, and C. K. Tedam) and that of Alhaji Osmanu, the MAP member. The remaining 2 seats of the 26 were won by Sumani Bukari, the CPP rebel, who later rejoined the party, and W. A. Amoro (Bongo) who was elected as an Independent, joined the NPP, and then (Aug. 1955) the CPP.

[53] Appointed district commissioner in the Trans-Volta region in 1957, and in 1959 an Ambassador.

[54] The Anlo Youth Organization member was M. K. Apaloo, a leading journalist, later to be a prominent member of the opposition, later again to be detained on grounds of complicity in the 'army plot' of 1958.

the seats and a narrow majority of the votes, a pattern that was to be reproduced in the country generally.

The Moslem Association fared reasonably well in the main towns, although its only successful candidate, at Tamale in the north, represented as much a victory for the NPP as a measure of support for Islam. Nevertheless, with a third of the vote in the Kumasi North and Accra West constituencies, the Association could fairly claim to exist in its own right.

Finally, the election results showed that the intelligentsia opposition was still shallow-rooted. The Congress Party was all but swept away, with K. A. Busia as its only successful candidate, by a margin of only eleven votes. Only in Akim Abuakwa, Cape Coast, and Wenchi was the party given a substantial share of the votes:

Akim Abuakwa Central:	J. B. Danquah, GCP	3,622[55]
	A. E. Ofori Atta, CPP	4,958
Akim Abuakwa West:	W. Ofori Atta, GCP	3,652
	S. W. Owusu Afari, CPP	4,963
Cape Coast:	N. A. Welbeck, CPP	7,665
	Kofi Amponsah-Dadzie, GCP	4,157
Wenchi West	K. A. Busia, GCP	3,765
	C. E. Donkor, CPP	3,754

If, too, the CPP had deserved to win because of its organization and the energy with which it contested the election, the Congress Party had often seemed to deserve to lose for precisely the same reasons. There was very little overall direction of the party, Busia actually being out of the country on polling day, while the appeal even of the more politically able of its candidates often looked inept. Thus the Kumasi South electorate had been told in an election leaflet[56]

Mrs Nancy Tsiboe

is your right candidate

VOTE FOR HER

She attended two world conferences, studied Red Cross work and

---

[55] Danquah's defeat was the more bitter in that he lost to Aaron Ofori Atta (a younger son of the Akim Abuakwa chief), who became a minister immediately following the election.

[56] Wife of John Tsiboe, owner manager of the *Ashanti Pioneer*; a prominent member later of the Ashanti NLM, and treasurer of the United Party until she crossed over to the CPP at the end of 1960. Voting in Kumasi South was: E. O. Asafu Adjaye (CPP) 11,232; Nancy Tsiboe (GCP) 2,104.

child delinquency in England, and specialized in problems about wayward girls. She is a Juvenile Magistrate.

VOTE FOR HER

—a recommendation which must have had, at best, an extremely limited appeal to the tough Kumasi voter. The intelligentsia might well be thought, therefore, to have played its final card, and to have lost. Yet this was by no means true. They joined forces with the NPP, and within months of the June election they were to be in the forefront once again in a new bid to overthrow the CPP.

In aggregate throughout the country, there was a considerable anti-CPP vote. The extent of the nationalist party's success in terms of seats exaggerated its strength at the polls, and when the election was looked at in terms of the actual votes cast the measure of the party's victory was greatly reduced:

	Seats	Per cent of 104	Votes	Per cent of total poll*
CPP	69	68·3	391,817	55·4
Non-CPP	32	31·7	314,903	44·6

* In 101 contested constituencies. There were 3 uncontested CPP seats.

The distribution of seats and votes between the parties was:

	Seats	Votes	Per cent of total poll
CPP	72	391,817	55·4
Ind.	11	156,401	22
NPP	15	68,709	9·7
MAP	1	21,172	2·9
GCP	1	32,168	5
TC	3	25,214	3·5
AYO	1	7,375	1
GNP	0	3,579	0·5
GAP	0	285	—

NOTE: the NPP figure includes the 3 nominal Independents, J. A. Braimah, the Tolon-Na, and C. K. Tedam. The Togoland Congress figure includes the Rev. F. R. Ametowobla. The CPP total includes Imoru Egala's votes and seat.

Or expressed regionally:

	Colony		Ashanti		TVT		North	
	Seats	Votes	Seats	Votes	Seats	Votes	Seats	Votes
CPP	38	178,226	18	95,845	8	46,547	8	71,199
Ind.	7	60,404	2	46,897	1	7,375	2	41,725
NPP	–	–	–	–	–	–	15	68,709
MAP	0	4,003	0	5,454	0	675	1	11,040
GCP	0	17,310	1	14,858	–	–	–	–
TC	–	–	–	–	3	25,214	–	–
AYO	–	–	–	–	1	7,375	–	–
GNP	0	3,579	–	–	–	–	–	–
GAP	0	285	–	–	–	–	–	–

What general conclusions could be drawn from these tables? First, surely, that the CPP was still the only political movement in the country capable of forming a government. No other party could equal its overall national character or match its skilful use of the techniques of mass action. With its 72 members in parliament, and a reserve of successful rebels who now waited hopefully to be taken back into favour as prodigal sons, the new government might well be thought impregnable. The party was once more in office, with a greater control of all the advantages of power: it was reasonable, therefore, to suppose that the leaders would be able, in time, to heal the divisions within the constituency executives, either by the threat of a withdrawal of government favour, or by the clever use of government patronage. Moreover, the opposition parties in the Assembly looked in poor shape. The intelligentsia group had lost its two ablest advocates in the 1951 Assembly—Danquah and William Ofori Atta. (It had, however, Busia and a new and forceful representative—M. K. Apaloo, for Anlo South.) The NPP members, though fiercely critical of the CPP, were likely to find it difficult to oppose the government on any national issue; the small number of Togoland Congress supporters were no less hostile to the CPP, but on the main issue which interested them and their supporters—Togoland unification—they were on opposite sides from the NPP, their nominal ally.

Nevertheless, it was also possible to see that the CPP had been forced to contend with a much greater challenge than any which had existed in 1951. The number of Independents, the NPP, the Muslims, the Togoland Congress, and local associations like the Anlo Youth Organization all pointed in the same direction, and showed the shift in emphasis that had taken place from national to local issues. The NPP in particular was a portent: its sudden formation, rapid growth, and unexpected success, showed how far the pendulum could travel away from the national appeal of Self-Government to a practical desire to see that local interests were safeguarded before independence was won. It was in keeping with British practice that such an election should have been held before independence in order to determine who should take working charge of the full grant of self-government: but its effect had been to demonstrate the truth of the maxim suggested in the opening paragraph of this account of the 1954 contest—that, while agitation may unite, elections tend to divide. The question remained therefore whether the CPP would be able to sustain its national appeal if faced with a widening of the attack launched by the NPP and the rebels. It was soon to be answered. For within months of the June election a movement was to be formed in Kumasi which brought together each of the main points of opposition to the CPP, and added new grievances of its own.

NOTE ON THE ELECTION CAMPAIGN

1. Lawra Nandom Constituency

Accounts of the 1954 campaign waged in the constituencies by one side or the other were difficult to come by. But the way in which the NPP was able to win one of its sixteen seats was recorded briefly for the writer by one of (four) candidates in the extreme north-west of the Northern Territories. The district—Lawra Nandom—was a remote one, delimited as a constituency by the Van Lare Commission which brought together three local chiefdoms, each grouped around an eponymous capital: Lawra, Nandom, and Birifu. The standpoint of the writer of the short extracts given below was that of an Independent candidate who misjudged his own chances. He begins by describing the several 'techniques' of electioneering in these remote parts, and then explains how the NPP candidate had all the local advantages on his side:

> The chiefs and headmen of each Division or village before polling day call together their subjects to discuss the support to be given to the candidates concerned. They present their views on this subject and rule out support for a particular candidate. During the general election of 1954 each chief in the Lawra-Nandom constituency had alternate views, and so the support given to the various candidates was split. But in Lawra, the Lawra-Na bade his subjects vote for his son Abayifaa Karbo.[57] All his sub-chiefs, headmen and householders were called into the palace and a big meeting discussed full support for Mr Karbo who contested on the NPP ticket. The Birifu people stood firm behind their chief Nonantuo Gandaa on the CPP ticket. In Nandom the Nandom-Na canvassed for his son K. P. Paul who stood as an Independent. His sub-chiefs and headmen were used in villages for this purpose. Sylvester also stood as an Independent because of the support of the Catholic teachers. Termaghre [a third Independent] had only his family to help him....
>
> The NPP had the support of the Lawra Confederacy Council staff, the office clerks, the foreman of works, the labourers in the camps, all had a hand. They competed for promotion in their various positions under the Council by supporting the Lawra-Na and the NPP. Labourers carried the word to their families; even the children at school were told to take the doctrines of the NPP home to their parents. Mr Karbo also had the use of the Lawra-

---

[57] Abayifaa Karbo, NPP and (later) United Party member for Lawra-Nandom. His father was one of the original members of the N.T. Council, and a member of the Coussey Committee.

Na's car. So in this way the propaganda of the NPP was wide, simple and successful. . . .

Because of Paul's support from the Nandom chief he did not lose his deposit. Neither did Sylvester because of the Catholics. The Catholic teachers, catechists and Catholic Action members were divided between Karbo and Sylvester except in Nandom town where they supported Paul. They regarded the CPP as a weapon leading to communism, restriction of religion and closing of their schools. The few who supported the CPP were disdained of their fellows. [58]

This interesting account showed quite clearly the interlocking structure of traditional and colonial authority, around which were woven other loyalties like those of the Catholics who supported Sylvester. What was missing here was the appeal of the CPP itself as a national force attracting support by its authority as a government and by its appeal as a nationalist movement. But the Lawra-Nandom constituency was a remote area in 1954, and the position began to change by the time of the third general election in July 1956, when there were only two candidates: NPP and CPP. Both the 'Catholic vote' and the 'Nandom vote' then went to Karbo who won a handsome victory. A. P. S. Termaghre also stood down, campaigned for the Birifu-Na and the CPP, and proved the generosity of the party towards its followers by being made District Commissioner for the north-west in 1958.

2. Sunyani West Constituency

A similar account was given the writer, in the form of answers to questions, by an unsuccessful 'rebel' candidate in western Ashanti:

Why were there three candidates, one CPP and two Independents?

'It is abundantly clear that, in 1954, Sunyani West Constituency which is a constituency of three Independent States agreed among

[58] Account given to the author by A. P. S. Termaghre. The result was: Abayifaa Karbo (NPP), 2,764; Nonantuo Gandaa (CPP), 2,434; Sylvester Sanziri (Ind.), 1,863; Konkun Polku Paul (Ind.), 1,569; and A. P. Sarvero Termaghre (Ind.), 508, who lost his deposit. Nonantuo Gandaa was the Birifu-Na, the chief of a historically important settlement, placed under Lawra by the British and continually petitioning for separation. He was a pleasant, eccentric character, a good farmer, genuinely attracted by the radicalism of the CPP, and astute enough to see the advantages of supporting the government. But Birifu was a small settlement of about 3,000 inhabitants, and it was difficult for the CPP to pick up support in the Lawra district as a whole. The party struggle was also a local struggle, as this short account made clear, and the conflict was renewed in the quarrel that broke out over a successor to the Nandom-Na who died shortly after the 1954 election. The NPP backed Paul, who was 'in the line of succession'. The CPP backed an unexpected candidate, Barrow Yuori, who claimed to have the support of the *tendanna* (called locally, the *tigansob*) and of the non-chiefly 'rural' compounds; and, eventually, the government approved the choice of Barrow Yuori.

other things to present three candidates based on three main factors:

1. Quality of the candidate.
2. Outspoken ability to secure his State's interests and the country as a whole.
3. Easy to be in touch for consultations on subject of interest to the Electorates for presentation in Parliament.

With these in view, the Electorates based their preference on a choice of a candidate who was primarily a native of the State and conversant with its problems rather than a Stranger ignorant of the knowledge of a state and hardly [available] to be consulted. By a process of party system CPP has succeeded to group and organise the whole country into constituencies administered by the executives headed by chairmen upon whom rests the solidarity of the Party. Therefore 'as no one can go to Heaven without Peter', so the question of nominations by the headquarters is ever done on the recommendations of the constituency chairman.'

[After a great deal of argument, the national headquarters in Accra decided to accept what was alleged to be the constituency chairman's partisan recommendation of one of the three; whereupon the two who were rejected decided to stand as 'rebels'].

How did you conduct Your Campaign?

'With its vast size coupled with the dilapidated aspect of the motor road, campaign in the Sunyani West Constituency was indeed a difficult problem when I was conducting my Campaign. From my well scrutinised plans I gave four days in every week of the Election period to travel to each of the three States accompanied by six specially selected eloquent speakers. Their subsistence and transport expenses were my responsibilities. For purposes of my Campaign, a taxi cab hired at £50 was ever at my disposal. Besides this, a fleet of 6 lorries were also engaged at £10 each in the last week of the election period to round up my Campaign, and were loaded with supporters both men and women. They enjoyed the round up Campaign with songs attributed to my qualities and meaning of my election symbol—'Fish for wisdom, integrity and experience'. I had two organising groups of men and flashing Girls in each of the three states for daily Canvas by house to house personal contacts. They were given drinks and cash for subsistence for services as Election Contractors, services which they happily accepted with interest and pride.

I did not of course make appeals for finances from anyone in connection with the campaign beside solemn and strong appeals for their votes. . . . To ease all problems of financial stringencies my Relatives who had agreed to support me, raised a loan of £700 for transport and other relevant expenses. From this picture it can be inferred that a Contestant is by all means a victim to debts and many afflictions of hunger and weariness. Conclusively, to stand for a parliament election is not a matter of utopian [enjoyment?].'

The result was:

Official CPP candidate	5,354
First Rebel	3,638
Second Rebel	2,283

A typical result at this time: each candidate picked up a sizeable vote from his own district, but the CPP candidate had, in addition, enough votes from party loyalists throughout the constituency to tip the balance.

VI

The Struggle for Power, 1954–6

THE year 1954 opened the second phase of the nationalist movement—the middle years of uncertainty and violence, when once
again a new party was formed and fresh demands raised of an extreme kind. It was noted in an earlier chapter that, despite the
confidence of the leaders as they renewed their demand for self-
government, the CPP in Ashanti 'trembled on the brink of
division', and indeed the June election was hardly over when discontent with the government grew to open revolt. A 'National
Liberation Movement', formed in Kumasi in mid-September,
was in full swing by the end of October. The threat to the CPP
was serious, for the NLM challenged the nationalist party at
several different points. Not only did it try—as the NPP had
done—to postpone the date of independence; it also proposed an
alternative, federal definition of the new Ghana state which drew
great political support from local grievances. Moreover, it met
the nationalist appeal of the CPP with a rival nationalism of its
own, through an impassioned demand for recognition of the
traditional unity of the 'Ashanti nation'. The newly elected
government was taken completely by surprise. Yet many of the
CPP members in Ashanti resisted the appeal of the new party
with the result that, by the end of 1954, a violent conflict developed in Ashanti between rival gangs which struggled against
each other wherever the CPP or the NLM was unable to establish a local stronghold of single-party rule. As the quarrel deepened, the colonial administration was drawn into the dispute, to
find itself in the uncomfortable position of a referee obliged to
interfere in a contest in which the participants declined to recognize any rules. And, no longer sure where the balance of power
lay in the country, the United Kingdom government also hesitated. It drew back from the prospect of surrendering control before this new threat to the stability of the nationalist régime. The
CPP leaders did everything they could to minimize the dispute

in order to reassure the British; the NLM, on the contrary, stressed the need for a new assessment of the political scene, and the argument continued into 1955 and 1956, violence spreading from Kumasi into the surrounding chiefdoms until, eventually, the United Kingdom government intervened and imposed its own solution—a third general election.

It is this struggle for power between the nationalist party and its enemies that forms the subject of this chapter. Between June 1954 and the July election of 1956 events crowded upon each other with great rapidity; and to enable the reader to view the conflict between the NLM and the CPP from more than one vantage point the narrative has been divided into three parts. The NLM is dealt with first; then the position of the CPP in relation to the new movement; and, thirdly, the failure of both sides to come to terms with each other. By way of introduction, however, to this triple account, something also needs to be said briefly of the immediate post-election scene.

In June and July 1954 there was hardly a sign of the conflict that was soon to break out. At the national level, all was quiet; and events took their expected course. Nkrumah submitted his list of names of the first all-African cabinet to the Governor.[1] The new parliament met for the first time under the 1954 constitution, and Emmanuel Quist was reappointed Speaker. The government then announced a detailed programme to prepare the country for the grant of self-government, now confidently expected. It included the reopening of 'negotiations with the United Kingdom Government with a view to the achievement of independence', an endorsement of the terms of the United Kingdom memorandum to the United Nations on the future of Togoland, the appointment of an Advisory Committee of Ministers 'to assist the Governor in the discharge of his responsibilities for defence and external affairs', and the speeding up of a policy of Africanization of the public service. These pronouncements

[1] Kwame Nkrumah, Prime Minister; Kojo Botsio, Minister of State; K. A. Gbedemah, Minister of Finance; A. Casely Hayford, Minister of the Interior; E. O. Asafu Adjaye, Minister of Local Government; J. H. Allasani, Minister of Education; J. E. Jantuah, Minister of Agriculture; N. A. Welbeck, Minister of Works; A. E. Ofori Atta, Minister of Communications; Ako Adjei, Minister of Trade and Labour; Imoru Egala, Minister of Health. Two were Ashanti; three were from Ashanti constituencies, Casely Hayford having been elected for Kumasi South. Krobo Edusei was appointed national propaganda secretary for the CPP in August.

were backed by an avowal of the government's intention to 'establish a firm basis of friendship with the other territories of West Africa' and, at home, to 'maintain freedom of speech, of thought and of the press', while refusing to 'tolerate violence in any form'.[2] The only point of friction in these early ceremonies came when the proposal was made that S. D. Dombo, Duori-Na (the leader of the NPP) should be recognized as Leader of the Opposition. Nkrumah objected, on the grounds that the NPP was a non-national party. The opposition members 'walked out' of the Assembly; Nkrumah was overruled by the Speaker, and order was restored.[3]

The new legislators were much like the party members of the 1951–4 Assembly, as may be seen in the analysis opposite.

The defeat of the UGCC leaders and the disappearance of the territorial council members made the Assembly still more uniform. Among its members there was no paramount chief or any representative of the once firmly established Colony intelligentsia who had given the earlier legislative councils so distinctive a flavour.[4] The 'young men' had come fully into their own, and party leaders and officials alike might well have thought that the revolution was over, now that control of the internal machinery of government was in the hands of the commoners. There was nothing either at national or local level to alarm the officials or disquiet the new ministers, and the country remained quiet throughout July and early August while the new parliament debated its affairs. Then, in September, there was a violent renewal of the Ashanti protest made during the 1953 debate on the Van Lare *Report*. This time it was centred not on parliament but in the constituencies, and with the suddenness of a tropical

---

[2] *The Speech prepared by the Ministers and delivered by H.E. the Governor and Commander-in-Chief on the occasion of the ceremonial opening of the Legislative Assembly of the Gold Coast on the 29th July 1954.*

[3] GC, LA Deb., 11 Aug. 1954. Nkrumah then warned the House that 'if we tolerate the formation of political parties on regional, sectional or religious bases, we shall not only be heading for political chaos but, worse still, we shall be sowing the seeds of the destruction of our national existence. Coming events cast their shadows before them, and the Government shall consider what steps should be taken to eradicate this emerging evil in our national life.' Something was clearly afoot, and Nkrumah at least had begun to sense it.

[4] Casely Hayford (from Cape Coast) and Asafu Adjaye (from Kumasi) might be said to belong to that earlier generation of reformist lawyers, but they were now relatively unimportant figures in the party; both looked out of place in the new cabinet of party radicals, and were later to withdraw from the front line of political action.

Assembly Members: Age and Education

	Ave. age at 1 July 1954	Education			
		Univ.	Secondary	Teacher training	Elementary
Ministers (11)	43·0	6	3	2	—
Ministerial Secretaries (11)	37·0	1	6	2	2
Other CPP members (50)*	37·4	4	15	17	14
Opposition members (32)	36·3	2	7	14	9

* Including the only woman member.

Assembly Members: Occupation

	Lawyers	Politicians	Teachers	Traders	Clerks	Local govt employees	Misc.
CPP	5	7	16	26	9	2	7
Opp.	–	–	15*	4	2	8	3

* Including 1 university teacher.

Source: Members' returns to the Speaker's Office and J. H. Price, 'The Gold Coast Legislators', *West Africa*, 26 May 1956.

storm, when the sky darkens and the clouds advance with astonishing speed over the horizon, opposition to the government drew together in Ashanti. From that point forward, the newly elected parliament was pushed into the background (although used occasionally as a weapon by the CPP against the new movement. For the NLM lay outside the framework of the 1954 constitution, and struggled to have it annulled.

THE NATIONAL LIBERATION MOVEMENT

The immediate origins of the NLM are clear. The starting-point was Gbedemah's introduction into the Assembly (10 August) of the Cocoa Duty and Development Funds (Amendment) Bill which sought to fix the price to be paid to farmers, per

load of 60 lb. of cocoa, at 72s. for a period of four years.[5] The
Ordinance was a sensible attempt to check an inflationary situation as the world price climbed to £450 a ton (or £12 10s. a load),
but ill timed. To fix the price at exactly the same level as the
previous year's, on so rapidly rising a market, would have been
poor tactics at the best of times; to do so immediately following
an election, when hopes had been raised, was folly. No doubt
there would have been complaints whatever course was followed,
but an immediate slight increase in the price, and the announcement (six months later, after the cocoa harvest was in) that prices
would continue to be maintained, might have reconciled the
farmers' representatives to the action taken by the government.[6]
But in August 1954 farmers in the cocoa constituencies could still
hear the arguments used by the CPP candidates that the recent
introduction of a new £5 note had been made to facilitate the
payment of 100s. a load price for the forthcoming main crop
season. And the more sophisticated of the government's critics
worked it out that, if it had been possible to pay 80s. a load in
1951–2 when the world price was £245 a ton, it was no crime to
ask for £5 or £7 a load now that the world price was over £450.[7]
The CPP leaders could protest that they were doing no more than

[5] Gbedemah was now Minister of Finance. His defence of the Cocoa Act was
that '. . . in 1950, out of a total export revenue of £77·4 million, cocoa constituted
£52·4 million; in 1951, out of a total export revenue of £92 million, cocoa constituted £60·3 million; in 1952, out of a total export revenue of £85·4 million,
cocoa constituted £52·5 million; and in the last year, that is, 1953, out of a total
export revenue of £89·7 million, cocoa constituted £66·1 million. All the other
export crops put together cannot form the basis of any major fiscal policy apart
from cocoa and therefore the Government is justified and is right in basing its
policy on the major crop which this country produces in order to stabilise its
economy, and in doing so to use the accumulated funds to the benefit of every
section of the community. . .' (GC, LA Deb., 13 Aug. 1954).

[6] This was the advice offered by Sir Patrick FitzGerald, then general manager of
the United Africa Company, who was attacked in the *Evening News* for his interference. The advice was sound; but it may well be that, coming from UAC, the
party was convinced of the rightness of its own course. The CPP was later to believe—they were ready by then to believe anything—that the European trading
firms were actively financing and promoting the NLM, on the grounds that the
firms had built up large stocks in mistaken anticipation of a high price. For the
connexion between the Asante Farmers' Union and Messrs Cadbury & Fry see
below, p. 344 n. 29.

[7] What did the cocoa farmer know of the world price? Not much, and 72s. a
load was still a very good price against the background of the pre-war years, when
in parts of Ashanti (e.g. in Dormaa in 1932) it fell to as little as 2s. 6d. But argument along these lines was well within the grasp of the local party executive member. The cocoa-price argument was always part of a wider Ashanti protest which
included farmers, traders, teachers, clerks, and so forth: its importance in September 1954 was that it brought into the open, and joined together, a deep-seated
grievance among many Ashanti about their relations with the south.

follow the policy on which they had been returned to office, in that their *Election Manifesto* 'Operation 104' had avoided any promise of a higher price. But promises of a general increase in cocoa prices had certainly formed part of the local propaganda carried on in a number of constituencies, and the farmers' disappointment was directed in the first place against the local party members who, in turn, complained to Accra. Nor was the position helped by a clumsy official statement, like the one issued by the Press Officer for the Cocoa Marketing Board, which pointed out—justifiably—that 'a rise in the price of a local raw product such as cocoa encourages inflation in the stores. . . . Increase cocoa prices abnormally today, and tomorrow prices in the stores will be sky-rocketted'—but added that: 'Should a farmer realise that a few loads of cocoa could yield sufficient income to keep him going all the year he might be encouraged to work less'. To this the Secretary of the United Ghana Farmers' Council, despite its CPP affiliation, retorted that 'it was not fair to offer a meagre price to the farmer who toils in the bush while the world market price has increased so steeply. . . . Also I would advise the CMB to pay [the Press Officer] less salary so that he might not work less.'[8]

It was popular argument carried on in these terms that turned discussion and complaints into angry, excited meetings of farmers throughout the cocoa-growing districts, but it was in Ashanti that protests began to take on a political character. This was hardly surprising, for cocoa was of paramount importance throughout the region, not only to the farmers but to the urban traders. Kumasi, in particular, was a boom-town, with great numbers of new two- and three-storied concrete houses, honey-combed with tenants, which now dominated even the traditional quarter, Manhyia, where the Asantehene had his palace and courts.[9] Nearly 50 per cent of the cocoa grown in the country

[8] *Ashanti Pioneer*, 21 Aug. 1954.
[9] Kumasi was—is still—different in this respect from Accra. The private-enterprise character of the town was borne out by a government *Kumasi Survey of Population and Household Budgets*, March 1956 (No. 5), when it was discovered that: 'Kumasi with only 34 per cent of all families having wage incomes was by far the least dependent of the three principal urban areas on employment'; its non-wage incomes were the 'principal source of livelihood in the city'. By contrast, in Accra, 57 per cent of all families depended on wage incomes, and in Sekondi-Takoradi the proportion was as high as 69 per cent. This meant a much greater dependence in Kumasi on fluctuations of local trade and its determinant—the cocoa price—and with it went a lively political activity.

came from the region, and much of its wealth was spent in the
regional capital:

	1936–7		1950–1		1951–2	
	Tonnage	Per cent	Tonnage	Per cent	Tonnage	Per cent
Eastern Province	128,000	43	56,147	21	47,585	24
Remainder of the Colony & Togoland	81,000	27	83,409	32	65,409	30
Ashanti	91,000	30	122,667	47	97,666	46

By the middle of August the demand had arisen in Kumasi for
£7 10s. a load,[10] and farmers began to meet in the local chiefdom
'capitals' up and down Ashanti to formulate complaints to the
United Ghana Farmers' Council. The 'Kumasi North-West
Farmers', for example, met at Offinso, some fifteen miles from
Kumasi, under the chairmanship of Opanin Kojo Kumadu, the
district Head Farmer. In characteristic language they 'sym-
pathized' with the government's desire to undertake development projects and 'totally disagreed' with its contention that the
farmers, if paid more, would waste the money on 'buying useless
commodities at the stores'.[11] Similar meetings were held in a
number of other towns, and on 15 August farmers from a number
of outlying districts travelled into Kumasi to meet at the Asawase
Community Centre where they protested against the price of
72s. a load and demanded the withdrawal of the Ordinance.
They met again a week later, when B. E. Dwira of the Farmers'
Council and the Cocoa Marketing Board tried to explain to them
the government's policy. He was shouted down, and it was at this
second meeting in Kumasi—on 22 August—that Kofi Buor, the
'Ashanti Chief Farmer', hitherto a loyal member of the Supreme
Council of the United Ghana Farmers' Council, 'swore the
Great Oath of Ashanti' before the assembled farmers that he had
not been consulted about the cocoa price.[12] It was these Asawase

[10] £7 10s. because this was (approximately) the price paid in the neighbouring
Togo Trust Territory and the Ivory Coast.
[11] *Ashanti Pioneer*, 13 Aug. 1954.
[12] The importance of 'swearing an oath' needs some explanation. The chiefs (as
will be seen) swore the Great Oath of Ashanti to support the NLM. In essence, an
oath consisted of breaking a taboo by the utterance of a particular word or phrase

meetings which marked the beginnings of a definite revolt against the CPP within the farmers' associations, for Kofi Buor and others now decided to back their demands for a higher cocoa price by a new movement. A 'Council for Higher Cocoa Prices' was formed with Kofi Buor as chairman; a cable was dispatched to the Queen in protest against the Cocoa Ordinance, and the farmers looked round for allies.

The cocoa issue was then quickly absorbed by more general complaints, and if the first step towards forming a new movement was made by the farmers' representatives, the second was taken by the CPP 'rebels' of the June election. The central committee had judged correctly when it chose Kumasi for its public ceremony of expelling the rebels; and although the results of the election might be thought to have allayed its fears—the party having won 18 of the 21 seats—the wide margin of its victory concealed the extent of opposition to the leaders. Over 41 per cent of the Ashanti electorate had voted against the party's candidates. Over a fifth of the votes—37,582 out of 163,054—had gone to the rebels. It was now that the effect of this was felt. For many of the disgruntled members of the local constituency executives were able to argue not only that Ashanti was misrepresented in the Assembly by party 'yes-men' who had voted for the Cocoa Amendment Bill against Ashanti interests, but that the fault lay in Accra where the central committee had forced its choice on the local branches. This was hardly the whole truth, but it was used as a ground of complaint, and it matched the general mood of dissatisfaction among the party members.

In much the same way, therefore, as those who claimed to

---

whose recital recalls an evil or tragic event. Thus a state may have lost its chief in battle on Thursday at such and such a place. To pronounce, as an oath, the word 'Thursday' or the name of the place was to recall the event; it was therefore a taboo, only to be broken when the speaker wished to emphasize the gravity of what he was saying or to secure public recognition of his statement. It could be used to bring a private injury into the open, before court for trial; to bind the swearer of the oath or others to follow a course of action: the penalty in each instance being the displeasure of the ancestral spirits who were disturbed by the recital of the forbidden names. For example, says Busia (p. 77): 'Captains going to war swore that they would never turn their back to their enemy. . . . A Captain swore on oath ordering that none of his men should retreat from the enemy. . . . A chief might swear an oath enjoining his men to observe a certain custom. . . '. The Great Oath of Ashanti might lie in the mere recital of the words: *me ka ntam kese* (I swear the Great Oath) or, more seriously, because it was more explicit, *me ka Kormante ne Memenada* (I swear by Kormantine and Saturday), supposedly the place and day of the death of the great Ashanti chief Osei Tutu. See also Rattray, ch. 13.

speak for the farmers had begun to divide into two camps—one led by Kofi Buor, and a small group which remained loyal to the Ghana Farmers' Council—so too the elementary-school-leavers in the constituencies began to quarrel among themselves. The CPP was not merely challenged in Ashanti: it began to fall apart. And, once again, as in the boycott of 1948 and the launching of the CPP a year later, the lead was taken by the Asante Youth Association. A number of its members were already offended by the government's disregard of their protests over the Van Lare *Report*, and phrases had been used then of an ominous cast, in which the expression 'the Ashanti nation' figured prominently.[13] They were now revived, and on Wednesday, 25 August—three days after the farmers' meeting at the Asawase Community Centre—the Kumasi branch of the AYA met in stormy debate at the Kumasi State Council Hall. The meeting was called to discuss the cocoa price, but other grievances were also raised, including the 1953 issue of the inadequacy of Ashanti representation in the Assembly. When Krobo Edusei, Osei Bonsu, and John Baidoo—all members of the Assembly who had voted for the Cocoa Bill—tried to justify the government's stand, they were roughly handled and forced to leave, and a committee of three was then ordered to frame a resolution in support of the farmers. The meeting was full of excited, emotionally-aroused members, not entirely sure what they wanted to do but determined to do something, urged on by a growing crowd of supporters outside the council chamber, some of whom began to chant the Ashanti war-cry—'Osei Ye', 'Osei Ye'—and to demand the election of new officers for the Association.[14] Eventually, the meeting was broken off, but the Association met again two days later (Friday, 27 August), this time with representatives from some of the outlying branches. Led by a small group of CPP rebels—Kusi Ampofo, Osei Assibey Mensah, and E. Y. Baffoe—the meeting now reached agreement on a number of points. Since the Cocoa Purchasing Company officials were getting good salaries (so it was argued), a price of 72s. a load for the cocoa farmer was un-

[13] e.g. in the *Statement* issued in August 1953, saying that: the AYA 'holds the view that in all things affecting the national interest it shall hold itself independent. It further holds the view that in the recent issue of electoral representation it shall support a national united front of the Ashanti nation.'

[14] The president was J. E. Jantuah, a loyal CPP Ashanti member of the Assembly, Minister of Agriculture.

fair: there had been 'a disregard and contempt' for the Ashanti representatives on the Cocoa Marketing Board and for the 'whole Ashanti nation'. *Ennye obi aburo nti na wofifi se*,[15] said one member, and they all agreed. The words 'federation' and *yeate ye ho*[16] were heard, and again there were wild scenes outside. This time the meeting ended with two resolutions: one endorsing a decision to support the farmers, the other demanding a 'federal constitution for the Gold Coast'. The following day there was a joint meeting of Kofi Buor and his Council for Higher Cocoa Prices with the AYA representatives at the Asawase Community Centre at which a number of well-known opposition leaders turned up: M. K. Apaloo, Kwesi Lamptey, and Ashie Nikoe.[17] The discussions were again confused, with heated exchanges between those who sought to restrain the members from directly challenging the government, and others who wanted to force a break. Once again the only definite resolution adopted was an expression of violent dissent with the Cocoa Amendment Ordinance, and a further memorandum of protest, sent this time to the Secretary of State.

Having thus openly linked themselves with the farmers' demands for a higher cocoa price, the AYA rebels then turned to the chiefs. Here, at first sight, was a curious *volte face* and, when the position of the CPP in these events is examined, it will be seen that not all the young men of the AYA or in the constituencies were prepared to join hands with their traditional rulers. Nevertheless those who saw the conflict that was arising between the farmers and the government as one affecting the rights and interests of Ashanti were also ready to see the chiefs as still the most potent symbol of Ashanti unity. The chiefs, in their turn, were willing allies in any movement against the CPP leaders, and their resentment against the government was easy to under-

[15] 'It is not for other people's corn that we grow teeth.'

[16] 'We have broken away': that is 'separation', 'federation', or whatever shade of meaning the user of the phrase liked to give it. This was to be the NLM party slogan in answer to the CPP's 'Freedom'.

[17] It was this meeting that led to the final break between Kofi Buor and the United Ghana Farmers' Council. Kofi Buor was 'removed from office' by Kwame Poku, the National President, and Martin Appiah Danquah, the acting secretary of the UGFC. 'As you are aware [Kofi Buor was told] this Council has pledged its loyalty to the CPP Government and therefore to meet with people who are against the Government and take decisions in the name of the Council is a grave constitutional issue' (unpubl. letter to Kofi Buor, 2 Sept. 1954, from Martin Appiah Danquah).

stand; they saw the power that had been theirs from time immemorial (which had not been greatly disturbed by British rule) now in the hands of their enemies. Although deprived of their independence by the British, the chiefs of the Ashanti Confederacy had been given considerable powers as a 'Supreme Native Authority'. They had received generous subsidies from the central government, and acted as deliberative body for the whole of the Confederacy area with substantive law-making powers.[18] The beginning of the end of these privileges had come in 1952 when the Asanteman Council, the Kumasi Native Authority, and the Chiefs' Councils within each Ashanti Division were pushed aside to make way for the new local authorities with their two-thirds elected membership. Government subsidies were still paid to the chiefs, and a State Council Ordinance in 1952 recognized the chief and his traditional advisers as having authority in customary matters, but the substance of their power, including the levying of the local rate, passed to the new urban and local councils. The future looked still more bleak, for the views of the CPP leaders were well known, and their refusal in 1953–4 to recommend the establishment of a second chamber confirmed the chiefs' forebodings. In short, they did not like Nkrumah, the CPP, the direction of reform, or the prospect before them.

The separate threads of support for a new party were now drawn swiftly together. The intermediary in September 1954 between the AYA spokesmen, the farmers, and the chiefs, was a local Kumasi leader of great enterprise: Bafuor Osei Akoto, a middle-aged, alert, energetic leader, a wealthy cocoa farmer, and a senior linguist (*okyeame*) of the Asantehene. When the CPP leaders learned of Bafuor Akoto's part in bringing the new movement into being, they liked to accuse the NLM in its early months of being led by a 'feudal illiterate': but this was by no means the case. Bafuor Akoto had attended the Kumasi Boys' School up to Standard VI (that is, nine years of schooling) before being apprenticed for six years as a motor mechanic to the important firm of Messrs Swanzy Transport. Eventually he had been made chief fitter for Messrs Cadbury & Fry in Kumasi; later again, in 1934–5, he had spent some thirteen months in Tamale as a fitter-driver in his own business until, with the

---

[18] For an account of the powers and functions of the Ashanti chiefs in pre-colonial times and under an NA system, see Busia.

restoration of the Ashanti Confederacy, he was called back to Kumasi and appointed one of the six senior linguists to the new Asantehene.[19] Brought up in the city as a child amidst stories of the 1900 rebellion and the past greatness of Ashanti, this was a post that he liked to fill (and filled very well); and in 1954 he was a man of great experience, widely known and respected by the chiefs who visited Kumasi to discuss state matters with the Asantehene, known and liked too by the Kumasi crowd of young men, not least because of his generous patronage of the Asante Kotoko football team. (He had, for example, accompanied the Gold Coast football team to England in 1951 at his own expense.) When, therefore, the rebel AYA leaders looked round for a leader, it was Bafuor Akoto whom they approached, and he immediately promised his help. Names were suggested—an 'Ashanti People's Party', the 'Ashanti Federal Party', the 'National Action Group', and—at the last—the 'National Liberation Movement'.[20] The AYA members—re-formed under a new president, G. K. Addai, a Kumasi pharmacist and cocoa farmer—undertook to spread the new party through the constituencies: to convert the CPP in Ashanti into an NLM just as they helped in 1949–50 to bring about the turnover of local branches of the UGCC to the CPP. Bafuor Akoto promised the help of the traditional leaders once the new movement was launched. When the Kumasi chiefs were in, the Asantehene could be approached; when the Otumfuo had given the party his blessing, the outlying paramount chiefs would declare their support. Kofi Buor would bring in the farmers, Alhaji Amadu Baba the Muslims. There were more distant allies in the north and Togoland who had already shown Ashanti the way. Then they could all turn their attention to the south; and if each played his part, it was hardly possible to fail. The chiefs, the farmers, the educated leaders, the young men, the spirits and ancestors of the entire Ashanti nation, would sustain and carry forward the work of liberation.

[19] 'Linguist' is misleading, although this is the usual English translation; more accurately, an *okyeame* is the 'spokesman' of the chief. Apart from his duties as a linguist, Bafuor Akoto employed some two dozen labourers on his farms which produced between 500–700 loads of cocoa a year. Thus to Bafuor Osei Akoto alone the difference between 72s. and £5 a load meant an overall difference in gross income of between £700 and £1,000 a year.

[20] A phrase hitherto used by the CPP of itself, borrowed from the vocabulary of communist writings.

Thus the pattern was designed; and thus it began to take shape. Early on Sunday, 19 September, at the large open space in Kejetia known as the Prince of Wales Park, a mammoth crowd began to collect, amidst the beating of drums, the singing of Ashanti war songs, the firing of muskets, and loud cries of *Mate me ho*! By midday the assembly was very large. Those who arrived late, to throng the outskirts of the crowd, could barely hear the proclamation of Bafuor Osei Akoto as chairman, or see the ritual slaughter of a sheep as the new chairman swore the Great Oath of Ashanti that he would not fail the movement; but they could see the flag of the party unfurled above the party platform, buy a membership card of the 'National Liberation Movement' with its printed motto, *Amanyopa* (Good Government), and hear the roars of the crowd as Bafuor Akoto was carried in triumph. Two other national officers were 'elected' with him—both of them members of the AYA–Kusi Ampofo, the party's first general secretary, and E. Y. Baffoe, its first national propaganda secretary. Thus the new party was launched, and argument went on that evening late into the night in the drinking bars and 'nightclubs' of Kumasi for and against it. But those who had seen the inauguration of the NLM did not doubt the importance of what had taken place.

Three weeks later the Kumasi chiefs declared their support— the more readily given because the NLM already had its first martyr. On 9 October a quarrel between CPP and NLM supporters in a house in Ashanti New Town led to blows, and E. Y. Baffoe was stabbed to death by K. A. Twumasi Ankrah who had recently been reinstated as regional propaganda secretary for the CPP.[21] The murder, and the name of the victim, aroused great emotion, and Bafuor Akoto carried the news to the Kumasi chiefs when he appealed for their support:

NATIONAL LIBERATION MOVEMENT

Bafuor Osei Akoto appeared before the State Council and explained that the National Liberation Movement was not a Party and that it was surely and honestly a National Movement with the following Aims and Objects:

(1) To banish lawlessness, intimidation, hooliganism, disregard

---

[21] Baffoe, a former Director of the CPC, had been a rebel candidate in the June election in Wenchi East.

for age and authority, suppression of individual conscience and all traces of communism.

(2) To establish respect for efficiency, integrity and honest labour.

(3) To honour, respect and be loyal to our traditional rulers and uphold the best in our culture.

(4) To secure due recognition of the economic, social and cultural background of the respective regions of the Gold Coast and work out a federal or any better form of constitution to give the country an effective voice in the regional and Central Government of the country.

(5) To encourage good neighbourliness among the people of the villages, towns and regions.

(6) To safeguard the interests of farmers and workers, and ensure proper incentives for their labours.

(7) To quicken the achievement of self-government and help build a prosperous, healthy, tolerant and God-fearing Gold Coast Nation.

(8) To foster friendly relations between the Gold Coast and the Commonwealth and other democratic nations.

The fifty-three chiefs of the Council listened in silence to what the senior linguist had to say: then, one after the other, led by Nana Bafuor Kwaku Gyawu II Bantamahene (the Krontihene or 'commander-in-chief' of the Kumasi army), they swore the Great Oath that 'they would give the Movement their maximum support'. They agreed:

(*a*) That the sorrowful incident culminating in the sad death of Mr E. Y. Baffoe be communicated to the Asanteman Council.

(*b*) That the State Council request the Asanteman Council to give to the new Movement their maximum support.

(*c*) That the sum of not more than £20,000 be drawn by the Kumasi State Council from the Asantehene's New Palace Building Fund for the support of this National Movement.[22]

The NLM then appealed direct to the Asantehene and the paramount chiefs of the Asanteman Council. A short memorandum outlined their case, saying that since 'cocoa producers have been alienated from the Cocoa Marketing Board and the Cocoa Purchasing Company which were set up primarily for their interests' their demand for a higher price was undeniably justified. This, however, was no longer the main objective. 'The cocoa

[22] Kumasi State Council *Proc.*, 11 Oct. 1954.

issue is only a facet of a larger problem', and the Movement was
appealing to the Asanteman Council 'for help in the campaign
against the larger issue, namely the stamping out of dictatorship
and communistic practices...'.[23] The chiefs were quick to respond
and, two days later, the Council was hastily summoned in
emergency session. The chiefs travelled in from their states, while
the crowds collected outside to raise an extraordinary hubbub,
yelling their approval at every sight of the enormous, brightly
coloured, tasselled umbrellas of the chiefs as they were escorted
to the Council chamber from their Buicks and Chevrolets. Inside,
the same performance took place as in the Kumasi State Council.
The chiefs who attended swore 'to support the NLM in so far as it
sought to further the establishment of a federal form of government for the Gold Coast', and pledged their loyalty to the Golden
Stool.[24] A 'Resolution to the Queen' was then unanimously
approved which, in more sober tones, prayed for the appointment of a Royal Commission to devise 'a federal constitution for
the Gold Coast', pointed out that 'the traditional constitution of
Ashanti is federal in nature', and declared that 'we firmly believe
that federation will benefit not only the component regions but
the country as a whole in that it will reduce the risk of undue
dictation from the Central Administration and the abuse of
power'. Both then and later the Asantehene publicly avowed his
support. 'I on my part have pledged myself unreservedly to this
cause', he told the Council early in August 1955, and was recorded as telling the chiefs that:

> The National Liberation Movement was a National Organisation.
> It was not a political party. .... People should not think that in sup-
> porting the Movement, they were assisting Bafuor Akoto or any other
> person. They were performing a duty to their nation. They were
> saving their nation from destruction. This was the gospel he wished to
> instil into the minds of all Ashantis. Their forebears through toil and
> sweat, through bitter experience had erected a Nation which was
> admired and respected by foreigners. It was the duty of the present
> generation to see that Ashanti was not lost through an unsuitable
> Constitution for the Gold Coast.[25]

The Asantehene's pledge was given in 1955; but the NLM was

---

[23] NLM memo., 19 Oct. 1954. [24] AC *Minutes* of emerg. sess., 21 Oct. 1954.
[25] AC *Minutes*, 17 & 18 Aug. 1955. It was at this meeting that the chiefs attacked
J. E. Jantuah, then Minister for Agriculture, for having said 'that the Golden Stool

already a power in Ashanti by the end of 1954, tripartite in form, single in appeal. The chiefs, the young men of the AYA, and the farmers' representatives acted together as a political party as, in former times, the Ashanti chiefs had worked together to make the state an unrivalled military power. So at least it seemed when the movement was at the height of its triumphant swing through the inner ring of 'cocoa states' within a 40–50-mile radius of Kumasi. In town after town, and village after village, the NLM flag went up and the CPP flag was pulled down, until, by the middle of 1955, the general secretary was claiming a distribution of 3,000 membership cards a week.

Where did the appeal of the new party really lie? How strong an organization was it? And what did its leaders and the constituency rank and file want?

Three separate groups supported the NLM in its early stages: the farmers who wanted more money for their cocoa, the AYA rebels who had turned against the CPP, and the chiefs who lived in hope of a reversal of their declining fortunes. To these dissatisfied elements should be added the UGCC–GCP leaders in the Colony and Ashanti who also sought revenge on Nkrumah and his People's Party; and in this catalogue of discontented groups alone there were reasons enough to trouble the CPP administration. But it does not wholly explain the force of the appeal made by the NLM. There were many non-Ashanti farmers who would have been glad of more money for their cocoa; there had also been a large number of rebel candidates in the June election in the southern constituencies; and even the faint-hearted chiefs in the Colony states gave their loyalty to the CPP more out of necessity than affection. Except in Akim Abuakwa, however, none of these southern groups was prepared to join the NLM. The explanation was not difficult to find. The fact is, the NLM was a Kumasi-centred, Ashanti movement, which appealed for support in the name of the Asantehene, the Golden Stool, Ashanti interests, Ashanti history, and Ashanti rights.

---

was like any ordinary stool; that it did not contain the spirit of any body, much less that of the Ashanti Nation; that it was a piece of wood carved by a wood carver and plated with Gold. It was therefore stupid for anyone to believe that it descended from Heaven.' The Kumasi State Council slaughtered six sheep in an attempt to expiate the crime, and the Asanteman Council tried to call Jantuah's family to account, without much success.

Countrymen, let us all rally to the struggle, and prayerfully bless the grandson of the great and unconquerable Osei Tutu, the warrior Opoku Ware and the invincible King Bonsu, to redeem their sons' grandsons and restore this beautiful land to her rich culture left us by the precious blood of our great ancestors. Arise dear Lord, for Thy children perish. . . . Countryman-Ashanti, whom will you serve beside Nana Osei Tutu, Otumfuo Sir Osei Agyeman Prempeh II K.B.E., Asantehene?[26]

This was typical of the appeal made by the NLM and those who responded came forward with their whole hearts. The strength of the new party was noted in November 1954 by the editor of the weekly paper *West Africa* who paid a brief visit to Kumasi, and accompanied an NLM procession from Kumasi to a small town some twenty miles west of the city. He heard

. . . Bafuor Akoto address a delegates' meeting from a large number of other villages. His speech was interrupted at intervals by an intense young man who led the crowd in booing CPP leaders one by one, and by the village chief leading them in war cries. Bafuor Akoto gave the usual list of Ashanti grievances—adding that the CPP had even made the youth disrespectful of their elders. He referred to the famous big house of Mr Krobo Edusei, for long the CPP 'boss' in Ashanti, which is now guarded by police since it is thought to be a standing provocation to people who accuse CPP leaders of having entered politics to enrich themselves.

But what really seemed to attract the audience were references to the military prowess of Ashantis, who met the British seven times, the special nature of Ashanti culture, the arrogance of coast men in dealing with Ashanti; once, said Nana Mensah Bonsu, the Hiahene, who was in the chair, one Ashanti gun could bring the submission of 100 men. And as in Kumasi itself the name of the movement's martyr, Emmanuel Baffoe, its propaganda secretary, killed in what is alleged to have been a political brawl, evoked deep emotion. How typical this village is I cannot say; the NLM officials there are simply the former CPP ones, who left the party in disgust because they felt they had been let down by the Government whose candidates, they say, promised an increased cocoa price during the election. Watching these ardent young men standing before the dignified Paramount Chief and the

---

[26] Ohennana John Kofi Poku, *Hints on Yeate Yen Ho, Yen Ara Asase Nii* (Kumasi, Abura Printing Works, 1955). J. K. Poku was general secretary of the Asante Farmers' Union; educated at the Roman Catholic primary school, Obuasi; he was part Fanti, and stood as an Independent candidate in the southern Colony constituency, Asin, in 1954.

movement's leader in his blue toga, I wondered how long the alliance could last; and as I turned to look at the noisy boys wearing jockey caps in NLM colours I wondered more. But while it lasts, and where it exists, it is a formidable alliance.[27]

Here was the inner dynamic of the new movement which drove it forward, fed by the more obvious grievances of the Ashanti farmers, traders, chiefs, and disappointed CPP members. The NLM gathered up an enormous variety of subsidiary discontents as it spread its organization through Ashanti—among those, for example, who were genuinely shocked by the evidence produced before the Van Lare Commission (and by rumours of far worse practices within the Cocoa Purchasing Company), or among the members of a particular local council whose estimates had been disallowed by the minister in Accra. But each local grievance was encompassed by a general resentment against the CPP, based on the belief that Ashanti as a whole—as a people in history—were being 'smothered' (to borrow an expression from the Togoland Congress) by a rival nationalist movement whose principal leaders were non-Ashanti. Hence the popularity at the time of the Ashanti saying: *Asante Kotoko, wokum apem a, apem beba* (the Ashanti porcupine—If you kill a thousand, another thousand will take their place).

How strong was its organization? This was a more difficult question to answer, and one that may be considered more easily after the 1956 election; but, on paper at least, the NLM was well equipped. The leaders formed an impressive group. They mirrored the triple base of the party: Kofi Buor and John Poku of the Asante Farmers' Union, Kusi Ampofo of the AYA, and (as representatives of the chiefs) Bafuor Akoto and the Nkofehene Opanin Antwi Bosiako—the latter a young, energetic, educated Kumasi sub-chief who succeeded E. Y. Baffoe as the party's propaganda secretary. Behind each of these three groups lay the local branches of the Farmers' Union, those of the AYA, and the state councils of the chiefs. In addition, there were the intellectuals. The leading figures of the Ghana Congress Party (which was soon to disappear completely before so vigorous a companion)—Busia, Danquah, William Ofori Atta, M. K. Apaloo, and others—had already promised their help. Then, in January 1955, the NLM received support from an unexpected quarter.

[27] *West Africa*, 27 Nov. 1954.

Three of the leading CPP Ashanti members—J. E. Appiah, R. R. Amponsah, and Victor Owusu—made public declarations on behalf of the new movement; they were joined by a fourth (non-Ashanti) ex-CPP, intellectual—Kurankyi Taylor. Appiah's announcement in particular was a remarkable one which raised the national stock of the NLM, and hurt the CPP's pride. Here was a former close companion of Nkrumah in England—a delegate to the fifth pan-African conference in Manchester, president of the West African Students' Union, and by 1952 the accredited representative of the Prime Minister and the CPP in London—who suddenly condemned the party in measured terms for being corrupt and dictatorial.[28] The parallel declaration by Amponsah a former education officer and liaison officer for the Cocoa Marketing Board in western Germany, and the lawyer Victor Owusu, hitherto an outspoken defender of the CPP, did not have quite the dramatic quality of Appiah's resignation: but the combination of all three was an impressive witness of the depletion of the CPP ranks in Ashanti. When the names of Kurankyi Taylor, Professor Busia (as he now was), his colleagues in the Ghana Congress Party, as well as those of Dr Kufuor,[29] and John Tsiboe[30] and his wife were added to those of the early leaders it was possible to measure the breadth of support that the NLM was given in Kumasi. Notwithstanding its narrow appeal—and setting aside for the moment the political aptitude (or lack of it) of its leaders (a very different quality from intellectual ability)—the NLM was undoubtedly equipped with spokesmen who were at least the intellectual equal of the CPP leaders.

[28] See e.g. the special mention of Joe Appiah in Padmore, app. 2, pp. 252–3. Appiah left to study law in London in 1944, was called to the bar ten years later, and returned to the Gold Coast in November 1954. He then watched the political scene in silence throughout the last weeks of 1954, and made his statement early in February 1955. Why did he leave the CPP for the NLM? There is no reason to doubt his statement that he disliked the corruption within the CPP and objected to the subservience of many of its leaders to Nkrumah. (He may also have been influenced by his father, J. W. K. Appiah, the chief secretary of the Asanteman Council.) Much of the dislike of the CPP by Appiah, Amponsah, and others came from its handling of the CPC. The former chairman of the Cocoa Marketing Board and the CPC, T. M. K. Mercer, had tried to get the CPP central committee to remedy the obvious abuses that existed, and had failed; he was now in London as Commissioner for the Gold Coast. Both Appiah and Amponsah knew of the complaints made by Mercer in December 1953, and that nothing had been done about them (see Jibowu Commission *Report*, 1956, app. 18).

[29] Lecturer in Chemistry at Kumasi College of Technology.

[30] Proprietor and Manager of the Abura Printing Works and the *Ashanti Pioneer*.

Around its inner council of leading members—Bafuor Akoto, Dr Busia, Joe Appiah, R. R. Amponsah (who replaced Kusi Ampofo as the general secretary), Nana Antwi Bosiako, Kofi Buor, John Poku, Kusi Ampofo, and others of the national executive—the NLM grouped a number of ancillary organizations in an attempt to rival those of the CPP: the Asante Farmers' Union,[31] the pro-NLM section of the AYA, a new Congress of Free Trade Unions, a paramilitary organization of 'Action Groupers' armed with cudgels, guns, and soda-water bottles,[32] and a fanatical Women's Section led by tough Ashanti market traders whose passionate advocacy of 'Federation' was certainly no less than that of the CPP Women's League's devotion to 'Freedom'. In mid-September 1955 the NLM produced its own daily newspaper, *The Liberator*, which was very much like its counterpart the *Evening News*—raucous, hard-hitting, and abusive;[33] the NLM Action Groupers were a deliberate copy and challenge to the Action Troopers of the CPP. The use of such methods by the NLM was a natural carrying over into the new movement of all the techniques of mass political action—flags, songs, propaganda vans, slogans and salutes—already acquired by many of the NLM officers during their membership of the CPP, while below the 'national' (that is, Ashanti) organization of the NLM there stretched the familiar network of constituency executives and local branches. The picture drawn by the editor of the weekly paper *West Africa* of the town where the 'NLM officials . . . are simply the former CPP ones, who had left the party in disgust' was by no means true of every town in Ashanti. But there were still enough deserters from the CPP to the NLM, even at constituency executive level, to transfer the pattern of organization from one to the other.

[31] That is, the (larger) section of the Ashanti farmers led by Kofi Buor and J. K. Poku. An attempt was now made to strengthen the old Asante Farmers' Union with (in 1955) the reissue of membership cards, a 1s. membership fee, and 'Aims and Objects' that included the NLM clause: 'To honour, respect and be loyal to our traditional rulers and to uphold the best in our culture'. The motto of the new Union was 'Labour and Honesty'; the slogan—'On with the Land'.

[32] It was not difficult to come by guns—of the sort used by farmers for hunting in the bush. A soda-water bottle, shaken violently and then hurled at an adversary, is a very nasty weapon. It had the further advantage that it could be made to appear innocuous: thus the usual defence offered by an Action Grouper (NLM) or an Action Trooper (CPP), if brought before the courts, was that the soda-water bottles were for 'refreshment'.

[33] The NLM was also supported, at a very different level, by the comparatively well-written, closely-argued editorials of the *Ashanti Pioneer*.

In the early stages of the movement the support of the pro-NLM chiefs was of great importance in helping to establish the party outside Kumasi. Within the municipality itself the Asanteman Council offices at Manhyia were a second party headquarters to the NLM office in Ashanti New Town, and Bafuor Akoto was as energetic at forwarding the aims of the NLM through the Kumasi chiefs as R. R. Amponsah, the general secretary, was in strengthening the movement through its more formal party organization. In the rural areas, the local paramount chief and his counsellors were powerful auxiliaries. Each Ashanti division had its state council consisting of the paramount chief, a number of traditional office holders, and the 'wing-chiefs' who commanded the outlying districts of the chiefdom. Each wing-chief was also the centre of a similar, subordinate array of lesser chiefs and village headmen. Thus, the authority of the chief spread down into the smallest village—although whether it was obeyed was another matter—and this finely spun web of power was placed at the disposal of the NLM leaders. The chiefs often liked to express their new-found party allegiance in military terms. 'You know', wrote Bafuor Akoto when soliciting the help of the chief at Attebubu in northern Ashanti, 'that the Ashanti nation is at war with Kwame Nkrumah and his Convention People's Party.' This was language the chiefs understood, liked, and responded to. The older, more experienced chiefs knew very well where their own strength and weakness lay in the state, and used this knowledge on behalf of the party. Many made intelligent use of the full panoply of traditional rule in visits to surrounding villages—beating gongs to summon the people, swearing oaths in support of the movement, and using the state drummers and horn blowers to sound out messages of defiance and exhortation, while the party's Action Groupers escorted the chief's palanquin in case trouble should arise or a village group prove recalcitrant.

The way in which the NLM raised the money it needed showed how effective this dual organization of the chiefs and the party could be. When, for example, the leaders wished to collect money for the 1956 election, Amponsah organized five groups of three members each—a chief, a commoner, and an educated leader—to 'tour the whole of Ashanti' in an attempt to raise

£30,000.[34] The assumption in the covering letter sent by the general-secretary that 'most people would subscribe £100', and the claim that 'one Ashanti has offered and paid £1,000', were not necessarily hope and bravado designed to encourage the others. Many of the NLM farmers and traders were generous donors, and it was by no means unusual at a party rally for a supporter to come forward on behalf of a local NLM group with a bundle of notes totalling £200 or £300 and hand them over to the platform with a great show of resolution. There were individual cocoa farmers and contractors who gave gifts in kind of considerable value, like the farmer in the Nkawie district west of Kumasi—a brother (or half-brother) of a CPP Assembly member who donated two propaganda vans to the party, each painted in the party's colours, complete with a loudspeaker apparatus, and (a pleasant touch) a full tank of petrol.

Many of the chiefs, too, were men of property on their own account, the democratic right of the commoners to prevail on the elders to destool the chief often leading to the rapid amassing of property by the chief lest he should be destooled. (This, of course, was often a cause of destoolment.) Moreover, they had an

---

[34] e.g.:

> The National Liberation Movement,
> The National Secretariat,
> P.O. Box 2004, Kumasi.
> 1 December, 1955.

Dear Nana [the form of address given to a chief],

You will recall that at the last meeting of the Asanteman Council Otumfuo announced that a delegation would be sent to each State to appeal for funds privately from individuals who would be willing to assist financially the cause for which the Asanteman Council and the National Liberation Movement have dedicated themselves.

Five groups of Chiefs and people, each group consisting of three have been selected to tour the whole of Ashanti for the above purpose. I have to inform you that you, Nana Anyinasehene, Dr I. B. Asafu-Adjaye and Panin Kwadjo Owusu Ansah (Kyedie) have been selected to tour the whole of *Sekyere East and West, Attebubu and Sekyedomase*.

I have to state that our target is £30,000 (Thirty thousand pounds) and each group will be expected to collect at least £6,000 (Six thousand pounds). It means that most of the people you will approach will need to offer £100 (One hundred pounds) and over with ONLY few offering £50 (Fifty pounds) and above.

As Otumfuo announced, all contributions, as well as those who make them, will be announced to the next meeting of the Asanteman Council. Also a special honours book for historic reference by Ashanti Nation will be kept of names of those who will make these offers. Already one Ashanti has offered and paid £1,000 (One thousand pounds) . . . Please collect receipt books from Bafuor Akoto.

I wish you the best of luck and God's protection and guidance while you tour.

> Yours very sincerely,
> R. R. Amponsah
> General Secretary

official 'stool income' drawn from timber concessions, rents of lands, cocoa tribute, and a proportion of the revenue raised by other local revenues which the new local authorities collected and then handed a third share to the state councils. The total income of the Asantehene and the Kumasi chiefs at this time was put at:

	Allowance to the Golden Stool (Asantehene)	Salaries to Clan Chiefs, Elders, & Queen Mother
1954–5	£15,000	£7,630
1955–6	£15,000	£8,357

Most of the paramount chiefs had a similar (though much less munificent) source of income; they no longer had any tax-levying power of their own, but they were still a long way from penury.[35] Traditionally, chiefs were said to have neither property nor income. They were merely the custodians of the wealth of the Stool, but from the earliest times they were quick to identify what they wanted to do with what the state could afford, and the resolution of the Kumasi Council of Chiefs has already been quoted that 'not more than £20,000' should be voted for the NLM from the 'Palace Building Fund'. (The actual sum handed over was £19,000, transferred from an account opened in March 1952 for the financing of a new *ahenfie* (or 'palace') from funds accumulated through the Ashanti National Levy of 2s. a man and 1s. a woman.) Because the Palace Fund was public money, collected for a specific purpose, the Commission of Inquiry set up by the government in 1958 to inquire into the affairs of the Kumasi State Council was able to conclude that there had been 'an abuse of power' on the part of the chiefs.[36] But the use of the Palace Fund was hardly seen in this light by the NLM leaders, even if they tried to keep the transfer away from public scrutiny. It was looked upon as a necessary counterpart to what was generally assumed to be the use by the CPP of the funds of the Cocoa Purchasing Company, the Industrial Development Corporation, and so on. The chiefs had agreed to support the NLM, they had access to the fund, and they did not hesitate. Similarly, in Akim Abuakwa (where the NLM had a staunch ally in the *okyenhene* Nana Ofori Atta) the state council resolved

[35] The salary of a paramount chief varied from state to state but it was usually not less than £60 a month.
[36] Sarkodee Addo Commission *Report*, 1958.

(20 April 1955) that 'one month's salary of each Chief should be deducted as a voluntary contribution for the National Liberation';[37] and it made no difference whether a chief supported the NLM or not.

There is little doubt also that some of the money raised was a deliberate by-product of the intimidation and violence that each side used against the other. In Kumasi, for example, in December 1955, 'Madam Abine (Abena?) Kumkumah' wrote to the NLM office having 'the honour to apply for some of the National Liberation cards to be distributed to all the tenants in my various houses in Kumasi to join the NLM and whoever will fail to enlist, will be put out or removed from my house at once, so help me to get some cards sufficiently'.[38] Kwame Gyamfi, a local CPP branch chairman in the Teppa-Ahafo district, told the Quist Committee (appointed in 1957 to investigate matters of this kind) that:

one early morning he was called by one Osei Kwadwo before the [local] chairman of the NLM, stripped naked and severely caned on the buttocks. . . . The chairman explained to him that he was the one who had diverted the minds of people from joining the NLM. He was also ordered to pay £8 to those who came to escort him to the chairman. The NLM chairman further invited NLM Action Groupers from Kenyasi who extorted an amount of £45 from him because the chairman said he had seen him, Gyamfi, standing under a CPP flag pole conversing with the CPP elements in the village about the punishment inflicted upon him. He failed to complain to the police because he thought he would be killed.

And again:

Kwame Apawu . . . a member of the CPP said in December 1955 that a group of NLM Action Groupers came to call him to the [chief]. There he was informed that they had been sent by the Asantehene to assemble all the villagers to discuss with them an important subject. . . . The villagers were told that the Asantehene wanted financial help from the villagers because Kwame Nkrumah wanted to capture the Golden Stool to Accra. . . . He [Kwame Apawu] said they were threatened that if they failed to contribute money the Asantehene would send Action Groupers to destroy the village. They became

---

[37] Jackson Commission *Report*, 1958. Between April 1955 and November 1957 over £10,000 went to the NLM from the State Council.
[38] Sarkodee Addo Commission *Report*, p. 119.

afraid. They collected the amount of £416 and handed it over to the chief.[39]

No doubt much of the violence and extortion that witness after witness for one side or the other recounted before the Quist Committee went on behind the backs of the leaders.[40] The CPP built up its 'Action Troopers'. The NLM retaliated with its 'Action Groupers'. The leaders turned a blind eye; and vied with each other in condemning violence. But the unsavoury side of the NLM (or of the CPP) should not be allowed to disguise the intensity of the struggle that was waged between the two parties. Within the limits of its appeal—and these will be discussed shortly—the NLM, by any reckoning, was a 'formidable alliance'.

If proof were needed, it was supplied in dramatic fashion in mid-1955. The CPP Assembly member for the Ashanti rural constituency, Atwima Nwabiagya, was killed in a lorry accident, and a by-election took place on 14 July. Here was the first opportunity of a direct trial of strength (of this kind) between the two parties, in a key constituency in the heart of the cocoa-farming country near Kumasi. Each side concentrated their efforts, bringing in registered voters by taxi and lorry from the western Ahafo districts where the Atwima farmers were planting new farms. N. A. Welbeck, Kojo Botsio, and Aaron Ofori Atta came up for the CPP from the south, Bediako Poku (now loans

---

[39] An account of evidence given before the Quist Committee published in the *Ashanti Pioneer*, 19 Aug. 1957. But there was evidence on the other side too:

'Kwabena Anto, NLM farmer of Kukuom, alleged that he was extorted £2.17.6d. about a year ago by Nana Yaw Frimpong, Kukuomhene, and his elders. The Chief sent Kwaku Manu to call him.

'When he went, the Chief told him that he would not be pleased with him if he was an NLM. The Chief then asked him to pay £4 to become a CPP. When he rendered apology it was reduced to £2.7.6d. He had money with him and he paid.

'Next day his brother told him that he was wanted by the Kukuomhene. When he went he met those he had mentioned. He asked for the Chief, but the people told him that in the absence of the Chief they were there.

'They then asked him to join the CPP and to pay £9 6s. for troubling them, otherwise they would beat him.

'Fofie said he therefore rendered apology through Twenetohene for reduction, but they never reduced it. His father went and fetched money and the money was paid. He was then allowed to go.

'He never reported to the police' (*Ashanti Pioneer*, 23 Sept. 1957).

The *Report* of the Quist Committee was submitted to the government but never published.

[40] Or, as Busia was reported telling the Sarkodee Addo Commission in connexion with the Palace Building Fund: 'I have the experience to know that a Leader puts himself in a very invidious position if he gets himself mixed up in the finances of the party' (*Report*, p. 131).

manager for the Cocoa Purchasing Company), and Joe Mainoo (provincial manager) were there with the Company's lorries and officials; B. E. Dwira campaigned for the party from Kumasi, with an escort of Action Troopers. The NLM mustered a large array against them: Bafuor Akoto, R. R. Amponsah, K. A. Busia, William Ofori Atta, Cobina Kessie, representatives of the NPP, the MAP, the local chiefs, and party members. The CPP had done what it could to make up lost ground by authorizing (in April) an increase in the cocoa price from 72s. to 80s. for the small mid-season crop; but this now went against the party, since what might have been accepted gratefully as a concession was now looked upon as weakness. The cocoa issue dominated the election. A local 'highlife' appeared, sung through the constituency by youths and schoolchildren with the farmers expressing their approval:

> If you want to send your children to school, it is cocoa,
> If you want to build your house, it is cocoa,
> If you want to marry, it is cocoa,
> If you want to buy cloth, it is cocoa,
> If you want to buy a lorry, it is cocoa.
> Whatever you want to do in this world,
> It is with cocoa money that you do it.[41]

Behind the cocoa price demand lay the Ashanti quarrel with the CPP. 'The election was not between [the candidates] but between the Ashanti nation and the forces that would like to disrupt the country', a speaker was reported as telling a large NLM crowd of supporters at a rally in the local 'capital town', Nkawie. The NLM sponsored the former GCP (and, in 1951, the CPP) candidate, B. F. Kusi, a local trader. The CPP candidate, B. K. Kufuor, was a cocoa broker and farmer.[42] Polling in the large, scattered farming area of thick bush and poor roads was low, although up on the 1954 general election figures by nearly 25 per cent. The NLM accused the CPP of using CPC lorries to carry voters to the polls, the CPP replied with charges that the NLM

[41] The song was written in *twi* (in which it goes with a much greater swing) by Fred Sarpong, a journalist and trader and NLM member.

[42] B. F. Kusi, merchant, nominated by a postal agent, a petty trader, and a local farmers' co-operative secretary; B. K. Kufuor, farmer, nominated by a farmer, a poultry keeper and a cashier. Kusi stood nominally as an Independent, since the NLM had not registered a party symbol, but the symbol used by Kusi—a cocoa tree—was the one adopted in 1956 by the NLM.

imported additional non-registered voters from Kumasi, but the police were there in great numbers, the polling agents on both sides were vigilant, and voting was orderly.

The NLM won decisively:

	Votes	Per cent
B. F. Kusi	3,998[43]	69·5
B. K. Kufuor	1,758	30·5

(Cf. 1954 result: John Baidoo (CPP) 3,203, B. F. Kusi (GCP) 1,708.)

The NLM rejoiced. Immediately the result was announced, Bafuor Osei Akoto handed a message to Dwira to give to Nkrumah saying that: 'My supporters and I have won our first victory, the forerunner of many more and crushing victories. We have defeated you and your supporters and we will continue to defeat you whenever and wherever we meet you at the polls.'[44] B. F. Kusi, the successful candidate, now re-entered the Assembly (where he had sat as a CPP member in 1951) declaring that he was 'grateful to the Ashanti nation for its wonderful support', and that he 'dedicated his life to the cause of Federation and the institution in this country of true democracy'.[45] The Asantehene congratulated the people of Atwima, and renewed his pledge to support the movement. The CPP could do nothing about it, although it might take some comfort from the fact that, if defeated, it was not completely routed even in the heart of the cocoa-growing district and an acknowledged NLM stronghold.

What, in fact, did the NLM hope to gain from its victory in the Atwima election? And, in more general terms, what did the leaders hope that the movement might accomplish?

The immediate objective of the NLM and its allies was to halt the negotiations between the CPP and the Colonial Office. They wanted a fresh start to the whole process of constitution making, one that would take into account the growing strength of the new movement. With these went a series of demands, from the original argument for £7 10s. for a load of cocoa, to the need for a Royal Commission to investigate the mounting volume of complaints about the Cocoa Purchasing Company. In sum, they amounted to two generally formulated demands: fresh elections

---

[43] The difference in votes was 'a ton of cocoa', 2,240 lb, and the NLM made use of the symbolism.

[44] *Ashanti Pioneer*, 18 July 1955.   [45] Ibid. 16 July 1955.

to take account of the changed political situation in Ashanti, and a federal constitution to prevent the 'abuse of power' and the 'growth of dictatorship'. The first of these demands, for new elections (which was greatly strengthened by the result of the Atwima Nwabiagya election and the refusal by the CPP to entertain the idea) will be discussed in detail later. The argument for federation is worth examining here since it included the main points of the general case advanced by the NLM against the CPP government.

The argument used in memorandum after memorandum to the Queen, the Secretary of State, the Governor, and the general public all turned on the need to prevent a concentration of power at the centre in order to safeguard local liberties. In this respect the NLM may be regarded as a true-to-form conservative party. But it also used arguments which must have come readily to a trained sociologist:

> The peoples of these territories, belonging as they do to different tribes, have different structures of society, and are at different stages of adaptation and adoption of western culture. In Ashanti the allegiance is to the Occupant of the Golden Stool; in other territories there are a large collection of states and allegiances.
>
> There is not enough consciousness of national identity to make possible easy and at the same time democratic unitary government. In the absence of this consciousness the safest course is to ensure that not all the powers of government are concentrated at the centre, but that a substantial part of them is retained in the component territories where people have learnt the habits and attitudes of living together for some time. . . .
>
> In our opinion it is not possible to secure in a unitary form of government such a division of powers that a despotic group of men cannot prevent the constitution and destroy the liberties of the people.[46]

In 1955 the NLM leaders believed that the weight of argument lay on their side. The country looked as if it had settled down into its 'natural' components: a Northern People's Party, a Togoland Congress, and an (Ashanti) Liberation Movement. Each was a political instrument (of a modern kind) which the 'people of these territories, belonging as they do to different tribes' had

[46] Preamble of *Proposals for a Federal Constitution for an Independent Gold Coast and Togoland, by Movements and Parties other than the Convention People's Party* (Abura Printing Works (n.d.)). The *Proposals* appeared in mid-1955.

fashioned, as it were, out of instinct once they had ceased to be beguiled by the CPP. So the NLM argument ran, and when the leaders accused the CPP of moving towards a dictatorial system of rule, the charge went a good deal farther than criticism of the intentions of the CPP government. The danger of dictatorship (the NLM argued), whether under colonial rule or party government, was always present once the decision had been taken to administer the country from a single centre of power: but the remedy was simple—to distribute power through a federal system, whereby protection would be given to local interests which, in turn, would safeguard local rights.

Such was the gist of the NLM case, and its *Proposals for a Federal Constitution* (published in 1955) outlined a familiar framework which may be paraphrased as:

1. An indissoluble federation of the Colony, Ashanti, Northern Territories and Togoland.[47]

2. A Governor-General, and regional 'Traditional Heads' or Governors.

3. A federal parliament consisting of a lower house directly elected on the basis of population, and an upper house based on the equality of the component states.

4. A Council of State of the Governor-General, heads of regions, the federal and regional prime ministers, and three other federal ministers.

5. Four bicameral regional parliaments.

6. Limited powers defined for the federal government covering defence, foreign affairs, commerce, higher education, communications, federal broadcasting, etc.; residual powers to go to the regions.

7. Revenue to be divided between the centre and the regions on the basis of derivation and needs. 'Applying, for example, the principles of derivation and population in the division of Revenue for cocoa only, the Colony shall be entitled to 35 per cent, Ashanti and the Northern Territories $27\frac{1}{2}$ per cent each, and Togoland 10 per cent.'

8. A machinery of constitutional change requiring the consent of a majority of the electors in a majority of the regions.

[47] Whether by 'Togoland' was meant the U.K. trust territory as a whole, or the southern section only, was left undecided, in view of the difficulty of getting the NPP and the Togoland Congress to agree on any precise statement.

9. A Constituent Assembly to be set up forthwith, its membership to be determined by a 'Preliminary Conference of all Political Parties and Movements'; its task would be to draw up a suitable Constitution on the above lines.

10. The future federal constitution to include a guarantee of fundamental human rights.

A number of these proposals (the finance clauses in particular) were obvious copies of the discussions then being conducted over reform of the Nigerian constitution.[48] They were open to the charge that, while a federal constitution might be a necessity for so large and diverse an area as Nigeria, it would be a grossly expensive and burdensome structure to impose on the smaller, compact area of the Gold Coast.[49] But the NLM argument went farther than an orthodox defence of federalism. The party also liked to pride itself on being 'of the soil'—an autochthonous movement of a distinctively African cast. The claim was implicit in the ample room found for the chiefs. 'We do not only seek to preserve chieftaincy', said the signatories; 'we consider that Chiefs should play an active and a definite part in the life of the country', and they proposed that the territorial councils should be metamorphosed into Upper Houses of the future regional parliaments. But the 'African claim' was also made explicitly, and the demand for federation was justified (as in the 1954 Asanteman Council resolution) as being in keeping with African customary rule. The intellectuals in the party argued that too much had been made—the CPP had made too much— of western political concepts and models, to the neglect of local African precepts and experience. The point was made at some length in the *Liberator* at the end of 1955.

The NLM is diametrically opposed to the view of the CPP. The NLM insists and maintains that we are Africans. The NLM insists that we as Africans must add something to the world's culture by formulating a constitution that is based on our own way of life and manners, traditions and culture. The NLM maintains, and rightly so, that we must not and cannot blindly copy European models. The NLM maintains that African genius is not lacking in the Gold Coast

---

[48] Nigeria, *Report of the Fiscal Commissioner on the Financial Effects of the Proposed New Constitutional Arrangements*, Cmd. 9026, 1953.

[49] The NLM reply to these charges was to point to Switzerland, a country smaller than the Gold Coast, but having a federal constitution.

and can be tapped for making a constitution on the African pattern. The NLM wants to bring out an African society that will be the admiration of the . . . civilised countries of the world. We don't want to make a constitution from text-books as the CPP seeks to do, without due regard for our customs and traditions.[50]

Were such arguments to be taken seriously? It was difficult to do so. Were the NLM leaders to be taken seriously in their demands for a truly federal constitution on the Nigerian or Swiss or Australian model? It was open to doubt. In the first place, the argument from African 'customs and traditions' was drawn more from the armoury of current political warfare than any established body of convictions. Thus the NLM accused the 'CPP demagogues' of 'suffering from blindness . . . caused by their claim of having a majority. It is high time to remind the CPP that "majority" is not the only thing which matters in discussing human relationships and running an African country'—but the precept was difficult to match with the party's behaviour towards minorities within its own areas of power. The actual phrases used by the *Liberator* were part of the common store of nationalist language used by both sides, and were of almost universal application. Indeed, they were to become part of the large and romantic category of similar expressions employed by Nkrumah and other African leaders to justify the single-party régimes of the newly independent states—and were capable of bearing whatever was thought politically expedient at the time. (They were also evocative of earlier arguments under colonial rule which appealed to an African past and defended native-authority government on the grounds that it grew out of and was based on custom and tradition.) Similarly, it was doubtful whether the NLM's demand for a federal constitution went much beyond the hope that it would provide an argument and a slogan around which it might be possible to rally a great deal of hitherto unfocused discontent against the CPP. For the picture drawn in the opposition's *Proposals for a Federal Constitution*—of a country divided tribally into separate areas—was a caricature of the actual

[50] *Liberator*, 20 Dec. 1955. So too the writer in *West Africa* who noted that the NLM was an 'extra-parliamentary movement, many of whose leaders openly repudiate the electoral method for Ashanti; even some highly educated young men speak of "our African way of doing things" ' (ibid. 27 Dec. 1954). The same young men, however, demanded fresh elections—as soon as they believed they could win.

situation, as the following section on the position of the CPP will
show. The intellectuals who were so prominent among the opposition leaders were fully conscious of the fact, and were careful to
balance the federal argument by stressing also their concern for
national issues. They encouraged a traditional Ashanti or Ewe or
Mamprusi patriotism while attacking the CPP for its inade-
quacies and malpractices as a national government. Indeed, by
1956 the growing strength of the opposition alliance had brought
a number of its leaders to the point where it became clear that
their primary aim was quite simply to replace the CPP government in Accra with one of their own making. Thus on the eve of
the July 1956 election Busia announced publicly that he and his
colleagues expected the Governor to call on them to form a
national government should they win a straight majority of the
votes.[51] And had they succeeded at the polls it seemed certain
that a great deal less would have been heard, both of the demand
for federation, and of the plea for an 'African constitution' based
on 'our customs and traditions'.

<h3 style="text-align:center">THE CPP</h3>

The sudden formation of the NLM took everyone by surprise,
including the CPP government which in the second half of 1954
was thrown off balance. It too was 'overtaken by events', much as
the colonial government had been in 1948. Notwithstanding the
unexpected appearance of the NPP before the 1954 election, and
the continued hostility of the bulk of the Ewe and Muslim communities, the CPP leaders refused to believe that the opposition
had any substance to it. Immediately after the June election had
taken place, the *Evening News* warned its opponents in characteristic language of the danger of further opposition:

Kwame Nkrumah, Man of Destiny, Star of Africa, Hope of

---

[51] Busia's statement (the writer was informed) was the result of 'a bitter debate
among the leaders:

'(*a*) should the NLM declare openly before the election that it was fighting
the cause of the Ashanti, the north and Togo in a federal constitution?
'(*b*) should the NLM act on the assumption that it would win and announce
its willingness to form a central government?

'The original intention was (*a*) but there was a change of policy because Kurankyi Taylor, R. R. Amponsah, Amponsah-Dadzie, and others gave such glowing
accounts of growing support in the south that an election victory was taken for
granted'. (Letter to the writer from a former NLM executive member. The effect
on the actual course of the 1956 election of the decision to fight nationally is discussed in the following chapter.)

Millions of down-trodden Blacks, Deliverer of Ghana, Iron Boy, Great Leader of Street Boys, personable and handsome Boy from Nzima, Kwame Nkrumah has given his answer to all the twaddle and tripe and the dirty scribblers of the [opposition papers] . . . and his answer is the People's Mandate. . . . For months past, the reactionaries have been pumping loathsome matter into the people of this country. We pointed out to them that they were mere children playing soldiers. Today, they see for themselves how very seriously the country takes them. Some of them we hear are weeping like mad! They need not weep yet—there is plenty of time ahead for weeping![52]

The Moslem Association Party, in particular, came under sharp attack, and there were demands in the newly elected Assembly, and the *Evening News*, that it be outlawed:

We seriously appeal to the Government to introduce legislation outlawing political parties based on religion, tribalism and racialism. . . . It is obvious from the total defeat by the politico-religious MAP even from the hands of Moslems all over the country that the necessary Socialist pre-requisites of such legislation . . . has really taken effect. But the legislation is necessary if the future of the country is to be saved. Ban the MAP NOW![53]

Two months later Dowuona Hammond (CPP) introduced a private member's motion in the Assembly urging the government to legislate against parties based on religion. It was passed by 72 votes against 14, although the government now held its hand as the sky began to darken over Kumasi.[54]

Even so the CPP was strangely slow in taking anything like the proper measure of the NLM. 'Separation, where is thy sting? Bafuor Akoto, where is thy federal illusion?' asked the *Evening News*, and the NLM leaders were derided as 'stooges, imperialist agents, arch-reactionaries, and ignorant infantile cocoa-season politicians'.[55] The CPP was prepared to admit that the new movement had been able to make local capital out of the Cocoa Duty (Amendment) Ordinance 'which at first sight engendered misunderstanding among a few of our friends of the peasant community but', said the *Evening News*, 'we are happy to note that all is now quiet.'[56] Nkrumah himself was on holiday at Amedzofe

[52] 19 June 1954.   [53] Ibid.
[54] GC, LA Deb., 12 Aug. 1954. The government did not act until November 1957 when it introduced the Avoidance of Discrimination Bill which forbade the existence of parties of a regional, religious, or tribal nature.
[55] 20 Sept. 1954.   [56] 23 Sept. 1954.

in the Togoland hills while the NLM gathered support in the Ashanti capital, and there was no direct mention of this new threat in his 'birthday message' to the nation. 'The Leader's Message to the Party on his 45th Birthday sent by the indefatigable Kwame Nkrumah, Hero and Generalissimo of the Ghana Liberation Army from Amedzofe, where the Osagyefo is at present on a brief retreat' announced that

it behoves us all to rededicate ourselves to the great task that lies ahead, namely, the attainment of national independence and the reconstruction of our dear Ghana. . . . Let us all rise above destructive criticism, inordinate ambition, selfishness and useless tribal prejudices and march forward like one to the victory that is inevitable. Bravo Comrades!—I salute you all—Freedom!

Thus when the local *Daily Graphic* stressed the danger of the situation in Kumasi, the paper was attacked as the vehicle of an imperialist propaganda. The NLM (to the *Evening News* in October and November) was still 'a few unruly tribalists'—led by 'a small clique of discredited and disgruntled bourgeois intellectuals' and encouraged by the 'blind Graphic imperialist stool pigeons'—while the situation in Kumasi was said to be 'not greater than can be dealt with by the normal machinery of administration'.[57]

The extravagance of the language apart, it was not difficult to sympathize with the CPP, or to understand its attempt to play the ostrich. The June election was over, Arden-Clarke had said that he would be the country's last Governor, the Secretary of State had talked of the 1954 constitution in terms of the 'final stage' before self-government. The Trusteeship Committee of the United Nations was even then discussing the Togoland question, and—as a dazzling prospect before the leaders—there lay the new world of international and pan-African relations. Nkrumah, in particular, was anxious to raise again the question of 'interterritorial solidarity' that he had once told the UGCC Working Committee he had laid aside in order to give priority to the immediate task of national self-government. Quotations had already begun to appear in the *Evening News* from the early panAfricanist, W. E. B. DuBois: 'Peoples of the Colonies UNITE! You have all freedom loving peoples of all countries behind you',

[57] 19 Oct. and 24 Nov. 1954. A series of attacks was made on the British-owned *Daily Graphic* during these weeks.

and there was a renewed emphasis on Nkrumah as a future 'architect of African unity'.[58] To equip itself for the task, the party had begun to push forward its ideological wing in an attempt to strengthen its somewhat shaky base of socialist theory. Branches of a 'National Association of Socialist Students' Organization' (NASSO) began to be opened in the main towns as centres of 'ideological training', and Cecil Forde, the former critic of the party, became its general secretary.[59] Meanwhile, the first steps were taken towards carrying out an African programme. It was announced that the party would open an office in Accra from which it would 'launch a Pan-African Movement', and bring about 'the federation of nationalist parties decided upon at a conference at the end of last year'. A former editor of the *Evening News*, James Markham, was brought back from the Anti-Colonial Bureau of the Asian Socialist Conference in Rangoon to be the secretary of the Pan-African Office; and the *Evening News* announced that the party hoped 'to call a conference of delegates from organisations all over Africa in August 1955'.[60] These proposals flowed logically from the announcement by Nkrumah that it was 'his aim that independence should be achieved within the lifetime of this Assembly'.[61]

By December these plans were so obviously placed in jeopardy that the government was forced to take notice of the NLM leaders, and the CPP was faced with a dilemma that it was unable to resolve until the 1956 elections. If the party ignored the Ashanti movement, it was in danger of losing the support it still had in the region; if, on the other hand, it acted against the NLM, it would have to admit that a serious problem existed—an admission that was bound to give the United Kingdom government doubts about the wisdom of surrendering control. Nevertheless, by the end of December the latter course—however unpalatable to the CPP—was beginning to be inevitable. Violence was spreading from Kumasi into the surrounding chiefdoms, and the Ashanti members who remained loyal to the party were pressing the need for action. In the early months of the NLM

---

[58] *Evening News*, 19 Oct. 1954.
[59] The ex-servicemen were also brought more closely within the party when R. M. Abbey, president of the Supreme Council of the Ex-Servicemen's Union, was elected to the Assembly in a by-election in Accra West on 28 September: R. M. Abbey (CPP) 5,247; Bankole Awooner Renner (MAP) 1,591.
[60] 26 Nov. 1954.   [61] GC, LA Deb., 9 Nov. 1954.

neither side in Ashanti had deliberately used violence as a weapon (although certainly violence occurred between individuals
and small bands of rival supporters) since each hoped to win or
retain support by an appeal to the Golden Stool or to nationalist
loyalties. Thus for a long time the two offices—the CPP regional
headquarters and the NLM party office—functioned side by
side in Ashanti New Town. By the end of 1954, however, the rival
movements were facing each other in Ashanti as opposed armies
and, early in December, the government hung out a flag of truce.
It offered to parley. In unusually dulcet tones the *Evening News*
ventured

> to suggest that the Government consider the feasibility of inviting the
> Asanteman Council and, say, the federalist party for a round table
> conference on the Kumasi issue. . . . To every negative there is a posi-
> tive. We are not intolerant of opposition parties or criticism as such;
> we are Democratic Socialists and are determined to live our faith. Let
> the Government invite the opposition elements concerned. [62]

This was a remarkable change of language and a clear illustration both of the growing strength of the Ashanti movement and
the impression it made on those who saw it grow. The government hesitated, and then offered to talk with the Kumasi leaders.
Invitations were sent first through the Ashanti members of the
Assembly and then, when these were ignored, by Nkrumah himself. Indeed, by the end of December Nkrumah had travelled a
long way from his party's initial contempt for the federalists. In a
Broadcast to the Nation, he offered to 'submit to the Legislative
Assembly, as a Government measure, legislation providing for
Regional Councils' so as to have 'the Regions more closely
associated by consultation and advice with decisions of the
Government'. [63] This was to no avail. The invitations and the
offer were first ignored and then rejected by the NLM leaders
who were now busily engaged in extending their appeal through
the Ashanti chiefdoms. Quite clearly, the government was at a
loss to know what to do. Independence, once almost within its
grasp, now looked a good deal farther off, and Nkrumah (during
his broadcast) had been compelled to add that the government
would take 'vigorous measures . . . against all who offend the
public peace'. For the nationalist party, therefore, this was a dark,
uncertain close to a year that had opened so full of promise.

[62] 2 Dec. 1954.   [63] Relayed on 30 Dec. 1954.

What could the CPP (at the beginning of 1955) oppose to the NLM in Ashanti? It fought on a double front. On the one hand it exercised its authority as a government to try and tempt the NLM into a compromise agreement (or, failing this, to expose its leaders as irreconcilables); on the other it used its powers as a party in office to weaken the NLM in its own stronghold. For although the CPP was at bay in Ashanti it was by no means without weapons.

There were three possible sources of support on which the CPP could hope to draw. In the first place, there were a number of non-Ashanti groups in the region many of whose members might be expected to prefer the wider nationalism of the CPP to the regionalism of the NLM. Secondly, the CPP might still hope to combat the Ashanti appeal made by the NLM by stressing its own programme of 'independence under the common man'. Thirdly, there were innumerable local disputes within the Ashanti chiefdoms which could yield a rich harvest if properly cultivated and turned to the advantage of the government party. Each of these three possibilities were explored by the CPP from the end of 1954, and together they helped it to regain some of the ground lost in September and October 1954. Each is examined in turn.

1. Scattered groups of immigrants (from other regions and from outside the country) were to be found throughout Ashanti, and concentrated in three main urban centres—Kumasi, and the two gold-mining towns—Konongo (in Ashanti Akim), and Obuasi. In Kumasi, the Ashanti were outnumbered in their own capital:

Kumasi Families by Origin

	Per cent
Ashanti	45
Fanti	16
Ewe	6
Ga	3
Northern	24
Nigerian & non-British	6

Source: *Kumasi Survey of Population & Household Budgets, 1955.*

Unfortunately for the CPP, the non-Ashanti families in Kumasi were not all hostile to the NLM. The crumbling tenements and compounds of the Zongo quarter to the north-east of the city were packed with northerners, many of whom were Muslims; they elected their own tribal heads, paid their respects to the Zerikin Zongo, and—following an ancient tradition—looked to the Asantehene for protection. 'You [the Zongo chiefs] are strangers sojourning in our midst. I have observed your demeanour in the present crisis and I have satisfied myself that you have given my Movement your unstinted support.' So the Asantehene told the tribal heads of the different northern communities in 1955.[64] In the southern wards of the municipality, however, the CPP was well supported. The Fanti, Ga, and even many of the Ewe, immigrants listened with growing alarm to the demand for recognition of Ashanti rights. They clung to the CPP therefore, even if—in the face of NLM hostility—they were not prepared to be very active on its behalf. Between 1954 and 1956 this pro-CPP southern element in the city was too small (and too subdued) to affect the dominant position held by the NLM, and when the 1956 election was held the NLM put up a southerner—Kurankyi Taylor—who had no difficulty in winning the seat. Nevertheless, the southerners resident in the city helped the CPP to retain a substantial minority position in the Kumasi South constituency from which it was able to advance after independence to regain control of the municipality as a whole.[65]

The prospect of carrying the battle into the NLM's own territory was still more hopeful in the Konongo (Ashanti Akim) and Obuasi mining centres. Not only were there sizeable numbers of southern clerks and storekeepers in both towns, but also a militant trade union force (employed on the companies' holdings) whose leaders were broadly sympathetic with the CPP.[66] More-

---

[64] Address given by the Asantehene to the Zongo chiefs, Kumasi State Council *Minutes*, 18 Apr. 1955. Most of the Muslims who had supported Mallam Mutawakilu against Alhaji Amadu Baba left Kumasi early in 1955 and sought refuge in Accra.

[65] The election study, 'Voting in an African Town' (Austin & Tordoff, *Political Studies*, June 1960) showed quite clearly the influence of the southern vote in many of the Kumasi wards. The CPP was given over 80 per cent of the vote among the Fanti, Ewe, and Ga compounds. After independence the CPP used its authority as a government to impose its will on the Muslim and northern immigrants, with such success that by 1958 the party had regained control of the municipal council. For further discussions of the basis of CPP-NLM membership in Kumasi, see the 'Note on NLM membership', p. 313 below.

[66] They were by no means integrated with the party, however, in 1954–6. The Mineworkers' Union under Daniel Fovie was very much an independent, though sympathetic, movement.

over, many of the cocoa farmers in the rural areas of the Ashanti
Akim and Obuasi constituencies spent the greater part of the
year away from their villages, working on new farms which they
had planted in western Ashanti. Their support—and votes—
were lost to the NLM therefore, and the Ashanti party was much
less securely based in these constituencies than the leaders believed it to be. The CPP, on the other hand, could look for substantial support from the more cosmopolitan and stable population of the mining towns.

In the rural areas also there were numbers of non-Ashanti—
among them, *abusa* labourers who tended the Ashanti owner's
land in return for a third share (*abusa*) of the cocoa crop, and
seasonal (migrant) labourers who were paid cash, plus food and
clothing, on a contract basis. Did these immigrant farmers, and
farm labourers, look to the CPP for support against the Ashanti
farmer-owner? Was it even possible to see a 'class' difference
among the rural population between the commoners' party and
the NLM? Such evidence as existed was difficult to assess but,
on balance, the differences between the two parties—as will be
seen—was territorial rather than social. Rich and poor farmers
(and both categories certainly existed at each end of a broad band
of 'middle' farmers) were to be found in both camps. Similarly,
the interests of the *abusa*, share-cropping labourer, for example,
were so closely bound up with the Ashanti owner-farmer, even
when the relationship was one of debtor and creditor, that these
two principal groups within the farming community were likely
to be in agreement on any issue affecting the locality: if a particular district opted for the NLM (or the CPP) both were likely
to be NLM (or CPP).[67] It might be thought that the immigrant

[67] On this question, Miss Polly Hill has some interesting comments. 'In West
Africa the indigenous relationship between 'employer' and 'employee' is not such
as leads to the creation of a class of impoverished and exploitable men and women. . . . The symbiotic relationship between the cocoa farmer and *abusa* man . . . is
not appropriately denoted by the employer/employee or the master/servant
terminology. . . . The *abusa* man [is] often left so free to get on with his work as he
thinks fit, as to be best regarded as selling the fruit of his labour. . . .' Miss Hill dis-
tinguishes five principal systems of employing labour in the cocoa-farming area:
abusa, by which the labourer is given a third share of the crop he tends and plucks;
nkotokuano—by which the labourer is paid a proportion of the load price received
by the farmer; the annual labourer—a wage employee engaged to clear new land
(at a cost which may be as high as £30 a year, plus food, clothing and tools; the
contract labourer; and the daily labourer who works under continual supervision. These divisions (it seems) are by no means absolute, since the *abusa* man
might also own farms on which he himself engages labour. See J. Brian Wills (ed.)

farm labourers at least would prefer the CPP to the NLM as a party which claimed to represent the under-privileged: but in practice it was doubtful whether they concerned themselves with political matters. They were migrants, who travelled south each year for employment and were engaged mainly to clear the bush for new farms; they were wholly dependent on the good will of the local chief and their farmer employer, and without any protective organization or union. Many also were from Upper Volta or Mali and, therefore, ineligible to vote in a general election.

2. Nevertheless, the CPP undoubtedly had its loyalist following in Ashanti, not only among the southerners resident in the region but among the Ashanti themselves. They were those who kept faith with the commoners' party in face of a challenge so closely identified with the chiefs. Precisely who these loyalists were, again it was difficult to say. The popular view (with which both the *Liberator* and the *Evening News* agreed, though in different language) was that the NLM was an 'aristocratic' (or, according to the CPP, a 'feudal') party which was supported by the 'better' element in society. Thus the *Liberator* declared that 'those who supported the CPP in Ashanti are those who belong to no family or clan, those who are strangers, not properly trained to appreciate the value of the true and noble Akan. These detribalised hooligans and hire-cut-throats are the only people who still remain CPP.'[68] As was shown, the observation was often true of many non-Ashanti groups in the towns. And, setting aside the abuse, there was some truth also perhaps in the claim that the NLM was more likely to be supported by the holders of important Stools and their kin—than by those whose family origins were at best obscure, and who may well have held back from a movement which stressed so strongly its devotion to Ashanti traditions. Admittedly, the distinction was nowhere clear-cut. For the NLM had its vigorous youth section (recruited from among the CPP) whose members saw profitable openings for their talents in any scheme of regional devolution; while the CPP had its wealthy Ashanti contractors, traders, and transport owners who wanted a strong central government and the contracts that would flow

Agriculture and Land Use in Ghana, 1962, chapter by Polly Hill on 'Social Factors in Cocoa Farming'.
[68] 20 Dec. 1955.

from a national development programme. Moreover, such social differences as existed between the two parties also tended to be obscured (as noted earlier) by the clash between rival territorial strongholds in the shape of districts, chiefdoms, sub-chiefdoms, and villages. Nevertheless, the fact remained that, throughout Ashanti, even within the NLM 'strongholds', the CPP retained the support of a number of party *militants*. And it could count on this small cadre force in almost every constituency. The remark quoted earlier from *West Africa* that 'the NLM officials . . . [were] simply the former CPP ones who left the party in disgust . . .' was not strictly accurate therefore. Many NLM officers were former CPP members; but many of the CPP constituency officers stopped their ears to the siren voices of the NLM. In Amansie, for example, most (though not all) of the village branches went over to the NLM. But of the thirty members of the constituency executive only one renounced his membership of the CPP. (Significantly, perhaps, he was one of the two better-educated members on the executive and may have been influenced by the old intelligentsia argument [which the NLM repeated] that the CPP was a party of nondescript leaders.) The CPP Ashanti members of parliament also stood firm, and although it was easy to explain their stand in terms of the advantages derived from their membership of a ruling party, it was (perhaps) too prosaic an explanation. Some at least felt a deep attachment to the revolution they had helped to bring about, and which they interpreted in terms directly opposed to the NLM. That is, they welcomed the centralization of power in a nationalist-directed party and the curbing of traditional authority.

As so often in Ghanaian politics, the stand of a particular individual was of great importance in this respect, namely, the former hero of the young men—Krobo Edusei. The resignation from the CPP of the 'unofficial party boss' in Ashanti would have had serious consequences. For more than any other leader Krobo Edusei typified the common-man element in the CPP—the local party loyalist who had opposed the officials and the chiefs in 1948 and the days of Positive Action. Yet his defection to the NLM— on the face of it—was not impossible. He had been brought up in a chief's house; he claimed descent from the great Ashanti warrior, Amakwatia; he had spoken no less vehemently than his associates in the Assembly in 1953 for an increase in the number of Ashanti seats, and even those who most disliked his toughness, or who experienced the rough edge of his tongue, never denied his courage (including the courage to change his allegiance). Yet he remained loyal to the CPP and, by doing so, almost certainly held many a wavering party member firm. Indeed, his services to the party went farther than this, for he was able to keep his constituency—Sekyere East—under party control. Alone of the great paramount chiefs of the inner ring of Ashanti chiefdoms, the Kumawuhene—chief of the most important state in Krobo Edusei's constituency—refused to support the NLM. And no one doubted that Krobo Edusei had a large say in the decision by the chief to support the government party.[69] Why did Krobo Edusei stand by the CPP, and use his influence over the Kumawuhene on behalf of the party? For the same reason (it was surely right to assume) as kept the Amansie executive and his fellow Assembly members loyal—namely, a binding self-commitment to a commoners' party which had brought wealth and power within reach of the 'ordinary man'.[70]

The number of the militant faithful—even when added to the non-Ashanti 'strangers'—was not sufficient, however, to turn the tables on the NLM, and Krobo Edusei's influence over Sekyere East was an exception to the general position in many of the constituencies where the CPP minority was harassed by the NLM. In Kumasi, for example, B. E. Dwira (the CPP leader in the New Tafo suburb) fortified his house, barricaded himself in the upper storey, and went into the main centres of the town only on quick sorties in a heavily protected jeep. In Amansie several of the executive fled to Accra or Kumawu, while others stayed in semi-hiding. E. H. Yeboah, the constituency secretary, led a hunted

[69] The decision was bitterly criticized by the other Ashanti chiefs, the Asantehene telling the Confederacy Council in August 1955 that 'the Kumawuhene . . . did not want to have anything to do with the National Liberation Movement which was fighting for the preservation of our traditions and culture. The Kumawuhene believed that a pipe-borne water supply was of more importance than the preservation of our culture' (*Minutes*, 18 Aug. 1955). But hard words broke no bones in Kumawu. The chief got his water supply—and much else—after independence. Tradition also played its part in the dispute between Kumawu and Kumasi: the two towns were said to have been rivals as potential capitals of the Ashanti confederacy at its foundation. It was believed that the high priest of Ashanti, Komfo Anokye, planted two *kum* trees, one in Kumasi, the other in Kumawu. The one grew, and gave shelter to the people—'Kumasi'; the other died—'Kumawu'. So Kumasi became the capital. So, at least, the legend ran.

[70] By the end of 1955 Krobo Edusei had a further strong motive for antipathy to the NLM when (in December) his sister was shot (and killed) by a gang of Action Groupers in an Ashanti village.

life, spending nights away from Bekwai when tension between
the NLM and the CPP reached breaking point, travelling to
Accra for consultations with the national headquarters by a
roundabout route through the bush to a distant railway station,
and having to answer (in the local Bekwai court) flimsy charges
brought by the pro-NLM chief.[71] The effect of this constant
harrying was generally to disrupt CPP organization in many of
the central Ashanti constituencies. Its daily paper—the *Ashanti
Sentinel*, managed by Dwira—was forced to close down, and the
executive in Kumasi found it difficult to maintain the bare outlines of an effective regional organization.

3. The CPP was still far from being eliminated, however, in
the region as a whole. There was still the third (and much the
most important) source of support—the existence of local
grievances against Kumasi, or against a pro-NLM chief, which
the party leaders were able to foster and turn to their advantage.
As the NLM itself liked to point out, Ashanti was itself a federation of many points of power, distributed in part hierarchically,
in part territorially, within which paramount chiefs quarrelled
with their subordinates, rival royal houses were divided over
succession claims, and neighbouring chiefdoms challenged each
other in the law courts over land and boundary rights. There was
a rich field of opportunity in these disputes not only for the CPP
but for the participants themselves. And from the end of 1954 onwards, throughout Ashanti, there began an intricate weaving of
party and local issues. Within the Adansi Division in south
Ashanti, for example, the chief (and his subordinates) of the small
Akrokerri chiefdom had for many years nursed a grievance over
their status within the Ashanti hierarchy. They claimed that they
had traditionally owed allegiance direct to the Asantehene until
1900 when the British placed them under the neighbouring
Adansi chief—a subordination confirmed at the restoration of
the Confederacy in 1935. There was little the Akrokerri people
could do about the relationship except complain—until 1954,
when the Adansi chief cast his lot with the NLM, whereupon the
Akrokerrihene sided with the CPP. Similarly, the chief of the

---

[71] One of the charges brought by the Bekwaihene was that Yeboah was trying
to kill him (at a distance) by playing a magic gramophone at dead of night.
Bekwai was a very troubled area, threatened with more serious weapons than
gramophones but, although the NLM dominated the area, there were local
enclaves of CPP support.

small town of Bechem in western Ashanti (traditionally subordinate to one of the chiefs of the Kumasi Division) seized the opportunity of the dispute between the parties to repudiate his allegiance to Kumasi in 1955, and declared his support for the CPP. In both instances, the chief acted with the consent of most of the elders and the commoners, while the minority which objected became NLM. In both instances, the CPP leaders hastened to give their blessing to the Akrokerri and Bechem 'rebels', and gave an undertaking of government support when the time was ripe.[72] Similar quarrels broke out throughout the region until, in every division, chiefdom, groups of villages, and even within a village, smouldering fires of controversy were rekindled by the dispute between the parties. The NLM had an advantage over the CPP in being able to evoke the name of the Asantehene (in addition to its initial propaganda for a higher cocoa price), but footholds of local dissent (shaped by traditional quarrels) remained for the CPP to cling to, and Ashanti became a battleground of warring party groups.

The most important of these territorial disputes lay to the west, among the Brong-Ashanti chiefdoms, where the roles of the two parties were often reversed: the CPP in the majority, the NLM in the minority. As the NLM advanced across the inner ring of cocoa states around Kumasi, and spread into the frontier area between central Ashanti and the Brong chiefdoms, it met with growing resistance. The appeal made by the leaders in the name of the Golden Stool and Ashanti rights revived a quarrel between Kumasi and the Brong chiefs which had already been ventilated in public. As elsewhere, the dispute was rooted in historical tradition.

The real strength of the Ashanti confederacy [before 1900] lay in the circle of 'true Ashanti states' within a fifty mile radius of its capital. . . . Outside this inner ring were a number of associated states which from time to time asserted their independence. Such were the Brong states to the north and north-west of Kumasi.[73]

---

[72] The CPP kept its promise. The Akrokerri and Bechem chiefs were recognized as paramount chiefs, and their states as paramount divisions, early in 1958. Apart from the prestige which paramountcy brought, there were material gains as well: e.g. in not having to refer traditional cases in customary law to the court of the paramount chief.

[73] W. Tordoff, 'The Brong Ahafo Region', *Econ. Bull.*, May 1959. The Brong were closely linked by language and culture to the Ashanti: both belonged to the Akan group of chiefdoms.

This historical distinction between the Brong and the 'true Ashanti' also lay at the heart of the CPP–NLM conflict in western Ashanti, and may be traced briefly in the political history of the two people. At the beginning of the nineteenth century the Brong chiefdoms were subject to Kumasi; later they joined with the British against Ashanti power, and were rewarded after 1901 by being recognized as separate states of a western Ashanti Province. In 1935, however, the Chief Commissioner brought pressure to bear on the Brong chiefs to join the newly restored Ashanti Confederacy: some agreed willingly, others reluctantly, and one refused absolutely.[74] The position then remained unchanged until 1948 when the chief of Techiman (an important Brong state) announced his intention of withdrawing from the Confederacy. The occasion of the quarrel was typical. The Techimanhene claimed (against the Kumasi chiefs) jurisdiction and the right to collect levy payments from nine villages (in the valley of the Tano-Subin rivers) which had been transferred from the Techiman Stool to Kumasi by a local Committee of Privileges in 1936. The chief had fought the case in a long chain of litigation from the Chief Commissioner's court to the Privy Council in London— and had lost. In 1948, however, he refused to attend meetings of the Confederacy Council, whereupon the Chief Commissioner punished the state by denying it the status of a Native Authority. But the Techiman secession was covertly supported by a number of Brong chiefs, and by March 1951 the Techimanhene thought he had sufficient support to form a Brong–Kyempem Federation'. The other leading figure in this dispute was Nana Agyeman Badu, the newly installed chief of the large Dormaa (Brong) state, an ex-government school teacher.[75] The grievances expressed by the Brong–Kyempem federation ran along familiar lines. It was said that the Ashanti chiefs looked on the Brong as inferior, that the Confederacy Council discriminated against the area by refusing its young men scholarships, that the organization of the Confederacy Executive Committee placed the Brong chiefs in a permanent minority, and that the 1938 Order of the

[74] Of the ten most important states, Banda, Wenchi, and Mo joined at the outset; Nkoranza, Drobo, Dormaa, Berekum, joined a few months later; Techiman agreed (under pressure) in April 1936, Abease in October 1938. Attebubu remained outside the Confederacy. Not all these chiefdoms were of Brong origin, but they had common grievances against Kumasi.

[75] The same Dormaahene who had stood for election in the February 1951 election against the CPP. See above, ch. II.

Council prohibiting the planting of new cocoa farms injured Brong interests:[76] in short, that the 'true Ashanti states' had concentrated the benefits of the Confederacy on themselves at Brong expense, much as the Ashanti in their turn were beginning to complain of their neglect by the Accra government.

The initial reaction of the CPP government to the Brong–Kyempem federation had been one of disapproval. The officials stressed the advantages of retaining Ashanti as a regional unit, the CPP added that it was opposed to tribalism. And in the early years of the new party administration after the 1951 election, the Brong question dropped into the background of events. It wilted from lack of adequate leaders, particularly when the Dormaahene left the country (as an adult student) to study at Ruskin College, Oxford. When he returned in 1954, however, the position was very different. For the NLM had already begun to make some headway with its demand for a higher cocoa price not only in central Ashanti, but in some of the Brong chiefdoms (notably Wenchi—K. A. Busia's home state). In reply, the Dormaahene and Techimanhene set about infusing new life in the still unrecognized Brong–Kyempem Council,[77] and this time the CPP were prepared to help, for here was a golden opportunity for the party to secure a base from which to attack. Admittedly, the policy was a somewhat dangerous one since it meant the encouragement of local, tribal demands at a time when the atmosphere was already charged with emotion. But the temptation was great, and in March 1955 Nkrumah informed the Assembly that the government was considering (1) the 'possibility of setting up a Brong–Kyempem traditional Council', (2) the 'desire of the Brongs for the establishment of a Development Committee for their areas', and (3) 'the case for the establishment of two administrative regions for Ashanti'.[78]

[76] The justification for the Order was the need to prevent the destruction of food farms. The Brong farmers were aggrieved because cocoa farming had been introduced at a later date in western Ashanti. In practice, however, the Order had very little effect.

[77] In view of the NLM demand for federation, the Brong chiefs changed the name of their own organization from 'federation' to 'Council'. As the dispute grew between the NLM and the Brong chiefdoms, the cocoa issue diminished in importance: a traditional animosity triumphed among the Brong farmers even over economic interests—a good index of the strength of Brong feeling towards Kumasi.

[78] GC, LA Deb., 25 Mar. 1955. The latent danger in any encouragement of the Brong states was already evident a fortnight earlier—on 8 March—when C. de Graft Dickson (CPP) had asked for a regional council for Ashanti Akim, the area *east* of Kumasi.

When nothing more happened, it was the turn of the Brongs to apply pressure. 'We shall be reluctantly compelled to betray our confidence in the government and the Prime Minister, Dr Kwame Nkrumah', said a petition from the (Brong) Bechem Youth Association, 'should the government defer our problem until the next Assembly session'.[79] The government was now ready to respond. It enacted (December 1955) a State Council (Ashanti) Amendment Ordinance which enabled subordinate chiefs, like the Bechemhene and others both in the Brong area and Ashanti proper, to appeal to the Governor against decisions of the Kumasi and Ashanti State Councils. The ordinance raised a storm of protest in Kumasi since it struck at the power of the Ashanti chiefs to depose a 'rebellious' subordinate, as they considered a number of pro-CPP chiefs—like the Bechemhene—to be.[80] In addition, the party leaders urged the leading Brong chiefs to remain patient until the Ashanti problem was dealt with satisfactorily when they would have their reward. The Brongs—chiefs and subjects alike—chafed under the restraint, but their dislike of Kumasi was such that—throughout these years—they remained loyal to the government.[81]

By giving its support to the Brongs, therefore, the CPP was able to strike back at the NLM with its own weapons. This line of attack on Kumasi was time-honoured—to outflank it by forming alliances with dissident groups to the west and north; it had been British policy at the end of the nineteenth century, and it was equally serviceable in 1955 to the CPP. As the year drew to a close, the importance to the CPP of Brong help became increasingly evident for—unpleasant though the prospect was to the leaders—a third election seemed likely to be forced on the government, and the Brong chiefdoms spread over six of the twenty-one Ashanti constituencies. Admittedly, the decision to secede from the Asanteman Council and establish a Brong-

---

[79] Quoted by Tordoff, *Econ. Bull.*, May 1959.

[80] The Act was of immediate help to the Bechem chief since the Kumasi State Council had declared him destooled (as it had a right to do). The government had refused to gazette the destoolment, and the chief remained in his little state, 47 miles from Kumasi; but there were enough local rivals to make his life unpleasant, and a demonstration of support for his stand by the government (through the State Councils Amendment Act) counted for a great deal in these battles of traditional rights and privileges.

[81] In 1958 they were indeed rewarded, when a separate Brong region, with its own administrative headquarters, Regional Commissioner and house of chiefs, was carved out of the western and northern districts of Ashanti. See below, ch. 7.

Kyempem Council had not been unanimous. The Wenchi and Berekum chiefs (among others) remained loyal to the Golden Stool, and the NLM (like the CPP in Ashanti proper) found numerous points of support among the intrigues and disputes of the Brong chiefdoms.[82] Nevertheless the majority of the chiefs and young men in the Brong states held steadfastly to the CPP, and thereby enabled it to recapture some of the initiative which it had lost in September 1954.

THE FAILURE TO NEGOTIATE

While these party struggles were taking place, a parallel series of constitutional manœuvres was conducted by the CPP in an attempt both to disarm the NLM and to persuade the United Kingdom government to fulfil its pre-1954 election undertaking. It failed on both counts, and the third general election followed. But for a long time the CPP leaders refused to accept such a solution of the Ashanti problem, not because they were sure the party would lose, but because they feared the margin of victory would be too narrow to permit the British government to surrender control. The NLM and its allies, on the contrary, pressed forward in hope—thinking they could win.

Nkrumah's invitation to the opposition leaders to take part in discussions in Accra at the end of December was rejected early in 1955. Two months elapsed; then, in April, the government appointed a Select Committee of the legislative assembly to 'examine the question of a federal system of government and the question of a Second Chamber for the Gold Coast. . . .'[83] The

[82] The NLM had a strong outpost in 'Brongland' in Berekum (101 miles from Kumasi) because of an ancient feud between Dormaa and the much smaller Berekum chiefdom. (The 'capitals' of the two states were only 30 miles apart.) It also had a 'fifth column' in Dormaa itself at Wamfie, a small town some fifteen miles from Dormaa Ahenkro. The Krontihene (the chief of the Dormaa army in pre-colonial days) lived at Wamfie, and claimed certain rights and privileges as a paramount chief in his own right (for which there was a shadowy historical justification). The Dormaa State Council denied him these rights, and declared him destooled, whereupon the Asanteman Council recognized the chief as a paramount and admitted him to its meetings in Kumasi. The dispute arose as early as April 1952 when the destoolment of the Krontihene was gazetted and the election of a successor recognized. Since the ex-Krontihene remained in his palace at Wamfie and refused to surrender the stool regalia, his successor had to live disconsolately in the Dormaa capital. The writer was in Dormaa Ahenkro when the Dormaahene threatened to 'march with all his forces on Wamfie' to expel the sub-chief, and a fine rumpus ensued. By 1955, therefore, Wamfie was an NLM outpost in a predominantly CPP state.

[83] GC, LA, Select Committee on Federal System of Government and Second Chamber for the Gold Coast, *Report*, 1955, from which the quotations that follow

parliamentary opposition—that is, the NPP, plus Dr Busia and M. K. Apaloo—was invited to take part in the Committee, and once again there were a number of abortive preliminary discussions between the two sides. Eventually the opposition declined. They wanted the government, said Busia, to consider the composition of a Constituent Assembly, and they believed it their 'duty in the highest interests of the country to refrain from participating in the farcical drama about to be enacted'. A committee of twelve CPP members was then formed under the chairmanship of the Deputy Speaker and began its discussions but, not surprisingly, 'all except two of the memoranda and other communications . . . received were against a federal system of government'. The Select Committee declared that this had not been allowed to influence its decisions, but it doubted 'the genuineness of the demand for federation', and declared against it. It also rejected the idea of an upper house: 'even if we [were to] recommend the creation of a Second Chamber', said the *Report*, 'the country does not possess its sinews of operation'. The Committee concurred with the view of one of its principal witnesses, J. H. Price, that 'the liberty which each individual in this country enjoys is greater than the liberty enjoyed by the individual in the United Kingdom',[84] dismissed current fears for minority rights as groundless but added that, to meet the present situation, the government might consider the establishment of 'such additional regional bodies as may be required to ensure full consultation and collaboration between itself and the various Regions'. This was simply to echo Nkrumah's December broadcast, and the *Report*, like the Committee itself, was totally disregarded by the opposition.

This first move by the government was so obviously a failure that there was a fresh pause while the CPP tried to gather itself together. The sixth anniversary of the party took place in Accra in June, and Nkrumah delivered a remarkable speech.[85] Some-

---

are taken. The adding of the question of an upper house was designed to placate the Colony Joint Provincial Council of Chiefs who never ceased to waver between being attracted by the idea of a Senate of Chiefs, and being alarmed by the thought that it might mean the dissolution of their own provincial councils.

[84] Ibid. J. H. Price was a lecturer in government at the University College; in June 1961 his contract was abruptly terminated by the government. The quotation is from the Proceedings of the Committee, 11 May 1955, p. 5 of the *Report*.

[85] *Text of Address by the Life Chairman to the Sixth Anniversary of the Party at Accra*, 12 June 1955.

thing was needed to revive the drooping spirits of the party members, and Nkrumah evoked memories of the days of Positive Action—the

beatings, the arrests, the imprisonments and the general persecution of Party members and supporters in those hectic days of our struggle. . . . All these difficulties have come and gone. We may yet be faced with difficulties, but these will also be overcome because we are determined and confident that victory will be ours.

The party was threatened by the violence of a 'feudal tyranny' led by 'certain intellectual snobs, traitors and saboteurs'. But there was no cause for alarm. 'The country is united', the delegates were told; moreover,

no less than twelve political parties have sprung up, and yet because they failed to produce any policy acceptable to the people none of them has succeeded. For the first and only time in the chequered history of this country, ours has been the only party to present a clear and bold programme for independence, freedom, democracy and justice.

Was all this, he asked, to be held up by a few 'Chiefs and disgruntled and disappointed politicians'? The party had won the 1954 election only a year ago, with 'an appeal to the nation [that] was simple and direct: "Give us the mandate to obtain independence for this country and develop our resources." The nation heard us and responded admirably.' There was criticism of the party for its supposed hostility to the idea of an opposition, but this was nonsense.

I have always expressed both in public and private that we need a strong and well organised Opposition Party in the country and in the Assembly. My advice to opposition parties has always been that they should organise themselves and choose reliable and trustworthy leaders—not saboteurs and political renegades and apostates—and that they should produce a national policy that the people can accept. . . . But unfortunately this seems beyond them because they seem incapable of direction and organisation; it appears that all they are capable of at present is abuse and vilification. . . .

While the audience expressed its approval, Nkrumah went on to explain that

the present political issue is a test as to whether parliamentary democracy will live and strive in this country or whether we shall revert to feudal tyranny and despotic rule. We must not forget that democracy means the rule of the majority, though it should be tempered by sweet reasonableness in the interests of the minority. In a parliamentary democracy legitimate constitutional opposition is a part of its fabric— but not opposition that breeds and fosters violence.

Was the CPP dictatorial? This was an 'iniquitous and vicious allegation'. Was Nkrumah himself a dictator? 'If I were a dictator', said the Life Chairman, 'the Opposition Party would have no place to stand to make the noise they are making'. The political record of the CPP was there to show its stand against dictatorship—against both the 'bondage of foreign colonialism and the tyranny of local feudal despotism'; and 'as a political party we expect criticism—we even enjoy it. . . '.

All this was in such contrast with the earlier attitude of the CPP that the NLM in Kumasi paid little attention to it. Moreover, a month later—on 14 July—the Ashanti party won the Atwima Nwabiagya by-election. The result understandably upset the CPP, and once again Nkrumah had to reassure his followers, this time at the annual Delegates' Conference which met at Kpandu in the Togoland Trust Territory at the beginning of August.[86]

You may have heard [he told the delegates] of the defeat of the party candidate at the Atwima Nwabiagya Constituency by-election. . . . I know that the result of the election came as a shock to all Party members especially to those Party members in the constituency who were very sure of victory. Many stories have been told in connection with the conduct of the elections but I assure you that in spite of our defeat our position is unshaken. It is darkest before the dawn; the battle is fiercest just before the cessation of hostilities.

All would be well provided there was 'loyalty, discipline and organisation . . . the three pillars on which is built the success of our Party'. The *Evening News* forgot the Leader's dislike of 'abuse and vilification' and, on the eve of the conference, came out with a scornful editorial: 'Asantehene: From Grace to Grass', saying that the by-election showed how 'the Golden Stool, itself desecrated by being dragged down into the mud of politics, continues to sink speedily into the mire within which the dignity of the Asantehene is drowning fast'. But there was very little except

[86] *Text of Address by the Life Chairman to the Sixth Annual Delegates' Conference held at Kpandu*, 31 July 1955.

abuse that the CPP could use in reply to the Atwima election, the NLM, the NPP, the Togoland Congress, or the Muslims. It was clearly beset with difficulties, and the note of disappointment that ran through the speeches of the delegates at the conference was easy to understand. It should, after all, have been the last conference before independence.[87] 'Renascent Africa' was stirring, and Ghana was to be its 'symbol and inspiration'.[88] The government had already sent an observer to the Afro-Asian conference at Bandung: Africa, Asia, and the world seemed to lie almost within reach. Yet the leaders were at a loss to know what to do.[89]

Following the Delegates' Conference, Nkrumah made a further effort to break the deadlock. The Secretary of State was requested to appoint a 'Constitutional Adviser' to assist the government and, in particular, to study the problem of a devolution of power from the central government to the regions. On 26 September 1955 Frederick Bourne arrived in Accra, and began a series of discussions with the Government, the Joint Provincial Council, the Trans-Volta Togoland Council, and a number of local government bodies.[90] Once again the opposition

[87] The sixth annual conference was originally arranged to take place at Saltpond—the town where the party had its origins, and where it would have made its last triumphant appearance before independence. But even the weather was hostile. Floods inundated the town—so the conference was transferred to Kpandu.

[88] Anniversary speech, 12 June 1955.

[89] The Kpandu conference also looked at the Ewe and Brong problems, and once again tried to improve party organization. Various resolutions were passed: one, recommending that the government 'withdraw all financial grants to the Asanteman Council forthwith', another calling for an amendment to the 1952 State Councils Ordinance 'to allow all chiefs in Ashanti to have a right of appeal to the Governor'. The conference also urged the government, 'having noted the demand of the Brong Kyempem people and their chiefs', to take steps immediately to establish a Brong Kyempem Traditional Council, a regional development committee, and a regional administration. On the Ewe problem, Nkrumah told the delegates, that the All-Ewe Conference movement, and even M. Olympio himself until 1951, had always meant Ewe unity within the Gold Coast, and he now 'invited the people of British Togoland to advance with the Gold Coast under the banner of the Convention People's Party'. Something was done, too, to overhaul the party's constituency organization where it was badly mauled by local disputes. New membership cards were issued, and branch officers urged to 'keep an up-to-date enrolment register of members [with] regular meetings to discuss current political, economic and social matters', and to 'keep in constant touch with the Constituency Headquarters, the Regional Headquarters and the National Secretariat'.

[90] Sir Frederick Bourne had served for many years in the Indian Civil Service and, more recently, in Pakistan. This caused a flutter in both parties' headquarters, but no one quite knew how to interpret the lesson Sir Frederick may have drawn from so extreme an example of secession. The *Report of the Constitutional Adviser* was submitted to the government in December 1955. The appointment was almost

parties refused to participate—the NLM and the Asanteman Council having been given an excellent excuse by the government not to do so. For it was while Bourne was in the country that the government introduced into the Assembly the amendment to the 1952 State Council Ordinance which enabled subordinate chiefs in Ashanti to appeal against decisions of their State Councils and the Asanteman Council. 'In the event', as the *Report of the Constitutional Adviser* recorded: 'the National Liberation Movement and its allies declared themselves unable to afford me the opportunity of consultation on the grounds that the recent State Councils (Ashanti) Amendment Bill directly attacked the heritage and culture of Ashanti and *pro tanto* stultified my mission.' This was very much Hamlet without the Prince, and Bourne had to confess that 'though [he was] aware of the Government's views on regional devolution . . . he had not had the advantage of discussing their own Federal proposals with the NLM. . . '. He submitted his recommendations, however, in December 1955 with the cautionary moral attached to them (which the NLM liked from time to time to repeat) that, 'Laws they are not, which public approbation hath not made so'.

The scheme of devolution propounded in the *Report* fell well short of the opposition's *Proposals for Federal Constitution*. It stated quite plainly that 'supreme legislative power' would have to remain at the centre, and that the opposition's *Proposals*, if adopted, would 'slow down development and introduce an intolerable handicap to the administration of the country'. There was, however, a certain broad sympathy for the opposition's stand. The particular grievances of the NPP were acknowledged in the recommendations of the need for a specific commitment by the government to a Ten-Year Plan for the north. The Brong demand for local autonomy was summarily dismissed: 'Whatever may be the result of the long standing difference between the Brong states of Western Ashanti and the Asanteman Council', wrote Bourne, 'I cannot see any administrative justification for

certainly suggested by the U.K. government. Busia had visited Britain (29 June–11 July); he had met officials at the Colonial Office, and in a *Report to Nana Asantehene on his Visit*, 16 July 1956, said that the U.K. government 'dug their toes in' over the suggestion of full federation, but might agree to the appointment of a Constitutional Adviser to work out the details of a devolution of power to the regions.

creating a separate region of this comparatively small area where-in local opinion on the subject is far from unanimous'. The *Report* then set out its main recommendations for five regional assem-blies, each to be entrusted with a wide range of delegated powers,[91] and for a form of guarantee to protect the powers and life of the assemblies once they were established.

Had both sides been interested in pursuing the argument there was a good deal in the detailed clauses of the *Report* for further de-bate. Its recommendations were handicapped from the start, however, in that they represented an attempt to devise an ad-ministrative answer for what was essentially a political problem, and as yet there was no suggestion in Kumasi of any readiness to compromise. The *Report* needed at least a minimum of trust in the good intentions of the government, and this the NLM refused to concede to the CPP since it had every hope, after the Atwima election, of gaining far more than control of a Regional Assembly. It dismissed the *Report* as irrelevant on the grounds that it failed to admit the need for regional legislatures of a strictly federal description. The CPP was less hostile to the recommendations in the *Report*, if only because the leaders recognized that, once a 'supreme legislative power' was retained at the centre, then the future at least was theirs. But a one-sided agreement was no agreement at all, and it was now that the United Kingdom government began to raise the possibility of a third general election.

The Secretary of State intimated that the British Government would hesitate to grant independence to the Gold Coast until a sub-stantial majority of the people had shown that they wanted inde-pendence in the very near future and had agreed upon a workable constitution for the country. If the Constitutional Adviser succeeded in recommending proposals which were generally acceptable to a majority, all well and good. If he failed, then there appeared no alternative but to call a general election in order to seek the views of the people.[92]

---

[91] They are given in s. 8 of the *Report*; they ranged from the approval of local-government authority estimates and precepts, control over local authorities' responsibility in respect of primary and middle education, responsibility for control over regional roads, rural housing projects, hospital sites and so forth, and appoint-ments to Statutory Boards and Committees. They were based in part on the earlier *Report on Regional Administration* in 1950 by Sir Sydney Phillipson which was not adopted by the CPP Government.
[92] Nkrumah, *Autobiography*, p. 245.

The choice was plain, therefore: either the government had to reach an accommodation with the NLM, or stake its future on the hazards of an election.

What was the CPP to do? And why should Nkrumah hesitate to risk an election? The simplest answer was surely the right one. The party was unsure of what the outcome might be. The leaders were doubtful, the party uneasy, the electorate unpredictable. CPP 'refugees' from Ashanti in Accra were pressing for further reprisals not elections, and the Ashanti Assembly members were all too aware, after the Atwima election, how narrow their own base of support had become. Thus to enter an election at the instigation of the Secretary of State, in the face of demands by the NLM that there should be one, and the categorical refusal of a majority of the party to entertain the idea, was, to say the least, an unpleasant prospect. The degree of uneasiness among the leaders may be seen even in Nkrumah's *Autobiography* when the worst (from the party's point of view) was almost over. 'The present transitional period had already given rise to difficulties; there [was] . . . criticism against the Government for not doing things which it was, in fact, not able to do, and a feeling by some that the Government had no power at all and could therefore be ignored.'[93] The 'members of my party executive were almost unanimous in voting against a general election and even to mention the subject was like waving a red rag before a bull'.[94] The CPP might yet win; it was even likely that it would: but—by what margin? And suppose the worst happened; suppose a second 'rebel election', as in 1954, took place among the party's own candidates in the south, while each of the regional parties— the NLM, the NPP, and the Togoland Congress—secured a majority of the seats in its own area? The prospect was at best uninviting, and the leaders refused to entertain it.

The outcome of these fears was a further effort to evade a final decision. At the beginning of January 1956 Nkrumah wrote to the four regional territorial councils and the four main political parties—the NLM, NPP, Togoland Congress, and his own party: each was invited to nominate delegates to attend a conference at Achimota School to discuss the proposals of the Bourne *Report*. Again the opposition decided to boycott the Conference, although the Asanteman Council and the NLM told the govern-

[93] Nkrumah, *Autobiography*, p. 244.   [94] Ibid. p. 248.

ment on 8 January that it would accept, provided a number of conditions (which they must surely have known were impossible) were observed: namely (1) any decisions arrived at should be considered by a freshly elected legislature; (2) the Moslem Association Party and the Aborigines Rights Protection Society should also be invited; (3) a preliminary Working Committee should meet to plan the agenda; and—finally—'the Government should as a sign of its good faith repeal the State Councils (Ashanti) Amendment Ordinance'.

At this point there was a wild flurry of argument, accusations, and threats. Nkrumah spoke at a rally in Accra and reminded his audience that though 'our opponents are forcing us into a General Election' he alone was 'the only man in the country at the moment to approve such a demand'.[95] Others of the party's central committee went a good deal farther than this. 'If Britain fails to announce the granting of independence', said N. A. Welbeck, 'the Gold Coast will be forced to declare itself independent and then invite Britain to participate in the celebrations when the time comes.'[96] K. A. Gbedemah told a party rally at Koforidua that

he believed everything would go as planned now for the achievement of independence by the Gold Coast this year or early in 1957, and that he didn't think the U.K. Government would refuse to give the Gold Coast independence. If they should refuse the Gold Coast might be forced to declare themselves independent as the Sudanese did recently, and many of the important countries like United States and India would immediately recognise the Gold Coast as an independent Sovereign State.[97]

These were wild statements which were not always accurately reported in the local press, but they matched the exasperation and despair of the CPP leaders. The NLM was quick to reply to these

[95] *Daily Graphic*, 28 Jan. 1956.

[96] *Ashanti Times*, 17 Feb. 1956, report of a rally in Accra. Welbeck was now Minister of Works.

[97] *Daily Graphic*, 27 Feb. 1956. Gbedemah was now Minister of Finance. Eventually, a *Statement* was issued from the Prime Minister's office saying that 'statements have been made alleging that the Gold Coast intends to adopt unconstitutional methods in order to achieve the complete transfer of power from the United Kingdom to the Gold Coast. These statements are incorrect. The Government has already demonstrated to the world its respect for constitutional methods and it will continue to pursue the achievement of full independence within the Commonwealth by constitutional means' (12 March).

reports with the equally wild threat of secession, Bafuor Akoto saying that 'if upon the strength of these CPP Ministers' statements the United Kingdom Government granted the Gold Coast independence without a general agreement on the constitution, Ashanti also would separate herself from the rest of the country'.[98]

Although there was no hope now of any general ground of agreement, the CPP did what it could to give the Achimota Conference the pretence of reality. It announced over the radio and in the press that, in addition to party representatives, members were being invited from the Ghana TUC, the Ex-Servicemen's Union, the Gold Coast Muslim Council, the Brong–Kyempem Council (and—as a 'concession' to the opposition—the Moslem Association Party). Later, the names of four local authorities in the north were added as having agreed to send representatives. Each of these additional bodies (the MAP apart) was directly hostile to the NLM and its allies.[99] Indeed, there were now no neutrals in the country, and although the Conference (arranged for 16 February in the Assembly Hall of Achimota School) was to meet under the chairmanship of a well-known and generally respected civil servant—C. W. (later, Sir Charles) Tachie Menson—he, too, was regarded by the NLM as 'a staunch member of the CPP and one of the Prime Minister's closest advisers in the CPP'. When, therefore, the opposition leaders met in Kumasi early in February, they rejected in forthright terms Nkrumah's invitation (renewed on 31 January with the additional suggestion that the points raised by the NLM and the Asanteman Council could be discussed at the Conference). There was little point, said the opposition,

in snatching the political advantage of going to a Conference so constituted and so doomed and then laying the blame for its failure

---

[98] *Liberator*, 6 Mar. 1956.

[99] The Ghana TUC was pro-CPP, in opposition now to a pro-NLM 'Congress of Free Trade Unions'; the CPP Gold Coast Ex-Servicemen's Union was opposed by a rival National (Gold Coast) Ex-Servicemen's Union; the Gold Coast Muslim Council was the pro-CPP minority association led by Mallam Mutawakilu in Kumasi and Z. B. Shardow in Accra; and the northern local council representatives were from western Gonja, northern Dagomba, Kassena-Nankanni south, and Builsa, where the chiefs and local leaders were pro-CPP. The composition of the Trans-Volta delegation, led by Togbe Tepre Hodo II of Anfoega and Wellington Kuma, was also such as to make it certain that the Togoland Congress would refuse to attend.

squarely at the door of its convenor, the Prime Minister. The position
in the Gold Coast is so grave that an abortive conference such as the
Prime Minister has planned may well destroy any remaining good
will and desire for cooperation. . . .[100]

The Conference opened (with Bourne in attendance) on
16 February and, as might be expected from so faithful a group,
quickly reached a broad measure of agreement. The only dis-
cordant note was sounded by two of the four members nominated
by the Joint Provincial Council who tried to mediate, and bring
in representatives of the NLM and the Asanteman Council, while
the Conference adjourned for a week. The opposition remained
hostile. Then the two members—Nene Mate Kole and Nana Otu
IX (Omanhene of the small Abura state in the western region)—
travelled to Kumasi after the Conference had resumed its discussions to meet the Ashanti leaders. This further effort also
failed, and the Conference concluded its work on 16 March, endorsing and filling in the proposals for a regional devolution of
power outlined in the Bourne *Report*. There was, however, one
significant amendment. The members of the Conference 'unanimously decided that the representations made by the Brong–
Kyempem Council delegation are weighty in material and fact
. . . and recommends to the Government, therefore, that, when
Regional Assemblies come to be set up, the case for a separate
Assembly for the Brong area should be given very careful
consideration'.[101]

The government solemnly accepted the Achimota Conference
Report, but the principal effect of the Conference was to extend
the hostility which already existed between the CPP and the
NLM. And already, by the middle of March—towards the end
of the Conference—tempers had risen to a point of hysteria on
both sides. The *Evening News* claimed to have knowledge of a
'secret meeting recently under the chairmanship of the Asantehene', at which the NLM decided 'to get rid of Kwame Nkrumah and if necessary Sir Charles Arden-Clarke', and an editorial

[100] 'Text of Statement issued by the NLM, the NPP, the MAP and the Togoland
Congress on February 5th 1956', *Ashanti Pioneer*, 7 Feb. 1956.
[101] Achimota Conference *Report*, 1956, para. 24. Nene Mate Kole of Manya
Krobo declined to sign the *Report*, having withdrawn four days before the end of
the Conference, saying: 'Are we discussing a constitution for the Gold Coast
Colony only or one for the whole Gold Coast?' (ibid. app. C).

warned the leaders of what their fate would be if they succeeded in their plan of 'assassination':

THEY WILL BE CRUSHED IF THEY DARE[102]

If anything happens to harm either Kwame Nkrumah or Sir Charles Arden-Clarke, death will be too merciful for this gang of traitors. We promise them that in their anguish and torture they will pray for death—but death will bide her time: the people of the Gold Coast will see to that. No single man will escape the justice that a nation cheated of its freedom will see fit to award.

To this extraordinary attack the *Liberator* replied in comparable language, saying that 'these homeless tramps and jackals ... are now haunted men and sorely afraid of their own shadows, otherwise they would not be fabricating such stories'; moreover, 'the Ashantis are thinking about better things and have no time to attempt the life of a damned Colonial Prime Minister'.[103]

Thus every attempt by the CPP to persuade the NLM that its points could be met within the framework of the 1954 constitution had failed. The government's overtures to the opposition had been rejected; Nkrumah himself had been outmanœuvred. These were unusual and unpleasant roles for the nationalist party to play. It hesitated, uncertain of itself, pleaded with the Governor and the Secretary of State, until—finally—the United Kingdom government forced the issue. Since the Achimota Conference 'had failed in providing the requisite agreement, there appeared to him [the Secretary of State] no alternative but to hold a general election'.[104] Nkrumah pleaded the risk of violence, warned Gordon Hadow (the Deputy Governor) and A. T. Lennox-Boyd (the Secretary of State) that 'if a general election were held in the near future, it appeared extremely doubtful that it would be conducted without violence', and pointed out that his own party executive was against it. None of these reasons was likely to impress the United Kingdom government as an argument in favour of granting independence. Even

[102] 12 Mar. 1956.
[103] *Liberator*, 14 Mar. 1956. The Asantehene issued an indignant rebuttal of the charges made in the *Evening News*, adding piously that 'a dishonest press to which truth is unknown, and whose main preoccupation is the fabrication and propagation of irresponsible, scurrilous and nearly always libellous information is a serious liability to any country'.
[104] This is the general account given by Nkrumah of his negotiations with London in the *Autobiography*, pp. 248–50, from which the quotations which follow have been taken.

now, however, Nkrumah did not give in without a final effort.
(None the less, it was probably fair to assume that a good part of
these last-minute negotiations were undertaken more to convince
his own party executive that there was no alternative to a third
general election than in the hope of persuading the Secretary of
State.) On 23 March Kojo Botsio was sent to England to put the
case for the immediate grant of independence on the grounds
that there was 'no need whatever to go back again to the country
to seek anew a mandate which was renewed only as recently as
June 1954', and that 'to impose new conditions on [the people]
would defeat the essence of parliamentary democracy'. A week
later Botsio returned to announce that the Secretary of State was
'genuinely out to help the Gold Coast gain its independence', but
that 'a general election [was] the only answer'.

Now at last Nkrumah was prepared for a third election, telling
the Governor that, given strict security precautions, he 'would be
prepared to declare a general election during the forthcoming
session of the Legislative Council, the date of the election being
in all probability towards the middle of July'. It was the Secretary of State, however, who made the first public announcement,
saying:

> I have been in close touch with the Prime Minister of the Gold Coast
> on these matters. It is the considered view of his Government that the
> time has now come for the Gold Coast to assume full responsibility
> within the Commonwealth for its own affairs. I have made my view
> clear to him that because of the failure to resolve the constitutional
> dispute we can only achieve our common aim of the early indepen-
> dence of that country within the Commonwealth in one way and one
> way alone; that is, to demonstrate to the world that the peoples of the
> Gold Coast have had a full and free opportunity to consider their
> Constitution and to express their views on it in a general election.
> I have told Dr Nkrumah that if a general election is held Her
> Majesty's Government will be ready to accept a motion calling for
> independence within the Commonwealth passed by a reasonable
> majority in a newly elected Legislature and then to declare a firm
> date for this purpose.[105]

A week later the Governor's 'Speech from the Throne' at the
ceremonial opening of the 1956 session of the Legislative Assembly in Accra announced that the government would 'seek a

[105] H.C. Deb., vol. 552, coll. 1557–8, 11 May 1956.

mandate from the people that they desire the immediate grant of independence' on the basis of detailed constitutional proposals to be submitted to the House.[106]

Thus the die was cast, in the hope that it would enable the remaining obstacles to independence to be overcome. No one, however, could be certain of the outcome of the election, and it was at least possible that the result would be not a resolution of the struggle between the two sides but continued deadlock. For the difficulties in arriving at a clear-cut solution had already been demonstrated, when, earlier in the year (on 9 May) the people of the trust territory had voted in the United Nations-held plebiscite in an effort to decide their future. The results were by no means straightforward, the northern section having voted for, and the southern section against, integration with the Gold Coast:

	Total	Southern section		Northern section	
For Union	98,761	43,976	42%	49,119	79%
For Separation	61,826	54,785	58%	12,707	21%

On closer analysis, it was possible to argue that only two of the six main districts in the southern section of the trust territory— Ho and Kpandu—had voted for 'the separation of Togoland under British administration from the Gold Coast and its continuance under trusteeship, pending the ultimate determination of its political future'.[107] It was unlikely, therefore, that the General Assembly of the United Nations would agree to the isolation of the Ewe areas of the trust territory, and certain that Britain would refuse to administer them. The United Kingdom government had made its own position unmistakably clear in this respect. On the other hand, the union of southern Togoland with French-speaking Togo—along lines of the settlement

---

[106] GC, LA Deb., 15 May 1956.

[107] Voters were asked to choose between 'union . . . with an independent Gold Coast' and 'separation' on this basis. The voting percentages on a district basis were (percentages):

	For Union	For Separation
Mamprusi	84	16
Dagomba	81	19
Gonja	79	21
Buem Krachi	60	40
Kpandu	34	66
Ho	28	72

For a more detailed appraisal of the results see the excellent monograph by J. S. Coleman, *Togoland*.

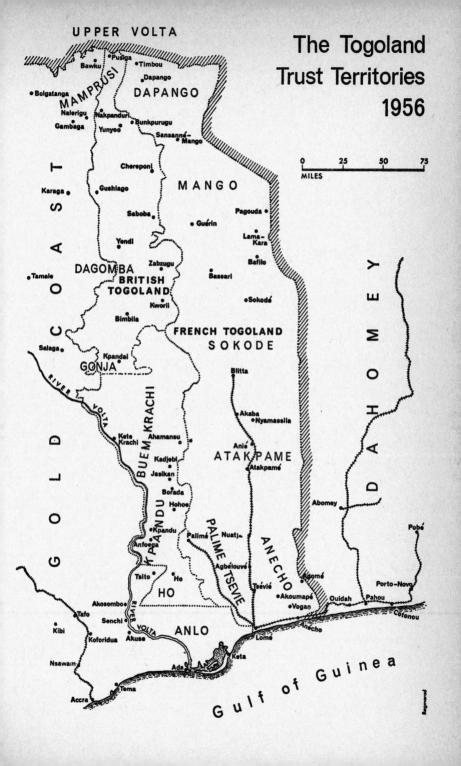

The Togoland
Trust Territories
1956

UPPER VOLTA

MAMPRUSI

DAPANGO

MANGO

GOLD COAST

DAGOMBA

BRITISH
TOGOLAND

FRENCH TOGOLAND
SOKODE

GONJA

BUEM

KRACHI

KPANDU

PALIME

TSEVIE

ATAKPAME

ANECHO

DAHOMEY

HO

ANLO

Gulf of Guinea

0   25   50   75
MILES

• Pusiga
• Timbou
Dapango
• Bawku
• Bolgatanga
Nalerigu
Nakpanduri• •Bunkpurugu
Gambaga
Yunyoo
Sansanné-
Mango

Cerepani

Karaga
• Gushiago
Saboba
• Guérin
Pagouda

Yendi
Lama-
Kara

Tamale
Zabzugu
Bafilo
Bassari
Kworli
•Sokodé

Bimbila

Salaga•
Kpandai
Blitta

RIVER VOLTA

Kete
Krachi
Ahamansu
Akaba
•Nyamassila

Kadjebi
Anie
ATAKPAME
Jasikan
•Atakpamé

Borada
Hohoe
Abomey•

•Kpandu
Nuatja•
Pobé•
Anfoega
Palimé

Tsito
Ho
Agbélouvé
•Tsévié

Akosombo
Tsévié
•Akoumapé
Ouidah•
Porto-Novo•
•Tafo
Senchi
•Vogan
Pahou•
Kibi
Koforidua
Akuse
Anecho
Cotonou•
Nsawam
Keta
Lome
Ada•
Accra•
Tema

Regmand

reached in 1960 over the question of the southern Cameroons and the Cameroun Republic—was also improbable, not only because of the strong objections that the CPP government would lodge against it, but because the Trusteeship Council itself was divided in its attitude towards French policy in the neighbouring trust territory.[108]

The Ewe question was thus seen to be part of the still wider problem of the relationship between the regions and the central government in the Gold Coast generally. And the uncertainty arising from the plebiscite results underlined the fear that the forthcoming general election—now scheduled for 17 July— would merely reproduce the north–south conflict in the trust territory on a national scale, namely a balance of interests between and within each region. One ray of hope was possible. The plebiscite had been remarkably peaceful, despite the violent antagonism between the Togoland Congress and the CPP. And this augured well for the July election. Nevertheless, what mattered was not the election but the result. By early July each side believed that it could either win or prevent its opponents from enjoying their victory. And if, indeed, the election led to further deadlock then it was difficult to see what more could be done, that had not already been attempted, to reconcile the CPP and the opposition.

[108] Universal suffrage was introduced in the French trust territory in June 1956 (under the *loi cadre*) but when the French government announced its intention of holding a referendum to enable the peoples of the territory to decide between 'full autonomy' under a new statute, and the continuation of the trusteeship, the seven non-administering members of the Trusteeship Council in New York rejected the invitation to send observers. They condemned the proposal and the invitation as merely a manœuvre to perpetuate French control. It was a time when every French move was suspect. The French went ahead however: Togo became an autonomous republic; Olympio came to power in 1958; and the territory became independent in 1960. But by then the Ewe areas of the former British Togoland had been integrated with Ghana. For an account of French policy in Togo up to 1956 see Coleman, *Togoland*, pp. 21–27, 80–85.

A NOTE ON NLM MEMBERSHIP

At the end of Chapter IV a general description was given of the members of a CPP constituency executive. The same may be done for the NLM in Kumasi:

NLM Constituency Executive, Kumasi South, 1957*

Office	Occupation	Education	Age	Whether former member of CPP	Origin
Chairman	Timber merchant	Secondary	48	No	
Vice-Chairman	Trader		45	Yes	
Secretary	Trader	Std VII	38	Yes	Ashanti
Prop. Secretary	Cocoa factor/ Councillor		39	Yes	
Treasurer	Teacher	Secondary	35	Yes	Akwapim
Committee Members:	Bailiff	Std VII	49	Yes	
	Farmer		50	Yes	Ashanti
	Trader		40	Yes	
	Plantain seller†		48	Yes	Banda
	Farmer	Illiterate	50	Yes	
	Trader		44	No	Ashanti
	Farmer		46	No	
	Goldsmith		40	No	
	Driver		37	Yes	Northerner
	Druggist		30	No	Fanti
	Letter-writer		39	No	
	Fitter	Std VII	40	Yes	Ashanti
	Storekeeper		38	Yes	Nigerian
	Carpenter		29	Yes	Ewe
	Farmer		46	No	Ashanti
	Trader	Illiterate	44	Yes	

* Information from Antwi Kusi, a Kumasi trader, later held in preventive detention. The analysis is of the NLM/United Party as it was in Kumasi South in 1957. No comparable table was possible for a rural area. An attempt in 1958 to reconstruct the NLM executive in Bekwai proved unsatisfactory. The figures of age and occupation in the table are approximate, but the general picture is accurate.

† The only woman member.

Several points of interest stand out from the table. First, the characteristically large number of Ashanti on the executive, despite the fact that many of the Kumasi South wards contained a majority of southerners. Second, the equally characteristic alliance between the 'intelligentsia leader' and the plebian rank and file; the chairman at this time was B. D. Addai, a prominent Kumasi merchant, a member of the 1946–50 legislative council and a former member of the UGCC Working Committee, whose large house at Adum was an early centre of anti-CPP activity. Third, the basic similarity—within the limits of the NLM Ashanti base—between the CPP and the NLM. The one shade of difference was perhaps (as might be expected) the slightly higher percentage of elderly illiterates in the NLM to whom an appeal for loyalty to the Golden Stool would have great emotional significance. Fourth, the extent to which the NLM was a break-away movement from the CPP—hence the similarity between them. Fifth, the broad base of the NLM: within its Ashanti limits, the NLM had many of the attributes of a 'mass party' despite the specific appeal made by the CPP to the Common Man.

The narrower limits of the NLM, compared with the CPP, were shown clearly in a survey in 1959 of voting behaviour in the town.[109] A pattern of voting was traced out from the 1956 election to the Kumasi South by-election in April 1959 (following Kurankyi Taylor's death); and the conclusion was reached that, whereas the NLM–United Party was largely confined to Ashanti and Muslim voters in the city, the CPP was able to attract support not only from the southern immigrants but from a substantial number of Ashanti voters as well. Thus the predominantly Ashanti wards were found to be divided between the opposition and the CPP roughly in the proportion 60 per cent for the NLM–UP, 40 per cent for the CPP; the southern immigrant wards voted overwhelmingly (80 per cent +) for the CPP. The only area of the city where the CPP was unable to muster any substantial support was in the Suame suburb—among the Ashanti Muslim (*asante nkramo*) compounds. The pro-CPP Ashanti vote was probably concentrated among the poorer compounds of the city (although, again, not among the very poor Muslim area). The wealthy Ashanti lawyers and businessmen, with their large houses and pleasant gardens in the Mbrom district, voted heavily against the CPP. (There were a number of individual exceptions: e.g. Krobo Edusei whose large house on the edge of Mbrom undoubtedly placed him with the new rich.) In sum, therefore, it was possible to make a reasonably accurate correlation between tribal origin and party affiliation and to draw the tentative conclusion that while the wealthier Ashanti families were likely to vote for the NLM, the poorer

[109] See Austin and Tordoff, 'Voting in an African Town', *Political Studies*, June 1960. The basis of the study was the ward results of the 1958 municipal elections.

compounds were likely to be divided between the two parties. Nothing, however, could be regarded as immutable. The fact that the NLM was in the ascendant in 1956, and the CPP on the defensive, helped to tilt the balance still farther on the side of the Ashanti party. The overall victory of the CPP in the election then saw the balance tilt back in favour of the ruling party. All power attracts and—in Ghana—the exercise of absolute power tended to attract absolutely. Or, in more homely terms: '*Obi nni sono akyi mmoro huasu*'—He who follows an elephant does not get wet from the dew.

The analysis sketched here referred only to Kumasi however, not to Ashanti as a whole. Both the NLM and the CPP drew the greater part of their support from one side or other in the disputes which divided the chiefdoms, the result being that the region became a battleground in which the parties operated from local, territorial strongholds.

VII

The 1956 Election

ELECTION studies must concern themselves with five principal questions: who were the competitors? What were the issues? How were the elections conducted? Who won? and What was the effect of the election on the general direction of politics at the time? The third general election in July 1956 was no exception, and these broad general headings may be used to discuss this final, pre-independence contest between the CPP and its opponents. Its importance could hardly be exaggerated. The result of the two days' voting would determine not only the timing of independence—a question raised by the United Gold Coast Convention in 1947 and still undecided—but the nature of the régime which would possess full control of the state. If the CPP won, by a comfortable margin of seats, then the direction taken by the nationalist movement since the end of the war was likely to continue, towards a unitary centralized state under a radical party leadership. A perceptive observer might have questioned the ability of Nkrumah and the CPP to maintain a liberal multi-party régime, but not their competence to use the resources of the country to carry still further the building of a modern African state. If, on the other hand, the NLM and its allies won, by whatever margin of votes and seats, it was difficult to see what the outcome might be. It was possible to question whether the leaders' commitment to a federal structure of government would survive the shock of victory. It was not easy to see how an effective government, whether federal or unitary, would emerge from the uneasy coalition of regional and minority groups whose principal bond of unity was a common dislike of Nkrumah and the CPP. Power, to be sure, is a marvellous cement of unity in the early years of victory. Nevertheless, it was open to doubt whether so mixed a body as the federation alliance would be able to cohere. (It was also doubtful whether the CPP would consent to play the part of a loyal opposition, although K. A. Gbedemah was soon to assure the country that it would.) Independence was certain, therefore, should the CPP triumph; much less sure should the NLM and its allies win the election. There was, however, a third possibility: namely, stalemate, and continued violence, until the growing disregard of law and order forced the colonial administration to intervene—to the dismay of the officials and CPP leaders alike—and the suspension of the 1954 constitution.

Was it possible that the CPP would lose? Had the NLM any chance of winning? The opposition leaders were convinced in 1955 and the early months of 1956 that they had the CPP at their mercy, and before turning to the five principal questions we might look at the general pre-election scene as it was viewed from the opposition headquarters.

First, the north, where the CPP had already met its first defeat. The Northern People's Party hoped to win twenty of the twenty-six constituencies in the region. They expected to lose Gonja West, where E. A. Mahama (a CPP member) and the Gonja paramount chief were in control of the village population throughout this vast constituency; three of the five Dagomba constituencies, because of the alliance between the Dagomba paramount chief (the Ya Na Abdulai) and J. H. Allasani, the Minister of Education; Kassena-Nankanni South, where the power of the chief of the important market centre at Navrongo had been placed behind L. R. Abavana, a ministerial secretary; and, possibly, Kusasi West, where Ayeebo Asumda, also a ministerial secretary, was similarly well entrenched.[1] But twenty out of twenty-six would be a major victory. The party had won sixteen seats in 1954 shortly after its inauguration; with the experience of that election, and two years' further campaigning behind it, the leaders were confident of improving the earlier figure.

In Ashanti the NLM was equally sure of its strength, particularly in the cocoa constituencies around Kumasi. It might lose Sekyere East, where Krobo Edusei and the Kumawuhene were still powerful figures. It might lose Wenchi East, where the Techimanhene was pro-CPP because of his dispute with the Asante-

[1] Why did these chiefs and their educated advisers support the CPP and not the NPP? Partly because of the long-sighted ability and ambition of individuals like J. H. Allasani, E. A. Mahama, and L. R. Abavana, partly also because of various local factors, shaped by disputes with neighbouring chiefdoms. Thus Kassena-Nankanni South was CPP not only because Abavana was already a ministerial secretary, but because the chief hoped to use government power to advance local ends of his own design. See the postscript to this chapter, p. 359 below.

man Council over the nine villages of the Tano–Subin valley and three other Brong constituencies—Sunyani West, Sunyani East, and Berekum (although the small Berekum chiefdom was a useful NLM enclave in the constituency as a whole). These were five doubtful constituencies out of twenty-one, but the NLM leaders saw no reason to doubt that the rest of Ashanti would follow the pattern already set by the Atwima Nwabiagya election in 1955.

In Trans-Volta the plebiscite results were naturally taken as a defeat for the CPP in the southern section of the trust territory. In addition, there was every chance that a 'Federated Youth Organization' (FYO)—a development from the Anlo Youth Association—would win two of the three Ewe-speaking constituencies of the south-east of the former Colony area. The Togoland Congress was sure beyond all possibility of doubt of its three strongholds in the trust territory—Kpandu North, Ho East, Ho West—and it had every hope of support from the Federated Youth Organization. This would give the opposition five out of the thirteen seats in the Trans-Volta region.

So far, then, the picture was promising:

North	20 out of 26 seats
Ashanti	16 ,, ,, 21 ,,
Trans-Volta	5 ,, ,, 13 ,,
	41

Forty-one seats out of 104 meant that the opposition needed at least a dozen of the forty-four seats in the Colony. This was thought to be quite possible. There were the three Akim Abuakwa constituencies, where Nana Ofori Atta and the State Council were campaigning for the NLM.[2] There were a number of local groups, like the Wassaw Youth Association, which were strongly anti-CPP. There was the hope that internal disputes within the local branch and constituency executives would damage the CPP, as had happened in 1954, and as was known to be taking place, for example, in Koforidua in the New Juaben constituency.[3] The CPP had lost six Colony seats to Independents in

[2] There were five Akim Abuakwa seats altogether, but the very large number of 'strangers' who were settled in Akim Abuakwa South and Akim Abuakwa East ensured that the CPP would have an easy win over the NLM in these two constituencies.

[3] The successful CPP candidate in 1954 in New Juaben was now changed. There was a sharp division in the local executive, and (if reports were to be believed) in the national executive where Gbedemah approved and others criticized the change.

the previous election and, given an extra weight of propaganda
from Kumasi, given the wealth of the NLM, given, too, the likelihood that the opposition would be able to reverse its narrow defeat in 1954 in three of the five Akim Abuakwa constituencies,
there seemed a reasonable chance of being able to take twelve
seats from the CPP. Thus, over the country looked at as a whole,
the position at the end of polling on 17 July might well be:

> NLM alliance 53 plus
> CPP 51 at most

This was the basis of the calculation which sustained the oppo-
sition leaders in their hope of ridding the country of the CPP. The
Proposals for a Federal Constitution had been published in 1955 on
behalf of a bewildering variety of leaders and parties—Bafuor
Osei Akoto for the NLM, S. D. Dombo for the NPP, S. G. Antor
for the Togoland Congress, B. E. A. Tamakloe for the Muslims,
W. E. G. Sekyi for the Aborigines Rights Protection Society in
Cape Coast (which still attempted a tremulous existence), Dr
Danquah in his own right, representatives of the Anlo Youth
Organization, the Asante Youth Association, a Ghana Youth
Federation, and the Ghana Action Party: 36 signatories alto-
gether, made up of 12 from the Colony, 3 from Togoland, 14 from
Ashanti, and 7 from the north. It was with this somewhat scat-
tered array of forces, flanked by a number of Independents, that
the opposition entered the election, and in a letter to Arden-
Clarke on the eve of the election Dr Busia set out the full list of
those who supported him as their leader, reminding the Governor that:

In accordance with constitutional practice in the United Kingdom,

---

The dominant figure was the New Juaben constituency chairman, I. K. Darko, a
wealthy (though not very well educated) trader, described to the writer as 'the
Mr Djin to Nkrumah in the constituency'. Darko put his weight behind a fellow
trader, M. O. Kwatia. The CPP Assembly member was the Rev. S. G. Nimako
who refused to stand down when the national executive nominated Kwatia, and
stood as an Independent. The NLM then put in its own candidate as well. Result:
M. O. Kwatia (CPP) 1,925, Rev. S. G. Nimako (Ind.) 916, M. K. Osei (NLM)
1,186.

A similar dispute disturbed the party in Kwahu North in the Colony, 'Nkrumah
himself supported Osafo but when he came here to meet the executive members
and the candidates, the majority chose E. I. Preko. So Nkrumah appealed to E. K.
Osafo to step down . . . . Osafo consented, and Nkrumah went away. On the following day, Osafo's supporters urged him not to withdraw, so he stood as an Independent candidate' (account given the writer by a research student). Result:
E. I. Preko (CPP) 2,890, E. K. Osafo (Ind.) 1,341.

the National Liberation Movement and its allies will expect Your
Excellency to call upon Doctor K. A. Busia, their Parliamentary
Leader, to form a Government should they (together with the
independents supporting them) win more than 52 seats at the election.[4]

The CPP was hardly likely to accept this forecast, even if some
of its members in Ashanti found it difficult to view the election
with anything like the confidence they had felt in 1951 and 1954.
The course open to the party, however, was quite clear. It had to
make sure of the south, while concentrating its forces against its
opponents' weak points—the Brong chiefdoms in Ashanti, the
Dagomba area in the north, and the non-Ewe constituencies in
the southern section of the trust territory. The leaders had to be
extremely careful also in the way that they handled the delicate
question of nominations. It was this issue that had produced the
large number of 'rebel Independents' in 1954, and a repetition of
those dangerous internal feuds might mean disaster. At the same
time the party needed to put up candidates in every constituency,
not only because it was necessary to maintain its reputation as a
national movement, but to secure as many seats and as large a
percentage of the total vote as possible. If these simple rules were
followed, the leaders saw no reason to doubt that the party would
win. The only question that troubled the national headquarters
was how wide the margin of victory would be: but this, no one
could foretell.

Who were the competitors? The distinguishing feature of the
election in this respect was the overwhelming importance of the
party candidates. The number of Independents fell from 156 in
1954 to 45, and of these 17 declared their 'independent support'
for Dr Busia. The distribution of candidates between the parties
was:

CPP	NLM	NPP	MAP	Togoland Congress	FYO	Wassaw Youth Ass.	Indep.	Total
104	39	23	3	3	6	2	45	225

The intensity of the struggle between the parties, particularly in
Ashanti, may be seen in the number of 'straight fights': 81 of the
99 contested constituencies:

[4] *Daily Graphic*, 15 July 1956.

	Total	*Ashanti*	*North*	*Trans-Volta*	*Colony*[5]
Unopposed	5	0	2	0	3
Straight fights	81	20	17	10	34
3-cornered	14	1	4	2	7
4-cornered	4	0	3	1	0
	104	21	26	13	44

There was little to choose between the parties in respect of the candidates they put up—just as there was very little difference between the CPP and NLM constituency executives; each side had a fairly wide range of occupations and professions, although heavily weighted still by the number of traders, local contractors, teachers, and clerks. Only in the north were the candidates of each main party a little different from each other, the NPP having a large number of local 'state secretaries' (former native-authority employees) and minor chiefs among its members—a reflection of its origins and conservative outlook. The overall position was:

1. *Seven Municipal Constituencies*

	CPP	*NLM*	*MAP*
Politicians	3	1	1
Company director	–	1	–
Lawyers	1	1	1
Ex-teacher/public corp. employee	1	–	–
Contractor	1	–	–
Clerk	1	–	–
State Secretary	–	1	–

[5] Note, too, the much smaller number of forfeited deposits: 49 out of 225, distributed among the CPP—4, NLM—10, NPP—1, FYO—3, and Independents—31, as follows:

	Colony	*Trans-Volta*	*Ashanti*	*North*	*Total*
CPP	0	1	3	0	4
NLM	9	–	1	–	10
MAP	0	0	0	0	0
NPP	–	–	–	1	1
TC	–	0	–	–	0
FYO	1	2	–	–	3
Indep.	18	6	1	6	31
	28	9	5	7	49

NOTE: 12 of the 31 Independents who lost their deposits had promised their support for Dr Busia.

2. *Ashanti Rural Constituencies*

	CPP	NLM	Ind.
Politician	2	–	
Lawyer	–	3	
Ex-public corp. empl.	–	1	
Contractor	2	1	
Clerk	1	2	
State Sec./Loc. Gvt	3	3	
Doctor	–	1	
Non-gradt teacher	3	2	
Trader/store-keeper	4	2	
Graduate teacher	1	1	
Cocoa buyer	3	1	
Farmer	1	–	
Letter-writer	–	1	
Surveyor	–	–	1

3. *Northern Territories*

	CPP	NPP	Ind.	MAP
Contractor	1	–	1	–
Clerk	1	–	1	–
State Sec./Loc. Gvt	4	10	5	–
Non-gradt teacher	11	6	5	–
Farmer	2	–	–	1
Trader/store-keeper	3	2	–	–
Agric. Asst	2	–	1	–
Nurse	1	–	1	–
Chief	1	3	–	–

4. *Trans-Volta Togoland*

	CPP	TC	Ind.	FYO
Politician	3	1	–	1
Clerk	2	–	2	–
Non-gradt teacher	6	1	4	2
Trader/store-keeper	–	–	2	1
Journalist	–	–	–	1
Artisan	–	–	1	–
Minister of relig.	1	–	1	–
Pharmacist	1	–	–	1

5. Colony Rural Constituencies

	CPP	NLM	MAP	Ind./WYA/FYO
Politician	3	–	–	–
Lawyer	3	3	–	2
Contractor	5	–	–	1
Clerk	–	2	–	2
State Sec./Local Gvt	–	1	–	2
Doctor	–	–	–	1
Graduate teacher	4	–	–	3
Non-gradt teacher	4	3	–	4
Trader/store-keeper	7	1	–	4
Farmer	5	2	–	–
Surveyor	1	–	–	–
Artisan	–	1	–	–
Pharmacist	2	–	–	2
Press proprietor	1	–	–	1
Journalist	1	–	–	2
Chief	–	1	–	2
Trade union off.	1	–	–	1
Bank employee	1	1	–	–
Accountant	1	–	–	–

Uncertainty over the outcome of the election, and the close rivalry between the parties saw the leaders exercise great care in the placing of their candidates. Thus the CPP moved Casely Hayford from Kumasi South to a safer seat in the south (although not to his home town, Cape Coast) and it was the NLM which put Kurankyi Taylor (a Fanti) in the constituency against a CPP Ashanti opponent. Nkrumah himself was nominated once more for Accra Central. But he and Kurankyi Taylor—and even Casely Hayford—were among the exceptions. The electoral regulations were in advance of general practice, and over most of the country the parties were careful to sponsor candidates who were not merely from the region but from the constituency itself (see table overleaf).

What were the issues? On the face of it, they were straight-forward: first, whether the United Kingdom government would hand over power in 1956 to the CPP; second, whether the constitution of an independent Gold Coast would be unitary or federal. This is what the leaders said the election was about, and one might look first at the way in which they presented their case.

Candidates' Origins 1956[6]

Area	Seats	Candidates	From the constituency	Outside the constituency but from the region	From outside the region
Accra	3	6	4	0	2
Colony	41	86	75	11	0
Ashanti	21	43	38	4	1
TVT	13	30	28	2	0
North	26	60	60	0	0
TOTAL	104	225	205	17	3

The NLM argument was ably set out by Dr Busia in a special 'Advertiser's Announcement' in the *Daily Graphic* on 6 July, eleven days before the main polling date. What Africa needed, said the opposition Leader, was 'constructive leadership', but where was it to be found? 'Many who most sincerely believed in the CPP and most devotedly supported the party or worked for it have been disappointed. Some because the achievements of the party have not come up to their expectations, and others because they have seen threats of dictatorship or evidence of corruption in the party.' The Cocoa Duty Amendment Ordinance in August 1954 (as Bafuor Akoto had said) 'forced into the open feelings which had been pent up for a long time', and the NLM had been formed with the demand 'for a federal form of government for the Gold Coast in order to safeguard the country against dictatorship, provide constitutional checks against centralization of power, and do justice to the legitimate and manifest desire of each region for a large measure of autonomy'. This was justified by Gold Coast history, and the NLM believed that the country's 'constitutional development should be based on our own traditions and culture'. The movement had been criticized by Nkrumah (said Dr Busia) as being the work of 'an irresponsible

[6] It was not always easy to say whether those who stood for election were local candidates, for a candidate's family ties with a constituency might be extremely strong although he was neither born nor went to school there. Thus Dr Danquah was born in Kwahu, but was very much an Akyem man of Akim Abuakwa; K. A. Gbedemah was an Ewe from the Keta area, and E. O. Asafu Adjaye an Ashanti, although both were born and spent their early years in Nigeria; and S. I. Iddrisu—son of Mallam Iddrisu Suleman of Yendi, the Dagomba capital—was elected unopposed for Dagomba North, although born in Kumasi.

minority' and as 'enemies of the people', but all attempts by the CPP to break the movement had failed. E. Y. Baffoe, the NLM propaganda secretary in Ashanti, and Kusi Ampofo, holding the same office in Akim Abuakwa, had been stabbed to death, there had been 'riots, the blowing up of houses, arson, murders and public disorders', and 'deplorable acts of violence all over the country perpetrated by both sides'. Yet the CPP government had refused to consider the calling of a Constituent Assembly. Instead, it had made a number of attempts to solve the constitutional issue to its own advantage, culminating in the Achimota Conference, when 'by their manner and content of their invitation they made it impossible for the Opposition to attend'. The NLM wanted independence: it had said so repeatedly, but it wanted independence as a 'happy unity of equals'. It did not want 'a Constitution in which it will be possible for a small coterie to dominate the country'.

This was the gist of the NLM argument on behalf of its constitutional proposals. But, said Dr Busia, there was a moral issue as well. 'During the last five years of CPP rule, we have had an increase in bribery and corruption on an unprecedented scale' a 'shameless self-aggrandisement or get-rich-quick policy, and a lying and deceit which members of the CPP, in spite of loud professions of patriotism, have encouraged or perpetrated'. Everyone knew why the CPP had resisted 'so strongly and vehemently' the appointment of a Commission of Inquiry into the Cocoa Purchasing Company, and the forthcoming election was an opportunity for the country 'to express its faith in probity, honesty, integrity and decent standards'. Furthermore, the CPP was not only corrupt: it was also inefficient. Money had been spent fruitlessly on the Dutch Shokbeton and Swedish housing schemes, and extravagantly on expensive roads, luxurious ministerial offices, cinemas, and a super-luxury hotel 'in order to titivate Accra'. Meanwhile, for want of an enlightened plan, standards of education had been lowered, the service conditions of teachers 'still cry for improvement', and 'parents pay more for a worse education in spite of fee-free primary schools'. There was a lack of proper planning which 'led to the expenditure of vast sums of money with little benefit to the people of the country'. 'The wealth of this country is in agriculture yet apart from the cocoa cutting out campaign the CPP has spent little on agriculture and

food is still far too dear.' Many people in the towns and villages
were 'drinking dirty water full of hookworm and guinea worm
and disease. Little wonder that there is so much debility and sick-
ness and death', and 'the money spent on luxuries or frittered
away could have been used for such things as preventing the disastrous floods of last year or on malaria prevention'.

Even on their own record, therefore—said Busia—the CPP
should be condemned. But 'what is at stake in the forthcoming
election is even bigger'. The Secretary of State had forced the
CPP into an election which it accepted as a 'challenge', 'thus be-
traying its grudging acceptance of a course of action which the
Prime Minister should have taken long ago'. Now the 'eyes of the
world are upon us; the rest of suffering Africa looks to us for an
inspired leadership and we dare not let them down.' The *Announcement* concluded: 'We believe in our cause, and we are confident that we can win.'

This was an eloquent well-mounted attack—although it was
possible to wonder how large an audience it hoped to reach—
and it took some time for the CPP to reply. On 11 July, however, in the *Evening News*, Gbedemah rebutted the charges made
by Busia, and raised an important question of his own: would Dr
Busia, would the NLM and its allies, agree to abide by the results
of the election?

Less elegantly worded than Busia's two-page advertisement,
Gbedemah none the less produced a competent summary of the
CPP case. Dr Busia (he said) had talked of corruption, and no
one denied that it existed or that it was there long before the CPP
came to office, but the wild accusations made against CPP ministers had always 'shrunk shamelessly' once the police had investigated the small number of charges that reached them. It would
be better, therefore, to await the outcome of the current inquiry
into the Cocoa Purchasing Company before drawing premature
conclusions. As for the outbreaks of violence that disfigured
political life in the country, why should Busia single out those
committed by the CPP against the NLM? What of the murder of
Krobo Edusei's sister, and of Kofi Banda—a CPP member—at
Ejisu, the attacks on CPP vehicles, and 'the NLM man named
Atta [who] spat into the Prime Minister's face last week at
Osino?'

Gbedemah then turned to the heart of the matter. Did the

NLM really want federation? The CPP doubted it. 'The answer is quite obvious. It is not federation that Busia or the NLM want because they know it will be unworkable and unacceptable to the whole country. What they want and have never been able to say so openly is that THEY should be in office and not the CPP.' The answer to this would be given on 17 July. The electorate would also be able to judge, too, whether the new roads that had been built, the new hospitals and health centres, new water supplies, new schools and colleges, new housing estates, and 'the many other signs visible to those who have eyes' were not sufficient proof of the efficiency and wisdom of the CPP administration. Busia had asked, were Nkrumah and the CPP Government dictatorial? 'If this was a dictatorship country could he have spoken such words a second time and found himself on the right side of a concentration camp?' 'If this were a dictatorship country could the foul things which have been written about this Government for many years now have been written time and again with impunity?'[7]

Finally, Gbedemah presented the CPP case in a number of affirmations: 'We believe that the Gold Coast with its small population of less than five million people and an economy which, although occasionally buoyant, is not generally so sound or so stable, can best exist as one nation with one government.' 'We believe that it will be madness to create four regional governments when with only one government it has been found so difficult to find personnel to fill all the vacancies in the administration.' 'We believe that . . . it will be possible to run a [unitary] government and have as well a loyal opposition.' 'We believe that the chiefs can continue to play an important role in this country so long as they do not take sides against some of their own subjects who do not accept their political viewpoint.' 'We believe that independence for Ghana this year can be achieved without bloodshed', and 'we the CPP do not threaten civil war if we lose the election'. By way of conclusion, Gbedemah repeated this last undertaking, and ended:

We the CPP give our assurance to the world that when the electors have given their verdict that verdict cannot be questioned by anyone.

---

[7] It was impossible to answer at the time, but by 1960 it was clear that neither Busia nor anyone else was free to act as Gbedemah said in 1956, and by 1961 Gbedemah had followed Busia into exile.

We declare that if we are defeated, those of us who will be elected—and already there are five [returned unopposed to] the [new] House—shall assume the role of a loyal opposition to the Busia Government and help him to usher in not only independence but also his new age of 'plenty for everybody and honesty in everything'.

But when the voters have judged and have given their verdict against Busia, what then? Dr Busia, I ask, what then?

Three days later, Gbedemah had his reply, this time in the *Ashanti Pioneer*:

Mr Gbedemah has asked me [said Dr Busia] to say what we will do if we lose this election and the CPP win. We have stated time and again that in our view victory for the CPP would be a national disaster, and we of the National Liberation Movement are prepared to meet it as such and to take all steps IN and OUT of the Legislative Assembly to mitigate the evil.

Mr Gbedemah gloats over the five CPP candidates returned unopposed because their opponents . . . have withdrawn their candidature, thereby depriving the population of the right to that free choice which Mr Gbedemah pretends to admire.

As I write, the Police are investigating a charge that one of the nominators of Mr Kojo Botsio . . . actually offered £60 to Mr Botsio's opponents in the Gomoa West constituency to withdraw. . . .

How could any self-respecting Movement accept such an election 'victory' and not appeal to law, justice and equity?[8]

Once more Gbedemah replied—just in time, since (he said) he would 'without doubt be returned to Ministerial Office and thenceforth the dignity of that office would restrain me from writing in this vein'; Busia would then be able to 'enjoy peace and tranquility from the acridity of my pen, and not be subject to the pungency and devastation of my argument'. He—Busia—had said that 'by the Grace of God he would not lose'; 'but . . . the GRACE OF GOD exists in abundant measure for us all, and does not descend on election day in the form of votes to fill ballot boxes'. The CPP would stand by its pledge to respect the wishes of the electorate, despite the fact that there were those who talked of 'armed rebellion and civil war and secession'; but 'if a civil war is started, does Busia not see that it is the majority that will win it?'[9]

---

[8] *Ashanti Pioneer*, 14 July 1956. In fact Kojo Botsio was not returned unopposed; one of the two opposing candidates withdrew, but not the NLM candidate, Nana Nkum. It was difficult, however, to believe that the latter was an active contestant: Kojo Botsio 3,317, Nana Nkum 79.

[9] *Evening News*, 16 July 1956.

On this unhappy note the correspondence closed and—the next day—polling was completed. Each statement was typical: for example, the very doubtful assumption by Busia that the NLM and its allies were—in general—a less violent, more honest body of men than the CPP, and his readiness to believe that, even if this were the case, the electorate would decide on this issue; and, on the CPP side, the indignation with which Gbedemah rebutted charges brought against the CPP which, whether those of corruption or a liking for dictatorial methods, seemed incontestable. Gbedemah's questioning of the NLM leaders' faith in federalism, and his assertion that what the opposition really wanted was quite simply to displace the CPP, was shrewd, even if it underestimated the limits of a strong Ashanti emotion within which the NLM leadership had to work. Busia's forthright disavowal of any automatic acceptance by the NLM of the results of the election was a remarkable admission. It showed (as the date of the election became imminent) that the NLM was less confident of its chances. It showed, too (as in the parting shots fired by each side) that those who had pinned their hopes for an immediate settlement of the CPP–NLM dispute on the outcome of the election might have cause to revise their judgement.

The argument conducted between Busia and Gbedemah in the press was somewhat limited in scope, and a broader view was presented by the *Election Manifestos* which both the NLM and the CPP distributed to their constituency organizations. Again, the coverage was small, but the constituency executives were the main centres of local propaganda, and it is worth looking at what the national headquarters thought would appeal to its local commanders.

The CPP appeal was short and direct:

THIS IS THE CPP'S HISTORIC CALL TO FREEDOM[10]

Reasons for Calling a General Election
In 1954 the country voted the Convention People's Party into power to obtain independence . . . and arrangements are being made for the actual transfer of power.
BUT—
The National Liberation Movement . . . with its allies have now declared No Federal Constitution, No Independence.

[10] CPP *Election Manifesto, 1956.*

Everyone is Aware

That several invitations were sent by the Prime Minister . . . for a
Round Table Conference in an endeavour to talk things over and
come to some mutual agreement on the constitution for the country,
but THEY TURNED EVERY ONE DOWN. . . .

What you are asked to Vote for is perfectly clear:

ALL YOU HAVE TO DO is to ask yourself two questions:

(1) Do I want FREEDOM and INDEPENDENCE NOW—THIS
YEAR—so that I and my children can enjoy life in a free and independent sovereign state of Ghana thereafter?

(2) Do I want to revert to the days of imperialism, colonialism and
tribal feudalism?

If you favour the first question—that is, if you want your INDE-
PENDENCE in 1956—then the ONLY WAY TO GET IT, IS BY
VOTING FOR KWAME NKRUMAH AND HIS CONVEN-
TION PEOPLE'S PARTY.

If you are faint-hearted and your spirit of nationalism is so pitiably
deficient that you incline your mind towards the second question,
then you are no concern of ours and you are an outcast as far as the
movement for Gold Coast Independence is concerned. You can vote
for those whose policy and avowed aim it is to split up this country
thereby delaying INDEPENDENCE.

The NLM document was a little more elaborate. It appeared
flanked by the cocoa tree symbol that the movement intended to
use during the election,[11] and dealt not only with the constitutional issue but the need for effective measures to raise living standards, improve existing social services, and protect minority
rights:

WHY YOU SHOULD VOTE FOR COCOA[12]

What the NLM and its Allies will by The Grace of God Do when
You Vote Them Into Power:

They will:

1. Call a National Constitutional Conference to frame the constitution of an Independent Gold Coast to report before the end
   of the year. . . .
2. Pass a motion in the Assembly calling upon the United Kingdom
   Parliament to grant this country independence.

---

[11] The CPP objected, on the grounds that the cocoa tree was a national emblem,
but were eventually overruled by the Electoral Commission established by the
Ministry of Local Government.
[12] Summarized from the *Liberator*, 25 June 1956.

3. Repeal the recent amendments to the State Councils Ordinance and thus take matters concerning the position of chiefs out of the hands of Politicians. . . .
4. Ensure the independence of the judiciary. . . .
5. Immediately start development schemes for the less developed areas. . . .
7. Take effective measures to keep down the cost of living by using such measures as price controls in particular on motor cars, motor spare parts and imported food stuffs and necessities. . . .
9. Re-organise the Industrial Development Corporation, the Cocoa Purchasing Company, Agricultural Development Corporation and other Statutory bodies. . . .
10. Ensure that farmers get full returns for their labour. . . .
11. Develop and extend Cooperative Societies. . . .
12. Set up light and heavy industries. . . .
14. Ensure that Trade Unions and Workers' Associations are free from Government control. . . .
15. Provide better living conditions for the Police and the Army. . . .
16. Make a special allocation of funds to development in the Northern Territories.
17. Encourage mechanisation of farming. . . .
19. Revise the educational system of this country. . . .
26. Ensure that minority interests are protected, and that minority rights are written into the constitution and guaranteed. . . .

It is difficult to believe that either of these declarations had any great effect on the electorate in general, but they were interesting statements which revealed certain characteristics of the leadership on each side. The CPP leaders wanted independence and full control immediately, and the party was probably right to present the issue in these simple terms. The NLM could claim that it too wanted independence as a 'partnership of equals', but there was also a strong element within the party—the 'Busia element' perhaps—which emphasized the need for reform and 'good government'. And over and above its demand for federation the NLM liked to stress this aspect of its case. The reader should not be misled, however, into thinking that these were the only issues which were presented to the electorate. They were important in so far as they helped to keep the second line of leaders in the constituency executives loyal to one side or the other, but one must also try and look a little farther than this, to see what happened when the parties translated their national message into constituency terms.

In his first reply to Busia, Gbedemah had quoted from an election leaflet of a local opponent in his own Trans-Volta constituency (Keta):

RED COCKEREL, THIEF[13]

Don't vote for the red cockerel which is the CPP

(1) CPP are thieves, rogues, traitors, double-tongued receivers of bribes, givers of bribes and gangsters.

(2) CPP introduced the following taxes: Local Rate, House Rate, Industrial Taxes, Taxes on domestic animals, cows, goats, sheep, and rates on bicycles.

(3) CPP introduced insubordination, tribal differences, disrespect, suppression, evil doing, lying, destruction of chieftaincy, greed and other such evils.

(4) CPP wants to divide the Ewes; give half to the Gold Coast and the other half to Dahomey. For these reasons don't vote for the red cockerel, the thief.

THE GOOD CROSSED PADDLE

Vote for the crossed paddle, vote for Anumu, the man who is a member of the party against the CPP. This party will remove the levy and other taxes. This party will stop extravagance, bribery, thieving and other evils which the CPP have introduced.

If you elect someone and he does not do your wishes you have the right to change him. Therefore use your discretion properly; vote for Anumu.

The NLM used much the same mixture of abuse, and an appeal to local interests:

VOTE FOR NLM[14]
& Allies on July 12 & 17
Reject the
Communist People's Party
(CPP)
A Party of
Crooks and Swindlers on
July 12 and 17
It is Your Money They Want.

In the heart of the NLM campaign country, over a wide area around Kumasi, the NLM leaders at their mass rallies, the

[13] Translated from Ewe—an uncommon example of the use of a local language.
[14] Propaganda leaflet of the NLM.

chiefs who ranged their state councils behind the movement, local speakers in the small market towns, and the constituency secretaries who made their propaganda tours through the villages, repeated over and over again the two main threads in the NLM appeal: cocoa and the Golden Stool. In the published programmes, the Ashanti appeal was understandably kept at a minimum since it was thought (quite rightly) that this might damage the party's alliances beyond Ashanti, but it was used again and again in its own region. Almost every NLM meeting emphasized the need for loyalty to the Asantehene and the Golden Stool in order to protect Ashanti interests. The familiar setting of the NLM campaign was an open clearing before the chief's palace or the nearby lorry park, where the start of a 'mass rally' was heralded by local propaganda vans playing the NLM highlife tune—*akoko suesue*.[15] The chief and his elders would arrive and take their seats on the platform, to be followed by a succession of local speakers who proclaimed their readiness to die for the Golden Stool while demanding a higher cocoa price, and used simple arguments to show the benefits to be gained from local control of one's own affairs.[16] There would then follow supporting speeches from an MAP leader in his long white Islamic gown, amidst cries of *Yate ye ho!* and *Islam!* the pouring of libations, the swearing of oaths, affirmations of loyalty to the NLM, and abuse of Nkrumah and the CPP, each item being punctuated by enthusiastic applause from the audience of young men, elders, market women, farmers, petty traders, teachers and clerks— looking exactly the same as any CPP audience (and there was

[15] i.e. Red Cockerel—shoo! In Kumasi, there was also the local song—*wobeto taxi a kokoo* (you need cocoa to buy a taxi).

[16] On the simple issue of the cocoa price, one may quote a typical extract from the *Liberator* late in April 1956:

'Cocoa Price'

'If ever the farmers of the Gold Coast have any opportunity to demonstrate their opposition against this CPP Government of swindlers it is now. Let the farmers ask for £5 a load for their cocoa this season. They should not compromise on this issue at all. . . . The money of the farmers has . . . been frittered away through . . . various Development Funds on ill-planned, ill-conceived and ill-executed projects. While the CPP Government shout from the housetops that they are developing the country, farmers in the rural areas who produce these millions of pounds sterling which the CPP have been using to finance their own party and the stomachs of their Ministers and Assemblymen, continue to live in squalor, disease, dirt, starvation and acute degradation. The cost of living continues to soar higher and higher, and the farmers receive lower and lower prices for their produce. Are the farmers forever to be the monkey that does the work and the CPP to be the baboon that eats?'

usually one not very far away in a rival town or state)—enjoying themselves, the songs, slogans and promises, amidst a general air of excitement and festivity.

The CPP, in its turn, spoke of the NLM and its allies in harsh terms as 'feudalists', 'saboteurs', 'tribalists'. It too attacked on a double front, proclaiming its nationalist beliefs while seeking to bring into its ranks as many local interests as it could promote. It retained its broad simple appeal as the party of independence and of the Common People, able to carry through government-financed development schemes, and ready to save Africa by its leadership; it still had its national hero, and it was able to bring to its propaganda in the constituencies—even in 1956—much of the early flavour, still, of an exalted revivalist movement:

WHY YOU SHOULD VOTE FOR NKRUMAH[17]

1. Because Nkrumah is a man of the Common People. . . .
3. Because Nkrumah is honest, straightforward, hardworking, vigilant and stainless. . . .
8. Because through Nkrumah's instrumentality Africanisation, free education, have been encouraged, building of hospitals, clinics, roads, bridges, harbours, Achiasi-Kotoku railway, the formation of IDC, ADC, CPC, Bank of the Gold Coast, the Volta River Project, Tema Development Corporation and many others. . . .
9. Because . . . on June 12th, 1949 the CPP was conceived and born and Nkrumah chosen by us to lead us for independence.
10. Because it was Nkrumah who asked the youth of Ghana . . . to make the Gold Coast a paradise so that when the gates of Heaven are opened by Peter we shall sit in heaven and see our children driving their aeroplanes, commanding their own armies.
11. Because in Africa today the sun is rising not in East but in West all through Kwame Nkrumah.
12. Because Nkrumah is talked about with surprise in Johannesburg, in Nairobi, Uganda, Alabama. . . .
13. Because if Nkrumah fails, a great hope will die in Africa. . . .

VOTE FOR NKRUMAH AGAINST THE MACHIAVELLIAN 'SOLO'. FREEDOM NOW AND FOREVER.

Like its rivals, however, the CPP also tried to bend to its use as many local issues as it could. The CPP–Brong alliance in western

---

[17] Election leaflet used in Accra, published in the *Evening News*, 13 July 1956. The 'Machiavellian Solo' was Solomon Odamtten, the Accra businessman who stood for the NLM against Nkrumah in Accra Central: Nkrumah, 11,119; S. E. Odamtten 1,865.

Ashanti was only the most conspicuous of a large number of un-written 'bilateral agreements', whereby the CPP leaders promised to further the local ambitions of chiefs and prominent individuals who, in return, gave the party their support. Outside the Fanti chiefdoms in the rural area of the Colony, where the CPP rested securely on an intense dislike of the Ashanti move-ment and had little need to buttress its support with particular local interests, the party manœuvred its way through the numer-ous disputes which riddled Ghanaian society—between rival lineages in a remote northern community, between Stool families in an Akan chiefdom, between state and state, district and dis-trict, village and village. In this delicate art of manœuvre the NPP and NLM had an advantage over the CPP. Within their own areas of control they had on their side the bulk of the tra-ditional leaders, whose knowledge and skill in exploiting these disputes was of a high order, sharpened by many years of prac-tice. But the CPP was by no means defenceless. Although re-stricted by the presence still of the Governor, it was able to de-ploy its powers as a government on behalf of its activities as a party. As will be seen in the account of the way in which the parties managed their election campaign, the CPP made good use of para-political organizations like the Cocoa Purchasing Company, whose access to government funds and a network of local agents stood the party in good stead in many of the Ashanti and Colony constituencies. The party was also able to hold out before a particular local council the promise of a generous de-velopment grant (or its withdrawal) or the dispatch of a 'com-munity development team' into (or from) the area. 'The king's wrath is as a roaring lion but his favour is as dew upon the grass'. Such was the burden of propaganda carried on by many CPP executives, the field officers of the CPC, and by emissaries from the party headquarters who brought with them the favour or displeasure of the 'party in power'.

These local features of the election were to be seen in any de-tailed examination of the way in which the parties fought each other in the field. But, before turning to the actual campaign, something needs to be said first of the administrative framework devised by the officials.

The most pressing problem was how to ensure a peaceful two days' polling. Violence had to be held in check and, at the very least, kept away from the polling booths. At first, however, in the last weeks before the election there seemed little hope that either side would call a halt to its campaign of violence and abuse, and the language of both the NLM *Liberator* and the CPP *Evening News* was replete with bloodcurdling accusations and threats of reprisals:

BROKEN PLEDGE[18]

If there is any notorious liar in this country whose word should never, never, never be trusted, that man is Mr Kwame Nkrumah, one man and one man alone, the arch exponent of democratic centralism. Nkrumah, the arch liar and his Cabinet gave a pledge in the Legislative Assembly recently that the forthcoming general election would be fought cleanly, without violence. The leader of the Opposition, Mr Dombo, also gave the same pledge on behalf of the Opposition.

Today, even before the election campaigning is officially launched, the hired thugs of Kwame Nkrumah, arch liar, have begun committing acts of violence in all parts of the country. Recently in Akyem Abuakwa some CPP thugs have been detained for alleged shooting incidents. Others are before the courts for similar acts of violence.

In Ashanti CPP hoodlums have begun committing very serious crimes. It is alleged that the hired CPP cut-throats have organised themselves into desperate gangs and have been stopping lorries on the Kumasi-Sunyani roads and at vantage points on the Kumasi-Accra roads attacking poor villagers.

Last Friday, some CPP hoodlums attacked a young man who entered a bar at Odum to buy. For about a whole week now, CPP hoodlums have been disturbing the peaceful atmosphere at Asawase Estate and intimidating people in the night, robbing them, all in the name of Kwame Nkrumah and his democratic centralism.

It is difficult to see why peaceful citizens should sit down to allow themselves to be mosted without any protection of any kind. If the present provocative acts are to continue then the citizens should be forced against their will to defend themselves. The NLM and their allies will not sit down to allow hired thieves and robbers of the CPP who are being paid out of Cocoa Purchasing Company Funds stolen by the CPP, to kill them. . . .

The present atmosphere is so tense that in absence of adequate Police protection, citizens would be forced to defend themselves. Self-preservation is the first law of nature and no one should be blamed when he is defending himself.

[18] *Liberator*, 4 June 1956.

REJECT THE SABOTEURS OF FREEDOM[19]

In the last couple of days, the whole country has been witness to the fact that the NLM and allies are unrepentant devils and brutes who are merely out to ruin the future of Ghana. Persons belonging to the opposition group attempted to poison the reservoir at Weija.[20] What could be more vicious and inhuman? It is frightful to behold that 'men with the best brains' could be so shockingly depraved. But this vile act stands as a monument to and a product of the 'best brains' of Ghana, the most 'honest men' in our world.

When we leave Accra and advert our attention to Kumasi we find that women who are pursuing their honest vocation in the markets are being beaten up and badly molested by thugs of the NLM and allies. Their only crime is that they are suspected of having pro-CPP sympathies. Certainly the intention of the murderous organisation is to intimidate the voters, especially in Kumasi South, so that they'll disperse in other parts of the country and reduce the CPP votes in the hope that the NLM candidate will win the Kumasi seats. . . .

But July 17 will soon be with us and it is for every right-thinking voter to cast his vote for the CPP which, on winning the election, will make it its first task to rid the country of cut-throats and gangsters who molest the lives of peaceful and peace-loving citizens. Apart from determining the constitutional issue this memorable date will determine whether Ghana shall continue to hear the explosions of dynamite and the shots of guns or whether everyone shall move about without fear of intimidation and violence.

When Baffour Akoto and other rumbuctious leaders of the opposition say they are against violence they are only engaging in maudlin talk, merely shedding crocodile tears. They actually plan and are actively encouraging the atrocities perpetrated by their Action Troopers who still enjoy their patronage. But we would warn these evil men that those who sow the wind will surely reap the whirl-wind.

To counter these threats, and to check the exuberance of the party *militants*, the Governor undertook publicly to 'discharge my responsibility for law and order with all the forces at my command'. Stringent police regulations controlled party attendances at rallies and the use of party vans in the more troubled areas of Akim Abuakwa and Ashanti.[21] However, it was still

[19] *Evening News*, 16 June 1956.
[20] Whence the Accra municipality drew its water supply. No evidence was produced for this very unlikely project.
[21] A letter was addressed by the Commissioner of Police to all political parties saying that 'it has become in certain areas of the country an unfortunate habit of certain political organisations to ensure the success of a political meeting by im-

thought that the duties which would rest on the local detachments of police and the Presiding Officers might prove too great a burden, and on these grounds—and because of a shortage of local administrative staff—the election was arranged to take place on 12 July in parts of the north, and on 17 July in the country generally. The officials were also instructed to take elaborate precautions to safeguard the actual conduct of polling. 'As the papers were full of rumours that it was intended to forge ballot papers for use in the election, extraordinary precautions were taken to ensure that no unauthorised printing should take place.'[22] The presses used were kept in a separate room in the government Printing Department under continuous police supervision, the serial number of the papers allocated to each electoral district kept secret until the actual day of polling, representatives of the parties encouraged both to attend the printing operation and to accompany the transport of ballot boxes and papers to the polling stations, and a right of search allowed at the polling booths.[23] There was a great deal of discussion also whether or not to change the actual machinery of voting. All manner of stories were in circulation of how easy it was to damage a ballot box (and the papers it contained) under the multi-box system used in 1959 and 1954. It was also commonly supposed that ballot papers were sold to party officials (or their accomplices) who deliberately voted late in the day and, once safely behind the voting screen, stuffed as many papers in the box as the time would allow. To meet these complaints, an official in the Ministry of Local Government devised a new form of polling booth in which 'the elector stood in full view of the public and placed his ballot paper

---

porting into the areas . . . lorry loads of supporters, many of whom are the organised bands known as Action Troopers or Action Groupers whose only role appears to be to intimidate persons to commit acts of violence and to instil fear into members of rival political organisations. The sudden invasion of an area by such persons has frequently led to outbreaks of violence' (*Daily Graphic*, 27 Apr. 1956). The organized movement of party supporters from one part of the country to another was therefore forbidden, and all 'troopers' were warned to stay away from rallies under penalty of the permit for the rally being withdrawn. This did not prevent clashes between the two parties which continued up to—and after—the election. Thus on 13 July, sixteen people were arrested after a battle with sticks, stones, and bottles at Kejetia (the main round-about in Kumasi) between CPP and NLM groups which had tried to pull down flags hoisted by each side in the market area.

[22] *Report on the 1956 Election.*

[23] It was rarely used but, as the Election Report commented, 'word went round that electors were liable to be searched' and this was probably almost as useful. There is no harm occasionally in implying rumour on the side of law and order.

in the box of his own choice through an opening in the side of the booth'—a 'Punch-and-Judy-stall' arrangement that the officials insisted would work. The scheme was rejected. It was argued that what was essential was not only that one side in the party struggle should win, but that it should also be accepted as the victor; if, however, the method of balloting were to be changed, the losing side might well claim that it had lost for that reason. So the method of balloting was left as it had been in 1954, and the officials concentrated, instead, on safeguarding the existing system.

Revision of the 1954 registers had started at the end of 1955–early 1956, and had been hastily completed in May–June. The final figures then showed that, of the total estimated adult population, some three-fifths were now enrolled:

Registration of Electors, Mid-1956

Estimated pop.	Aged 21 & over	Registered	Per cent
4,676,000	2,450,224	1,459,743	59·6

(Based on the *Digest of Statistics* for mid-1956.)

This was higher than in 1954, but still not very good, and if the estimate of population for 1956 were taken backwards from the 1960 census figures (rather than forward from what was probably an underestimate in 1948) the percentage was seen to be very low. The maximum number of people in the country were now entitled to register and vote. For the 1954 requirement that

Registration by Regions, 1956

Region	Estimated pop.	Aged 21 & over	Registered	Per cent
Ashanti	964,000	505,136	389,153	77
TVT	528,058	276,702	197,195	71
Northern	1,147,000	601,028	359,330	60
Colony	2,036,942	1,067,358	514,065	48
TOTAL	4,676,000	2,450,224	1,459,743	60

Source: Based on the *Digest of Statistics* for mid-1956. Figures for TVT taken from the 1948 Census and adjusted for 1956 on the basis of the *Digest's* percentage increase for the whole country 1948–56.

an elector should have paid his local levy had been dropped, and the 1957 Ghana Nationality Act had not yet been passed to deprive British subjects not of Ghanaian birth of the vote. The low registration figure was not, however, as might be supposed, the result of the disturbed conditions that existed in the Ashanti or Akim rural areas, but of an indifference towards the election in areas where the CPP was dominant, and the contest a foregone conclusion. Thus Ashanti and Trans-Volta registered over 70 per cent of the adult population, the north did well, and the two Colony regions badly.

The main polling day—17 July—dawned fair and dry, a favourable omen in the middle of the rainy season, and as the day lengthened towards evening, it was unmarred by any serious clash between the two sides. Polling closed early at 5 p.m. to enable the ballot boxes to be started on their way to the counting stations in good time before dusk, but the crowds were everywhere orderly, and the police escorts unmolested. The explanation of this unexpected truce, however, was not difficult to find. In part, it was because of the confidence each side had in its ability to win by fair means, thus lessening the temptation to use other methods; in part, the peaceful conduct of the election was due to the vigilance of the colonial government—the officials and the police—as a well-armed neutral supervisor. It was the last full-scale effort on the part of the colonial administration to hasten its own departure in as orderly a manner as the parties would allow, and by the evening of 17 July, as the first results began to be broadcast over the wireless before the crowds which gathered to watch the public election screens in the municipalities, the officials could congratulate themselves once again on having accomplished successfully what was now their third general election.

How had the parties fared? In the last weeks of the campaign each side struggled to press home whatever advantage it thought it possessed over its rivals: but, as the date appointed for the election drew near, the NLM began to falter. This was the conclusion reached by the writer, drawing partly on observation, partly on accounts by those who belonged to the party's national executive. It began to falter as the result of uncertainty where best to concentrate its efforts. The problem it faced, though simple to state, was difficult to resolve. To win a national victory, the opposition parties had to break through their regional boundaries: neither the NPP nor the Togoland Congress could hope to do this, while the Moslem Association was ineffective outside the immigrant wards of the municipalities. The task was entrusted, therefore, to the NLM. It was this that gave rise to a dispute which was to have a disastrous effect on the party's fortunes. The southerners on the national executive—Kurankyi Taylor, M. K. Apaloo, John and Nancy Tsiboe—were confident that dissatisfaction with the CPP in the south had reached breaking-point. They could point to three particular grievances—the increased cost of living at the end of 1955,[24] the tales of corrupt practices being unfolded before the Commission of Inquiry into the affairs of the Cocoa Purchasing Company,[25] and the residual

[24] The index of retail prices of imported goods began to rise steeply at the end of 1955, and was 10 per cent higher by February 1956 compared with the relatively stable period between 1952 and 1955. The daily-rated unskilled labourer was still on 4s. 6d. a day—the level fixed in April 1952—until April 1956 when the government increased the rate to 5s. 2d. See W. B. Birmingham, *Econ. Bull.*, Mar. 1960.

[25] The (Jibowu) Commission of Enquiry into the Affairs of the Cocoa Purchasing Company opened its hearings in May and closed them on 21 June 1956, and the *Report* (signed by Olumuyiwa Jibowu, Federal Justice of the Supreme Court in Nigeria, R. F. George, a Chartered Accountant, and J. W. de Graft Johnson, a lawyer) was submitted in August. It may be helpful to summarize its findings here, from paras. 203–16:

(1) The 'allegation that the CPP controlled the CPC is justified'.
(2) No direct proof was produced that CPC funds were used to finance the CPP but 'we cannot be satisfied that loans monies might not have been used for other purposes'.
(3) Loans were only given to farmers who were members of the pro-CPP United Farmers' Council.
(4) Loans were given in excess of the fixed limits, and without regard to the authorized procedure.
(5) Bribery, corruption, and extortion among some CPC officials existed.
(6) Repayment of loans had fallen greatly into arrears.
(7) There was some truth in the allegation that CPC vehicles had been used for the Atwima Nwabiagya by-election campaign by the CPP.
(8) Some CPC staff were 'inefficient, unqualified and dishonest'.
(9) A. Y. K. Djin, Managing Director of the CPC, 'connived at irregularities committed by certain employees', 'took undue advantage of his position as Managing Director to reduce freight charges made by the Company for transporting goods of his firm', 'managed his personal business while full-time Managing Director . . . contrary to his agreement', and 'made full use of CPC staff to sell wares of his private firm'. The *Report* concluded that 'in view of our findings on the allegations of irregularities made against Mr Djin we do not consider him to have been a fit and proper person to have been in what was virtually sole control of the affairs of a quasi-public concern whose assets, and those of the Loans Agency at 30th September, 1955, totalled over £6,000,000'. It added: 'Mr Djin's case does not, in our view, reflect any credit on the Government. . . . It has been suggested that [Dr Nkrumah] failed to see that Mr Djin was properly dealt with as he deserved because he [Dr Nkrumah] was indebted to Mr Djin. This is denied, but he failed to erase from our mind the impression that he had

bitterness left by the quarrel within the CPP over the nomination of candidates during the 1954 election. These, it was argued, pointed to a definite swing away from the CPP, and the NLM should encourage this trend—inaugurate branches in the south, recruit members, hold rallies, put up its own candidates, stress the poor quality of the CPP leaders, play on the hardship of the ordinary consumer, and hold out the vision of an intelligent, well-ordered administration under Dr Busia. After some hesitation, Bafuor Osei Akoto and Busia agreed. Others—Dr Kufuor, the Nkofohene, R. R. Amponsah, Joe Appiah, Jacob Fordwo (the young Kumasi trader who was in charge of the NLM's 'Operation 21' in Ashanti), and even the Asantehene himself—were critical, and urged instead the prior need to make absolutely sure of the movement's own Ashanti base. This division between the leaders, deepened by personal quarrels, was never fully healed. And the decision to move openly and directly into the Colony— for Kurankyi Taylor and Bafuor Akoto had their way—proved doubly dangerous. It united the Colony constituencies behind the CPP as nothing else could have done while, at the same time, it prevented the NLM from concentrating the full weight of its money, propaganda, and organization in a number of marginal Ashanti constituencies.[26]

The difficulty which faced the NLM in trying to spread its appeal into the Colony may be illustrated by an account of its failure even in the southern cocoa constituencies where its demand for higher load prices was echoed by local complaints among the Akim and Akwapim farmers. The NLM was rebuffed here, as it had been by the Brong chiefdoms. The CPP made skilful use of a local suspicion of Ashanti intentions, and countered the NLM demand for a higher cocoa price with the offer of loans through the Cocoa Purchasing Company. Thus the goodwill of the local farmers became a prize disputed between the CPP act-

---

unfortunately placed himself in such an embarrassing position in relation to Mr Djin that he could not take or cause to be taken steps which might displease or be unpleasant to Mr Djin.'

[26] The account given here is based on accounts given to the writer by those who took part in these events. That a division took place within the NLM executive was common knowledge at the time. Thus the point was reached immediately before the election where the executive members were so unsure of Kurankyi Taylor's attitude that they nominated a 'reserve' candidate for Kumasi South— A. S. Y. Andoh—who filed his nomination papers as an Independent, and then withdrew when Kurankyi Taylor managed to reassure the executive of his loyalty.

ing through the CPC, and the NLM using (so it was said) the European buying firms. According to the account of a local CPC agent, farmers in the Swedru area of the Colony became 'disappointed as no loans could be given any longer' (under restrictions imposed on the CPC) and were approached

by underground workers of the National Liberation Movement . . . who succeeded to get Messrs Cadbury and Fry to grant loans to farmers. . . . This action of the NLM was breaking down our centre and others. It was a real threat to the general organisation of the CPP and the CPC. It became an appaling danger to our Party in power and our dear Company—CPC.

It was decided therefore to 'combat the situation'.

We began to hold meetings and devised ways and means of rubbing shoulders with farmers in their villages and even farms. By this means we came to learn that most of them had taken heavy advances from Cadbury & Fry for which each Farmer had secured his farm. . . . We were able to convince most of them to restore confidence in the CPP upon our assurance that we shall move Heaven and Earth to get their loans paid. . . . Although we had no power to use purchase money for this campaign, yet as the position was such that little delay on our part would cause heavy damages to our party in power and the CPC so we became compelled to storm the weather by giving out the advances in question and we saw well that they are paid to Cadbury as refund of the advances. . . . Thus we captured Farmers and villages some of which we at once transferred . . . into sub-centres.[27]

This candid tale may be matched with a very similar account by the pro-NLM Asante Farmers' Union to show how, in an Ashanti cocoa growing district, the NLM was able to claim that it had thwarted attempts by the Cocoa Purchasing Company to win over the farmers:

The Ashanti Chief Farmer Opanin Kofi Buor in company of [others] visited Goaso-Mim [to the west of Kumasi]. . . . The Union, upon the untiring and initiative effort of Opanin Kofi Buor . . . contacted Messrs Cadbury and Fry for financial assistance. Upon strong negotiation coupled with some very outstanding immovable and strong securities of which Nana Kofi Asenso Antoahene gave a quota, Farmers within the Union have been advanced (according to their

---

[27] Letter, dated 20 Feb. 1955, from a local CPC agent to the Acting Managing Director, printed in part in the Jibowu Commission *Report*, para. 72.

cocoa supply output per farm or farms). A total of about £70,000 have been advanced up to date to the following areas. . . . Other areas are to follow. Thus the farmers within the Union so far advanced will automatically deliver cocoa to the nearest Cadbury and Fry centre within each area in full liquidation of the advances so received. By this, the Union have been able to liberate the farmers from the depressive and deceptive clutches of the CPC.[28]

One may see in these two accounts how the NLM was unable in the Colony to repeat its rapid success in Ashanti.[29] The fact is that the Asante Farmers' Union succeeded in the Goaso area not because the villages were cocoa-farming communities but because they were Ashanti. It was possible to argue that, had the NLM limited its campaign to the simple issue of the cocoa price, the Ashanti, Colony, and even the Brong farmers, would have joined forces, as they succeeded in doing during the great cocoa hold-up of 1937–8. When, however, the Council for Higher Cocoa Prices was turned into a Kumasi-based National Liberation Movement, the Colony farmers refused their support. And as they listened to the propaganda coming out of the Ashanti capital, and saw the preparations being made for the extension of the party into the Colony, they saw the NLM not as the farmers' friend but as the spearhead of a new Ashanti invasion of the south.[30]

[28] 'Progress Report of the Asante Farmers' Union', given to the Asanteman Council on 2 Aug. 1955 (*Minutes*, 2–9 Aug. 1955). The Union had been active in the campaign during the Atwima Nwabiagya by-election in 1955. It was always short of money, and the instalments on its propaganda van were 'overdue for two months'. It wanted, therefore, a subvention from the Council, professing 'unflinching loyalty to the Throne and the person of Otumfuo the Asantehene, the Ashanti Nation and the Gold Coast at large'. The NLM helped to finance it as a useful ancilliary organization, and John Poku, the general secretary, was a member of the NLM executive. The Union had a celebrated officer: 'Mami Ataa Adjoa, an outstanding woman farmer at Akwasiasi, [who] was elected and installed (in 1955) as Asante Akuafo Baapanin'—Ashanti Chief Women's Farmer—a title that not even the CPP had thought of.

[29] Neither account needed to be taken literally. It was difficult to accept the picture of the Swedru farmers being influenced by 'underground NLM workers on behalf of Messrs Cadbury & Fry': this was, after all, merely what the CPC official told the Managing Director, although the farmers doubtless had a well-established habit of dealing with Cadbury & Fry which the CPC agents liked to ascribe to NLM activities. Similarly, in Goaso, it may be that Cadbury & Fry took advantage of the Asante Farmers' Union to secure its hold in the buyers' market against competition from the CPC, although this too is only what the Union told the Ashanti chiefs.

[30] One further example of the importance of local disputes whereby the CPP managed to keep a substantial foothold in Ashanti: the Farmers' Union confessed to the Asanteman Council that it had not been able to hold any rallies in the Kukuom and Hwidiem area of Ashanti, not far from Goaso, because the villages

This alarm was widespread in the western area of the Colony, which stretched from Ashanti through Assin to Cape Coast, where cocoa was of secondary importance and stories of the havoc wrought by Ashanti armies in the nineteenth century were not yet forgotten.[31] It was true that for half a century Fanti and Ashanti had lived together in friendly neighbourly fashion. As already noted, there was a large Fanti population in Kumasi (among them some of the leaders of the NLM), and the two Akan groups were intermingled throughout the southern half of the country. But a lurking suspicion remained of Ashanti intentions whenever political questions were raised. Nothing could have been better calculated than the NLM to arouse these suspicions. And those who were present in the municipality when the NLM made a determined effort to influence the Cape Coast electorate early in June 1956 told how the local townspeople hung back (despite a strong core of opposition voters among them) as a long cavalcade from Kumasi of lorries, propaganda vans, taxi-cabs, and cars flying the NLM flag moved slowly in to the town park led by Alhaji Amadu Baba, mounted on a white horse (brought by rail from Kumasi to Sekondi); how anxiety mounted too not only in Cape Coast but in many other southern constituencies at this sudden appearance of the Ashanti movement. On Sunday, 10 June, the NLM was inaugurated in Accra where it linked itself with the small opposition group led by the Ga lawyer, Obetsibi Lamptey, the journalist, K. Y. Attoh, the businessman Solomon Odamtten, and the Muslim communities of the Accra Zongo. It attracted a large audience, but again there must have been many who turned up more out of wonder at, than in support of, what was inevitably regarded as an Ashanti movement. In a number of southern constituencies, therefore, sus-

---

there were 'CPP infested'. There was an ancient dispute between Kumasi and the local Kukuom chief over the nature of the allegiance between the Ashanti capital and the local chiefdom. The area remained a small CPP enclave therefore in a strongly NLM part of Ashanti, and the CPC was active among the farmers. After independence, the CPP government raised Kukuom to the status of a 'paramount chief state'.

[31] 'Every town and village south of Kumasi was overawed by a dread of the vengeance of Ashantee, or in strict alliance with that powerful nation', and 'from the [river] Pra southward, the progress of the sword down to the very margin of the sea may be traced by mouldering ruins, desolated plantations and osseous relics. . . . Little kingdoms have thus been annihilated, as in the case of Denkyira, Akim, Wassaw, and many others, whose names have almost become obsolete.' This was Dupuis' account in 1824 (pp. 33 and 45).

picion of the NLM grew until it reached a point of almost complete unanimity in favour of the CPP. Nor was the electorate deceived when the NLM candidate registered as an Independent. In the rural western area of Abura Asebu, John Tsiboe—a Fanti member of the NLM executive—stood as an Independent, and claimed to have the support of the Abura State Council in his own home area; but a little before the election, 'the chiefs changed their mind after being told for a long time that the NLM would make the Aburas the servants of the Ashantis'.[32]

To have united the south against it—by its own exertions—was condemnation enough of NLM policy, but the damage extended still farther. Those on the executive who had argued that they should leave the south to its own quarrels and concentrate on Ashanti were soon to have further evidence for their fears. For while the leaders were parading in the south, the CPP carried the battle into the NLM camp with a full-scale rally on 1 July in the Prince of Wales Park at Kejetia. The joint chairmen were Nana Agyeman Badu Dormaahene, the Brong chief, and Barima Otuo Acheampong Kumawuhene; local CPP speakers, who had hitherto led a harassed life in the town, were reinforced by a strong contingent from Accra. The rally was not as successful as the party had hoped it would be. It was originally intended that Nkrumah and a number of national party figures should arrive by air to liberate the Ashanti capital from what the *Evening News* called 'a pall of political terrorism and oppression',[33] but although the large crowd waited patiently in the hot sun in relatively good order (under strong police surveillance) nobody had arrived by midday.[34] The Kumasi CPP leader, Atta Mensah,

[32] So at least the author was told in a letter from a research student. The 1954 election had been closely fought in the constituency between the CPP and two rebels. Now the voting was almost entirely one-sided: J. E. Hagan (CPP) 4,848, J. W. Tsiboe (Ind.) 216. One other example must suffice to show how dangerous it was to stand for the NLM in the south. In the Agona rural constituency the CPP candidate had lost in 1954 to a rebel candidate—A. D. Appea—who refused to rejoin the party; the CPP now had a new candidate, and Appea stood for the NLM. The chiefs turned against him, as did many of his associates, and his vote slumped from over 3,000 in 1954 to 877, giving his CPP opponent—W. A. C. Essibrah—an easy victory. There were CPP rebel candidates in Koforidua and Kwahu North, but nothing on the scale of 1954. In both these constituencies the fault was the national executive's in substituting one candidate for another and so confusing the electorate.

[33] 30 June 1956.

[34] There was one new speaker—the Queen Mother of Juaben who had remained obdurately CPP in defiance of the Juabenhene and most of his elders. When the chief was destooled in 1958, the Queen Mother was elected to the paramount Stool.

then telephoned the national headquarters, only to be told that the aeroplane by which the leaders had planned to travel had developed a leak in one of the petrol tanks. Eventually K. A. Gbedemah, Kojo Botsio, Aaron Ofori Atta, and N. A. Welbeck arrived by road late in the afternoon without Nkrumah (who had thought it wiser to stay in Accra), addressed the crowd briefly, and the rally broke up quickly—as the regulations demanded—before dark. The NLM mocked its organizers, and derided Nkrumah for failing to appear. Nevertheless, the rally and the crowds which attended were a portent: they showed that the CPP was by no means routed in Ashanti, even in Kumasi. The NLM leaders had no call to be complacent, and—as the results were to show—the monies and energies expended in the south might well have been put to better use within their own region.

Who won? The answer is plain: the CPP, with 71 seats out of the 104, and in terms of votes:

$$\left.\begin{array}{l} \text{CPP} - 398{,}141 \\ \text{Non-CPP} - 299{,}116 \end{array}\right\} \text{ in 99 contested constituencies}$$

There was a slight increase in the votes per constituency from 6,997 in 1954 to 7,043 in 1956, but the poll was only 50 per cent of the registered electorate and probably something under 30 per cent of the total adult population.[35] As in the previous elec-

---

The rally was not entirely peaceful. Explosions were heard in the adjoining Ashanti New Town area. Some of the crowd rushed to the scene, to find (it was said) an 'executioner's hat'—the skull-cap traditionally worn by the Asantehene's executioners (*abrafo*). It was handed to the Dormaahene and the Kumawuhene, and the chiefs agreed to exhibit it periodically in turn in their local state capitals.

[35]

Year	Aged 21 & over	Registered	Voters	Voters as % of regist.	Voters as % aged 21 & over
1956	2,338,210	1,392,874	697,257	50	29·8

NOTE: Those aged 21 and over, and the registered electorate do not include the five uncontested constituencies. Calculations based on the 1948 census and the annual *Digest of Statistics*.

The very different nature of the campaign in the south from that in Ashanti and the north can be seen in the variation in the size of the vote-per-constituency:

Colony	—	4,780
Ashanti	—	10,166
TVT	—	7,814
North	—	6,228

tion, the effect of the voting was once again to distort the actual picture of party strengths: to him that hath was given. For every four voters who cast their vote for the CPP, there were three who voted for alternative candidates; but, with 57 per cent of the votes, the CPP won 67 per cent of the contested seats.[36] Nevertheless, when the five unopposed seats were added to its gains, it was clear beyond all doubt that the CPP had secured the 'reasonable majority in a newly elected Legislature' which the Secretary of State had asked for in May, and it could legitimately claim 'to be the only party able to speak in the national sense'.[37]

The opposition was defeated. It was hardly possible (though its leaders were to make a bold attempt to do so) to interpret the results any other way. There had been times when the NLM and its allies had been over-sanguine in supposing they could win an overall majority. There had also been moments of understanding when the leaders were justly apprehensive of the strength of the ruling party: but they had never doubted their ability to hold the CPP to a narrow margin and prevent it from achieving the two-thirds majority which it was generally assumed the Secretary of State would require. (Indeed, the CPP itself was doubtful whether it could reach such a figure: hence its stubborn resistance to the idea of a third election.) In fact, the CPP had succeeded beyond its own expectations. The opposition was unlucky: it had, after all, won considerably more than a third of the votes cast. But the United Kingdom government was hardly likely to look beyond the formal requirement that one side or the other should command un unmistakable majority in the newly elected Assembly. Moreover, the failure of the opposition went beyond its national defeat by the CPP; it was clear from the way the votes had run that not only had its various sections been driven back in their own regions and districts, but that it had suffered heavy losses even within its own local strongholds.

The NPP, for example, failed to win its twenty seats. It won a majority of the votes and seats in the region; but the CPP— largely because of its ability as a party in office to attract support from leading 'notables' in a number of constituencies—won

[36] In other words, it had taken over 9,000 votes to elect an opposition M.P. and only 6,000 to elect a CPP member.

[37] Nkrumah, *Autobiography*, p. 273.

eleven of the twenty-six seats. The northern party actually lost Tamale, the regional capital, where rival factions within the CPP had shelved their differences during the election campaign under an agreement, among northerners and southerners alike, to support the Dagomba transport owner, R. S. Iddrisu against Alhaji Osmanu. It also lost the Talensi and Bongo constituencies because it backed the weaker side in a struggled between, and within, rival lineages; it lost Builsa where the chief and his candidate wavered from one side to the other and finally came down on the side of the CPP government;[38] and, much to its surprise, it lost Bawku largely because of a dispute over the succession to the vacant Skin. On the other hand, it could claim a number of notable successes. In the central Mamprusi constituencies, for example, where the paramount chief the Na Yiri, and his state secretary Mumuni Bawumia, still held staunchly to the party they had done so much to promote, its candidates won easily. Similarly in the Wala and Lawra-Nandom constituencies, the party had no difficulty thanks to the support of the chiefs and state councils, and in Tumu it succeeded in overthrowing Imoru Egala, Minister of Health in the 1954–6 cabinet.[39] The overall picture in the Protectorate was:

	Seats	Votes
NPP	15	74,172*
CPP	11	66,641
Ind.	0	8,665

* Including 1,732 votes cast for the only MAP candidate, Alhaji Osmanu, in Tamale.

NOTE: two of the CPP seats were unopposed.

In the thirteen Trans-Volta constituencies the pattern was very much as it had been in 1954. The CPP again won eight seats, and again lost (as was generally forecast) the three Ewe-dominated constituencies in the southern trust territory to the Togoland Congress (aided by the pro-Congress Independent candidate, the Rev. F. R. Ametowobla). M. K. Apaloo of the Federated Youth Organization was also successful in Anlo South in an area of deep feeling against the CPP Government dating back to the

[38] The successful candidate was A. Afoko, who was later to leave the CPP for the opposition and then to change back again to the CPP. The Builsa constituency was a remote one, even in the north, and detached from NPP and CPP alike.
[39] E. K. Mummuni Dimbie (NPP), 3,866, Imoru Egala (CPP), 3,488.

1951 tax riots. The only major surprise of the election came in South Tongu where a rebel CPP candidate defeated an Assembly member, W. M. N. Djetror.[40] The CPP actually increased its vote in the southern trust territory (and in the Trans-Volta Region as a whole) over that of 1954, both absolutely and relatively, and had every right to congratulate itself so soon after its setback during the plebiscite.

	Seats	Votes
CPP	8	55,508
Togoland Congress & FYO	4	30,946
Independents	1	15,130

The opposition was totally eclipsed in the Colony. It had hoped to win up to 12 seats: it failed to gain one. The CPP won all 44, sweeping the board with contemptuous ease. Admittedly, there were more votes cast in the 21 Ashanti constituencies than in the 41 contested Colony seats, but this, too, was an indirect measure of the dominant position which the party enjoyed in the south. In 20 constituencies the CPP candidate was given over 3,000, his opponent less than 1,000 votes; and in many, the opposition vote shrank to a truly derisory figure.[41] Once again Danquah went down to defeat, although by the narrow margin of under 600 votes in a total poll of nearly 9,000,[42] and, again, the most likely explanation was the pro-CPP combination of sub-chiefs hostile to Nana Ofori Atta, and a general resentment against the authority of the Akim Abuakwa chiefs among the immigrant Akwapim, Shai, and Ga farmers. Besides Akim Abuakwa, the only other serious challenge to the CPP came from dissident movements of a local nature like the Wassaw Youth Association which almost (but not quite) repeated its 1954 success—an indication once more of what the picture might have been but for the direct intervention in the Colony of the NLM.[43] Thus every hope of the opposition alliance—of the Ga vote in Accra, of the intelligentsia vote in Cape Coast, of a possible

---

[40] The 'rebel' was B. A. Konu who, as soon as he was elected, announced his support for the CPP, thus bringing its total to 72. Voting was very low in this large rural area, Ind. 2,069, CPP 853, out of 6,904 registered electors.

[41] e.g. Denkyira (Western Region): CPP 6,621. Ind. pro-NLM 476. Yilo Krobo (Eastern Region): CPP 2,619. Ind. pro-NLM 54.

[42] Akim Abuakwa North: C. E. Nimo (CPP) 4,679. J. B. Danquah (NLM) 4,122.

[43] E. K. Dadson (CPP) 3,279. K. Ocran (WYA) 3,239.

'anti-corruption' vote among the Sekondi-Takoradi workers—proved chimerical.[44]

The overall result in the Colony was:

	Seats	Votes
CPP	44	179,024*
Opposition	0	33,066
Inds.	0	9,536

* Including 3 seats unopposed.

These figures may be subdivided to show the relatively close voting in the five Akim Abuakwa constituencies:

	CPP		Opposition		Independents	
	Seats	Votes	Seats	Votes	Seats	Votes
Akim Abuakwa	5	19,932	0	13,419	0	374
Rest of the Colony	39	159,092	0	19,647	0	9,162

Finally, there was Ashanti where the NLM, winning 13 of the 21 constituencies, had also secured a regional majority of both votes and seats. Despite the large southern element in Kumasi South, Kurankyi Taylor was elected with the highest vote in the whole election—11,882 against 7,740.[45] Together with the Moslem Association the party won both Kumasi seats, and in many of the 'inner' Ashanti rural constituencies the CPP was trounced. The lawyer Victor Owusu in Agona Kwabre had 8,984 against the CPP's 1,354; Joe Appiah in Atwima Amansie was given 8,811 against 1,557; B. F. Kusi in Atwima Nwabiagya retained his seat for the NLM with a vote of 8,334 against his opponent's 1,390. Nevertheless, although the leaders publicly proclaimed

[44] e.g. Accra East: Ako Adjei (CPP) 8,834; Nai Tete (NLM) 1,085; Cape Coast: N. A. Welbeck (CPP) 5,744; K. Amponsah-Dadzie 3,437; Sekondi-Takoradi: J. Arthur (CPP) 8,310; D. K. Sam (Ind. pro-NLM) 220.

The CPP was very strong in Sekondi-Takoradi at this time. The NLM campaign against corruption fell on deaf ears, the railway and harbour workers allegedly telling the local opposition speakers: 'We know the CPP has squandered money; we will vote for them to squander even more.' And: 'it is the hungry man who eats. The present Assembly members are now satisfied. So we will vote them again.' It was a different story by September–October 1961, however, when there was an extended strike in Sekondi-Takoradi over the 1961 budget. But by then the right to vote as well as the right to strike had been virtually extinguished.

[45] The next highest was Nkrumah in Accra Central, with 11,119.

these victories, in private they lamented bitterly their lack of judgement. For, routed in the Colony, they had also erred badly in three and possibly four of the inner ring of Ashanti constituencies: Obuasi, Ashanti Akim, Adansi Banka, and Sekyere East. It was possible to explain the first two in straightforward terms in view of the anti-NLM 'strangers' vote in the constituencies, the one dominated by the large gold-mining town of Obuasi, the other by the mining centre at Konongo in Ashanti Akim.[46] Adansi Banka could be explained away in view of the quarrel between the Adansi paramount chief (supported by the Asantehene) and the subordinate chiefdom of Akrokerri which voted solidly for the CPP, and Sekyere East by the rivalry between the Asantehene and Kumawuhene. But Ashanti Akim and Adansi Banka were lost by the narrowest of margins.[47] Neither defeat was inevitable. And those who had argued against the party's intervention in the south were now convinced that they had been right, that an all-out effort in Ashanti itself could have saved Ashanti Akim, Adansi Banka, and possibly Obuasi. (It was argued too that had the large number of pro-NLM farmers been conveyed back from their farms in the western Ahafo districts to their villages in Sekyere East, even Krobo Edusei's constituency might have been snatched from him.) This was the price (it was argued) of extending the election campaign to the south, and the money which had been allowed to soak into the pockets of local agents who promised everything, and did nothing, might have turned the tide in these marginal Ashanti constituencies.[48] As it was, the movement which claimed to represent Ashanti had lost four constituencies within sixty miles of Kumasi—half the

[46] Many of the underground workers in the mines were from the north and might have been expected to vote for the opposition. But this was not necessarily the case. The northerner who voted for the NPP in the north was quite likely to vote for the CPP in the south which he recognized as the 'party of the underdog'; many were also disqualified on grounds of insufficient residence, or as non-British subjects from Upper Volta and Mali. The very small vote in Obuasi—CPP 3,551, NLM 1,170—suggested that the constituency was won partly on the votes of the anti-NLM southern clerks and teachers, partly on the pro-CPP vote among the small number of miners who managed to get onto the register. The Mine-Workers' Union at this time might justly be regarded as 'independent pro-CPP'. It had staged a successful strike in 1955, but against the overseas mining companies, not the CPP government.

[47] Adansi Banka: CPP 2,937; NLM 2,603. Ashanti Akim: CPP 5,918; NLM 5,191.

[48] The most often quoted example was the money paid out for an NLM propaganda van in Sekondi-Takoradi, which remained locked in a garage throughout the election campaign because of local hostility.

CPP's total in the region. The importance of the Brong issue could also be seen clearly, the remaining four CPP seats all being located in western Ashanti—Wenchi East, Sunyani West, Berekum, and Sunyani East.[49] In sum, the Ashanti results were:

	Seats	*Votes*
NLM/MAP*	13	127,098
CPP	8	96,968
Ind.	0	503

* The only MAP candidate was the Ashanti lawyer Cobina Kessie in Kumasi: 7,565 against 4,216.

To show the Kumasi–Brong balance, the figures may be sub-divided:

VOTES AND PERCENTAGES

	NLM/MAP		*CPP*	
15 Ashanti seats	101,465	63·4	58,597	36·6
5 Brong seats	22,663	38·7	35,806	61·3

Excluding the Attebubu constituency which overlapped Ashanti and the Brong area.

Thus, the NLM won nearly two-thirds of the vote in the 'true Ashanti' states; the CPP won nearly two-thirds of the vote in the Brong area. The full results were as shown on p. 354.

Finally, what effect did the election have on the general direction of politics? The answer is plain. It cleared the way for the grant of independence eight months later since it produced the alignment of forces which the United Kingdom government had asked for: namely, a 'reasonable majority in a newly elected legislature'.[50] In particular, the results forced the CPP and the

[49] Dr Busia, on the other hand, was safely home in Wenchi West—also a Brong constituency but having close ties with Kumasi: 4,884 votes against 3,125. Voting in the Attebubu constituency was very close. The CPP was unlucky here, for its candidate (and Assembly member) died shortly before the election, a squabble arose over the nomination, and the NLM candidate squeezed through on a minority vote: NLM—2,970; CPP—2,565, rebel CPP—503. This was the only three-cornered fight in Ashanti.

[50] 'Her Majesty's Government considered that the outcome of the General Election . . . fulfilled the conditions of the Colonial Secretary's undertaking of the 11th May 1956' that 'a motion calling for independence within the Commonwealth' should be passed by 'a reasonable majority in a newly elected legislature' (*The Proposed Constitution of Ghana*, presented by the Secretary of State for the Colonies to Parliament . . . February 1957, Cmnd. 71).

1956 Election Results

	Colony		TVT		Ashanti		North		Total		Per cent of total votes cast
	Seats	Votes	Seats	Votes	Seats	Votes	Seats	Votes	Seats	Votes	
CPP	44	179,024	8	55,508	8	96,968	11	66,641	71	398,141	57
Non-CPP	0	42,602	5	46,076	13	127,601	15	82,837	33	299,116	43
NLM	0	26,124	—	—	12	119,533	—	—	12	145,657	
MAP	0	1,814	—	—	1	7,565	0	1,732	1	11,111	
NPP	—	—	—	—	—	—	15	72,440	15	72,440	
TC	—	—	2	20,352	—	—	—	—	2	20,352	
FYO	0	1,230	1	5,617	—	—	—	—	1	6,847	
WYA	0	3,898	—	—	—	—	—	—	0	3,898	
Inds.	0	9,536	2	20,107	0	503	0	3,665	2	38,811	
	44	221,626	13	101,584	21	224,569	26	149,478	104	697,257	100

NOTE: the Independents include Rev. F. R. Ametowobla in support of the Togoland Congress, and B. A. Konu who later joined the CPP. The 5 unopposed seats have been added to the CPP total.

opposition alliance (at least for the time being) to accept the need for compromise. A further intervention by the Secretary of State, Lennox-Boyd, was necessary to persuade the leaders of both sides of the fact: but when the timetable of negotiations was set out, the chronology told its own tale:

3 August: a motion introduced by Nkrumah calling for independence was passed by 72 votes to 0. The opposition boycotted the Assembly.

18 September: announcement by the Secretary of State that the United Kingdom government would introduce a Bill to accord independence to the Gold Coast on 6 March 1957.

October: talks began between the CPP government and the opposition, without reaching agreement.

10 November: the government published its *Revised Constitutional Proposals*; debated 12–14 November, and approved by 70 votes to 25.

24–30 January: visit by the Secretary of State, and agreement reached between the CPP and the opposition leaders on a new United Kingdom White Paper which set out a *Proposed Constitution of Ghana.*

6 March: Independence.

Immediately following the July election, the opposition attempted to argue that the outcome had justified their demand for federation.

The results of the election show that the National Liberation Movement and its Allies won 1 out of 51 seats in that part of the country called the Gold Coast Colony proper, 13 out of the 21 seats in Ashanti, 15 out of the twenty-six seats in the Northern Territories, and 3 out of 6 seats in the Southern part of the Trust Territory of Togoland. . . . When the results are looked at regionally, as they must be, since the issue of the election was one of a Unitary or Federal Constitution, it would be seen that the case for the National Liberation Movement and its Allies has been established.[51]

Employing these and similar arguments, the Asante Youth Association, the Asanteman Council, the Kumasi State Council,

---

[51] Statement by Dr K. A. Busia at a press conference on 20 July published in the *Ashanti Pioneer*, 21 July 1956. The use of the words 'Colony proper', and the 'southern part of the Togoland trust territory', ignored the setting up of a Trans-Volta region, and the fact that some of its 13 constituencies lay partly in the trust territory, partly in the Colony.

the Zongo chiefs, and various bodies allied to the opposition, began to demand the summoning of a 'Constitutional Conference, Constituent Assembly or Constitutional Convention';[52] and when, in August 1956, Nkrumah introduced his motion calling for independence, the opposition withdrew from the Assembly.

> Since it is apparent that the Government has decided to impose the will of the Colony region on the other three regions despite the fact that the majority of peoples of these three other regions have voted for a federal constitution, we decided to withdraw from the Legislative Assembly and to consult with our regions to find ways and means of achieving their expressed aim of an agreed constitution before independence.[53]

In the immediate post-election months, therefore, it looked as if the 1956 election had failed in its purpose. Unrest continued in Kumasi and the *Evening News* and the *Liberator* renewed their abuse of each other. In truth, however, the opposition leaders had been dismayed by the results of the election, and knew that the case for federation was lost.[54] One may indeed doubt—with K. A. Gbedemah—whether they had ever passionately believed in its ideals. The demand for a federal constitution had constituted an effective challenge to the CPP, and the NLM/NPP had used it as such; but when the election put the CPP back in power with a more than two-thirds national majority of the seats, and nearly 40 per cent of the seats in Ashanti and the north, the opposition leaders were soon brought to the conference table. Argument, and apparent deadlock, followed the first attempts to compromise, and again the Secretary of State was obliged to act as mediator. But Lennox-Boyd was able to succeed in January 1957, where Bourne had failed the previous year, not because the proposals he put forward for a compromise constitution were essentially different from those of the Bourne *Report*, but because the circumstances in which the CPP and the opposition found themselves had been changed fundamentally by the elec-

---

[52] *Liberator*, 20 July 1956.

[53] Statement issued by Dr K. A. Busia on behalf of the opposition members of parliament, 3 Aug. 1956, published in the *Ashanti Pioneer*, 4 Aug. 1956.

[54] The change of tone in the *Liberator* was easily noticeable: e.g. 'The NLM and NPP Opposition allies still stand by their demands, and will certainly press in the new legislature with a higher and more stronger voice and persistence for a Constituent Assembly to draw up a constitution for the country. . . .' And: Nkrumah must 'come to an understanding with the NLM, NPP and the Togoland Congress' (20 July 1962).

tion. The opposition was now on the defensive, and its leaders knew they had to secure the best terms they could. (They also prided themselves on their ability to outwit the CPP in devising constitutional limits to the power of the new government.) The CPP leaders, on the other hand, were confident once more of their position. They were in office again, and independence was certain; and now that the substance of power was theirs, they were content in the meantime to enter into intricate arguments over the detailed proposals of a new Order in Council.

Thus, on the surface, early in 1957 an unexpected harmony was achieved after the violent discords of the past three years. Nkrumah told the Assembly members:

> Mr Speaker, I have great pleasure in announcing . . . the results of the consultations that I have had with the Leader of the Opposition on the United Kingdom Government's White Paper on the proposed constitution of Ghana which was published a few days ago. The Leader of the Opposition and I are at one in accepting the White Paper, to our general satisfaction. [*Hear, hear*] We consider the White Paper, and the Order in Council to be based on it, acceptable as a basis for the working of our Independence Constitution. [*Hear, hear*] With mutual confidence and cooperation we are certain that the foundation of our Independence which is now being truly laid, will support firmly the superstructure of our political and economic life and lead to the greater happiness and progress of all sections of our nation.[55]

Dr Busia concurred.

> Mr Speaker, as stated by the Prime Minister, the Opposition have agreed to accept the United Kingdom's White Paper and the Order-in-Council to be based on it as a workable compromise. It does not indeed provide all we asked for but we are prepared to cooperate to make it a successful foundation for the democratic life which we all desire to see established and practised in this country. [*Hear, hear*] . . . I am painfully conscious of the deep divisions among the representative supporters of the Opposition and the Government which have resulted from our differences over the constitutional issue. I would appeal to all on both sides of this House to join together to work for the success and greatness of our nation. [*Hear, hear*][56]

Three weeks later Nkrumah addressed the last meeting of the Gold Coast Assembly on the last day of colonial rule, tracing the

---

[55] GC, LA Deb., 12 Feb. 1957: 'Statement on Ghana Constitution'.
[56] Ibid.

history of the nationalist struggle since 1951 to the point where: 'By twelve o'clock midnight, Ghana will have redeemed her lost freedom'.[57] His speech was endorsed by S. D. Dombo, Deputy Leader of the Opposition. At midnight, before the Legislative Assembly building, the Union Jack was lowered: and a red, green and gold flag, overprinted with a black 'lodestar of African freedom', was hoisted in its place.

[57] GC, LA Deb., 5 Mar. 1957.

A NORTHERN ELECTION CAMPAIGN IN 1956

The 1956 election was fought out at very different levels, with so close an interweaving of local and national disputes that it was not always easy to see their relevance one to another. Start an election in Ghana, and so many battles are joined that the main armies are lost to view or, more accurately, they appear to dissolve into smaller and smaller groups of combatants each fighting for local ends seemingly unrelated to each other. But to see the election in this light is to confuse the local tactics of the lieutenants with the broader strategy of the generals. Each side will use every local device it can to secure an advantage for itself, and the parties will be exploited in their turn by chiefs, elders, and young men to further local ambitions; but, however fitful the overall power of the party's leaders may be, its presence is there, and influences the course of even the most local of electoral battles. Thus the illiterate peasant farmers of the remote chiefdoms, who knew very little of what was happening beyond the boundaries of the Protectorate, were drawn into the national struggle in 1954 and 1956 as local ambitions (and fears) were stirred by disputes between the politicians. In 1954, for example, the extreme northern constituency, Kassena-Nankanni North, had voted solidly for an Independent pro-NPP candidate because he had led a local protest movement (within the native authority and the new District Council) against the pretensions of the pro-CPP chief in the neighbouring constituency, Kassena-Nankanni South.[58] Thus the northern constituency was pro-NPP because Kassena-Nankanni South was CPP. By 1956, however, the long arm of the CPP had reached still farther north, and had succeeded in splitting the Kassena-Nankanni North constituency into rival groups. One was led by the chief of the small settlements around the frontier town, Paga (whose brother had been the successful pro-NPP candidate in 1954), the other by the chief of a nearby settlement of scattered compounds grouped around the small market centre at Chiana, whose brother now agreed to stand for the CPP.[59] Thus the great national issues of federation or unitary government, the form and timing of independence, the reform of the Cocoa Purchasing Company, the cocoa price, and the moral issues raised by

[58] The Kassena-Nankanni South chief and candidate, L. R. Abavana, supported the CPP because of their shrewd appraisal of the advantages of such a decision. Both were able men, and both were proved right. Abavana became a ministerial secretary after the 1954 election, later a minister, and by 1960, Regional Commissioner for the whole of northern Ghana; the Navropio was made a 'paramount chief' and, by 1960, President of the Northern House of Chiefs.

[59] Why did the Chiana chief—the Chianapio—and his half-brother—Ayagitam —suddenly agree to support the CPP in 1956? Because of the example before their eyes of the benefits bestowed on the Navropio and Abavana in Kassena-Nankanni South.

Busia and Gbedemah, were reduced to a simple struggle between rival chiefdoms for control of their own area. This did not mean however that the election was meaningless in local terms, or that it was any the less strongly fought. On the contrary, the struggle raged furiously throughout the constituency; and—fortunately—a detailed account is available of what took place:

Things were not as easy in the election as they were in 1954. It was very difficult to forecast the winner. . . .

We got to work at once, called all the councillors in Paga, got bicycles from the NPP Tamale headquarters. One jeep was given to us to use in Kassena-Nankanni North and South constituencies. . . . We had little use for the jeep as it was not easy to travel to the remote places with a car. The councillors and some young men of Paga helped us a great deal, expecting no reward. We made it an issue that it was a fight between the Chianas and the Pagas. We will not like the Chianas to be paramount over us. We would have to walk to Chiana for court cases and pay our levies to them; we made it known that if we allowed the Chianas to win, that means Chianapio [the chief] would be paramount and would dictate to our chief in Paga.

Owing to this news the whole of Paga went haywire. Enthusiastic representatives from all sections volunteered to help Paga win the election so that we might not become servants to the Chianas but masters of our own.

Here was one element at least that the Kassena-Nankanni election had in common with the electoral struggle at regional and national levels: the desire to be 'masters of our own'—the CPP nationally, the NLM in Ashanti, the Paga in their own little territory. The way in which they set about securing it in Kassena-Nankanni was as follows:

Kola was sent out per leaders of groups for customary greetings; drinks, cloths and even money were given to convince the headmen in the district to plead for us. In the Nankanni area our aim was to convince the headmen who were very influential. In —— especially we had an assurance from the chief of support. We were not sure in ——until the last two days to the elections. Most of the headmen in —— supported us, but were waiting for a word from the chief who had not made up his mind as to whom to vote for. The reason why he does not want to tell us his mind was, he said: 'the highest bidder will win the election'. He said he heard that when they elect M.P.s to the Assembly, we rather go to find fortune for our benefits. That for every mile we travel we claim allowance and because of this he would not tell us his mind. We spent heavily in these wards so I think we were the highest bidder. We got more votes than our opponents here. On market day [in a neighbouring chiefdom] we had a rally in the market with the —— chief as chairman. We invited all the Headmen, young men and some influential leaders in the area. We bought about three pots of pito costing about £2.10/– and about £1.10/– worth of kola. The rally was a success. After the rally, we made them drink, gave them kola, and spent almost £40 in the market alone. We slept in the town[60] for two days and at night called on the Headmen and explained what [the CPP candidate] was trying to do, tipped them heavily, gave out Kola and drinks, i.e. spirits, cloths etc. Before leaving —— we left two of our men and a native who helped us a great deal, we gave them about £5 each for canvassing, i.e. buy kola and tipping them etc.

We spent heavily in this constituency. The other side also spent heavily. In one case, a headman who was supporting us turned later to be our enemy. We understood the other side gave him about £40 cash as he was a popular man in this area and having many subjects under his command.

In most of the area our issue was that the [pro-CPP] Chianapio wanted to be made paramount chief over the other chiefs in Kassena-Nankanni North area, and that would mean that we would have to leave and attend his calls and were going to be under Chiana, pay our levies to them for the development of the town. . . . You could see that the chief is doing the canvassing, riding bicycle here and there through rain or shine. . . .

On the 17th was the last date; we made sure that our electorate came out to vote. Early in the morning we sent lorries to the far places which were very far from the polling stations. . . . One influential chief who was supporting the CPP had told his subjects to vote for the CPP. He came with his headmen and, after voting, sat in front of the polling booth just by the door. . . . So his presence there made some of our supporters afraid to vote. They feared that the chief might know what they were voting for. I complained about this and the chief was asked to go home. . . .

The register of voters' list was very inaccurate that it was difficult for some to cast their votes as the names and the serial numbers were inaccurate. About 5% were unable to vote owing to this mistake in each of their respective wards. Voting was very heavy, about 99% cast their vote in Paga town.[61]

[60] 'Town' is an exaggeration. It was usual to refer to Paga or Chiana as 'towns' but, properly speaking, they were market centres which had grown in the shadow of the chief's compound.

[61] Account of the NPP election campaign in 1956 as seen by one of the candidate's agents, A. Lobaza, to whom the writer is deeply indebted. Voting was not, of course, 99 per cent throughout the constituency, but it was high, and the NPP only narrowly beat its opponent. Registered electors, 17,422; voters—10,605: a

This lively account is a good measure of the earnestness with which the candidates and their agents carried out their campaign. There was no law restricting the amount each candidate could spend, and the regulations prohibiting 'treating' were wholly ineffective. But money was needed not so much to buy votes as to ensure, and retain, good will. Party loyalties in an area like Kassena-Nankanni were decided by customary and personal allegiances, and it would have taken a great deal to persuade a 'Paga man' to vote for someone from Chiana. (The customary practice of bestowing a gift as a ritual act of good will, however, became extremely expensive when translated into 'pito for the masses and whisky for the elder'.) None of this expenditure spared the party agents the task of conducting their propaganda through the maze of dusty paths which stretched between the separate home-steads, each with its thirty or forty relatives living inside a walled compound of neatly thatched huts, and tilling a small acreage of farmland. They had to sit down patiently with the elders, drink and explain matters to them. They had to win their approval by coming as the emissary of the chief (or as the emissary of his leading opponent), enlist their sympathies by using familiar, local lines of argument, and prove to them in material ways that the candidate was a generous, open-handed person, worthy of their support.

67·4 per cent poll. Party votes: NPP, 5,775; CPP, 4,528. An Independent candidate put up by the CPP in the hope of splitting the Paga vote had only 302 votes.

VIII

Independence and the New Republic

Was it reasonable in March 1957 to be optimistic about the future of the new state under the terms of the agreed constitution? How strong—or how weak—were national ties after the party disputes of the previous decade? How seriously was the country threatened by internal quarrels which required harsh methods of control? These were questions that were soon to be answered by Nkrumah in practical terms. The constitution was abolished, and political life reduced to a narrow struggle for power within the single party—steps which followed logically from the premise stated in the preface to the *Autobiography* that new states may need underpinning by 'emergency measures of a totalitarian kind'. Thus neither he nor the other CPP leaders at that time were prepared to act on the assumption that the state was sufficiently united to support the inter-party relationship envisaged in the new constitution. And, at first sight, there seemed ample justification for a line of policy which was shortly to be followed by a number of independent African governments. True, self-government had been attained, and a considerable degree of social revolution achieved whereby a new class of educated commoners had come to power without destroying completely the framework of a traditionally well organized society: but the very success of the CPP removed from the leaders the main ground of their appeal since 1949. Meanwhile, the country appeared dangerously divided. Regional parties were backed by strong local interests which, in the very heart of Accra, were shortly to throw up a new protest movement among the Ga community, and throughout the five regions which the constitution was designed to preserve as separate administrative units there could be seen that excessive concern for local issues which was so marked a feature of Ghanaian politics.

Nevertheless, there was much to be said on the other side. A line of argument which justified the course of events after 1957 on the grounds that it was inevitable (and therefore right) paid little respect to the evidence available from which quite different conclusions could be drawn. And something also needs to be said of the credit side of the political balance sheet after ten years of nationalist politics. Three main arguments could be adduced:

1. It was (in the first place) wholly inadequate to measure the degree of national unity by political considerations only. The economy, for example, continued to grow, and to contribute to the national strength of local society, whether in the form of the new metalled highways which replaced the earlier trunk roads, or in the export of cocoa, production of which continued to increase steadily throughout the period of party conflict in Ashanti and the Colony. By 1960 exports exceeded pre-war, pre-swollen-shoot figures. The price per ton on the world market still dipped and soared from month to month and from year to year, but it averaged a high level in the opening years of independence. It was £221 a ton early in 1957 compared with £208 early in 1951 when the CPP first took office; it continued at well over £200 for the main crop season 1957–8 and climbed to £350 the following year. It was not until 1961–2—that is, a year after the inauguration of the republic—that the price tumbled sharply to catch the government unawares at a time when it was over-committed on development expenditure: even then the rate of growth of the economy was checked rather than halted. The overall position of cocoa exports and prices during these years may be set down as follows:

Cocoa Production, 1956–61

	1956–7	1957–8	1958–9	1959–60	1960–1
'000 long tons	264	207	255	317	430
Per cent of world production	29·6	26·9	28·4	30·6	37·2

World Cocoa Price, 1949–61 (£ per ton)

1949	1950	1951	1952	1953	1954	1955	1956	1957	1958	1959	1960	1961
190	208	285	301	287	467	302	221	247	352	285	225	177

Source: Economic Survey 1962, table 7, p. 24; table 8, p. 25.

The attempt to force the pace of economic development, and the large increase in government expenditure after 1960, were later to bring the economy under pressure both internally and externally.[1] But in 1957 the balance-of-payment difficulties lay in the future: they belonged to the period of personal presidential rule, and they could hardly be adduced to explain (still less to justify) the shift away from the parliamentary system agreed to at independence.

Any attempt to assess the overall strength of the country in 1957 also had to consider the position of the civil service (including the police), which by that date was staffed almost wholly by Ghanaian officers. It had remained virtually unaffected by the pre-independence struggle between the CPP and the opposition, and it continued to serve the new state loyally in face of a great deal of unmerited criticism. Shortly after independence, for example, at the height of his triumph over the opposition, Nkrumah widened his attack on what were said to be 'neo-colonialist forces' at work in Ghana to include both the civil service and the university from which the administrative grade of the service was recruited. In his speech during the tenth anniversary celebrations of the party he condemned the university at Legon in harsh terms as 'a breeding ground for unpatriotic and anti-Government elements'. He found it 'intolerable that we should be training people most of whom will eventually come into Government service who will be permeated with an anti-Government attitude, that is to say, an anti-Convention People's Party attitude.... How can these people serve loyally the Government and the State?' A note of warning was then sounded that 'if reforms do

[1] A large part of the financial difficulty that overtook the country in 1961 was brought about by a sharp increase in spending on the part of the government itself:

(£ million)

	1956–7	1957–8	1958–9	1959–60	1960–1
Capital expend.	19·1	19·0	27·3	34·6	44·5
Consumptn expend.	38·8	38·1	44·5	49·3	65·5
Financ. claims, interest & trfrs abroad	2·6	6·7	6·6	4·1	3·6
TOTAL	60·5	63·7	78·3	88·0	113·7

The heaviest items of government expenditure in 1960–1 were: education, 13·2 per cent; general administration, 12·4 per cent; communications, 12·2 per cent; agriculture, 10·2 per cent; defence, 8·8 per cent (*Economic Survey 1962*, tables 89–90, pp. 106–7).

not come from within, we intend to impose them from outside, and no resort to the cry of academic freedom (for academic freedom does not mean irresponsibility) is going to restrain us. . . .'[2] The upshot early in 1960 was that the university was subject to a special review by an international Commission appointed by the government. The Commission made a number of moderate recommendations concerning the intake of students, the rate of Africanization among the teaching staff, and the promotion of African studies in the college, which the government accepted (although it also acted contrary to the Commission's statement in the *Report* that non-Ghanaians on the staff of the university 'should enjoy a sense of security' when, in mid-1961, it abruptly terminated the contracts of one Ghanaian and five European members).[3] Meanwhile the college continued to produce graduates who held aloof from the party without ceasing to be loyal to the new republic. Similarly, in May 1960 the government issued *A New Charter for the Civil Service* which declared (p. 3) that: 'With the achievement of independence the position of the Civil Service in Ghana was drastically altered but these revolutionary changes did not become immediately apparent partly because of the continuity of personnel.' But in fact very little was changed. The service remained under the control of a Civil Service Commission, and the New Charter itself recognized that 'the principle of loyalty to the State and to the Government . . . does not imply participation in party politics. Perhaps the most important feature of the Civil Service is its non-political character.' The most important administrative difference after 1957 was at local level where party district commissioners replaced the cadre of Government Agents (a number of whom remained in their districts as advisers to the party bosses). In general, the civil service, the police, the university at Accra, and the Kumasi College of Technology[4] weathered a great deal of abuse without being greatly affected by it.[5] Similarly, the courts remained free under

[2] Address to 10th Party Anniversary Rally, 12 June 1959 (*Evening News*, 14 June 1959).
[3] Ghana, Commission on University Education, Dec. 1960–Jan. 1961, *Report*, para. 34.
[4] Later, the Kwame Nkrumah University of Science and Technology.
[5] The difficulties which arose between the party and the civil service always sounded worse than, in practice, they were: they did, however, result in a small number of senior Ghanaian officers leaving the country to take appointments with international organizations.

magistrates and judges who were appointed by a Judicial Service Commission. The laws were harsh, and the government was able to by-pass the courts under legislation of a special nature, like the Preventive Detention Act, but where the courts had jurisdiction the laws were impartially administered. Thus the framework of law and administration which had kept the nationalist movement within bounds after 1949, and which had enabled elections and the plebiscite to be held fairly, was still there in 1957. Indeed it was to the leading figures in the civil service that Nkrumah was later to turn as the effective instruments of his own personal rule after the inner party quarrels, assassination plots, and detentions of 1961. Flagstaff House (where the President established his offices) became a centre of budgetary and economic planning directed by Nkrumah and an able group of economists, statisticians, and administrators. This efficient, neutral sector of government was there at independence in 1957 and it was reasonable to suppose that it was as capable then, as it had been earlier, of functioning alongside the open party disputes between the CPP and its opponents.

2. In the second place, it was by no means certain, because the country was divided territorially between the CPP and the opposition, that it was threatened by piecemeal fragmentation. Neither side had succeeded in monopolizing local opinion even within its own strongholds. The CPP was strongly supported in Ashanti. The opposition had some following in the south. Togoland and the north were a patchwork of CPP and non-CPP villages. Admittedly, the rank and file on each side were strongly tempted to assert a total hold wherever they were in the majority; but they took their cue from the leaders. And, provided the leading figures were prepared to co-operate at national level, there were reasonable grounds for hope that such an accord between the parties might be extended locally. It required no more of the constituency executives and the electorate than was common practice in an Akan chiefdom where the various factions engaged in the struggle for the Stool between rival royal houses, and for offices under the Stool, had long learnt to live together in perpetual (yet limited) conflict. The doubt in 1957 was whether such a pattern of orderly conflict could be reproduced in modern terms. Yet it was noticeable that the number of party incidents in which violence was used—of the kind which had ruptured the

normally close-knit pattern of social life in a number of Ashanti districts—greatly diminished in the early months of 1957. The party leaders were beginning to come to terms nationally, and tension was correspondingly reduced in the country at large.[6] It was also possible to point to large areas of the country where political differences existed peacefully alongside ties of mutual economic interest, marriage, church fellowships, and social groups of one kind and another over a wide field of private interests.[7] If one added to these forces making for cohesion a growing awareness (born of the 1954–6 conflict) of the power of the Accra government and the national role of the civil service and police, it was not unreasonable to argue that the possibility of a working compromise between the parties existed—provided the leaders on both sides were prepared to co-operate to achieve it.

How did the opposition (in particular) stand in this respect? The CPP may have been expected to look with confidence at its own strength. But what likelihood was there that the alliance of opposition parties would survive, even supposing the CPP did not try to hasten its end? Were there genuine differences between Busia and his colleagues on one side, and the CPP on the other? And would the opposition be content to act within the limits of

[6] The CPP and opposition members were often able to collaborate in the advantages of membership of the National Assembly. viz:

G.V. Cars (Allocation)

Mr E. I. Preko asked the Minister of Finance how many of the [Government Vehicle cars bought for use during the independence celebrations] had been sold to Members of Parliament. . . .

Mr Bensah: Of the cars purchased by the Government . . . seventy-six have been allocated to Members of Parliament on application; forty-seven to Government supporters, twenty-eight to members of the Opposition, and one to an Independent Member.

Mr Preko: How many cars were allocated to Members of the Opposition?

Mr Bensah: The cars available for distribution included Jaguars, Chevrolets, Wolseleys, but the majority of the Jaguars went to the Opposition (Ghana, Parl. Deb., 2 May 1957).

They also worked together, and got through a great deal of useful work, in important committees of the House, such as the Public Accounts Committee which had 8 government and 4 opposition members.

[7] Even at the height of the NLM–CPP controversy, there was very little hostility between individuals on tribal grounds alone. One particular incident stands out in the writer's mind. Late in 1955 he was travelling from Kumasi to Accra, and gave a lift to a young primary-school-educated Fanti girl whose mother was a market trader in Kumasi. She was not only young but pretty. During the journey he asked the girl whether she would be willing to marry someone not necessarily from her own Fanti community, but an Ashanti, or a Ga, or an Ewe. To each question she replied, 'Yes, she would'. Only when the question was put: would she marry a northerner? was there any hesitation; then she confided that she would—provided he was 'a Christian and had money'.

the constitution if faced with an indefinite period of opposition? Here were real problems to which no immediate answer was possible. Indeed, it might be thought that, if the CPP were to make no other move against the opposition alliance than to offer its members inducements to join the government party, the uneasy coalition of regional and local parties would quickly fall victim to its own internal differences. Against such a view, on the other hand, it could be said that the CPP leaders at least did not believe that such tactics were sufficient in themselves to dislodge the opposition, and that they recognized the strength of an inherent stubbornness in the attitude of many of the opposition leaders. It was even possible to indicate certain broad differences of principle and policy between the two sides. Thus the CPP was in favour of a centralization of authority, the opposition of a greater regionalization of powers. The CPP was a radical, vaguely socialistic, commoners' party, the opposition had a more tender regard for traditional interests. Nkrumah was an ardent pan-Africanist, Busia was sceptical of such programmes. These differences lent a sharp edge to debates in the opening year of the new parliament. Admittedly, it was doubtful whether the opposition leaders objected to the CPP primarily on these grounds. There were many occasions when they and their CPP counterparts seemed no more than participants in 'a conflict without principle', one party 'occupying office, the other seeking to dislodge it'.[8] But many opposition leaders also had a deep, instinctive dislike of everything that Nkrumah and the CPP stood for. They continued the old intelligentsia attack on the commoners' party as being both unfit and unworthy to govern. And, on this basis, they drew support from a broad section of educated opinion which disliked the quality of leadership provided by the CPP. In addition, the different components of the opposition alliance were able to root themselves in the multitude of local interests in the constituencies, for it was beyond the powers of any government in the country to satisfy every local interest—between the Paga and Chiana chiefdoms in the north, rival market groups in Kumasi, traditionally opposed groups in this or that particular state, or the warring factions of the Muslim communities in the urban 'Zongos'. As long as an open opposition was allowed to

---

[8] Maurice Duverger's description of the differences between parties in the United States (*Political Parties* (1954), p. 418).

exist, therefore, it was likely to find some support for itself. And when its leaders looked back over the previous decade of party conflict they could at least draw the conclusion that the electorate as a whole was by no means committed irrevocably to the CPP.

Thirdly, there was the 1957 constitution itself. Was it possible to see in the agreement reached between the leaders the base for a workable majority-minority system? The constitution had at least one advantage over its predecessor in that the National Assembly (unlike that of 1954–6) now included the full range of both government and opposition opinion. The dispute between the CPP and its rivals had been put to the test in 1956; each party group had entered the election in full strength, and neither side— at independence—doubted that the results, and the division of seats in the new parliament, were a reasonable measure of the strength of the competing groups. The constitution was, indeed, built on this assumption. It was not of course difficult to understand why the regional assemblies that were to replace the interim bodies set up in March 1957 were unpalatable to the CPP leaders (particularly in view of their commitment to the Brong demand for a separate region and assembly). But, however cumbersome the regional bodies may have seemed in CPP eyes, they were the seal of an agreed settlement between the parties or, at their lowest rating, the price of reconciliation. (It may be worth noting here that when the CPP government abolished the assemblies they left untouched the regional houses of chiefs: what went by the board were regional bodies of a popularly elected kind.) Provided, therefore, that the party leaders refrained from pressing their right to govern or to oppose beyond mutually acceptable limits, it was possible to argue that the structure of the new constitution was capable of providing both an efficient and a tolerant form of parliamentary rule.

The argument set out in the foregoing paragraphs rested on the basic assumption that it was possible to limit the conflict between the parties to 'mutually acceptable limits'. It was on this basis, however, that it foundered, for compromise required caution and prudence—qualities essential to the 1957 constitution if it was to function effectively: without them, there was little hope of its survival. And so it proved. The reasons for its failure were those given in the introductory chapter, namely, a profound dislike by Nkrumah of any open criticism of his rule, the nationalist zeal of a recently formed People's Party which (under Nkrumah's leadership) sought to identify itself with the state, and the rash behaviour of the opposition which supported every group and cause that it thought might overthrow the government. Evidence of the breakdown of the temporary truce achieved in 1957 was soon forthcoming. As the first year of independence came to an end, it was clear that whatever nominal recognition the CPP gave to the advantages of an opposition—and its leaders had not yet formulated their belief in single-party rule as a necessary feature of the African landscape—there was little taste for it in practice. And within six months of independence, the CPP had begun to repeat the argument tentatively advanced in Nkrumah's *Autobiography* that, since the party's opponents were 'violent, waspish and malignant', there was need for a 'temporary benevolent dictatorship'.[9] On the basis of arguments of this kind the leaders began to augment and consolidate the power of the party by whatever means they could devise. For their part—in the face of such pressures—the opposition hastened all the more anxiously to sponsor every outbreak of discontent with CPP rule, rashly confident (despite the outcome of the 1956 election, and beyond all the evidence available) of bringing about its downfall. It was a disastrous policy (from its own point of view) for the simple reason that the ruling party was far better placed and armed for an all-out struggle between the two sides.

There was also a more immediate explanation of the failure of the 1957 constitution. Because it was designed to function on the basis of compromise and tolerance, it required at least an initial period of convalescence after the turmoil of the 1954 struggle. The nationalist temper of the government, and the antipathy of the leaders towards each other, meant that the temporary accord reached between them was open to every breath of suspicion fanned by one side or the other. And, unfortunately, there was ample material for such suspicions in the actual course of events after March 1957. Indeed, the warmth of the independence celebrations was very quickly chilled, first by a renewal of local

---

[9] Speech by Cecil Forde, when general secretary of the CPP, at the Arena in Accra on 13 August 1957. 'Perhaps there may be much to be said for a temporary dictatorship than a democratic state where the Opposition is violent, waspish and malignant' (*Ashanti Pioneer*, 14 Aug. 1957).

violence in the Ewe Togoland area, and then by a sudden outburst of rowdy discontent in Accra. And something must be said of
both these events in order to understand the action subsequently
taken by the CPP and the opposition.

Even while the formal independence ceremonies were being
held in Accra, rumours reached the capital that matters had
taken a very different course in the thick bush of the Alavanyo
district among small groups of supporters of the Togoland Congress. They had banded themselves together in camps, marched
up and down in ragged military formation, and practised with
shotguns in the hope that they might thereby hasten the day of
Togoland unification. The government acted promptly by moving troops and police into the area—a large force to deal with a
minor revolt—and the camps were quickly broken up. The
casualties reported were three people killed in rioting in Kpandu
town early in March, and a number of further victims in the
action taken by the police and army to restore order. (The final
toll may well have been very much higher.) Two months later
there was an inconclusive debate in parliament on the government's action in quelling the riots. It was defended by the ministerial secretary F. Y. Asare (a CPP Ewe), and opposed—on the
grounds that the action taken was unnecessarily harsh—by Kojo
Ayeke, the Togoland Congress executive member.[10] There for
the moment the matter rested, although the disturbances were
not forgotten, for Ayeke and S. G. Antor (general secretary of the
Togoland Congress) were later to be arrested and charged with
complicity in the plot. The effect of the Alavanyo riots on the
attitude of the main party groups towards each other at this time
was less perhaps (at least on the surface) than might be supposed
from the measures taken by the government to suppress them.
For it was generally recognized that the Ewe question was in a
special category of difficulty since it involved relations with a
neighbouring country. Whereas the Ashanti, or northern, or any
of the myriad of local grievances were an issue of domestic politics, the Ewe demands raised much wider questions touching the
actual frontiers of the state. Moreover, the rebels were quickly
suppressed. Nevertheless, the disturbances were important in
their long-term effects. They added to the tension which existed
beneath the surface goodwill and confirmed the CPP's belief in

[10] Ghana, Parl. Deb., 3 May 1957.

the need to introduce extreme measures of control to curb its opponents.

Three months later further disturbances took place following the formation of a new party, the Ga Adangme Shifimo Kpee— the Ga Standfast Association. The Accra movement and the other forms of discontent which took shape around it are worth discussing in some detail for they provided the material for a new phase of the conflict between the CPP and the opposition. And it was against their background that the CPP began to extend its power over the country as a whole.

The complaints of the Ga community in the capital were first voiced within the CPP itself through a memorandum submitted to the central committee at the beginning of 1956 by the Accra regional executive:

Resolutions Passed at Meetings of the Accra Region held at Orgle Street on 5–12 January 1956 and forwarded to the Hon. Dr Kwame Nkrumah, Prime Minister, Life Chairman of the Convention People's Party.[11]

That this Council comprising the three Municipal Constituencies (East, West and Central Accra), the Ga-Rural Constituency and the Dangme-Shai Constituency having had occasion to discuss various topics affecting the welfare of the Party resolved:

1. Whereas it is known that we find it difficult to criticise and it is improper to criticise our party in public.

2. And whereas it is known that we are given no opportunity to criticise our Party internally.

3. And whereas it is known that any attempt to offer suggestions or to make any criticism against the Party is misconstrued and accepted by the power that be as disloyalty.

4. And where it is known that criticisms are never known to have been invited by the powers that be from us, though directives are from time to time issued to us concerning organisational work. ...

7. And whereas it is known that the Fantis, Ashantis, and Ewes in the past, principally Fantis, though preaching against tribalism and nepotism are actually practising these administrative vices as witnessed by the number of them who are employed in the Ministries. ...

9. And whereas it is rumoured that a Fanti Minister, Fanti Ministerial Secretaries and some of their wealthy friends are busily engaged in paying for and thereby acquiring for themselves some of

---

[11] Resolution of the Accra Regional Council; CPP, signed (nominally at least) by leading CPP figures in the Accra region—E. C. Quaye, C. T. Nylander, R. A. Hammond, E. W. Note Dowuona, 49 members in all.

the Estate buildings taken from defaulting members of the Party....

12. And whereas the Ga-Adangmes have deceived themselves into thinking that tribal barriers were broken down for ever....

22. And whereas this discrimination has weakened some of our members creating defections and making organisational work difficult....

27. And whereas in spite of everything else the Ga-Adangmes are being treated by the powers that be of no consequence....

38. And whereas Sir Tsibu Darku who once said 'who are the people' was appointed chairman of the Tema Development Corporation, earning allowances averaging £150 a month....

48. And whereas it is the prevailing practice of party leaders to refuse interviews with accredited members ... (as witness the refusal of the Life Chairman to meet representatives of the Accra Region (CPP) recently.

49. Therefore BE IT RESOLVED AND IT IS HEREBY RESOLVED that while this feeling in the Ga-Adangme area ... gathers and engenders a ferment for an eruption likely to blow up any time, the Hon. Dr Kwame Nkrumah be made known of it before it is too late if he seems not to know it or does not know it....

At the beginning of 1956 (when these resolutions were handed to the central committee) the times were dangerous, and the rank and file remained loyal to the nationalist aims of the party. In 1957, however, the complaints were revived; and, although many of the CPP members refused their support, others attempted to re-cast them in a more overtly tribal form. A decision was taken among a small group of young men—in a room rented by Attoh Quarshie (a government transport driver) in the slum area around Bukuom Square, Accra—to form a 'non-political association' to 'protect the interests of the Ga people'.[12] The name chosen was the Ga Adangme Shifimo Kpee. Help was enlisted from the drivers of the local taxi station at the corner of Zion Street and Bannerman Road who began to spread the new movement quickly through the central wards of the municipality—Nkrumah's own constituency. Its most ardent supporters were the unemployed elementary-school-leavers, popularly known as 'Tokyo Joes', who already had their own leader—'Zorro'.[13] But the rallying cry of *Ga Shikpon* (Ga Lands) brought

---

[12] The founder members were: Attoh Quarshie, Acka Nettey (teacher), Charles Lamptey (motor mechanic), E. O. Pobby (store-keeper), Tete Addy (bicycle repairer), J. T. Nartey (clerk), Nikoi Kotey (clerk).

[13] Emmanuel Oko Bruce.

in other groups. The Ga students of the University College, for
example, met at the Accra Community Centre in May and June
to support the demand for an inquiry into the allocation by the
government of the estate houses.[14] The chiefs also lent their support, taking part in an appeal for funds, and in a formal procession to the Okai Hill shrine outside Accra—supposedly the last
resting place of the migrant Ga people before they moved to the
coast. The formal inauguration of the party took place in Bukuom Square on Sunday, 7 July, in pouring rain when a tumul-
tuous crowd collected to cheer the leaders dressed in red shirts
and headkerchiefs. A senior traditional ruler—Nii Amunakwa II,
Otublohun Manche—presided over the rally; the leading fetish
priest—the Nai Wulomo—poured libation and slaughtered a
white sheep. A flag was unfurled—an elephant and palm tree
within a red and blue circle;—and Nkrumah was publicly and
formally denounced three times as the leader who had 'betrayed
the common man'. On the platform sat S. G. Antor of the Togoland Congress, J. B. Danquah, and a number of opposition party
leaders. The Tokyo Joes stood round the platform as an unofficial
guard, and slogans—*Ga Shikpon* and *Gboi mli gbewo* (Strangers are
crushing us)—were shouted out to the crowd, which cheered
every speech by the leaders, and ignored the heavy rain which
streamed through the rough awning of neem trees and palm
branches.

As the Ga movement gathered momentum, it touched off unrest among other discontented groups. The day of the inauguration of the new party, an emergency meeting was held of the Supreme Council of Ex-Servicemen, at which protests were recorded against the government's handling of the allocation of the
estate houses, and a declaration issued to the effect that its members would 'march on the castle' (where Nkrumah had now taken
up residence) unless they were afforded proper recognition. (One
of the complaints made by the Ex-Servicemen's Union concerned

[14] The housing problem in Accra lay at the heart of the Ga case, and dated back
to the earthquake of 1939 which destroyed a large number of houses in the Ga area.
The leaders were promised new houses, but the war intervened, and housing
accommodation was still very short ten years after the war ended. Estate houses
were built for renting, on Ga traditionally-owned land, but there were widespread
accusations against the CPP leaders that they had allocated many of the newer
houses to their wives and relatives in preference to those really in need. Something
was done through the setting up of a Housing Corporation in 1955–6, but building
operations were slow, and the completed houses expensive.

the proposal made by the government to start a 'Builders' Brigade' which was seen as a possible rival organization.) The Motor Drivers' Union also was up in arms over the introduction of a new ordinance designed to limit the issue of licences, and threatened to strike on 23 July unless the ordinance was withdrawn beforehand. And—to add to the discomfort of the government—Akantigsi Afoko, the CPP member for the northern Builsa constituency, announced his resignation from the party prior to joining the NPP.[15] Nkrumah at this time was out of the country attending the Commonwealth Prime Ministers' meeting, and it was to these troubles that he returned on 22 July, to meet with a very mixed reception. The Ga chiefs dissembled their earlier opposition and gathered to welcome the Prime Minister, the Nai Wulomo again pouring libation—this time for Nkrumah as he left the railway station: but the Tokyo Joes gathered at a number of points on his way to the castle, shouting their slogans and waving placards variously inscribed: 'Welcome Mr Dictator'. 'We are Verandah Boys Still'. 'You can't fool Ga's all the time'. 'No rooms, no jobs, but taxes: Why?' And: 'P.M.! Is Goldsmith Your Father's Name?'[16] The following day (23 July) the threatened drivers' strike took place. The lorry parks were idle and, as food became scarce, prices rose: a tuber of yam went up from 2*s.* 6*d.* to 5*s.* 6*d.*, plantain from 6*d.* to 2*s.*, garden eggs were 4*d.* instead of a penny each. Meanwhile, the Ga Shifimo Kpee continued to hold its rallies in the Ga wards, although less peacefully and uninterruptedly now, for the CPP leaders had recovered from their initial dismay to launch a rival movement—the Ga Ekomefeemo Kpee—whose supporters clashed violently with those of the Shifimo Kpee.[17]

It was in these circumstances that the CPP leaders began to exercise their power. One may suppose that the Ga movement, following the Alavanyo riots, not only strengthened Nkrumah's

[15] He rejoined the party within the year.

[16] An obscure reference to Nkrumah's *Autobiography* in which he described his father as being a goldsmith, without mentioning his name: the implication was that Nkrumah was not wholly Ghanaian—the rumour being that his father was from Liberia.

[17] e.g. on 21 August when there was rioting between the two rival factions in Bukuom Square: 53 arrests were made. The following day five of the leading Ga Shifimo Kpee members were set upon and attacked with knives and bottles by a CPP gang. Twelve were arrested and sentenced to short terms of imprisonment, including Kwatelai Quartey—a Ga—at this time national propaganda secretary for the CPP.

determination to introduce his 'emergency measures of a totalitarian kind', but persuaded the rank and file of the party of the need to reinforce their hold on the electorate. The first steps were taken at the end of July when it was announced that deportation orders had been issued against the Muslim leaders in Kumasi, Alhaji Amadu Baba, and Alhaji Othman Larden.[18] The deportations were the prelude to a series of measures introduced by Krobo Edusei whom Nkrumah appointed Minister of the Interior on 29 August 1957 (until 16 November 1958).[19] They may be grouped in a number of categories, and listed briefly:

1. Those designed to deprive the opposition of the basis of their support in the regions: e.g. by the passage of an Avoidance of Discrimination Act in December 1957, which forbade the existence of parties on a regional, tribal or religious basis.[20] In addition, there was a carefully mounted attack on the pro-opposition chiefs. Commissions of inquiry were set up to examine the conduct between 1954 and 1957 of Nana Ofori Atta and the Akim Abuakwa State Council, and the Kumasi State and Asanteman Councils. Pressure also began to be exerted through the use of administrative powers governing the status and functions of chiefs and their state councils. Early in 1958 a number of Ashanti chiefdoms (e.g. Duyaw Nkwanta, pro-NLM) were 'downgraded' from the position of a paramount chief state; others (e.g. Bechem, pro-CPP) were upgraded. The effect was easily predictable: destoolment charges were brought by the pro-CPP element in a state from which government recognition had been withdrawn. They were approved by those who feared the further consequences of government disapproval. The government then recognized the charges as valid, the chief was 'gazetted' as being destooled, and a (pro-CPP) candidate from a rival royal house took his place. Once the chief was changed, pressure was exerted

[18] A deportation order was also served against Bankole Timothy, a Sierra Leone journalist working for the *Daily Graphic*, author of a biography of Nkrumah. The deportations of the two Muslim leaders provoked a storm of protest in Kumasi. It was argued in court that the two Alhajis were Ghanaian citizens, whereupon the government passed the Deportation (Othman Larden and Amadu Baba) Act on 23 August, empowering the minister to deport them despite the fact that the case was still being heard. They were deported to Nigeria the following day. Then the government had to pass another act indemnifying Krobo Edusei (as the minister responsible) from any contempt of court ruling.
[19] Helped by Geoffrey Bing who was appointed Attorney-General on 7 September 1957, until 1 October 1961.
[20] Originally, the Political Parties Restriction Bill: a more appropriate title.

in a variety of subtle, indirect ways to bring other sections of the chiefdom into line; then, after an interval of time, recognition was accorded, and paramount status restored, to both chief and state. By such means, every pro-NLM chief in Ashanti was removed from office with the exception of the Asantehene who was spared only after he had made a public declaration of support for 'the government of the day'. Similar steps had been taken in respect of the Zerikin Zongo—the Muslim leader—in Kumasi. The government secured the appointment at the end of 1957 of Mallam Mutawakilu in place of the deported Alhaji Amadu Baba, although at the cost of a local declaration of emergency in the municipality (December–January) when protests were staged by supporters of Amadu Baba among the Muslim communities.

2. Measures taken to emphasize and augment the power of the party in the regions. The same day (16 October 1957) as the announcement of a Commission of Inquiry into the affairs of the Akim Abuakwa State Council (1957) it was also stated that Regional Commissioners would be appointed from 1 November as 'representatives of the Government in their regions . . . personally and directly responsible to the Government for the administration of their regions and for seeing that this policy is carried out'.[21] The number appointed included a Commissioner for Western Ashanti (i.e. the Brong areas) despite the provisions in the 1957 constitution which had sought both to limit the regions to five (North, Ashanti, Trans-Volta, and two southern regions), and to make it extremely difficult to increase the number. When the names of the regional (and, subsequently, of district) commissioners were announced, they were of party members and not administrators. The fusion of party and government power was thus demonstrated as clearly as it could be at local and regional level: the party boss sat in the former colonial commissioner's office, and presided over an administrative hierarchy arranged much as in colonial times, which he now placed at the service of the party.[22]

[21] *Ghana Gazette*, 16 Oct. 1957.
[22] The similarity between colonial and CPP times may be seen in the following extracts:

'*Chief Smokes Peace Pipe with Party Executives*

The Regional Commissioner of Ashanti, Mr R. O. Amuako-Atta settled a dispute existing between the omanhene of Kuntanase State, Nana Kofi Boateng and the executive of the Kuntanase branch of the CPP. . . . The Regional Com-

3. Measures taken to centralize the authority of the government, involving the systematic dismantling of the 1957 constitution. In April 1958 the *Report* of the Regional Constitutional Commission appeared, making precise, detailed recommendations for the establishment of elected regional assemblies to replace the interim assemblies appointed in 1957.[23] The *Report* set out the range of powers the Commission thought appropriate for such bodies, and chartered a careful course between the grant of 'wide and extensive powers over numerous fields of activity' (such as the opposition were demanding), and their reduction to 'advisory, rather than . . . executive bodies' (as the CPP wanted).[24] It was signed by Mr Justice Van Lare as Chairman, and 21 members of whom 13 were CPP and 8 supported the opposition.[25] However, the government's *Statement on the Report* severely restricted the range of powers suggested, in effect reducing them to advisory bodies; and it was in this form that they were introduced in 1958. The opposition protested in strong terms. And, apprehensive now of their position in areas where the chiefs had

---

missioner appealed to them to forget the events of the past and co-operate for the benefit of the state.

He also requested that the Kuntenasehene should arrange to re-instate the destooled Queen Mother of Kuntenase before the end of March this year and to present her to him after her re-installation' (*Ghana Times*, 27 Jan. 1960).

'*Regional Commissioner Warns Against Subversion in Kokofu.*

Mr R. O. Amoako Atta, Regional Commissioner for Ashanti, warned a large gathering of chiefs, elders and people at Kokofu on his tour of the Amansie district recently against subversive acts. He said he knew all that was going on in the State, and in his capacity as the Regional Commissioner for Ashanti, he would deal with anyone who would in any way worry the Kokofuhene [the Chief]. . . .

'He also asked the people to co-operate with the District Commissioner for the area, Mr Kofi Akowuah, because that would enable them to have regular communication with the government. He asked everybody to give assistance to the Census officials.

'At Bekwai, he visited places like the Destitute Home' (*Ashanti Pioneer*, 15 Feb. 1960).

[23] The interim assemblies set up at independence consisted of the members of parliament in each region.

[24] Para. 8. The CPP view was expressed by the *Ghana Times*: e.g. in the issue of 27 June 1958 which considered that the Regional Assemblies should have 'effective powers of advising the Government in specified fields', and in the government's White Paper No. 4 of 1958: 'The Government considers that it would be wasteful, cumbersome and altogether unsound, administratively, to have in the proposed local government structure another tier in the form of Regional Assemblies where would be exercised powers and functions which have normally been exercised by local Authorities. . . '.

[25] Among them, E. H. T. Karboe, Regional Commissioner for the Eastern Region, E. K. Dadson, Government Chief Whip, the Rev. S. A. Dzirasa, Ministerial Secretary, and (for the opposition) Joe Appiah, A. S. Andoh, J. A. Braimah.

been brought under government control, or where the party commissioners were active, they declared that they would boycott the elections to take place in October. The result was that the CPP gained control of all five assemblies, thus opening the way for revision of the 1957 constitution. The CPP-dominated assemblies and houses of chiefs met briefly in September 1958 and approved a Constitutional (Repeal of Restrictions) Bill which sought to remove the restrictions governing constitutional change in the 1957 Order in Council; the Bill was presented in parliament in October and passed by the required two-thirds majority. A Constitution (Amendment) Act followed in March 1959, and the dismemberment was complete: the regional assemblies (but not the regional houses of chiefs) were abolished, and an unrestricted power vested in a simple majority of the National Assembly. The following April Ashanti was divided by the creation of a new Brong–Ahafo region, and the CPP debt to the Brongs was paid in full.

4. Measures taken against individual members of the opposition, under a succession of repressive acts: e.g. the Deportation Act of August 1957, the Emergency Powers Act of December the same year, and—on 18 July 1958—the Preventive Detention Act under which it was possible to detain a person for five years (without right of appeal to the courts) for conduct prejudicial to the defence and security of the state and its foreign relations. The threat of a Preventive Detention Act, to 'empower the Government to imprison, without trial, any persons suspected of activities prejudicial to the State's security', had been held over the opposition from the middle of December 1957 when Krobo Edusei announced in parliament that he proposed to introduce such a Bill the following February.[26] The immediate causes of its enactment and use, however, were almost certainly twofold. One was the discovery of an opposition plot. Sometime in June 1958 R. R. Amponsah, general secretary of the combined opposition parties, had bought those relatively harmless pieces of military accoutrement—Sam Brown belts, canes, badges of rank, and hackles—which were later to figure at the Granville Sharp inquiry into the alleged plot to assassinate Nkrumah.[27] Hence

[26] Ghana, Parl. Deb., 11 Dec. 1957.
[27] See App. B for a summary of the inquiry. A 'hackle' was the green feather worn by officers of the former West African Frontier Force.

Nkrumah's defence of the Bill on the grounds that it would injure only the wicked.

Firstly, the only persons who need be alarmed about it are those who are either attempting to organise violence, terrorism, or civil war, or who are acting as fifth columnists for some foreign power interested in subversion in Ghana. Secondly, the Bill has been deliberately drafted so that the Government can deal with any attempt to subvert the State by force. Thirdly, the Government is determined to preserve in Ghana both justice and freedom.

At which Amponsah injected: 'We do not believe a word of that.'[28] Secondly, the readiness of the CPP leaders to introduce such measures was almost certainly due to their growing impatience with the ordinary machinery of law. In November 1957 S. G. Antor and Kojo Ayeke were arrested, and charged with complicity in the Alavanyo riots in the former trust territory; they were sentenced to six years' imprisonment, but acquitted on appeal because of certain misdirections to the jury by the trial judge. A year later there was a similar case. Amponsah too was charged with sedition, not because of his activities (whatever they were) in London that summer, but because he had accused the police of aiding and abetting the government in the printing of false ballot papers for the forthcoming regional assembly elections.[29] The charges levelled at the police by Amponsah were shown to be false: but he too was acquitted on the grounds that the prosecution had preferred the wrong charge against him.

It was then that the government began to use the Preventive Detention Act. In November 1958 it detained some thirty-eight members of the opposition, among them Attoh Okine (lecturer at Kumasi College of Technology) and K. Y. Attoh, a leading Accra journalist.[30] Then, in December, Amponsah and M. K. Apaloo were detained. Captain Awhaitey, the Commandant of Giffard Camp in Accra, declared that he had been approached

[28] Ghana, Parl. Deb., 14 July 1958.

[29] It was found during the trial that Amponsah had said at a rally on 18 September 1958: 'The Ghana police, in particular the most senior officers, are conniving and condoning at the very serious crime by the Government of printing extra ballot papers in order to set up a one party dictatorship in the country' (Ghana, *Statement on the Report* (of the Granville Sharp Commission), 1959, p. 32).

[30] They were nearly all Ga leaders. The charge (never proved) was that they had formed a subversive organization known as 'Zenith Seven' whose members had plotted to assassinate Nkrumah.

by two people on 18 December, one of whom was introduced to him as R. R. Amponsah MP, and that they had sought to enlist his aid (and of the n.c.o.s under his command) to overthrow the government. Nkrumah was to be arrested (or possibly assassinated) on his way to the airport where he was to fly on 20 December to India. The story recounted by Awhaitey was hardly credible; yet it was sufficiently alarming for the army, cabinet, and police to take action.[31] It was from this point forward that Nkrumah began to use the Detention Act on a widening scale, and on much more slender evidence of guilt than was produced against Amponsah, first against the opposition and then against a number of the CPP leaders themselves.

In the early years after independence the party increased its power primarily at the expense of the opposition. And if it was not difficult to understand the nervous reaction by the government to plots and intrigues against it, it was also easy to see why the opposition should have felt a growing fear as the CPP asserted its authority. A web of power was spun over the country, its threads reaching out from the central committee of the party into the constituencies through a number of satellite organizations. The United Ghana Farmers' Council was given statutory recognition as the sole representative of the farmers in September 1957, the TUC was recast under an Industrial Relations Act which established a centralized structure of a limited number of national unions under CPP control,[32] and a National Co-operative Council was created at the expense of the genuinely independent Alliance of Co-operatives. The Women's Section of the party, a youth movement, the Builders' Brigade, and a multitude of local organizations were similarly knit into the main body of the CPP. The overall spread of power was described graphically by Nkrumah himself in 1959:

And now I would like to explain the relationship of our Party, the Convention People's Party. It is a nation-wide political party containing the vast majority of our country. It is likened to a mighty tree with many branches. The Convention People's Party constitutes the root and the trunk, and its branches include such organisations as the United Ghana Farmers' Council, the Trades' Union Congress, the

---

[31] Awhaitey's evidence (two versions of it) is given in Appendix B.
[32] An account of the 1958 Industrial Relations Act will be found in the *Econ. Bull.*, Apr. 1959.

Cooperative Movement, the Ex-servicemen, Women's Organisations, the Kwame Nkrumah Kurye Kuw, the National Associations of Socialist Students Organisation, the League of Ghana Patriots and other patriotic organisations which in their various ways are giving support to our Party. . . .[33]

Nor was it enough that the party should be powerful: it also had to be seen to be so. Nkrumah's statue stood outside Parliament House in party guise.[34] His profile appeared both on the new issue of independence stamps and a new coinage, the latter inscribed 'Kwame Nkrumah, civitatis Ghaniensis conditor'. A cluster of imposing buildings began to be constructed in the heart of Accra to house the party headquarters, the Farmers' Council, and the TUC; the party commissioners kept as close a watch over the rank and file members in the constituencies as they did over the electorate, the Regional Commissioners were given cabinet rank, and the general secretary of the TUC and the Farmers' Council were ranked as Ambassadors in dignity and salary, in order to raise the party above government.

I want it to be known categorically and unequivocably [Nkrumah told his audience at the 1959 rally] that since the Party forms the Government the members of its Central Committee, the leading Directorate of the Party, will in future take precedence over non-Central Committee Ministers at all public and civic functions. I want it to be firmly understood that it is the Convention People's Party which makes the Government and not the Government which makes the Convention People's Party and we intend to give public acknowledgement to this fact by raising the prestige of our Party to its proper status in our national structure.[35]

The expense of maintaining this enormous apparatus of party power was obviously heavy; but many sources were tapped. For example, the 1958 Industrial Relations Act imposed a compulsory levy of 2s. a month on all wage- and salary-earners in the country which was deducted on behalf of the TUC by every employer, whether private or government. The regional and district commissioners, though recruited from party members, were paid from party funds. And as the power and prestige of the ruling

[33] Prime Minister's speech to 10th annual Delegates' Conference, *Evening News*, 3 Aug. 1959.
[34] i.e. in a northern smock (*batakali*), and with an uplifted arm in the party's Freedom salute.
[35] 10th Anniversary Address (*Evening News*, 14 June 1959).

party increased, money poured into its coffers from private sources. An appeal fund for the new CPP headquarters in Accra, launched at the sports stadium at the beginning of 1958, set a target of £500,000, and by June 1959 the amount collected was said to have reached £200,000.[36] What sums were raised by less public channels could only be conjectured.

Confronted with this impressive array of power, the opposition did what it could to draw together and formulate its own arguments. On 3 November 1957 a United Party was inaugurated in Bukuom Square, Accra, at a rally presided over by Busia. Its executive was drawn from its component groups—the NLM, NPP, MAP, the Togoland Congress, the Anlo Youth Organization, and the Ga Shifimo Kpee.[37] The chairman for the occasion was Ashie Nikoe (who had performed the same function for the CPP at its first meeting on 12 June 1949); the first speaker was Attoh Quarshie of the Ga movement. The inauguration was well attended, the Ga movement then being at its height, and there was a succession of opposition rallies throughout its areas of support to proclaim the change of name and the renewal of the attempt to resist the CPP. Nevertheless, the leaders found it difficult to match the government party in terms of agents, money, and organization. The pro-United Party section of the trade unions, the Asante Youth Association, the farmers, the market women, and other groups were overshadowed now by the government-backed TUC, the United Ghana Farmers' Council, the CPP Women's Section and allied bodies.[38] The sense of defeat bred by the growth and assertion of CPP power began to be seen in 1958 first in a series of election defeats and then in the defection of a number of northern (opposition) members of parlia-

[36] The appeal was made during the weekend of the announcement of the recognition of eight new paramount chief states in Ashanti. The Bechemhene donated 800 guineas to the Fund, Nkrumah promised 1,000 guineas, W. M. Q. Halm (chairman of the Black Star Shipping Line) £500, Gbedemah and Botsio £500 each, Krobo Edusei and his wife £250. The Muslim Council in Accra presented £500 to Botsio as secretary to the CPP.

[37] The officers were: national chairman—Dr J. Hutton-Mills, retired medical officer; deputy chairman—J. A. Braimah; national treasurer—Mrs Nancy Tsiboe; working committee—Dr Busia, S. D. Dombo, E. O. Obetsibi Lamptey, M. K. Apaloo, Joe Appiah, Attoh Okine, Bankole Awooner Renner, K. Y. Attoh, Ashie Nikoe, Kwesi Lamptey, Dr I. B. Asafu Adjaye, and Dr Danquah.

[38] The most important of the unions which opposed the pro-CPP TUC was the United Africa Company Employees' Union. It was independently run and financed, but because of the position and history of the UAC itself the union was vulnerable to the charge (however undeserved) that it was simply the agent or 'stooge' of overseas, capitalist interests.

ment. In February came the loss of the Kumasi municipal elections; in June the failure of the Ga vote in the Accra elections, while the growing power of the CPP even in the rural areas of Ashanti could be seen in a number of local-government elections:

Council	CPP	UP	Ind.
Konongo-Odumase urban	12	1	1
Mampong local	5	12	0
Nsutaman	7	5	–
Berekum	8	2	0
Kwamang	4	2	0
Bekwai urban	3	3	–
Ejisu	6	3	–
Atwima Mponua	2	20	–
Obuasi	10	0	–
Jamasi	1	10	–
Abease	6	0	–

Source: Ghana Gazettes, Feb. 1958—random selection.

The UP still had its local strongholds, but the drift was towards the CPP under steady pressure in the form of inducements and threats by the newly appointed Regional and District Commissioners. Thus in April 1959, the UP lost a parliamentary by-election in Kumasi itself. In June it lost Sekyere West (Amponsah's constituency in Ashanti); in October Wenchi West, Busia having gone into exile at the end of June. It managed to win Anlo South, but only two of the four municipal by-elections in the Accra central wards.[39] After this succession of disappoint-

---

[39] The 1959 by-elections were a good pointer to the future not only in the results but in the way they were contested. The Kumasi South election was of particular interest because of the intervention of B. E. Dwira, hitherto a leading CPP loyalist in the municipality, as a rebel Independent. A full account of the election will be found in *Political Studies*, June 1960. The result was: CPP 9,032; UP 8,653; Independent 1,339. In the Accra municipal by-elections the UP won a majority of the votes (UP 3,707; CPP 3,292) in the four contested wards. The elections were rowdy, the 'UP Women's League, dressed in shorts and blouses, paraded the streets within the various wards to compete with the Builders' Brigade and to bolster up the morale of the male UP members. . . . The women's section shouted *CPP dzuloi e* (CPP are a gang of thieves). . . . Mr Osei Baidoo, assistant general secretary of the UP, escaped bodily harm when he was attacked by CPP thugs through the timely intervention of the Tokyo Joes who repulsed the attack. . .' (*Ashanti Pioneer*, 1 Oct. 1959). The Wenchi West and Sekyere West elections were more violent, and the police and administrative staff were bewildered by the party commissioners who campaigned energetically against the opposition candidate. Ballot boxes arrived late, polling officials were chased into the bush, and agents

ments (momentarily checked by local successes) its decline was swift. In an attempt to forestall their defeat some of its members began to contemplate other measures of resistance, of a kind later to be examined by the Granville Sharp Commission. But the effect was to bring more quickly upon them the fate they had hoped to prevent, for the CPP redoubled its efforts to suppress the United Party and could plead that the safety of the state demanded it. By 1960 the effect of a combination of threats and blandishments was plain to see: of the 32 opposition members at independence, 3 were being held in detention, 1 was in exile, and 12 had crossed to the government side. A number more were to take the same road under the republic, some to prison, some abroad, others to the sanctuary of the ruling party.

The relative strength and weakness of the CPP and the opposition in 1960 was seen when the government announced that it intended to seek approval for a draft republican constitution and to hold an election for the office of president. The United Party hesitated, then decided once again to challenge the CPP and turned to Nkrumah's early opponent—Danquah. Thus the two men were brought face to face again. Nkrumah was now 50, Danquah 64; Nkrumah had been in office since 1951; Danquah in opposition all his life. When the plebiscite was held, the opposition lost once again and the CPP had its way with the constitution, transforming the 1951–7 structure of government into a presidential system which placed very great power in Nkrumah's hands. Yet, when all due respect had been paid to the power of the nationalist party, the fact remained that in 1960 the opposition was still in existence. The intellectuals and their local followers persisted in their dislike of Nkrumah and the CPP, and rallied as best they could within the limits allowed them by the ruling party. How effective in practice this dislike was, and the extent to which the government was prepared to go to suppress it, became clear when the results were known of the last of the electoral contests to be held during these years.

---

were beaten by rival party supporters. The UP candidate withdrew from the contest at midday. The result was CPP 10,840; UP 5,153. The UP won the by-election in Anlo South in July 1959 which followed the detention of M. K. Apaloo: UP 3,086; CPP 2,531. Three years later the UP member was detained, and the CPP took the seat unopposed.

THE 1960 PLEBISCITE

The chief interest in the plebiscite lay less in the outcome than in the means adopted to secure a result favourable to the CPP's view of the position it held in the country. Not only was the full weight of the government brought to bear on the electorate, but—when the size of the 'yes' vote for Nkrumah and the proposed republican constitution was thought to be insufficient—the party officials (so the evidence suggests) tampered with the actual conduct of polling on the two subsequent days of the plebiscite.[40] Although they were suspicious that this might happen, the United Party leaders decided none the less to oppose both the government's draft constitutional proposals and Nkrumah's candidature as President. Busia had left the country in 1959; others were in prison: but the remaining members of the national executive of the party called upon the electorate to reject the constitution, while sponsoring Danquah as a rival presidential candidate. This somewhat contradictory policy did not appear to puzzle the electorate (the number of votes for Danquah being roughly the same as those against the constitution). The decision by the opposition to take part, however, almost certainly helped the CPP to muster its own supporters.

The appeal made by the CPP to the electorate had very little to do with the proposed constitution. It stressed instead the determination of the party to mount a programme of national welfare within which every section of the community would find its reward:

VOTE NKRUMAH AND 'YES' BECAUSE[41]

In education, the CPP offers free university education: more secondary schools for girls; more technical schools.

If you are a worker, the CPP offers security, better, cheaper houses for renting and eventual ownership; plans for cheaper prices for foodstuffs.

If you are a farmer or co-operator, the CPP offers loans to develop; more feeder roads, better marketing facilities; a canning factory.

If you are a fisherman, the CPP offers a hire purchase scheme for

---

[40] The plebiscite was held on three days—19, 23, & 27 April, the results being announced at the close of each day's poll. Electors were asked to vote twice: once for or against the draft constitutional proposals, and again for Nkrumah or Danquah as president.

[41] *Evening News*, 18 Apr. 1960: reprinted from a party handbill.

motorised vessels; a modern market at Takoradi; a canning factory. For every citizen, the CPP offers a fair share of produce; more and better equipped hospitals; economic security; social security.

If you are a market woman, the CPP offers liberal loans; expanded market space. If you are a chief, the CPP offers you dignity and social security under the constitution including the possibility of an appointment as Ambassador. If you are a businessman, the CPP offers extended guarantee corporation facilities and economic prosperity.

The ability of such a programme to win support was hardly in question, particularly when backed with threats of what might follow opposition to the CPP. A typical example appeared in the *Evening News* on the third day of voting.

> Already our opponents have been virtually pulverised in many constituencies which have voted and whose results have been announced. It must be made still worse for them today. Our opponents and traducers should be reduced to a really abject situation. It is then that they will realise in the fullest measure that the people support Comrade Kwame Nkrumah and utterly reject their crazy policies and wicked methods. As for their threats, in spite of their magnitude, they remain what they are—threats. Whoever ranges himself against the CPP and Comrade Nkrumah will soon discover to his bitter chagrin that he is a mere butterfly on the great wheel of our party machine whose velocity is terrific.[42]

Evidence not only of the intention, but of the ability, of the CPP to enforce its authority lay all about the electorate—in the recently acquired fleet of white Fiat cars bought for its officers by the TUC, in the lorries which carried groups of uniformed Builders' Brigaders across the constituencies, in the procession of large cars which accompanied the District Commissioners and CPP members of parliament from polling booth to polling booth, in the activities of the constituency agents who urged electors to 'vote red' for the letters YES and for Nkrumah, and the flood of propaganda leaflets and posters which appeared during the weeks before the first day's polling. Every effort was made to impress upon the electorate that the CPP was, in fact, as it was intended to be in theory: 'a powerful force, more powerful . . . than anything that has yet appeared in the history of Ghana . . . more

[42] *Evening News*, 27 Apr. 1960.

than a political party . . . the living embodiment of the whole glory of our lives'.[43]

At first sight, the United Party had very little to offer against this massive onslaught. It could hardly hope to compete in terms of promises of economic welfare,[44] and had nothing like the resources of money or party agents commanded by its rival. Instead, it fell back on the two lines of attack it had formerly used. It repeated the old intelligentsia argument that the CPP was a dangerous, dictatorial party which intended to suppress still further the constitutional rights of the people; and it did what it could to turn local issues to its advantage. Joe Appiah, for example, called upon the electorate to vote for Danquah in order 'to re-dedicate the nation to a new sense of true liberty making justice and the rule of law the cornerstone of such a re-dedication'.[45] The executive issued a number of pamphlets opposing the draft constitutional proposals on the grounds that they 'will bring to an end the responsibility of Parliament to the people', that 'Article 2 of the Draft betrays the hard won sovereignty of Ghana',[46] that 'the President's absolute power without check (1) to grant loans, (2) to appoint judges, (3) to control the Civil Service and the Armed Forces' would lead to dictatorship, and 'because the economic ideology of the Draft Constitution savours of communism'.[47] Outlets for such criticism in the opposition were now beginning to narrow. For example, permission to reply over the Ghana broadcasting network to Nkrumah's recommendation of the draft constitutional proposals was refused to Danquah. Local chiefs and district commissioners in the south were hostile to the point of refusing Danquah's travelling propaganda van entry into a number of districts. But the *Ashanti Pioneer* was still unrestricted,[48] and it was still possible to obtain police permits to hold rallies. The UP also drew support from a

[43] Report of Nkrumah's speech at the opening of the party's new headquarters in Accra, *The Times*, 14 Apr. 1960.
[44] Local agents of the UP however still demanded £5 for a load of cocoa.
[45] *Daily Graphic*, 19 Apr. 1960.
[46] Art. 2 of the Draft (and final) constitution: 'In the confident expectation of our early surrender of sovereignty to a union of African states and territories, the people now confer on Parliament the power to provide for the surrender of the whole or any part of the sovereignty of Ghana'.
[47] Quotations taken from pamphlets issued at the time by members of the UP.
[48] In February 1961 the *Ashanti Pioneer* was placed under the supervision of a government-appointed censor; in October 1962 the government announced that it proposed to take over the paper and the Abura printing works.

familiar array of local discontents—among the Ewes in Trans-
Volta, among the Ga in Accra, among the trade unionists who
disliked the 1958 Industrial Relations Act, among rival factions
in the dispute over the succession to the Royal Dagomba Skin in
Yendi, among cocoa farmers who were disgruntled at the lower
price (60s. a load) fixed by the Marketing Board (nominally with
the support of the farmers through the Ghana Farmers' Council), among Danquah's local supporters in Akim Abuakwa, and
those who were still loyal to the thirteen UP members of parliament. It had sufficient support to enable Danquah to tour a number of constituencies in every region, and sufficient protection
from the police in the large towns to hold a number of rallies
although not everywhere the UP organizers wished. The stubborn opposition to CPP propaganda in many local areas brought
the only serious incident of the three days' voting when a quarrel
between irate villagers and a Builders' Brigade team in Ashanti
on the eve of the first day's polling led to the shooting of two
Brigaders.

The results of the plebiscite were declared at the end of each
day's polling. The first to be announced were those for Accra,
where two tendencies were noticed immediately. The first was
that the poll was very low:

Voters in the 3 Accra constituencies	25,946
Registered electorate	57,208
Poll 45 per cent.	

The percentage was surprising in view of the efforts made by the
leaders during rallies held by each party, and the known hostility
towards the government among a large section of the Ga community, many of whose leaders had been placed in preventive
detention. Nor were there any restrictions on the electorate of a
kind which might have prevented a high vote. Polling was
orderly throughout the municipality thanks to a number of mobile police squads and the stationing of a police constable at every
polling station. The parties' agents were allowed to carry out
their tasks of checking and scrutinizing electors; and the crowds
which gathered to watch the day's events, although boisterous
and poised always on the edge of violence, were held in restraint
by the police except for an occasional scuffle. Yet less than half
the electorate voted. The commonest (and most probable) ex-

planation of the low poll was indifference among the general
public to the question of a republic, plus a sense of disbelief
among some UP supporters that the CPP would allow the vote to
go against them, and a corresponding belief among CPP members that since the issue was not in doubt there was no paramount
need to vote.

The other point of interest was the substantial UP minority
vote. Those who had thought that the UP might win on the Ga
vote in the city underestimated the extent to which the Ga community was divided between those who accepted the need to co-
operate with the government, and those who refused to do so;
they underestimated, too, the large number of southern (non-
Ga) compounds in the municipality. But those who expected an
easy win for the CPP, in the light of its massive appeal as a government party, also discounted too readily the antipathy not only of
many of the Ga community but of the considerable numbers of
civil servants and 'intellectuals' in Accra who had little liking
for Nkrumah, the CPP, or the proposed presidential system. The
result was:

	Nkrumah		*The Constitution*
For	16,804	For	16,739
	Danquah		*The Constitution*
For	9,035	Against	9,207

Danquah had succeeded in winning 35 per cent of the vote.
Nkrumah had won comfortably, with 65 per cent of the vote in a
45 per cent poll of the registered electorate. The numbers of
electors in Accra (after re-registration in 1957) had fallen well
below the 1956 figure—from 86,603 to 57,208. Thus the number
who were prepared to vote for Nkrumah and the republican constitution in Accra was extremely small: 16,804 in a city of well
over 200,000 and (approximately) 100,000 adults. There had
been, it was clear, a massive abstention, and a surprisingly high
opposition vote.

Thanks to the administration and the police the vote in Accra
was free from interference in the actual manner of polling. The
party agents watched each other closely, like the small African
hawks which circle the area where the hunter is closing on his
quarry; and the police watched the agents and the polling
queues. However, the two days' polling which followed—in

Ashanti and the Volta region on 23 April, and the rest of the country (Brong Ahafo, the south, and the rest of the north) on 27 April—showed a very different pattern. The vote swung up— to over 80 per cent in a number of constituencies, and over 90 in three of the 104. The UP percentage dropped to a negligible figure in a number of constituencies where there were good grounds for supposing that it still had a substantial minority support. Consider, for example, the Ashanti rural constituency Atwima Nwabiagyia—the scene of the NLM by-election in 1955 and B. F. Kusi's triumph in 1956. In the third general election, the Atwima Nwabiagyia vote had been

	Voters	*Electors*	
NLM	8,334	13,937	70 per cent poll
CPP	1,390		

The plebiscite figures were:

	Electors	*Pro-CPP*	*Pro-UP*	
Constitutional proposals	25,461	22,738	155	90 per cent poll
Presidential election	„	22,676	137	

The plebiscite results were hard to accept as valid. B. F. Kusi, the United Party member, campaigned energetically in the constituency where he was permitted to do so. And although it was possible to see that the United Party had lost support in an area where many of the chiefs had been replaced by pro-CPP rivals, and where the district commissioner was particularly active, it was reasonable also to suppose that the UP still had at least a fair minority following. The area consisted largely of cocoa farmers, it had been a famous opposition stronghold, and in the local government elections the previous October (1959) the UP candidates had been given a substantial vote.[49] Yet—when the votes were counted in 1960, it was found that Danquah, using the NLM/UP cocoa tree symbol, had received only 137. It was difficult to believe.

Other constituencies showed similar discrepancies.[50] And it

[49] e.g. for the large Kumasi West Local Council (covering an area larger than the Atwima Nwabiagyia opposition constituency): CPP 17,129; UP 7,853. There was considerable doubt about the size of the CPP vote here too. The Atwima constituency in 1959 had large areas where the UP was so strongly supported, despite the activities of the district commissioners, that a pro-UP vote could still be recorded until the full weight of government power was brought to bear in the plebiscite.

[50] The 90 per cent and over 80 per cent poll in some constituencies was, in itself,

was at least possible to surmise that the combination of a low poll and a substantial opposition vote in Accra on the first day of the plebiscite had led a number of regional and district commissioners (with or without the authority of the central committee) to ensure not only that the right people voted but that the right number of ballot papers were placed in the boxes.[51] How widespread malpractices of this kind were it was difficult to say, but it was possible to arrive at three tentative conclusions. (1) Voting in the municipalities was conducted fairly (setting aside the propaganda advantages of the ruling party) because the police were vigilant and a number of foreign observers present. The parties' agents were allowed to do their work unmolested. The voting figures were reasonably accurate therefore. The poll was low, and the balance of opposition to Nkrumah and the draft constitution in the order of 30 to 70 per cent.[52] (2) In many southern Fanti constituencies the CPP was so obviously predominant (as in 1956) that the local party officials had little cause to interfere except to brush aside a number of scattered groups of UP supporters. The plebiscite thus became a 'race with one horse', and again polling was light. (3) Where it was difficult not to express doubts of the validity of the results was in the disputed rural constituencies in Ashanti, Trans-Volta, and Akim Abuakwa, and in the Brong Ahafo constituencies where the CPP chiefs and party commissioners were determined to prove their gratitude to the government which had given them a region. The poll went up in Ashanti, Trans-Volta, and Akim Abuakwa—as might be expected in view of the conflict between the parties: but—con-

---

suspicious: the only precedent in Ghana was in Akim Abuakwa Central in 1956 where the election was bitterly fought between the CPP and the NLM. The poll was 91 per cent—but of a much lower registration figure. High votes were obtained in Nigeria in the federal elections of 1959, and in Malaya in 1955 but not in Ghana in three general elections and numerous by-elections before 1960. Neither a proxy nor a postal vote was available; and the constant ebb and flow of the population could be observed at any lorry park or main road on any day in the month.

[51] Once the opposition polling agents were chased away, and the polling staff brought under the orders of the regional commissioner, there was no limit to the ability of the CPP officials to interfere. There were many stories of votes being found in the ballot boxes in thick wads—where the local party agent was flustered (or indifferent), and neglected even to make it look as if votes had been cast in the orthodox way.

[52] Seven municipal constituencies:

For Nkrumah	.. ..	55,167
For Danquah	.. ..	22,366
For the constitution	..	54,818
Against the constitution	..	23,023

trary to previous experience—the opposition vote dropped, and dropped far below what most observers expected. On the other hand the poll was also abnormally high in Brong Ahafo despite the virtual elimination of any open opposition to the CPP. And in both instances the explanation seemed clear—that the vote was artificially increased by over-zealous agents of the ruling party.

The overall results (taken at face value) showed that an overwhelming number of constituencies had voted for Nkrumah and the draft constitution: 102 of the 104.[53] Anlo South persisted in its opposition to the CPP, defying every form of pressure brought by the CPP; Ho West (the Ewe stronghold) voted *for* the constitution, and for Danquah.[54] The overall poll was only 54 per cent, the suspiciously high vote in a number of rural areas being matched by the low poll in the municipalities, the two southern regions, and many of the northern constituencies:

Registered electors	2,098,651
Voters (constitutional issue)	1,140,165
Voters (presidential candidates)	1,140,699

The overall vote showed a nearly 90 per cent vote for Nkrumah and the draft constitution:

	Votes	Per cent
For the constitution	1,008,740	88·5
Against the constitution	131,425	11·5
For Nkrumah	1,016,076	89·1
Against Nkrumah	124,623	10·9

In view of the power of the CPP, and the readiness of the leaders to use state authority to back their appeal, the results were hardly surprising. The issues at stake had not been whether the CPP would find support for its constitution, or whether Nkrumah would be elected President, but how successful the party would be in getting its supporters to the polls. And it was in this sense—in the swelling of the size of the poll beyond what was plausible in a number of constituencies that the CPP almost cer-

[53] Figures taken from *Ghana Today*, May 1962. The regional percentage poll was: Northern Region 43 per cent, Western Region 50 per cent, Eastern Region 50 per cent, Volta Region 50 per cent, Ashanti 70 per cent, Brong Ahafo 80 per cent. Municipalities 49 per cent.

[54] The division between the parties in both constituencies was narrow:

	For the constitution	Against	For Nkrumah	For Danquah
Anlo South	3,450	3,577	3,470	3,563
Ho West	5,816	5,660	5,673	5,794

tainly manipulated the voting. Thus deceit was added to force where both were probably unnecessary. In view of its power and prestige as a governing party the CPP would no doubt have succeeded in persuading the electorate by more gentle methods to endorse the leaders' desire for a republic. But the poll was likely then to have been low, and the difference in votes between the two candidates less extreme—a result, in effect, out of keeping with the picture of the CPP drawn by Nkrumah at the tenth anniversary celebrations.

THE POLITICS OF THE REPUBLIC

It is impossible to do more than sketch the general direction of politics after Nkrumah assumed office on 1 July 1960. The régime appeared triumphant. The opposition was reduced to no more than a token force, the CPP dominated the unicameral assembly, and Nkrumah was President with very great executive authority.[55] A 'positive neutralist' policy was pursued with vigour abroad, and pan-African theories continued to flourish. Nevertheless, the first years of the republic were as disturbed as those of the previous decade; and by 1964 Nkrumah's policy was in ruins. The CPP was in disarray, the state itself damaged by attacks on the judiciary, police, the civil service, and the universities. The economy was under restraint. Ghana was isolated within the pan-African movement; and the government was under attack not merely in the West but in Africa itself for its suppression of civil liberties. The following section attempts to explain why this was so.

Pan-African Myths

It is necessary to go back a long way to trace the origins of Nkrumah's passionate interest in African unity. It was rooted in his Negro college days and the works of Marcus Garvey; it could be seen in his activities in the West African secretariat in London and the 1945 Manchester conference. Attempts to kindle this interest in the Gold Coast in 1954 had had to be abandoned following the rise of the NLM, but they were revived after independence by Nkrumah and Padmore whom he appointed as his Adviser on African Affairs (until Padmore's death in 1959). The

---

[55] See Pt III of the constitution. For full text see App. C and also L. Rubin and P. Murray, *The Constitution and Government of Ghana* (1961); S. A. R. Bennion, *The Constitutional Law of Ghana* (1962).

first major step forward was taken in 1958, when the first Conference of Independent African States was held in Accra. Eight states were represented—Ethiopia, Sudan, the UAR, Libya, Tunisia, Morocco, Liberia, and Ghana—and a joint declaration was issued whereby the leaders pledged themselves to 'assert an African Personality' in the world. In December, the first All-African People's Conference assembled in Accra, bringing together nationalist leaders from colonial territories as well as the independent states. The resolutions adopted included the proposal to establish a permanent secretariat in Ghana to 'accelerate the liberation of Africa from imperialism and colonialism' and 'the emergence of a United States of Africa'. In this way the early conferences held by DuBois found a new life and—it would seem —a greater reality. Meanwhile, other plans were formulated. On 23 November 1958 Nkrumah and Sekou Touré, President of the newly independent Republic of Guinea, announced the formation of a Ghana–Guinea Union. Membership, as defined on 1 May 1959, was to be open to 'all independent African States or Federations adhering to the principles on which the Union is based'. Each country was to 'preserve its own individuality and structure' until both were able to 'decide in common what portion of sovereignty shall be surrendered'. Resident ministers were to be exchanged, and an economic relationship explored—stimulated by the promise of a grant of £10 million by Ghana to its poorer partner. At the end of 1960 the union was joined by the Mali Republic after the latter's break with Senegal, and on 1 July the following year the three republics issued a Charter setting out fourteen articles of a 'Union of African States' as the 'nucleus of the United States of Africa'. Nkrumah's election as President and the opening months of the Republic thus coincided with a great stirring of African hopes, and Ghana was in the forefront of a new pan-Africanism firmly placed in Africa itself.

In the latter half of 1960, however, the anti-colonial tide began to run faster and faster, beyond the control of any single leader. Nkrumah was swept along with it, but he was a great deal less successful now than in the early years of independence. Two events in particular saw him unable to retain the initiative. First, there was the dramatic volte face in French and Belgian policy whereby the whole of French-speaking Africa (except French

Somaliland) became independent by the end of 1960. Ghana acquired independent neighbours—and rivals. The ex-French colonies (Guinea and Mali excepted) held together, first in the 'Brazzaville group' and then in the Union Africaine et Malgache. In addition, they retained their links with France, in terms of aid, currency, and trade, and with Europe by their attachment as associated states of the Common Market. Here was a new group of African states under leaders like Senghor and Houphouët-Boigny who were very unlike Nkrumah, and who were either hostile or indifferent to his warnings of the dangers of too close a relationship with France. Secondly, there was the plight of the Congo. Nominally an independent African state, it was harassed by rival provincial and tribal parties which, in Katanga, were encouraged by outside interests. To Nkrumah, the Congo was evidence writ large of those neo-colonialist forces which he now began to see at work throughout the African continent. Ghana had a direct interest in the huge republic where its troops were among the first to arrive, and where Lumumba and Gizenga were looking to Accra for help. Moreover Lumumba's failing struggle in the latter half of 1960 was interpreted by Nkrumah as a re-enactment on a wider scale of the earlier conflict between himself and the NLM–NPP alliance.[56] Lumumba's murder on 17 January 1961[57] and the death of Hammarskjöld in September fed in him a bitter emotion, and he saw in the death of the Secretary-General of the United Nations 'a terrible example of the iniquity of colonialism which will go to any lengths to achieve its criminal aims'.[58]

It is true that the caution which had held him back from uncertain adventures in the past was still not wholly missing. Among the radicals of the 'Casablanca group' of states which met in January 1961 to discuss the Congo, and to draw up an 'African Charter', he appeared as almost a moderate.[59] And in March he

[56] q.v. Nkrumah's comments on the 'dangers of federalism': 'The people of Ghana decisively rejected a federal form of constitution at the General Election in 1956 and the reasons why they did so were equally applicable to other African states. . . . The Congo indeed provides a striking example of how federation can be used as a cloak to conceal new colonialism' (Presidential Address to parliament, Ghana, Parl. Deb., 21 Apr. 1961). At this time Nkrumah was preparing to transfer the Ghana diplomatic mission from Léopoldville to Stanleyville and Gizenga's 'legal government of the Congo'.
[57] Announced on 13 Feb. 1961.   [58] *Ghana Today*, 27 Sept. 1961.
[59] e.g. over the question of withdrawing troops from the U.N. command in the Congo.

acted with remarkable restraint (it would seem) over the question of South Africa's withdrawal from membership of the Commonwealth.[60] Throughout 1961 and 1962, however, he found himself opposed by the majority of the African leaders. Rival groups of states appeared, not only among the French-speaking countries, but among those which preferred a more tentative approach to African unity than the absolutist view taken by Nkrumah. In January 1962 twenty states met at Lagos in an effort to heal the breach between the rival 'Casablanca', 'Monrovia', and 'Brazzaville' groups.[61] Ghana and the other Casablanca powers refused to attend: but they were now in a minority. Moreover, the Ghana–Guinea–Mali union was all but dead, and the two French-speaking republics began to move towards a closer association with France and the Union Africaine et Malgache. A year later there were new moves. Algeria was now independent, the French-speaking states were beyond all reasonable doubt truly independent, and a conference at Addis Ababa in May 1963 brought all thirty-two African states together. Nkrumah hastened to avail himself of the opportunity. He had written his *Autobiography* to mark the occasion of independence; *I Speak of Freedom* had saluted the dawn of the new republic; now Nkrumah's third book appeared: *Africa Must Unite*.[62] It was an inelegant mixture of rambling argument and unrelated comment on Ghanaian politics, but remarkable for its obsession both with 'neo-colonialism'—the 'sinister chain of interests which unites events in the Congo and Angola to East and West Africa'—and its *simpliste* belief in the possibility of 'a major political union of Africa'.[63] Both these themes were expanded at the Conference in his speech to the delegates. Nkrumah declared that 'we have already reached a stage where we must unite or sink into that condition which has made Latin America the unwilling and distressed prey of imperialism'.[64] There was among the western powers 'a carefully calculated pattern working towards a single end: the continual enslavement

[60] See N. Mansergh, ed., *Documents and Speeches on Commonwealth Affairs, 1952–62* (1963), p. 399.

[61] 'Monrovia'—the Conference of Independent African States in Liberia, May 1961, minus the Casablanca powers; 'Brazzaville'—the group of French-speaking states formed in 1960–1 minus Guinea and Mali.

[62] London, 1963.   [63] Ibid. p. 191.

[64] 'United We Stand', *Address at the Conference of African Heads of State and Government in Addis Ababa on May 24, 1963*.

of our still dependent brothers and an onslaught upon the independence of our sovereign African states'. Africa—'the milch cow of the Western world'—must end its dependence. There should be 'a formal declaration that all the independent African states here and now agree to the establishment of a Union of African states' and to the working out of 'a machinery for the Union Government of Africa'. Such a government, said Nkrumah, might be located at Bangui or Léopoldville. Meanwhile, there should be plans for an African common market, currency, monetary zone, a central bank, a common foreign policy, citizenship, and a joint system of defence. Here was vision indeed! But Nkrumah was in a minority of one. The Addis Ababa states drew up a modest 'Charter of the Organization of African States' which stressed the sovereignty of the individual members, and reached agreement on the principle of non-interference in the territorial integrity of the existing states. Indeed, in August 1963, when the Conference took the practical step of establishing in Dar-es-Salaam a Liberation Committee of representatives of nine African states to assist nationalist groups in colonial and South Africa, Ghana was excluded. The first of the pan-Africanists was ignored.

Nor did Ghana fare better in its relations with its neighbours. Togo became independent on 27 April 1960 and the two governments quickly began to quarrel. Nkrumah and Olympio accused each, with justification on both sides, of subversion. The frontier was more often than not closed, trade reduced to smuggling, and political refugees from Ghana gathered in Lomé as if to compensate for those who fled, opposed to Olympio's rule, from Togo to Accra. The assassination of Olympio in January 1963 eased the relationship between the two countries for a time, although the sober-minded Grunitzky (Olympio's successor) was hardly likely to feel much sympathy with Nkrumah's interpretation of pan-African ties. Early in 1964, however, the frontier was again closed. There was a latent hostility also between Nkrumah and Houphouët Boigny, not least because of Nkrumah's encouragement of the Sanwi rebel leaders in the south-east of the Ivory Coast.[65] To the north, the government of Upper Volta found it convenient to balance the Ivory Coast against Ghana, and President Yameogo agreed in July 1961 to abolish customs duties be-

[65] See the map in the *Autobiography*, p. 263.

tween the two states. It was a useful agreement, but hardly a significant step towards the achievement of the United Africa that
Nkrumah urged so continually on his colleagues.

The effect of Nkrumah's isolation within the movement he had
virtually re-created in 1958 had to be taken into account when
assessing the course of events within Ghana itself. It must have
exaggerated that aspect of Nkrumah's character which was
quick to see any criticism of himself as motivated by sinister forces
seeking to overthrow the true revolutionary. In his student days
and in London he had fed on Marxist, anti-imperialist dogmas
which had been laid aside in the practical struggle for self-
government: they must hardly have seemed relevant during
the partnership established between himself and Arden-Clarke.
They were now revived, however, to explain not only the African
scene in which Ghana found itself under attack by a number
of African governments, but the increasingly troubled state of
affairs within the country itself.

Economic Difficulties

In 1961 there was a serious check to the economy. At a time
when the government was heavily committed on its capital expenditure the cocoa price began to fall, and it was obliged to
draw heavily on its reserves.[66] As part of the measures taken, a
harsh budget was introduced in mid-July. Government expenditure was left untouched but increased duties were levied on a
wide range of consumer goods in an attempt to raise additional
revenue. A new system of purchase tax was also adopted, and a
compulsory savings scheme imposed whereby a levy of 5 per cent
was deducted from all salaried and wage incomes over £120 a
year. Prices rose sharply, and the net income of farmers and
wage-earners alike fell. The budget bore heavily in particular on
the skilled and semi-skilled worker, and a major strike took place
in September among the railway and harbour workers in
Sekondi-Takoradi. It was the first large-scale stoppage since the
miners' strike of 1955–6 and was based on genuine grievances.
But because such action was now illegal under the 1958 Industrial
Relations Act, a state of emergency was declared in the town.
Violence broke out between the strikers and police as party
leaders travelled back and forth from Accra to Sekondi, some to

---

[66] The figures are given above, p. 364.

appeal, others to admonish. Those on strike held out for two to three weeks, but were gradually forced back to work as funds ran out. Nkrumah was on his way back to Ghana from a visit to Eastern Europe, the Soviet Union, Peking, and (on 2 September) the Conference of Non-Aligned Nations at Belgrade when the first stoppages occurred. He remained in Accra on his return, and issued a stern warning. The men should return to work or bear the consequences. He saw in the strike sinister forces at work. The strikers had asked 'that our Republican Constitution should be abolished and that we should go back to the system of having a Governor General. . . . This clearly exposes the purposes of this strike and those behind the strikers.' There was no need for such action, Nkrumah continued, since

if the railway workers disagreed with the policies of their constitionally-elected Government, they had every right to make their views known . . . through their Members of Parliament . . . or the TUC. . . . But what is the nature of these supposed grievances which have prompted these workers to take this illegal and disgraceful action? They object to the compulsory savings scheme, to the monthly deduction of income tax and to the Government's taxation policy as a whole, in fact to the whole budget.[67]

He was not content with warnings. After the men had returned to work, their leaders and a number of market women who had helped the strikers were arrested. On 3 October Danquah, Joe Appiah, S. G. Antor, Victor Owusu, and—a new omen— P. K. K. Quaidoo, a former CPP Minister of Trade, were also detained together with some fifty members of the United Party opposition.

The Sekondi strike was not perhaps a major threat to the régime, but it was one that might well become so. It is true that the compulsory savings scheme was abolished two years later in the 1963 budget; but the high import duties on petrol and consumer goods were retained and increased in both 1962 and 1963. It was difficult, indeed, to believe that the cocoa farmers were content with their 54s. a load, or that the 'common man' was eager to respond to the argument that he should accept higher prices and a shortage of consumer goods in the interests of the Volta River

[67] *Ghana Today*, 27 Sept. 1961.

Scheme or the Kwame Nkrumah steel works at Tema. Ministers, regional and district commissioners, party officials, and the leading figures in the party's auxiliary organizations, still lived a life of obvious plenty: the sacrifices fell on those least able to protest about them. Moreover, there was a very important difference between the ability of the CPP before 1960 to meet such criticisms and its position some three or four years later. At the time of the plebiscite, the party was still an organized force under leaders who continued to work together under Nkrumah. It could even be said—the point was made at the close of the section of the plebiscite—that the party was still a popular force (though far less so than Nkrumah pretended). From 1961 onwards, however, the CPP leaders began to quarrel violently among themselves and with Nkrumah.

The Break in Party Unity

There had been quarrels within the party before at rank and file level: the NLM had been formed out of dissident party members. There had also been the minor inner party revolt of 1951–2. But Nkrumah, Gbedemah, Kojo Botsio, Krobo Edusei, and a majority of the founders of the CPP had stayed loyally together. Now the party was torn apart. Part of the explanation was a very simple one: the disappearance of the United Party opposition. Hitherto, the CPP had always had to face an external, open opposition, whether it was the colonial administration in 1949, the NLM–NPP alliance in 1954, or the UP after 1957. After 1960 it turned in on itself. Thus the belief that the problems of the previous decade could be conjured out of existence by bringing them within a single party proved a dangerous illusion. It was not the only explanation, however. The break in party unity was also the result of Nkrumah's own actions and neglect. As already recounted, he was absorbed in pan-African schemes and the pursuit of non-alignment during the greater part of 1960 and 1961. Such time as he gave to the party was spent in an equally fruitless search for a source of radicalism among his followers which would match his own belief in the need for a 'full-scale intellectual, educational and organisational attack on all aspects of colonialism, neo-colonialism and imperialism'.[68] The effect was to increase the quarrels among the leaders. The extent to

[68] See below, p. 409.

which the CPP had begun to divide into warring sections—the assembly members, the bureaucracy, the trade unions, the Farmers' Council, the Co-operative Movement—was revealed by Nkrumah himself on his return from the Commonwealth Prime Ministers' Meeting early in 1961. On 8 April he delivered a warning 'Dawn Broadcast to the Nation':

While I was away certain matters arose concerning the Trades' Union Congress, the National Assembly, the Cooperative Movement and the United Ghana Farmers' Council. These matters created misunderstanding... Some Parliamentarians criticised the Trades Union Congress and the other wing organisations of the Convention People's Party. The officials of these organisations objected to the criticism and made counter-criticisms against certain Parliamentarians and this started a vicious circle of criminations and recriminations. ...

Nkrumah began his criticisms with the 'parliamentarians' and their attempt to become a 'new ruling class of self-seekers and careerists':

Any Party Member of Parliament who wishes to be a businessman can do so, but he should give up his seat in Parliament. ... This tendency [to pursue private interests] is working to alienate the support of the masses and to bring the National Assembly into isolation. Members of Parliament must . . . on no account . . . regard constituency representation as belonging to them in their own right. In other words, constituencies are not the property of Members of Parliament. It is the Party which sends them there. ...

He then turned to the ancillary organizations:

This is not the time for unbridled militant trade unionism in our country. ... At this stage I wish to take the opportunity to refer to an internal matter of the Trades Union Congress. It has come to my notice that dues of 4s. per month are being paid by some unions, whereas others pay 2s. ... I have therefore instructed . . . that Union dues shall remain at 2s. per month.

Coming to the integral organisations of the Party I consider it essential to emphasise once more that the Trades Union Congress, the United Ghana Farmers' Council, the National Cooperative Council and the National Council of Ghana Women are integral parts of the Convention People's Party, and in order to correct certain existing anomalies the Central Committee has decided that separate membership cards of the integral organisations shall be abolished. In all Regional Headquarters, provision will be made for the Central Party and these integral organisations to be housed in the same building. . . . Also the separate flags used by these organisations will be abolished and replaced by the flag of the Convention People's Party. . . .

It was also possible to see from the Dawn Broadcast and other speeches why it was that the Sekondi-Takoradi strikers were so incensed. The CPP was now a very profitable source of wealth for those who held power within it. It had always been corrupt: but it had also fought for self-government. Now however that the political kingdom was complete, the opportunities for private gain were very great:

I come now to a question of the highest importance and one which affects our good name. I have received several reports that some of our Party officers are demanding sums of money from would-be members before they admit them into the local branch. . . . The Central Committee view this matter very seriously and are taking steps to check it.[69]

I have stated over and over again, that members of the Convention People's Party must not use their party membership or official position for personal gain or for the amassing of wealth. . . . In other words, no Minister, Ministerial Secretary or Party Member of Parliament should own a business or be involved in anyone else's business. . . . Some Party members in Parliament . . . are tending . . . to become a social group of self-seekers and careerists. . . .[70]

A great deal of rumour-mongering goes on. . . Abine stated that Ekua said that Esi uses her relations with Kweku to get contract through the District Commissioner with the support of the Regional Commissioner and the blessing of a Minister in Accra. . . .[71]

One of the most degrading aspects of Party conduct is the tendency on the part of some Comrades to go round using the names of persons in prominent positions to collect money for themselves. Equally degrading is the tendency on the part of some persons in prominent positions to create agents for collecting money.[72]

The limits that Nkrumah tried to impose on his followers were in themselves a measure of the wealth available to them. It was

[69] 10th Anniversary Address (*Evening News*, 14 June 1959).
[70] Dawn Broadcast, 8 Apr. 1961.   [71] Ibid.   [72] Ibid.

ruled from the President's office that party members should not own:

(a) more than two houses of a combined value of £20,000;

(b) more than two motor cars;

(c) plots of land (other than those covered by (a) above) with the present total value greater than £500.[73]

A similar generosity was extended to the party leaders in the regions. The chairmen of the municipal and city councils, for example, were paid £1,800 plus an entertainment allowance of £250 a year and free accommodation.[74]

These were the circumstances in which Nkrumah began his search for new leaders. The 'old guard' were easy victims of any general accusation of corruption that Nkrumah, through the *Evening News*, might bring against them, and he began a search for followers who shared his own taste for dialectic—or who were at least willing and able to learn the language of 'Nkrumaism'. The first signs of this shift away from the established leaders could be detected in the tenth anniversary speech. 'Comrades', Nkrumah told his audience, 'it seems to me that maybe from complacency or exhaustion, some of our older party members seem to have lost the early spirit of zeal and self-sacrifice which once imbued our Party.' What was required was a new philosophy. 'We, as an organised Party, need a central ideology to inspire us in our actions. And unless we are so armed and inspired we shall find ourselves rudderless. From the lowest member to the highest we must arm ourselves ideologically.'[75] In January 1960 Nkrumah replaced Kojo Botsio as secretary of the central committee of which he was already chairman. The plebiscite and the inauguration of the republic intervened. The Congo erupted into chaos. Then in May 1961, following the Dawn Broadcast, Nkrumah made two further moves. He became general secretary of the party as a whole, of which he was already Life Chairman, and he moved Gbedemah from the Ministry of Health. It was the first open split between Nkrumah and the ablest of his lieutenants. More drastic steps followed. Beginning on 28 September—immediately after the Sekondi strike had been suppressed—the party was purged of a number of its leading figures on the

[73] *Ghana Today*, 11 Oct. 1961.
[74] Address to Kumasi City Council, 24 Mar. 1962.
[75] *Evening News*, 14 June 1959.

grounds that they had abused their position by amassing too great a fortune even by party standards. Gbedemah, Botsio, S. Y. Yeboah (Commissioner for the Brong Ahafo Region), E. K. Dadson and W. A. Wiafe (ministerial secretaries), and Ayeh Kumi (Executive Secretary of the Development Secretariat) were asked to resign. Others were asked to surrender property in excess of the limits laid down earlier in the year. Among them were Krobo Edusei (Minister of Communications and Transport), E. K. Bensah (Minister of Works), A. E. Inkumsah (Minister of the Interior), C. de Graft Dickson (Minister of Defence), E. H. T. Karboe (Commissioner for the Eastern Region), and J. E. Hagan (Commissioner for the Central Region). A little later Krobo Edusei was asked to resign. It was a direct attack on a large section of the party's leaders.

Gbedemah protested his innocence in the National Assembly, and spoke vehemently against the use of the Detention Act. The occasion of the debate was the second reading of the Criminal Code (Amendment) Bill to establish a Special Criminal Division of the High Court from which there would be no appeal, introduced by Kwaku Boateng (Minister of the Interior) as containing 'the seed of the true welfare of the people of Ghana'. For who could believe 'that Kwame Nkrumah who is so constitutional in all his deeds, so wise and kind as he always has been . . . could create a system of Court offensive to our motto: Freedom and Justice?' To which Gbedemah replied:

In 1958, this House in order to ensure that the hard won freedom of the people of this country should be safeguarded, in all sincerity, passed the Preventive Detention Act so that those who would by revolt and not through the ballot box overthrow the Government might be prevented from doing so. [*Interruption.*]—I say this Bill was passed in all sincerity. What do we find in the application of the provisions of that Act? How many people are languishing in jail today? [*Uproar.*]—How many people are languishing in jail today detained under this Act?

If we are to learn from experience, this is a Bill which when passed into law would soon show that the liberty of the subject is extinguished for ever. To-day, there are many people whose hearts are filled with fear—fear even to express their convictions. When we pass this Bill and it goes on the Statute Book, the low flickering flames of freedom will be for ever extinguished. We may be pulled out of bed to face the firing squad after a summary trial and conviction. There is no appeal and hon. Members of the Parliament of Ghana are being asked to pass this Bill into law. To-day, we may think that all is well, it is not my turn, it is my brother's turn, but your turn will come sooner than later. [*Hear, hear.*][76]

Immediately Gbedemah finished speaking he left the country before action could be taken against him. Others, however, were less fortunate, for it was now that Danquah and his colleagues were detained, allegedly for their participation in the Sekondi strike.

By the end of 1961, therefore, the CPP was bereft of its early leaders. In their place were those who had very little power or authority in their own right, but who were able to use Nkrumah —and the cloudy tenets of 'Nkrumaism'—to bolster their own position. Eager to establish their authority, they echoed Nkrumah's attacks on colonialism, neo-colonialism, and the hidden enemies within the state who were said to be saboteurs of 'African socialism'. They were led by Tawia Adamafio—Busia's former colleague, and general secretary of the CPP since 1960—as Minister of Information, Coffie Crabbe, executive secretary of the party, Kwaku Boateng, H. S. T. Provencal (later Deputy Minister of the Interior), and a number of their followers.[77] The

---

[76] Ghana, Parl. Deb., 16 Oct. 1961. Gbedemah was supported only by the 'Minority Group' of eight UP members: S. D. Dombo (Jirapa-Lambussie, Northern Ghana); B. K. Adama (Wala South, Northern Ghana); Dr I. B. Asafu-Adjaye (Juaben-Edweso, Ashanti); Jatoe Kaleo (Wala North, Northern Ghana); Abayifaa Karbo (Lawra-Nandom, Northern Ghana); B. F. Kusi (Atwima-Nwabiagya, Ashanti); A. W. Osei (Ahafo, Ashanti); R. B. Otchere (Amansie West, Ashanti).

[77] A list of such members was given by the Attorney-General in his Opening Address at the Treason Trial on 9 August 1963 after Tawi Adamafio's fall from power. Printed as a supplement to *Ghana Today*, 14 Aug. 1963.

'The Group was composed of: Mr Kwaku Boateng, Minister of the Interior; Mr Dowuona-Hammond, Minister of Education; Mr J. K. Tettegah, Secretary-General of the TUC; Mr K. Amoako-Atta, Deputy Governor of the Bank of Ghana; Mr T. O. Asare, Chairman and Managing Director of the Ghana Commercial Bank; Mr Eric Heymann, Editor of the *Evening News*; Mr T. D. Baffoe, Editor of the *Ghanaian Times*; Mr Z. B. Shardow, Head of the Ghana Young Pioneers; Mr Cecil Forde, attached to the President's Publicity Secretariat; Mr H. P. Nelson, Principal Secretary of the Ministry of Trade; Mr Kweku Akwei, Head of the Party's Education Wing at the Party Headquarters; Mr S. B. Ofori, part of the time at the Agricultural Development Corporation and thereafter the Chairman of the Ghana Fishing Corporation; Mr E. N. Omaboe, Government Statistician; Mr D. S. Quarcoopome, at the time in charge of security in the country; and Mr A. C. Kuma, then State Professor at the University of Ghana.

'This group met either in Tawia Adamafio's house or in the house of Kweku Akwei. A considerable amount of their time was spent in attacking Ministers whom Tawia Adamafio did not like. An examination of the personalities of the group and

initiative in these moves was clearly Nkrumah's who had already
(on 22 September) abruptly dismissed General Alexander (Chief
of the Ghana Defence Staff since January 1960). But where
Nkrumah led, Tawia Adamafio followed eagerly, and aped his
master with a zeal that outran even his own imitators. It was during these feverish months also that the first bomb explosions took
place in Accra, presumably intended to bring about a cancella-
tion of the Queen's visit in November. In this respect at least they
failed. For, after an initial hesitation by the United Kingdom
government and two hurried visits by Duncan Sandys, the visit
went forward and the Queen travelled peacefully through the
country. But it was a brief lull in the storm. Once the Queen left,
further explosions occured. They led to a total break in the relations between Ghana and Togo, and the issue of a Government
White Paper in which Britain was accused of complicity in the
attempt to subvert the Ghana government.[78]

Parallel with these developments went a further effort to instil
in the party the rudiments of a crude ideology. For the junior
members a new development was given to the youth section
through a Ghana Young Pioneers' organization for schoolboys
and schoolgirls. For the senior echelons of the party, a Kwame
Nkrumah Ideological Institute was opened at Winneba, some
forty miles west of Accra, where seminars on 'Nkrumaism' were
held for ministers, the party's national headquarters' staff, civil
servants, and assembly members. The level of discussion may be
judged from Nkrumah's own address (*Guide to Party Action*) to the
first seminar of an Ideological School at the Institute on
3 February 1962:

Let us not forget that Marxism is not a dogma but a guide to
action.... The Party has defined a social purpose and it is committed
to socialism and to the ideology of Nkrumaism. And I take it that
when you talk of Nkrumaism, you mean the name or term given to

---

their functions would immediately show that Tawia Adamafio had gathered
around himself men in key positions in the country.... It is not suggested that the
members of this group did anything wrong. The fact which needs to be empha-
sised is that Tawia Adamafio could call upon them and by misrepresentation of
the President's wishes use them for his own purposes if he so desired. Under the
guise of the indoctrination of a hard core of party cadre, he placed himself in a
position of command with personal support through these personalities from a wide
section of the population and from very sensitive and important organs of Government.'

[78] *Statement by the Government on the Recent Conspiracy*, Dec. 1961.

the consistent ideological policies followed and taught by Nkrumah. These are contained in his speeches, in his theoretical writings and stated ideas and principles. You also mean that Nkrumaism, in order to be Nkruma-istic, must be related to scientific socialism. To be successful, however, this ideology must:

(*a*) Be all-pervading, and while its theories in full can only be developed in and around the Party leadership, it must influence in some form all education and, indeed, all thinking and action.

(*b*) Be not only a statement of aims and principles, but must also provide the intellectual tools by which these aims are achieved, and must concentrate on all constructive thinking around these aims; and,

(*c*) Offer the ordinary man and woman some concrete, tangible and realisable hope of better life within his or her lifetime.

Within this ideology there should be a full-scale intellectual, educational and organisational attack on all aspects of colonialism, neocolonialism and imperialism.

Nkrumah told the assembled ministers, central committee members, party officials, regional and district commissioners, that 'periodical educational meetings' were needed to 'inculcate in the minds of the nation's youth the ideology of the Party'. Party members must be

imbued not only with a keen sense of patriotism but also with a sense of lofty ideals. . . . All this will lead to one useful result—discipline. The whole nation from the President downwards will form one regiment of disciplined citizens. In this way, we shall move forward with great confidence, stepping ahead ever firmly with a keen sense of purpose and direction.[79]

Alas, for the principles of Nkrumaism. The new era of radical leadership, 'stepping ahead ever firmly with a keen sense of purpose and direction' was short-lived. A little over a year after his

[79] *Guide to Party Action*, address by Osagyefo Dr Kwame Nkrumah to the first seminar of the Ideological School at the Kwame Nkrumah Institute of Ideological Studies, 3 Feb. 1962, issued by the CPP central committee. A similar account of 'Nkrumaism' by Kofi Baako will be found in *The Party* (the fortnightly journal which appeared at the beginning of 1961), the theme being that 'Nkrumaism' is 'a non-atheistic socialist philosophy which seeks to apply the current socialist ideas to the solution of our problems . . . by adapting these ideas to the realities of our every-day life. It is basically Socialism adapted to suit the conditions and circumstances of Africa' (issue no. 4, Apr. 1961). The amateurism of the language should not deceive the reader. There was a minority of would-be Marxists who attended the Winneba Institute who were willing to respond to, and to avail themselves of, Nkrumah's taste for party theorizing.

rise to power, Tawia Adamafio was in prison under the Detention Act which he had made the chief instrument of his power. The occasion of his fall was an attack on Nkrumah's life on 1 August 1962. The President was returning from a visit to President Yameogo of the neighbouring Republic of Upper Volta, when he stopped at the small northern Ghanaian village of Kulungugu. As he alighted from the car, a hand-grenade exploded, killing those near him and wounding many more. The immediate outcome was a tightening of security measures throughout the country, but the principal victims were Adamafio and his followers. On 29 August he, Coffie Crabbe, and Ako Adjei (Minister of Foreign Affairs) were detained on grounds of their participation in the attempted assassination.[80] Their arrest did not prevent further outrages in Accra where a series of explosions occurred in September. Nevertheless, the Kulungugu affair saw the temporary eclipse of the extreme anti-western, anti-neo-colonialist wing of the party. It was not altogether unexpected, since changes in this direction had been made earlier in the year. For example, Danquah, Victor Owusu, and a number of former CPP members had been released in June, a step that Adamafio apparently tried to resist.[81] After Kulungugu, however, there was a hurried reinstatement of the old guard. Krobo Edusei became a minister again; N. A. Welbeck, a former minister who had been obliged to take second place to Coffie Crabbe in the party bureaucracy, became its executive secretary. A little later in time Botsio was appointed Minister of Foreign Affairs. Later again Joe Appiah was released from detention. This lightening of

[80] The immediate grounds of suspicion against Adamafio were that he and his followers hung back and kept away from Nkrumah as the procession of cars approached Kulungugu. 'On the journey . . . to the place of the incident they isolated themselves from the Leader to whom they had clung previously all along as if they were his lovers. They rode in different cars and were hundreds of yards away leaving the President behind. These rascals had evil plans' (F. E. Tachie-Menson, Ghana, Parl. Deb., 6 Sept. 1962). The detention of Ako Adjei was puzzling. Like Adamafio he had once been opposed to the CPP (though at an earlier date). Like Adamafio (and Adamafio's protégé, Coffie Crabbe) he was a Ga, and it was rumoured that a Ga movement still existed known as the *Emashi Nonn* ('It still survives'). But although their common tribal origin may have helped the three to act in concert it does not explain why Ako Adjei should want to join the other two. After all, there were many Ga still loyal to the CPP. Ako Adjei showed few signs of a militant attitude towards pan-Africanism, neo-colonialism, socialism, or any of the causes to which the others devoted themselves.

[81] There is some evidence for this. 'At Tamale [after the Kulungugu incident] Adamafio said, "we told Osagyefo not to release the detainees and he refused. Look at what has happened" ' (W. A. Amoro, Ghana, Parl. Deb., 6 Sept. 1962).

the political scene was matched on the economic side by new promises to foreign investors. The verbal attacks on neo-colonialism continued, but practical overtures were made to overseas companies which were once again offered guarantees against expropriation, the right of transfer of profits abroad, and a number of tax allowances. The guarantees were restated by Nkrumah in his 'Address to the National Assembly' on 2 October 1962, and then embodied in a new Capital Investments Bill in April 1963.[82] The extremist element in the party was still there in the party press which continued its venomous attacks on individuals within the party, and on 'neo-colonialist forces' within the country; it was likely to remain in active existence since it reflected a fundamental characteristic of Nkrumah's own character. Nevertheless, by the middle of 1963, the 'ideological wing' of the party—created in Nkrumah's own image—was relatively subdued compared with its ascendancy twelve months earlier.

The change was reflected in the greater freedom of debate in parliament:

Minister of Agriculture (Mr Krobo Edusei): Many of us have suffered at the hands of persons who say 'Osagyefo says'. The Press of Ghana has been saying that Osagyefo says we must remove this Minister. Osagyefo says we must remove that Minister, and many people have been shamefully disgraced. . . .

. . . I beg your pardon, Sir, we know that the people of this country are not fools. They are not fools. They know who are the enemies of the State. They know who have been condoning and conniving at the actions of Tawia Adamafio. They know the members of the inner circle and you cannot arrest Adamafio, Ako Adjei and Cofie Crabbe and leave the other members of the inner circle of Adamafio.

I am therefore appealing to the Minister of the Interior—

Mr Iddrisu: Maybe he is one of them!

Mr Krobo Edusei: If the Minister of the Interior is one of them, then he must get up and go to Osagyefo and ask for his sins to be forgiven him. We want our Minister of the Interior to uncover the other members of the inner circle of Adamafio. It is therefore time for him to tell the Police—[A Member: 'To tell us!']—to tell the Police that if we have not rounded up all members of this inner circle the country is not safe. If you know them, come out and name them. . . .

. . . There are a lot of innocent people in the country who have been

---

[82] The Bill was generously worded, but many of its benefits were offset by the higher rate of company taxation levied in the budget that followed.

locked up by the Minister of the Interior. Innocent people who may not know anything have just been locked up by the Minister of the Interior for questioning. Why is it that up till now the Minister has not been bold enough to go to the Guinea Press and close it down? The country has entirely been disappointed by what is going on at the Guinea Press. [*Uproar.*][83]

There was a further tendency to be noted. Although the National Assembly continued to meet, and ministers were still in charge of departments, the cabinet was often manipulating a machine whose primary motive lay elsewhere. Nkrumah now placed his immense power behind the administrators. He worked long hours each day in the presidential offices in Flag-staff House where there was a capable administrative machine controlling the Office of the Budget, the Planning Commission, the Development Secretariat, the Volta River Project, and a proliferation of departments. If many of the ministers and junior ministers were of poor quality, it was not a criticism that could be brought against the senior civil servants. It was possible, there-fore, to hope that a further element had been added to the political structure of control which might help to keep it steady for some time to come.

The hope was illusory. Under a fair sky, the political scene appeared steady: it was ill equipped to withstand rough weather. And a new crisis suddenly confronted Nkrumah. Throughout 1963 the trial had proceeded of those arrested after the Kulun-gugu attack before a special court consisting of Sir Arku Korsah, the Chief Justice, and W. B. Van Lare and Akufo Addo, judges of the Supreme Court. In April five of the first seven to be tried were found guilty of treason and sentenced to death; their two companions (one a woman) were given terms of imprisonment. The decision to hold a trial—in itself a sign of more liberal views —must have appeared justified to Nkrumah. Then the court re-sumed in August to hear the case against Tawia Adamafio, Ako Adjei, Coffie Crabbe, R. B. Otchere (the former Ashanti UP assembly member), and Yaw Manu, a government clerk. A strange muddled tale was unfolded of intrigue, fraud, party quarrels, witchcraft, and 'money doubling' by resort to the magic world of the 'spirit Zebus from the kingdom of Uranus'. (So Ako Adjei pleaded in defence of his misuse of government

[83] Ghana, Parl. Deb., 5 Oct. 1962.

funds.) That plots had been hatched in Lomé and elsewhere by former opposition members—notably by Obetsibi Lamptey—was clear. And, indeed, Otchere pleaded guilty. But that Tawia Adamafio, Ako Adjei, or Coffie Crabbe had anything to do with the Kulungugu attack became increasingly doubtful as the trial continued. And on 9 December all three were acquitted. No one who examined the evidence could have supposed the verdict would be otherwise. Nevertheless, on 11 December, Nkrumah—acting within the terms of the constitution—dismissed Sir Arku Korsah as Chief Justice. On 23 December the National Assembly met in special session and passed the Law of Criminal Procedure (Amendment No. 2) Act empowering the President to quash any decisions of the Special Court; and on 25 December Nkrumah declared the judgment null and void. The dismissal of the Chief Justice was welcomed eagerly by the *Ghanaian Times* which declared that Sir Arku Korsah had 'failed in his duty, let his leader down and betrayed his country' by not telling Nkrumah beforehand what the verdict would be.[84]

At the end of 1963 Nkrumah announced his intention of seeking approval through a referendum to be held from 24 to 31 January on two amendments to the constitution. One would 'invest the President with power in his discretion to dismiss a Judge of the High Court at any time for reasons which appear to him sufficient'. The other would 'provide that . . . there will be one national party in Ghana [and] that the one national party shall be the Convention People's Party'. Further shocks were to come. For on 2 January 1964 police constable Seth Ametewee, on duty in Flagstaff House, fired five shots at Nkrumah. The range was close, the marksmanship poor; and Nkrumah was unhurt, although the last two shots killed Salifu Dagarti, a special security guard officer. Six days later E. R. T. Madjitey, Commissioner of Police, S. D. Amaning, Assistant Commissioner, and eight other police officers were dismissed; on the 8th Preventive Detention Orders were served against Amaning, M. K. Awuku, a police superintendent, and—once again—J. B. Danquah. Later again, it was the turn of the university to come under attack. De Graft Johnson, now Director of the Institute of Public Education (the former Institute of Extra-Mural Studies) was detained, Dr Osborne, a British physicist, held for questioning, and six senior

[84] *Ghanaian Times*, 12 Dec. 1963.

members deported; N. A. Welbeck headed a rowdy procession of party loyalists through the university compound, breaking windows and shouting abuse at the students. The *Ghanaian Times* moved back to the centre of political activity in full cry:

> It is clear that the imperialist networks left behind have not yet been sufficiently assailed and assimilated into the revolution, and we find ourselves in the state of what Lenin once called the 'irreconcilability of class antagonisms'. The sins of these enemies have long been known to us. They desire the failure of our revolution because its socialist objectives run counter to their gregarious, greedy, avaricious natures. They seek the blood of Osagyefo because he is the major block to the continued exercise of their class privileges in the exploitation of the African masses, to the triumph of neo-colonialism and monopoly capital, not only in Ghana, but throughout Africa.[85]

The Eclipse of the Opposition

When the referendum was held at the end of January, it resulted in an impressive demonstration of government power.

Yes votes —	2,773,920[86]
No votes —	2,452
Registered electorate —	2,877,464 92.8 per cent poll

Results of this kind were nonsensical. Malpractices were reported as being so widespread that the referendum was an administrative exercise by the party rather than a test of public opinion. The most common device used by the party officers was that of sealing (or removing) the 'No' box. Even so, there must have been a very large number of fictitious votes to produce a 93 per cent poll.[87] None the less, in February 1964 Ghana became a Convention People's Republic. The party flag, overprinted with a black star, replaced the national flag; the Minority Group in parliament, and the United Party outside the assembly, were finally extin-

[85] *Ghanaian Times*, 3 Jan. 1964.
[86] Ibid. 4 Feb., 1964. Regional results were said to be:

	Yes	No
Upper Region	325,859	186
Northern Region	201,781	30
Brong Ahafo	368,369	0
Ashanti Region	425,022	0
Western Region	217,947	0
Central Region	441,041	0
Eastern Region	390,938	0
Volta Region	261,393	677
Accra District	141,570	1,559

[87] See the two articles in *The Guardian*, 3 and 4 Feb. 1964.

guished. It was hardly unexpected, despite the apparent brightening of the political scene in 1963. Indeed, the referendum was the logical outcome of an earlier private member's motion calling for the establishment of a single-party state which the assembly had approved in September 1962.[88] In a broader sense still, it was the logical outcome of the nationalist demands put forward by Nkrumah and the CPP in 1949. In their beginning was their end. The Leader who was sentenced—in open court—in 1950 was now in control of the judiciary; the nationalist party which had led the attack on colonial rule had become the state.

Looking back from 1964 over the previous decade and a half, it seemed doubtful whether the nationalist régime begun in 1949 would be able to survive as long a period again. It had held together until the attainment of independence. But from 1957, more particularly after 1960, it had lurched from crisis to crisis, governed by caprice and having to use the cruel weapon of the Preventive Detention Act to silence its opponents. The structure of representative government was still there, and it was still possible (even in 1964) to argue that it would not require a great deal of nursing by tolerant competent leaders to re-establish it as a parliamentary system. It seemed unlikely, however, that such an initiative would be forthcoming. Why? Because of the quality of leadership provided by Nkrumah, and the nature of the CPP as a nationalist party—characteristics examined in the introductory chapter. And by way of conclusion to this study, it may be helpful to restate here what they were.

A major responsibility must lie with Nkrumah for the smothering of what might have become an openly competitive society. The peculiar form of the Republic cannot be said to derive directly from the attitude to power shown by Nkrumah in 'The Circle' or in the verses he placed at the head of his *Autobiography*.[89] There were long periods, in the early 1950s especially, when he was prepared to reflect the more tolerant outlook of his colonial partners. Nevertheless, the emotional view of himself as a revolutionary leader, rich in charismatic appeal, was always there. After 1957 it was openly expressed and compulsive. And it cast great doubt even on the years of relative stability. Consider, for example, the turn of events between 1962 and 1964. There were

[88] Ghana, Parl. Deb., 11 Sept. 1962.
[89] See above, p. 41.

difficulties and dangers enough to make any leader apprehensive of his position. Yet in 1963 it began to look as though Nkrumah would be able to maintain a delicate balance, not only among the warring sections of the party, but between the party itself and the efficient, neutral sectors of the state. Then the acquittal of Tawia Adamafio—who had owed his position entirely to Nkrumah's encouragement of a vociferous, extremist element within the party—threw everything awry once more. The subsequent dismissal of the Chief Justice was a wholly unnecessary act of anger and spite. It had no political justification, any more than had Nkrumah's continued support of those who managed and wrote for the party press. Yet he can hardly have hesitated before taking his revenge.

Here was a principal source of anxiety—the volatile, unpredictable nature of Nkrumah himself, who fashioned the myth that Ghana was engaged in a perpetual revolution against hidden enemies, believed in it himself, and imposed it on his followers. Certainly there were dangers that threatened the régime, particularly after 1961 when opposition took the form of indiscriminate acts of public murder. But to suppose that such attacks could be avoided by forcing the country into a single-party mould, or by subordinating the police, civil service, judiciary, and the universities to party control in the name of a wholly mythical revolution, was both naïve and dangerous. Such measures were likely to prove a greater threat to the régime than the difficulties they were supposedly intended to avert.

Secondly, there was the nature of the CPP itself. Its leaders and the rank and file had welcomed the enforced destruction of the opposition without reckoning the cost to themselves: they thus helped to sharpen the knife which many of them were later to feel against their own throats. But it was in the nature of the CPP as a commoners' movement led by the elementary-school-leavers that its members should have been unable to make the calculation themselves. Although a more empirical leader might have led them along a more tolerant path, they were also readily open to suggestions that power was there not only to be used but used to the utmost. They followed Nkrumah willingly, therefore, when he made extravagant claims for the party. A more sophisticated movement might then have insisted on retaining a share of power with the leader: but, again, the CPP lacked any understanding of the dangers of an extreme concentration of power. What they knew best was the colonial system, or traditional chieftaincy rule: in each case an autocracy tempered by restraint. Indeed, apart from their passionate belief in 1949 in self-government, they were often remarkably easy-going. They were in no sense a party of stern theoreticians; as commented earlier, there was often a strong sense of social unity even between party opponents. Totalitarian power was alien to them—until they felt its authority, and it was then too late to do more than deplore its misuse.

Thirdly, there were the particular difficulties of the republican era. The African scene became bewilderingly complex, and increasingly unstable, as plots, counter-plots, assassinations, and seizures of power by army commanders took their toll of the early leaders. Within the country itself, the economy lost much of its buoyancy as cocoa prices fell; and, as the cost of living went up, and goods became scarce under a clumsily administered system of import controls, people grumbled. By the 1960s the excitement of self-government had receded; independence was taken for granted, and numerous private interests were reasserted by sectional groups within the regions. It was easy to exaggerate these differences: Nkrumah himself was over-ready to condemn all minority interests as 'tribalism'. In practice, though grievances were frequently expressed in community terms they were as much the reflection of local needs and rival interests as of tribal conflict. Nevertheless, Ghanaian society *was* quarrelsome, and the CPP mirrored its nature at every level of its organization.[90] In addition, there was the threat of sudden outbursts of muderous violence by aggrieved relatives, clandestine opposition groups based on Lomé, or single-minded individuals who set themselves the task of overthrowing the régime. It was not difficult to understand, therefore, why Nkrumah and the CPP leaders should be nervous, and inclined to impose blanket measures of control over the whole country whenever danger was thought to be imminent. Restraint and a cool head were needed in these circumstances, and they were virtues which eluded both the party and its leader.

[90] As Nkrumah complained: 'Here and there a chief's stool becomes vacant. Two Party comrades contest for enstoolment; one succeeds. Immediately the loser turns against the Party and the Government' (Address to Kumasi City Council, 24 Mar. 1962).

In sum, the effect of the measures imposed, and the opposition it provoked, isolated Nkrumah within the CPP, and the party from the general public. The President secluded himself in Christiansborg Castle guarded by soldiers, having disarmed the police after the second assassination attempt at the beginning of 1964. The parliamentary wing of the CPP could no longer be said to be directly representative of the electorate, the last general election having been held in 1956. The last contested by-election was at the end of August 1960. 'Candidates' thereafter were selected and approved by the central committee and then declared elected unopposed; and the Detention Act made sure that the boldest rebel was deterred from standing.[91] The party as a whole was still nominally an impressive structure of authority throughout the country. It had actually met in conference in 1962 in Kumasi to approve its draft programme of 'Work and Happiness' as the basis of a national Seven-Year Development Plan, although the 'debates' among those who attended were taken up very largely with avowals of loyalty to Nkrumah and the party. In sum, it was becoming increasingly difficult to distinguish between the façade and reality of its power. Its officials went about their work of exhortation in the constituencies, but they left the actual running of the regions to their administrative secretaries and executive officers in the civil service. The CPP was now a massive propaganda machine without an effective appeal to sustain it. Nevertheless, it continued in existence since on its survival hung the privileges of a large number of beneficiaries—the assembly members, the regional district commissioners, the sizeable bureaucracy in the national headquarters, and the officials of the numerous ancillary organizations.

It might be thought that this isolation of the régime was not in itself important. So long as the government provided employment and an adequate wage structure, and Nkrumah escaped assassination, would the CPP not be able to continue to 'lurch

[91] Between 1956 and the end of 1963 there were 33 by-elections, 13 caused by the Detention Act, and others by the self-imposed exile of opposition or CPP members. The last contested by-election was in Accra Central (Nkrumah's former constituency) when the UP candidate gave up in protest four days beforehand because of the restrictions put upon him. The result was: H. S. T. Provencal (CPP) 11,545; Solomon Odamtten (UP) 165. A little before the election, Osei Baidoo, assistant general secretary of the UP, J. E. Vanderpuije, chairman of the Accra UP, and three others were detained.

from crisis to crisis'? The administrative framework of the state was strong. Could it not uphold the party still, as it had done since 1951 when it first took office? There was also an immense political capital invested in the party by those who held office under its auspices: could they not reach a working compromise with Nkrumah in order to safeguard the régime and themselves? Other states, other régimes, have survived along much the same lines. Why should the CPP not be equally successful?

Certainly it was possible. Nevertheless, if comparisons were to be made with other countries, the omens were by no means favourable. Nkrumah frequently warned his fellow African rulers of the need to avoid a 'Latin American situation'. But was there any reason to suppose that the African states would be able to escape the conflicts and frequent overthrow of governments in that other post-colonial continent, either in their relations between themselves, or in their domestic policies?[92] There were also particular grounds for apprehension in Ghana. On the one hand there was the frightened obstinacy of Nkrumah, a romantic African Marxist, determined to play the part of a revolutionary, and leader of a docile party most of whose active members were bemused and dazzled by their own success. On the other hand there was the greater wealth and sophistication of Ghanaian society (compared with the majority of its African neighbours): these qualities were likely to increase rather than diminish the demand, certainly for a more effective, and possibly for a more liberal, régime. The Sekondi strike in 1961 was of particular interest in this respect. Many of those who had protested were earning £20 or more a month, and had been hard hit by the budget precisely because they had a great deal to lose by any fall in wages. Moreover, they had demanded not only an end to the restrictions imposed by the budget, but a restoration of the greater freedom of political expression which had existed in the

[92] Consider, for example, the erratic course of government in Peru between 1931 and 1962 through a number of presidential elections—some distorted, others suspended when the radical opponents of the ruling party appeared to be winning, others again providing an unexpected change of government until the military turned out the civilians. The 1933 constitution declared that the President 'personifies the nation', the 1945 amendments to the constitution 'combined in an unusual form features taken from the presidential and parliamentary forms of government'—as in Ghana. The source material will be found in R. A. Humphreys, *Latin American History* (Oxford, 1957), R. H. Fitzgibbon, *The Constitutions of the Americas* (Chicago, 1948), and H. Kantor, *The Ideology and Program of the Peruvian Aprista Movement* (California, 1953), from which the quotation in this note is taken.

1950s. Similar unrest was surely likely to be provoked over a wide range of occupations. In 1960, for example, it was estimated that between 1961 and 1965 nearly 200,000 would be leaving the elementary schools and some 20,000 finishing their secondary education.[93] They would almost double the existing number of unskilled and semi-skilled workers, and increase by a third 'the administrative, managerial, professional, technical and skilled occupations in the country'. Whatever government existed in Ghana over the decade would have to meet the problem of absorbing this new generation of educated leaders. And it seemed more and more doubtful whether Nkrumah and the CPP would be equal to the task. Indeed, the party's capacity to meet such problems was almost certainly less in 1964 than at any time previously. It had lost much of its former popular base as a commoners' party. It had never been able to recruit more than a handful of the university graduates and secondary-school-leavers (and seemed unlikely to do so in the future). And by early 1964 it had considerably weakened its authority as a government, and therefore its ability to act in an emergency, by its attacks on the judiciary, the civil service, and the police.

With these long-term prospects in view, and the growing danger that power might be seized with very little effort by a determined minority,[94] it was impossible to be confident about the future. Nor could one draw comfort from what had happened in the past. The abrupt reversal of the fortunes of the colonial government in 1948, the CPP in 1954, the opposition in 1957, and many of the CPP leaders after 1960, held little promise that the future would avoid similar crises, in any one of which the

---

[93]   *Output between 1961–5 from*

Elementary schools	180,000
Secondary schools	20,000
Teacher Training Colleges	13,000
Universities (abroad & at home)	7,750

Of the 180,000 elementary-school-leavers, it was estimated that 146,000 would receive no further education. Of the 20,000 secondary-school-leavers, 7,000 would have no additional qualification (Ghana, *Survey of High Level Manpower*, 1960).

[94] One possibility was a coup d'état by the army, for which there were a growing number of precedents in Africa. It was small—between 7,000–10,000 men—but well equipped, and its officers were educated, capable leaders. Once having seized power in Accra, the replacement of the CPP commissioners in the regions by junior and senior officers was not likely to present any great difficulty to a determined army commander. Whether the British-trained officers could reach a decision to intervene was another matter.

régime might founder. To express such fears was not to question the underlying strength of the country in terms of the administration, the ability of a skilled labour force, and the enterprise of the Ghanaian farmer and trader. The uncertainty lay in the political scene which, in the opening years of the Republic, had been as troubled as at any time during the whole period of this study. And it is on this note of uncertainty of what the political future would hold that this account must close.

Appendix A

THE GOLD COAST/GHANA PRESS

The earliest newspaper in the country was the *Royal Gold Coast Gazette & Commercial Intelligence* which appeared handwritten in 1822; the first regular newspaper was James Brew's *The Gold Coast Times* in 1874. By the end of the nineteenth century some nineteen papers had existed at one time or other, limited in circulation to a few hundred but of a high standard of journalistic writing, a tradition continued by J. E. Casely Hayford's *The Gold Coast Leader* between 1902 and his death in 1929. A new development began in 1931, the year of Danquah's *West African Times* (later the *Times of West Africa*) when Danquah, Nnamdi Azikiwe, Wuta Ofei, and C. S. Adjei attacked different aspects of colonial policy in flamboyant language. When the restrictions imposed during the war on the import of newsprint were lifted, and nationalist demands gathered force, newspapers, news-sheets, weekly journals, pamphlets appeared in great number—including Nkrumah's Accra *Evening News* (3 September 1948)—hard-hitting, raucous, simply-written, crudely-printed. A mass circulation was not achieved until the appearance at the end of 1950 of the *Daily Graphic*, a subsidiary of the London overseas *Daily Mirror* Group, which was at first boycotted, then copied and, after independence, largely ignored by nationalist opinion except on the rare occasion when it ventured to comment on local political issues.

At independence, the position had been reached when, compared with the twenty daily papers of 1950, there were only five of any political importance: the *Evening News* (CPP – 1948), the *Liberator* (NLM – 1954), the *Ashanti Pioneer* (Independent-opposition – 1939), the *Daily Graphic* (neutral – 1950), and the twice-weekly *Ashanti Times* (owned, written, and published since 1947 by the Ashanti Gold Fields Corporation). The rise and decline in the number of papers may be set down as:

	1870–1900	*1901–30*	*1937*	*1948*	*1950*	*1959*
Daily	2	–	1	6	20	5
Weekly*	5	7	4	8	7	5
	7	7	5	14	27	10

* including 1 vernacular weekly.

Source: *Report on the Press in West Africa* (Ibadan, 1960), p. 38.

After 1957 the *Liberator* disappeared, and the *Ghana Star*—later the *Guinea Times*, later again the *Ghanaian Times*—appeared to supplement the *Evening News*, both published by the Guiness Press under government surveillance. The *Ashanti Pioneer* was muzzled in 1960, leaving the CPP press in undisputed sway. There were also papers of special interest like the weekly *Ghanaian Worker*, the weekly *Catholic Voice*, and the (Catholic) *Standard;* there were also a number of English and vernacular papers and magazines of a limited circulation.

The circulation claimed by the party and neutral papers in 1960 was: *Evening News*, 50,000 per issue, *Ghanaian Times*, 30,000; *Ashanti Pioneer*, 25,000; *Daily Graphic*, 75,000; *Ashanti Times*, 20,000. These figures were very approximate, and ranged from well audited accounts to what the editors said were printed and sent to local agents. When the writer was last able to make some inquiries in the field in 1962, the figures of newspapers actually sold were probably: *Daily Graphic*, over 100,000; *Evening News*, 15,000–20,000; *Ghanaian Times*, 8,000–12,000; *Ashanti Pioneer*, 10,000.

See the useful *Report on the Press in West Africa* prepared for the International Seminar on 'Press and Progress' held at Dakar, May–June 1960, and distributed by the Department of Extra-Mural Studies, Ibadan, Nigeria, especially pp. 32–38 ('The Ghana Press', by K. A. B. Jones Quartey). See too Jones Quartey's articles in *Universitas*, University of Ghana publication, June and December 1958.

Appendix B

Extracts from the *Proceedings and Report of the Commission appointed to enquire into the matters disclosed at the trial of Captain Benjamin Awhaitey before a Court Martial and the surrounding circumstances*

1. *First Statement by Major Awhaitey, 19 December 1958*[1]

I am Camp Commandant of Giffard Camp. I know Mr R. R. Amponsah and have known him for the past 25 years. We were teachers together at one time. At 6.30 p.m. yesterday a driver whose name I do not know called at my house and told me that I was wanted by my Uncle the Chief of Dodowa at Labadi in order to accompany him to a Lawyer. I went with the driver and he took me to a house opposite the Shell Station on the Labadi Road which I can point out. We stopped and I saw Mr R. R. Amponsah outside the house. The driver stopped the car and Amponsah introduced himself to me. Amponsah called me aside and told me that the Opposition had helped us a lot. He told me that he had heard that I was the Camp Commandant and that we should try to be grateful to the Opposition and that the only way we could do that was to support them to come into power. I asked him how we could do that as we are non political and he said that we should support them by organising a *Coup d'Etat*. I said that this is too serious and I do not think I can do it. He said that I should not have any fear at all as Lt Kattah was supporting them. He then pulled out of his pocket a bundle of currency notes and said—'Here is £50 if you could give this to the N.C.O.s to support us they would be better off when we come to power.' He then opened a suitcase in which I saw some khaki uniforms—I did not touch the money or the uniforms. He told me that they intended to go to the Airport on the 20-12-58 and arrest the Prime Minister and any other Cabinet Ministers who might be there to see him off and they then intended to seize power and that the N.C.O.s would then be better off. I told him that I could not do this as if my G.O.C. were to hear of this I would be in trouble. I then started to leave the place and he told the driver to take me home. He asked me to think if over and to meet him at the Labadi Road–Giffard Camp Road T Junction at 6.30 p.m. on the 19-12-58. I then left him.

I was worried throughout the night and at 1.30 p.m. today the 19-12-58 I rang up Lt Amenyah in Records Office and told him the

[1] App. A, p. iii.

whole story and asked him to meet Amponsah for me and to tell Amponsah to keep out of my way as I was not prepared to have anything to do with it. The Lt agreed to do this and left.

When I met Amponsah there was another man with him who was introduced to me as the brother of the Prof. Busia. I do not think I could recognise him again.

The only other information I can give is that in June I was invited to a wedding by Capt Tevie. At the reception I saw Mr M. K. Apaloo, M.P., who called me aside and asked me if the army personnel were happy. I told him that I was all right and asked him if he had any complaints from the Army. He said no and I left him as I thought he was trying to make approaches to me.

I have no knowledge of any other N.C.O.s or officers who might be concerned in this plot.

2. *Second Statement by Major Awhaitey, 2–3 January 1959*[2]

At 18.30 hours on 18th December, 1958, a gentleman called at my house No. 18 Giffard Villas, Giffard Camp, and told me that my uncle, the Chief of Dodowa, had asked him to bring me to Labadi to accompany him to a lawyer. I went with him in a car. At Labadi, opposite a Shell Co. Petrol Station the driver stopped, opened the door for me and when I got out a tall gentleman met me. He said 'Good evening, Major. It was I who sent for you and not your uncle. By the way, do you remember me? I am R. R. Amponsah. We met at Wesley College Kumasi some 20 years ago.' I said 'Oh yes. I do remember. What can I do for you?' He said 'You know we, the Opposition, have helped the Army a great deal and the only way we expect you to express your gratitude is to come to our support.' I asked him in what way we could help as we in the Army are entirely non-political. He said 'Oh, you know. *Coup d'etat*. The Prime Minister will be leaving for India on Saturday 20th December, 1958, and if you could induce your N.C.O.s to help in arresting him and other Cabinet Ministers who are going to see him off at the Airport, we might overthrow the Government and come into power. All of you in the Army would then be better off.' He dipped his right hand into his pocket, showed me a bundle of money and said 'Look, take this £50 to your N.C.O.s and induce them by all means to support us.' I said 'Don't be silly, I am not prepared to take this.' He then took me to the back of the car, flung open a suitcase and said 'Look, all these uniforms will be given to your men if they come to our support.' I said 'Why come to me with this suggestion? Why did you not go to any of the senior Ghanaian officers, like Major Otu?' He said 'You see, we

[2] App. A, p. ii.

understand you are the Camp Commandant in charge of all the troops in Accra. That is why I sent for you.' I said 'It is a fact that I am the Camp Commandant but all my men are non-infantry and know nothing about fighting.' He said 'Look, Major, do please remember what we, the Opposition have done for the Army in the way of increasing pay, car loans, etc., and by all means think of this. Meet me at Junction Giffard Camp and Teshie Road at 6.30 p.m. tomorrow.' I looked round for a taxi to leave. He said 'Oh no I'll let the driver take you back'. On the return journey I got annoyed with the driver and asked his name. He said his name is Kofi Gyamfi. I said 'This should be your first and last time of calling me in my uncle's name'. He answered in Pidgin English 'He be Master say make I talk so'. We arrived in my house and throughout the night I was greatly worried.

I decided to report, but I had no one to bear out my story. If Mr Amponsah was arrested, the other two men, that is the driver and another short man who had been standing by when I arrived at the meeting place, would all deny. Probably also Mr Amponsah, being a M.P., could sue me for defamation of character and claim heavy damages. On the other hand I felt that if I did not report and the meeting between Amponsah and me became known to the Army authorities I might be penalised. At 13.00 hrs on 19th December I decided to tell somebody. I rang Major Michel three times but there was no reply. Major Aferi came to my office when I was taking orders. The next name that came to my mind was Lt Amenyah whom I have known for a long time. I phoned him to come to see me when he closed. At 13.45 hours Lt Amenyah arrived at my office and I told him the story I have already given. We spoke in Adangbe. I did not use a single English word. When referring to the Prime Minister I remember using the word 'Anu' meaning 'arrest' which was the exact word used by Mr Amponsah. With regard to the money, I told Lt Amenyah that Mr Amponsah showed me a bundle of currency notes which he said was £50 but I did not take it. I sent Lt Amenyah to meet Mr Amponsah at the rendezvous to tell him that I was not interested in his request and that I was not meeting him. Moreover if the G.O.C. were to hear of it I would be in trouble. Lt Amenyah agreed to go on the errand. At 15.45 hours while in my house the G.O.C. and some police officers called in and invited me to an office where I was asked to make a statement. At 23.00 hours my house and my office were thoroughly searched but nothing was found. At about 01.00 hours 20th December I was placed under close arrest and at 10.00 hours on 21st December I was released to open arrest. At 11.00 hours on 22nd I was asked to make another statement to the Police.

3. *Statement by Lt E. R. Amenyah*[3]

I am Officer i/c Records, Ghana Army. At about 13.00 hours on 19th December 1958 I was in my office when the accused, whom I now recognise, telephoned me. He asked me to come to his office at 13.30 hours. I agreed. I arrived at about 13.45 hours. The accused said 'I have information of a confidential nature to tell you'. The accused and I were speaking in the Adangbe language which is his native tongue. I understand it perfectly. The accused said that on 18th December two Members of Parliament had visited him in his house at night. He said they were Mr Amponsah and Mr Apaloo. These two men, the accused said, had brought some Army uniforms with badges of rank and £50 in cash. The accused then showed me a brief case on the table in his office and said that at that very moment the money was in the case. The accused then continued to relate the events of the previous night to me. He said that the two M.P.s had requested him to call round some Ghanaian N.C.O.s and induce them with the £50 to cause a *coup d'etat*, and to assassinate the Prime Minister when he was to emplane for India. The accused told me that he had thought about the whole thing and he had decided that he would not do it. The accused then said that the M.P.s had arranged to meet him that night at 19.00 hours at the T-junction Labadi Road and Giffard Camp. He said he did not want to meet them and asked me to meet them and say he would not be coming. He asked me to say that his reason for not coming was that when he was discussing the arrangements with some N.C.O.s a British officer came to tell him he was wanted by the G.O.C. and that the G.O.C. had asked for a statement. The meeting should therefore be called off. I told the accused that I would go to the T-junction and do as he asked. I left his office at about 14.15 hours. I went to my house to change and then drove to Major Trumper's house. I told him what the accused had told me.

At about 18.20 hours, acting on instructions, I drove to the T-junction. At about 19.00 hours a car approached from Accra direction, passed me and stopped a short distance down a sandy track leading to the beach. I approached the car. There was only one man in it. I asked him if he were Mr Amponsah and he said he was. I got into the car with him and clearly recognised him. I gave him the message from the accused. He then told me to go to the accused and ask him what time it would be convenient for them to meet. He said he would wait there for the answer. I returned to Giffard Camp and reported the meeting to my senior officers.

On instructions I returned to the meeting place at about 19.45

[3] App. A, p. i.

hours. I met Mr Amponsah at the same place in his car. Just as I was getting into the car another car turned into the track. A Police officer came out and arrested Mr Amponsah. My conversation with Mr Amponsah was in English throughout. He speaks it well.

4. *Unanimous Report by the 3 Commissioners*[4]

Lt Amenyah, the originator of the report on which the Police and the Army acted, was, on the whole, an unsatisfactory witness. He in fact gave false evidence when he stated on oath that he had never been a member of the C.P.P. . . . It would be dangerous for us to act, as we said in the course of the proceedings, on his evidence when any part of it is not supported by other testimony or circumstances.

Summary of Findings[5]

(1) That Mr Amponsah was in June and July, 1958, engaged in the purchase of military accoutrement referred to in our Report in connection with his own designs, using for this purpose his own moneys withdrawn by him from the Osei-Bonsu Overseas Study Account at Barclays Bank, 108 Queen's Gate, London. . . .

(3) That in this and together with Mr Amponsah in Lome, Mr Apaloo was engaged in the purchase of West African Frontier Force officers' hackles, and that Mr Apaloo knew of the materials which Mr Amponsah purchased in London. . . .

(6) That Mr Amponsah and Mr Apaloo since June, 1958, were engaged in a conspiracy to carry out at some future date in Ghana an act for an unlawful purpose, revolutionary in character.

(7) That there is no evidence whatsoever that Dr Busia, Mr Appiah, Mr Owusu and Mr Dombo were involved in these transactions. . . .

(20) That neither Mr Apaloo nor Mr Amponsah met Awhaitey at Mr Koney's house on the 18th December, 1958, as alleged by Awhaitey at the time suggested by him.

5. *Majority Report*[6]

(2) That Lt Amenyah's version of what took place between himself and Mr Amponsah on the night of the 19th December, 1958, at the Labadi Road T-junction is the correct one. . . .

(6) That Awhaitey, Mr Amponsah, Mr Apaloo and Mr John Mensah Anthony, were engaged in a conspiracy to assassinate the Prime Minister, Dr Kwame Nkrumah, and carry out a *coup d'etat*. . . .

(8) That neither Mr Amponsah nor Mr Apaloo abandoned their

---

[4] *Proceedings and Report*, pp. 478–9.   [5] Ibid. pp. 478–9.   [6] Ibid. p. 495.

original plan to carry out at some future date an act for an unlawful purpose which was revolutionary in character.

6. *Minority Report by the Chairman*[7]

(1) That there was no conspiratorial association between Mr Amponsah and Mr Apaloo in association with Awhaitey.

(2) There did not exist between Mr Amponsah, Mr Apaloo and Awhaitey a plot to interfere in any way with the life or liberty of the Prime Minister of Ghana on the airport before his departure for India on the 20th December. . . .

(7) That Mr Amponsah and Mr Apaloo had as soon as they knew that the Badges & Equipment transaction had been disclosed to the Police abandoned any idea of associating further with anything connected with that transaction and had no intention of involving themselves further in any such exploits. . . .

(13) That . . . persons unknown . . . secured Mr Amponsah's presence at the Labadi Road T-junction at 7 p.m. on the 19th December and put Mr Apaloo to the trouble of searching for Mr Amponsah at that place after Mr Amponsah had been arrested.

[7] *Proceedings and Report*, pp. 505–6.

Appendix C

THE CONSTITUTION
OF THE
REPUBLIC OF GHANA

WE THE PEOPLE OF GHANA, by our Representatives gathered in this our Constituent Assembly,

IN EXERCISE of our undoubted right to appoint for ourselves the means whereby we shall be governed,

IN SYMPATHY with and loyalty to our fellow-countrymen of Africa,

IN THE HOPE that we may by our actions this day help to further the development of a Union of African States, and

IN A SPIRIT of friendship and peace with all other peoples of the World,

DO HEREBY ENACT and give to ourselves this Constitution.

This Constitution is enacted on this twenty-ninth day of June, 1960 and shall come into operation on the first day of July, 1960.

Part I

POWERS OF THE PEOPLE

1. The powers of the State derive from the people, by whom certain of those powers are now conferred on the institutions established by this Constitution and who shall have the right to exercise the remainder of those powers, and to choose their representatives in the Parliament now established, in accordance with the following principle—

> That, without distinction of sex, race, religion or political belief, every person who, being by law a citizen of Ghana, has attained the age of twenty-one years and is not disqualified by law on grounds of absence, infirmity of mind or criminality, shall be entitled to one vote, to be cast in freedom and secrecy.

2. In the confident expectation of an early surrender of sovereignty to a union of African states and territories, the people now confer on Parliament the power to provide for the surrender of the whole or any part of the sovereignty of Ghana.

3. The power to repeal or alter this Part of the Constitution is reserved to the people.

Part II

THE REPUBLIC

4. (1) Ghana is a sovereign unitary Republic.

(2) Subject to the provisions of Article Two of the Constitution, the power to provide a form of government for Ghana other than that of a republic or for the form of the Republic to be other than unitary is reserved to the people.

5. Until otherwise provided by law, the territories of Ghana shall consist of those territories which were comprised in Ghana immediately before the coming into operation of the Constitution, including the territorial waters.

6. Until otherwise provided by law, Ghana shall be divided into the following Regions, which shall respectively comprise such territories as may be provided for by law, that is to say, the Ashanti Region, the Brong-Ahafo Region, the Central Region, the Eastern Region, the Northern Region, the Upper Region, the Volta Region, and the Western Region.

7. The Flag of Ghana shall consist of three equal horizontal stripes, the upper stripe being red, the middle stripe gold and the lower stripe green, with a black star in the centre of the gold stripe.

Part III

THE PRESIDENT AND HIS MINISTERS

Head of the State

8. (1) There shall be a President of Ghana, who shall be the Head of the State and responsible to the people.

(2) Subject to the provisions of the Constitution, the executive power of the State is conferred upon the President.

(3) The President shall be the Commander-in-Chief of the Armed Forces and the Fount of Honour.

(4) Except as may be otherwise provided by law, in the exercise of his functions the President shall act in his own discretion and shall not be obliged to follow advice tendered by any other person.

(5) The power to repeal or alter this Article is reserved to the people.

9. The term of office of the President shall begin with his assumption of office and end with the assumption of office of the person elected as President in the next following election, so however that the President may at any time resign his office by instrument under his hand addressed to the Chief Justice.

First President

10. KWAME NKRUMAH is hereby appointed first President of Ghana, having been chosen as such before the enactment of the Constitution in a Plebiscite conducted in accordance with the principle set out in Article One of the Constitution.

Election of President and Assumption of Office

11. (1) An election of a President shall be held whenever one of the following events occurs, that is to say—
    (*a*) the National Assembly is dissolved, or
    (*b*) the President dies, or
    (*c*) the President resigns his office.

(2) Provision shall be made by law for regulating the election of a President, and shall be so made in accordance with the following principles—
    (*a*) any citizen of Ghana shall be qualified for election as President if he has attained the age of thirty-five years;
    (*b*) the returning officer for the election shall be the Chief Justice;
    (*c*) if contested, an election held by reason of a dissolution of the National Assembly shall be decided by preferences given before the General Election by persons subsequently returned as Members of Parliament, or, if no candidate for election as President obtains more than one-half of the preferences so given, by secret ballot of the Members of the new Parliament;
    (*d*) if contested, an election held by reason of the death or resignation of the President shall be decided by secret ballot of the Members of Parliament.

(3) If an election is to be decided by balloting among the Members of Parliament and a President has not been declared elected after five ballots the National Assembly shall be deemed to be dissolved at the conclusion of the fifth ballot.

(4) Where a person has been declared by the Chief Justice to be elected as President his election shall not be questioned in any court.

12. (1) The President shall assume office by taking an oath in the following form, which shall be administered before the people by the Chief Justice—

    I.....................do solemnly swear that I will well and truly exercise the functions of the high office of President of Ghana, that I will bear true faith and allegiance to Ghana, that I will preserve and defend the Constitution, and that I will do right to all manner of people according to law without fear or favour, affection or ill-will. So help me God.

(2) Instead of taking an oath the President may if he thinks fit make an affirmation, which shall be in the like form with the substitution of *affirm* for *swear* and the omission of the concluding sentence.

13. (1) Immediately after his assumption of office the President shall make the following solemn declaration before the people—

On accepting the call of the people to the high office of President of Ghana I............................solemnly declare my adherence to the following fundamental principles—

That the powers of Government spring from the will of the people and should be exercised in accordance therewith.

That freedom and justice should be honoured and maintained.

That the union of Africa should be striven for by every lawful means and, when attained, should be faithfully preserved.

That the Independence of Ghana should not be surrendered or diminished on any grounds other than the furtherance of African unity.

That no person should suffer discrimination on grounds of sex, race, tribe, religion or political belief.

That Chieftaincy in Ghana should be guaranteed and preserved.

That every citizen of Ghana should receive his fair share of the produce yielded by the development of the country.

That subject to such restrictions as may be necessary for preserving public order, morality or health, no person should be deprived of freedom of religion or speech, of the right to move and assemble without hindrance or of the right of access to courts of law.

That no person should be deprived of his property save where the public interest so requires and the law so provides.

(2) The power to repeal this Article, or to alter its provisions otherwise than by the addition of further paragraphs to the declaration, is reserved to the people.

Official Seals

14. There shall be a Public Seal and a Presidential Seal, the use and custody of which shall be regulated by law.

Ministers and Cabinet

15. (1) The President shall from time to time appoint by instrument under the Presidential Seal persons from among the Members of Parliament, who shall be styled Ministers of Ghana, to assist him in his exercise of the executive power and to take charge under his direction of such departments of State as he may assign to them.

(2) The power to repeal or alter this Article is reserved to the people.

16. (1) There shall be a Cabinet consisting of the President and not less than eight Ministers of Ghana appointed as members of the Cabinet by the President.

(2) Subject to the powers of the President, the Cabinet is charged with the general direction and control of the Government of Ghana.

(3) The appointment of a Minister as a member of the Cabinet may at any time be revoked by the President.

(4) The power to repeal or alter this Article is reserved to the people.

17. The office of a Minister of Ghana shall become vacant—

(*a*) if the President removes him from office by instrument under the Presidential Seal; or

(*b*) if he ceases to be a Member of Parliament otherwise than by reason of a dissolution; or

(*c*) on the acceptance by the President of his resignation from office; or

(*d*) immediately before the assumption of office of a President.

Supplemental provisions as to President

18. (1) The office of the President shall be executed, in accordance with advice tendered by the Cabinet, by a Presidential Commission consisting of three persons appointed by the Cabinet—

(*a*) during an interval between the death or resignation of a President and the assumption of office by his successor; and

(*b*) whenever the President is adjudged incapable of acting.

(2) Any functions of the President which, by reason of the illness of the President or his absence from Ghana or any other circumstance, cannot conveniently be exercised by him in person, may, so long as he is not adjudged incapable of acting, be delegated by the President to a Presidential Commission consisting of three persons appointed by him:

Provided that nothing in this section shall be taken to prejudice the power of the President, at any time when he is not adjudged incapable of acting, to delegate any exercise of the executive power to some other person.

(3) A Presidential Commission may act by any two of its members, and if any vacancy arises by reason of the death of a member the vacancy shall be filled by the Cabinet or by the President, according to which of them appointed the deceased member.

(4) The President shall be deemed to be adjudged incapable of acting if the Chief Justice and the Speaker—

    (*a*) have jointly declared that, after considering medical evidence, they are satisfied that the President is, by reason of physical or mental infirmity, unable to exercise the functions of his office, and

    (*b*) have not subsequently withdrawn the declaration on the ground that the President has recovered his capacity.

(5) If, at the time when a Presidential Commission falls to be appointed under section (1) of this Article, the number of Ministers in the Cabinet is less than eight or there are no Ministers in the Cabinet, then, for the purpose of the appointment of a Presidential Commission and the tendering of advice to the Commission as to the membership of the Cabinet in the first instance, one or more persons shall be deemed to be included in the Cabinet as follows:—

The person or persons who last ceased to be in the Cabinet shall be deemed to be included and, if the number remains less than eight, the person or persons who before him or them last ceased to be in the Cabinet shall also be deemed to be included, and so on until the number is not less than eight.

Persons shall be deemed to be included whether or not they are still Ministers, and persons who ceased to be members of the Cabinet on the same day shall be treated as having ceased to be members at the same time whether or not the fact that they are all deemed to be included raises the number above eight.

19. (1) The President shall receive such salary and allowances, and on retirement such pension, gratuity and other allowance, as may be determined by the National Assembly.

(2) The salary and allowances of the President shall not be reduced during his period of office.

(3) Salaries and allowances payable under this Article are hereby charged on the Consolidated Fund.

Part IV

PARLIAMENT

20. (1) There shall be a Parliament consisting of the President and the National Assembly.

(2) So much of the legislative power of the State as is not reserved by the Constitution to the people is conferred on Parliament; and any portion of the remainder of the legislative power of the State may be conferred on Parliament at any future time by the decision of a majority of the electors voting in a referendum ordered by the President and conducted in accordance with the principle set out in Article One of the Constitution:

Provided that the only power to alter the Constitution (whether expressly or by implication) which is or may as aforesaid be conferred on Parliament is a power to alter it by an Act expressed to be an Act to amend the Constitution and containing only provisions effecting the alteration thereof.

(3) Subject to the provisions of Article Two of the Constitution, Parliament cannot divest itself of any of its legislative powers:

Provided that if by any amendment to the Constitution the power to repeal or alter any existing or future provision of the Constitution is reserved to the people, section (2) of this Article shall apply in relation to that provision as if the power to repeal or alter it had originally been reserved to the people.

(4) No Act passed in exercise of a legislative power expressed by the Constitution to be reserved to the people shall take effect unless the Speaker has certified that power to pass the Act has been conferred on Parliament in the manner provided by section (2) of this Article; and a certificate so given shall be conclusive.

(5) No person or body other than Parliament shall have power to make provisions having the force of law except under authority conferred by Act of Parliament.

(6) Apart from the limitations referred to in the preceding provisions of this Article, the power of Parliament to make laws shall be under no limitation whatsoever.

(7) The power to repeal or alter this Article is reserved to the people.

21. (1) The National Assembly shall consist of the Speaker and not less than one hundred and four Members, to be known as Members of Parliament.

(2) The Members shall be elected in the manner provided by a law framed in accordance with the principle set out in Article One of the Constitution, and the Speaker shall be elected by the Members.

(3) There shall be freedom of speech, debate and proceedings in the National Assembly and that freedom shall not be impeached or questioned in any court or place out of the Assembly.

(4) The President may attend any sitting of the National Assembly.

(5) The power to repeal or alter this Article is reserved to the people.

22. (1) There shall be a new session of the National Assembly once at least in every year, so that a period of twelve months shall not elapse between the last sitting of the Assembly in one session and the first sitting thereof in the next session.

(2) The President may at any time by proclamation summon or prorogue the National Assembly.

(3) The power to repeal or alter this Article is reserved to the people.

23. (1) The President may at any time by proclamation dissolve the National Assembly.

(2) The President shall in any case dissolve the National Assembly on the expiration of the period of five years from the first sitting of the Assembly after the previous General Election.

(3) If an emergency arises or exists when the National Assembly stands dissolved, the President may by proclamation summon an assembly of the persons who were Members of Parliament immediately before the dissolution and, until the majority of results have been declared in the General Election following the dissolution, the assembly shall be deemed to be the National Assembly.

(4) The power to repeal or alter this Article is reserved to the people.

24. (1) Every Bill passed by the National Assembly shall be presented to the President who shall—

    (*a*) signify his assent to the Bill, or

    (*b*) signify his assent to a part only of the Bill and his refusal of assent to the remainder, or

    (*c*) signify his refusal of assent to the Bill.

(2) On the signifying by the President of his assent to a Bill passed by the National Assembly or to a part thereof, the Bill or that part thereof, as the case may be, shall become an Act of Parliament.

25. (1) At the beginning of each session of the National Assembly the President shall deliver to the Members of Parliament an address indicating the policies proposed to be followed by the Government during that session.

(2) At least seven days before each prorogation of the National Assembly the President shall deliver to the Members of Parliament an address indicating the manner and results of the application of the policies of the Government during the preceding period and otherwise setting forth the state of the Nation.

(3) If circumstances render it impracticable for the President himself to deliver any such address, he may instead send a message to the National Assembly embodying the address.

(4) In addition to delivering any address or sending any message under the preceding provisions of this Article, the President may at any time deliver an address to the Members of Parliament or send a message to the National Assembly.

(5) Every message sent by the President to the National Assembly shall be read to the Members of Parliament by a Minister.

Part V

PUBLIC REVENUE AND EXPENDITURE
Taxation

26. (1) No taxation shall be imposed otherwise than under the authority of an Act of Parliament.

(2) The power to repeal or alter this Article is reserved to the people.

Custody of Public Money

27. There shall be a Consolidated Fund and a Contingencies Fund, together with such other public funds as may be provided for by law.

28. (1) The produce of taxation, receipts of capital and interest in respect of public loans, and all other public revenue shall be paid into the Consolidated Fund unless required or permitted by law to be paid into any other fund or account.

(2) The President may, in relation to any department of State, direct that a separate public account be established for the department and that the revenue of the department be paid into that account.

29. (1) Expenditure shall not be met from any public fund or public account except under a warrant issued by authority of the President.

(2) Whenever a sum becomes payable which is charged by law on a public fund or on the general revenues and assets of Ghana, the President or a person authorised by him in that behalf shall cause

a warrant to be issued for the purpose of enabling that sum to be paid.

(3) A warrant may be issued by authority of the President for the purpose of enabling public money to be applied—

    (*a*) as part of moneys granted for the public service by a vote of the National Assembly under this Part of the Constitution, or

    (*b*) in defraying, in the manner provided by Article Thirty-four of the Constitution, urgent expenditure authorised under that Article, or

    (*c*) in performance of an agreement to grant a loan made under Article Thirty-five of the Constitution.

30. Where—

    (*a*) money is drawn out of a public fund or public account for the purpose of being applied as part of moneys granted for a particular public service by a vote of the National Assembly, but

    (*b*) the money so drawn proves to be in excess of the amount granted for that service,

particulars of the excess shall be laid before the National Assembly and, if the National Assembly so resolve, the amount originally granted for the service in question shall be treated for accounting purposes as increased to include the amount of the excess.

Moneys granted by Vote of the National Assembly

31. (1) The President shall cause to be prepared annually under heads for each public service estimates of expenditure, other than expenditure charged by law on a public fund or on the general revenues and assets of Ghana, which will be required to be incurred for the public services during the following financial year; and, when approved by the Cabinet, the estimates so prepared (which shall be known as "the annual estimates") shall be laid before the National Assembly.

(2) Each head of the annual estimates shall be submitted to the vote of the National Assembly but no amendment of the estimates shall be moved.

(3) A vote of the National Assembly approving a head of the annual estimates shall constitute a grant by the Assembly of moneys not exceeding the amount specified in that head to be applied within the financial year in question for the service to which the head relates.

32. (1) If it appears that the vote of the National Assembly on any heads of the annual estimates will not be taken before the commencement of the financial year to which they relate, the President shall cause to be prepared under those heads estimates of the expenditure which will be required for the continuance of the public services in question until the said vote is taken; and, when approved by the Cabinet, the estimates so prepared (which shall be known as "provisional estimates") shall be laid before the National Assembly.

(2) If, after the National Assembly has voted upon the annual estimates for any financial year, it appears that the moneys granted in respect of any heads thereof are likely to be insufficient or that expenditure is likely to be incurred in that year on a public service falling under a head not included in the annual estimates, the President shall cause to be prepared under the relevant heads estimates of the additional expenditure; and, when approved by the Cabinet, the estimates so prepared (which shall be known as "supplementary estimates") shall be laid before the National Assembly.

(3) Sections (2) and (3) of Article Thirty-one of the Constitution shall apply in relation to provisional and supplementary estimates as they apply in relation to the annual estimates:

Provided that, where an item of expenditure is included both in provisional estimates and in the annual estimates, a grant in respect of that item shall not by virtue of this section be taken to have been made more than once.

33. In addition to granting moneys on estimates of expenditure the National Assembly may, if satisfied that it is necessary in the public interest to do so, make any extraordinary grant of money for the public service, including a grant on a vote of credit, that is a grant of money to be used for a purpose which, for reasons of national security or by reason of the indefinite character of the service in question, cannot be described in detailed estimates.

Expenditure out of Contingencies Fund

34. (1) Where in the opinion of the President—

    (*a*) money is urgently required to be expended for a public service, and

    (*b*) the payment thereof would exceed the amount granted by the National Assembly for that service or the service is one for which no amount has been so granted, and

    (*c*) it is not practicable to summon a meeting of the National Assembly in sufficient time to obtain the necessary grant,

the President may by executive instrument authorise the money required to be drawn from the Contingencies Fund.

(2) An executive instrument made under this Article shall

specify the head under which the expenditure in question would have been shown if it had been included in the annual estimates.

(3) As soon as is practicable after an executive instrument has been made under this Article—

(*a*) the instrument shall be laid before the National Assembly, and

(*b*) a resolution authorising the transfer to the Contingencies Fund from a public fund specified in the resolution of an amount equal to the amount of the expenditure to which the instrument relates shall be moved in the National Assembly by a Minister authorised in that behalf by the President.

(4) In addition to sums transferred under section (3) of this Article, the National Assembly may from time to time authorise the transfer from the Consolidated Fund to the Contingencies Fund of sums required to maintain an adequate balance therein.

Public Loans

35. (1) The President may on behalf of the Republic enter into an agreement for the granting of a loan out of any public fund or public account if he thinks it expedient in the public interest so to do.

(2) If the National Assembly so resolve, agreements entered into under this Article for amounts exceeding the amount specified in the Assembly's resolution shall not become operative unless ratified by the Assembly.

(3) As soon as is practicable after an agreement has been entered into under this Article, particulars of the agreement, and of the borrower and the purpose for which the loan is required, shall be laid before the National Assembly.

36. No loan shall be raised for the purposes of the Republic otherwise than under the authority of an Act of Parliament.

37. (1) The public debt, interest thereon, sinking fund payments in respect thereof, and the costs, charges and expenses incidental to the management thereof are hereby charged on the general revenues and assets of Ghana.

(2) The power to repeal or alter this Article is reserved to the people.

Audit of Public Accounts

38. (1) There shall be an Auditor-General, who shall be appointed by the President and who shall not be removable except by the President in pursuance of a resolution of the National Assembly supported by the votes of at least two-thirds of the total number of Members of

Parliament and passed on the ground of stated misbehaviour or of infirmity of body or mind.

(2) The Auditor-General shall retire from office on attaining the age of fifty-five years or such higher age as may be prescribed by law.

(3) The Auditor-General may resign his office by writing under his hand addressed to the President.

(4) The salary of the Auditor-General shall be determined by the National Assembly, is hereby charged on the Consolidated Fund and shall not be diminished during his term of office.

39. (1) The accounts of all departments of State shall be audited by the Auditor-General who, with his deputies, shall at all times be entitled to have access to all books, records, stores and other matters relating to such accounts.

(2) The Auditor-General shall report annually to the National Assembly on the exercise of his functions under section (1) of this Article, and shall in his report draw attention to irregularities in the accounts audited by him.

Part VI

LAW AND JUSTICE

Laws of Ghana

40. Except as may be otherwise provided by an enactment made after the coming into operation of the Constitution, the laws of Ghana comprise the following—

- (*a*) the Constitution,
- (*b*) enactments made by or under the authority of the Parliament established by the Constitution.
- (*c*) enactments other than the Constitution made by or under the authority of the Constituent Assembly,
- (*d*) enactments in force immediately before the coming into operation of the Constitution,
- (*e*) the common law, and
- (*f*) customary law.

Superior and Inferior Courts

41. (1) There shall be a Supreme Court and a High Court, which shall be the superior courts of Ghana.

(2) Subject to the provisions of the Constitution, the judicial power of the State is conferred on the Supreme Court and the High Court, and on such inferior courts as may be provided for by law.

(3) The power to repeal or alter this Article is reserved to the people.

Provisions as to Superior Courts

42. (1) The Supreme Court shall be the final court of appeal, with such appellate and other jurisdiction as may be provided for by law.

(2) The Supreme Court shall have original jurisdiction in all matters where a question arises whether an enactment was made in excess of the powers conferred on Parliament by or under the Constitution, and if any such question arises in the High Court or an inferior court, the hearing shall be adjourned and the question referred to the Supreme Court for decision.

(3) Subject to section (2) of this Article, the High Court shall have such original and appellate jurisdiction as may be provided for by law.

(4) The Supreme Court shall in principle be bound to follow its own previous decisions on questions of law, and the High Court shall be bound to follow previous decisions of the Supreme Court on such questions, but neither court shall be otherwise bound to follow the previous decisions of any court on questions of law.

43. Provision shall be made by law for the composition of superior courts in particular proceedings:

Provided that no appeal shall be decided by the Supreme Court unless the court hearing the appeal consists of at least three Judges, of whom at least one is a Judge of the Supreme Court; and no question whether an enactment was made in excess of the powers conferred on Parliament by or under the Constitution shall be decided by the Supreme Court unless the court considering the question comprises at least three Judges of the Supreme Court.

Judges of the Superior Courts

44. (1) The President shall by instrument under the Presidential Seal appoint one of the Judges of the Supreme Court to be Chief Justice of Ghana.

(2) The Chief Justice shall be President of the Supreme Court and Head of the Judicial Service.

(3) The appointment of a Judge as Chief Justice may at any time be revoked by the President by instrument under the Presidential Seal.

45. (1) The Judges of the superior courts shall be appointed by the President by instrument under the Public Seal.

(2) Provision shall be made by law for the form and administration of the judicial oath, which shall be taken by every person appointed as Judge of a superior court before the exercise by him of any judicial function.

(3) Subject to the following provisions of this Article, no person shall be removed from office as a Judge of the Supreme Court or a Judge of the High Court except by the President in pursuance of a resolution of the National Assembly supported by the votes of not less than two-thirds of the Members of Parliament and passed on the grounds of stated misbehaviour or infirmity of body or mind.

(4) Unless the President by instrument under his hand extends the tenure of office of the Judge for a definite period specified in the instrument, a Judge of the Supreme Court shall retire from office on attaining the age of sixty-five years and a Judge of the High Court shall retire from office on attaining the age of sixty-two years.

(5) A Judge of a superior court may resign his office by writing under his hand addressed to the President.

(6) The power to repeal or alter this Article is reserved to the people.

46. (1) The salary of a Judge of a superior court shall be determined by the National Assembly and shall not be diminished while he remains in office.

(2) The Chief Justice shall be entitled to such additional allowance as may be determined by the National Assembly.

(3) All salaries and allowances paid under this Article and all pensions and other retiring allowances paid in respect of service as Chief Justice or other Judge of a superior court are hereby charged on the Consolidated Fund.

Attorney-General

47. (1) There shall be an Attorney-General, who shall be a Minister of Ghana or other person appointed by the President.

(2) Subject to the directions of the President, there shall be vested in the Attorney-General responsibility for the initiation, conduct and discontinuance of civil proceedings by the Republic and prosecutions for criminal offences, and for the defence of civil proceedings brought against the Republic.

(3) The office of the Attorney-General shall become vacant—
    (*a*) if his appointment is revoked by the President; or
    (*b*) on the acceptance by the President of his resignation from office; or
    (*c*) immediately before the assumption of office of a President.

President's powers of mercy

48. (1) The President shall have power, in respect of any criminal offence—

(*a*) to grant a pardon to the offender, or

(*b*) to order a respite of the execution of any sentence passed on the offender, or

(*c*) to remit any sentence so passed or any penalty or forfeiture incurred by reason of the offence.

(2) Where the President remits a sentence of death he may order the offender to be imprisoned until such time as the President orders his release.

Part VII

HOUSES OF CHIEFS

49. There shall be a House of Chiefs for each Region of Ghana.

50. A House of Chiefs shall consist of such Chiefs, and shall have such functions relating to customary law and other matters, as may be provided by law.

Part VIII

THE PUBLIC SERVICES

51. (1) The Public Services of Ghana shall consist of the Civil Service, the Judicial Service, the Police Service, the Local Government Service, and such other Public Services as may be provided for by law.

(2) Subject to the provisions of the Constitution and save as is otherwise provided by law, the appointment, promotion, transfer, termination of appointment, dismissal and disciplinary control of members of the Public Services is vested in the President.

52. All pensions, gratuities and other allowances payable on retirement to members of the Civil Service, the Judicial Service and the Police Service are hereby charged on the Consolidated Fund.

Part IX

THE ARMED FORCES

53. (1) Neither the President nor any other person shall raise any armed force except under the authority of an Act of Parliament.

(2) The power to repeal or alter this Article is reserved to the people.

54. (1) Subject to the provisions of any enactment for the time being in force, the powers of the President as Commander-in-Chief of the Armed Forces shall include the power to commission persons as officers in the said Forces and to order any of the said Forces to engage in operations for the defence of Ghana, for the preservation of public order, for relief in cases of emergency or for any other purpose appearing to the Commander-in-Chief to be expedient.

(2) The Commander-in-Chief shall have power, in a case where it appears to him expedient to do so for the security of the State, to dismiss a member of the Armed Forces or to order a member of the Armed Forces not to exercise any authority vested in him as a member thereof until the Commander-in-Chief otherwise directs; and a purported exercise of authority in contravention of such an order shall be ineffective.

Part X

SPECIAL POWERS FOR FIRST PRESIDENT

55. (1) Notwithstanding anything in Article Twenty of the Constitution, the person appointed as first President of Ghana shall have, during his initial period of office, the powers conferred on him by this Article.

(2) The first President may, whenever he considers it to be in the national interest to do so, give directions by legislative instrument.

(3) An instrument made under this Article may alter (whether expressly or by implication) any enactment other than the Constitution.

(4) Section (2) of Article Forty-two of the Constitution shall apply in relation to the powers conferred by this Article as it applies in relation to the powers conferred on Parliament.

(5) For the purposes of this Article the first President's initial period of office shall be taken to continue until some other person assumes office as President.

(6) The power to repeal or alter this Article during the first President's initial period of office is reserved to the people.

Select Bibliography

Note: This list covers the main sources used in the text and a small number of works of general interest which have a bearing on Ghanaian politics between 1946 and 1960.

1. BOOKS

Acquah, Ioné. *Accra Survey*. London, 1958.

Almond, Gabriel and J. S. Coleman, eds. *The Politics of Developing Areas*. Princeton, 1960.

Amamoo, H. E. *The New Ghana*. London, 1958.

Apter, David E. *The Gold Coast in Transition*. Princeton, 1955.

Arden-Clarke, Sir C. Eight Years of Transition in Ghana. *African Affairs*, January 1958.

Bennion, S. A. R. *The Constitutional Laws of Ghana*. London, 1962.

Bonne, Nii Kwabena. *Milestones in the History of the Gold Coast*. London, 1953.

Bourret, F. M. *Ghana; the Road to Independence*. London, 1960.

Bowdich, T. E. *Mission from Cape Coast Castle to Ashantee*. London, 1819.

Buell, Raymond L. *The Native Problem in Africa*. New York, 1928.

Burns, Sir Alan. *Colonial Civil Servant*. London, 1949.

Busia, K. A. *The Position of the Chief in the Modern Political System of Ashanti*. London, 1951.
— The Prospects for Parliamentary Democracy in the Gold Coast. *Parliamentary Affairs*, v/4 (1952).

Cardinall, A. W. *The Gold Coast, 1931*. Accra, 1932.

Casely Hayford, J. E. *Gold Coast Native Institutions*. London, 1903.

Coleman, James S. *Togoland*. New York, 1956.

Danquah, J. B. *Liberty of the Subject*. Kibi, n.d.
— *The Doyen Speaks: Some Historical Speeches by Dr J. B. Danquah*. Accra, n.d.

Dupuis, J. *Journal of a Residence in Ashantee*. London, 1824.

Duverger, M. *Political Parties*. London, 1954.

Dzirasa, Stephen. *Political Thought of Dr Nkrumah*. Accra, n.d.

Emerson, Rupert. *From Empire to Nation*. New York, 1960.

Fortes, M. *The Web of Kinship among the Tallensi*. Oxford, 1945.

Guggisberg, Sir Gordon. *The Gold Coast: a Review of Events of 1920–6 and the Prospects of 1927–8*. Accra, 1927.

Hailey, Lord. *Native Administration in the British African Territories*, Pt 3. London, 1951.

Hancock, W. K. *Survey of British Commonwealth Affairs*. London, 1942.

Hill, Polly. *The Gold Coast Cocoa Farmer*. London, 1956.

Hodgkin, Thomas. *Nationalism in Colonial Africa*. London, 1956.

—— *African Political Parties*. London, 1961.

Johnson, J. W. de Graft. *Towards Nationhood in West Africa*. London, 1928.

— The Fanti Asafu. *Africa*, 1932.

Kimble, David. *A Political History of Ghana, 1850–1928*. London, 1963.

Legum, Colin. *Pan-Africanism; a Short Political Guide*. London, 1962.

Mackenzie, W. J. M. *Free Elections*. London, 1950.

— and K. E. Robinson, eds. *Five Elections in Africa*. London, 1960.

Nkrumah, Kwame. *Ghana; the Autobiography of Kwame Nkrumah*. Edinburgh, 1957.

— *I Speak of Freedom*. London, 1961.

— *Africa Must Unite*. London, 1963.

Padmore, George. *The Gold Coast Revolution*. London, 1953.

—— *Pan-Africanism or Communism?* London, 1956.

Pedler, F. J. *West Africa*. London, 1951.

Ramseyer, F. and J. Kühne. *Four Years in Ashantee*. London, 1875.

Rattray, R. S. *Ashanti Law and Constitution*. Oxford, 1929.

Rubin, L. and P. Murray. *The Constitution and Government of Ghana*. London, 1961.

Saloway, Sir R. The New Gold Coast. *International Affairs*, October 1955.

Sarbah, J. M. *Fanti Customary Laws*. London, 1904.

Timothy, Bankole. *Kwame Nkrumah*. London, 1955.

Tordoff, W. The Ashanti Confederacy. *Journal of African History*, iii/3, 1962.

Trimingham, J. Spencer. *Islam in West Africa*. Oxford, 1959.

Wallerstein, Immanuel. *Africa; the Politics of Independence*. 1960.

Ward, W. E. F. *A History of the Gold Coast*. London, 1948.

Wight, Martin. *The Gold Coast Legislative Council*. London, 1947.

Wills, J. B. *Agriculture and Land Use in Ghana*. London, 1962.

2. OFFICIAL PUBLICATIONS

1. *Great Britain*

Colonial Office

Annual Report on the Gold Coast. 1920–1955.

Report by His Majesty's Government in the United Kingdom . . . to the Trusteeship Council of the United Nations on the Administration of Togoland for the year 1947. (Annually, to 1954.)

1948. Commission of Enquiry into Disturbances in the Gold Coast. *Report.* (Chairman: Aiken Watson.) Col. no. 231.

1948. *Statement by His Majesty's Government* [thereon]. Col. no. 232.

1949. Committee on Constitutional Reform. *Report to H.E. the Governor.* (Chairman: J. H. Coussey.) Col. no. 248.

1949. *Statement by His Majesty's Government* [thereon]. Col. no. 250.

1954. *Despatches on the Gold Coast Government's Proposals for Constitutional Reform exchanged between the Secretary of State for the Colonies and H.E. the Governor, 24th August, 1953 to 15th April, 1954.*

Command papers

1938. Commission on the Marketing of West African Cocoa. *Report.* (Chairman: W. Nowell.) Cmd. 5845.

1943–4. *Report on Cocoa Control in West Africa, 1939–43 and Statement on Future Policy, 1944.* Cmd. 6554.

1946. *Statement on Future Marketing of West African Cocoa.* Cmd. 6950.

1952. *The Volta River Aluminium Scheme.* Cmd. 8702.

1957. *The Proposed Constitution of Ghana.* Cmnd. 71.

Orders in Council

The Gold Coast (Constitution) Order in Council, 1950. S.I. No. 2094.

Gold Coast Colony and Ashanti (Legislative Council) Order in Council, 1954. S.R. & O. No. 353.

The Ghana (Constitution) Order in Council, 1957. S.I. No. 277.

2. *Gold Coast/Ghana*

Reports of Committees and Commissions, &c.

1948. Commission of Enquiry into Disturbances. . . . *See under* Great Britain.

1949. Committee on Constitutional Reform. *See under* Great Britain.

1950. Legislative Council. Select Committee appointed to Examine the Questions of Elections and Constituencies. *Report, with the Legislative Council Decisions Thereon.* (Chairman: F. K. Ewart.)

1951. Commission for Regional Administrations. *Report by the Commissioner* (Sir S. Phillipson).

1953. Commission of Enquiry into Representational and Electoral Reform. *Report.* (Chairman: W. B. van Lare.)

1952. Commission of Enquiry into Wenchi Affairs. *Report,* by J. Jackson.

1954. Commission of Enquiry into Mr Braimah's Resignation and Allegations arising Therefrom. *Report.* (Chairman: K. A. Korsah.)

1955. Legislative Assembly. Select Committee on the Federal System of Government and Second Chamber for the Gold Coast. *Report.*

1956. Conference to consider the Report of the Constitutional Adviser, Achimota. *Report of the Achimota Conference.* (Chairman: C. W. Tachie-Menson.)

1956. Commission of Enquiry into the Affairs of the Cocoa Purchasing Co. Ltd. *Report.* (Chairman: O. Jibowu.)

1958. Regional Constitutional Commission. *Regional Assemblies; Report to . . . the Governor-General.*

1958. Committee of Enquiry . . . into Affairs of the Kumasi State Council and the Asanteman Council. *Report* by Mr Justice Sarkodee Addo.

1958. Commission appointed to enquire into the Affairs of the Akim Abuakwa State. *Report,* by J. Jackson.

1959. Commission appointed under the Commissions Enquiry Ordinance. Enquiry into the Matters Disclosed at the Trial of Captain Benjamin Awhaitey before a Court Martial and the Surrounding Circumstances. *Report.* (Chairman: G. Granville Sharp.)

1959. *Statement* [thereon].

Other

Gold Coast, Census Office. *Census of Population 1948, Report and Tables.* London, 1950.

— Government. *Constitutional Proposals for Gold Coast Independence and Statement on the Report of the Constitutional Adviser and the Report of the Achimota Conference.* 1956.

—— The Government's Proposals for Constitutional Reform. 1953.

—— The Government's Revised Constitutional Proposals for Gold Coast Independence, 1956.

— Legislative Assembly. *Debates,* 1951–7.

— Legislative Council. *Debates,* 1919–50.

— Ministry of Finance. *Economic Survey.* 1953–6.

— Office of the Constitutional Adviser. *Report,* 1955. (Constitutional Adviser: F. C. Bourne.)

— Office of Govt Statistician. *Digest of Statistics.* (Period.)

—— *Sekondi-Takoradi Survey of Population and Household Budgets,* 1955 and *Kumasi Survey of Household Budgets and Population,* 1955. 1956.

Ghana. Governor-General. *The Ghana Constitution, Order in Council, 1957, the Referendum, Voting Regions,* 1957.

— Ministry of Finance. *Economic Survey,* 1957–61.

— Office of the President. *Statement by the Government on the Recent Conspiracy.* December 1961.

— Parliament. *Debates,* 1957–

Regional Councils

Asanteman Council (until 1950 The Ashanti Confederacy Council). *Minutes.*

Joint Provincial Council of Chiefs. *Minutes.*

Northern Territories Council (until 1950 The Northern Territories Territorial Council). *Minutes.*

3. *United Nations*

UN Visiting Mission to Trust Territories in West Africa. *Reports and Related Documents,* 1952–5.

—— *Special Report on the Ewe and Togoland Unification Problem,* 1952 (*TCOR,* 11th sess., suppl. 2).

Report of the UN Plebiscite Commissioner, 19 June 1956 (T/1258 & Add. 1).

3. NEWSPAPERS AND PERIODICALS

NEWSPAPERS*

Evening News
Morning Telegraph
Ashanti Pioneer
Liberator
Daily Graphic
Ashanti Times
Togoland Vanguard
West Africa
Ghana Today

PERIODICALS

Africa.
African Affairs.
International Affairs.
Journal of African History.
Journal of Commonwealth Political Studies.
Parliamentary Affairs.
Political Studies.
Transactions of Ghana (formerly *Gold Coast and Togoland*) *Historical Society.*
Economic Bulletin (Economic Society of Ghana).

* See above, p. 422.

Index

Botsio, Kojo: education, 16; argues
need for single party, 33, 42; helps to
form CYO, 81; —and CPP, 84-5;
released from prison (1950), 115;
minister, 155 n., 169, 219; apptd
Min. of State, 251 n., 274; appeals to
Sec. of State against 3rd elect., 309,
328, 247; resigns, 406; reinstated,
410

Bourne, Sir Frederick, 301-3

Bowdich, T. E., 18 n., 21 n.

Braimah, J. A.: apptd to leg. co.
(1950), 105; elect. (1951), 148;
—(1954), 232 n., 236, 240-1, 243 n.,
379 n.; defines northern position
(1951), 155; confesses to receiving
£2,000, 164-5; resigns, 164, 184;
supports NPP, 186; deputy chairman UP, 384

Brong Ahafo: defined, xi; Brong-
Kumasi dispute, 293 f., 301 n.; and
Bourne *Report*, 302-3; elect. results
(1956), 353; region estab., 380

Builders' Brigade, 382, 385 n., 388, 390

Bukari, Sumani, 222, 240 n., 241 n.

Buor, Kofi: swears Ashanti Great
Oath, 256; forms Council for Higher
Cocoa Prices, 257-9, 261, 267, 343

Burns, Sir Alan, 3, 7 f.; relations with
Danquah, 10 n., 11, 24

Busia, K. A., xiii; apptd to admin. service, 8, 15 n., 18 n.; quoted 24 n.,
29, 45, 57, 257 n., 260 n.; elect.
(1951), 146-7, 155; —(1956), 353;
Social Survey Sekondi, 165 n.; leader
Ghana Congress Party, 180-3; warns
of danger of Nkrumah as charismatic leader, 181 n.; criticizes
Krobo Edusei, 182 n., 227; elect.
(1954), 242, 244; supports NLM,
267-9; rejects Sel. Committee on
Fed. Syst. Govt, 298, 303; opposes
Achimota Conference, 306-7; sub-
mits list of opposition to Governor
(1956), 319-20, 321 n.; elect. appeal
(1956), 324-6; agrees to extend
NLM to Colony, 342; claims elect.
results justified fed., 355-6; welcomes
grant of indep., 357; leader of
United Party, 384-5; leaves Ghana,
385

Cadbury & Fry, 254 n., 260, 343-4

Chiefs; defined, xiii; and 'young men',
18 ff.; and 1948 riots, 78 ff.; in
Bekwai, 95 ff.; arrange Joint Territorial Council movement, 135; defended by NPP, 230; elect. support
(1954), 246; support NLM in
Ashanti, 259-65; income, 272

'Circle, The', 76, 81, 87 n., 000

Cocoa: (1937) hold-up, 10, 25;
swollen shoot and 1948 riots, 59-66;
prices, 66 n., 157; CPP control
measures v. swollen shoot, 159-61;
price fixed at 72s. a load, 253-4;
regional prodn, 256; and 1955 by-
election, 275; prodn and price
(1956-61), 364, 400

Cocoa Purchasing Co.; establ., 72-3;
Jibowu Inquiry summarized, 341 n.
and 1956 elect., 343

Coleman, J S., 189 n., 310 n., 312 n.

Colony, the: defined, xi; elect. results
(1954), 244; —(1956), 347 n.,
350-1, 354

Committee on Youth Organization
(CYO), 81, 84

Congo, 397; death of Lumumba, 397;
—of Hammarskjöld, 397

Convention People's Party (CPP): defined, xii, 3; as a 'commoners' party,
12; as a nationalist party, 42-3;
inaugurated, 85; in Bekwai, 99;
elect. appeal (1951), 130-1; —(1954)
212-15; —(1956), 329-30, 334; in-
experience of assembly members,
153; const. examined, 162-3; inner
party revolt (1951-2), 164-70; central ctee membership (1949), 167;
reorganized (1952-3), 171-6; challenged by Ashanti members (1953),
176 ff.; analysis of Ass. members
(1951), 195; —of constituency organizations, 197-9; Independents'
revolt (1954), 215-25; wins 1954
elect. 238 ff.; —1956 elect., 347;
resists NLM, 281 ff.; described by
Nkrumah, 382-3; (1960) pleb. appeal, 387-8; break in party unity
(1961), 402-7; equated with the
state, 415; re-examined, 416 ff.

Coussey Committee, 80 ff.; *Report* publ.,
85-6.

Coussey, Henley, chairman of Ctee on
Const. Reform (1948), 80-1

*Set by The Broadwater Press Ltd
and reprinted lithographically by
Fletcher & Son Ltd, Norwich*